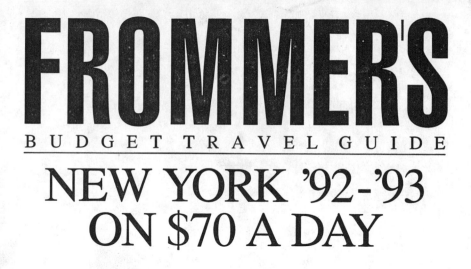

FROMMER'S

BUDGET TRAVEL GUIDE

NEW YORK '92-'93 ON $70 A DAY

by Joan Hamburg and
Norma Ketay

PRENTICE HALL TRAVEL

NEW YORK • LONDON • TORONTO • SYDNEY • TOKYO • SINGAPORE

The walking tours on pages 241, 252, 255, 260, 266 and 276 are courtesy of
John Foreman.

FROMMER BOOKS

Published by Prentice Hall General Reference
A division of Simon & Schuster Inc.
15 Columbus Circle
New York, NY 10023

ISBN 0-13-333469-4
ISSN 8755-5433

Design by Robert Bull Design
Maps by Geografix Inc.

Manufactured in the United States of America

FROMMER'S NEW YORK on $70 a Day '92-'93

Editor-in-Chief: Marilyn Wood
Senior Editors: Judith de Rubini, Alice Fellows
Editors: Sara Hinsey, Paige Hughes, Lisa Renaud, Theodore Stavrou
Assistant Editors: Peter Katucki, Lisa Legarde
Managing Editor: Leanne Coupe

CONTENTS

10 NEW YORK CITY NIGHTS 337

Index 376

LIST OF MAPS

INVITATION TO THE READERS

In researching this book, I have come across many wonderful establishments, the best of which I have included here. I am sure that many of you will also come across appealing hotels, inns, restaurants, guesthouses, shops, and attractions. Please don't keep them to yourself. Share your experiences, especially if you want to comment on places that have been included in this edition that have changed for the worse. You can address your letters to:

Joan Hamburg/Norma Ketay
Frommer's New York on $70 a Day '92–'93
c/o Prentice Hall Travel
15 Columbus Circle
New York, NY 10023

A DISCLAIMER

Readers are advised that prices fluctuate in the course of time and travel information changes under the impact of the varied and volatile factors that affect the travel industry. Neither the author nor the publisher can be held responsible for the experiences of readers while traveling. Readers are invited to write to the publisher with ideas, comments, and suggestions for future editions.

SAFETY ADVISORY

Whenever you're traveling in an unfamiliar city or country, stay alert. Be aware of your immediate surroundings. Wear a moneybelt and keep a close eye on your possessions. Be particularly careful with cameras, purses, and wallets, all favorite targets of thieves and pickpockets.

CHAPTER 1

INTRODUCING NEW YORK CITY

- **WHAT'S SPECIAL ABOUT NEW YORK CITY**
- **1. GEOGRAPHY, HISTORY & POLITICS**
- **DATELINE**
- **2. CULTURAL & SOCIAL LIFE**
- **3. RECOMMENDED BOOKS & FILMS**

With this printing, *New York on $70 a Day* is thirty-two years old. Every two years since it first came out in 1960, it has been revised or rewritten to make sure its information is accurate, up-to-date, and in keeping with the philosophy of the book: to provide reliable descriptions, prices, and directions so that visitors to our city can enjoy it as we do—without spending a fortune while savoring the countless pleasures New York has to offer.

New York has weathered many changes in the intervening years: Steel skyscrapers have given way to glassy postmodern corporate palaces; the Spanish barrios of the West 60s gave way to the opulence of Lincoln Center; nouvelle cuisine and health food have, for many, edged out the heavier cuisine of old.

But in this city of constant change, one thing remains the same. Whether you are a seasoned New Yorker or a first-time visitor, New York never exhausts its ability to surprise. Most New Yorkers are not born or brought up here. They become New Yorkers when the city's magic spell of excitement, intrigue, and glamour makes them realize that it's the most exciting place in the world.

It's not true that New York is a city only for the rich. No other city in the world offers the diversity in price range for a variety of goods and services. New York has been called the world's number-one performing arts city, providing both residents and visitors with a dazzling array of unusual and exciting events. Some of the best cultural events in the city are free or available at low cost. For example, Shakespeare in the Park (Central Park) is presented by the New York Shakespeare Festival every summer, and stars such as Meryl Streep, Kevin Kline, Morgan Freeman, Dustin Hoffman, and Christopher Walken have played on the stage of Central Park's open-air Delacorte Theatre. Tickets, available on a first-come, first-served basis, are absolutely free.

Restaurants can be found to fit any budget. This book will provide you with enough choices to keep you busy eating out for years. Hotels, on the other hand, are another thing altogether. New York has more than its share of good ones, with correspondingly high prices—the Helmsley Palace, the Regency, the Waldorf, the Plaza, among others—but finding the smaller, off-beat hotels with satisfactory rooms at lower cost takes a lot of looking. We have nonetheless uncovered a number of hotels with adequate accommodations at budget prices.

If it's nightlife you've come for, there are offerings galore—the widest range of nighttime entertainment possibilities in the world! You can spend evenings on end without exhausting the supply of bars, dance clubs, country-music haunts, jazz clubs, showcase theaters, and concert halls.

For food, the selections are even better: hundreds upon hundreds of restaurants where good meals are still in the budget to moderate range. These are not so easy to find for the inexperienced visitor, but every New Yorker knows that these low-cost finds exist. We've collected scores of those "little places around the corner" into one volume.

WHAT'S SPECIAL ABOUT NEW YORK CITY

World-Class Attractions
- The Statue of Liberty is an awesome sight for first-time visitors as well as those who live here.
- Ellis Island, the beginning of freedom for 12 million immigrants from 1892 to 1954, is now open to tourists.

Museums
- The Metropolitan Museum of Art. No other American museum can match it.
- MOMA (Museum of Modern Art). Captures the excitement of 20th-century art.
- The Guggenheim Museum displays modern art in Frank Lloyd Wright's equally modern, snail-shaped building.

Nightlife
- Scores of nighttime activities include theater, film, music, and dance, as well as a club scene that is beyond compare.

Shopping
- Macy's. It's the world's biggest department store and an attraction in itself.
- The Lower East Side. A bargain hunter's dream, riddled with novelty shops as well as discount stores.

- Madison Avenue and SoHo for international designers, art, and antiques.

Architectural Highlights
- The New York Public Library (1898–1911), an example of Beaux Arts design, with the lions Patience and Fortitude flanking the steps.
- Grand Central Terminal (1903–1913), one of Manhattan's most beautiful interiors.
- Empire State Building (1931). No longer the tallest building in the city, but still the most famous.
- The Flatiron Building (1902), interestingly shaped like a 19th-century flatiron.

Zoos
- The Bronx Zoo, one of the biggest and best in the world.
- Central Park Zoo, a great place for kids and adults alike.

Public Gardens
- Central Park, a stunning example of landscape design.
- New York Botanical Garden, located in the Bronx, with a unique acre of gardens under glass.
- Brooklyn Botanical Garden. One of the most splendid gardens in the area.

1. GEOGRAPHY, HISTORY & POLITICS

GEOGRAPHY

New York is made up of five boroughs: **Manhattan, Brooklyn, the Bronx, Queens,** and **Staten Island.**

The island of Manhattan—in the very center of New York City—is where the key public buildings are located, and where the most important commercial, industrial, and cultural activities take place. Here you'll find virtually all the sights you've come to see, all the hotels and restaurants that we'll recommend, and most of the famous places and landmarks that are customarily identified with New York. That's not to say that the other boroughs don't have attractions of their own, but you'll have more than enough to do if you try to canvass merely the sights of Manhattan. (We have, however, included several sights in other boroughs.)

Manhattan, with its skyscrapers, is only a small section of greater New York.

Most New Yorkers live in the other boroughs and travel back and forth each day to their jobs in Manhattan. If you take a trip into Brooklyn, the Bronx, Queens, or Staten Island, you'll find streets with trees, private homes, little community centers, schools, fields, and parks similar to those you'd find in the residential districts of any other town.

HISTORY/POLITICS

New York is the world's capital for commerce and trade. And it's always been that way, ever since Peter Minuit landed with a small group of Dutch settlers and drove a shrewd bargain with the Indians, purchasing Manhattan for $24 worth of trinkets (that was perhaps the last time Manhattan real estate could be called cheap).

Established as a trading post in 1624, Nieuw Amsterdam was always run as a business. To attract new settlers, the Dutch offered land inducements to merchants willing to stay. As the population increased, outposts were established in Staten Island, Queens, and the Bronx. The town earned an early reputation for dissipation that it's never quite shaken—liquor stores lined the streets, much to the chagrin of Governor Peter Stuyvesant, and drunkenness was rampant.

Though thoroughly autocratic, Stuyvesant was well regarded. Under his administration Nieuw Amsterdam got its first city hall (a converted tavern), a city government, ferry service, and a police department. A fortified wall was built along what is now Wall Street to keep out the Indians and the British.

When British troops attacked in 1664, however, Stuyvesant was in no position to fight—so Nieuw Amsterdam became New York. Though it was recaptured by the Dutch in 1673 and held for over a year, it was returned to the British in exchange for Java, which was considered a more valuable asset.

New York saw its first civil liberties battle in 1734, when John Peter Zenger, editor of the *New York Weekly Journal*, was prosecuted for libel for articles he had written criticizing British rule. Public opinion led to his acquittal, and freedom of the press was born.

During most of the American Revolution, the British were headquartered in New York, but a victorious George Washington rode into town to cheering crowds. At Fraunces Tavern, still a New York landmark, he bade farewell to his troops "with a heart full of love and gratitude." For a time, New York was the capital of the new United States—George Washington was inaugurated at Federal Hall.

The City Planning Commission, organized in 1811, designed Manhattan's present-day grid system of streets; and in 1815, a Board of Health was established in further anticipation of the needs of a burgeoning city. New York boomed after 1812, largely due to the opening of the Erie Canal, which gave the city a virtual monopoly on transportation to the west. In 1858, Frederick Law Olmsted, a landscape designer, and Calvert Vaux, an architect, won the

DATELINE

- **1625** Nieuw Amsterdam becomes the first permanent settlement in lower Manhattan.
- **1626** Peter Minuit appointed governor of Nieuw Amsterdam; he purchases Manhattan Island from the Indians for $24.
- **1630–1639** Staten Island purchased from the Indians; Brooklyn and the Bronx settled.
- **1647** Peter Stuyvesant becomes governor.
- **1652** A fortified wall to keep out the British replaces the old fence on Wall Street.
- **1664** British invade Nieuw Amsterdam and rename it New York.
- **1667** British and Dutch sign Treaty of Breda, giving New York to Britain.
- **1709** The Wall Street Slave Market opens for business.
- **1710** Population nears 30,000.
- **1713** Ferry service started between New York and Staten Island.
- **1725** The *New*
(continues)

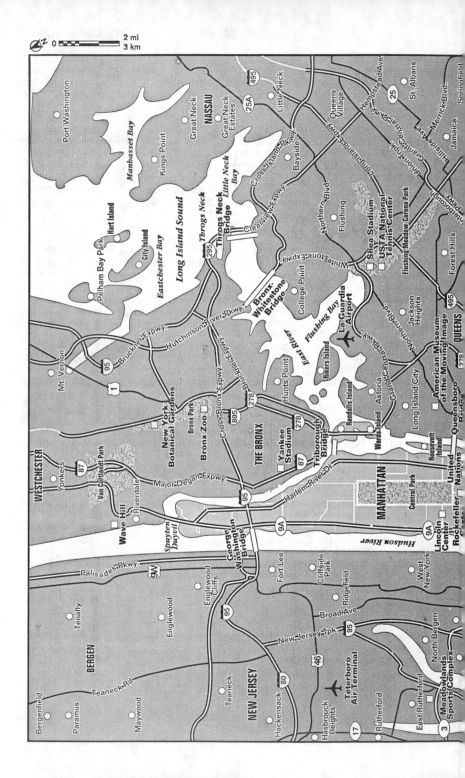

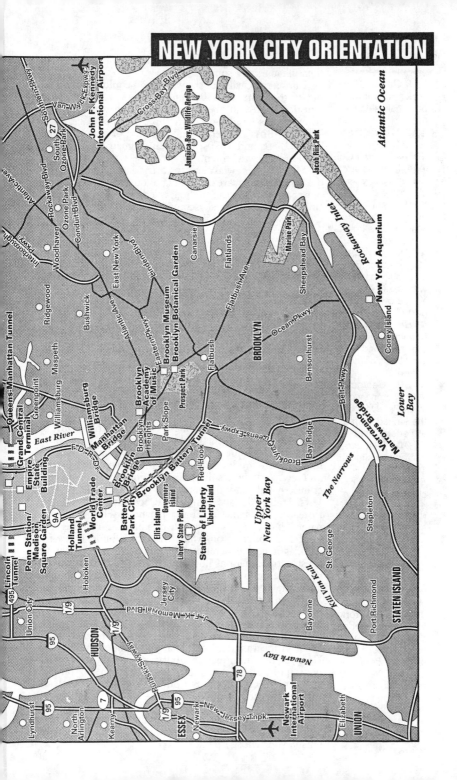

NEW YORK CITY ORIENTATION

York Gazette, New York's first newspaper, makes its debut.

• **1732** First theater is built.

• **1754** King's College, later Columbia University, is chartered.

• **1761** Oil lamps hung on posts are Manhattan's first street lights.

• **1774** Townspeople turn back English ship loaded with tea in New York's own "tea party."

• **1784** New York becomes capital of the state, and, a year later, of the nation.

• **1789** George Washington sworn in as President of the United States at Federal Hall.

• **1790** First census counts almost 100,000.

• **1791** Stock Exchange started.

• **1797** Capital of New York moved to Albany.

• **1811** City Planning Commission designs the city's present-day grid layout of streets and avenues.

• **1831** New York University founded.

• **1848–1850** A huge influx of immigrants from Ireland and Germany raises New York's population to 696,115.

• **1851** The *New*
(continues)

competition to design Central Park out of a swampland then inhabited by squatters.

During the Civil War the well-to-do could buy their way out of the draft for $300, and the poor, resentful of the injustice, rioted in the streets. After the war, economic recovery was rapid, and corruption commonplace. Under William "Boss" Tweed's administration of Tammany Hall in the 1860s and 1870s, it's been estimated that perhaps $200 million was stolen.

Millions of new Americans arrived at Ellis Island, and the tremendous waves of immigration produced the manpower for building the city's elevated railway, the Brooklyn Bridge, and the first skyscrapers. In 1898, Brooklyn and Queens were annexed into Greater New York.

The twentieth century has seen stupendous expansion in New York only temporarily interrupted by economic depressions and two world wars. After the debacle of the Tammany Hall political regime, Mayor Fiorello La Guardia restored color, character, and optimism to an office lacking all three. La Guardia saw his city through the Depression years, creating jobs, improving buildings and parks, and securing federal aid for the poor. In 1952, the United Nations moved to Manhattan, making New York a political sounding board for the world.

2. CULTURAL & SOCIAL LIFE

New York vies with Mexico City and Tokyo for the distinction of being the world's most populous city. Some 7½ million people live within the city limits, and 5½ million more are located in the surrounding suburbs.

New York prides itself on its polyglot mix. It is an ethnic, racial, and religious smorgasbord. Italians, Irish, Jews, Arabs, Haitians, Hungarians, Scandinavians, Chinese, Koreans, Vietnamese, Thais, Japanese, Hispanics—you name it, New York's got it. The rich blend of cultures is the solid underpinning on which the city is built. Every few decades a new generation of immigrants emerges as the latest entrepreneurial hotshots. Everyone gets a turn and the city respects, even salutes, the hard workers who make it to the top. New York is the personification of the American Dream. Just looking at any list of who's who in the city clearly confirms that the strength of New York lies in the sons and daughters of its immigrants.

New Yorkers have also always prided themselves on being in the vanguard of social and political movements. Here you find headquarters for various civil rights organizations; political organizations from far right to far left; sexual rights organizations, both gay and heterosexual; and women's organizations.

New York offers groups for whatever your interest, problem, or cause may be. And the "live and let live" attitude of most residents guarantees you freedom to pursue your chosen path.

No other American city, with the possible exception of Washington, D.C., has the importance of New York. The city is the center of America's communications industry and the advertising and public relations world. The offices of the major fashion houses and magazines are located here, as is virtually the entire book-publishing industry. New York is the home base of America's commercial theater, the nation's major opera company, and key art galleries and museums. Many of the country's major industrial concerns maintain headquarters in the skyscrapers of Manhattan. The city is so full of celebrated public figures and important cultural, political, and economic events that most New Yorkers remain blasé and unconcerned about things that would dazzle and excite the residents of almost any other town. We admit, of course, the many flaws and inconveniences of New York, but as you can see, we love our city and grow more aware of its endless opportunities and gifts with every passing day.

Tourists may not be tempted to savor all the unusual neighborhood areas of New York, but to us there is nothing more interesting than the people who live here. Everyone knows us for our culture, but the huge ethnic population is what makes this city great. We will give you a rundown on these neighborhoods in Chapter 4. Visit them and meet real New Yorkers. New Yorkers are friendly, open people, and they are proud of their city.

3. RECOMMENDED BOOKS & FILMS

BOOKS

GENERAL

Cudahy, Brian J., *Over and Back* (Fordham University Press, 1989).

Dolkart, Andrew S., *The Texture of Tribeca* (TriBeCa Community Association, 1989).

Dunlap, David W., *On Broadway* (Rizzoli International, 1990).

Furia, Philip, *The Poets of Tin Pan Alley* (Oxford University Press, 1990).

Kinkead, Eugene, *Central Park: The Birth, Decline, and Renewal of a National Treasure* (Norton, 1990).

Kisseloff, Jeff, *You Must Remember This* (Schocken Books, 1989).

Miller, Terry, *Greenwich Village and How It Got That Way* (Crown Publishers, 1990).

Morris, Jan, *Manhattan '45* (Oxford University Press, 1987).

Schermerhorn, Gene, *Letters to Phil* (New York Bound, 1982).

Snyder, Robert, *The Voice of the City: Vaudeville and*

DATELINE

York Times is founded.

• **1858** Frederick Law Olmsted and Calvert Vaux win competition to design Central Park.

• **1863** Draft riots against law allowing the rich to avoid conscription during the Civil War by paying $300.

• **1880** Grand opening of the Metropolitan Museum of Art.

• **1882** Power plant built by Thomas Edison provides city with electricity.

• **1883** Brooklyn Bridge opens to traffic.

• **1885** United States receives Statue of Liberty as a gift from France.

• **1890** Population reaches 1,441,216.

• **1891** Tchaikovsky conducts opening concert at newly completed Carnegie Hall.

• **1892** Immigration center established on Ellis Island.

• **1898** Greater New York formed by incorporation of all five boroughs.

• **1899** Bronx Zoo opens.

• **1900** Construction of subways begins.

• **1901** Macy's department store opens for business.

• **1911** New York
(continues)

Popular Culture in New York (Oxford University Press, 1989).

Trager, James, *Park Avenue: Street of Dreams* (Atheneum Publishers, 1989).

Trager, James, *West of Fifth: The Rise and Fall of Manhattan's West Side* (Atheneum Publishers, 1987).

ECONOMIC, POLITICAL & SOCIAL HISTORY

Allen, Oliver E., *New York, New York: A History of the World's Most Exhilarating & Challenging City* (Macmillan, 1990).

Asbury, Herbert, *The Gangs of New York* (Capricorn Books, 1989).

Baldwin, James, *Notes of a Native Son* (Beacon Press, 1990).

Blackmar, Elizabeth, *Manhattan for Rent, Seventeen Eighty-five to Eighteen Fifty* (Cornell University Press, 1988).

Brandt, Nat, *The Man Who Tried to Burn New York* (Syracuse University Press, 1986).

Cohen, B., Heller, S., and Chwast, S., *New York Observed* (Harry N. Abrams, 1987).

Gambee, Robert, *Wall Street Christmas* (Norton, 1990).

Jacobs, William Jay, *Ellis Island* (Macmillan, 1990).

Kazin, Alfred, *Our New York* (Harper & Row Publishers, 1989).

Kessner, Thomas, *Fiorello H. La Guardia and the Making of Modern New York* (McGraw-Hill Publishing Co., 1989).

Kotker, Norman, *Ellis Island* (Macmillan, 1990).

MacKay, Ernst A., *The Civil War & New York City* (Syracuse University Press, 1990).

Marshall, Richard, *Fifty New York Artists: A Critical Selection of Painters & Sculptors Working in New York* (Chronicle Books, 1986).

Patterson, Jerry E., *The Vanderbilts* (Harry N. Abrams, 1989).

Rink, Oliver A., *Holland on the Hudson* (New York State Historical Association, 1986).

Plunz, Richard A., *A History of Housing in New York City* (Columbia University Press, 1990).

Sharp, Robert M., *The Love and Legends of Wall Street* (Down Jones-Irwin, 1989).

Whitman, Walt, *Walt Whitman's New York* (Macmillan, 1963).

ARCHITECTURE & THE ARTS

Bogart, Michele H., *Public Sculpture and the Civic Ideal in New York City 1890–1989* (University of Chicago Press, 1989).

Boyer, M. Christine, *Manhattan Manners: Architecture & Style 1850–1900* (Rizzoli International, 1985).

Goldberg, Paul, *Skyscraper* (Knopf, 1981).

Lieberman, Nathaniel, *Manhattan Lightscape* (Abbeville Press, 1990).
Mackay, Donald A., *The Building of Manhattan: How Manhattan Was Built Overground & Underground, from the Dutch Settlers to the Skyscrapers* (Harper & Row Publishers, 1987).
Orkin, Ruth, *More Pictures From My Window* (Rizzoli International, 1985).
Rajs, Jake, *Manhattan: An Island in Focus* (Rizzoli International, 1985).
Rosen, Laura, *Top of the City: New York's Hidden Rooftop World* (Thames & Hudson, 1990).
Silver, Nathan, *Lost New York* (American Legacy, 1982).
Stern, Robert A. M., Gilmartin, Gregory, and Massengale, John M. *New York 1900: Metropolitan Architecture and Urbanism 1890–1915* (Rizzoli International, 1983).
Valenzi, Kathleen D., ed., *Private Moments: Images of Manhattan* (Howell Press, 1989).
Watson, Edward B., *New York Then & Now: Eighty-three Manhattan Sites Photographed in the Past & Present* (Dover Publications, 1976).
Willensky, Elliot, and White, Norval, *AIA Guide to New York City* (Harcourt Brace Jovanovich, 1989).

FICTION FOR ADULTS

Cooper, James F., *The Last of the Mohicans* (State University of New York Press, 1983).
Finney, Jack, *Time and Again* (Simon & Schuster, 1986).
Fitzgerald, F. Scott, *The Great Gatsby* (Macmillan, 1981).
James, Henry, *Washington Square* (G. K. Hall & Co., 1980).
Liebling, A. J., *The Telephone Booth Indian* (North Point Press, 1990).
Powell, Dawn, *The Locusts Have No King* (Yarrow Press, 1989).
Wharton, Edith, *The Age of Innocence* (Macmillan, 1983).

FICTION FOR KIDS

Barracca, Sal, *The Adventures of Taxi Dog* (Halcyon Books, 1990).
Gangloff, Deborah, *Albert and Victoria* (Crown Publishers, 1989).
Macaulay, David, *Underground* (Houghton Mifflin Co., 1976).
Selden, George, *The Cricket in Times Square* (Dell Publishing Co., 1970).
Swift, Hildegarde H., *The Little Red Lighthouse and the Great Gray Bridge* (Harcourt Brace Jovanovich, 1974).
Thomson, Kay, *Eloise* (Simon & Schuster, 1969).
Waber, Bernard, *Lyle, Lyle, Crocodile and the House on East 88th Street* (Houghton Mifflin Co., 1965).
White, E. B., *Stuart Little* (Harper & Row Publishers, 1973).

FILMS

Hundreds of movies have been made about New York and in New York—it's one of the most familiar movie sets in the world. Woody Allen's films, perhaps more than any

IMPRESSIONS

To Europe she was America, to America she was the gateway of the earth. But to tell the story of New York would be to write a social history of the world.
—H. G. WELLS, *THE WAR IN THE AIR*, 1908

To any person who desires such queer prizes, New York will bestow the gift of loneliness and the gift of privacy.
—E. B. WHITE, *HERE IS NEW YORK*, 1949

other, catch the humor and angst of current-day New Yorkers, especially *Annie Hall, Manhattan,* and *Hannah and Her Sisters.* Nobody tells about growing up in the city better than Neil Simon in *Brighton Beach Memoirs.* Italian family life in New York is portrayed in *Moonstruck; Godfather III, Prizzi's Honor,* and *Goodfellas* deal with the world of organized crime in New York. Several scenes in *Ghostbusters* were shot at Columbia University; *Ghost* took place in SoHo, Brooklyn, and downtown Manhattan. *Tootsie* deals with New York's television world. *Crossing Delancey* shuttles between the old-world Jewish culture of the Lower East Side and Manhattan's uptown literary set. Spike Lee portrays the seamy streets of Brooklyn in *Do the Right Thing,* and then there's the black comedy *After Hours.* Of course, there's the all-time New York classic, *Breakfast at Tiffany's.* And the list goes on.

PLANNING A TRIP TO NEW YORK CITY

This chapter is devoted to the when, where, and how of your trip—the advance-planning details of getting it together and taking it on the road.

After deciding where to go, most travelers have two fundamental questions: What will it cost? and How do I get there? This chapter will answer both of those questions and resolve other important issues, such as when to go and where to obtain more information about New York.

1. INFORMATION & MONEY

SOURCES OF INFORMATION

Before you leave home, you can direct your questions about New York to the **New York Convention and Visitors Bureau,** 2 Columbus Circle, New York, NY 10023 (tel. 212/397-8222—and be patient). The bureau will provide a guide and map to New York in six languages, loads of brochures, guides to restaurants and stores in all boroughs, a list of free New York activities, bus maps, subway maps, tickets for TV shows, and twofers (two-for-the-price-of-one theater tickets), plus a complete listing of seasonal attractions. For a recorded message about current free events in New York, call 360-1333.

A good travel agent can also be a source of information. Make sure your agent is a member of the American Society of Travel Agents (ASTA).

WHAT THINGS COST IN NEW YORK CITY	U.S. $
Taxi from LaGuardia Airport to Manhattan	25–30
Bus from LaGuardia Airport to Manhattan	8.50
Local telephone call	25¢
Double at the Days Inn–New York (expensive)	114–164
Double at the Hotel Wentworth (moderate)	80–85
Double at West Side YMCA (budget)	45–55
Dinner without wine at Capsouto Freres (expensive)	14–24
Dinner without wine at All State Café (moderate)	8.95–14.95
Dinner without drinks at Happy Burgers (budget)	5–7.95
Beer at a bar or restaurant	2.50–4.50
Soda	75¢–1.50
Cup of coffee	45¢–85¢

	US$
Roll of ASA 100 Kodacolor film, 36 exposures	5.75
Suggested admission to the Metropolitan Museum of Art	6
Movie ticket	7.50
Broadway theater ticket	30–65

2. WHEN TO GO — CLIMATE & EVENTS

THE CLIMATE

An old saying about New England's weather holds true for New York's as well: If you don't like the weather, just wait a few minutes and it'll change. To be prepared for any contingency, always check the forecast in the morning. Phone 976-1212 for up-to-the-hour forecasts.

New York's temperature swings from the low average of 32° Fahrenheit in January to a high of 86° Fahrenheit in July. However, those are just averages; any New Yorker will tell you that it gets much warmer and colder than that.

Average Monthly Temperatures (in degrees Fahrenheit)

Jan	Feb	Mar	Apr	May	June	July	Aug	Sept	Oct	Nov	Dec
38	40	48	61	71	80	85	84	77	67	54	42

NEW YORK CITY CALENDAR OF EVENTS

These New York celebrations can be one of the highlights of a visit. The dates vary, so call or write ahead for details to the New York Convention and Visitors Bureau, 2 Columbus Circle at West 59th Street, New York, NY 10023 (tel. 397-8222).

JANUARY–FEBRUARY

☐ **Winter Antiques Show,** at the Seventh Regiment Armory, Park Avenue at 67th Street.
☐ **Chinese New Year** celebrations in Chinatown, on the first full moon after January 21.

MARCH

☐ **New York Flower Show,** Pier 92, 51st Street and Twelfth Avenue.
☐ **St. Patrick's Day Parade** on Fifth Avenue, when the whole city becomes Irish for a day.
☐ **Easter Parade,** Fifth Avenue, in front of St. Patrick's Cathedral, Fifth Avenue at

50th Street, on Easter Sunday, late morning. Wear your finest spring outfit and join in.

APRIL

✪ *OPENING DAY FOR THE NEW YORK METS AND NEW YORK YANKEES* *A grand old tradition lives on—there are few things more satisfying on a spring day than to munch on a hot dog in the House That Ruth Built. Hope springs eternal every spring.*
    Where: *Shea Stadium and Yankee Stadium.* ***How:*** *Buy tickets at the stadium, or play it safe and reserve tickets through Ticketmaster (tel. 307-7171).*

MAY

☐ **Ukrainian Festival,** 7th Street between Second and Third avenues.
☐ **Ninth Avenue International Festival,** 37th to 57th streets on Ninth Avenue, featuring food, music, and crafts.

JUNE

☐ **Belmont Stakes,** Belmont Racetrack.
☐ **Gay Pride Parade,** Fifth Avenue.

✪ *SHAKESPEARE IN THE PARK* *The best free theater offerings you've ever dreamed of seeing begin every June and run through September. Big names like Morgan Freeman, Raul Julia, and Christopher Walken have brought the Bard's works to life in Joseph Papp's annual gift to the city.*
    Where: *The Delacorte Theatre in Central Park.* ***When:*** *Tuesday through Sunday evenings.* ***How:*** *Line up at the Delacorte early in the afternoon to claim a voucher for the tickets, which are given out at 6:15pm.*

☐ **JVC Jazz Festival,** at various locations.

JULY–AUGUST

☐ **Macy's Fireworks Celebrations,** over the East River. July 4.
☐ **New York Philharmonic Free Parks Concerts,** all five boroughs.
☐ **Mostly Mozart Festival,** Lincoln Center.

SEPTEMBER

☐ **U.S. Open Tennis Championships,** Flushing Meadows, Queens.
☐ **Feast of San Gennaro,** Little Italy.

OCTOBER

☐ **Halloween Parade** in Greenwich Village.

NOVEMBER

✪ *RADIO CITY MUSIC HALL CHRISTMAS SPECTACULAR* *An extravaganza complete with Rockettes and Santa. A must for the kids.*
    Where: *Radio City Music Hall, Sixth Avenue and 50th Street.* ***When:***

November through early January. **How:** *Call 757-3100 for tickets and information.*

- ☐ **New York City Marathon.**
- ☐ **Christmas window displays** go up in all the major department stores.

○ **MACY'S THANKSGIVING DAY PARADE** *Nowadays the giant balloons floating by are just as likely to be Bart Simpson or Garfield the Cat as Rocky and Bullwinkle, but the magic is still the same.*
  Where: *Central Park West and Broadway.* **When:** *Thanksgiving morning.* **How:** *Push and shove for space on the sidewalk with everyone else.*

DECEMBER

- ☐ **Lighting of the giant Rockefeller Center Christmas tree.**
- ☐ **New Year's Eve celebrations,** with the lighted ball atop Times Square marking the stroke of midnight and First Night celebrations with music and performances in and around Grand Central Station. December 31.

3. WHAT TO PACK

The most important thing to bring is a comfortable pair of shoes—you're going to be doing plenty of walking.

In winter, dress in layers. Not only will you be warmer, but you'll be able to take off layers when you go inside the frequently overheated restaurants and museums. A comfortable pair of warm, winter boots are essential if you want to take any winter walks, as are a hat, scarf, coat, and gloves.

Summer in New York can be downright blistering. Be sure to bring plenty of lightweight clothing, along with a light sweater or jacket, since many restaurants and theaters keep a heavy hand on the air-conditioning switch.

If you dress for moderate weather in the spring and fall, you can't go wrong. And bring an umbrella in all seasons!

4. TIPS FOR THE DISABLED, SENIORS, SINGLES, FAMILIES & STUDENTS

FOR THE DISABLED

All public buildings and many hotels and restaurants are wheelchair accessible. Most buses in the public transportation system are also wheelchair accessible. There is no wheelchair accessibility to the subways and few subway stations have escalators; using the subways usually means a good deal of stair climbing. Services and programs are available through the **New York Association for the Blind,** 111 East 59th St., New York, NY 10021 (tel. 355-2200); **Deafness Information and Referral Service,** 30th Avenue and 75th Street, Jackson Heights, NY 11730 (tel. 899-8800); and the **Mayor's Office for the Handicapped** (tel. 566-3913).

FOR SENIORS

Members of the **American Association of Retired Persons (AARP),** 1909 K Street NW, Washington, DC 20049 (tel. 202/872-4700), are often eligible for discounts at hotels and sightseeing attractions. Seniors with Medicare cards can ride the buses or subways for half fare.

For $1 you can get a booklet entitled *Travel Tips for Senior Citizens* (No. 8870), published by the Superintendent of Documents, U.S. Government Printing Office, Washington, DC 20402 (tel. 202/783-5238). Another useful publication is *101 Tips for the Mature Traveler*, distributed by Grand Circle Travel, 347 Congress St., Suite 3A, Boston, MA 02210 (tel. 617/350-7500 or toll free 800/221-2610).

Information on senior travel is also available from the **National Council of Senior Citizens,** 1331 F Street NW, Washington, DC 20004 (tel. 202/347-8800).

FOR SINGLE TRAVELERS

Unfortunately, the travel industry is geared to twosomes, and singles may wind up feeling out in the cold when it comes to hotel bills. **Travel Companion,** P.O. Box P-833, Amityville, NY 11701 (tel. 516/454-0880), tries to match single travelers with compatible companions. For $36 to $66, you'll get a six-month listing of potential companions of either sex.

FOR FAMILIES

New York is loaded with attractions for kids—this is one place where you'll never hear "But, Mom, there's nothing to *do*." Just be sure to sit your kids down and explain that since New York is a big city, they've got to be alert and stay close to you. If you live in a small town, your kids may not have ever seen the kind of poverty they're going to encounter in New York, so you may want to prepare them for the people living or begging on the streets.

Children under 17 can usually stay in their parents' hotel room for free; if you're traveling with two or three children, you may want to check out prices for a suite.

We've listed baby-sitting services in the "Fast Facts" section found in Chapter 4. There are special recommendations for kids in the hotel and restaurant chapters that follow, and we've put together a special section on sightseeing and entertainment called "Cool for Kids." If you need even more guidance, Frommer's also offers a special guide called *The Candy Apple: New York with Kids*.

FOR STUDENTS

Students can take advantage of cheap lodging in New York's hostels by joining the **International Youth Hostel Federation (IYHF);** contact American Youth Hostels, P.O. Box 37613, Washington, DC 20013-7613 (tel. 202/783-6161). Carry a valid student ID with you at all times; you'll often be eligible for discounts on theater and concert tickets and admission to museums.

5. GETTING THERE

BY PLANE

Almost every major international airline flies into New York (international flights usually arrive at Kennedy). Domestic carriers serving New York include **America West** (tel. toll free 800/247-5692), **American** (tel. toll free 800/433-7300), **Continental** (tel. toll free 800/525-0280), **Delta** (tel. toll free 800/221-1212), **Northwest** (tel. toll free 800/225-2525), **TWA** (tel. toll free 800/221-2000), **United** (tel. toll free 800/241-6822), and **USAir** (tel. toll free 800/428-4322). See Chapter 4, "Getting to Know New York City," for information on the airports.

In general, the lowest fares are **APEX** fares, which may have restrictions, such as a 21-day advance purchase or a Saturday-night stay requirement. APEX fares are usually nonrefundable. If you can live with these restrictions, the savings are considerable.

Keep an eye out in the travel section of your local newspaper for promotional rates. Airlines engage in cutthroat competition, and any promotional fare announced by one will probably be quickly matched by its competitors.

For really rock-bottom fares, try flying standby, hoping that a seat will become available at the last minute. **Travel Avenue,** 641 W. Lake St., Suite 201, Chicago, IL 60606 (tel. toll free 800/333-3335), also offers deeply discounted fares.

BY TRAIN

Amtrak (tel. toll free 800/USA-RAIL) has frequent service to New York. If you're coming from Washington, for example, the trip will take about 3½ hours, and will cost you around $89 round trip. From Boston, the fare is usually $77 round trip and travel time is about 4½ hours. For information on arriving in Penn Station or Grand Central Terminal, see Chapter 4, "Getting to Know New York City."

BY BUS

If you've got the time, traveling by bus will be kind to your wallet. **Greyhound** (tel. 212/971-6363, or check your local listings) offers service to New York's Port Authority (see Chapter 4 for information on arriving). From Boston, round-trip fares may be less than $60, and the trip might take 4 to 5 hours; from Chicago round-trip fares are $230 and travel time is 16 to 24 hours.

BY CAR

From the south, the New Jersey Turnpike (I-95) leads to the Holland Tunnel, the Lincoln Tunnel, and the George Washington Bridge. From the north, the New York Thruway (Rtes. 287 and 87) leads to Manhattan's East and West Sides; the New England Thruway (I-95) leads via connecting roads to Manhattan and the other boroughs. From the west, the Bergen-Passaic Expressway (I-80) leads to Manhattan.

We don't recommend having a car in Manhattan. Parking on the street is a hassle, and if you bring a car radio into the city, you may not have it for long. Rates for garage parking, especially in hotels, are astronomical. Don't drive here if you can avoid it.

6. ENJOYING NEW YORK CITY ON A BUDGET

THE $70-A-DAY BUDGET

Our main goal is to show you how to enjoy New York without spending a fortune. To do that you have to begin with a moderate per-day cost of living. By living costs we refer to basic necessities: your hotel room and three meals. Obviously your transportation, sightseeing, and entertainment costs will all be in addition to this, but we will show you how to enjoy these and other activities with a reasonable expenditure of money.

Ⓕ FROMMER'S SMART TRAVELER: AIRFARES

1. Shop all the airlines that fly to New York.
2. Do your homework and be persistent—fares change daily (sometimes hourly), so if you keep calling, you won't necessarily have to pay the first amount you're quoted.
3. Ask if there's a lower fare if you travel on a weekday rather than on a weekend or holiday.
4. Remember that discounted fares may be available if you're able to purchase the ticket 21 days in advance.

Inflation, as we all know, has become a way of life across the nation, and New York City is no exception. Good values in hotels are, alas, becoming almost impossible to find. You can just about squeak by on food for $20 a day and, by traveling with a companion and sharing a double-occupancy room, spend $40 to $50 a day for your lodgings. For those of you with a little more to spend, we have included more expensive choices; your flexibility will make it a bit easier.

The $70-a-day standard won't bring you to a Hilton or a Plaza, but it will usually produce an adequate room, plus very good meals—and this we say without reservation—for our many small foreign restaurants especially offer what we consider gourmet-quality food.

By cataloging all the choices, *New York on $70 a Day* hopes to service the entire range of visitors and residents: from the extremely cost-conscious to those who have more to spend but want to get the best value for every penny.

SAVING MONEY ON ACCOMMODATIONS

1. Look for unconventional lodgings—from the city's bed-&-breakfast agencies to its hostels and Y's.
2. *Always ask* for weekend packages and other special discounts from your hotel when you make your reservation—there may be special rates available that weren't advertised.
3. Ask to see a cheap room before you commit to staying there. If you're disappointed, ask to see other units; sometimes they vary considerably in budget lodgings.
4. Ask to see if you qualify for any reduced rates if you belong to a special group—you may be eligible for corporate, military, or senior-citizen discounts.

SAVING MONEY ON MEALS

1. Check to see which restaurants have special early-bird dinners or fixed-price meals. Many establishments participate in "Tuesday Night Out," offering special discounts on this traditionally slow night.
2. If you have your heart set on dining in an expensive restaurant, have lunch there instead of dinner. The cuisine and ambience will be the same; the prices won't.
3. Watch those drink tabs—they'll get you every time.
4. This is your great opportunity to try new cuisines. New York is full of informal ethnic eateries offering gourmet-quality meals at reasonable prices.
5. Remember that New York's delis, street vendors, and pizza shops are lifesavers—the food's terrific, the prices are right, and the kids love 'em.
6. Stock up on snacks for your hotel room. A quick stop into the nearest supermarket can save you a call to room service or a trip to the high-priced 24-hour deli when you have the late-night munchies.

SAVING MONEY ON SIGHTSEEING & OTHER ENTERTAINMENT

1. Read the sightseeing chapter carefully and note any days with free or discounted admission when you're planning your itinerary.
2. Carry any student, senior-citizen, or military ID with you in case you qualify for reduced admission at museums or for cheap theater and concert tickets.
3. Take advantage of New York's wealth of free entertainment in the parks, museums, and public plazas.

SAVING MONEY ON SERVICES & OTHER TRANSACTIONS

1. Don't overtip—15% is standard for good service in restaurants (a good rule of thumb in New York is to double the tax on your bill). Here are some additional general rules for tipping: bellhops, 50¢ per bag; taxis, 15%, 50¢ minimum;

chambermaid, $1 to $1.50 per night (for double or single room); barbers and hairdressers, 15%; manicurists, $1. Naturally, if any of the above provide extra services, your tip should be increased accordingly. Do not tip hotel desk clerks, theater ushers, employees of cafés where a "No Tipping" sign is displayed, and subway or bus operators.

2. Your hotel might offer laundry and dry cleaning services, but that will usually cost you a fortune. Find the neighborhood Laundromat instead.

CHAPTER 3

FOR FOREIGN VISITORS

1. **PREPARING FOR YOUR TRIP**
2. **GETTING TO THE U.S.**
* **FAST FACTS: THE FOREIGN TRAVELER**

Although American fads and fashions have spread across Europe and other parts of the world so that America may seem like familiar territory before your arrival, there are still many peculiarities and uniquely American situations that any foreign visitor will encounter.

1. PREPARING FOR YOUR TRIP

ENTRY REQUIREMENTS

DOCUMENTS Canadian nationals need only proof of Canadian residence to visit the United States. Citizens of Great Britain and Japan need only a current passport. Citizens of other countries, including Australia and New Zealand, usually need two documents: a valid passport with an expiration date at least six months later than the scheduled end of their visit to the United States and a tourist visa available at no charge from a U.S. embassy or consulate.

To get a tourist or business visa to enter the United States, contact the nearest American embassy or consulate in your country; if there is none, you will have to apply in person in a country where there is a U.S. embassy or consulate. Present your passport, a passport-size photo of yourself, and a completed application, which is available through the embassy or consulate. You may be asked to provide information about how you plan to finance your trip or show a letter of invitation from a friend with whom you plan to stay. Those applying for a business visa may be asked to show evidence that they will not receive a salary in the United States. Be sure to check the length of stay on your visa; usually it is six months. If you want to stay longer, you may file for an extension with the Immigration and Naturalization Service once you are in the country. If permission to stay is granted, a new visa is not required unless you leave the United States and want to reenter.

MEDICAL REQUIREMENTS No inoculations are needed to enter the U.S. unless you are coming from, or have stopped over in, areas known to be suffering from epidemics, especially of cholera or yellow fever.

If you have a disease requiring treatment with medications containing narcotics or drugs requiring a syringe, carry a valid signed prescription from your physician to allay any suspicions that you are smuggling drugs.

CUSTOMS REQUIREMENTS Every adult visitor may bring in, free of duty: one liter of wine or hard liquor; 200 cigarettes or 100 cigars (but no cigars from Cuba) or three pounds of smoking tobacco; $400 worth of gifts. These exemptions are offered to travelers who spend at least 72 hours in the U.S. and who have not claimed them within the preceding six months. It is altogether forbidden to bring into the country foodstuffs (particularly cheese, fruit, cooked meats, and canned goods) and plants (vegetables, seeds, tropical plants, and so on). Foreign tourists may bring in or take out up to $10,000 in U.S. or foreign currency with no formalities; larger sums must be declared to Customs on entering or leaving.

INSURANCE

Unlike most European countries, there is no national health system in the United States. Because the cost of medical care is extremely high, we strongly advise every traveler to secure health coverage before setting out. Therefore, you may want to take out a comprehensive travel policy that covers (for a relatively low premium) sickness or injury cost (medical, surgical, and hospital); loss of, or theft of, your baggage; trip-cancellation costs; guarantee of bail in case you are sued; costs of accident, repatriation, or death. Such packages (for example, "Europe Assistance" in Europe) are sold by automobile clubs at attractive rates, as well as by insurance companies and travel agencies.

2. GETTING TO THE U.S.

Travelers from overseas can take advantage of the **APEX (Advance Purchase Excursion) fares** offered by all the major U.S. and European carriers. Aside from these, attractive values are offered by **Icelandair** on flights from Luxembourg to New York and by **Virgin Atlantic** from London to New York/Newark.

Some large American airlines (for example, TWA, American Airlines, Northwest, United, and Delta) offer travelers—on their transatlantic or transpacific flights—special discount tickets under the name **Visit USA,** allowing travel between any U.S. destinations at minimum rates. They are not on sale in the U.S., and must, therefore, be purchased before you leave your foreign point of departure. This system is the best, easiest, and fastest way to see the U.S. at low cost. You should obtain information well in advance from your travel agent or the office of the airline concerned, since the conditions attached to these discount tickets can be changed without advance notice.

The visitor arriving by air, no matter what the port of entry, should cultivate patience and resignation before setting foot on U.S. soil. Getting through immigration control may take as long as two hours on some days, especially summer weekends. Add the time it takes to clear Customs and you will see that you should make very generous allowance for delay in planning connections between international and domestic flights—an average of two to three hours at least.

In contrast, for the traveler arriving by car or by rail from Canada, the border-crossing formalities have been streamlined to the vanishing point. And for the traveler by air from Canada, Bermuda, and some points in the Caribbean, you can sometimes go through Customs and Immigration at the point of departure, which is much quicker and less painful.

For further information about travel to and arriving in New York see "Getting There" in Chapter 2, and "Arriving" in Chapter 4, Section 1.

FAST FACTS THE FOREIGN TRAVELER

Business Hours   Banks open weekdays from 9am to 3pm; although there's 24-hour access to the automatic tellers at most banks and other outlets. Generally, **offices** open weekdays from 9am to 5pm. **Stores** are open six days a week with many open on Sundays, too; department stores usually stay open until 9pm on Thursday.

Climate   See Chapter 2, Section 2.

Currency and Exchange   The U.S. monetary system has a decimal base: One American dollar ($1) = 100 cents (100¢).

Dollar bills commonly come in $1 ("a buck"), $5, $10, $20, $50, and $100 denominations (the last two are not welcome when paying for small purchases and are not accepted in taxis or at subway ticket booths).

There are six denominations of coins: 1¢ (one cent or "penny"); 5¢ (five cents or "nickel"); 10¢ (ten cents or "dime"); 25¢ (twenty-five cents or "quarter"). Two other coins do exist, but are almost never seen, the 50¢ piece (fifty cents or "half dollar"); and the rare—and prized by collectors—$1 piece (both the older, large silver dollars and the newer, small Susan B. Anthony coin).

Travelers checks denominated in dollars are accepted without demur at most hotels, motels, restaurants, and large stores. But as any experienced traveler knows, the best place to change traveler's checks is at a bank.

Credit cards are the method of payment most widely used: VISA (BarclayCard in Britain), MasterCard (EuroCard in Europe, Access in Britain, Diamond in Japan), American Express, Diners Club, Carte Blanche, and Discover. You can save yourself trouble by using "plastic money," rather than cash or traveler's checks, in 95% of all hotels, motels, restaurants, and retail stores. A credit card can also serve as a deposit for renting a car, as proof of identity (often carrying more weight than a passport), or as a "cash card," enabling you to draw money from banks that accept them.

For **currency exchange** in New York City, go to **Thomas Cook Currency Services** (formerly Deak International), which offers a wide variety of services, over 100 currencies, commission-free traveler's checks, drafts and wire transfers, check collections, and precious metal coins and bars. Rates are competitive and service excellent. They are located at the JFK Airport International Arrivals Building (tel. 718/656-8444), daily from 8am to 9:30pm; at Rockefeller Center at 630 Fifth Ave. (between 50th and 51st streets) (tel. 757-6915), Monday through Friday from 9am to 5pm, and on Saturday from 10am to 3pm; at Grand Central Terminal, 41 East 42nd St. (tel. 212/883-0400), Monday through Friday from 9am to 5pm, and on Saturday from 10am to 3pm; at Herald Center Shopping Mall at 1 Herald Square (between 33rd and 34th streets on Sixth Avenue) (tel. 736-9790), Monday through Friday from 9:30am to 5:30pm, and on Saturday from 10am to 3pm; and downtown at 29 Broadway (tel. 820-2470), Monday through Friday from 9am to 5pm.

Many midtown hotels will exchange currency if you are a registered guest.

Note: The "foreign-exchange bureaus" so common in Europe are rare even at airports in the U.S., and nonexistent outside major cities. Try to avoid having to change foreign money, or traveler's checks denominated other than in U.S. dollars, at a small-town bank, or even a branch in a big city; in fact, leave any currency other than U.S. dollars at home—it may prove more nuisance to you than it's worth.

Drinking Laws   See "Fast Facts: New York City" in Chapter 4.

Electric Current   The U.S. uses 110–120 volts, 60 cycles, compared to 220–240 volts, 50 cycles, as in most of Europe. Besides a 100-volt converter, small appliances of non-American manufacture, such as hairdryers or shavers, will require a plug adapter with two flat, parallel pins.

Embassies and Consulates   All embassies are located in the national capital, Washington, D.C.; some consulates are located in major cities, and most nations have a mission to the United Nations in New York City.

Listed here are the embassies and New York consulates of the major English-speaking countries—Australia, Canada, Ireland, New Zealand, and Britain. If you are from another country, you can get the telephone number of your embassy by calling "Information" in Washington, D.C. (tel. 202/555-1212).

The **Australian embassy** is at 1601 Massachusetts Ave. NW, Washington, DC 20036 (tel. 202/797-3000). The **consulate** is located at the International Building, 636 Fifth Ave., NY 10111 (tel. 212/245-4000).

The **Canadian embassy** is at 501 Pennsylvania Ave. NW, Washington, DC 20001 (tel. 202/682-1740). The **consulate** is located at 1251 Ave. of the Americas, NY 10020 (tel. 212/586-2400).

The **Irish embassy** is at 2234 Massachusetts Ave. NW, Washington, DC 20008 (tel. 202/462-3939). The **consulate** is located at 515 Madison Ave., NY 10022 (tel. 212/319-2555).

The **New Zealand embassy** is at 37 Observatory Circle NW, Washington, DC 20008 (tel. 202/328-4800). There is no consulate in New York.

The **British embassy** is at 3100 Massachusetts Ave. NW, Washington, DC 20008 (tel. 202/462-1340). The **consulate** is located at 845 Third Ave., NY 10022 (tel. 212/752-8400).

Emergencies Call **911** for fire, police, and ambulance. If you encounter such travelers' problems as sickness, accident, or lost or stolen baggage, call **Traveler's Aid,** an organization that specializes in helping distressed travelers, whether American or foreign. Call 944-0013 in Manhattan or 718/656-4870 at Kennedy International Airport. See Chapter 4, Section 1, for more details.

Holidays On the following legal national holidays, banks, government offices, post offices, and many stores, restaurants, and museums are closed: January 1 (New Year's Day), Third Monday in January (Martin Luther King Day), Third Monday in February (President's Day, Washington's Birthday), Last Monday in May (Memorial Day), July 4 (Independence Day), First Monday in September (Labor Day), Second Monday in October (Columbus Day), November 11 (Veteran's Day/Armistice Day), Last Thursday in November (Thanksgiving Day), and December 25 (Christmas Day).

The Tuesday following the first Monday in November is Election Day; it is a legal holiday in presidential-election years.

Information See Chapter 2, Section 1.

Legal Aid If you are stopped for a minor infraction (for example, of the highway code, such as speeding), never attempt to pay the fine directly to a police officer; you may be arrested on the much more serious charge of attempted bribery. Pay fines by mail, or directly into the hands of the clerk of the court. If accused of a more serious offense, it is wise to say and do nothing before consulting a lawyer. Under U.S. law, an arrested person is allowed one telephone call to a party of his choice. Call your embassy or consulate.

Mail If you aren't sure of your address, your mail can be sent to you, in your name, **c/o General Delivery** at the main post office at Eighth Avenue and 33rd Street. The addressee must pick it up in person, and must produce proof of identity (driver's license, credit card, passport, and so on).

Mailboxes are blue with a red-and-white logo, and carry the inscription "U.S. MAIL." A first-class **stamp** is 29¢.

Newspapers and Magazines see "Fast Facts: New York City" in Chapter 4.

Post Office The main Post Office is at Eighth Avenue and 33rd Street (tel. 212/967-8585).

Radio and Television There are dozens of radio stations (both AM and FM), each broadcasting talk shows, continuous news, or a particular kind of music—classical, country, jazz, pop, gospel—punctuated by frequent commercials. Television, with three coast-to-coast networks—ABC, CBS, and NBC—joined in recent years by the Public Broadcasting System (PBS) and a growing network of cable channels play a major part in American life. New York has 7 network and local channels transmitting 24 hours a day, plus a large number of cable channels and a few pay-TV channels showing recent movies or sports events.

Safety Whenever you're traveling in an unfamiliar city or country, stay alert. Be aware of your immediate surroundings. Wear a moneybelt and don't flash expensive jewelry and cameras in public. This will minimize the possibility of your becoming a crime victim. Be alert even in heavily touristed areas. New York City has a reputation for crime and you should observe proper precautions. Avoid Central Park and other deserted areas at night. If you ride the subway after midnight stand in the area of the platform marked for off-hours waiting. (Also see "Fast Facts: New York City" in Chapter 4.)

Taxes In the U.S. there is no VAT (Value-Added Tax) or other indirect tax at a national level. Every state, and each city in it, is allowed to levy its own local tax on all purchases, including hotel and restaurant checks, airline tickets, and so on. In New York City the sales tax rate is 8¼%.

Telephone, Telegraph, Telex, and Fax   Pay phones can be found on street corners, as well as in bars, restaurants, public buildings, stores, and service stations. Local calls cost 25¢.

For **long-distance** or **international calls,** stock up with a supply of quarters; the pay phone will instruct you when, and in what quantity, you should put them into the slot. For long-distance calls in the U.S., dial 1 followed by the area code and number you want. For direct overseas calls, first dial 011, followed by the country code (Australia, 61; Republic of Ireland, 353; New Zealand, 64; United Kingdom, 44; and so on), and then by the city code (for example, 71 or 81 for London, 21 for Birmingham) and the number of the person you wish to call.

Before calling from a hotel room, always ask the hotel phone operator if there are telephone surcharges. These are best avoided by using a public phone, calling collect, or using a telephone charge card.

For **reversed-charge** or **collect calls,** and for **person-to-person calls,** dial 0 (zero, not the letter "O") followed by the area code and number you want; an operator will then come on the line and you should specify that you are calling collect, or person-to-person, or both. If your operator-assisted call is international, ask for the overseas operator.

For local directory assistance ("Information"), dial 411; for long-distance information dial 1, then the appropriate area code and 555-1212.

Like the telephone system, **telegraph** and **telex** services are provided by private corporations like ITT, MCI, and above all, Western Union. You can bring your telegram to the nearest Western Union office (there are hundreds across the country), or dictate it over the phone (a toll-free call, 800/325-6000). You can also telegraph money, or have it telegraphed to you very quickly over the Western Union system.

Most hotels have **fax** machines available to their customers (ask if there is a charge to use it). You will also see signs for public faxes in the windows of small shops.

Time   The U.S. is divided into six time zones. From east to west, these are: Eastern Standard Time (EST), Central Standard Time (CST), Mountain Standard Time (MST), Pacific Standard Time (PST), Alaska Standard Time (AST), and Hawaii Standard Time (HST). Always keep the changing time zones in mind if you are traveling (or even telephoning) long distances in the U.S. For example, noon in New York City (EST) is 11am in Chicago (CST), 10am in Denver (MST), 9am in Los Angeles (PST), 8am in Anchorage (AST), and 7am in Honolulu (HST). When it is noon in London (GMT, or Greenwich Mean Time), it is 7am in New York.

Daylight Saving Time is in effect from 1am on the first Sunday in April until 2am on the last Sunday in October, except in Arizona, Hawaii, part of Indiana, and Puerto Rico.

Tipping   See Chapter 4, "Fast Facts: New York City."

Toilets   Often euphemistically referred to as rest rooms, public toilets are nonexistent on the streets of New York City. They can be found, though, in bars, restaurants, hotel lobbies, museums, department stores, and service stations—and will probably be clean (although ones in the last-mentioned sometimes leave much to be desired). Note, however, that some restaurants and bars display a notice that "Toilets are for use of patrons only." You can ignore this sign, or better yet, avoid arguments by paying for a cup of coffee or soft drink, which will qualify you as a patron. The cleanliness of toilets at railroad stations and bus depots may be questionable; some public places are equipped with pay toilets that require you to insert one or two dimes (10¢) or a quarter (25¢) into a slot on the door before it will open. In rest rooms with attendants, leaving at least a 25¢ tip is customary.

Yellow Pages   The local phone company provides two kinds of telephone directories. The general directory, called "White Pages," lists subscribers (business and personal residences) in alphabetical order.

The second directory, the "Yellow Pages," lists all local services, businesses, and industries by type, with an index at the back. The listings cover not only such obvious items as automobile repairs by make of car, or drugstores (pharmacies), often by geographical location, but also restaurants by type of cuisine and geographical location, bookstores by special subject and/or language, places of worship by religious denomination, and other information that the tourist might otherwise not readily find. The Yellow Pages also include city plans or detailed area maps, often showing postal ZIP Codes and public transportation.

THE AMERICAN SYSTEM OF MEASUREMENTS

Length

1 inch (in.)	=	2.54cm				
1 foot (ft.)	=	12 in.	=	30.48cm	=	.305m
1 yard	=	3 ft.	=	.915m		
1 mile (mi.)	=	5,280 ft.	=	1.609km		

To convert miles to kilometers, multiply the number of miles by 1.61 (for example, 50 mi. × 1.61 = 80.5km). Note that this conversion can be used to convert speeds from miles per hour (m.p.h.) to kilometers per hour (km/h).

To convert kilometers to miles, multiply the number of kilometers by .62 (example, 25km × .62 = 15.5 mi.). Note that this same conversion can be used to convert speeds from km/h to m/h.

Capacity

1 fluid ounce (fl. oz.)	=	.03 liter				
1 pint	=	16 fl. oz.	=	.47 liter		
1 quart	=	2 pints	=	.94 liter		
1 gallon (gal.)	=	4 quarts	=	3.79 liter	=	.83 Imperial gal.

To convert U.S. gallons to liters, multiply the number of gallons by 3.79 (example, 12 gal. × 3.79 = 45.48 liters).

To convert U.S. gallons to Imperial gallons, multiply the number of U.S. gallons by .83 (example, 12 U.S. gal. × .83 = 9.95 Imperial gal.).

To convert liters to U.S. gallons, multiply the number of liters by .26 (for example, 50 liters × .26 = 13 U.S. gal.).

To convert Imperial gallons to U.S. gallons, multiply the number of Imperial gal. by 1.2 (example, 8 Imperial gal. × 1.2 = 9.6 U.S. gal.).

Weight

1 ounce (oz.)	=	28.35 grams				
1 pound (lb.)	=	16 oz.	=	453.6 grams	=	.45 kilograms
1 ton	=	2,000 lb.	=	907 kg	=	.91 metric ton

To convert pounds to kilograms, multiply the number of pounds by .45 (example, 90 lb. × .45 = 40.5kg).

To convert kilograms to pounds, multiply the number of kilos by 2.2 (example, 75kg × 2.2 = 165 lb.).

Temperature

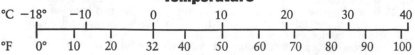

°C	−18°	−10	0	10	20	30	40
°F	0°	10 20	32 40	50	60 70	80	90 100

To convert degrees Fahrenheit to degrees Celsius, subtract 32 from °F, multiply then divide by 9 (example, 85°F − 32 × 5/9 = 29.4°C).

To convert degrees Celsius to degres Fahrenheit, multiply °C by 9, divide by 5, and add 32 (example, 20°C × 9/5 + 32 = 68°F).

CHAPTER 4

GETTING TO KNOW NEW YORK CITY

1. **ORIENTATION**
2. **GETTING AROUND**
- **FAST FACTS: NEW YORK CITY**
3. **NETWORKS & RESOURCES**

To the first-time visitor, New York can be overwhelming. But there is, believe it or not, a method to the madness. The city's layout is sensible and easy to grasp. If you take just a few minutes to figure out the lay of the land, you'll soon be able to negotiate your way around like a native.

1. ORIENTATION

ARRIVING

BY PLANE

New York is served by three major airports—John F. Kennedy International Airport, LaGuardia Airport, and Newark International Airport. Find your way to the Ground Transportation Center nearest your terminal; the personnel there will help you arrange transportation into the city.

Unfortunately, none of the airports is linked directly and easily to the city's public transportation network, but resist the urge to hop into a cab, as fares are beyond our budget (as much as $30 or $35 plus tunnel or bridge tolls from Newark). If you really must take a taxi, try to cut costs by sharing. Be sure that you have an authorized yellow cab, and that the meter starts running accurately after you get in. It's also a good idea to get a fare receipt (you have to ask for one) so you can track down the taxi if you leave behind any of your belongings. Any problems or complaints about taxi service or fares should be reported: call 869-4237.

Buses are a much better bet than taxis. **Carey Airport Express** (tel. 718/632-0500) is a reliable company, charging $8.50 from LaGuardia, $11 from Kennedy, with service into Manhattan every 20 to 30 minutes. You'll be dropped off at Grand Central Terminal or any one of several midtown hotels. From Newark, **Olympia Trails** (tel. 201/589-1188 or 212/964-6233) charges $7 for the ride to the downtown World Trade Center or to Grand Central. **New Jersey Transit** (tel. 201/589-1188) will take you to the West Side's Port Authority Terminal for $7.

Minibus service is available from all airports via **Gray Line Air Shuttle** (tel. 212/757-6840), with departure schedules varying according to passenger demand. Fares are $11 from LaGuardia, $14 from Kennedy, and $16 from Newark.

BY TRAIN

If you're taking the train, you'll arrive at **Grand Central Terminal,** on the East Side at Park Avenue and 42nd Street, or at **Penn Station,** on the West Side at 34th Street and Seventh Avenue. Both stations have taxi stands and easy connections with the subway system.

BY BUS

Bus travelers will arrive at New York's **Port Authority Terminal,** at Eighth Avenue and 42nd Street. The area around the terminal can be dangerous at night, so keep your wits about you. There's a taxi stand out front on Eighth Avenue, and the station is connected to several subway lines.

BY CAR

If you're driving into the city, our best advice is to find a reasonably priced place to park your car and keep it there. Street parking can be tough to find, and you may find yourself having to move your car for street cleaning every day or two.

Garages can be expensive, but one cheap alternative is **Auto Baby Sitters** in Brooklyn (tel. 718/493-9800). They will pick up your car from the city for $15 and store it for $50 a week or $85 a month (plus tax). They pick up and deliver to local airports as well.

TOURIST INFORMATION

Stop by the **New York Convention and Visitors Bureau** at 2 Columbus Circle (West 59th Street and Broadway), open from 9am to 6pm Monday through Friday. The staff is cooperative and knowledgeable, and there's a wealth of brochures and pamphlets and information on attractions and special events.

If you're a stranger in the city and in any kind of trouble, **Traveler's Aid** can help. They have three offices: 2 Lafayette St., near City Hall (tel. 577-7700); 158–160 W. 42nd St., near Broadway (tel. 944-0013); and at the International Arrivals Building at JFK Airport (tel. 718/656-4870).

We also suggest that you get a copy of the *New York Times, New York* magazine, or the *Village Voice*. All are packed with timely listings of what's going on in the city's cultural life.

CITY LAYOUT

NEIGHBORHOODS IN BRIEF

Lower Manhattan/Financial District This is where you'll find Wall Street along with some of Manhattan's most historic buildings and stunning architecture. Visit during the day when the financial markets are going full tilt; the area tends to be deserted at night.

TriBeCa The "*Triangle Below Canal Street*" has followed in SoHo's footsteps as a haven for artists and a trendy, revitalized neighborhood.

Lower East Side A stroll through the Lower East Side will take you back to the turn of the century—waves of immigrants who entered the United States at Ellis Island made their first homes here. Today an Orthodox Jewish population still thrives below Houston Street, but it shares the area with new immigrants from Latin America and Southeast Asia. Great budget shopping.

Chinatown For street shopping and divine dining, there's no place like Chinatown, loosely bounded by Canal Street to the north, Worth Street to the South, Broadway to the West, and Bowery to the East. It's a bustling hodgepodge of small streets lined with exotic shops and restaurants.

Little Italy Just north of Chinatown, centered on Mulberry Street, this is the ultimate ethnic neighborhood for locals and tourists alike. The area's Italian character is reflected in its many bakeries, sidewalk cafés, restaurants, and food shops.

SoHo/NoHo "*South of Houston Street*" is an area extending south from Houston to Canal Street between Broadway and the Avenue of the Americas. An industrial area in the 19th century, its old cast-iron factory and warehouse buildings now house influential art galleries, and an ever-increasing number of fashionable restaurants and shops. The best sightseeing streets are West Broadway, Greene Street, Prince Street, and Spring Street. "North of Houston" has developed just north of SoHo, mainly along Broadway and Lafayette Street between Houston and Eighth streets.

Greenwich Village This area, still remembered for the Bohemian life of the 1920s and 1930s, reflects the special diversity that is New York. The area is bounded north and south by 14th and Houston streets, and on the east and west, respectively, by Broadway and the West Side Highway. Centered on Washington Square Park and including New York University, it is both frenetic and serene, commercial and residential, the center of New York's gay community and home to world-famous jazz clubs. Between Seventh and Broadway you'll find Sheridan Square, honky-tonk West 4th and 8th streets, and the whirl of Washington Square Park. Farther west it still offers quiet, intimate streets lined with trees and town houses.

The park is the hub of the Village—especially on a sunny weekend or a warm summer night, when it's peopled by magicians, musicians, street artists, mothers and toddlers, men bent intently over chess boards, young people on roller blades, hustlers, and hundreds of spectators soaking up the scene.

East Village In the last few years the East Village and Alphabet City, farther east, have become a magnet for artists, musicians, and punk and avant-garde style in general. It's also the center of the city's Ukrainian community. In the 1960s St. Marks Place (an extension of 8th Street) became the center for New York's counterculture movement—the East Coast's Haight Ashbury. Since then, each new avant-garde crowd has paraded its style through the East Village's streets. Home to the New York Public Theater and other off-Broadway companies, it's also a great hunting ground for budget restaurants.

Chelsea An old residential area with the streets graced with brownstones, Chelsea has been transformed in the last two decades by trendy restaurants, theaters, and stores.

Penn Station/Herald Square/Garment District Penn Station (downstairs) and Madison Square Garden (upstairs), are located at West 34th Street between Seventh and Eighth avenues. A couple of blocks away is Macy's in Herald Square, at the junction of Sixth Avenue, Broadway, and 34th Street. And one block farther east on Fifth Avenue stands everyone's favorite skyscraper, the Empire State Building, with the Guinness World Records Exhibit Hall down in the concourse. The wholesale shops and racks of clothes being wheeled along the street in the West Thirties are a giveaway that you're in the Garment District, where a huge percentage of America's clothing is made and distributed.

Gramercy Park/Murray Hill These two East Side neighborhoods stretch from 15th Street to bustling Grand Central Terminal on 42nd Street, bounded by Park Avenue South. You'll find towering apartment complexes near the East River, and bucolic surprises like the Third Avenue Organic Garden—a community effort between 31st and 32nd streets complete with summertime scarecrows and zinnias. There are traces of very old New York—like Irving Place, where Washington Irving used to meet with a literary salon; the Players Club, founded by Edwin Booth, still stands in all its Gothic splendor at 16 Gramercy Park South. There are contrasts—exclusive Gramercy Park, and grimy commercial areas in the 20s between Madison and Third avenues. The Lexington Avenue section is home to many Indian and Pakistani restaurants and shops.

Midtown West/Times Square The area west of Fifth Avenue, north of 34th Street to Central Park, is Midtown West. The Times Square area, which occupies the blocks west of Broadway between 42nd Street to 49th Street, is, of course, home to New York's famed Broadway theater district. But it is also crammed with porno shows, pinball emporiums, pizza and souvlaki shops, and sleazy movie houses. The area is nothing if not colorful, but it can be dangerous, especially at night after the theater-going crowd has cleared off. Avoid 42nd Street between Seventh and Eighth avenues after dark, unless you're doing a sociological study on New York's lower depths. The area is undergoing redevelopment, but all you can see of that so far is an

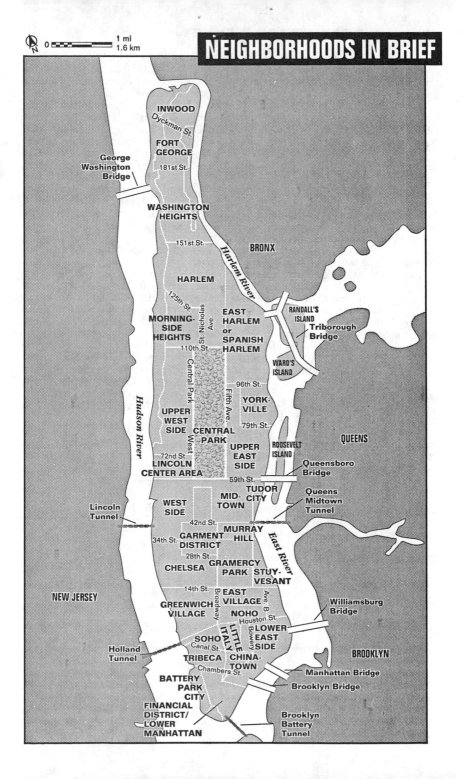

abundance of construction sites. You'll certainly see an array of human types—clergy and streetwalkers, performers, cops, supersalesmen, pimps, office workers, out-of-towners, photographers, and just plain New Yorkers. And then of course there are the lights and billboards—block for block more here than anywhere else in the world.

Midtown East   The area east of Fifth Avenue and north of 34th Street to Central Park is home to countless office buildings. Walk east on 42nd Street from Grand Central Terminal and you'll pass the Chrysler Building, the Daily News Building, the Ford Foundation, en route to the United Nations at the East River's edge. A stroll up Fifth Avenue will take you close to such world-famous landmarks as Rockefeller Center, St. Patrick's Cathedral, Tiffany's, Steuben Glass, F. A. O. Schwarz, Saks Fifth Avenue, Elizabeth Arden, and more.

Central Park   This huge leafy oasis runs from Fifth Avenue to Central Park West (continuation of Eighth Avenue) and from 59th to 110th streets—840 acres of boating, tennis, gardens, playgrounds, bridle paths, and statuary smack in the middle of some of the world's most expensive real estate. Do spend an afternoon in Central Park. You'll experience a microcosm of city life in the park, from English nannies and their charges and East Side types sunning themselves behind the Metropolitan Museum to the sounds of salsa, reggae, and rap.

Upper West Side   A former ethnic area full of mom-and-pop shops that's been yuppified. Some welcome the change; others deplore it. You'll find an exciting and energized neighborhood with a large student population and ethnically varied residents. Columbia University, at 116th Street between Broadway and Amsterdam Avenue, is the city's only Ivy League institution and wields considerable influence despite its distance from downtown Manhattan.

Upper East Side   East of Central Park over to East River, between 61st and 96th streets, this quiet and elegant section of the city is home to New York's "old money" as well as the many exclusive shops, art galleries, and fine antiques shops of Madison Avenue. "Museum Mile" along Fifth Avenue stretches from the Metropolitan Museum of Art at 82nd Street, to El Museo del Barrio at 104th Street. In the 80s along First and Second avenues is the area still known as Yorkville, where you'll find traces of old German New York.

Harlem   For many the name is synonymous with racial tension, but for those willing to explore, there's a wealth of black culture, history, architectural restoration, and musical heritage to be found north of 110th Street.

MAIN ARTERIES & STREETS

Laid out on a grid system, Manhattan is the easiest of the boroughs to negotiate. Avenues run north (uptown) and south (downtown), while the streets run east to west (crosstown) with Fifth Avenue as the East Side/West Side demarcation. Broadway runs north to south diagonally across the grid.

Both avenues and streets are numbered consecutively, streets from south to north (1st Street is downtown just above Houston street), and avenues from east to west, from First Avenue near the East River to Twelfth Avenue near the Hudson. The only exceptions are the three named avenues on the East Side: Madison, next to Fifth Avenue, Park, and Lexington. Sixth Avenue is also called the Avenue of the Americas; you will see both names in these pages.

IMPRESSIONS

New York is the greatest city in the world—especially for my people. Where else, in this grand and glorious land of ours, can I get on a subway, sit in any part of the train I please, get off at any station above 110th Street, and know I'll be welcome?
—DICK GREGORY, *FROM THE BACK OF THE BUS*, 1962

A few West Side avenues acquire names as they move uptown: Eighth Avenue becomes Central Park West above 59th Street, Ninth Avenue becomes Columbus Avenue above 69th Street, and Tenth Avenue becomes Amsterdam above 72nd Street.

This pattern changes in the older, downtown sections below 14th street on the West Side, and below Houston Street on the East Side. Downtown streets have names rather than numbers, and in the oldest sections, streets follow the outlines of original cowpaths and old village streets. They twist and turn in no defined fashion and give such neighborhoods as Greenwich Village, Chinatown, and the Wall Street area their particular charm, but they are not as easy to negotiate.

FINDING AN ADDRESS

To find the nearest cross street on an avenue address, drop the last digit of the number of the address and divide the remaining number by two. Then add or subtract the appropriate number from the list below.

For example, if you were trying to locate 645 Fifth Avenue, you would drop the 5, leaving 64. Then you would divide 64 by 2, leaving 32. According to the list below, you would then add 20. Thus 645 Fifth Avenue is at about 52nd Street.

Avenue A, B, C, or D	add 3
First Avenue	add 3
Second Avenue	add 3
Third Avenue	add 10
Fourth Avenue (Park Avenue South)	add 8
Fifth Avenue	
1 to 200	add 13
201 to 400	add 16
401 to 600	add 18
601 to 775	add 20
776 to 1286	cancel last figure and subtract 18
Sixth Avenue	subtract 12
Seventh Avenue below Central Park	add 12
Eighth Avenue below Central Park	add 10
Ninth Avenue	add 13
Tenth Avenue	add 14
Eleventh Avenue	add 15
Amsterdam Avenue (Tenth Avenue above 72nd Street)	add 60
Broadway	
1 to 754 below 8th Street	
754 to 858	subtract 29
858 to 958	subtract 25
Above 1000	subtract 31
Central Park West (Eighth Avenue above 59th Street)	divide number by 10 and add 60
Columbus Avenue (Ninth Avenue above 69th Street)	add 60
Lexington Avenue	add 22
Madison Avenue	add 26
Park Avenue	add 35
Riverside Drive	divide number by 10 and add 72
West End Avenue (Eleventh Avenue above 57th Street)	add 60

All east-west street addresses in New York are counted from Fifth Avenue and increase in number as they move away from Fifth Avenue. Thus the address 2 West 44th Street would denote a building on 44th Street just a few steps to the west of Fifth Avenue; 56 West 44th Street would indicate a building that is even farther west, and so on. The address 12 East 45th Street would denote a building just a little to the east of Fifth Avenue, while 324 East 45th Street would indicate a building on 45th Street that is way, way east of Fifth Avenue.

MAPS

We've included maps to make orienting yourself easier. For more detailed color maps, we recommend the *"I Love NYC" Travel Guide,* available free from the New York Convention and Visitors Bureau, 2 Columbus Circle, New York, NY 10019 and at Times Square on 42nd Street, between Broadway and Seventh Avenue. Or get (our favorite) the *Flashmaps Instant Guide to New York,* which has maps showing restaurant, theater, hotel, and museum locations, as well as subway and bus routes. Another popular map is *Hagstrom's Quick and Easy Metropolitan Area.*

2. GETTING AROUND

BY PUBLIC TRANSPORTATION

Visitors 65 years old and older can ride city transportation at half fare by showing a Medicare card or a half-fare card issued by the NYC Department for Aging. Call 577-0819 for details.

For information about the transit system, call 718/330-1234.

BY SUBWAY

Despite the noise and occasional discomfort, especially during the hottest days of summer, the quickest, cheapest, and most efficient way to move around the city is by subway. We recommend that every visitor ride the subway at least once: If you haven't ridden the subway you haven't seen New York.

Tokens cost $1.15 apiece, allow you to ride anywhere on the extensive system, and are obtained at token booths inside the stations. Purchase tokens with small bills; anything larger than a $20 bill will not be accepted.

To the stranger, the system might appear extremely complex and mysterious, so the first thing to do is to obtain a good map, available free at most token booths. Because it is complex, you may want to supplement it with a copy of the aforementioned *Flashmaps Instant Guide to New York,* which contains excellent maps not only of the subway system, but of everything in town. Almost every bookstore carries it, as do large newsstands.

A number of subway lines run through Manhattan. Once the subway was separated into several systems, but today there is only one metropolitan system. The lines are the Seventh Avenue/Broadway line (1, 2, 3, and 9 trains), the Eighth Avenue line (A, C, and E trains), the Sixth Avenue line (B, D, F, and Q trains), the BMT (formerly Brooklyn-Manhattan Transit, still known by its acronym; N, R, J, M, and Z trains), and the Lexington Avenue line (4, 5, and 6 trains). Three subway lines run crosstown: the Grand Central–Times Square shuttle, the Flushing line (7 train), and the Carnarsie–14th Street line (L train). Each train is clearly numbered or lettered, indicating its specific route.

There are many crossover points from line to line; these will be indicated on your subway map. Most lines, as they pass through midtown stop at roughly similar cross streets: for example, all lines stop at 59th, 50th/51st, 42nd, 33rd/34th, 23rd, and 14th streets on their respective avenues and routes.

The subway is not difficult to negotiate, and is a great time saver. Avoid the rush hours—8 to 9:30 am and 4:30 to 6pm. Pushing and shoving is the rule then—as is is most other times—but at rush hour there are at least 100 people per car pushing and shoving (feels more like a thousand).

To avoid waiting in line to buy tokens, purchase a ten-pack for $11.50. Tokens can also be used on the bus.

It is not a particularly good idea to ride very late at night. If you do, avoid empty cars, and on the station stand in the clearly designated waiting area. Transit policemen patrol the trains at all times, and the conductor rides in either one of the center cars in a tiny compartment. Some station entrances are closed and these are marked with a red light; open entrances are marked with a green light.

Do not hesitate to ask questions. Subway personnel (token sellers, conductors, transit police officers) are the best sources of information on exactly which train goes where—and how to negotiate the maze of underground passageways to find the train you're looking for, or to the exit to the street.

BY BUS

The bus is the most interesting way to travel and routes are not hard to understand. Free bus maps are available. Buses require exact change in coins; the driver does not make change or take bills. Subway tokens may also be used. Transfers are free.

NORTH OR SOUTH BUSES   Virtually every avenue in Manhattan has buses that go either up or down the entire length of that avenue, in one direction since most of the avenues have one-way traffic restrictions. Buses go north (uptown) only on First Avenue, Third Avenue, Park Avenue (to 40th Street only), Madison Avenue, Sixth Avenue (Avenue of the Americas), Eighth Avenue, and Tenth Avenue.

Buses go south (downtown) only on Second Avenue, Lexington Avenue, Fifth Avenue, Broadway (below 59th Street), Seventh Avenue (below 59th Street), and Ninth Avenue.

Along York Avenue, Riverside Drive, and Broadway and Central Park West above 59th Street, buses go in both directions (uptown and downtown).

East or West in Manhattan

There are also a number of crosstown buses that go east or west across the entire island. Buses go east on 8th Street, 50th Street, and 65th Street. (*Important note:* This last bus travels along 65th Street on the West Side of Manhattan; after it crosses Central Park to the East Side, it continues along 65th Street to Madison Avenue, turns north for 3 blocks and continues east.) Buses go west only on 9th Street, 49th Street, and 67th Street. (*Another important note:* This last bus travels along 67th Street on the East Side of Manhattan only; after it crosses Central Park to the West Side, it continues its westbound route on 66th Street.)

Buses go in both directions (east and west) on 14th Street, 23rd Street, 34th Street, 42nd Street, 57th Street, 59th Street, 79th Street, 86th Street, 96th Street, 116th Street, 125th Street, 145th Street, and 155th Street.

Free transfers can only be used where routes intersect (ask for your transfer when you pay your fare as bus drivers often get cranky if asked later). Senior citizens, those 65 and over, who are New York City residents pay half fare, except during rush hours.

BY TAXI

Obviously the most convenient way to travel around town is by cab, but it's not cheap. At press time, fares start at $1.50 the minute you step into a cab, and thereafter the charge is $1.25 for each additional mile, and an additional 20¢ for every minute of waiting time in traffic. The rider pays bridge, tunnel, and/or highway tolls. Also, as of this writing there is a 50¢ surcharge tacked on each fare from 8pm to 6am.

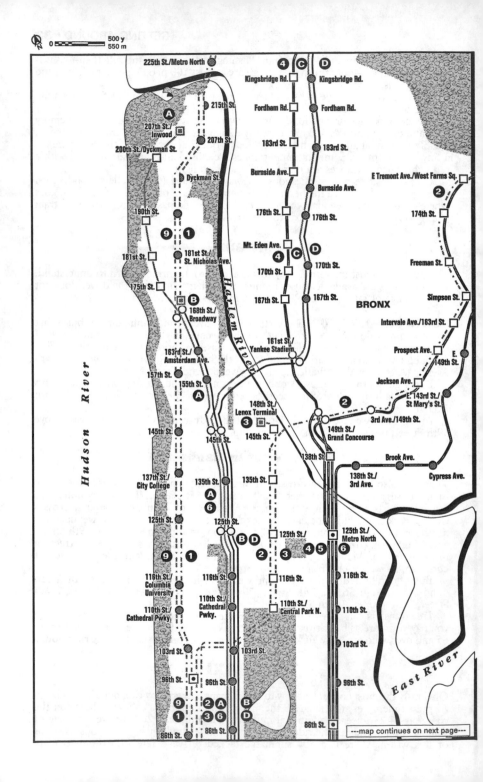

NEW YORK CITY SUBWAY SYSTEM

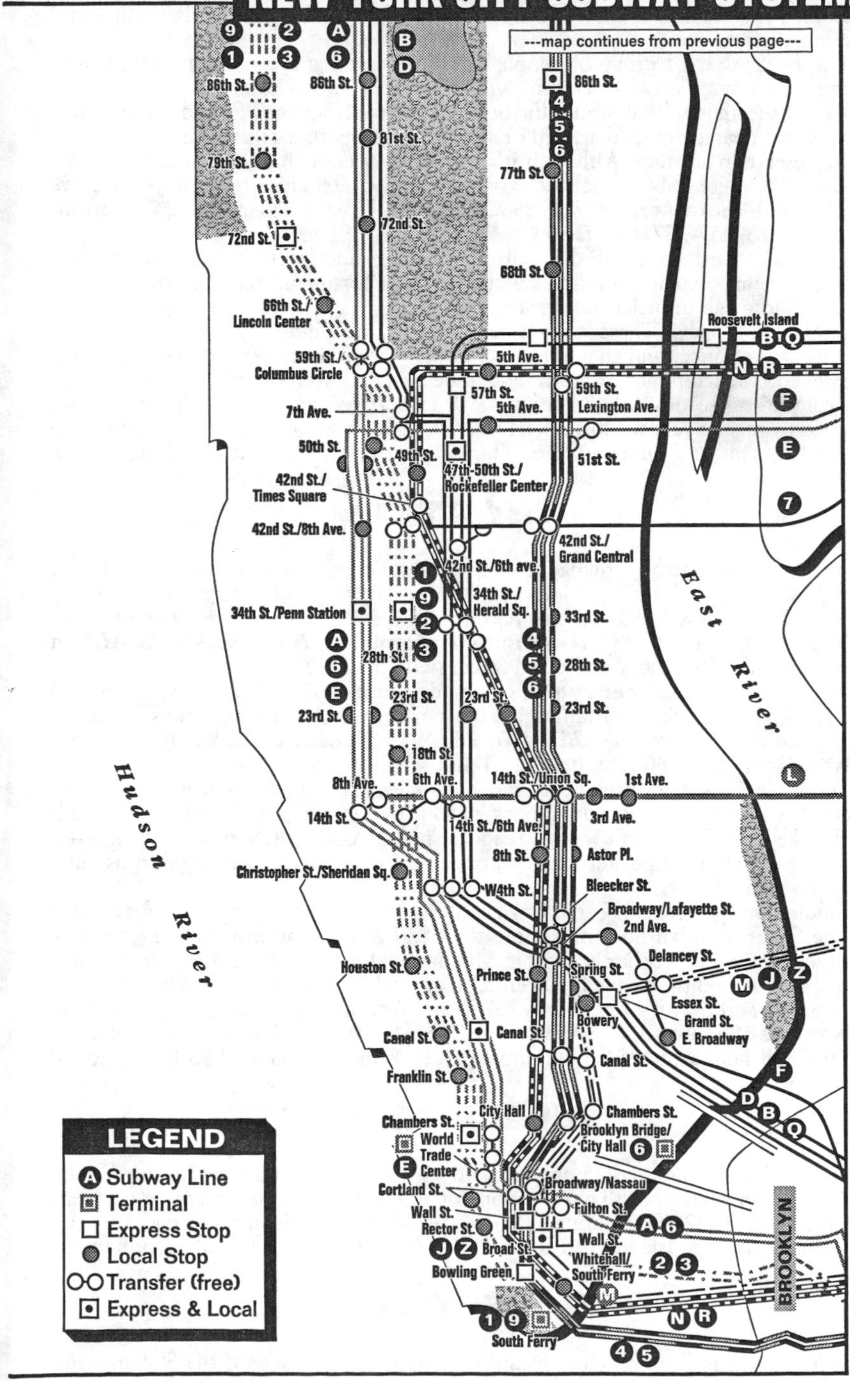

Of course you are also expected to tip, but don't let any driver intimidate you—give 15% on all fares.

On short rides, if a group of people hop a cab together it can often cost less than taking a subway. You can often find willing cab sharers at bus stops.

Check the Yellow Pages under the heading "Taxicab Service" for radio-dispatched cabs, which operate on regular meter rates, though sometimes there's an extra charge if you reserve in advance. Although it's usually easy enough to walk out and hail a passing cab, there may be occasions when you'd prefer door-to-door service. We usually call **MinuteMen** (tel. 718/899-5600, or toll free 800/345-6636), **Communicar** (tel. 718/457-7777), or **Bell Radio Taxi** (tel. 691-9191).

Cabs are hard to come by during morning and evening rush hours, and furthermore any trip at these times will cost you a fortune in waiting time. It's also hard to find a cab in inclement weather.

Avoid gypsy cabs. These cabs do not have a medallion on top, many have a battered appearance, and they offer somewhat questionable service—we ourselves have been taken for more than a ride. There are, however, some fine private-car services with radio-dispatched late-model sedans. If you find yourself in an area not serviced by regular yellow cabs, ask a local person for a recommendation or check the Yellow Pages under "Car Service" or "Taxis." Ask for the rate when booking service.

BY CAR

We do not recommend driving in Manhattan. Drivers are aggressive; streets are potholed, street parking nigh impossible, and garage parking expensive. Illegally parked cars are towed and you will have to pay a stiff fine to recover your vehicle.

The main office of the **American Automobile Association (AAA)** in Manhattan is at Broadway and 62nd Street (tel. 757-2000).

The major **national car rental** companies, such as Avis, Budget, National, and Hertz, all have branches in Manhattan, but be prepared for sky-high rates. Discount rentals are available from **AAM CAR,** 303 W. 96th St. (tel. 222-8500), and **USA Rent a Car,** 30 W. 60th St. (tel. 427-1800).

People in New York have been known to have fistfights over street-side parking places. If you're very lucky, you may catch someone leaving a spot; otherwise, you'll need to keep circling. Don't wait to see a car pulling out. Watch for telltale signs—a person reaching into a pocket for keys, opening a car door, or walking purposefully toward a vehicle.

Finding inexpensive garage parking is not easy either. The average price for a space can be $5 or more an hour and more than $20 a day. The **municipal garages** managed by the city are the cheapest in Manhattan. In the midtown area, for instance, there's one on Eighth Avenue between 53rd and 54th streets (tel. 997-8901). Parking costs $2.40 an hour; it's open daily 24 hours. Another municipal garage is on the **Lower East Side,** at 105–113 Essex St., near Delancey (tel. 475-9814). Parking is 50¢ per half hour with a $4 minimum between 7am and 7pm and $6 for 24 hours.

SUBURBAN TRANSIT

New York has excellent rail connections to its suburbs and other major cities in the Northeast. For Metro North information (for Westchester County and other northern suburbs), phone 532-4900; phone 718/454-5477 for Long Island Rail Road information (for all of Long Island); call toll free 800/USA-RAIL for Amtrak information.

BY FERRY/BOAT

New Yorkers who live on Staten Island commute to work aboard the Staten Island Ferry, and visitors should take the trip from the southern tip of Manhattan and back

IMPRESSIONS

What else can you expect from a town that's shut off from the world by the ocean on one side and New Jersey on the other?
—O. HENRY, "GENTLE GRAFTER" IN A *TEMPERED WIND*, 1908

---

just for the view. It's a great bargain, too. The other "must," although it's not a bona fide mode of local transportation, is a trip around Manhattan aboard the Circle Line's boats. It will really help you orient yourself and provide great photo opportunities.

Area Code Manhattan and the Bronx 212; Queens, Staten Island, and Brooklyn 718; Long Island 516; Westchester and Rockland counties 914; Connecticut 203; New Jersey 201 and 609.

Baby-sitters Try the **Gilbert Child Care Agency** (tel. 921-4848), the **Lynn Agency** (tel. 874-6130), or the **Babysitter Guild** (tel. 682-0227). Barnard College women also run a small baby-sitting service (tel. 854-2035). At most agencies, you should be prepared to pay the sitter's cab fare home after a certain hour.

Business Hours Standard office hours are 9am to 5pm. Banks in Manhattan keep relatively short hours, closing at 3pm or 3:30pm on most weekdays. Department stores are usually open until 6pm, with late closings (around 8:30pm) on Mondays and Thursdays.

Car Rentals See "Getting Around" in this chapter.

Climate See "When to Go—Climate & Events" in Chapter 2.

Consumer Complaints To report any problems with merchants or ask consumer-related questions, call the Better Business Bureau (tel. 533-6200) or the Department of Consumer Affairs (tel. 577-0111).

Dentist Call the **New York University College of Dentistry,** 345 E. 24th St. near First Avenue (tel. 998-9976). The **Dental Emergency Service** (tel. 679-3966, or 679-4172 after 8pm) is a 24-hour answering service that will try to refer you to a dentist.

Doctor Call the **Doctor's Home Referral/Home Call** service of the New York Medical Society (tel. 718/745-5900 or 718/238-2100). **Immediate Medical Care of Manhattan,** 116 W. 72nd St. (tel. 496-9620), charges about $75 for a basic office visit, and walk-ins are accepted.

Drugstores **Duane Reade** stores offer discount prices. A good drugstore open 24 hours a day is **Kaufman's,** 50th Street and Lexington Avenue (tel. 755-2266). Many **Love's** stores throughout the city are also open round the clock.

Emergencies Call the police, the fire department, or an ambulance at 911.

Eye Care An inexpensive place to get a general eye examination or referral is the **Optometric Center,** the clinic of the State College of Optometry, State University of New York. The offices are located at 100 E. 24th St., between Park Avenue South and Lexington Avenue. Call 420-4900 for information and appointments.

You can get 1-hour service at **Cohen's Optical Company.** With many branch locations, Cohen's has some of the lowest prices in New York. **Lenscrafters** has two centrally located branches, at 901 Sixth Avenue at 33rd Street and 2040 Broadway at 70th Street, both offering 1-hour service.

Hairdressers/Barbers **Salon Ziba,** 200 W. 57th St. (tel. 767-0577) offers reasonably priced hair styling for men and women 7 days a week, with no appointment necessary. **Dramatics** and **Jean Louis David** also accept walk-ins, with locations all over the city charging inexpensive rates.

Hospitals See "Doctors," above, if your problem is not critical. If there's a real crisis, emergency wards are always open at **St. Vincent's Hospital,** Seventh Avenue and 11th Street (tel. 790-7000); **New York Hospital,** Cornell School of Medicine, East 70th Street at York Avenue (tel. 472-5454); and **Mt. Sinai Hospital,** at Madison Avenue and 100th Street (tel. 241-7171).

Hotlines   For gay and lesbian concerns, see "Networks and Resources" in this chapter. For serious problems call **Helpline** (tel. 532-2400), **Victim Services** (tel. 577-7777), or **The Samaritans** (tel. 673-3000) for help and counseling daily 24 hours. The **Childhelp National Child Abuse Hotline** (tel. toll free 800/422-4453) is staffed 24 hours a day by trained psychology professionals and social workers. Call **Alcoholics Anonymous** at 473-6200. The **Drug Abuse Information Line** (tel. toll free 800/522-5353) is staffed around the clock to provide referrals for anyone with a drug problem. Call the **Rape Hotline** at 267-7273.

Information   See "Tourist Information" in Section 1 of this chapter.

Laundry/Dry Cleaning   New York City seems to have a dry cleaner on every block, and most of them can provide express service on the same day, if you bring in your things in the morning. Such speedy service, however, does cost more. If your clothes are just rumpled from a suitcase, try this old trick: Hang the offending item in your hotel bathroom, shut the door, and run a hot shower (preferably with you in it to conserve water). In a few minutes the wrinkles should be steamed out and the garment ready to wear.

Libraries   The main branch of the New York Public Library is at Fifth Avenue and 42nd Street.

Liquor Laws   Hard liquor is sold only in licensed package stores, which are closed on Sunday. Beer is sold in delis and grocery stores. The legal drinking age in New York is 21, though the city is notorious for serving alcohol to anyone old enough to see over a bar.

Luggage Storage   Grand Central Terminal and the Port Authority have luggage storage facilities, charging small fees to keep your bags if you'd like to leave your stuff behind while you search for a place to stay.

Maps   See "Orientation" in this chapter.

Newspapers/Magazines   New York City has four daily newspapers, the *New York Times,* the *Daily News,* the *New York Post,* and *New York Newsday.* The Friday "Weekend" and the Sunday "Arts and Leisure" sections of the *Times* are especially good resources. Weekly publications with good entertainment and cultural listings include the *New Yorker, New York* magazine, and the *Village Voice* (particularly strong for music, cheap events, freebies, and off- and off-off-Broadway performances). You'll find newsstands on practically every corner.

Photographic Needs   Dozens of cut-rate photo-supply stores dot the West Side. One of the best known is 47th Street Photo, 67 W. 47th St., between Fifth and Sixth avenues (tel. 260-4410), plus its other branches—see Chapter 9, "New York City Shopping." Try to bargain with the cut-rate places.

If you have your own equipment already, try to bring more than one lens—a 35-mm, 50-mm, and 135-mm lens should cover any photographic opportunity. Also, don't attract attention to your camera equipment by carrying it in a flashy, expensive camera bag. Bring a nondescript, surplus-type bag if you can.

For a week's stay, you might want to bring 14 rolls of film, about two per day. Ten rolls (black-and-white or color) should be slow speed (ASA 64 or 100) and the remainder fast speed (ASA 400 or 1000) for taking either indoor photos without flash or night photos.

Police   Call 911 for life-threatening emergencies only; call 374-5000 for normal matters.

Post Office   The General Post Office, 33rd Street and Eighth Avenue (tel. 967-8585), is open daily 24 hours.

Radio   Local AM stations include 660 (WFAN for sports); 710 (WOR for talk and news); 880 (WCBS for all news); 1010 (WINS for all news); and 1560 (WQXR for classical music). FM radio stations include 88.3 (WBGO for jazz); 93.1 (WPAT for easy-listening music); 93.9 (WNYC Public Radio for classical music); 95.5 (WPLJ for pop, rock, and dance music): 98.7 (WRKS, or KISS 98, for pop and dance music); 99.5

(WBAI, a nonprofit station); 101.1 (WCBS for "golden oldies" rock); 102.7 (WNEW for progressive rock); 104.3 (WNCN for classical music); 107.5 (WBLS for urban contemporary).

Religious Services   Saturday's *New York Times* runs a list of Sunday services.

Rest Rooms   If you don't want to spend money in a restaurant, there are many buildings with well-maintained public rest rooms. All the major retail stores are good bets: Bloomingdale's (1000 Third Ave., at 59th Street), Bergdorf Goodman (Fifth Avenue, at 58th Street), Tiffany's (727 Fifth Ave., near 57th Street), Saks Fifth Ave. (Fifth Avenue at 50th Street), Lord & Taylor (Fifth Avenue at 39th Street), and Macy's (Broadway at 34th Street). You can also use the facilities at most of the better hotels, many open 24 hours: the Pierre (Fifth Avenue at 61st Street; on the second floor and in the rotunda), the Essex House (160 Central Park South, near Seventh Avenue; in the lobby and on the second floor), the Waldorf-Astoria (Park Avenue at 50th Street; in the lobby), the Grand Hyatt New York (Park Avenue, at Grand Central Terminal; in the lobby), the Parker Meridien (118 W. 57th St., near Sixth Avenue; downstairs), the Plaza (Fifth Avenue at 59th Street; in the lobby), and the Marriott Marquis Hotel (1535 Broadway, near 45th Street; with a bathroom on every one of its eight floors).

Amid the steel and concrete are also a number of atriums that have lavatories and places to sit: Olympic Tower (connects 51st and 52nd streets, east of Fifth Avenue), Citicorp Center (153 E. 53rd St.; lower level), the Park Avenue Plaza (55 E. 52nd St.), 875 Third Ave. (at 52nd Street; ask the guard to unlock the rest rooms), the Crystal Pavilion (805 Third Ave., at 50th Street), the IBM Garden Plaza (590 Madison Ave., near 55th Street; lower level), Trump Tower (725 Fifth Ave., near 57th Street; downstairs), and the RCA Building (30 Rockefeller Plaza; concourse level).

Safety   Stay alert. It is your responsibility to stay alert even in what may seem the safest situation. When strolling New York streets alone at night stay in busy areas where there are other people. Some areas should be avoided entirely at night. These include Harlem, Spanish Harlem, Times Square (except during theater-going hours), the East Village between First Avenue and the river ("Alphabet City"), and the Lower East Side or any area deserted at night. Traveling in a group is always safer.

During the day or night, walk purposefully. Wear a moneybelt or keep your purse tucked under your arm. Wear your wallet in front, not back, pockets. Don't wear expensive jewelry or keep passports and all your money in a single place.

In the subway at night, don't stand close to the tracks; choose crowded, not empty, cars, and once riding, stay alert. We don't recommend using the subways for late-night travel; the buses are usually safer. But also keep in mind that at rush hour, the heavy jostling crowd provides a good camouflage for pickpockets. Don't leave passports and money in hotel rooms, and be aware that some criminals view department-store customers as lucrative and easy targets.

In some parts of the city, people play card or dice games in the streets. Never join them—these games are illegal and they are rigged. The person you see winning is a plant.

Also, be careful of the traffic. Cars and trucks and especially the cabs move very fast and don't always stop for pedestrians. Also watch out for bicycles.

Taxes   New York sales tax is 8¼%.

Taxis   See "Getting Around" in this chapter.

Telegrams/Telex   Call 800/325-6000 for Western Union.

Television   Local stations include Channel 2 (WCBS, network), Channel 4 (WNBC, network), Channel 5 (WWNY, Fox network), Channel 7 (WABC, network), Channel 9 (WWOR, local), Channel 11 (WPIX, local), Channel 13 (WNET, public television), Channel 31 (WNYC, public television), and Channel 47 (WNJU, mostly Spanish).

Time   New York is on Eastern Standard time, three hours ahead of the West Coast.

Transit Info   For bus or subway information, dial 718/330-1234.

Useful Telephone Numbers   For telephone information for Manhattan and the Bronx, dial 411; for other boroughs, dial 718/555-1212. For the time, call

976-1616. For immediate 24-hour first-aid—or hospital referral if necessary—at the **Poison Control Center** call 340-4494 or **P-O-I-S-O-N-S** (764-7667). **Weather** Dial 976-1212.

3. NETWORKS & RESOURCES

FOR STUDENTS

The **Council on International Educational Exchange (CIEE)**, 356 W. 34th St. (tel. 661-1450), is a major student travel organization that may be able to help you obtain discounts on travel arrangements or an international student ID card. It's especially helpful if you're a foreign student visiting the U.S.

New York has a large student population, and it may be worth your while to check the bulletin boards at Columbia University and the Loeb Student Center of NYU for information on casual work and sublets.

FOR GAY MEN & LESBIANS

New York has a huge gay and lesbian community, with many clubs, bars, businesses, and community events centering in Greenwich Village. The Gay Pride celebration each June is a major event, drawing thousands of participants from all over the world.

The *Village Voice* is a good source of information on gay nightlife and cultural events. Manhattan also boasts excellent bookstores carrying titles by, for, and about gays—two of the best are the **Oscar Wilde Memorial Bookshop**, 15 Christopher St. (tel. 255-8097), and **A Different Light**, 548 Hudson St. (tel. 989-4850).

The **Gay/Lesbian Switchboard** (tel. 777-1800) operates daily from 10:30am to midnight and has listings of more than 100 organizations and agencies that deal with gay issues. There's also a **Lesbian Switchboard** (tel. 741-2610), in operation Monday through Friday from 6 to 10pm. A number of organizations meet at the **Lesbian and Gay Community Services Center**, 208 W. 13th St. (tel. 620-7310), which also sponsors dances and social events.

FOR WOMEN

It's important for women in New York to look confident and walk purposefully on the streets. If you don't look like a victim, the odds are that you won't become one. Keep tabs on your purse and be aware of who's walking near you on the streets at all times. Ask local women where they feel safe to travel late at night, and don't ever hesitate to take a cab if you're going out alone in the evening—it may be the most worthwhile splurge you ever make.

If you're looking for safe but low-cost accommodations, try the women-only **Martha Washington Hotel** or **Allerton House.**

Resources include **Womanbooks**, 201 W. 92nd St. (tel. 873-4121), a feminist bookstore; **Women's Roommate Referrals** (tel. 972-9899); and the national headquarters of the **National Organization for Women (NOW)**, 15 W. 18th St. (tel. 807-0721). If you need help, call the **Rape Hotline** at 267-7273, the **Women's Counseling & Psychotherapy Referral Services** (tel. 996-3939), or the **Women's Counseling Project** at Barnard College (tel. 280-3063).

FOR SENIORS

The Manhattan branch of the **American Association of Retired Persons (AARP)** is located at 919 Third Ave. (tel. 758-1411).

WHERE TO STAY IN NEW YORK CITY

You're planning your first trip to New York, or maybe the first one in some years. When it comes to choosing a hotel, confusion reigns. You've heard rumors that Manhattan hotel rooms are vastly overpriced and that some neighborhoods are not safe. Should you choose to stay in midtown near Times Square, in the Lincoln Center area, or over on the East Side? What about that big new hostel uptown? And how much will you have to pay for a decent room? Finding a suitable budget hotel is the most difficult task, and the trickiest job of all.

Like many other major cities, New York has an area noted for the cluster of good, inexpensive hotels: the midtown theater district and the West 50s. Other budget hotels are widely scattered. Some, of course, have no fancy doormen or brocaded lobbies, but they do have adequate accommodations whose prices can still be considered reasonable in today's highly inflated hotel market.

RATES

And what does a reasonable, budget-minded hotel cost in New York these days? More than it does in most other cities. Plan on spending around $100 for a double if you wish to stay in one of the regular tourist hotels (see Section 2, "Hotels," below). High as these rates may seem, they are actually budget by New York standards—in many hotels, rates of $150 and more per night are commonplace, and luxury hotels start at $200 and go up. If you stay in a hostel, a Y, or a women's hotel, or are a student or young working person and can qualify at certain places, you will, of course, pay much less. Weekly stays bring down the rates. A bed-and-breakfast can save you money. And the best deal of all is to plan your trip for a weekend when first-class and luxury hotels often have special packages, with meals and maybe theater tickets, for not much more than the cost of a budget hotel.

DISCOUNTS

Finding the best bargains in rooms is an art, so here are a few tips that all tourists on a budget should know. First of all, the rates that hotels quote, known as "rack rates," are not necessarily what you will have to pay. When you make reservations, always ask if there are special discounts that might apply: corporate rates, family rates, package deals, senior-citizen rates (almost all hotels have these), rates for students, military personnel, government employees, clergy, or airline employees, or whatever is appropriate. If you call a hotel directly, rather than a toll-free "800" number, you have a better bargaining position. We do suggest advance reservations, of course, but sometimes you can walk into a hotel late in the afternoon and if it is not completely booked, you may luck into a room at a considerably reduced rate. (*Warning:* Don't try this unless you have relatives or friends with an extra bed to fall back on.)

In order to take advantage of the special discount rate that some hotels offer to readers of this book, you must write well in advance stating specifically what price room you require. You may not get the same discount if you arrive without advance reservations, even if you flash a copy of this book upon registering. And if you haven't written for reservations, call from a phone booth before rushing to the hotel.

A few New York hotels still have some rooms available without private baths —which means you share a connecting bath with the adjoining room or trek down the hall a few doors to a bath. Request them when you can: savings are great.

It also cuts costs to travel in threes. A triple is usually a large double-occupancy room with one double bed and one twin—three for little more than the price of two.

If you're a couple traveling with another couple you can share a suite, which usually consists of two well-furnished bedrooms and one bathroom. Some even have kitchen units. By sharing a bathroom, you'll discover that the cost of a luxury suite is less than the cost of two private rooms with bath.

TAXES

Note that the rates we quote for rooms do not include the dismaying hotel taxes: On hotel rooms under $100 a night, it is 16¼%, plus $2 per room per night. On hotels over $100, it is even more—21¼%, plus $2 per room per night. Try to stay under the $100 rate if you can.

TELEPHONE TRAPS

Before you pick up the phone in your hotel room, beware. Phone calls can add enormously to your bill. Hotels, seeing phone service as an easy source of revenue, often add extra charges onto regular long-distance calls, credit-card calls, and even local calls—and they may charge you for calls that have not been completed. Also, you may find yourself linked up with a phone company you've never heard of that charges exorbitant rates. The safest and cheapest way to make phone calls is to use public phones in the lobby. If you do make calls from your room, be sure to look for the card outlining the costs: by law it must be posted by the main phone in your room.

(F) FROMMER'S SMART TRAVELER: HOTELS

1. Make a deal. Always inquire when making reservations for any special discounts that might apply: corporate rates, family rates, weekend packages, senior-citizen rates (almost all hotels have these), rates for students, military, government employees, clergy, airline employees, or whatever is appropriate.
2. When dealing with a national chain, call the hotel directly rather than phoning an 800 number: you have a better chance of negotiating a discount rate.
3. Consider a bed-and-breakfast accommodation; rates are about half of what they are in a hotel. Sometimes complete apartments, without hosts, are available.
4. Try to schedule your trip for a weekend: Weekend package deals, even at some of New York's best hotels, are incredible bargains.
5. Inquire about weekly rates: If you're staying for a week or longer, you can usually get a cheaper rate.

If it isn't, check with the front desk. And keep a record of all calls you make, case things get out of hand when you get your bill.

1. NEW YORK ON A SHOESTRING — HOSTELS, Y's & DORMS

MIDTOWN EAST

CARLTON ARMS HOTEL, 160 E. 25th St. (at Third Ave.), New York, NY 10010. Tel. 212/679-0680. 54 rms (shared and private baths). **Subway:** 6 to 23rd St.

$ Rates: With private bath: $48 1 person, $62 2 persons, $74 3 persons. Without private bath: $40 1 person, $54 2 persons, $65 3 persons. Students and foreign tourists receive a discount of roughly 10%. MC, V. **Parking:** Side streets or nearby garages, around $20.

Is it an avant-garde art gallery pretending to be a hotel, or is it a hotel pretending to be an avant-garde art gallery? The answer is a little bit of both. Surely, there is no other hostelry in New York quite like this one. The artistic inventions of a friendly staff and their friends in the art community have turned this once rather decrepit hotel on a shabby street into a congenial place for young travelers. Especially popular with counterculture types and students from Europe and Asia, this four-story hotel has ancient furniture, but the beds are all new and good, and the place is kept clean, safe, and comfortable.

The amazing thing is the decor: vivid color schemes (some halls and doors are painted in black accented by vivid fluorescent colors); hallway and wall murals climb the staircase, filling every inch of wall space and reaching up to the ceilings; and theme rooms (like the Roses and Car Crashes room, for example) create an atmosphere unlike anything to be found at your neighborhood Holiday Inn. The management has hit upon a brilliant decorating scheme: every 3 months they turn over four rooms to aspiring artists and give them a free hand; when all four rooms are completed, an art opening is held. Their wall murals then become a permanent part of the decor. As of this writing, 49 of the hotel's 54 rooms have been done. These rooms have attracted so much attention (some are lovely, some verge on the grotesque) that they have been used as backdrops for fashion shots in one of Europe's most prestigious fashion magazines. Advice to those who want peaceful dreams: Have a look at your room when you register to see if the art agrees with you. Some 40% of the rooms have private baths; others share communal facilities. Every room has its own sink. There is no air conditioning, but all have fans. The Carlton Arms shows what can be done with little money but lots of imagination—it's one of a kind.

To make reservations, first call as far in advance as possible. Then call at least 2 weeks in advance of arrival to confirm.

INTERNATIONAL STUDENT HOSPICE, 154 E. 33rd St. (between Lexington and Third aves.), New York, NY 10016. Tel. 212/228-7470 or 228-4689. 20 accommodations (none with bath). TV **Subway:** 6 to 33rd St.

$ Rates: $30 per night. No credit cards. **Parking:** None.

Despite its name, this place is not for internationals only: this reconverted Murray Hill town house is a place where Oxford scholars swap stories with Ohio collegians, where students from St. Louis stay across the hall from those from the Sorbonne. Sponsored by a nonprofit foundation and in business since 1958, ISH can house 20 guests (students are preferred, but others are sometimes accepted) and houses them in rooms for four; there are just a few tiny private rooms. Bathrooms and showers are down the hall. Rooms are small but clean, and there's a library for studying, and even a tiny lounge with color TV. Guests must observe a midnight curfew. The hospice is within

500 m
550 y

Columbus Circle

THEATER DISTRICT

Port Authority Bus Terminal

Bryant Park

Eleventh Ave.
Tenth Ave.
Ninth Ave.
Eighth Ave.
Seventh Ave.
Broadway
Avenue of the Americas
(6th Ave.)
Rockefeller Center

W. 55th St.
W. 54th St.
W. 53rd St.
W. 52nd St.
W. 51st St.
W. 50th St.
W. 49th St.
W. 48th St.
W. 47th St.
W. 46th St.
W. 45th St.
W. 44th St.
W. 43rd St.
W. 42nd St.
W. 41st St.
W. 40th St.
W. 39th St.
W. 38th St.

MANHATTAN
Midtown

Allerton House **1**
Ameritania Hotel **2**
Best Western's Milford Plaza **3**
The Chelsea Hotel **4**
The 3684-MChelsea Inn **5**
Hotel Consulate **6**
Days Inn–New York **7**
Doral Inn **8**

Hotel Edison **9**
Grand Hyatt New York **10**
Helmsley Middletowne **11**
Hotel Iroquois **12**
Journey's End Hotel **13**
Mansfield Hotel **14**
New York Helmsley **15**
New York Hilton & Towers **1**
Novotel New York **17**

MIDTOWN MANHATTAN ACCOMMODATIONS

E. 58th St.

E. 57th St.

E. 56th St.

E. 55th St.

E. 54th St.

E. 53rd St.

TURTLE BAY

E. 52nd St.

E. 51st St.

E. 50th St.

E. 49th St.

E. 48th St.

E. 47th St.

E. 46th St.

E. 45th St.

E. 44th St.

E. 43rd St.

E. 42nd St.

E. 41st St.

E. 40th St.

E. 39th St.

E. 38th St.

Sutton Pl.

Sutton Pl. So.

Beekman Pl.

Mitchell St.

Park Ave.

Lexington Ave.

Third Ave.

Second Ave.

First Ave.

Fifth Ave.

Madison Ave.

Vanderbilt Ave.

Tudor City Pl.

FDR Drive

East River

Parker Meridien 18
Pickwick Arms Hotel 19
Portland Square Hotel 20
President Hotel 21
Quality Inn Midtown 22
Ramada Hotel 23
Hotel Remington 24
The Roger Williams 25
Travel Inn Motor Hotel 26

Travelodge Hotel Skyline Manhattan 27
Vanderbilt YMCA 28
Hotel Wellington 29
Hotel Wentworth 30
The Westpark Hotel 31
The Wyndham 32

walking distance of Grand Central Terminal, Penn Station, Madison Square Garden, and the United Nations, in a mixed residential-business neighborhood, right in the shadow of the Empire State Building. Write or call in advance; you can call at any hour: the phone is on 24 hours a day.

**VANDERBILT YMCA, 224 E. 47th St. (between Second and Third aves.).
Tel. 212/755-2410.** Fax 212/752-0210. 415 rms. A/C **Subway:** 6 to 51st St.
$ Rates: $38–$48 single, $48–$58 double, $63–$67 triple, $84 quad. MC, V.
Parking: Nearby garages, around $20.

For the young and young at heart (men, women, even families), this is the best of the city's Y's. The 10-story building offers excellent athletic facilities (including a large indoor pool, gym, and sauna), plus a cafeteria and a self-service laundry. The atmosphere is like that of a European youth hostel—relaxed, young, and friendly—but visitors of any age can stay. The cafeteria offers big, filling meals from $4 to $5. Guests are given automatic Y membership for the length of their stay and can use all Vanderbilt Y facilities. Rooms are small and spartan, but very clean, located off attractive hallways with carpeted walls. All accommodations have single or bunk beds, dressers, and desks. Some have sinks in the room, but baths are down the hall. Phones are also in the hall; the desk takes messages.

Considering the East Side location and the facilities, this Y is a bargain. It's also the kind of place where parents can feel at ease sending young sons and daughters.

UPPER WEST SIDE

**INTERNATIONAL HOUSE OF NEW YORK, 500 Riverside Drive (at 122nd
St.), New York, NY 10027. Tel. 212/316-8400.** Fax 212/316-1872. 750
rms (shared baths). TEL **Subway:** 1 to 116th St.
$ Rates: $25 single; monthly rates average $18 per day. No credit cards. **Parking:**
Only after stays of 2 weeks.

University students aged 21 or above (with student IDs) and those with academic affiliations should consider the vacation-time (May 15 to August 15 and December 15 to January 15) accommodations here. During the academic year, International House, which overlooks the Hudson River, accommodates more than 500 students from all over the world. About 65% are foreigners, and though many of the American residents attend Columbia University, over 45 educational and training institutes are represented each year. But when the permanent residents leave on vacation, the house rents its rooms to students visiting New York.

Accommodations are just part of the offerings. There's a low-priced cafeteria, a small dining room and kitchen for informal parties, a laundry, music practice rooms, a general store, and several public lounges including a TV room and study rooms. There's also a gym with volleyball, basketball, and table tennis facilities, and there are dance and aerobics classes. Special activities for students and newcomers to New York occur almost daily.

Rooms are simple but neat and clean, with linoleum-tile floors, linens, and the necessary furnishings. They are all singles, two-thirds of which have sinks; bath and toilet facilities are shared in the hall. There is no maid service, but linens can be exchanged for fresh ones for a small fee. Vacuum cleaners and irons are available at no extra cost.

Applications are required for stays of longer than a month. Extra cots costs $10 a night for a maximum period of two weeks. Rooms are occasionally available to transient students during the academic year, but advance reservations cannot be confirmed more than a week in advance.

**INTERNATIONAL STUDENT CENTER, 38 W. 88th St. (between Central
Park West and Columbus Ave.), New York, NY 10024. Tel. 212/787-
7706.** Fax 212/580-9283. 46 beds (shared baths). **Subway:** B, C to 85th St.
$ Rates: $10 per day. No credit cards.

With all the backpacks around, this place for those between the ages of 18 and 30

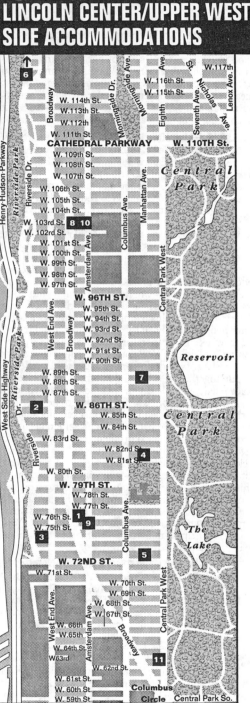

0 ▭▭▭ 600 m
660 y

MANHATTAN

Upper
West
Side

Broadway
  American Hotel
Cambridge
  House Hotel **1**
Esplanade Hotel **2**
  and Suites **3**
Excelsior Hotel **4**
Hotel Olcott **5**
International House
  of New York **6**
International
  Student Center **7**
Malibu Studios
  Hotel **8**
The Milburn **9**
New York
  International
  AYH-Hostel **10**
West Side YMCA **11**

feels like a student hostel the moment you set foot in the door. Sponsored by the Association for World Travel Exchange, ISC has been hosting students and travelers since 1956. They've converted an old brownstone in a pleasant residential neighborhood into seven single-sex dormitory rooms, each of which has four to ten beds and its own bath. Downstairs is an old community kitchen and a TV lounge, where everyone socializes. It's a good place to meet a traveling companion. Most summer guests are from Western Europe; in winter most guests are from New Zealand, Australia, and Japan. Manager Robert Tesdell advises that reservations are not accepted; call as soon as you arrive in town. Passports are required.

MALIBU STUDIOS HOTEL, 2688 Broadway (at 103rd St.), New York, NY 10025. Tel. 212/222-2954. Fax 212/678-6842. 150 rms (shared and private baths). **Subway:** 1, 9 to 103rd St.

$ Rates: $50 single, $60 double nightly; $150 weekly small studio without bath; $60 single, $70 double larger rooms with private baths and TV; large family rooms and suites, rates on request. No credit cards. **Parking:** Nearby garages, around $20.

Just around the corner from the New York International AYH Hostel, these offbeat budget lodgings are practically its unofficial annex. It's decorated in a California palm tree motif, and is always packed with singles new to New York: would-be actors and actresses, performers and entertainers, students from nearby Columbia University as well as businesspeople on budgets, European and American tourists, all in search of clean, comfortable, and safe no-frills lodgings at excellent prices. The very best bargains are for those who stay at least a week. Small studios are freshly painted and decorated with quilted spreads and drapes, a desk/dresser and chair, and a small refrigerator topped by a two-burner electric hotplate, plus a sink. The immaculate bathrooms, shared with three or four other people, have both tub and shower. Fans are available, and TVs can be rented for $15 a week. Then there are the larger rooms, which have private baths, air conditioning, and color TV. Rooms in an adjoining building are quite large and have double beds and a sofa bed, and are suitable for families. Families and large groups can also be put together in adjoining rooms. Call the reservations manager to explain your exact needs; most likely he will be able to work something out for you.

There are 24-hour switchboard and message service and pay phones in the lobby. Bathrooms are cleaned by the housekeeping staff, but guests are expected to care for their own rooms (they'll loan you a vacuum cleaner at the desk). And there's a laundry next door. Security is no problem, since they use a closed-circuit-TV security system, have someone on duty at the front desk 24 hours a day, and keep the front door locked (guests must be buzzed in). There is no elevator. The hotel has no restaurant, but you can choose from dozens of ethnic and fast-food restaurants nearby—or have Chinese food delivered from the restaurant on the corner. A travel agency is next door. Midtown is about 15 minutes by subway or 30 minutes by bus.

Guests often become friends. (Recent guests have included a 40-member French contingent who arrived to take part in the New York Marathon and a group from the BBC.) The helpful management provides free passes to local clubs and discos. Write or call for advance reservations.

NEW YORK INTERNATIONAL AYH–HOSTEL, 891 Amsterdam Ave. at 103rd St., New York, NY 10025. Tel. 212/932-2300. Fax 212/932-2574. 480 beds (shared baths). A/C **Subway:** 1, 9 to 103rd St.

$ Rates: $18.75 per night for members of AYH; nonmembers may purchase a membership on the premises (around $25) or pay a guest membership of $3 a night. Linen rental (if necessary): $3 a night. MC, V. **Parking:** Nearby garage, around $20.

This may well be New York's best budget lodging choice. For little more (sometimes less) than the cost of parking a car in the midtown area, you can park yourself in a clean, comfortable, and secure hostelry. And the new hostel, which opened in the spring of 1990, is not just for international students and others traveling with a pack on their back and a bicycle on the rack (although they make up the largest percentage of guests): couples, families, people of all ages are welcome.

And all are guaranteed an experience unlike that of the average, impersonal New York hotel.

The hostel is unique on many counts. It was the first American Youth Hostel in New York, is the largest in the country, and is one of the most ambitious hostel projects in the world. It is housed in a century-old city landmark listed on the National Register of Historic Places, which was designed by the famed 19th-century architect Richard Morris Hunt (who was also responsible for the Metropolitan Museum of Art). The four-story, Victorian Gothic building, which had been abandoned and had fallen into disrepair, has been given a $15-million renovation, and superbly restored, following the most minute (and costly) city, state, and federal landmark requirements. It offers handsome common rooms (one for quiet pursuits, another for television), a spacious garden for dining and sunning, a common kitchen, a self-service cafeteria, meeting and conference rooms, and a full-service travel agency. The hostel is located one block away from the subway station at 103rd Street and Broadway in a multiethnic neighborhood that is undergoing gentrification. Seven blocks north is the Cathedral of St. John the Divine, and four blocks farther north begins the campus of Columbia University. Midtown is about a 15-minute subway ride or a 30-minute bus ride away.

The sleeping rooms are spacious and sunny, with high (8- or 10-foot) ceilings and either two, three, or four bunk beds with drawer space underneath. Rooms are carpeted and have individual heat/air-conditioning controls. Baths are down the hall (a ratio of 8 people to one bathroom), and have individual showers and dressing rooms. There are four hotel-quality family rooms that have queen-size beds and two bunk beds. Security is excellent; rooms have electronic key locks, and only those with keys are allowed access to the bedroom floors.

There are no curfews or closing times, making the hostel fully accessible to guests 24 hours a day. No chores are required. All the facilities have been designed to bring people together, to promote a lively cross-cultural exchange in a relaxing atmosphere, to give people "an alternative to the sterile environment of New York hotels." Advance reservations are suggested.

WEST SIDE YMCA, 5 W. 63rd St. (between Central Park West and Broadway), New York, NY 10023. Tel. 212/787-4400. Fax 212/580-0441. 525 rms (shared and private baths). A/C TV **Subway:** 1, 9, A, C, D to 59th St.

$ Rates: $35–$45 single; $45–$55 double. AE, MC, V. **Parking:** On side streets or at nearby garages, $10–$20.

The West Side YMCA has an excellent location, seconds away from Lincoln Center and Central Park, and 10 minutes from midtown by bus or subway. Students and tourists can feel comfortable here. Single and double rooms for both men and women 18 years or older are offered, with special rates for students and groups. There's daily maid service, mail and message service, and 24-hour uniformed security guards. Television is available in some of the rooms, and air conditioners can be rented for $3.25 per day.

All guests of the West Side YMCA are members for as long as they stay. That means free use of the excellent Health and Fitness Center, which features two gyms, two pools, a banked and cushioned indoor running track, Nautilus and Universal weight systems, plus handball, racquetball, and squash courts, a steamroom, sauna, and much more. A good choice if you need to stay in shape while visiting New York! For more details, call the reservations office at extension 120 or 121.

IN NEARBY NEW JERSEY

STEVENS INSTITUTE OF TECHNOLOGY, c/o Campus Holidays USA, Inc., 242 Bellevue Ave., Upper Montclair, NJ 07043. Tel. 201/744-8274 or toll free 800/526-2915. Fax 201/744-0531. 400 rms (shared and private baths) in summer, 40 rms in winter.

$ Rates: Standard dormitory rooms $36 for single occupancy, $24.50 per person for double occupancy; deluxe rooms $50 for single occupancy, $32 per person for double occupancy. Family suites for up to 4 persons $120. **Parking:** On premises, free.

Some of New York's best budget accommodations are not in New York at all. They're 10 minutes away, across the Hudson River, at the campus of Stevens Institute of Technology in Hoboken, New Jersey. From the scenic, 55-acre campus sitting on a high bank of the Hudson known as Castle Point, guests can view New York's fabled skyline from myriad viewpoints; enjoy safe, secure, and clean accommodations at very low prices; and pop into Manhattan in all of 10 minutes via convenient PATH trains that travel beneath the Hudson River. In addition, they have access to a low-cost cafeteria for meals, and can partake of all the sports and leisure activities on campus—tennis courts, an indoor track, indoor swimming pool, sauna, weight machines, and squash, basketball, and racquetball courts—free.

Here's how it works. Visitors live right in the dorms alongside regular students; the dorms are very quiet, we're told (these are serious students who usually spend their time glued to their computers). Rooms are scrupulously clean. Visitors may choose a standard dorm room, which consists of a bunk bed (beds may be placed side by side on the floor), a desk, and a chair; baths are down the hall, and the rooms are not air-conditioned. If you want the room to yourself, you pay more. Technology Hall has comfortable deluxe rooms, with regular twin beds, air conditioning, carpeted floors, and private baths. Families should know about the beautiful suites, complete with two twin beds (two rollaways can be added), a full bath with tub and shower, TV, air conditioning, and a fully equipped kitchen with utensils provided. If you stay three or more nights, there is no charge for linens; for one or two nights, the linen package is $4.50.

You can save money even on these low rates. Campus Holidays, the rental agent of Stevens Institute residence halls, has agreed to offer readers of this book a 10% discount, which also applies to their 3-day "Big Apple on a Budget" tour; inquire when you make reservations.

Hoboken is a working-class waterfront town currently being gentrified by New Yorkers. Its major claims to fame are that it was the birthplace of the game of baseball, the hometown of Frank Sinatra, and the site of the classic Brando film, *On the Waterfront*. The campus is a seven-block walk, a 40¢ bus ride, or a $2 taxi ride to the PATH trains, which run to the World Trade Center, Greenwich Village, and midtown Manhattan (near Madison Square Garden) for $1.15, 24 hours a day. Public buses also make frequent runs into New York. The campus is convenient for motorists, since it's halfway between the Lincoln and Holland tunnels.

FOR INTERNATIONAL STUDENTS & TRAVELERS

THE CHELSEA CENTER, 511 W. 20th St. (between Tenth and Eleventh aves.), New York, NY 10011. Tel. 212/243-4922. 14 beds (shared baths). **Subway:** C, E to 23rd St., then crosstown bus west.
$ Rates: $19 per night (including linens and blankets) and breakfast (bread, butter and jam, tea, coffee, and milk). No credit cards.

The Chelsea Center, circa 1981, is perhaps the homiest hostel in town. The teakettle is always on and a warm welcome is available from hostess Heidi Dubose of Germany and her staff, who have remodeled the first floor of an old loft building and turned it into a home-away-from-home for wandering students and travelers from abroad. The two large coed rooms, one with six double-decker beds, the other with eight bunk beds, are sunny and very clean, with whitewashed walls; sheets and blankets are included. The center welcomes backpackers, hikers, and other travelers, and always gives first preference to foreigners. The location, although it seems a bit out of the way in a mixed residential/light industrial area, is actually excellent. It's a 2-minute walk to the 23rd Street crosstown bus that takes you to the heart of Manhattan, and a short walk to Greenwich Village. Several nearby discos are open until the wee hours (free or low-cost admission passes are usually available).

Guests have the use of the cozy kitchen, where they can be found having a snack, chatting with Heidi or the staff about goings-on in New York, or perhaps celebrating a birthday. One student from Australia wrote in the guestbook: "Definitely the most friendly place in the U.S.A. and a 'secure' place to feel welcome in New York." The house is closed between 11am and 4pm, but the office remains open for check-in and check-out. Reserve far in advance or at least call before your arrival.

Note: If they can't put you up, the people at the Chelsea Center will do their best to find you another good, low-cost accommodation.

FOR WOMEN ONLY

ALLERTON HOUSE, 130 E. 57th St. (corner of Lexington Ave.), New York, NY 10022. Tel. 212/753-8841. 369 rms (shared and private baths). TEL **Subway:** 6 to 59th St.

$ Rates: $35–$45 single, with community bath; $50 with private bath. $76 double with private bath. No credit cards. **Parking:** Nearby garages, around $20.

Allerton House is a dowdy but doughty dowager among its kind. Its lobby looks more like that of an office building than a hotel, with only a plaque to mark its entrance. The location is excellent, in a busy midtown business and shopping neighborhood, with Bloomingdale's just two blocks away. The atmosphere is sedate (about three-quarters of the rooms are occupied by permanent residents, mostly older women), but there are also enough 20- to 30-year-old guests for younger women to feel at home. Pluses include a wraparound rooftop terrace and a laundry. Tommy Makem's atmospheric Irish Pavilion restaurant, with candlelight, beamed ceilings, and a popular bar, adjoins the hotel. And there's usually a crowd lined up waiting to gain access to the Living Well Lady Figure Salon on the mezzanine floor (hotel guests are usually entitled to one free visit) or to the Beverly Bridge Club, one of the city's busiest and best (lunch and an afternoon's worth of bridge for under $10), on the third.

Almost half the rooms have been redecorated; they are small but pleasant, with high ceilings, sinks, and dressers. The other rooms are clean, but without much charm. Rooms on the 17th floor, however, are attractive, with twin beds, private baths, air conditioning, and nice furnishings.

2. HOTELS

Whatever hotel you choose, be sure to write well in advance for a reservation. The average price of a double room will be around $100, and advance reservations are your best guarantee for getting the lowest rates possible.

Please note that hotel parking rates are on a 24-hour basis and usually do not include in-and-out privileges.

MIDTOWN EAST

PICKWICK ARMS HOTEL, 230 E. 51st St. (between Second and Third aves.), New York, NY 10022. Tel. 212/355-0300. Fax 212/355-0300. 380 rms (with shared and private bath). A/C TV TEL **Subway:** 6 to 51st St.

$ Rates: $40 single without bath; $50–$60 single with bath; $80 double or twin with bath; $95 studio with bath; extra person $12. AE, MC, V. **Parking:** Nearby garages, around $20.

You simply can't beat this location—a few blocks from major shopping, cinemas, and restaurants in a lovely East Side residential neighborhood. It's a surprise to find a budget hotel here. This half-century-old hotel, which is being spruced up all the time, offers an attractive lobby with a Tudor-style fireplace, a rooftop sun deck, and airport limousine service. It's one of the busiest hotels on the East Side, and definitely the most reasonable.

The Pickwick Arms is one of the few hotels left in New York where you can save money by sharing the bath down the hall. Some of the older singles, small but quite cozy, have washbasins only, and share a bath/shower with five or six other rooms; some baths are shared by only two rooms. Many of the smaller, older rooms, however, have been converted into large guest rooms (most with twin beds; only 40 have doubles), with attractive furniture, cable TVs, AM/FM radios, and in-room safes. The management prides itself on excellent mattresses, careful housekeeping, and good security; guests must be buzzed in late at night.

Families who don't mind living in one room can take advantage of the eight family rooms. They're furnished with one or two double beds or twin beds and a sofabed, and have their own bathrooms. I especially liked the ones in the rear, overlooking the garden.

Although there are many nearby restaurants, the Pickwick Arms has a few of its own. On one side of the building is the Beekman Deli, open daily from 7am to midnight, which delivers to the rooms. On the other is the world-famous (and expensive) Spanish restaurant Torremolinos.

Many of your fellow guests at the Pickwick Arms will be South Americans or Europeans on tour. Be sure to reserve well in advance.

THE ROGER WILLIAMS, 28 E. 31st St., New York, NY 10016. Tel. 212/684-7500 or toll free 800/637-9773. Fax 212/576-4343. 211 rms (with bath). A/C TV TEL **Subway:** 6 to 33rd St.
$ Rates: $55–$65 single, $60–$70 double, $65–$75 twins, $75–$80 triples, $80–$90 quads. AE, MC, V. **Parking:** At nearby garage, $17.70.

Bringing the family to New York? Need a place to stretch out, cook a meal, or bring in food? The Roger Williams could be the answer to a prayer. This is an older building, recently renovated and remodeled, in the quiet, safe, and central Murray Hill neighborhood. Most rooms are large and all are comfortable, with simple but new furnishings, firm new mattresses, and bathrooms with both tub and shower. Some of the rooms even have terraces. Every room has a kitchenette (two-burner gas stove, sink, refrigerator, cabinet space), and a "Kitchen Kit" sets you up with a tea kettle, paper plates and cups, plastic cutlery, and tea, coffee, sugar, and salt; pots and pans will be provided on request. There's a 24-hour deli–salad bar across the street, and Chinese restaurant adjoining the hotel.

Manager Peter Arest and his staff, mainly old-timers, are very friendly and informal, with lots of good tips for guests.

MIDTOWN WEST

TIMES SQUARE & THE THEATER DISTRICT

BEST WESTERN'S MILFORD PLAZA, 270 W. 45th St. (at Eighth Ave.), New York, NY 10036. Tel. 212/869-3600, or toll free 800/221-2690, 800/522-6449 in New York State. Fax 212/944-8357; telex 177610. 1,300 rms (with bath). A/C TV TEL **Subway:** A, C, E, to 42nd St.
$ Rates: $95–$135 single, $110–$150 double. Weekend packages available. Daily "Lullabuy of Broadway" package around $50 per person in a double room. AE, DISC, EU, JCB, MC, V. **Parking:** Valet parking at nearby garage $11.

One of the most convenient of New York theater hotels, this place has an air of excitement that begins in the graceful marble lobby, with its three-story-high ceiling, so pretty with red carpets and black chairs, and extends right up the 28 floors to the rooms, 211 of which have a star on the door and views of Broadway's theater marquees. Guest rooms have new carpeting and attractive spreads and wallpaper, and the bathrooms have been handsomely retiled. Rooms are compact rather than large, but have everything you need, including AM/FM radios and individually controlled air conditioning and heat; there is free ice on every floor. Security is excellent, since everyone coming up to the rooms must show a key.

Milford guests can enjoy a lavish breakfast buffet (with eggs cooked to order) for under $10, from 7 to 11am. The Stage Door Canteen specializes in barbecued food and nostalgia: Its walls are decorated with photos of the original Stage Door Canteen. Mama Leone's, one of the city's most famous Italian restaurants, is now on two levels of the Milford Plaza. The Celebrity Deli is popular with just about everybody, especially with traveling Texans, who fall in love with the corned-beef sandwiches. The lobby also offers a travel and theater-ticket desk, a sundry shop, and a unisex hair salon.

The "Lullabuy of Broadway" deal, available daily, includes a room plus continental breakfast, a meal, and a welcoming cocktail for the rate of around $50 per person in a double. And on regular rates, the management will extend a 10% discount if you reserve directly and identify yourself as a reader of this book.

HOTEL CONSULATE, 224 W. 49th St. (west of Broadway), New York, NY 10019. Tel. 212/246-5252 or toll free 800/346-8006. Fax 212/245-2305; telex 427035. 225 rms (with bath). AC TV TEL **Subway:** 1, 9 to 50th St.
$ Rates: $70–$105 single, $90–$135 double, suites $110–$150 for 2; extra adult $15. Children under 16 free in parents' room. 10% discount for readers of this book. AE, DC, DISC, ER, MC, V. **Parking:** On premises, $14.

With the Eugene O'Neill Theater next door, and the Ambassador and the Actor's Church across the street, the Hotel Consulate is in the heart of the theater district. This remodeled old-timer (once the Forrester Hotel, home to the likes of Walter Winchell and José Greco) offers sedate, but tasteful rooms furnished with color-coordinated spreads and drapes, reproduction prints, and AM/FM radios. The Consulate is popular with both businessmen and tourists, and with many Europeans and Canadians; they take Canadian money at par, which means very respectable savings of about 15% (other discounts do not apply in this case). The hotel is very careful about security; the staff keeps an eye on everyone who comes in, and the owner surmises that the Consulate "probably has less theft than any hotel in New York City." A moderately priced coffee shop, open from 7am to 7pm, will provide room service; Columbus on Broadway, a popular grill and bar, is on the premises.

The management has agreed to offer those readers who contact them directly and mention this book a discount of 10% on rates.

HOTEL EDISON, 228 W. 47th St. (west of Broadway), New York, NY 10036. Tel. 212/840-5000, or toll free 800/637-7070. Fax 212/719-9541, telex 23887 EDIS. 900 rms (with bath). A/C TV TEL **Subway:** 1, 9 to 50th St.
$ Rates: $94–$99 single, $99–$110 double, $110 triple, $120 quad; $130–$150 suites. AE, CB, DC, DISC, MC, V. **Parking:** Nearby garage, $15.66.

When a hotel has been doing business for over 50 years and is still going strong, you know they must be doing something right. Such a one is the Edison, where the management works hard at pleasing guests. What I like best here is the feeling of spaciousness that the newer hotels, even the most expensive ones, cannot afford to have. You'll sense it in the large lobby, handsomely renovated in the style of its Art Deco heritage, the wide halls, and the nicely decorated rooms. The lobby bustles with guests (many of them theater groups from Europe, South America, and Japan), and has a theater-ticket broker (the hotel is in the very heart of the theater district), a gift shop, and a transportation desk.

The rooms themselves are large and comfortable, many with two double beds and two large closets, and fashionable laminated "shipboard furniture." Double-paned windows help control noise. The one-bedroom suites are warm and homey and beautifully furnished; they are an excellent buy.

Right on the premises is Café Edison, open from 7am to 8pm daily, which serves homemade cheese blintzes, bread pudding, and cabbage soup, among other offerings; the owner makes fresh corn muffins every morning. A bit of a legend in the area, it's been dubbed the "Polish Tea Room" by its regular crowd of Broadway moguls, television actors, successful and aspiring thespians, and a group of retired magicians who have their regular table in the back; it's reputed that as many deals are made here over the gefilte fish and chopped liver as at the more glittering Russian Tea Room on 57th Street. The owners are a Polish immigrant couple; most of their East European Jewish dishes are not listed on the regular menu, so ask. Sofia's, on the other side of the lobby (once the Green Room, home to the big bands and names like Blue Baron), serves elegant continental cuisine, and the Rum House Bar and Lounge is a popular theater-district watering hole with a West Indian accent.

HOTEL IROQUOIS, 49 W. 44th St. (off Fifth Ave.), New York, NY 10036. Tel. 212/840-3080 or toll free 800/332-7220. Fax 212/827-0464. 100 rms, 60 suites (with bath). A/C TV TEL **Subway:** B, D, F to 42nd St.

$ **Rates:** $75 single, $85 double; $99 suite for 2, $125 suite for 3, $135 suite for 4, $145 suite for 5 people. AE, DC, MC, V. **Parking:** Nearby garage, about $14.

Just a few doors away from the famed Algonquin Hotel, the Iroquois boasts an excellent location, outside the noisy, congested theater district, yet only a short walk away. The small lobby has seen better days, but the rooms are inviting, especially the suites, which offer good value for several people traveling together. Most have recessed kitchenettes (all-in-one units complete with a small refrigerator topped by two burners, a sink, and an oven), are large and very nicely furnished. All rooms and suites have acoustic windows. Judy's Restaurant is right off the lobby.

HOTEL REMINGTON, 129 W. 46th St. (between Sixth and Seventh aves.), New York, NY 10036. Tel. 212/221-2600. Fax 212/221-2600. 80 rms (shared and private bath). A/C MINIBAR TV TEL **Subway:** 1, 9 to 50th St.

$ **Rates:** $75 single with bath, $60 without bath; $80 double with bath, $60, $65 without bath; $85 triples with bath; $90 quads with bath. AE, MC, V. **Parking:** Nearby garage, around $12.

With its central location, cheerful and clean accommodations, plus a very friendly staff, the Remington is a fine budget choice. Most of the guests here seem to be from Brazil, Venezuela, or other South American countries. They—and the large numbers of Europeans who frequent the hotel in summer—recognize the value it offers. The small hotel was totally renovated a few years ago and is continually improving itself. The lobby looks larger than it really is, thanks to its mirrored walls and crystal chandelier; there is one small elevator to navigate the nine floors of the hotel. Rooms are nicely decorated with white furniture and floral wallpaper; all have radios and insulated windows, which makes for quiet. Bathrooms are new, and some are quite special, with colored tubs and marble vanities. Rooms without private bathrooms have a sink and use of a very clean bathroom, shared by three rooms.

HOTEL WENTWORTH, 59 W. 46th St. (between Fifth and Sixth aves.), New York, NY 10036. Tel. 212/719-2300. Fax 212/768-3477. 194 rms, 20 suites (with bath). A/C TV TEL **Subway:** 4, 5, 6 to 42nd St.

$ **Rates:** $70–$80 single, $80–$95 twin, $80–$85 double, $85–$105 two double beds, $100–$150 suites. AE, DC, JCB, MC, V. **Parking:** Nearby garage, $20.

If you can't get into the Remington, consider a larger establishment run by the same management, where the rates are a bit higher but also reasonable by New York standards. The Wentworth offers pleasant rooms, cheerfully decorated with flowered wallpaper and spreads. A coffee shop provides room service. The Wentworth is well located, close to Fifth Avenue and the charming People Plaza, a minipark between 45th and 46th streets, laced with interlocking gardens, outdoor sculpture, and cascading waters. In spring and fall, midtown workers pause here for lunch and free noontime entertainment. The hotel's winding, crystal-chandeliered lobby boasts its own 60-booth Jewelry Exchange. Many guests are South American or European.

MANSFIELD HOTEL, 12 W. 44th St., New York, NY 10036. Tel. 212/944-6050 or toll free 800/255-5167. Fax 212/764-4447, telex 421348. 200 rms (with bath). A/C MINIBAR TV TEL **Subway:** 4, 5, 6 to 42nd St.

$ **Rates:** $65–$70 single; $75–$80 double or twin; $85, $95, $100 junior suite for 2, 3, or 4 people; $100, $120, $140 large suite for 4 to 6 people. AE, DISC, MC, V. **Parking:** Nearby garage, $15 minus 10% discount for hotel guests.

Just a few steps from Fifth Avenue, the Mansfield is a modest but acceptable budget choice, popular with European, South American, and Japanese guests. What it has going for it is a good location, on the same block as the Harvard Club and the New

York Bar Association; a friendly staff; and a small lobby that adjoins O'Lunney's, a delightful Irish pub offering country music and folk singing 4 nights a week. Limited room service is available via the Sandwich Shop. What it lacks—aside from the splendid staircase intact in this Stanford White 1907 building—is charm. Rooms are clean, but small with minimal decoration. The cozy suites are perhaps the best buy here, and refrigerators can be furnished on request.

PORTLAND SQUARE HOTEL, 132 W. 47th St. (between Avenue of the Americas and Seventh Ave.), New York, NY 10036. Tel. 212/382-0600 or toll free 800/388-8988. Fax 212/382-0684. 104 rms (with shared and private bath). A/C TV TEL **Subway:** 1, 9 to 50th St.

$ Rates: $40 single with shared bathroom facilities; $60 single with private bath; $75 double, one bed, private bath; $85 double, two beds, private bath; $90 double for 3 persons, private bath; $95 double for 4 persons, private bath. AE, MC, V. **Parking:** Nearby garages, from $20.

Here's a delightful budget oasis in the midst of the busy Times Square area. The Portland Square Hotel has been, under another name, a theater hotel since 1904 (James Cagney was one of the famous who stayed here). Now, with all new electricity and plumbing, it's been totally transformed, boasting a small-but-stylish lobby decorated with old Broadway photographs and other memorabilia of the 1920s and '30s, and tiny, tidy, comfortably furnished guest rooms. The Puchall family management (which has also transformed the Herald Square Hotel and the Washington Square Hotel) likes to treat their guests with old-fashioned hospitality. They provide lockers where guests may store luggage after they've checked out, and a comfortable sitting area, a rarity in many budget hotels. The Portland Square describes itself as a "classic limited-service budget hotel." There's no room service and the rooms are small, but if you want clean and central, this is a great buy.

PRESIDENT HOTEL, 234 W. 48th St. (between Broadway and Eighth Ave.), New York, NY 10036. Tel. 212/246-8800, or toll free 800/826-4667. Fax 212/974-3922. 369 rms, 14 suites (with bath). A/C TV TEL **Subway:** 1, 9 or C, E to 50th St.

$ Rates: $65 single, $75 twin, $150 suite, only for readers of this book who reserve directly; regular rates are about $20 higher. AE, DC, DISC, ER, JCB, MC, V. **Parking:** Nearby garage, $12.

Total remodeling has created a handsome 16-story hotel with a spectacular postmodern lobby, complete with its skylit Atrium Court and waterfall and floors of Italian marble. La Primavera is a stunning room for Italian and continental cuisine, and the piano bar is a popular spot for drinks and conversation. Brasserie D'Artiste Coffee Shop offers deli-style meals. Guest rooms are most attractive, with mauve spreads and drapes and handsome bathrooms with luxury personal-care items. Room sizes vary, but all are respectable; some of the smaller rooms even have little balconies. Beds are twins or doubles, with some queen-size beds. There's concierge service and a multilingual staff. This building is corporate headquarters for the Chatwall company, which operates this hotel and Quality Inn Midtown (see below).

QUALITY INN MIDTOWN, 157 W. 47th St. (between Sixth and Seventh aves.), New York, NY 10036. Tel. 212/768-3700, or toll free 800/334-4667. Fax 212/768-3403. 210 rms, 100 suites (with bath). A/C TV TEL **Subway:** 1, 9, B, D, F to 50th St.

$ Rates (for readers of this book who reserve directly): $75 single, $85 double, $90 triple, $95 quad. AE, DC, DISC, ER, JCB, MC, V. **Parking:** Nearby garage, $11.

A residential atmosphere pervades this "olde New York–style" hotel. On one side of the attractive lobby is La Veranda, a tasteful restaurant for northern Italian cuisine. The guest rooms, of decent size, are done in a maroon-and-white color scheme and have handsome beige tile or marble bathrooms. Guests are served complimentary continental breakfast in the lobby atrium.

Regular rates are about $20 higher than those quoted above.

**RAMADA HOTEL, W. 48th St. and Eighth Ave., New York, NY 10019.
Tel. 212/581-7000,** or toll free 800/228-2828. Fax 212/974-0291, telex
147182. 336 rms (with bath). A/C TV TEL **Subway:** C, E to 50th St.
$ **Rates:** $98, $108, $118, $128, $138 single; $110, $120, $130, $140, $150 family
rooms. AE, CB, DC, DISC, ER, JCB, MC, V. **Parking:** On premises, $7.75.

The redecorated Ramada Hotel looks very handsome, with its chrome-and-glass,
hi-tech modern lobby, softened by comfortable furniture and a marble terrazzo floor.
The attractive rooftop pool on the 15th floor has an open-air cocktail lounge and
skyscraper views. The sunny, plant-filled Jerry's Metro restaurant is a New York–style
deli and cocktail lounge. Rooms have been redecorated in mauve and teal, and come
with such amenities as oversize closets with safe (at nominal charge), AM/FM radios,
and in-room movies. Beds are either double, double doubles, or king-size. The
Ramada boasts a tight security system: Security guards in and out of uniform patrol
the hotel constantly. Rates go a bit high for our budget, but since the hotel is large,
you can usually get something at the lower rates.

**TRAVEL INN MOTOR HOTEL, 515 W. 42nd St. (between Tenth and
Eleventh aves.), New York, NY 10036. Tel. 212/695-7171** or toll free
800/869-4630. Fax 212/967-5025. 160 rms (with bath). A/C TV TEL **Subway:** A,
C, E to 42nd St.
$ **Rates:** $90 single, $105 double, $115 triple, $135 quad. Rollaways $10. Children
16 and under stay free in parents' room. AE, DC, MC, V. **Parking:** On premises,
free.

⭐ The Travel Inn Motor Hotel has always been popular with visitors who want
the convenience of a central location, free parking, and a refreshing swim when
they come home from a hard day's sightseeing or business. A total renovation
was completed a few years ago, making the hotel better than ever, and still an
excellent value for New York. Even standard rooms are enormous, most are furnished
with two double beds, desks, imported white furniture from France, matching
draperies and spreads done in seashell motifs. The halls are handsome, with marble
and glass panels on the walls. The lobby is small, but the gathering places here are an
Olympic-size outdoor swimming pool (reserved strictly for guests of the hotel), several
pretty courtyards, and sunbathing areas decked out with garden furniture. All of this
makes the hotel an excellent choice for families with children. On the premises is the
Bistro 42nd Restaurant.

The location is excellent—one block from the Off-Broadway 42nd Street Theater
Row and just a few blocks from Times Square (easily accessible by crosstown bus).
The Travel Inn is very popular, so try to reserve at least 2 weeks in advance if possible,
especially in the summer.

The Travel Inn offers several package deals. The most popular, which is called "Big
Apple by Air, Land & Sea," includes accommodations for 3 days, a helicopter ride, a
Circle Line boat cruise, a full American breakfast every day and a complete
dinner—all for $360 single, or $240 per person in a double. This and other packages
are available daily.

**TRAVELODGE HOTEL SKYLINE MANHATTAN, 49th to 50th sts. on
Tenth Ave., New York, NY 10019. Tel. 212/586-3400,** or toll free
800/433-1982, 800/327-6542 in Canada. Fax 212/582-4604, telex 262559. 230
rms, 10 suites (with bath). A/C TV TEL **Subway:** A, C, E to 42nd St.
$ **Rates:** $90 single, $98 double; $150, $200, $250 suites; extra person $20. Up to
2 children under 14 can stay in parents' room free. AE, CB, DC, ER, MC, V.
Parking: On premises, complimentary (with a $2 in-and-out charge).

Things are looking very good indeed at this place, which has recently become part of
the Travelodge chain and was completely redone several years back, from its skylit
glass-and-marble lobby with its comfortable seating areas, to the new coffee
shop–restaurant–cocktail lounge and piano bar called Clinton Bar & Grill. This is a
large hotel, with the rooms spread out over two buildings, and best of all, a beautiful
glass-enclosed rooftop swimming pool, complete with sun deck and sauna, heated

and open all year. There's exercise equipment—a rowing machine, bikes, a treadmill, and so on—in the pool area, too, so guests need never miss their daily workouts. The rooms are very large, done in attractive color schemes, with radio and wakeup alarm clocks, individual climate control, and large desks; modern tile baths have tub/shower combinations. Comfortable suites, with a sofabed in the living room, make good family choices.

HOTEL WELLINGTON, 871 Seventh Ave. at 55th St., New York, NY 10019. Tel. 212/247-3900, or toll free 800/652-1212. Fax 212/581-1719, telex 66297UW. 700 rms, 100 suites (with bath). A/C TV TEL **Subway:** N, R to 57th St. or D, E to Seventh Ave.

$ Rates: Standard rooms: $89–$94 single, $99–$104 double. Tower Rooms: $99–$104 single, $109–$114 double. Family Rooms: $120–$125, $130–$175 1-bedroom suite. AE, DC, MC, V. **Parking:** Nearby garage, around $19.

Your fellow guests at the Wellington are apt to be a varied crowd: perhaps dancers from a ballet company appearing at the nearby City Center, visitors from Scandinavia and Western Europe, businesspeople and tourists—all attracted by a good location and a good price. One of New York's older hotels, the Wellington consists of three buildings, some of which house both visitors and long-term guests. Standard rooms, which have either twin or double beds, are small but pleasant, with bamboo headsteads and perhaps rose-colored spreads (color schemes vary from floor to floor). Many rooms have been completely redone, with laminated furniture and a more modern decor. Most rooms have both tub and shower, though some have shower only. Very nice indeed are the Tower Rooms, quite large, with space for a table and chairs. And nicest of all are the large suites, lovely, with double convertible sofas in the living rooms; some have stoves and refrigerators. Family rooms have two double beds and two bathrooms. The Park Café coffee shop adjoining the attractive lobby, open from 6am to 1am, also provides room service.

THE WESTPARK HOTEL, 308 W. 58th St., New York, NY 10019. Tel. 212/246-6440 or toll free 800/248-6440. Fax 212/246-3131. 100 rms, 10 suites (with bath). A/C TV TEL **Subway:** 1, 9, A, B, C, D to 59th St.; N, R to 57th St.

$ Rates (including continental breakfast): $70–$100 single, $80–$110 double; $140–$180 suites; 10% discount for readers who contact the hotel directly. AE, MC, V. **Parking:** Nearby garage, $10.

Just opposite Central Park, around the corner from Carnegie Hall and a short walk from Lincoln Center, the Westpark is a quiet, nine-story hotel with plenty going for it. It's an old, well-insulated building that has been charmingly renovated.

The Westpark is popular with businesspeople, tourists, and small groups. The modernistic lobby, with glass doors, mirrored columns, a fireplace, and soft-green velvet chairs, adjoins the Café Comedy next door. The rooms are decorated with maroon quilted bedspreads, ginger-jar lamps, and other nice touches; of course, all have AM/FM radios and other amenities. The higher-priced rooms have views of Central Park. Especially handsome are the one-bedroom suites: One of our favorites has pink drapes, a four-poster bed, two television sets, velvet sofas, a desk, and lovely lamps and prints. Guests can use the facilities of a nearby health club with a large indoor swimming pool for $10 a day. Free continental breakfast is served in a nearby restaurant. Many languages are spoken at the Westpark, and service is helpful and friendly.

AROUND HERALD SQUARE

HERALD SQUARE HOTEL, 19 W. 31st St., New York, NY 10001. Tel. 212/279-4017, or toll free 800/727-1888. Fax 212/643-9208. 115 rms (shared and private baths). A/C TV TEL **Subway:** B, D, F, N, R to 34th St.

$ Rates: $40 single with shared bathroom facilities; $50–$55 small single or double with private bath with shower; $65 standard single with bathroom with shower and tub; $70–$75 standard double with bathroom with shower and tub; $85 large double room; $90 large double room with three beds; $95 large double room for 4 with two doubles or four twins; all large doubles with private bathrooms. AE, DISC, JCB, MC, V. **Parking:** Nearby garage, around $20 to $30.

This landmark Beaux Arts building, built in 1893 by Carrère and Hastings, served as *Life* magazine's offices until 1936; upstairs lived such renowned New Yorkers as illustrator Charles Dana Gibson. Decades later it had become a run-down hotel. But now, the Puchal family, who have a passion for history and nostalgia, have transformed the building into a small, charming hotel, and it's been an instant success, especially with European tourists and South American buyers. The small, limited-service establishment is perfect for the budget traveler. And while the location is no longer fashionable, it is certainly convenient— around the corner from Macy's Herald Square, three blocks south of the Empire State Building, and close to the Fifth Avenue department stores. The nine-story building has been restored and renovated from top to bottom, inside and out, beginning with Philip Martiny's *Winged Life*, the gilded sculpture over the entrance. A small, sparkling lobby is decorated with reproductions of old *Life* magazine covers, as are the halls and guest rooms. All rooms are nicely done in pastel tones, and have brand-new bathrooms.

HOTEL STANFORD, 42 W. 33rd St., New York, NY 10001. Tel. 212/563-1480. Fax 212/629-0043. 135 rms (with bath). A/C TV TEL **Subway:** B, D, F, N, R to 34th St.

$ Rates: $80 single, $90 double, $100 twin; $120 larger doubles with extra bed; $130 larger twins; $180 and up, suites for 4 to 6 persons. Children under 12 free; extra person $15. AE, DC, JCB, MC, V. **Parking:** Nearby garage, $34.

Practically next door to Macy's and Abraham & Straus, and a block away from the Empire State Building, the Hotel Stanford offers quality at a good price. Korean-owned, the hotel caters to an international trade and maintains high standards, offering many of the amenities of a larger hotel while maintaining the friendliness and security of a smaller one. The bright, compact lobby boasts a small Japanese garden with a miniature pond and bridge, and the Garden coffee shop for all three meals. A door at the right leads to Sorabol, an inexpensive and authentic Korean restaurant, and on the second floor is Maxim's, a cozy piano bar. Rooms are tastefully decorated, and each has a small refrigerator. Bathrooms are all new. Suites, with lovely Oriental partitions dividing the space, are especially good for families.

HOTEL WOLCOTT, 4 W. 31st St., just off Fifth Ave., New York, NY 10001. Tel. 212/268-2900. Fax 212/563-0096. 250 rms (shared and private baths). A/C TV TEL **Subway:** B, D, F, N, R to 34th St.

$ Rates: $40 single or double, $45 triple, $50 quad, all with shared bath; $55 single or double, $65 triple, $75 quad, all with private bath. AE, MC, V. **Parking:** Nearby garage, about $16.

When it was completed in 1904, the Wolcott was one of the grandest in the city; for many years, the inaugural balls of New York's mayors were held here; its marvelous classical facade and ornate lobby are still intact. The Wolcott is now one of the best basic/budget bets in the area. Its location (across the street from the Herald Square Hotel) is convenient to Fifth Avenue shops and Broadway theaters. Rooms, kept up to snuff over the years, have all the basics, although some are small; try to get one of the larger rooms if you can. Shared bathrooms are well kept. Many long-term residents still live here. The hotel is very popular with Europeans, especially Scandinavians, and with South American visitors.

CHELSEA

THE CHELSEA HOTEL, 222 W. 23rd St. (between Seventh and Eighth aves.), New York, NY 10011. Tel. 212/243-3700. Fax 243-3700, ext. 2171. 400 rms (with bath). TEL **Subway:** 1, 9, C, E to 23rd St.

$ Rates: $65–$85 single, $75–$125 double, from $85 up kitchenette rooms, $150–$165 suites for 4, with kitchenette. AE, MC, V. **Parking:** Nearby garage, about $15.

In a city where the old is often torn down to make way for the new, the Chelsea has stood since 1882, catering to the bohemian, the creative, the offbeat, and those who thrive among them. It was the first hotel in the United States to be proclaimed a national landmark. This is the place where Andy Warhol made the movie *Chelsea Girls;* where Dylan Thomas, Brendan Behan, Lenny Bruce, Jane Fonda, and Elliot Gould all came to rest, retreat, and get inspiration; where the composer Virgil Thompson lived for years. Among the works that have been written at the Chelsea are Arthur Clarke's *2001,* Thomas Wolfe's *You Can't Go Home Again,* Arthur Miller's *After the Fall,* and William Burroughs's *Naked Lunch.* Manager Stanley Bard reigns over the scene, and his art collection (including many works from grateful tenants) turns the lobby here into a veritable art gallery. Note especially the sculpture called *Chelsea People*—you'll recognize many of the celebrities who have called the Chelsea home. A half-million-dollar renovation a few years back has spruced up the French Louisiana facade of the building with its wrought-iron balconies and made it more attractive than ever. A good Spanish restaurant, El Quijote, adjoins the hotel.

Many of the guests stay here for a long time—or forever—attracted by the soundproof walls (three feet thick!), the friendly family feeling, and the enormous rooms, each with unique features (perhaps working fireplaces or kitchens). Short-term visitors come from all over the world, attracted by the legend of the hotel. Even the smallest of the transient rooms is large by New York hotel standards. The furnishings are not luxurious (there are, for example, no pictures on the walls, since most tenants want to hang their own; bedspreads and drapes can be a bit somber, and the furniture is not new), but the rooms are adequate, and usually kept up. About half the rooms have air conditioning, and color TVs can be rented for $15 per week.

Readers of this book will be given the seventh night of a week's stay free if the week is prepaid. Request this when making reservations.

THE CHELSEA INN, 46 W. 17th St. (west of Fifth Ave.), New York, NY 10011. Tel. 212/645-8989, or toll free 800/777-8215. 13 rms (with bath). A/C TV TEL **Subway:** F to 14th St. or 1, 9 to 18th St.

$ Rates: $70 singles with shared bath; $78 double with shared bath; $105 studio with private bath: $135 suite with private bath. AE, MC, V. **Parking:** Nearby garage, $14.

This "urban inn" is designed especially for businesspeople and family vacationers who prefer an intimate, small establishment in a quiet part of town, complete with kitchenette. Close to the "Photography District," the "Flower Market," the Toy Center, the Gift Building, and the Garment Center, Chelsea Inn is very popular for long-term stays. Owners Linda Mandel, Mindy Goodfriend Chernoff, and Harry Chernoff bought this old building a few years ago, totally renovated it, and created rooms that offer homey comforts and more than a touch of charm. The nicely decorated rooms all have kitchenettes and AM/FM radios. Bathrooms have murals on the walls, and some rooms have a garden view. Families do best in the two-room suites, with a double bed in one room and a highrise that opens into two separate beds in the other. Rollaways can be added to any room for $10 a night. Those rooms on the first three floors are all walk-ups. The front desk closes every night at 9pm, so guests are given their own front-door keys.

GREENWICH VILLAGE

WASHINGTON SQUARE HOTEL, 103 Waverly Place (between Sixth Ave. and Washington Square Park), New York, NY 10011. Tel. 212/777-9595 or toll free 800/222-0418. Fax 212/979-8373, telex 12-6909. 200 rms (with bath). A/C TV TEL **Subway:** A, B, C, D, E, F, Q to West 4th St.

$ Rates: $52 single, $74–$95 double standard (unrefurbished); $60 single, $83–$105 deluxe (refurbished). AE, MC, JCB, V. **Parking:** Nearby garage, $19.

★ There's only one tourist hotel in the Village, and luckily for us, it's a budget hotel. The Washington Square Hotel couldn't have a better location. It's steps away from Washington Square Park and in the very heart of the Village scene, with its restaurants, shops, clubs, and lively street life. The hotel, built in 1902, has been thoroughly renovated, and work on the rooms continues steadily. Most are tastefully decorated, with hand-painted walls with muted floral designs, and well-coordinated drapes and bedspreads. The deluxe (refurbished) rooms cost a bit more and are much nicer. The new lobby is a beauty, with tile floors, a wrought-iron gate, and a winding staircase. Guests, who may be European or Japanese tourists or musicians who play the local clubs, get lots of friendly service and sightseeing tips here. They have the use of fax and telex machines in the office, and there's a room with lockers where they can store their belongings if they must check out early. In the works at this writing are a fitness center and a coffee shop.

LINCOLN CENTER/UPPER WEST SIDE

This is one of the most congenial areas in New York for the budget-minded. Not only are rates invariably lower and values much greater than in midtown hotels, the location could not be more convenient. The 104 bus, which runs along Broadway, goes directly to the midtown theater district. Subway connections are also quick and easy.

BROADWAY AMERICAN HOTEL, 2178 Broadway at 77th St., New York, NY 10024. Tel. 212/362-1100 or toll free 800/445-4556. Fax 212/787-9521, telex 6790802 BWAY UW. 200 rms (shared and private baths). A/C TV TEL **Subway:** 1, 9 to 79th St.

$ **Rates:** $45 single, $65 double, $75 triple, with shared bath; $79 single, $89 double, $99 triple, with private bath. Children under 12 stay free in parents' room. AE, MC, V. **Parking:** Nearby garages, $15–$20.

Ⓢ Built in 1919 and treated to a smashing multimillion-dollar renovation in 1990, this hotel is good news for budget travelers. Although about half the rooms are still used by long-term residents, the renovation has created a handsome new lobby, three high-speed elevators, all new bathrooms, and new guest rooms that are small, streamlined models of efficiency: Decorated in soft gray and black, with cut-out black headboards, each boasts a small refrigerator, safe in the closet, and an individual temperature control. Most rooms, even those with private baths, have sinks. There are at least seven bathrooms on each floor; some have tubs as well as showers. Rooms for nonsmokers are available. There are washers and dryers and vending machines on alternating floors. Adjoining the hotel are a Chinese restaurant and a bagelry; dozens of other restaurants are within walking distance.

CAMBRIDGE HOUSE HOTEL, 333 W. 86th St., New York, NY 10024. Tel. 212/873-8800. Fax 212/873-8926. 75 rms, 35 suites (with baths). A/C TV TEL. **Subway:** 1, 9 to 86th St.

$ **Rates:** $60 single, $85 double; $125–$185 suite. Extra person $10.
This is an older Upper West Side residential apartment hotel that's gradually being converted into accommodations for visitors. So far, about half of the rooms are available for short stays. They are a good buy, very large and well decorated, with spacious closets, new marble bathrooms, and small kitchenettes in almost all units (ask at the desk for cooking equipment). My favorite here is the top-of-the-line one-bedroom suite, with parquet floors, handsome modern furniture, a sofa bed in the living room, a full kitchen, and a terrace overlooking the Hudson River. Up to four could settle in comfortably here; monthly rates are available. The halls and lobby were scheduled for renovation as we went to press. La Mirabelle, a charming and popular French bistro, is right on the premises.

ESPLANADE HOTEL AND SUITES, 305 West End Ave. (at 74th St.), New York, NY 10023. Tel. 212/874-5000, or toll free 800/367-1763 from U.S. and Canada. Fax 212/496-0367. 50 rms, 150 suites (with baths). A/C TV TEL **Subway:** 1, 2, 3 to 72nd St

$ Rates: $90–$100 single, $99–$120 double. $140 for up to 4 in a one-bedroom suite, $210 for up to 6 in a two-bedroom suite. Inquire about special promotions and weekly rates. AE, CB, DC, DISC, MC, JCB, V. **Parking:** Discounted at nearby garage, $10.

Some of the largest hotel accommodations in New York can be found here. Move into one of the suites and you'll be inclined to throw a party! More than 60 years old, in a neighborhood of landmark buildings and tree-lined streets, this fine residential hotel now has rooms available to short-term visitors. Fellow guests are liable to be from London or Paris or next door—people who are having their apartments painted or redecorated often move in for a while. Many performers from nearby Lincoln Center stay here.

The lobby has been redecorated in an elegant design. You'll be in heaven if you can get one of the suites with a view of the Hudson River. Rooms are lovely, spacious, and nicely furnished, and many have walk-in closets. All have small kitchenettes. Suites are enormous; the bedroom has two double beds; the huge living room has an open-up couch; and all have kitchenettes. Considering the number of people they can hold in comfort, they are among the best bargains in town.

There's an exercise room and a laundry on the premises. And small pets are allowed. A modest $3.50 charge brings a continental breakfast and a daily newspaper to your room.

EXCELSIOR HOTEL, 45 W. 81st St. (off Central Park West), New York, NY 10024. Tel. 212/362-9200. Fax 212/721-2994. 300 rms (with bath). A/C TV TEL **Subway:** 1, 9 to 79th St.
$ Rates: $65–$75 single, $75–$85 double; $94–$108 kitchenette suite for 4; $130–$150 2-bedroom suite. AE, MC, V. **Parking:** Nearby garage, around $24.
Across the street from the American Museum of Natural History, in a residential block, the Excelsior is a charmer in the European manner. In fact, European visitors, including consular people and titled types, are frequent guests. Curators and couriers from the Metropolitan Museum of Art and the Museum of Modern Art stay here.

Three marble steps lead down to a graceful, high-ceilinged lobby, with an accommodating coffee shop off to one side that provides room service at breakfast. Rooms, constantly being updated and renovated, are done in pale tones, nicely if not lavishly furnished in light woods, quilted bedspreads, and matching draperies; and they have large closets. Upper-floor rooms at the front of the house offer views of the museum's park and the midtown skyline; those in the rear offer views of the gardens of houses on 82nd Street. They do not book wedding parties, and quickly dispense noisy guests. It's easy for families to save money by cooking in the suites' fully equipped kitchens. The hotel is at the top of the Columbus Avenue shopping-and-restaurant neighborhood, 16 blocks from Lincoln Center and a short bus ride to midtown shops and theaters. The management is helpful and security is excellent.

HOTEL OLCOTT, 27 W. 72nd St. (between Columbus Ave. and Central Park West), New York, NY 10023. Tel. 212/877-4200. Fax 212/580-0511. 45 rms, 55 suites (with bath). A/C TV TEL **Subway:** C to 72nd St.
$ Rates: $80 daily, $475 weekly studio for 1 person; $90 daily, $535 weekly studio for 2 persons; $110 daily, $650 weekly one-bedroom suite for 1 or 2 persons; $15 daily, $70 weekly for extra person sharing. No credit cards. **Parking:** Nearby garage, $20.

Many guests here are performers at nearby Lincoln Center, diplomats, and U.N. personnel. The Royal Ballet of London calls it their New York home, and so do half a dozen singers from the Metropolitan Opera and other celebrities. This residential hotel also has plenty of space for transients. It is very well located, close to Lincoln Center, across the street from Central Park, and in the very heart of the exciting Columbus Avenue scene. Its Dallas BBQ Restaurant is inexpensive, serving meals averaging $6 or $7 in a pleasant setting.

Studios and suites are spacious, clean, and homey, with attractive furnishings, big closets, and carpeted floors. All have cable, AM/FM radios, and fully equipped kitchenettes with hotplates and refrigerators. The suites have living rooms, and two-bedroom suites have two baths.

The management advises that you reserve 4 weeks in advance for an extended stay of a week or more; for 3 or 4 days, a week in advance; and for 1 night only, call during that week.

THE MILBURN, 242 W. 76th St., New York, NY 10023. Tel. 212/362-1006 or toll free 800/833-9622. Fax 212/721-5476. 70 rms (with bath). A/C TV TEL **Subway:** 1, 2, 3 to 72nd St.
$ Rates: $85–$100 single or double; $120–$160 suites. AE, CB, DC, MC, V.
Parking: Nearby garage, $14.

Once just another gracious West Side apartment building, the Milburn is now one of the nicest hotels in the area, thanks to management's converting 70 of its 120 apartments into guest rooms. Some $3 million was spent on the renovation of lobby and rooms; the lobby is small but handsome, with an Oriental carpet, chandeliers, and original paintings. Concierge service is available 24 hours a day. Studios are spacious, done in a cheerful modern mode, with a queen- or king-size bed or twins. All rooms have glass tables with chairs, carpeting, and new bathrooms. Best of all, each has a modern, fully equipped kitchenette with microwave oven and utensils. Suites are impressive, with the living room sofa opening into a queen-size bed. And all the rooms are quiet—there's no midtown construction noise here. Many international and corporate clients are frequent return guests.

3. WORTH THE EXTRA BUCKS

MIDTOWN EAST

JOURNEY'S END HOTEL, 3 E. 40th St., New York, NY 10016. Tel. 212/447-1500, or toll free 800/668-4200. Fax 212/213-0972. 189 rms. A/C TV TEL **Subway:** B, D, E or 4, 5, 6 to 42nd St.

 FROMMER'S COOL FOR KIDS
HOTELS

The Roger Williams (see p. 52). Try to get a large room with a terrace here and give the kids some space to stretch out. It will have a kitchenette, so you can fix their favorite snacks.

Travel Inn Motor Hotel (see p. 56). An Olympic-size outdoor swimming pool, a large recreation area, and plenty of space in which the kids can let off a little steam make this a family favorite.

Days Inn–New York (see p. 64). Kids adore the open-to-the-sky rooftop swimming pool at this hotel. They may not want to go anywhere else!

Travelodge Hotel Skyline Manhattan (see p. 56). Even if the weather is cool, the kids will love the glass-enclosed rooftop swimming pool, with sun deck and sauna, heated and open year round.

Stevens Institute of Technology (see p. 49). Older children can get the feeling of what it's like to live on a college campus. They'll also enjoy the indoor swimming pool, the tennis courts, and other sports facilities.

$ Rates: $125.88 single, $135.88 double (the 88¢ is a company tradition). Extra person $10. Children under 12 free. AE, DC, MC, V. **Parking:** Nearby garage, $25.

A value-oriented hotel in a superb location, just off Fifth Avenue and across the street from the New York Public Library, near Grand Central Station, and within walking distance of Broadway theaters, Journey's End is a welcome new addition to the New York hotel scene. It is the first entry in New York of the popular Canadian corporation that has achieved phenomenal success by offering "limited service lodging." They have no meeting rooms, swimming pools, or valet or room service—what they do have are handsome new buildings; clean, comfortable rooms; and plenty of friendly and personal service.

A good bet for both families and business travelers, the 29-story high rise has a small, attractive lobby and a mezzanine where guests can have complimentary coffee and read the local newspapers in the morning. Rooms are of average size and attractively furnished, most with queen-size beds and a sofa that converts to a small bed; some rooms have two double beds. Each room has a worktable, a large desk where a businessperson can spread out. The telephone is on a nonrestrictive 14-foot cord. Rooms also have wheelchair access.

UPPER EAST SIDE

THE HOTEL WALES, 1295 Madison Ave. (between 92nd and 93rd sts.), New York, NY 10028. Tel. 212/876-6000 or toll free 800/223-0888 U.S. & Canada. Fax 212/860-7000. 55 rms, 39 suites (with bath). A/C TV TEL **Subway:** 6 to 86th St. or 4, 5, 6 to 96th St.

$ Rates (including continental breakfast and afternoon tea): $125–$145 single or double; $175–$225 suite. Extra person $20. AE, MC, V. **Parking:** Valet, $21 a day.

Carnegie Hill, which begins at 86th Street and Madison Avenue, is one of New York's most agreeable residential areas, dotted with art galleries, lovely shops, and a plethora of sophisticated restaurants. The Hotel Wales has long been a standby here, offering gracious rooms at good rates. The owners have recently renovated the venerable building, redoing all the rooms with handsome traditional furniture, installing new windows that enhance the views of Central Park available from many rooms, and stripping the painted wood surfaces down to their original beauty. New lighting, carpeting, and bedspreads have all been installed, and the petite lobby, with its vaulted ceiling and colonnaded winding marble staircase, is prettier than ever. All rooms are of good size. The lovely suites have either queen- or king-size beds, plus a sofabed in the living room. Some of the rooms and suites have refrigerators.

In the lobby are two enjoyable restaurants: Sarabeth's Kitchen, a New York favorite for quiches, omelets, and other light food, serving three meals a day, beginning with a luscious breakfast; and Busby, a popular bistro offering well-priced lunches and dinners. An attractive breakfast room is on the second floor; guests can read the local and international newspapers with their morning coffee. Afternoon tea is also available.

For a fee of $12 a day, guests at the Wales may use the facilities, including a lovely swimming pool, at the nearby Olympic Spa.

MIDTOWN WEST

AMERITANIA HOTEL, 1701 Broadway, at 54th St., New York, NY 10019. Tel. 212/247-5000 or toll free 800/922-0330. Fax 212/247-3316. 250 rms, 12 suites (with baths). Weekend packages available. A/C TV TEL **Subway:** D, E to Seventh Ave.; 1, 9 to 50th St.; N, R to 57th St.

$ Rates: $99–$139 single or double; $125–$175 suite. Extra person $10. Children 17 and under free in parents' room. AE, MC, JCB, V. **Parking:** Nearby garage, discounted rate of $12.

★ You say you've always wanted to be on Broadway? Well, here's your chance. Not only will the sparkling new Ameritania Hotel give you a lodging right on Broadway itself, in the heart of the entertainment district, but a very respectable price. A total remake of an old theatrical hotel (Frank Sinatra and the Rat Pack used to hang out here way back when), the Ameritania has a graceful lobby with a waterfall, and clublike atmosphere. The guest rooms are of good size and decorated elegantly, with rose carpeting, soft pastel spreads and drapes, clock radios, a sitting area in each room, and gorgeous bathrooms completely done in Italian marble. The TV (color cable with HBO and in-room movies) is discreetly hidden in an armoire. Most of the rooms have two double beds; there are a few with queen-size beds or twins. Junior suites, with two doubles in one room and a regular bed or sofa bed in the adjoining room, are well set up for family living. Free coffee and rolls are available in the breakfast room, and Valentino's, a stylish Italian restaurant, adjoins the hotel. There's a well-equipped exercise room and a gift shop. Guests receive complimentary admission to the nearby Ritz nightclub.

COMFORT INN MURRAY HILL, 42 W. 35th St., New York, NY 10001. Tel. 212/947-0200, or toll free 800/228-5150. Fax 212/594-3047. 120 rms (with bath). A/C TV TEL **Subway:** B, D, F, N, R to 34th St.

$ Rates: $99–$109 single, $114–$124 double; $129–$139 room with double bed and pullout sofa; $109–$119 room with queen-size bed; $119–$139 room with king-size bed (no rooms with two doubles or twins available). Extra person $12. Weekend packages available. AE, CB, DC, DISC, ER, JCB, MC, V. **Parking:** Nearby garage, $20.

A small luxury hotel at modest prices, Comfort Inn Murray Hill boasts European charm, personal service, and a handy location just around the corner from Fifth Avenue department stores and near Seventh Avenue's Garment District and not far from Jacob Javits Convention Center; no wonder it's a hit among fashion industry buyers and other smart business and vacation travelers. This older building with its thick walls was recently given a $4.5-million renovation. The charming small lobby, with its winding marble staircase, Greek columns, and plush furnishings, is the scene of complimentary morning coffee and Danishes. There are no more than 12 rooms on each floor, which makes for a cozy feeling (women traveling alone seem to feel especially safe here), and these rooms are very pleasantly decorated in soothing pastel tones; all have newly tiled baths. A floor for nonsmokers is available. Manager Shirley Solomon advises that you call the hotel directly, rather than the 800 number; you may qualify for AARP, AAA, senior-citizen, corporate, fashion industry, or other discounts.

DAYS INN–NEW YORK, 440 W. 57th St., between Ninth and Tenth aves., New York, NY 10019. Tel. 212/581-8100, or toll free 800/325-2525; from Canada, call collect 416/964-3434. Fax 212/581-8719, telex 960413. 590 rms and suites (with bath). A/C TV TEL **Subway:** 1, 9, A, C, D to 59th St., then 57th St. crosstown bus.

$ Rates: $99–$139 single, $114–$164 double; $225–$275 suite. Discounts of 10% to 50% for senior citizens who are members of "September Days Club" ($12 membership fee; phone 800/241-5050). AE, DC, DISC, MC, V. **Parking:** On premises, $7; free for corporate guests.

This New York member of the Days Inn chain has a lot going for it: an excellent location, comfortable rooms, an attractive plant-filled lobby, an on-site garage, and, best of all, an open-air rooftop swimming pool and café. The attractive Greenery Restaurant offers all three meals plus room service. Rooms, quite large by New York standards, are attractively decorated in pastel and earth colors; bedding can be either two double beds or a king-size bed. More expensive King Leisure and Deluxe rooms also have sofas. Definitely worth trying for is their "Bonanza Days" package: for $55 per person in a double, two people get a room, continental breakfast, free newspaper, and free parking; up to 2 children under 17 can stay in their parents' room free (breakfast not included). An extra night is $49.50 per person.

THE WYNDHAM, 42 West 58th St. between Fifth and Sixth aves, New York, NY 10019. Tel. 212/753-3500. 152 rms, 60 suites. A/C TV TEL **Subway:** B to 57th St.; N, R to Fifth Ave.

$ Rates: $115–$125 single, $130–$140 double, $175–$210 1-bedroom suite, $285–$325 2-bedroom suite. AE, DC, MC, V. **Parking:** Nearby garage, $28.

★ The Wyndham is one of New York's best-kept secrets, a hotel cherished by those who appreciate old-fashioned warmth, charm, and graciousness; staying here is like being a guest in a club where everybody knows your name. Resident owners John and Suzanne Mados and their staff create an atmosphere that has long attracted visiting film, theater, and literary folks; Sir Alec Guiness, Eva Marie Saint, Peter O'Toole, Philip Roth, and Eva Gabor are some of the famous guests, and it was always Sir Laurence Olivier's home when he was appearing on Broadway. The plush lobby that looks like the living room of a European country inn leads to the rooms and suites, each with its own distinctive personality. All are done with a tasteful mixture of antiques and one-of-a-kind pieces, good paintings on the walls, and graceful touches throughout, as well as the expected individually controlled air conditioning, cable color TV, and good-sized baths. If you can afford a super-splurge, indulge yourself with one of their exquisite suites: Sir Laurence's favorite was Suite 1401 with handsome chandeliers, huge bed, gilt-edged mirrors, and Persian carpets.

Jonathan's Restaurant, right on the premises, offers three reasonably priced meals a day. And, oh yes, the Plaza Hotel is right across the street.

4. WEEKEND & OTHER PACKAGES

Many New York hotels and travel companies offer weekend package deals that prove to be relatively inexpensive. During the week, most of the city's top hotels are occupied by out-of-town business executives. When the weekend comes, the rooms are empty. To fill the gap, many hotels offer couples excellent rates for a 2- or 3-day period, and throw in a few breakfasts and dinners, and sometimes a few theater tickets as well. Some packages are also available during the week.

For a complete rundown on hotel packages, pick up or write for a free pamphlet called *New York City Tour Package Directory*, available from the New York Convention and Visitors Bureau, 2 Columbus Circle, New York, NY 10019. Your travel agent will also know of many packages. If you can get copies of the *New York Times*, check the Sunday Travel Section where many packages are advertised.

Keeping in mind that all rates are subject to change, and that bookings are based on availability, here are some examples. The hotels, of course, can be approached directly.

⑤ ✪ If you'd rather stay in a suite with a kitchen, you can't do better than to reserve one of the extraordinary weekend packages offered by the **Manhattan East Suite Hotels.** This company manages (among many others) eight of the city's most prestigious luxury suite hotels, including the **Shelburne Murray Hill,** 303 Lexington Ave., at 37th Street; the **Beekman Tower,** 49th Street and First Avenue, opposite the United Nations Plaza; the **Eastgate Tower,** 222 E. 39th St.; the **Dumont Plaza,** 150 E. 34th St.; **Lyden Gardens,** 215 E. 64th St.; **Lyden House,** 320 E. 53rd St.; **Plaza Fifty,** 155 E. 50th St.; and the **Southgate Tower,** 371 Seventh Ave., at 31st Street, opposite Madison Square Garden and Pennsylvania Station. When corporate guests go home for the weekend, their exquisite apartments become available at much lower prices. A studio for two people, normally renting for $150 to $220, is $115; a junior suite (a very large, L-shaped room with a dining area) that usually rents for $160 to $220 for up to three people, is $125; a one-bedroom suite for up to four people, normally renting for $185 to $255, is $140. Weekend rates at the Beekman Tower range from $140–$295. This has to be one of the best deals in town, especially for a large family or two couples traveling together. The suites are large, gracious, and exquisitely furnished, and all have fully equipped kitchens. Of course, all the usual hotel services and amenities are available.

Which of these hotels to choose is your only problem. The Eastgate Tower and Southgate Tower have on-premises garages. Lyden House and Southgate Tower have no two-bedroom suites. Reservations can be made up to 2 months in advance. Some fall weekends may not be available. For reservations, call 212/465-3690, or toll free 800/ME-SUITE.

Note: Rates are good on Friday, Saturday, or Sunday night, but you must arrive on Friday or Saturday to qualify for the Sunday rate.

Good-value "No Frills" weekends are offered at the five pricey Helmsley hotels in New York. Best deals of all are at the **Helmsley Windsor,** 100 W. 58th St., New York, NY 10019 (tel. 212/265-2100), and the **Helmsley Middletowne,** 148 E. 48th St., New York, NY 10017 (tel. 212/755-3000), where the price of a double room is $114 per night for a Friday and/or Saturday arrival. The Middletowne has kitchenettes. The **New York Helmsley,** 212 E. 42nd St., New York, NY 10017 (tel. 212/490-8900), has deluxe accommodations for $140 per double room per night for Friday and/or Saturday arrival. All these can be booked by calling their toll-free number: 800/221-4982.

"Weekend à la Carte" offers luxury with a French touch at the lovely **Parker Meridien,** 118 W. 57th St., New York, NY 10019 (tel. 212/245-5000, or toll free 800/543-4300). One or two nights' (Friday or Saturday arrival) accommodations and membership in the hotel's health club (year-round pool, Nautilus equipment, sauna, and so on) are included for the price of $150 per night for two people.

The attractive **Doral Inn,** 541 Lexington Ave. (at 49th Street), New York, NY 10022 (tel. 212/755-1200, or toll free 800/223-5832), has a "No Frills" package for a neat price: $99 per room per night, for single, double, or triple occupancy.

The **Doral Park Avenue,** 70 Park Ave. (at 38th Street), New York, NY 10016 (tel. 212/687-7050, or toll free 800/847-4135), is a European-style hotel with the only sidewalk café on Park Avenue. All rooms have refrigerators, premier movie channels, and marble baths with dryers. Their "Weekend in the Big Apple" package for 1 or 2 nights (Thursday to Sunday arrival) offers accommodations in deluxe rooms plus continental breakfast, parking, and health club privileges for $130, single or double.

The **Grand Hyatt New York,** Park Avenue at Grand Central (tel. 212/883-1234 or 800/228-9000), offers a honeymoon package called "Romance Honeymoon": deluxe king-bedded accommodations, champagne and chocolate-dipped strawberries, and free parking, all for $185 per room. Alas, this honeymoon only lasts 1 night: Friday, Saturday, or Sunday.

The "Hilton Bounce Back" is a popular program at the **New York Hilton & Towers** at Rockefeller Center, 1335 Avenue of the Americas (between 53rd and 54th streets), New York, NY 10019 (tel. 212/586-7000 or 800/HILTONS). Stays of 1 to 3 nights, Thursday through Sunday, are available for $165 in the regular hotel, $195 in the Towers, and that includes accommodations, continental breakfast, and two children staying free in their parents' room.

The stylish **Novotel New York,** 226 W. 52nd St., New York, NY 10019 (tel. 212/315-0100 or toll free 800/221-3185) offers a good deal with its "Broadway Bed & Breakfast" plan: the price of $147.75 single, $80.25 per person in a double, includes accommodations and a full American breakfast buffet in Café Nicole. Children under 16 can stay free in their parents' room and also get the free breakfast.

Note: Packages are subject to availability and prices are subject to change.

5. ROOMS FOR FAMILIES

Many of our hotels cater specifically to families traveling with children, or possess unusually large rooms in which additional cots can be placed.

MIDTOWN AREA

The renowned but offbeat **Chelsea Hotel,** 222 W. 23rd St. (between Seventh and Eighth avenues), New York, NY 10011 (tel. 212/243-3700), has family apartments for four—two rooms with kitchen—from $150–$165 a night, and less for weekly stays and longer.

There are kitchenettes in all the units at the cozy little **Chelsea Inn,** 46 W. 17th St. (just west of Fifth Avenue), New York, NY 10011 (tel. 212/645-8989). Families can enjoy one-bedroom suites at $135 for two ($10 for each additional person, up to four).

In the Herald Square area, families can share a good-sized room with two double beds for under $100 at the newly renovated **Herald Square Hotel,** 19 W. 31st St. (just west of Fifth Avenue), New York, NY 10010 (tel. 212/279-4017, or toll free 800/727-1888).

The **Hotel Consulate,** 224 W. 49th St. (west of Broadway), New York, NY 10019 (tel. 212/246-5252), has suites that can sleep up to four people, at $110 to $150 (for two).

Very large rooms with two double beds can easily house you and the kids, and there's a swimming pool too, at the **Travel Inn Motor Hotel,** 515 W. 42nd St. (between Tenth and Eleventh avenues), New York, NY 10036 (tel. 212/695-7171). Doubles are $105, and $10 for each extra person.

The kids will enjoy the pool and all of you can bunk in rooms with two double beds for $98 to $115 (or in a suite starting at $150) at the **Travelodge Hotel Skyline Manhattan,** 49th to 50th streets on Tenth Avenue, New York, NY 10019 (tel. 212/586-3400, or toll free 800/433-1982, 800/327-6542 in Canada).

Family rooms with two double beds, sleeping three or four, run $110 to $120, and suites are $130 to $150 at the **Hotel Edison,** 228 W. 47th St. (just west of Broadway), New York, NY 10036 (tel. 212/840-5000, or toll free 800/367-7070).

Large, beautifully furnished suites cost $95 for two, $125 for three, $135 for four, $145 for five at the **Hotel Iroquois,** 49 W. 44th St. (between Fifth and Sixth avenues), New York, NY 10036 (tel. 212/840-3080).

Doubles and family rooms cost from $110 to $150 at the **Ramada Hotel,** 48th Street and Eighth Avenue, New York, NY 10019 (tel. 212/581-7000, or toll free 800/2-RAMADA). The kids will love the rooftop pool.

Cozy suites sleep four to six at the **Hotel Mansfield,** 12 W. 44th St. (just west of Fifth Avenue), New York, NY 10036 (tel. 212/944-6050), and cost $100 for four, $120 for five, or $140 for six.

Family rooms are a good buy at the **Hotel Wellington,** Seventh Avenue at 55th Street, New York, NY 10019 (tel. 212/247-3900, or toll free 800/652-1212). Rooms with two double beds and two bathrooms are $120 and $125; elegant one-bedroom suites go for $130 to $175.

A pretty room with two double beds costs $90 at the **Hotel Remington,** 129 W. 46th St. (between Sixth and Seventh avenues), New York, NY 10036 (tel. 212/221-2600, or toll free 800/223-1900). And similar rooms are $85 to $105, while suites rent for $100 to $150, at a sister establishment, the **Hotel Wentworth,** 59 W. 56th St. (between Fifth and Sixth avenues), New York, NY 10036 (tel. 212/719-2300).

Children under 12 can stay free with their parents at the **Hotel Stanford,** 42 W. 33rd St., New York, NY 10001 (tel. 212/563-1480); large suites for 4 to 6 persons begin at $180.

At Columbus Circle, luxurious one-bedroom suites for up to four people can be found for $140 to $180 at the **Westpark Hotel,** 308 W. 58th St. (between Eighth and Ninth avenues), New York, NY 10019 (tel. 212/246-6440). A 10% discount is offered to our readers.

The **Roger Williams,** 28 E. 31st St., New York, NY 10016 (tel. 212/684-7500 or toll free 800/637-9773), offers large family rooms with kitchenettes and maybe even a terrace: $75 to $85 for triples, $80 to $90 for quads.

Families who don't mind sharing the bath can stay at the **Vanderbilt YMCA,** 224 E. 47th St. (between Second and Third avenues), New York, NY 10017 (tel.

212/755-2410). Triples and quads (with bunk beds) rent for $63 and $84, respectively, and full use of all health-club facilities—including a terrific pool—is included. (Summer rates are slightly higher.)

The **Pickwick Arms Hotel,** 230 E. 51st St. (between Second and Third avenues), New York, NY 10022 (tel. 212/355-0300), is a budget hotel in a fashionable location. Studios with a double plus a sofabed go for $95. A few rooms in the rear overlook a garden.

UPPER EAST SIDE

The **Hotel Wales,** 1295 Madison Ave. (between 92nd and 93rd streets), New York, NY 10028 (tel. 212/876-6000), has newly redone suites that can sleep up to four people for $175 to $225 for two, plus $5 each for the third or fourth guests. There's a sofabed in the living room, and queen- or king-size beds in the sleeping room.

On weekends only, several luxurious residential hotels managed by **Manhattan East Suite Hotels** offer studio apartments and suites at reduced rates: $115 for a studio, $125 for a junior suite, and $140 for a one-bedroom suite accommodating up to four people. For full details, see "Weekend and Other Packages," above.

UPPER WEST SIDE

A very good bet is the **Hotel Olcott,** 27 W. 72nd St. (between Columbus Avenue and Central Park West), New York, NY 10023 (tel. 212/877-4200). Two to four people in a spacious one-bedroom suite with fully equipped kitchenette and living room pay from $100 to $130. Larger suites are sometimes available in summer, and weekly rates are especially good here.

Another Upper West Side favorite is the sedate **Excelsior Hotel,** 45 W. 81st St. (off Central Park West), New York, NY 10024 (tel. 212/362-9200), across from the American Museum of Natural History, which offers beautiful suites with full kitchens, housing two to five people, for $94, $108, $130, and $150.

You and the kids can all stretch out in the very large suites at **Esplanade Hotel and Suites,** 305 West End Ave. (at 74th Street), New York, NY 10023 (tel. 212/874-5000, or toll free 800/367-1763, U.S. and Canada). One-bedroom suites are $140 for up to four; two-bedroom suites run $210 for up to six people.

At the attractive **Hotel Milburn,** 242 W. 76th St., New York, NY 10023 (tel. 212/362-1006), families can relax in bedroom and parlor suites, at $130 to $160 for two people; children under 12 stay free with their parents.

Cambridge House Hotel, 333 W. 86th St., New York, NY 10024 (tel. 212/873-8800), is a homey place with large rooms; suites are $125 to $185.

NEW JERSEY

On the campus of the **Stevens Institute of Technology** in Hoboken, N.J. (tel. toll free 800/526-2915), families can enjoy a suite with two twin beds, two rollaways, and a fully equipped kitchen, for all of $120 per night.

6. ROOMS FOR SERVICE PERSONNEL

While the USO does not have hotel rooms, it can help service personnel on active duty, and their families, get New York hotel rooms at rates of 20% to 40% off regular prices. The **Gen. Douglas MacArthur Memorial Center** is at 151 W. 46th St. (between sixth and seventh avenues), New York, NY 10036 (tel. 212/719-5433). They often have free tickets to movies, Broadway shows, and sports events on a day-to-day basis, and provide information on New York sightseeing and nightlife. Free refreshments are often available, too, with volunteers doing the cooking.

THE SOLDIERS' SAILORS' AND AIRMEN'S CLUB, INC., 283 Lexington

Ave., between 36th and 37th sts., New York, NY 10016. Tel. 212/
683-4353 or 800/678-TGIF. 28 rms (shared baths). **Subway:** 6 to 33rd St.
$ Rates: $30 Fri, Sat, and hols; $25 Sun–Thurs for semiprivate rooms. Lower rates
for couples and groups of 3 or more. MC, V. **Parking:** Nearby garages, around
$20.

This facility rents semiprivate rooms for enlisted servicemen and servicewomen and
warrant officers, active, reserve, National Guard, service academy and R.O.T.C.
students, dependents (at least 12 years old), allied forces, and all retirees (officers
included). Separated personnel (six months or less) are also welcome; they must show
a copy of DD 214 or separation papers. The rooms are homey, neat, and cheerful,
with nice furnishings, cream-colored walls adorned with framed prints, and very high
ceilings; many have shuttered windows. Phones are in the hall; the front desk takes
messages. The building itself is like a gracious old home with elegantly furnished
lounges (one houses a jukebox and a piano), a library/writing room, a pool room, and
a TV room. Free breakfast and lunch on Saturday and free continental breakfast on
Sunday are served in the budget cafeteria. The club also provides free tickets (when
available) to movies, plays, and other events.

7. BED & BREAKFAST

With the unusually high cost of New York hotel rooms, the bed-and-breakfast
concept of staying in a private residence and receiving breakfast as part of your rent is
growing more popular. New York has at least three major B&B organizations. The
oldest and largest is **Urban Ventures,** which offers comfortable, carefully chosen
rooms in private apartments—mostly on Manhattan's Upper West Side, Upper East
Side, and Greenwich Village, and close-to-Manhattan areas of Brooklyn—at rates
that are often less than those at budget hotels. Singles cost from $45 to $70, doubles
run from $65 to $90. A studio apartment costs from $70 to $90 and a one-bedroom
apartment costs from $95 to $145. Stays usually average several nights to 2 weeks
(there is a 2-night minimum). This is a good bet if you'd like not only to save money,
but to establish some personal contact with New Yorkers, since Urban Ventures' hosts
tend to be outgoing types who genuinely like people. Contact Mary McAulay at
Urban Ventures, P.O. Box 426, New York, NY 10024 (tel. 212/594-5650).

Another popular outfit is **City Lights Bed and Breakfast Ltd.,** P.O. Box
20355, Cherokee Station, New York, NY 10028 (tel. 212/737-7049), which makes
placements in Manhattan, Brooklyn, Queens, and even Long Island and Westchester.
Owner Dee Staff Neilsen usually has singles for $60 to $75, doubles for $70 to $90,
and unhosted apartments for $95 to $250 and up. City Lights also offers settings for
small business meetings and conferences, a personalized shopping service for B&B
clients, and individualized art and architecture tours.

Many people in the arts and related professions are hosts at **Judy Goldberg's
Bed, Breakfast (& Books),** 35 W. 92nd St., New York, NY 10025 (tel.
212/865-8740), which got its name from her husband, who is in the book business;
city guides and B&B directories are also available. Mrs. Goldberg works with each
client and host personally; she has units available all over Manhattan, from SoHo to
uptown locations. Most rooms in hosted apartments go for $65 to $75 single and $80
to $85 double with private bath, $70 with shared bath. Unhosted apartments start at
$100 for studios and go up to about $120 and $130 for a one-bedroom apartment.
Two-bedroom apartments for four people could be $160 a night.

None of these three agencies requires a membership fee. They do, however,
request that you make reservations in advance (the farther in advance the better), and
there is a cancellation charge. All accommodations and hosts are inspected and
screened, and an attempt is made to bring together people of similar interests. And the
letters of appreciation all these groups have received from satisfied guests are truly
impressive.

8. LONG-TERM STAYS

RESIDENCES FOR STUDENTS & YOUNG WORKING PEOPLE

THE DE HIRSCH RESIDENCE AT THE 92nd STREET YM–YWHA, 1395 Lexington Ave. (at 92nd St.), New York, NY 10128. Tel. 212/427-6000. Fax 212/415-5578. 403 beds (shared baths). **Subway:** 6 to 86th St. or 4, 5, 6 to 96th St.

$ Rates: Shared rooms start at about $400 per month per person for a minimum stay of 3 months; singles begin at about $560. For short-term stays (available at certain times of the year), rates are on a weekly basis, starting at $168 per week per person in a shared room. Group rates available for other ages and lengths of stay. AE, MC, V. **Parking:** Nearby garages, around $20.

⭐ This highly recommended Y is a cultural paradise for those young men and women who plan to stay at least 3 months. Not only does it offer pleasant rooms with light housekeeping privileges, but it has long presented outstanding cultural programs, ranging from top-flight classical music groups to lectures and appearances by such writers as John Updike and Nobel Prize–winner Elie Weisel. Residents often get reduced-price or free tickets to these events. Residents also have the use of a splendid health club facility with gymnasium and pool; social, TV, and study lounges; a library; art and photo galleries. The Y is located in one of New York's finest residential neighborhoods—the Upper East Side—and is convenient to public transportation.

Rooms are clean and comfortable, furnished with a single bed or beds, dressers, bookshelves, and lamps. Most rooms are air-conditioned; baths are communal; public phones are in the hall. Each floor has its own large self-service kitchen and dining room, as well as laundry room. Each room has a phone jack so phones can be installed at regular New York City rates.

The Y accepts young men and women between the ages of 18 and 30, regardless of race or religious belief, but only if full-time students or employees, or a combination of the two. Every applicant is required to have a personal interview (by appointment) prior to admission. (Special arrangements can be made for those coming from another part of the country or from overseas). Long-term residents are required to purchase a residence membership ($75 annually), and a $35 fee is payable upon submission of a completed application.

When writing for an application form, specify that you are between the ages of 18 and 30 and are employed or in school; otherwise, you will first get a letter explaining eligibility requirements. Write as far in advance as possible, as space is limited. Highly recommended.

RESIDENCES FOR WOMEN

JOHN AND MARY MARKLE EVANGELINE RESIDENCE, 123 W. 13th St. (between Sixth and Seventh aves.), New York, NY 10011. Tel. 212/242-2400. 205 rms (all with bath and shower). TEL **Subway:** 1, 2, 3, 9, F to 14th St.

$ Rates: On a weekly basis, minimum stay 30 days, including two meals a day: single, $191.25; in a double, $122.95 and $143.50 per person; in a triple, $117.20 per person; in a quad, $101.50 per person. Short-term guest rooms at daily or weekly rates, from $60 per night. No credit cards. **Parking:** Nearby garages, around $20.

Here, on one of the prettiest tree-lined streets in Greenwich Village, the Salvation Army runs a superb facility. Rooms are divided equally among college students, businesswomen, and senior citizens; you might find students from Parsons School of Design and NYU, nurses from St. Vincent's Hospital, and even an octogenarian retired professor from Columbia! During the summer months, when the college students have gone home, rooms are often taken by young ballet students (accompanied by chaperones) who have come to New York on scholarships.

A $7-million renovation has made the 60-year-old building better than ever. Rooms are attractively furnished in colonial style; weekly maid service is provided; and everyone has use of a typing room, a TV room, a piano studio, a lounge, study halls, and a beautiful roof bath. No men are allowed in the rooms.

A personal interview or two letters of recommendation are required, and you must show that you work or go to school full time. A visiting female friend or female family member can get a cot in your room for $15/$20 a night; occasionally rooms for family members are available on a daily basis for $35, meals extra. A few double rooms are available. The minimum stay is 90 days (during the summer, 30 days or 6 weeks). Contact Miss Barbara Shaw or Maj. James Miller.

PARKSIDE EVANGELINE, 18 Gramercy Park South (at Irving Place), New York, NY 10003. Tel. 212/677-6200. 300 rms (shared and private baths). TEL **Subway:** 6 to 23rd St.

$ Rates: On a weekly basis, including two meals a day: $146 single, $140 double per person. No credit cards. **Parking:** Nearby garages, about $20.

Located right off lovely Gramercy Park in one of New York's most exclusive neighborhoods (some of the rooms overlook the park, and residents can use this private locked facility), the Evangeline (also run by the Salvation Army) houses women students and working women aged 18 to 35. It's the kind of a place where a parent would feel comfortable having a daughter stay. Facilities include a fireplace lounge off the lobby, two outdoor rooftop terraces with chaise longues for sunbathing, a sewing room, music practice rooms, washing machines (irons and ironing boards available), exercise machines, old-fashioned hairdryers, two TV rooms, and a very attractive second-floor lounge where women can entertain visitors. There's also a lovely dining room.

Rooms (singles and doubles) are small, but clean and charming, with curtained windows and maple furnishings, switchboard phones, and sinks. Most have a bath in the room; some share a connecting garden. In addition to the cafeteria/dining room, which provides two meals a day included in the price of the room (a third meal is available for a fee), there's also a snack bar and counter on the first floor. Single, double, triple, and quad rooms are available. There is a waiting list, but rooms are also assigned on the basis of need. Several guest rooms are available on a nightly or weekly basis, including two meals. Inquiries should be directed to Maj. Daniel Moore.

TEN EYCK–TROUGHTON MEMORIAL RESIDENCE, 145. E. 39th St. (between Third and Lexington aves.), New York, NY 10016. Tel. 212/490-5990. 333 rooms (all shared baths). TEL **Subway:** 4, 5, 6 to 42nd St.

$ Rates: $133 or $138 single, on a weekly basis, including two meals a day.

Another Salvation Army facility for women, Ten Eyck–Troughton is superbly located in the midtown, Murray Hill area. This one is for women ages 30 to 60 who are employed full time. Attractive facilities include a TV lounge, piano and practice room, typing room, study hall, a lovely solarium and roof garden, a snack bar and counter in addition to the dining room, which provides two meals a day. All rooms are single; there are no private bathrooms. Rooms are small, and each is simply furnished with bed, chest, a secretary desk, and a chair. Individual air conditioners may be installed. All applicants must have a personal interview.

THE WEBSTER APARTMENTS, 419 W. 34th St. (between Ninth and Tenth aves.), New York, NY 10001. Tel. 212/967-9000. 400 rms (with shared bath). TEL **Subway:** A, C, E to 34th St., then crosstown bus.

$ Rates: Between $100 and $160 per week, depending on salary, on a weekly basis, including two meals a day. $25 per person per night, including breakfast only, for visitors (check with manager for qualifications). No credit cards. **Parking:** Nearby garages, around $20.

This outstanding hostelry offers permanent-residence accommodations. Heavily endowed by Charles and Josiah Webster (Charles was a partner in R. H. Macy & Co.), who founded the residence in 1923 and left means to fund the enterprise, it provides the comforts of home (a very stately and elegant home) to young working women at low cost. Facilities of the 13-story brick structure include a gracious lobby, a handsome library with deep leather chairs, an elegant drawing room, a practice room with piano, television rooms, a charming wicker-furnished garden room, a card-playing room, and even a series of small intimate rooms for entertaining "gentleman callers" (the latter are not permitted upstairs). Other amenities include a lovely garden (quite a luxury in Manhattan) and a rooftop garden as well, sewing machines, typewriters, laundry, and daily maid service.

The rooms themselves, all singles, are pretty and quaint, with freshly painted walls, carpeting, and all necessary furnishings, including a sink. Baths are in the hall. Rooms have electric fans; air conditioning is available at extra cost.

Although most of the residents are young, women of any age who have a job or are looking for one in New York should come in or call to arrange a visit. You can write to the above address, but if you're in the city, come in or call during business hours.

APARTMENTS

The market is so tight in New York that finding an apartment can take weeks or months of tracking down leads and combing real estate ads. Try the Sunday real estate section of the *New York Times,* which comes out late Saturday night. Check the ads in the *Village Voice* (at the newsstands on Wednesday), and in the *Chelsea Clinton News* and other neighborhood papers.

WHERE TO EAT IN NEW YORK CITY

New York's melting pot has produced the world's largest array of cuisines. Here you can sample everything from hearty Polish fare to refined French cooking, take in the friendly atmosphere of a family-run trattoria, or sip wine in chic Art Deco surroundings. The biggest problem is deciding where you want to go—there are more than 17,000 restaurants in the city.

Pick up the *New York Restaurant Guide,* a new 50-page guide to eating spots in all five boroughs compiled by the New York Convention and Visitors Bureau. For a free copy, write to: Restaurant Guide, New York Convention and Visitors Bureau, Inc., 2 Columbus Circle, New York, NY 10019.

This chapter will introduce you to nearly 400 restaurants, arranged by geographic location. At the end we have included some special suggestions— where you'll find the things New York does best (pizza, deli food, and bagels), where to have dessert, and those places worth a once-in-a-blue-moon splurge.

1. LOWER MANHATTAN/ TRIBECA

LOWER MANHATTAN

CHRISA II, 76 Fulton St., near Gold St. Tel. 964-4136.
   Cuisine: GREEK. **Reservations:** Not needed. **Subway:** A, C to Broadway/ Nassau St.
$ Prices: All items under $8. AE, DC, MC, V.
   Open: Mon–Fri 10:30am–9:30pm; Sat 10:30am–8pm.
Located a few blocks from the South Street Seaport, Chrisa II offers Greek specialties in a coffee shop atmosphere, brightened by island scenes painted on the walls and Greek music in the background. The prices are definitely right for the budget traveler. You might lunch on pita-bread sandwiches filled with souvlaki, shish kebab, or sausage; or Greek antipasto. There's also cheese or spinach pie and a Greek salad.

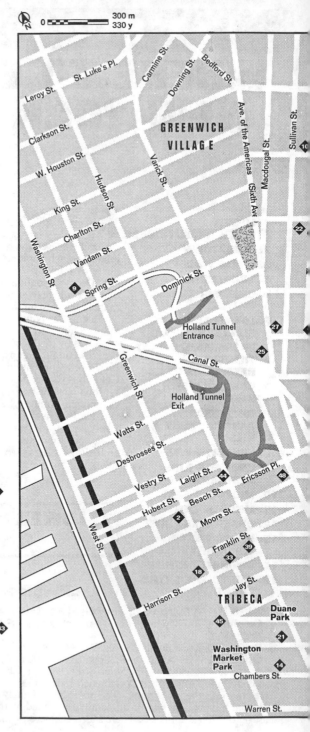

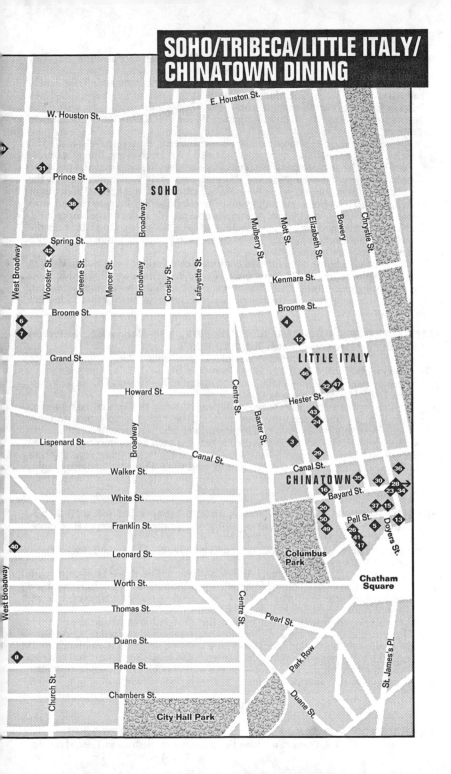

SOHO/TRIBECA/LITTLE ITALY/ CHINATOWN DINING

HAMBURGER HARRY'S, 157 Chambers St., near Greenwich St. Tel. 267-4446.
  Cuisine: AMERICAN/BURGERS. **Reservations:** Recommended for lunch.
  Subway: 1, 9, 2, 3, A, C, E, N, R to Green St.
$ **Prices:** Burgers and main courses $5–$12. AE, MC, V.
  Open: Mon–Thurs 11:30am–11:30pm, Fri–Sat 11:30am–1am, Sun noon–11:30pm.

 For some of the city's most acclaimed hamburgers, drop into "Ha-Ha." The decor is a functional mix of butcher block and Art Deco—just the right setting for Harry's hefty but lean hamburgers, broiled over live charcoal and mesquite (the wood that gives these burgers their distinctive taste). If you want to watch the red-capped chefs in action, ask to be seated at the counter. You'll have 17 varieties of hamburgers to choose from, ranging from a "number 10" to burgers topped with béarnaise sauce, Gorgonzola cheese, guacamole and pico de gallo, or the works (chili, cheddar cheese, chopped onion, guacamole, and pico de gallo). Don't pass up the fresh curlicue french fries, which have received top marks from New York's discriminating restaurant reviewers.

Try the fajitas—a house specialty that combines char-broiled beefsteak or chicken with pico de gallo, refried beans, guacamole, and steaming flour tortillas. Other items on this surprisingly eclectic menu: chili, and specials such as the shrimp plate, corn chowder, and desserts such as Mississippi mud cake with whipped cream. Ha-Ha's serves wine and beer.

KATIE O'TOOLE'S PUB AND RESTAURANT, 134 Reade St., between Hudson and Greenwich sts. Tel. 226-8928.
  Cuisine: PUB GRUB. **Reservations:** Recommended for parties over 10.
  Subway: 1, 2, 3, 9, A, C, E, N, R to Chambers St.
$ **Prices:** Appetizers $2.95–$3.95; main courses $6.95–$9. AE, DC, MC, V.
  Open: Daily 11am till "the wee hours."

★ The chatty Irish staff will make you feel at home in this quaint, oak-paneled pub with its tree-shaded outdoor terrace. The fare is simple pub grub—a specialty is bangers and mash (sausages and mashed potatoes). You can also get sandwiches and burgers, as well as standard appetizers such as potato skins and fried zucchini sticks. Main course specials are a good buy at $6.95, including vegetable and potato. There's authentic English beer on tap, and on a Thursday or Friday night, you'll find a gathering of 40 or 50 area musicians playing the blues—not what you'd expect for a pub, but you won't find anyone complaining.

PIPELINE, 2 World Financial Center, at 225 Liberty St. Tel. 945-2755.
  Cuisine: AMERICAN. **Reservations:** Accepted only for parties of 6 or more.
  Subway: 1, 9, N, R to Cortland St.
$ **Prices:** Appetizers $4.95–$6.50; main courses $7.95–$17.50. AE, MC, TR, V.
  Open: Daily 10am–midnight.
Head here for a taste of "Nouveau American Grill." The decor is hi-tech, with steel-pipe sheeting and walls painted in neon colors. Multiple television screens above the bar play diners' selections from the video jukebox. Outside is a tree-lined dining terrace with a great view of the Hudson River and Jersey City.

The menu is a little pricey for our budget, but the food is good and the portions large. The fettuccine with arugula, mushrooms, asparagus, and roasted peppers tossed in lemon, garlic, and olive oil is excellent. There's a good selection of sandwiches, all served on fresh baguettes with cottage fries and tomato salad. For dessert you can't go wrong with the Pipeline Banana Split—vanilla and chocolate ice cream, chocolate syrup, Heath Bars, and whipped cream.

TRIBECA

BEACH HOUSE, 399 Greenwich St., at Beach St. Tel. 226-7800.
  Cuisine: MEXICAN. **Reservations:** Recommended. **Subway:** 1, 9 to Franklin.

$ Prices: Main courses $9–$11. AE, DC, MC, V.
Open: Daily 11:45am–11:00pm.

TriBeCans come here for true south-of-the-border taste. The interior of this Civil War–era building is dark and warm; large fans spin lazily from the high ceiling, painted mirrors adorn the walls, and customers sit at booths or candlelit tables near the bar. You can order burritos, enchiladas, tacos, and tostadas, served with refried beans and rice, separately or in combinations of two or three. For something unusual, try the flautas (deep-fried corn tortillas filled with chicken and topped with guacamole and sour cream), or the pollo mole poblano (half a chicken sautéed in mole sauce).

DELPHI, 109 W. Broadway, at Reade St. Tel. 227-6322.
Cuisine: GREEK. **Reservations:** Recommended for parties of 6 or more.
Subway: 1, 2, 3, 9, A, C, E, N, R to Chambers St.; J, M, Z, 4, 5, 6 to St. Andrews Place.
$ Prices: Appetizers $3–$7.25; main courses under $10. AE, D, MC, V.
Open: Daily 11am–11:30pm.

This bustling Greek restaurant is well worth a visit. Delphi has an enclosed terrace and a small room on the ground floor; the upstairs room is full of hanging plants and travel posters advertise Greece from nearly every wall. Try the stuffed grape leaves appetizer or the Delphi specialty, spinach cheese pie; then move on to a hearty Greek salad or tomatoes stuffed with pignola nuts, raisins, and rice, and cooked with herbs and spices. For filling meat dishes, you might turn to the souvlaki platter (roasted marinated beef and lamb) or the golden-baked pastitsio (macaroni layered with ground beef, cheese, and tomato sauce). The meat dishes all include a small Greek salad, rice or baked potato, and fresh broccoli. Definitely a good deal.

HOW'S BAYOU, 355 Greenwich St., at Harrison St. Tel. 925-5405.
Cuisine: CAJUN. **Reservations:** Recommended. **Subway:** 1, 2, 3, 9 to Chambers St.
$ Prices: Lunch appetizers $2.95–$3.95, dinner appetizers $3.95–$5.95; main lunch courses $4.25–$8.95, main dinner courses $6.95–$13.95. AE.
Open: Sun–Thurs 11:30am–midnight; Fri–Sat 11:30am–1am.

This neighborhood hangout is a festive Cajun place, housed in a former meat market whose many doors stay open on summer nights to give diners the feeling they're eating al fresco. Fans hang from the pressed-tin ceiling, as does a large neon sign that spells out the restaurant's name. Paper bags of tortilla chips adorn every butcher-block table—a clue that the kitchen produces Mexican as well as Cajun specialties. The staff makes you feel like an instant regular by snapping Mardi Gras beads around your neck.

The good home-cooking won't win accolades from restaurant critics, but it's hearty, and served in generous portions. For lunch you can have chunky chili or a "Bayou Po' Boy" on fresh hero bread, filled with cold cuts or chicken fried steak. Also featured is a Bayou pesto turkey burger. Specialties include a chicken, sausage, shrimp, and crayfish jambalaya, enchiladas, and southern fried chicken. Evenings, you can also choose Creole meatloaf and grilled chicken from the Cajun offerings, fajitas from the Mexican list, and chicken fried steak and barbecued pork ribs from the menu section labeled "Southern Hospitality." Round out the meal with homemade apple pie or Creole bread pudding with whiskey sauce. Weekend brunch offers items from lunch and dinner plus corned-beef hash and eggs, omelets, and side orders of grits or corn and blueberry muffins.

RIVERRUN, 176 Franklin St., between Greenwich and Hudson sts. Tel. 966-3894.
Cuisine: AMERICAN. **Reservations:** Suggested on weekends for the clam-bake. **Subway:** 1, 9 to Franklin St. **Bus:** M10 to Franklin, or M22 to Greenwich Ave.
$ Prices: All items under $10. AE, DC, MC, V.
Open: Sun–Thurs 11:30am–midnight; Fri–Sat restaurant 11:30am–1am, bar until 2am.

Healthful food, manageable prices, friendly service, and rotating artwork done by neighborhood artists are three good reasons for this cozy restaurant's popularity, especially with the local crowd. At lunch you can choose among several meal-size salads, including a mixed seafood salad, a hearty niçoise, and a bracing mixture of lettuce, chicken, apples, walnuts, Swiss cheese, and onion. Perhaps you'd prefer the full smoked trout with bean salad, chicken and vegetables in spicy garlic sauce with rice, or a mound of steamed mussels floating in a zesty sauce of garlic, white wine, and tomatoes. Omelets with french fries are less expensive, as are sandwiches such as the avocado on whole wheat and the cheeseburger with french fries.

Many lunch items reappear on the dinner menu at slightly higher prices. Among additional main dishes are shrimp with snowpeas in a spicy garlic sauce; fried chicken with cornbread and homemade potato salad; and angel-hair pasta Fra Diavola with mixed seafood. If you've a yen for something sweet, try the riverrun's three-berry pie.

Their unlimited-champagne brunch, on weekends, features eggs florentine or Benedict, French toast with bacon or ham, and a selection of omelets. Also available are items from the regular lunch menu: salads, burgers, and quiche with french fries.

THE SPORTING CLUB, 99 Hudson St., between Harrison and Franklin sts. Tel. 219-0900.

Cuisine: AMERICAN. **Reservations:** Recommended. **Subway:** 1, 9 to Franklin St.

$ Prices: Main courses $7.95–$14.95. AE, DC, MC, V.

Open: Daily 11:30am–midnight or 2am. **Closed:** Summer weekends.

The main draw at this unique TriBeCa restaurant is a 10-foot video screen and a computerized scoreboard, which tower above the oval bar and can be seen from every table in this mahogany-paneled, multilevel restaurant. TV monitors dotted around the restaurant enable Bill Rose, the owner, to show from three to six events simultaneously. (Call ahead and he'll tell you if he'll be able to pull your favorite team off a satellite or cable link. The scoreboard keeps almost instantaneous track of every game being played in the nation.) Sports lovers flock to this restaurant, and the clientele, about two-thirds male, often includes well-known sports figures, sometimes working behind the bar. The menu is eclectic and moderately priced, running from "O.J.'s Buffalo Wings" to the "Larry Bird roast chicken" and a "George Steinburger." On Saturday and Sunday from noon to 5pm, brunch is popular—only partly because every home run will earn you a free drink during baseball season.

SQUARE DINER, 33 Leonard St., corner of West Broadway. Tel. 925-7188.

Cuisine: GREEK. **Reservations:** Not accepted. **Subway:** 1, 9 to Franklin St.; N, R to Canal St.

$ Prices: All items under $10. No credit cards.

Open: Mon–Fri 6am–9pm, Sat–Sun 8am–5pm.

The Square Diner offers friendly, unpretentious atmosphere and good-quality Greek and American food at very low prices. On a street full of chic new restaurants, this handsome aluminum diner seems an anomaly.

This is one of the few places left in Manhattan where you can still get a deluxe hamburger or cheeseburger for under $6. The chopped sirloin steak platter is served with soup or salad. The Greek salad platter is a good buy, as is the lamb shish kebab. Omelets and sandwiches are also on the menu here, and for dessert you might want to regress with a malted with double ice cream.

THE THAI HOUSE CAFÉ, Hudson St., at Hubert St. Tel. 334-1085.

Cuisine: THAI. **Reservations:** Not needed. **Subway:** 1, 9 to Canal St.

$ Prices: Appetizers $3.95–$5.75; main courses $5.95–$10.95. No credit cards.

Open: Mon–Sat 11:30am–11:30pm.

A simple, unpretentious spot, the Thai House Café serves up reasonably priced spicy delicacies, with lots of vegetarian selections. Start off with the delicate house spring rolls, with a sweet, zesty sauce for dipping. Two can share a dish of mee krob: savory, crisp vermicelli with dried shrimp and bean cake. We were in ecstasy over the roast chicken in a fiery red curry sauce, with coconut milk, bamboo shoots, green peas, and carrots—if you like things spicy, this is the dish for you. We also recommend the roast duck with mixed vegetables (it comes with broccoli, snow peas, baby corn, Chinese cabbage, and mushrooms). Singha beer is, of course, the beverage of choice.

TOMMY TANG'S, 323 Greenwich St., near Duane St. Tel. 334-9190.
   Cuisine: THAI. **Reservations:** Recommended. **Subway:** 1, 2, 3, 9, A, C to Chambers St.
$ Prices: Main courses $8.95–$21. AE, DC, MC, V.
   Open: Lunch Mon–Fri 11:30am–3pm; dinner Mon–Thurs 6–11pm, Fri–Sat 6pm–midnight.
At Tommy Tang's, traditional Thai cuisine is prepared with a creative flourish. Despite the spotless white linen and the exotic flower arrangements, a friendly, intimate atmosphere permeates the restaurant. The dining room, painted in pastels and tastefully lighted, has a sort of "new-wave deco" feel.
   Main dishes include such exotic offerings as shrimp panang (sautéed shrimp and red-pepper points in a strongly spiced curry sauce), and rad na noodles (sautéed with chicken, pork, or beef with broccoli in an oyster sauce). The ginger chicken with scallions and shiitake and straw mushrooms, served in a mild black-bean sauce, is a nice counterpoint to many of the spicier items on the menu.

WALKER'S RESTAURANT, 16 N. Moore St., at Varick St. Tel. 941-0142.
   Cuisine: AMERICAN. **Reservations:** Recommended for Friday lunches. **Subway:** 1, 9 to Franklin St.
$ Prices: Main course specials $9–$14. AE, DC, MC, V.
   Open: Daily 12:45pm–1am.
Walker's used to be Vic's Bar, a rough-and-tumble tavern, and the space still retains a cozy tavern-like atmosphere. In the front half of the restaurant is a beautiful old oak bar with 19th-century beveled mirrors. The place is frequented by local TriBeCa loft dwellers and is usually quite busy for dinner.
   The food, though basic, is satisfying. Daily specials are written on a blackboard; the night we dined here they included grilled lamb with rosemary, Louisiana fried chicken, spinach linguine with seafood, and broiled grouper. Main dishes are excellent and reasonably priced. The lunch menu includes a variety of low-priced sandwiches as well as an 8-ounce sirloin steak sandwich that will cost a bit more. On weekends Walker's has an à la carte brunch that includes a free drink.

2. CHINATOWN

Chinatown's main attraction is its restaurants. Cantonese-style food predominates, but Cantonese, Szechuan, Hunan, Mandarin, and Shanghai—all varieties of Chinese fare from the country's different provinces—are represented in force.
   Characterized by specialties that include fried wontons or wonton soup, roast pork, and shrimp with lobster sauce, unfortunately, the cuisine has been given a bad name by restaurants that serve overcooked cliché dishes full of cornstarch. In Chinatown, less Westernized versions of Cantonese favorites prove that at its best, Cantonese food can meet the standards of the most sophisticated and demanding gourmet. *A word of caution:* Some restaurants will doctor dishes served to Westerners, so if you want to sample something Chinese style, make that clear to your waiter.
   Szechuan, the hot-pepper province in southwestern China, is a center for savory, spicy cooking where dishes are seasoned with generous portions of garlic and scallions. Shanghai cuisine—a combination of Chinese regional cuisines—was

created by chefs from every part of China who were drawn to that sophisticated city in days of yore.

Many of these restaurants offer a unique treat called **dim sum,** the traditional Chinese tea lunch, which is an economical way to sample some of Chinatown's most interesting dishes.

What you'll find lacking in most Chinese restaurants is ambience. The Chinatown standard of interior design is hard Formica furnishings placed under harder fluorescent lighting. Plastic tablecloths and simple spindleback chairs complete the spartan style of decor. But don't be put off: it's a Chinatown truism that some of the plainest places serve some of the most memorable meals.

There are a few other rules of thumb to remember while scouting out an authentic Chinese meal. Once seated, you can point to tasty-looking dishes en route to other tables—most restaurants have many dishes not listed on the menu. And don't go to Chinatown expecting intimate or quiet dining. In fact, you'll often share a large round table with other diners. Relax, enjoy, and concentrate on your main goal: serious eating at a very reasonable price.

We've made a few selections below, but you'll have the best time if you relax and wander—bargain-hunt in the curio and craft shops, soak up the sights and sounds, and scan the menus for a place that looks like a likely candidate for your dining adventure.

BOW LUCK RICE SHOPPE, 17 Doyers St., near Pell St. Tel. 571-1375.
  Cuisine: CANTONESE. **Reservations:** Recommended. **Subway:** J, M, Z to Chambers St.
  $ Prices: Main courses $4.50–$16. No credit cards.
  Open: Daily 11am–10:30pm.
A Chinatown institution with superior Cantonese fare, located on a charming curved side street, Bow Luck was for years an out-of-the-way favorite among Chinatown residents and in-the-know tourists. Then the food critic for the *New York Times* gave the 150-seat restaurant her seal of approval with a rare three-star (excellent) rating. Now it's hard to find a seat for lunch. Among the house specialties are crabs Cantonese style, stir-fried with a sauce of pork, ginger, black beans, and scallions; and treasurer duck, garnished with jumbo shrimp, roast pork, chicken, mushrooms, and snowpeas. The much-raved-about steamed flounder and steamed bass are not on the menu, so ask your waiter.

Our favorite nonseafood dishes are steak with jade tree, meat that melts in your mouth served on a bed of broccoli; beef with mixed vegetables; and watercress soup. The thick, chewy noodle dishes are quite good, and the roast duck lo mein is near nirvana for noodle nuts. Bring your own wine or beer, since the house serves no liquor.

FOUR FIVE SIX, 2 Bowery, corner of Doyers St. Tel. 964-5853.
  Cuisine: SHANGHAI. **Reservations:** Recommended for large groups. **Subway:** 6, J, M, Z to Canal St.
  $ Prices: Appetizers $1–$4.95; main courses $5.95–$12.95. AE, DC, MC, V.
  Open: Sun–Thurs 11:30am–10pm; Fri–Sat 11:30am–11pm.
Under the same ownership and bearing the same name, but in English, as Say Eng Look (see below), this place offers a similar menu in slightly less appealing surroundings. It's also more touristy, with Westernized versions of Shanghai specialties; so if you want the real thing, talk to your waiter or go to Say Eng Look.

HONG YING, 11 Mott St., near Chatham Square. Tel. 962-9821.
  Cuisine: CANTONESE. **Reservations:** Not accepted. **Subway:** 6, J, M, Z to Canal St.
  $ Prices: Appetizers $1.25–$4.95; main courses $5–$11. No credit cards.
  Open: Sun–Thurs 11am–1am; Fri–Sat 11am–3am.
The menu here boasts that "all our Chinese food is delicious, the price reasonable." Critics and customers agree. Here you can find offbeat Cantonese seafood delicacies like mussel casserole with black beans and garlic, and eggplant with garlic.

Our favorite meal is wor shu opp—fried duck with a thin coating of finely chopped almonds under skin as crisp as parchment and topped with a delicate sauce. Also interesting yet inexpensive is lor hon jai, mixed vegetables in bean-curd sauce topped with sesame seeds; Canton-style crabs or snails; steamed fish; and a unique dish called fun gone har kew, fried chicken livers and jumbo shrimps with water chestnuts, bamboo shoots, snowpea pods, and other vegetables. Hong Ying also offers many low-priced basic Chinese noodle dishes.

KAM BO RICE SHOPPE, 51 Bayard St. Tel. 233-5440.
Cuisine: CANTONESE. **Reservations:** Not accepted. **Subway:** 6, J, M, Z to Canal St.
$ Prices: All items under $10. No credit cards.
Open: Sun–Thurs 11am–3am, Fri–Sat 11am–midnight.
Here's another place to go for quality Cantonese food. In addition to inexpensive yet filling noodle dishes ($3.25 to $5.25), you can get stir-fried vegetable and beef dishes with rice. For seafood lovers, there are mussels in a black-bean sauce served in a hot clay pot, or the "Three Stars Sea Food Pot," with lobster, crabmeat, jumbo shrimp, and mixed Chinese vegetables.

LITTLE SZECHUAN, 31 Oliver St., off Chatham Square, between Henry and Madison sts. Tel. 349-2360.
Cuisine: SZECHUAN. **Reservations:** Not accepted. **Subway:** 4, 5, 6 to Brooklyn Bridge/City Hall.
$ Prices: Appetizers $1–$4.95; main courses $4.95–$10.95. No credit cards.
Open: Sun–Thurs 11:30am–10pm; Fri–Sat 11:30am–10:30pm.
Little Szechuan is hard to find, but well worth the search. The name is appropriate: the tiny place has only eight tables. A golden dragon covers most of one wall, and newly installed track lighting adds a touch of modernity.
The service is extremely hospitable, the food is superlative, and the prices are unbeatable. Most dishes cost under $8. We've feasted on ginger shrimp, sautéed hot pork shreds, orange beef, ta-chien chicken, hot-and-spicy vegetables, and the cold noodle appetizer with sesame sauce. You'll be hard-pressed to find either better or cheaper fare.

MANDARIN INN PELL, 34 Pell St., corner of Mott St. Tel. 267-2092.
Cuisine: CHINESE. **Reservations:** Not accepted. **Subway:** 6, J, M, Z to Canal St.
$ Prices: Appetizers $1.25–$4.95; main courses $8–$14; fixed-price dinners $12–$18. AE, DC, MC, V.
Open: Sun–Thurs 11am–1pm; Fri–Sat 11am–midnight.
Mandarin Inn Pell is one of the best of the mixed-bag genre. It's one of the largest restaurants in Chinatown, with seating on two floors for 300 people. The decor is wild, especially upstairs, and there are wine-red carpeting, scarlet drapes, and crystal chandeliers.
Among the chef's prize recipes are those for lobster and black-bean sauce, and Mandarin spareribs. The house offers a complete family dinner or a gourmet dinner that includes soup, appetizer, main dish, and dessert. When ordering à la carte, we like to begin by sharing an order of sizzling rice soup, almost a meal in itself, containing shrimp, chicken, pork, and snowpeas, or perhaps an order of scallion pancakes. Exciting main dishes include lemon chicken, Mongolian lamb, spicy Kung Pao shrimp, and spicy sautéed string beans or eggplant. For dessert there's no other choice but the Peking honey crisp banana, deep-fried in batter and then dipped in honey, sugar, and sesame seeds ($4.50 for two).

PEKING DUCK HOUSE, 22 Mott St. Tel. 962-8208.
Cuisine: PEKING DUCK. **Reservations:** Not accepted. **Subway:** 6, J, M, Z to Canal St.
$ Prices: Appetizers $1.50–$5.75; main courses $5–$10; whole duck $26. AE.
Open: Sun–Thurs 11:30am–10:30pm; Fri–Sat 11:30am–11:30pm.

It's easy to see why the Peking Duck House is on former mayor Ed Koch's list of his ten favorite restaurants. When the chef carves the roast duck with surgeon-like skill at your table, the skin has been browned to a golden lacquer. The moist, tender meat folds neatly into the paper-thin crepes served with the meal. A velvety hoisin sauce and cool cucumbers and scallions make the roasted duck sandwich a succulent taste sensation. Other house favorites include sliced pork double sautéed with chili sauce, the spiced cold beef appetizer, or the sliced beef with watercress in hot garlic sauce. Although the duck is expensive, a host of vegetable, beef, chicken, and seafood dishes are available under $10, with noodle and vegetable dishes the best buys.

PHOENIX GARDEN, 46 Bowery Arcade, between Bowery and Elizabeth sts. Tel. 962-8934.
   Cuisine: CANTONESE. **Reservations:** Not accepted. **Subway:** 6, J, M, Z to Canal St.
$ **Prices:** Appetizers $1.25–$4.95; main courses $7.50–$9.95. No credit cards.
   Open: Daily 11:30am–10:30pm.
This bustling and friendly restaurant is frequented by many uptowners. The real challenge here is picking only a few dishes from the extensive menu—for starters, Phoenix Garden offers more than 26 soups (about $5.50). Other specialties include roast squab, pepper-and-salty shrimp, sizzling chicken with ginger and scallions in casserole, and pan-fried noodles.

SAY ENG LOOK, 5 E. Broadway, off Chatham Square. Tel. 732-0796.
   Cuisine: SHANGHAI. **Reservations:** Required for large groups. **Subway:** 6, J, M, Z to Canal St.
$ **Prices:** Appetizers $1.50–$5; main courses $7–$13.95. AE, DC, MC, V.
   Open: Sun–Thurs 11:30am–10:30pm; Fri–Sat 11:30am–11pm.
This restaurant is one of the best places in Chinatown to sample Shanghai delicacies. Say eng look means "four, five, six" in Shanghai dialect—an unbeatable combination in Chinese games of chance. Indeed, owner/chef A. K. Chang leaves nothing to fate as he fixes such surefire winners as finely sliced deep-fried pork cutlets, special mixed vegetables, shrimp with sizzling rice, sweet-and-sour sliced fish, and shrimp with kidney. You might also try the casseroles—another Shanghai specialty—particularly the fishhead casserole or the chicken with cashew nuts.
   Say Eng Look's interior is spotless and attractive. Subdued lighting tones down the flamboyant red walls, and the beamed ceiling gives the restaurant a homey charm.

SIU LAM KUNG, 18 Elizabeth St. Tel. 732-0974.
   Cuisine: CHINESE SEAFOOD. **Reservations:** Recommended. **Subway:** 6, J, M, Z to Canal St.
$ **Prices:** Appetizers $1.25–$5.95; main courses $6.95–$14.95. No credit cards.
   Open: Daily 11am–midnight.
Here, crisply uniformed waiters serve fresh seafood in a refined atmosphere. The tank in the window of the restaurant is home to such future dinner fare as frogs, served with black-bean sauce, and eels, served sliced and sautéed in a mild sauce (prices vary seasonally). You can also get a delicious sizzling dish of sang kang scallops in a spicy brown sauce, or lobster prepared in either black-bean sauce or with ginger and scallions (with prices depending on the season). Another highly recommended house specialty is shrimp with cashew and steamed crab.

SUN LOK KEE, 13 Mott St., near Chatham Square. Tel. 285-9856.
   Cuisine: CANTONESE. **Reservations:** Not accepted. **Subway:** 6, J, M, Z to Canal St.
$ **Prices:** Appetizers $1–$5.95; main courses $5.95–$11. No credit cards.
   Open: Daily 11am–midnight.
Sun Lok Kee has the freshest Cantonese-style seafood in Chinatown. This small, nondescript restaurant is always packed, but service is fast and so is the line. The menu offers hefty main dishes. Some of our favorite dishes are mussels in black-bean sauce, steamed fish, steamed shrimp, and crabs Cantonese style. The fresh vegetable and pork dishes make delicious accompaniments.

WONG KEE RESTAURANT, 113 Mott St. Tel. 966-1160.
   Cuisine: CANTONESE. **Reservations:** Accepted for large groups. **Subway:**
   6, J, M, Z to Canal St.
$ Prices: Appetizers $1.50–$6; main courses $2.50–$11.95. No credit cards.
   Open: Daily 11am–9:45pm.
This tiny but top-notch establishment provides delicious, cheap noodle and soup
dishes without the frenetic fast-food atmosphere found in other Chinatown noodle
houses. The place is cheerily decorated in shades of steely gray, lemon yellow, and
dark turquoise.
   Wong Kee's hearty dishes over rice, such as beef with green peas, and main dishes
like sizzling chicken—beans, chunks of chickens, garlic, and scallions—can feed two
people. There are other more expensive house specialties, such as Wong Kee spiced
pork and any of Wong Kee's fresh vegetable dishes. A Chinese friend told us about this
place and we can understand why it's his favorite. BYOB.

DIM SUM

Many Cantonese and larger Chinese restaurants offer a dim sum brunch, usually
served from 10am to 3pm. Waiters bring trays of Chinese delicacies and other food in
bite-size portions; you choose what you like and are charged by the number of plates
on your table at the brunch's end. A satisfying dim sum brunch generally costs
between $6 and $8 per person.
   All the popular places for dim sum are very crowded on weekends, but this real
Chinese eating experience is worth the wait, and weekend crowds are part of the fun.

**HEE SEUNG FUNG or HSF, 46 Bowery, between Canal St. and Chatham
   Square. Tel. 374-1319.**
   Cuisine: DIM SUM. **Reservations:** Accepted. **Subway:** 6, J, M, Z to Canal St.
$ Prices: Dim sum courses $1.60–$3. No credit cards.
   Open: Dim sum daily 7:30am–5pm; dinner 7:30pm–midnight.
      HSF prides itself on offering the largest choice of dim sum in the city. Plates of
      dim sum are continuously wheeled around the restaurant from 7:30am to 5pm.
         The à la carte menu of Cantonese fare offered by the restaurant after noon
presents some interesting possibilities for the demanding palate; try the snail with
black-bean sauce or the shark fin with shredded chicken soup.
   Hee Seung Fung is decorated in gold and chrome, and, because of many favorable
write-ups, enjoys a large tourist and uptown crowd along with Chinatown locals.
Especially helpful are the pictorial brochures at each table that describe various
dishes. The restaurant has become so popular in recent years that it now has a branch
uptown at 578 Second Ave., at 32nd Street (tel. 689-6969).

THE NICE RESTAURANT, 35 E. Broadway. Tel. 406-9510.
   Cuisine: DIM SUM. **Reservations:** Not accepted. **Subway:** 6, J, M, Z to
   Canal St.
$ Prices: Dim sum courses $1.70–$4.50. AE.
   Open: Dim sum daily 8am–4pm; dinner daily 4:30–11pm.
In recent years, this place has become a favorite for dim sum. Its two floors seat more
than 400 people, and the restaurant is often full. This is Hong Kong–style dining at its
best: the bigger, the better.
   Don't be intimidated by the hustle and bustle. You can take cues from other diners,
and don't be shy about asking what's in a dish. Many dim sum dishes are some kind of
dumpling with shrimp, pork, vegetable, or fish fillings. Some favorites are steamed
buns filled with pork, shrimp dumplings, pork wontons, and beef balls. There are also
sweet confections to end the meal—typical are small cakes filled with custard,
coconut, almond, or red-bean paste.

SILVER PALACE, 50 Bowery, near Canal St. Tel. 964-1204.
   Cuisine: DIM SUM. **Reservations:** Not accepted. **Subway:** 6, J, M, Z to
   Canal St.
$ Prices: Dim sum courses $1.75–$5. No credit cards.

Open: Daily 8am–4pm.

Dim sum at the Silver Palace has become a Chinatown tradition. An escalator brings you to the second-floor dining room, which looks roughly the size of a football field and is decorated in bright red with many large tables—necessary for its hordes of devoted customers. In fact, the management claims there's seating for 800. Reservations aren't accepted, they say, because they'll always find room for you. The food at Silver Palace is fast, fresh, and delicious. There are more than 58 kinds of dim sum available.

NOODLE HOUSES

Throughout Chinatown are many small places specializing in Chinese noodle dishes served with pork, shrimp, chicken, duck, fish, vegetables, and beef. These noodle meals are filling, delicious, and a budget traveler's dream.

HONG FAT, 63 Mott St., between Bayard and Canal sts. Tel. 962-9588.
   Cuisine: CHINESE NOODLES. **Reservations:** Not accepted. **Subway:** 6, J, M, Z to Canal St.
   $ Prices: Noodle dishes $3.95–$5.50. No credit cards.
   Open: Daily 10am–5am.
This place is a premier noodle emporium, but it resonates with the noisy atmosphere of a fast-food burger chain. It's a good eatery for a quick lunch, if not the place for a relaxing dinner.

China's four basic noodles are served: lo mein (soft noodles), show fon (broad noodles), chow mai fon (fine rice noodles), and special noodles with gravy. You can also order your noodle dish fixed "your way," with any combination of roast pork, beef, shrimp, fish, chicken, or duck.

The restaurant also serves several non-noodle Szechuan specialties, including beef with Szechuan-preserved vegetables, dried sautéed string beans with minced pork, and lemon chicken, all priced under $7.

SHANGHAI SNACK BAR, 14 Elizabeth St. Tel. 964-5640.
   Cuisine: CHINESE NOODLES. **Reservations:** Not accepted. **Subway:** 6, J, M, Z to Canal St.
   $ Prices: Noodle dishes under $7.50. No credit cards.
   Open: Daily 10:30am–10pm (approximately).
For some of the best soup in Chinatown, try this spot at the end of the covered Elizabeth Street mall walkway. Offering more than 25 varieties of soup and noodle dishes, it's the perfect place for a quick yet filling meal. Try the Shanghai noodles in a bowl of hearty broth, with diced chicken and pork, shrimp, bamboo shoots, green peas, and Chinese mushrooms, or the several appetizing dumpling dishes under $3.50.

WO HOP, 15 and 17 Mott St. Tel. 766-9160 or 406-3973.
   Cuisine: CHINESE NOODLES. **Reservations:** Accepted only at 15 Mott.
   Subway: 6, J, M, Z to Canal St.
   $ Prices: Noodle dishes $2.95–$7.25. No credit cards.
   Open: 15 Mott St. daily 11am–5am; 17 Mott St. daily 24 hours.
   Wo Hop is actually two restaurants, which are different in decor but similar in menu. Devotees of both restaurants recommend the chunky, meat- and seafood-filled soups and noodle dishes. The Wo Hops offer over 50 noodle dishes priced under $6. Many of the steamy plates of silky noodles, such as roast pork chow fon and beef chow fon, cost $3.50 or less. Other low-priced Cantonese fare includes roast pork with green peppers and onions, beef with beansprouts, and kam loo wonton—fried wonton, breaded with seafood, roast duck, chicken, pork, pineapple, and sweet-and-sour sauce.

Number 15 is the more attractive place to eat. Decorated with bright-red tiles and electrically lit photomurals of the Chinese countryside, the 50-seat restaurant is cheerful and pleasant. Number 17, located at the bottom of a flight of stairs, has been in that location for over 40 years.

3. LITTLE ITALY

See also Section 14, "Specialty Dining," for details on Ferrara's and other favorite coffee-and-pastry spots in Little Italy. No experience of this neighborhood is complete without ample time spent nursing a cappuccino and a cannoli in one of the many charming cafés.

BENITO'S I, 174 Mulberry St. Tel. 226-9171.
> **Cuisine:** ITALIAN. **Reservations:** Recommended for large parties. **Subway:** 6 to Spring St.
> **$ Prices:** Pasta courses $6–$10.75; main courses $9.25–$13.95. MC, V.
> **Open:** Sun–Thurs noon–10:30pm, Fri–Sat noon–midnight.

No longer affiliated with Benito's II (see below), this small restaurant features delicious Sicilian cuisine in a charming, intimate atmosphere.

We found the scaloppine alla Benito excellent (veal with prosciutto and mushrooms sautéed in marsala wine). An unusual and tasty dish is broccoli di rape, bitter broccoli cooked with garlic and herbs. Also recommended is the fettuccine Giulio Cesare, veal-based red cream sauce, with mushrooms, prosciutto, and freshly ground parmesan.

BENITO'S II, 163 Mulberry St., between Broome and Grand sts. Tel. 226-9012.
> **Cuisine:** SICILIAN. **Reservations:** Not needed. **Subway:** 6 to Spring St.
> **$ Prices:** Pasta and main courses $9.25–$13. No credit cards.
> **Open:** Daily noon–midnight.

Benito's II is a good bet for first-rate, southern-style Sicilian cuisine. It's a rustic restaurant, with a dark wood–paneled ceiling and exposed-brick walls punctuated by floor-to-ceiling wood beams. Tables are covered with white linen tablecloths, and waiters are sharply dressed in white and black.

The veal, seafood, and pasta are excellent, as are the antipasti. You'll get the best deal if you order in courses, Italian style, and share. Two people might begin with the pepper stuffed with vegetables in marinara sauce or the popular mozzarella in carrozza (fried cheese sandwiches); or go on to share one of the pastas, such as spaghetti carbonara style or homemade manicotti; then perhaps a main dish, octopus Sicilian style (with tomatoes, capers, garlic, and black olives), veal scaloppine, or the delicious striped bass, broiled and served in a light tomato sauce with capers and anchovies. If you decide to splurge on dessert, try the zabaglione with strawberries, a popular Benito II custard dessert.

FLORIO'S, 192 Grand St., between Mott and Mulberry sts. Tel. 226-7610.
> **Cuisine:** ITALIAN. **Reservations:** Not accepted. **Subway:** B, D, Q to Grand St.; N, R, 6 to Canal St.
> **$ Prices:** Appetizers $3.95–$7; main courses $10.75–$17. AE, D, DC, MC, V.
> **Open:** Daily 11am–midnight.

What would a visit to Little Italy be without a thick slice of pizza or a hefty cheese calzone? For both, Florio's is the place. Entered via an alcove with large plant-filled windows, the interior has exposed-brick and stucco walls decorated with oil paintings, a beamed ceiling, and tables covered with red tablecloths under glass. There's a very comfortable backroom with a skylight and thriving potted trees and plants.

Try a thick-crust pizza or a piece of cheese calzone (think of it as a fried, rolled slice of pizza with filling); you can also get cheese and sausage or cheese and prosciutto varieties. Florio's offers huge hero sandwiches. There are also homemade pasta dishes, and fish, chicken, and veal main dishes. Italian ice creams and pastries are available for less than $3.50.

LUNA, 112 Mulberry St., between Canal and Hester sts. Tel. 226-8657.

Cuisine: ITALIAN. **Reservations:** Not accepted. **Subway:** N, R, 6, J, M, Z to Canal St.

$ Prices: All items under $10. No credit cards.

Open: Daily noon–midnight.

Family-owned and family-run, Luna is one of Little Italy's more reasonably priced restaurants. It has a justifiably loyal clientele and at dinnertime the 12 booths fill quickly, so be prepared to wait.

The antipasto is very good, and comes with stuffed pepper, mushrooms, scallops, and clams. Pasta dishes include spaghetti, lasagne, ravioli, and linguine, and there are also seafood and veal dishes. But seafood steals the show; we favor calamari oreganato, a tender, sliced squid baked with a topping of breadcrumbs, garlic, oregano, and olive oil. There are also healthy platters of steamed mussels and clams, wine by the glass, and a full complement of bar drinks.

PUGLIA, 189 Hester St., near Mulberry St. Tel. 966-6066 or 226-8912.

Cuisine: ITALIAN. **Reservations:** Not accepted. **Subway:** 6 to Canal St.

$ Prices: Pasta and main courses $7–$11.95. No credit cards.

Open: Tues–Sun noon–1am.

No one should miss the experience of eating at Puglia. Although the food is excellent, the main attraction is the atmosphere: crowded, casual, rowdy (in a friendly way); on weekends the house singer and organist often leads the customers in a sing-along. Puglia is a venerable New York institution in which patrons have been partying since 1915. The festive diners sit at long tables out front, and there's an adjoining garden-like backroom with a bar. In the summer a few tables grace a small garden outside.

The food is inexpensive (with most dishes under $11) and the portions are hefty. An order of garlic bread or a glass of wine with your meal can be had for less than $2. Good food, great fun.

TERESA'S OF MULBERRY STREET, 117 Mulberry St. Tel. 226-6950.

Cuisine: ITALIAN. **Reservations:** Recommended at dinner and on weekends.

Subway: N, R to Prince St.; 6 to Spring St.; J, M to Kenmare St.

$ Prices: All items $3.75–$18.50. AE, MC, V.

Open: Daily noon–11:30pm.

Right down the street from Umberto's (below) is a pretty and intimate little place with barely enough room for its 11 indoor tables and 4 patio tables. It has plant-filled windows, beautiful latticework over room-length mirrors, and tables covered with green oilcloth. The entire effect is charming and very Italian. The menu is the same at lunch and dinner, and the prices are extremely reasonable: Most pastas are under $8; a favorite is the filette de pomadoro—red sauce, onion, fresh tomatoes, Italian ham, and a dash of red wine.

UMBERTO'S CLAM HOUSE, 129 Mulberry St., corner of Hester St. Tel. 431-7545.

Cuisine: ITALIAN. **Reservations:** Not needed. **Subway:** N, R, 6 to Canal St.

$ Prices: Main courses $8.75–$18. AE.

Open: Daily 11am–6am.

Umberto's is perhaps the best known of Little Italy's restaurants. Even during the wee hours, the place is filled with actors, actresses, and other restaurateurs. One whole wall is devoted to autographed pictures of the celebrity clientele—among them Frank Sinatra, Johnny Carson, Cher, Jackie Gleason, and Fellini. Nevertheless, Umberto's is an attractive and unpretentious place with butcher-block tables, large windows, and blue-tiled floors. In good weather a row of umbrella tables is placed outdoors on a small patio.

Umberto's is most renowned for its clams and its linguine in hot sauce. Seafood, such as calamari (squid), scungilli (conch), and mussels are served with a choice of hot, medium, or sweet sauces and biscuits. House favorites include the fish salad combination—shrimp, calamari, mussels, and scungilli with lemon, oil, garlic, and parsley—and fish and chips or a plate of smelt with french fries, lemon, and tartar sauce. You can get a dozen cherrystone or littleneck clams and most of the traditional Italian pastries.

Interestingly enough, Umberto's has its menu in six languages besides English— Spanish, Japanese, Chinese, Italian, French, and German.

VINCENT'S CLAM BAR, 119 Mott St., corner of Hester St. Tel. 226-8133.

Cuisine: ITALIAN. **Reservations:** Not accepted. **Subway:** B, D, Q to Grand St.; 6 to Canal St.

$ Prices: Main courses $6.95–$14; seafood combination platters $13–$15. AE.

Open: Sun–Thurs 11:30am–2am; Fri–Sat 11:30–5am.

This is the only Little Italy restaurant that has been around longer than Puglia. Giuseppe and Carmelo Siano established the place in 1904, and the Siano family has been running it ever since. The front room houses a bar and a long counter, behind which Vincent's chefs cook up steaming pots of their famous hot sauce. The main dining room in the back is informal but pleasant, with beamed walls, two big arched windows, and fresh flowers on every table. On the wall, watching over it all, is a large oil painting of the Siano brothers.

Fresh fish, seafood, and pasta are the specialties here: you can get an order of linguine and clams, calamari, or shrimp with medium or hot sauce; baked mussels; littleneck clams; or an Italian seafood combination platter.

4. SOHO/NOHO

SOHO

ABYSSINIA, 35 Grand St., corner of Thompson St. Tel. 226-5959.

Cuisine: ETHIOPIAN. **Reservations:** Not needed. **Subway:** 1, 9, A, C, E to Canal St.

$ Prices: Main courses average $9.95–$12.95. AE.

Open: Mon–Fri 6–10:30pm, Sat–Sun 1–10:30pm.

Abyssinia offers adventurous cuisine in an intriguing ethnic setting. Diners are seated on tiny stools around a short round table decorated with a dome of straw. When the meal is served, the dome is removed and hung on the wall.

The exotic variety of vegetarian, beef, and fish dishes are all accompanied by an ample serving of "injera," the porous Ethiopian pancake that takes the place of knife and fork and can be used to soak up every last bit of the spicy red-pepper sauce known as "berbere." Doro wot, a popular Ethiopian dish of chicken marinated in berbere, is exceedingly tender and spicy. Also excellent is kitfo, a national dish of steak tartare seasoned with spiced butter and hot chile powder.

Desserts are equally unusual, from a simple plate of papaya with lime to a rich dark African chocolate-chip cake. For those who can never get enough chocolate there's even a trio of handmade chocolate truffles. Cocoa beans never tasted so good.

BROOME STREET BAR, corner of Broome St. and West Broadway. Tel. 925-2086.

Cuisine: AMERICAN/CONTINENTAL. **Reservations:** Not accepted. **Subway:** N, R to Prince St.

$ Prices: Main courses $5.50–$7.50. No credit cards.

Open: Sun–Thurs 11am–1:30am; Fri–Sat 11am–2:30am.

From late morning until early morning, this pub is filled with an eclectic crowd of artists, writers, and musicians. Broome Street is especially attractive in the late afternoon when jazz plays on the sound system, and you can sit over a beer or coffee and study the passing SoHo scene through the plant-filled front windows. There are a venerable old mahogany bar, small tables with comfortable bentwood chairs, and old-fashioned fans overhead.

The menu is posted: salads, quiches, burgers, sandwiches, and omelets. There's a wide assortment of desserts at around $3, and the ice cream is Häagen-Dazs. Try the pineapple fizz.

THE CUPPING ROOM CAFÉ, 359 West Broadway, between Broome and Grand sts. Tel. 925-2898.
   Cuisine: AMERICAN. **Reservations:** Not needed. **Subway:** N, R, A, C, E to Canal.
$ **Prices:** Main courses under $11. AE, DC, MC, V.
   Open: Mon–Thurs 7:30am–1am, Fri 7:30am–2am, Sat 8am–2am, Sun 8am–1am.
This charming restaurant is simply one of the most comfortable places in town for a leisurely breakfast or brunch. The decor creates a rural feel, with exposed-brick walls, captain's chairs, blackboard menus, and a working pot-bellied stove. A huge vase of colorful flowers sits on an oak counter and more flowers adorn marble-topped tables. The skylight-lit back room is a perfect place to enjoy excellent croissants and delicious freshly brewed coffee, while jazz or classical music plays in the background. There is live jazz on Friday and Saturday nights.

You can get a homemade muffin and a cup of coffee, chicken tarragon salad, or a hot waffle topped with raisins, nuts, fresh fruit, and homemade whipped cream. For dessert, try the delicious Austrian plum cake or perhaps the fruit torte.

LA DOLCE VITA, 195 Spring St., between Sullivan and Thompson sts. Tel. 431-1315.
   Cuisine: ITALIAN. **Reservations:** Suggested for large parties. **Subway:** C, E to Spring St.
$ **Prices:** Appetizers $3.25–$9; main courses $8–$14.95. AE.
   Open: Mon–Fri 11am–midnight; Sat–Sun 10am–midnight.
Here you'll find a true sampling of "the good life." Owner/chef John Mazzocchi's special touch is evident everywhere, from the exposed-brick walls lined with stars' photographs from the 1930s, '40s, and '50s, to the blue-and-white-checked table-cloths, ceiling fans, and carved-oak bar, to the delicious and innovative food. In warmer weather the restaurant expands for al fresco dining at tables on the sidewalk.

You'll find an exciting assortment of northern Italian specialties. For an appetizer, try the mussels marinière served in a white wine and cream sauce in a small or large portion, or the fresh roasted peppers and mozzarella. Main dishes include spinach fettuccine with four cheeses and walnuts, shrimp, clams, and mussels Fra Diavola in a spicy red sauce, and chicken breast scarparella in a light garlic sauce. If you're lucky, papardelli will be a special. Make sure you leave room for the mouthwatering homemade desserts, all $4. We recently enjoyed the amaretto cheesecake and the tartuffo, an Italian chocolate truffle. Ask your waitress for the daily offerings.

EAR INN, 326 Spring St., between Washington and Greenwich sts. Tel. 226-9060.
   Cuisine: INTERNATIONAL. **Reservations:** Not accepted. **Subway:** 1, 9 to Canal St.; C, E to Spring St.
$ **Prices:** Main courses $3.50–$9; daily specials $4.75–$9. AE, DC.
   Open: Daily noon–1am; Sun brunch noon–5pm.
Although slightly west of SoHo proper, the Ear Inn is well worth the few extra blocks of walking. This small, casual restaurant in a landmark building dating from 1817 is a beloved neighborhood hangout whose outstanding feature is its clientele of writers, musicians, and artists. While dining, you'll probably be reading about the building's interesting history, which includes originally being the home of James Brown, who was a black man and an aide to George Washington. Poetry readings are offered every Saturday at 3pm, live music Sunday and Wednesday at 10pm, and tables covered with butcher paper and crayons, should the creative urge strike while dining. The restaurant's decor is minimal—a collection of old glass bottles on the bar, a few fish on the walls, and a wood floor. Tables with blue-and-white-checked tablecloths are

located in the front and in a small back room. The jukebox, which plays the latest in New Wave, reggae, and jazz, is very, very good.

The Ear Inn's specialty is "international home cookin'" and the food is inexpensive and imaginatively prepared. You might sample the cowboy chili—an excellent hot-and-spicy offering—along with a mixed green salad or salade niçoise. Or there are sirloin burgers, pasta of the day, and daily specials. The large desserts are all homemade, and there's a full bar.

ELEPHANT AND CASTLE, 183 Prince St., between Sullivan and Thompson sts. Tel. 260-3600.

> **Cuisine:** AMERICAN. **Reservations:** Not accepted. **Subway:** N, R to Prince St.; C, E to Spring St.; 1, 9 to Houston St.
>
> **$ Prices:** Appetizers $2.75–$6; main courses $7.50–$12. AE, CB, DC, MC, V.
>
> **Open:** Mon–Thurs 8am–midnight; Fri–Sat 8am–12:30am; Sun 10am–midnight.

Early risers who want to breakfast in SoHo before taking on the galleries should head here. You'll find 22 different kinds of omelets, including a delicate fines-herbes omelet and smoked salmon with dill; fresh-squeezed orange juice is also available. Jam jars decorate the shelves mounted on mirrored walls and give the place a cozy, early-morning feel.

Hamburger lovers may want to lunch at Elephant and Castle; there are 12 different toppings for the juicy thick burgers, including guacamole with cheddar and tomato and sour cream with horseradish. For the famished, there's even the Elephant burger—a colossal creation of chopped beef served with curried sour cream, bacon, scallions, cheddar, and tomato.

FANELLI'S, 94 Prince St., corner of Mercer St. Tel. 226-9412.

> **Cuisine:** INTERNATIONAL. **Reservations:** Not accepted. **Subway:** N, R to Prince St.; 6 to Spring St.; B, D, F, Q to Broadway/Layfayette St.
>
> **$ Prices:** Main courses $5–$7. No credit cards.
>
> **Open:** Mon–Sun 10am–2am; Sun noon–2am.

Fanelli's, the last of the neighborhood taverns, has been around for over a century. It's a small place with a handful of tables and an eclectic clientele. The original owner, Mike Fanelli, was a boxer in his youth, and the walls are lined with photographs of old fights and famous boxers. The food is simple, but filling. You can have linguine with marinara sauce, lasagne, shepherd's pie with salad, New England clam chowder, or a thick sandwich.

I TRE MERLI, 463 West Broadway, between West Houston and Prince sts. Tel. 254-8699.

> **Cuisine:** ITALIAN. **Reservations:** Accepted. **Subway:** R to Prince St.; C, E to Spring St.
>
> **$ Prices:** Main courses $7.50–$24. AE, DC, MC, V.
>
> **Open:** Mon–Fri noon–1am, Sat noon–2am.

A young, sophisticated crowd is already flocking to the SoHo cousin of a wine bar and restaurant in Genoa, Italy. Indeed, the Genovese owners have taken pains to give their New York hangout a sleek Italian look. The trendy interior is a highly glossed black and features a clever modular bar with movable sections. Wine and champagne come by the glass or bottle and are imported exclusively from the I Tre Merli vineyards in northern Italy.

The cuisine, like the wine, is Genovese, and the fragrant and spicy dishes served at brunch evoke lazy afternoons in Italy. Try the delicious artichoke salad with parmesan cheese; gnocchi, potato pasta with a basil-and-garlic sauce; or breast of chicken with herbs. Lunch is slightly less expensive than dinner, but the view from the mezzanine of the late-night action at the crowded ground-floor bar may make the splurge worthwhile.

LUPE'S EAST L.A. KITCHEN, 110 Sixth Ave., at Watts St. Tel. 966-1326.

> **Cuisine:** MEXICAN. **Reservations:** Not accepted. **Subway:** C, E to Spring St.; 1 to Canal St.

$ Prices: Appetizers $1.50–$4; main courses $6.95–$7.75; Sun brunch: to $7.25. No credit cards.
Open: Lunch daily 11:30am–4pm; dinner Sun–Thurs 4–11pm, Fri–Sat 4pm– midnight; Sun brunch 11:30am–4pm.

It's little more than a hole in the wall, but Lupe's exudes cheer with bright colors, background jazz tapes, and old album covers displayed on the walls. All the usual Mexican standbys are here; you might start with the cazuelitas, little corn-flour cakes fried and filled with beef or chicken, beans, cheese, and salsa, and follow with chili Colorado, spicy beef and onions in red chili sauce served over rice. You'll find several variations of burritos on the menu, along with a good selection of Mexican beers.

We came for Sunday brunch, and although service was a bit indifferent, the food, atmosphere, and prices made up for it. The banana pancakes were delicious, and we also enjoyed the spicy Anaheim omelet, with green chiles and sour cream. The huevos batidos are another good bet—scrambled eggs with tomato, cheese, chilis, and shredded corn tortillas.

MOONDANCE DINER, 80 Ave. of the Americas (Sixth Ave.), at Grand St. Tel. 226-1191.
Cuisine: AMERICAN. **Reservations:** Not accepted. **Subway:** 1, 9, A, C, E to Canal.
$ Prices: Hamburgers and sandwiches $6.25–$10; full meal $8–$10. No credit cards.
Open: Sun–Thurs 8:30am–midnight; Fri–Sat 24 hours.

Traditional deco diners were easy on the eyes and difficult on the digestion. At SoHo's Moondance Diner you can have the best of both worlds. Under a revolving electric moon, in a pre–World War II railway car, you can eat tasty well-prepared food served by friendly waiters. Try the grilled mozzarella with basil and tomato on garlic challah, or the popular chicken-salad sandwich. The patrons are an interesting blend of blue-collar and art-world chic. During warmer months, streetside tables are set out. Breakfast is served all day.

PRINCE STREET BAR AND RESTAURANT, 125 Prince St., corner of Wooster St. Tel. 228-8130.
Cuisine: INTERNATIONAL. **Reservations:** Not needed. **Subway:** R to Prince St.; 6, C, E to Spring St.
$ Prices: Appetizers $2–$3.50; main courses $6.50–$12.50. No credit cards.
Open: Sun–Thurs 11:30am–1am; Fri–Sat 11:30am–2am.

The crowd here is an interesting cross section of the SoHo populace. The back of the dining room is dimly lit by pink overhead bulbs and houses a bar covered with framed mirrors; up front, light streams in through high, plant-filled windows. The menu offers over 80 separate dishes, including many Indonesian specialties. A small sampling includes guacamole dip; tofu parmigiana with french fries or rice, and bread (for the somewhat health-conscious); mixed vegetables with lemon butter; and a roast beef and creamed horseradish sandwich in toasted pita.

Then there are the hot toddies for the winter months, refreshing piña coladas for the summer, and a slew of fresh-baked desserts—try the "tunnel of fudge" cake.

THE SOHO KITCHEN, 103 Greene St., between Prince and Spring sts. Tel. 925-1866.
Cuisine: AMERICAN/CONTINENTAL. **Reservations:** Not accepted. **Subway:** R to Prince St.; 6 to Spring St.
$ Prices: Appetizers $2.75–$7.25; main courses $5.75–$15.75. AE, CB, DC, MC, V.
Open: Mon–Thurs 11:30am–2am, Fri–Sat 11:30am–4am, Sun 11:30am–10pm.

Lovers of wine and imaginatively prepared food should head for this large loft space. You'll find a varied clientele clustered at the raised tables along both walls or relaxing at the enormous horseshoe bar. Adding to the atmosphere are the huge contemporary artworks hanging on exposed-brick walls.

The menu offers anything from a light snack to a full meal. Try the gourmet pizzas—perhaps the mozzarella with sun-dried tomatoes. Grilled trout is good, and fettuccine with peas, smoked salmon, and caviar in a cream sauce is excellent.

After ordering food, have a taste of the grape from their incredible wine list—with 110 selections, it is said to be the most extensive in the world. You can have a 5-ounce glass, starting at $4, or a full bottle. For those who want to sample wine of a particular variety or region, have a "flight" tasting—a serving of four to eight 1.5-ounce tastings, beginning at $7.75.

TENNESSEE MOUNTAIN, 143 Spring St., at the corner of Wooster St. Tel. 431-3993.
    Cuisine: AMERICAN/RIBS. **Reservations:** Recommended. **Subway:** C, E to Spring St.
$ **Prices:** Appetizers $3.50–$6.95; main courses $8.95–$14.95; rib platters $12.95–$14.95. AE, CB, DC, MC, V.
    Open: Mon–Wed 11:30am–11pm, Thurs–Sat 11:30am–midnight, Sun 11:30am–10pm.

For a convivial atmosphere, friendly service, and hickory-smoked ribs that melt in your mouth, Tennessee Mountain's the place. You'll keep down your tab if you stick to the burgers ($5.95 to $7.25) or the chili ($5.95 to $6.95), or if you order half a barbecued chicken for $8.95. But the lean, tender ribs are worth the extra few dollars—they come with the best fries we've had in a while, and are served with a tangy homemade Tennessee barbeque sauce or a spicy black jack sauce. And this is no time to worry about your cholesterol count—have an order of batter-fried onion rings on the side.

Monday is usually barbeque and brew night—your main course platter will come with fries, coleslaw, fresh-baked muffins, and all the beer or wine you can drink, all for $13.99. When we were there during the summer, Tuesdays and Wednesdays were picnic nights, with $1 drafts, and complimentary corn-on-the-cob and watermelon with your rib combo. Delivery service is available, and there's a happy hour at the bar on weekdays from 4:30 to 7pm.

NOHO

Caramba!, 684 Broadway, at the corner of Great Jones Street (tel. 420-9817), is a favorite hangout for the young professional crowd, who come on weekend nights to enjoy the giant slush margaritas. See Section 9 for a complete review of the Midtown West branch of Caramba!

ACME BAR & GRILL, 9 Great Jones St., corner of Lafayette St. Tel. 420-1934.
    Cuisine: CAJUN. **Reservations:** Not accepted. **Subway:** 6 to Bleecker St.; B, D, F to Broadway/Lafayette St.
$ **Prices:** Main courses $5.25–$12. No credit cards.
    Open: Mon–Fri lunch 11am–4pm; Mon–Fri dinner 4pm–midnight, Sat–Sun 4pm–1am; brunch Sat–Sun 11:30am–3:45pm.
Now that New York's Cajun fad has died down, the serious business of Cajun food can proceed with less fanfare and more truly good eating at places like Acme Bar & Grill. A big, dark space hung with old gas-station signs, its modest motto is "An Okay Place to Eat."

Its menus, identical for lunch and dinner but with a $1 to $2 price difference, are made up of a modest number of dishes that focus on fish and average under $12. Catfish and trout loom large, whether pan-fried, blackened, or spicy. Oyster lovers can feast on a robust plate of fried or steamed oysters, and non-fish-eaters can console themselves with crisp chicken-fried steak.

Brunch features such hearty fare as catfish and eggs.

BAYAMO, 704 Broadway, between East 4th St. and Astor Place. Tel. 475-5151.

Cuisine: CUBAN. **Reservations:** Not needed. **Subway:** 6 to Astor Place.
$ Prices: Appetizers $3.95–$8.95; main courses $5.95–$17.95. AE, DC, MC, V.
Open: Sun–Thurs noon–midnight, Fri–Sat noon–2am.

The owners call it a Cuban restaurant with Chinese overtones, but the decor is pure New Wave.

You can get almost anything at Bayamo. In the mood for a salad? Try ensalada de pollo escabechado, which is spiced chicken mixed with cold vegetables. If maybe you want eggs, order the huevos revueltos con camarones—scrambled eggs with shrimp, tomato, and chili. For a taste of the East, sample any of the spring rolls, made to order with your choice of filling, and filling enough to be a whole meal. There's also a large dessert menu. The homemade flan with pecans and macadamia nuts gets rave reviews. Or try the mandarin orange sorbet.

BLUE WILLOW, 644 Broadway, corner of Bleecker St. Tel. 673-6480.
Cuisine: AMERICAN. **Reservations:** Recommended. **Subway:** B, D, F to Broadway/Lafayette St.; 6 to Bleeker St.
$ Prices: Most items under $12. AE, DC, MC, V.
Open: Sun–Thurs 11:30am–midnight, Fri–Sat 11am–2am.

Housed in an old 20th-century bank (there's a vault downstairs), Blue Willow offers American cuisine with a twist. Its main dining room is decked with marble walls, an antique wooden bar, and lofty tin ceilings. If you can wade through the sea of Persian rugs and antique furniture in the back room, you can listen to local jazz musicians perform nightly.

A little pricey in the seafood and meat department, Blue Willow offers a variety of other dishes at reasonable prices. Begin with steamed mussels in Spanish garlic sauce with garlic bread, and then move on to the roast leg of lamb with mint, spinach, and pecan stuffing. Or try any of the pasta dishes, like shrimp, mussels, crabmeat, and scallops on fettuccine or the handmade wild-mushroom ravioli.

EDDIE'S, 14 Waverly Place, near Broadway. Tel. 420-0919.
Cuisine: TEX-MEX. **Reservations:** Not accepted. **Subway:** 1, 9 to Sheridan Sq.; A, C, E, B, D, F, Q to West 4th St.
$ Prices: Burgers and main courses under $8. AE.
Open: Mon–Sat 11am–11pm.

Heapin' helpings are the rule at Eddie's, where the burger platters and salads weigh more than most people do when they're born. The crowd at Eddie's is likely to be mostly college kids from New York University, which perhaps explains the sturdy, no-nonsense decor. Eddie's provides good solid food at a low price in a simple place. It's a fine spot for a weary traveler who has spent the day exploring New York's oddities and is not in the mood for any more surprises.

Besides the basic burgers and Tex-Mex fare, Eddie's offers omelets and bountiful vegetarian selections, including tofu salads, stir-fried vegetables with brown rice, and fried tofu fajitas. The prices are more than reasonable, especially given the portion size. Burger platters include a pile of fries and a healthy salad. If you ask, Eddie's will grace your table with a bowl of fresh popcorn. Eddie's does not serve hard liquor.

GONZALEZ Y GONZALEZ, 625 Broadway, between Bleecker and Houston sts. Tel. 473-8787.
Cuisine: MEXICAN. **Reservations:** Recommended Thurs–Sat. **Subway:** 1, 9, B, D, F, Q to Houston St.; R to Prince St.
$ Prices: Appetizers $4.95–$6.75; main courses $6.95–$13.95. AE, CB, DC, MC, V.
Open: Sun–Thurs noon–midnight, Fri–Sat noon–2am.

While people may be surprised by the high cost of Mexican food in New York, this place is worth a visit. You get the real thing at Gonzalez y Gonzalez. The restaurant's motto is "Comida tipica de Mexico"—that is, "typical Mexican food." And the south-of-the-border decor, with its murals, piñatas, and sombreros, completes the theme. The menu is in both Spanish and English.

To start, you might try roast cheese with tomatillo sauce or roast mushrooms with chiles and salsas. Marinated chicken in banana leaves, rice with seafood, and whitefish with garlic are excellent main-course selections. If you have a light appetite, the seafood soup, thick and spicy with plenty of squid and fish, and a side order of plantain fritters or fried plantains is more than a meal. There's a tantalizing array of Mexican desserts—try banana and mango flambé with ice cream.

If the authentic food doesn't make this restaurant famous, maybe its 100-foot-long bar will. A waiter told us that it's the longest bar in New York and the second longest in the country. It's a good place to sip margaritas to live Latin rhythms (see Chapter 10, "New York City Nights" for details).

MINAMI, 27 Waverly Place, between University Place and Greene St. Tel. 529-2198.
    Cuisine: JAPANESE. **Reservations:** Recommended. **Subway:** A, C, E, B, D, F, Q to West 4th St.; 1, 9 to Sheridan Sq.
$ **Prices:** Sushi rolls $5.50; full dinner $11–$16.50. AE, MC, V.
    Open: Sun–Thurs 11am–11pm, Fri–Sat 11am–midnight.

Minami serves the standard New York–Japanese fare in attractive, clean surroundings. The waiters are warm without being intrusive. Here you can try fresh sushi and sashimi, chicken teriyaki, and the more unusual yellowtail teriyaki. Full dinners include soup, salad, and rice.

THE NOHO STAR, 330 Lafayette St., corner of Bleecker St. Tel. 925-0070.
    Cuisine: CHINESE/AMERICAN. **Reservations:** Not accepted. **Subway:** 6 to Bleecker St.; B, D, F, Q to Broadway/Lafayette St.
$ **Prices:** Appetizers $5–$6; main courses $10.75–$14. AE, CB, DC, MC, V.
    Open: Mon–Fri 8am–12:30am; Sat 10:30am–12:30am; Sun 10am–11:30pm.

The window panes are slanted, and every column and wall sports a different design. Despite the initial feeling of vertigo, however, few eating places could be more comfortable or more satisfying.

The menu is Chinese and American. For breakfast, one might have eggs Nepal, scrambled with cream and a touch of curry, and served with flaky papadum bread, or yogurt frou-frou, with fresh fruit, hazelnuts, and Vermont maple syrup. The regular dinner menu features particularly good Chinese dishes—among them, crispy jumbo shrimp with pan-blackened stringbeans, and the vegetarian delight.

5. GREENWICH VILLAGE

See also Section 4, "SoHo/NoHo," for a description of Elephant and Castle; there's a branch at 68 Greenwich Ave., between West 10th Street and Seventh Avenue (tel. 243-1400).

A POY LAUNG, 210 Thompson St., between Bleecker and West 3rd sts. Tel. 533-7290.
    Cuisine: THAI. **Reservations:** Accepted. **Subway:** A, B, C, D, E, F to West 4th St.
$ **Prices:** Main courses $4.95–$11.95. AE ($25 minimum), MC, V ($15 minimum).
    Open: Mon–Sat noon–11pm; Sun 5–11pm.

If you've never eaten Thai food, we highly recommend trying it here; some people swear it's the best in town. It's a small, unassuming place (only nine tables), and simply decorated. The location couldn't be better (the restaurant's big front window provides a fine view of a delightful stretch of Thompson Street), nor could the food.

Many dishes are hot and spicy, but you may order mild. Those that come with Thai sauce are especially hot, but milder dishes include pork, shrimp, beef, or chicken with eight kinds of vegetables. We tried one of each—beef with eight vegetables and chicken with spicy Thai sauce—and both were excellent. It's a bargain of a meal. A glass of house wine or a refreshing glass of Thai iced tea complement the meal nicely.

BENNY'S BURRITOS, 113 Greenwich Ave., at Jane St. Tel. 633-9210.
   Cuisine: MEXICAN. **Reservations:** Not accepted. **Subway:** 1, 2, 3, 9 to 14th St.
   $ Prices: Appetizers $1.50–$5; main courses $4.25–$7.95. No credit cards.
   Open: Sun–Thurs 11:30am–midnight, Fri–Sat 11:30am–1am; Sun brunch 11:30am–3pm.

Benny's is the best budget find we've seen in many moons. There's good reason why the crowds line up to get in: delicious Cal-Mex fare, with nothing on the menu over $8. Kitschy 1950s and '60s memorabilia sets the breezy tone, with a St. Joseph's aspirin clock, B-movie posters, and tacky antique lamps.

But you're not here for decor—you're here for the huge burritos. Loosen your belt and get down to business—we loved the vegetarian Mission burrito, a fresh flour tortilla stuffed with beans, rice, Monterey Jack cheese, guacamole, and sour cream. The Bay burrito adds beef or chicken to the mix; you might prefer the fresh spinach or chicken fajita versions. Pick your own chili combination, mixing the two-bean, three-chili basic with beef, chicken, Monterey Jack cheese, onions, and/or sour cream. All this noshing is of course accompanied by the appropriate beverages: plain, strawberry, or raspberry margaritas (for a bit more you can have yours made with Cuervo); Tecate or Dos Equis beer; jalapeño vodka; a Red Hot Shot (cinnamon Schnapps with a dash of Tabasco); Benny's fresh lemonade; and apple cider. Brunch is served on Saturdays and Sundays, with Mexican-style omelets among the offerings.

BLUE MILL TAVERN, 50 Commerce St., west of Seventh Ave. Tel. 243-7114.
   Cuisine: AMERICAN. **Reservations:** Not accepted. **Subway:** 1, 9 to Sheridan Square.
   $ Prices: All items under $15.
   Open: Dinner Mon–Thurs 5–10pm; Fri–Sat 5–11pm.
Located on one of the quietest and quaintest streets in the Village, the Blue Mill Tavern is around the corner from the famous Edna St. Vincent Millay House. It's a little difficult to find but definitely worth the search.

Alcino Neves, whose family has run the place for more than 50 years, was raised (and still lives) in an apartment above the restaurant. The restaurant was established in the 1920s and was a speakeasy during Prohibition. It once did a thriving tourist business, but now caters mainly to locals who know the place.

Inside, one can sit at leather booths, and across from a mahogany bar, or in the main dining room, where three huge murals, painted to look like Delft tile, establish the Dutch theme.

The food is traditional—the kind your mom used to make. Chopped sirloin, caldeirada (a Portuguese fish stew), liver and bacon, or a small steak all come on a platter with a potato and either two vegetables or a salad.

BOOSTAN, 85 MacDougal St., between Bleecker and Houston sts. Tel. 533-9561.
   Cuisine: MIDDLE EASTERN. **Reservations:** Recommended. **Subway:** 1, 9 to Houston St.; A, C, E, B, D, F, Q to West 4th St.
   $ Prices: Appetizers $3–$4.50; sandwiches and salads $3–$6.95; main courses $5.95–$11.95. No credit cards.
   Open: Daily noon–1am.
If you're tired of rich sauces and meat main dishes, Boostan is your solution. It prides itself on large helpings of extremely healthy foods based on Middle Eastern and Mediterranean recipes. The decor includes lacquered tree-trunk tables adorned with flower-filled vases, guitars and wooden flutes, and weavings. If weather permits, you can sit outside at small Formica tables.

Boostan's vegetarian dinners are widely appreciated for their freshness. A favorite

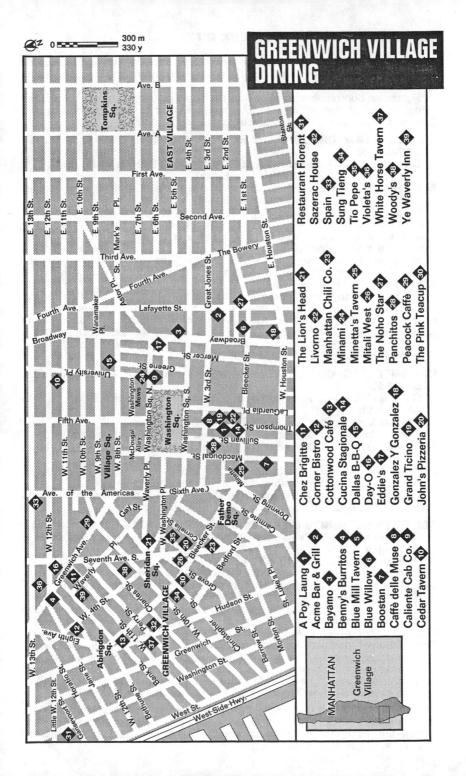

GREENWICH VILLAGE DINING

Restaurant Florent 31
Sazerac House 32
Spain 33
Sung Tieng 34
Tio Pepe 35
Violeta's 36
White Horse Tavern 37
Woody's 38
Ye Waverly Inn 39

The Lion's Head 21
Livorno 22
Manhattan Chili Co. 23
Minami 24
Minetta's Tavern 25
Mitali West 26
The Noho Star 27
Panchitos 28
Peacock Caffè 29
The Pink Teacup 30

Chez Brigitte 11
Corner Bistro 12
Cottonwood Café 13
Cucina Stagionale 14
Dallas B-B-Q 15
Day-O 16
Eddie's 17
Gonzalez Y Gonzalez 18
Grand Ticino 19
John's Pizzeria 20

A Poy Laung 1
Acme Bar & Grill 2
Bayamo 3
Benny's Burritos 4
Blue Mill Tavern 5
Blue Willow 6
Boostan 7
Caffè delle Muse 8
Caliente Cab Co. 9
Cedar Tavern 10

MANHATTAN

Greenwich Village

among regulars is couscous topped with stewed vegetables, but you might go for the whole-wheat spaghetti primavera, the baba ghannoush sandwich, the special Boostan moussaka, or the stuffed zucchini.

Desserts at Boostan should not be ignored. Baloza pudding, homemade with fresh orange or apricot, low-fat milk, and whipped cream, is particularly popular, as is Boostan's carrot cake. Try a Turkish coffee to top it all off.

CAFFÈ DELLE MUSE, 76 W. 3rd St., at the corner of Thompson St. Tel. 982-3120.

Cuisine: ITALIAN. **Reservations:** Recommended. **Subway:** A, B, C, D, E, F, Q to West 4th St.; or 1, 9 to Sheridan Square.

$ Prices: Appetizers $2.50–$5.75; pasta courses $5.75–$8.75; main courses $6.95–$10.95. Credit card minimum $30. AE, MC, V.

Open: Mon–Thurs 11:30am–11pm; Fri–Sat 11:30am–midnight.

Candles flickering on the lovely dark floral tablecloths and swinging jazz or soothing classical tapes in the background set the tone at this casual but romantic Village spot. Our cordial waitress started us off with one of the chef's specialties, ribollita—a hearty, perfectly spiced vegetable and bean soup. The caprese, fresh homemade mozzarella with tomatoes and basil, was artfully presented and came with oil and vinegar in tiny hand-painted pitchers.

We moved onto a wonderful cheese ravioli, with a delicate meat sauce, and well-prepared rings of chicken breast stuffed with ham and mozzarella in a wine and mushroom sauce, accompanied by a small serving of white lasagne. The dessert menu is full of temptations like zabaglione and tiramisu, but we split a concoction called a Marilyn: vanilla and strawberry ice cream topped with bananas, whipped cream, and light-as-a-feather sugar cookies—heavenly stuff.

CALIENTE CAB CO., 21 Waverly Place, corner of Greene St. Tel. 529-1500.

Cuisine: MEXICAN. **Reservations:** Not needed. **Subway:** A, B, C, D, E, F to West 4th St.

$ Prices: Main courses $6.95–$13.95. MC, V.

Open: Mon–Thurs noon–1am, Fri–Sat noon–3am, Sun noon–midnight.

Those who like to take their meals in a party atmosphere will love Caliente Cab Co. You'll be able to spot the restaurant from a distance—the huge, tipped-over margarita above the door is a Village landmark. The crowd-pleasing menu and the decorating scheme convey a futuristic interpretation of a Tijuana taxi garage.

Popular items include a choice of quesadillas and Mexican pizzas, combination platters of taco, enchilada, tostada, and burrito, or sizzling fajitas.

CALIENTE'S BURRITO BAR, 305 Church St. Tel. 219-9200.

Cuisine: MEXICAN. **Reservations:** Not needed. **Subway:** 1, 9, A, C, E, N, R to Canal St.

$ Prices: All items under $10. MC, V.

Open: Mon–Thurs 11am–midnight, Fri–Sat 11am–1am.

This brand new restaurant is a spinoff of the above-mentioned Caliente Cab Co., and has been described as a restaurant with "60's decor and 60's prices."

To start you might try meatless nachos, prepared with Monterey Jack and Colby cheeses, and then move on to smoked chargrilled BBQ Chicken or the "Speedy Gonzalez" burrito—a blend of chili, rice, cheese, onions, sour cream, and red sauce. The "Okie from Muskogee" burrito is delicious, with its filling of grilled chicken, rice, onions, lettuce, tomatoes, guacamole, and sour cream. They also have a burrito for the vegetarian—"Grazin'-in-the-Grass." The Burrito Bar has a variety of frozen drinks, including the "Tie-Dye Margarita"—a tall strawberry drink with Blue Curaçao swirled in—as well as nonalcoholic ones for those who don't drink.

CEDAR TAVERN, 82 University Place, between 11th and 12th sts. Tel. 929-9089.

Cuisine: AMERICAN. **Reservations:** Accepted for large groups only. **Subway:** 4, 5, 6 N, R, to Union Square.

$ Prices: Appetizers $4.50–$4.75; main courses $5–$11.75; specials from $6.25 and up. AE, MC, V.

Open: Sat–Tues 11:30am–2am, Wed–Fri 11:30am–3:30am; Sat–Sun brunch noon–4:30pm.

The Cedar Tavern is a comfortable joint, as the manager likes to say. Downstairs it's dark and woody. In the back there are cozy booths lit by lantern-like lamps; up front there's an elaborate maple bar, which is over 100 years old, with panes of stained glass; and on the second floor there's a garden under a peaked glass roof. In the late 1950s and early '60s the tavern, then located around the corner on 10th Street, was a hangout for abstract expressionist artists like Mark Rothko, Franz Kline, and Jackson Pollock. Now the clientele is more likely to be the neighborhood crowd—antique dealers, professionals, and students.

Meals here are tasty, simple, and cheap. You can order a cheese, mushroom, or ham omelet, served with a vegetable, potato, and salad, or pork chops and broiled scallops—two of the more popular items, served with a salad and potato. At the weekend brunch, you get a cocktail, coffee, home fries, and a choice of eggs Benedict, French toast, or eggs with ham, bacon, or sausage.

CHEZ BRIGITTE, 77 Greenwich Ave., between Bank and 11th sts. Tel. 929-6736.

Cuisine: FRENCH. **Reservations:** Recommended. **Subway:** 1, 9 to Sheridan Square.

$ Prices: Main courses under $12. No credit cards.

Open: Mon–Sat 11am–9pm.

This tiny restaurant is easy to overlook. It has two counters, 12 seats, minimal decor, and a sense of humor: A sign in the window declares, "Chez Brigitte will seat 250 persons at one time." If you don't mind the luncheonette ambience, you'll be pleased with the Provençal fare at reasonable prices.

You can begin with pea, onion, or soup du jour, and then choose a daily special (served with a vegetable and potato, rice, or macaroni) or main dishes like beef bourguignon, filet of sole meunière, veal cutlet, or chicken fricassée. Omelets, sandwiches, and fresh homemade desserts—such as chocolate chiffon or banana pie—are also available.

CORNER BISTRO, 331 W. 4th St., corner of Jane St. and Eighth Ave. Tel. 242-9502.

Cuisine: AMERICAN. **Reservations:** Not accepted. **Subway:** A, C, E to Jackson Sq.; 1, 2, 3, 9 to 14th St.

$ Prices: Hamburgers $3.75–$6. No credit cards.

Open: Mon–Sat 11:30am–4am, Sun noon–4am.

This quiet, friendly place is a true neighborhood bar, with big wooden booths and sporting events on TV. The menu is short and to-the-point: The burgers are enormous, the chili is two-alarm, the sandwiches are basic grilled cheese and BLT's, and the shoestring fries are crisp and plentiful.

COTTONWOOD CAFÉ, 415 Bleecker St., between West 11th and Bank sts. Tel. 924-6271.

Cuisine: TEX-MEX. **Reservations:** Necessary for parties of 10 or more. **Subway:** 1, 9 to Sheridan Square.

$ Prices: Main courses under $10. No credit cards.

Open: Daily lunch 11am–3pm; dinner Mon–Sat 5pm–11:45pm, Sun 5pm–11pm; Sat brunch 10am–3pm, Sun brunch 10am–4pm.

A bank of windows facing Bleecker Street lends a bright and breezy air to the front dining room. The back dining room, just as large but darker, is where the music begins at about 10:30pm on weekdays and 11:30pm on Saturday. Most of the performers are original songwriters, often playing folk or country-and-western music on acoustic guitar. Performances continue until the bar closes, between 12:30 and 2am.

The menu is limited but excellent, offering such Tex-Mex culinary delights as chicken and cheese enchiladas with refried beans and rice, and chicken fajitas—marinated chicken pieces wrapped in a tortilla. Other main dishes include chicken-fried steak, pork chops, or smoked barbecued ribs; all come with a choice of two vegetables (also available à la carte). We recommend the mashed potatoes—cooked with their skins and slathered with creamy gravy—and fried okra or blackeyed peas. Come hungry; the portions are huge. For brunch, try the huevos rancheros (hot Mexican eggs), fresh fruit pancakes, or grits.

CUCINA STAGIONALE, 275 Bleecker St. Tel. 924-2707.

Cuisine: ITALIAN. **Reservations:** Not accepted. **Subway:** 1, 9 to Sheridan Square.
$ Prices: Appetizers $2–$5.95; main courses $5.95–$10.95. No credit cards.
Open: Mon–Fri 11:30am–10:30pm; Sat–Sun noon–10:30pm.

The line outside this small, down-to-earth restaurant may be a bit daunting, but it's well worth the wait—legions of New Yorkers have overeaten here. Cucina Stagionale packs in the crowds with imaginative dishes (such as a cold strawberry soup) and traditional Italian favorites. There's a changing list of daily specials; the night we stopped by, we enjoyed a heaping plate of marinated mussels, and the seafood fettuccine was nothing short of spectacular. It's BYOB, so you'll save significantly on your drink tab.

DALLAS B-B-Q, 21 University Place, off 8th St. Tel. 674-4450.

Cuisine: AMERICAN/BARBECUE. **Reservations:** Not needed. **Subway:** A, C, E, B, D, F, Q to West 4th St.; 4, 5, 6 to Union Square; R to 8th St.
$ Prices: All items $2.95–$8.95. AE, MC, V.
Open: Sat–Thurs noon–midnight; Fri noon–2am.

Dallas B-B-Q is our candidate for the best budget buy in the Big Apple. From the glass-enclosed dining room you can look out on a colorful Village street scene. Inside, the dining room is decorated in black and white—the walls and chairs are zebra-striped, and the table tops black lacquer.

At B-B-Q you'll get some of the best barbecue and cornbread in the Village. To start (but only if you're really hungry, as the portions are indeed Texas-sized), you shouldn't miss the vegetable tempura. Try the baby back spareribs, served with a choice of potato and a generous slab of cornbread. You can get a smaller portion of the same meal at lunchtime. The finger-licking quarter chicken comes with a potato and cornbread. A giant Dallas burger with a generous (and we mean generous) portion of french fries might do the trick. B-B-Q offers other tidbits—such as corn on the cob or their famous onion loaf (an incredible "loaf" of wonderfully greasy onion rings). B-B-Q serves wine and beer, and some of the biggest margaritas you can imagine. If you need lots of food for just a little money, Dallas is the place.

DAY-O, 103 Greenwich Ave., near W. 12th St. Tel. 924-3160.

Cuisine: CAJUN/CARIBBEAN. **Reservations:** Recommended Thurs–Sat nights. **Subway:** 1, 2, 3, 9, A, C, E to 14th St.
$ Prices: Main courses $6.95–$12. No credit cards.
Open: Mon–Tues 4–11pm, Wed–Thurs 4pm–midnight, Fri 4pm–1am, Sat 2pm–1am, Sun 2–11pm.

This combination of Southern and Caribbean cooking results in distinctively spicy dishes. Many of the recipes come from Small's Paradise—a reknowned Harlem eatery. Eventually, the owners hope to work a little Italian into the menu to stay true to the restaurant's geographic roots—for 30 years this was the home of La Marionetta restaurant.

Four different artists were hired to paint tropical murals on the walls from floor to ceiling. The palm trees really sway and motorized mobiles bob and swing overhead to a reggae soundtrack. This "urban jungle" caters to a young, trendy, Greenwich Village crowd.

Main dishes include Dolores's chicken Dixie, Beryl's best (a house secret—Jamaican-seasoned minced sirloin), codfish fritters, West Indian peppersteak, and gumbo Day-O (a hearty portion of seafood stew with Cajun seasonings). The "side stuffers" continue the Cajun/Caribbean theme. You can also get healthy portions of collard greens, black-eyed peas with rice, fried plantains, sweet-potato chips, and cornbread. Fluorescent and pastel-colored drinks are an important part of the Day-O menu: flavored margaritas, daiquiris, Day-O rum punch, and flying baboons. Drinks are served only from 1am to 4am.

RESTAURANT FLORENT, 69 Gansevoort St., between Washington and Greenwich sts. Tel. 989-5779.
    Cuisine: FRENCH. **Reservations:** Recommended at dinner. **Subway:** A, C, E to 14th St. **Bus:** M14 to Gansevoort St. We recommend taking a cab.
$ Prices: Appetizers $3.50–$9.50; main courses $8.50–$15.00. No credit cards.
    Open: Daily 24 hours: Breakfast 8–11am; lunch 11am–3:30pm; dinner Mon–Sat 6:30pm–midnight, Sun 6:30–11:30pm.

Located in the desolate meat market district, in the far western reaches of the Village, Restaurant Florent is a clattering, glittering diamond in the rough. The kitchen serves excellent bistro food at reasonable prices. Coquilles St-Jacques; a wonderful goat cheese salad; and a charcuterie plate, offering three different meat pâtés, are among the more popular dishes. Florent does not serve mixed drinks, but does offer a good selection of wines, beers, and cognacs. Though the prices are low and the decor diner-hip, take care to dress sharp; behind a deceptively humble storefront, an artsy and fashion-conscious crowd has come to Florent to talk, flirt, and scheme. Très hip.

GRAND TICINO, 228 Thompson St. Tel. 777-5922.
    Cuisine: ITALIAN. **Reservations:** Recommended. **Subway:** A, C, E, B, D, F, Q to West 4th St.
$ Prices: Appetizers $7–$9; main courses $14–$19. AE, DC, MC, V.
    Open: Lunch Mon–Sat noon–3pm; dinner Mon–Sat 5–11pm.

You may recognize this place as the gracious restaurant with an understated elegance and friendly service that was featured in the hit movie *Moonstruck*. Established in 1919, it's the oldest Italian restaurant in the Village. A few steps below street level, it's entered via a small alcove of plant-filled windows. The tables are covered with white linen, softly lit with individual lamps, and surrounded by simple black chairs. A few pieces of pottery line a shelf that runs across the room and a huge vase of flowers sits beside the bar.

    The dinner and lunch menus are essentially the same, with prices running about $1 less at lunch. Most of the soups are priced at about $3 for dinner. Main dishes come with a vegetable of the day or spaghetti. A typical dessert is tiramisu, a sweet pudding with whipped cream, espresso, and ladyfingers.

JOHN'S PIZZERIA, 278 Bleecker St., between Cornelia St. and Seventh Ave. South. Tel. 243-1680.
    Cuisine: PIZZA. **Reservations:** Recommended for parties of 10 or more. **Subway:** 1, 9 to Sheridan Square; A, C, E, B, D, F, Q to West 4th St.
$ Prices: Pizza $8.25–$12.50. No credit cards.
    Open: Sun–Thurs noon–midnight, Fri–Sat noon–1am.

Located in the middle of an Italian neighborhood that has stubbornly maintained its identity through decades of bohemia, commercialization, and gentrification, John's represents an older, more traditional style of pizzeria that is hard to find in New York. John's serves only whole pizzas, for take-out or on-the-spot consumption.

    The decor is resolutely featureless, but we (and most New Yorkers) think the pies are among the best in town. A list of some 40 variations ranges from the small cheese-and-tomato pizza to the giant six-ingredient extravaganza. It is a popular place, so expect to wait.

THE LION'S HEAD, 59 Christopher St., just off Seventh Ave. South. Tel. 929-0670.
    Cuisine: CONTINENTAL. **Reservations:** Needed for dinner. **Subway:** 1, 9 to Sheridan Square. **Bus:** M10 to Seventh Avenue South.
$ Prices: Appetizers $3.50–$7.50; main courses $8–$17. AE, DC, DISC, MC, V.

Open: Daily lunch noon–4pm; dinner 5:30pm–1am.

The Lion's Head is known as a writers' hangout, the sort of place where at the bar you might meet the body behind a famous byline or the author of one of the books whose jacket covers line one wall. A hand-carved lion's head of oak, dating from the turn of the century, looms above the bar. With its low ceilings, dark-wood paneling, exposed-brick and amber lighting, the place is dark and cozy. Dinners like grilled ribeye steak in Irish whiskey can easily break a budget, but for a low-priced alternative, order the spinach and fettuccine with pesto sauce, pan-fried brook trout, or the chicken pot pie.

The Lion's Head serves a reasonably priced brunch including eggs Benedict with fries; walnut pancakes with bacon, ham, or sausage; or a chef's salad.

LIVORNO, 216 Thompson St. Tel. 260-1972.

Cuisine: ITALIAN. **Reservations:** Recommended. **Subway:** A, C, E, B, D, F, Q to West 4th St.

$ Prices: Appetizers under $5; main courses $8–$14. AE, DC, MC, V.

Open: Daily noon–11:30pm.

A few doors away from Grand Ticino you'll find this charming, festive restaurant. In the front room there's a bar under a shingled eave, and the walls are decorated with prints, paintings, and maps of Italy. Pass through a latticework arbor with plastic grapes to enter the main dining room in the back, where trompe-l'oeil windows are framed by wood shutters and boxes of plastic geraniums. Tables are covered with white linen over deep-green cloths.

Appetizers such as spinach or escarole in broth, or a hot antipasto are a good bet. Try the homemade pasta dishes and main dishes such as veal scaloppine, veal cutlet, or chicken cacciatore. All include a side order of vegetables or pasta.

MANHATTAN CHILI CO., 302 Bleecker St., right off Seventh Ave. Tel. 206-7163.

Cuisine: TEX-MEX. **Reservations:** Not accepted. **Subway:** 1, 9 to Sheridan Square.

$ Prices: All items $6–$10. MC, TR, V.

Open: Sun–Thurs 11:30am–midnight, Fri–Sat 11:30am–1am.

The Manhattan Chili Co. boasts a mouthwatering selection of chilis. What they call the "Real McCoy" is the way they make it in the Lone Star State, with chunks of beef and two kinds of chili powder—no beans, no tomatoes, no bull. For variety, you may want to try the "High Plains Turkey" chili, or if you like spicy food, choose the "Texas Chain Gang" chili. All the chilis come with rice and your choice of three toppings.

Besides chili, the menu includes a few other Tex-Mex favorites like chunky gazpacho or chicken and steak fajitas served on a sizzling platter with onions and red peppers. For dessert, sample the Chocolate Banana Tortilla Cake or the Margarita Pie. The restaurant also has a full bar. During warm weather months, ask to be seated in the wonderful outdoor garden. Brunch is served Saturday and Sunday.

MINETTA'S TAVERN, 113 MacDougal St., at Minetta Lane. Tel. 475-3850.

Cuisine: ITALIAN. **Reservations:** Recommended. **Subway:** A, C, E, B, D, F, or Q to West 4th St.; 1, 9 to Sheridan Square.

$ Prices: Main courses $8.95–$15.95. AE, DC, MC, V.

Open: Daily noon–midnight.

Located in the heart of Greenwich Village, Minetta's Tavern offers Italian dishes in a cozy and casual atmosphere. The decor includes small paned windows, a dark wooden bar, a dessert case filled with pastries, and small tables covered in white linen.

Minetta's is affordable and serves an array of vegetable, poultry, veal, and pasta dishes. We enjoyed the petto di pollo alla fiorentina—breast of chicken sautéed with spinach—and the tortellacci, pasta filled with basil, Fontina, and ricotta. Delicious desserts and coffees are also available.

MITALI WEST, 296 Bleecker St., corner of Seventh Ave. South. Tel. 989-1367.

Cuisine: NORTHERN INDIAN. **Reservations:** Recommended. **Subway:** 1, 9 to Sheridan Square; A, C, E, B, D, F, Q to West 4th St.
$ Prices: Appetizers 90¢–$5.50; main courses $6.95–$16.95. AE, MC, V.
Open: Lunch Fri–Sun 11am–3:30pm; dinner daily 4:30pm–midnight.
While Indian restaurants can be found everywhere, there are few as satisfying as Mitali West. This two-story red palace is done up in classic Indian style—or the local version thereof—with red-jacketed waiters, low lights, and printed fabrics on the walls. The food is abundant at fairly low prices, and the savvy diner can feast for very little.

Main dish such as Dopiaz curry will do the trick, filled out with side orders of paratha, a savory flat bread, and perhaps mango chutney. For a splurge, a meal might begin with chicken tandoori or lobster curry. The budget-minded might also look into the combination platters.

PANCHITO'S, 105 MacDougal St., between Bleecker and West 3rd sts. Tel. 473-5239.
Cuisine: MEXICAN. **Reservations:** Recommended. **Subway:** 1, 9 to Houston St.; A, C, E, B, D, F, Q to West 4th St.
$ Prices: Appetizers $4.95–$9.95; main courses $6–$13. AE, CB, DC, MC, V.
Open: Daily 11am–4am.
A casual, crowded, noisy place, Panchito's is so popular at peak hours that the lines of hungry customers snake back through the long grotto-like hallway.

The newly renovated restaurant is bright and lofty, with room for over 200. It runs the width of a block; in the back, plant-filled windows open onto a quiet street. The floors are concrete set with marble, and the main dining room is lined with black-walnut booths and Mexican folk art. Overhead, large ceiling fans whir gently. Many evenings a local musician plays Spanish classical guitar.

Panchito's may be as popular for its drinks as for the food it serves. The bar boasts 101 different double-rum piña coladas and frozen margaritas, 25 types of rum, 15 cognacs, and 12 premium tequilas. Food is good and affordable, and the portions are generous. In fact, unless you're simply ravenous, an order of Panchito's popular platters—fajita, Chicken Luis, or Big Burrito served with rice and beans—should be plenty.

PEACOCK CAFFÈ, 24 Greenwich Ave., off West 10th St. Tel. 242-9395.
Cuisine: ITALIAN. **Reservations:** Not accepted. **Subway:** 1, 2, 3, 9 to 14th St.
Bus: M13 to Sixth Ave.
$ Prices: Main courses $5–$9. No credit cards.
Open: Sun–Thurs 1pm–1am, Fri–Sat 1pm–2am.
Bring a good book and a thin wallet to the Peacock Caffè. It's a quiet, romantic place, with classical music playing in the background, baroque columns, anonymous busts, a life-size statue of Pan playing his flute, and a carved-wood peacock perched over what was once a fireplace.

The Peacock is mainly a coffeehouse, offering an array of coffees with pastry, but during the day a variety of sandwiches on Italian bread, such as prosciutto and provolone, and salami and provolone are served.

At night you can choose a pasta dish like gnocchi with butter sauce, or tortellini or fettuccine with meat sauce. Try the homemade Florentine apple torte served with whipped cream, or the Milanese coffeecake served with butter.

THE PINK TEACUP, 42 Grove St., near Bleecker St. Tel. 807-6755.
Cuisine: SOUL FOOD. **Reservations:** Not accepted. **Subway:** 1, 9 to Sheridan Sq.; A, C, E, B, D, F, Q to West 4th St.
$ Prices: Main courses $8.50–$14.
Open: Mon–Thurs 8am–midnight; Fri–Sun 24 hours.
This luncheonette is one of the few eateries in the Village where a yearning for true southern cooking can be satisfied. Nearly everything is pink, including the walls, curtains, menu, and shirts worn by the waitresses and waiters.

The place is small, with ten counter stools and seven oilcloth-covered tables. The walls are adorned with an assortment of photographs of Stevie Wonder, Martin Luther King, Jr., John F. Kennedy, and the Supremes. The menu is remarkable for bounteous fare at budget prices. Begin your morning with a breakfast of eggs, grits, and bacon; or dine in true southern style on pecan or blueberry pancakes and a grilled pork chop or fried chicken with a biscuit. Dinner offerings are equally generous: All come with hot bread, soup, salad, two vegetables—such as black-eyed peas, yellow turnips, or okra—and dessert. All are homemade, hearty, and deliciously authentic.

SAZERAC HOUSE, 533 Hudson St., corner of Charles St. Tel. 989-0313.
   Cuisine: AMERICAN/CREOLE. **Reservations:** Not needed. **Subway:** 1, 9 to Sheridan Square. **Bus:** M13 to Hudson St.
$ **Prices:** Lunch and brunch appetizers $3.25–$8.25, dinner appetizers $3.50–$8.25; main lunch and brunch courses $4.50–$13.95, main dinner courses $8.95–$18.95. AE, DC, MC, V.
   Open: Mon–Fri lunch noon–4:30pm, Sat 11am–4:30pm; dinner daily 5pm–midnight; Sun brunch 11am–4:30pm.

⭐ A glassed-in sidewalk café hides the fact that this is the oldest structure on Charles Street. The 1826 landmark building was once part of a farm.

Sazerac's interior is old-style Village, with an old mahogany bar, rough hardwood floors, oak booths and tables, and a working fireplace. The theme is old New York with a taste of New Orleans, the atmosphere is cozy and attracts primarily a neighborhood crowd.

The menu offers moderately priced favorites, such as plantation chicken with peanut sauce and grilled vegetables, or BBQ shrimp with black beans, or you can get the traditional shepherd's pie or meatloaf and mashed potatos. Sazerac is a favorite Village spot for brunch, serving à la carte pain perdu (Louisiana-style French toast), a variety of gourmet egg dishes, hash and eggs, and quiche. There are also burgers for the ravenous.

SPAIN, 113 W. 13th St., west of Sixth Ave. Tel. 929-9580.
   Cuisine: SPANISH. **Reservations:** Recommended, especially on weekends.
   Subway: 1, 2, 3, 9, F to 14th St; L to Sixth Ave.
$ **Prices:** Main courses $7–$16. No credit cards.
   Open: Daily noon–1am.
This unpretentious and friendly restaurant has been run by the same family for two generations. The fare is northern Spanish, and seafood the specialty. You might want to split one of the extra-large portions between two people. The menu at lunch and dinner is the same, with prices running about 50¢ to $1.50 more at dinner. The most popular dish is mariscada with green sauce—a medley of shellfish (clams, lobster, shrimp, mussels) served in a huge metal pot. Main dishes are served with Spanish rice, a tossed salad, and bread. A half carafe of sangría is a good bet, and for dessert, try the caramel custard.

SUNG TIENG, 334 Bleecker St., between Christopher and W. 10th sts. Tel. 924-8314.
   Cuisine: CHINESE. **Reservations:** Not needed. **Subway:** 1, 9 to Sheridan Square; A, C, E, B, D, F, Q to West 4th St.
$ **Prices:** Appetizers $1–$5.95; main courses $6.95–$14. AE, CB, DC, MC, V.
   Open: Daily 1pm–2am.
This large, airy place has white walls and picnic tables in a little terrace out front. It serves unusual Cantonese, Szechuan, and Hunan dishes with flair, and minimal MSG. The Fisherman's Nest consists of scallops, prawns, fish cakes, and crab prettily served in a wonton basket. The Dragon and Phoenix is a succulent combination of lobster and chicken. The house favorites include ginger chicken and orange beef or chicken—served with orange rinds, dried chile peppers, and garlic.

TÍO PEPE, 168 W. 4th St., between Sixth and Seventh aves. Tel. 242-9338.
   Cuisine: SPANISH/MEXICAN. **Reservations:** Not needed. **Subway:** 1, 9 to Sheridan Square; A, C, E, B, D, F, Q to West 4th St.

$ Prices: Appetizers $3.50–$6.95; main courses $10.95–$15; Sun brunch buffet $11.95. AE, DC, MC, V.

Open: Sun–Thurs noon–1am; Fri–Sat noon–2am.

Tío Pepe is a family-style restaurant serving traditional Spanish and Mexican cuisine. There is a lovely glass-enclosed garden and a guitarist adds romance to the atmosphere.

The best buys are the Mexican "all-you-can-eat" combo platters—tacos, enchiladas, tamales, burritos—served with soup, salad, rice, and beans. At lunch, most of the same main dishes—paella, shrimp in green sauce, filet of sole molinera, and others—are recommended. There is also an "all-you-can-eat" Sunday brunch buffet, which comes with a cocktail.

VIOLETA'S, 220 W. 13th St., between Seventh Avenue and Greenwich St. Tel. 255-1710.

Cuisine: MEXICAN. **Reservations:** Recommended for parties of 5 or more.
Subway: 1, 2, 3, 9, A, C, E to 14th St.
$ Prices: Lunch specials $5.95–$10.50; main dinner courses $4.95–$12.50; dinner specials $6.95–$8.95. No credit cards.
Open: Lunch daily 1–4pm; dinner daily 5pm–midnight.

A cozy, rustic atmosphere is created with candlelit wooden tables, recorded guitar music, and large posters of Mexican movie stars. The owner, Violeta, is nearly always on hand to oversee the kitchen.

In addition to the regular Mexican offerings—burritos, enchiladas, and tamales—there are house specialties that include lamb tacos and mole poblano (chicken in a nonsweet chocolate sauce). Mexican beer and pitchers of fruity sangría are available to quench your thirst. The lunch menu offers lighter versions of the regular dinner menu.

WHITE HORSE TAVERN, corner of West 11th and Hudson sts. Tel. 243-9260.

Cuisine: AMERICAN. **Reservations:** Not needed. **Subway:** 1, 9 to Sheridan Square. **Bus:** M10, M11 to Abington Square.
$ Prices: Main courses $3.95–$7.75. No credit cards.
Open: Daily 11am–2am; weekend brunch served 11am–4pm.

This legendary Village hangout has long been a haven for writers and artists, including Dylan Thomas, who died several days after downing 18 shots of whiskey here in less than 20 minutes.

The place is loud and roomy, and the food is simple and cheap—burgers, fish and chips, and the like. The weekend brunch is a bargain and you can get French toast, omelets, corned beef hash, and basic eggs and bacon.

WOODY'S, 140 Seventh Ave. South, between West 10th and Charles sts. Tel. 242-1200.

Cuisine: AMERICAN. **Reservations:** Required for parties of 8 or more.
Subway: 1, 9 to Sheridan Square; A, C, E, B, D, F, Q to West 4th St.
$ Prices: Appetizers $3.95–$6.95; main lunch courses $4.95–$8.95, main dinner courses $7.95–$16.95; brunch $8.95. Lunch specials $4.95–$7.95, dinner specials $9.95–$14.95. AE, DC, DISC, MC, V.
Open: Mon–Fri lunch noon–5pm, Sat 11:30am–4pm, Sun 11am–4pm; Mon–Thurs dinner 5pm–midnight, Fri 5pm–1am, Sat 4pm–1am, Sun 4pm–midnight. Bar open a half hour later during the week, an hour later on weekends.

Seated in either the glass-enclosed front porch or the sidewalk café, you can watch the parade of passing pedestrians. Inside there's an elaborate 150-year-old hand-carved mahogany bar from Bavaria and a pleasant lounge area with a view of the street. The bar crowd is always casual, and on weekends it gets rowdy.

Woody's international menu is extensive. You can order Santa Fe guacamole cruda with blue corn chips and "snakebite salsa," Jamaican jerk-spiced chicken salad with a light mango pineapple dressing, or just a classic chef salad. There are also plenty of sandwiches and hamburgers to choose from, including a Middle Eastern pita sandwich, which is vegetable salad with tabouli and Feta served in a warm whole-wheat pita pocket—scrumptious! There are also daily specials that change frequently.

Saturday and Sunday brunch includes a drink, a choice of eggs Benedict, eggs Florentine, three-beef hash and eggs (roast beef, corned beef, and pastrami), French toast, and fresh fruit, and chicken and vegetable quiche plus unlimited coffee at a bargain price.

The bar, which stays open until 4am, boasts an impressive list of 91 international beers. You can sample 50 different beers and receive a Woody's T-shirt, or you can sample all 91 and get a sweatshirt, baseball hat, your own personal Woody's stein for your next visit, and a six-pack of your favorite beer (if you can still remember what that was).

YE WAVERLY INN TAVERN AND RESTAURANT, 16 Bank St., at Waverly Place. Tel. 929-4377.
  Cuisine: AMERICAN/CONTINENTAL. **Reservations:** Recommended for weekends and Tues. **Subway:** 1, 2, 3, 9, A, C, E to 14th St.
$ **Prices:** Appetizers $3.25–$6; full meal $16. AE, DC, MC, V.
  Open: Mon–Thurs 5:15–10pm; Fri–Sat 5–11pm; Sun 4–9pm (brunch 11:30am–3pm).

This quaint little inn has been making customers happy since the 1920s, and the building that houses them dates to over a century ago. You can almost smell the age in the yellowing, cracking wallpaper, dark-wood wainscoting, oaken booths, and pendulum clocks. There's even an 1868 engraving of Manhattan to really take you back in time. In spring and summer there's patio dining in the back. In winter, two of the four dining rooms are heated by working fireplaces.

Dinner prices at Ye Waverly Inn have begun to climb over budget, but an early-dinner special, served Monday through Thursday from 5:15 to 6:30pm, is worth scheduling your evening around. Lunch is also a good deal. You can order soup, fresh muffins, salad, and a variety of sandwiches, like a hearty grilled Cheddar or Swiss with ham or bacon. And the inn makes its own desserts—pecan pie, Wellesley fudge cake, and carrot cake.

Perhaps the best time to head for Ye Waverly Inn is on Sunday, when a classical guitarist serenades partakers of a champagne/cocktail brunch. Choose from eggs Benedict, fluffy omelets, quiche, French toast, or apple fritters with bacon and maple syrup. Complete with drink or juice, homemade rolls or muffins, and coffee or tea.

6. LOWER EAST SIDE/EAST VILLAGE

The food here is some of the best and cheapest in the city. A word to the wise: While the East Village is filled with streets that bustle with activity into the wee hours of the morning, some side streets are deserted and unsafe. Don't miss the excitement here, but exercise caution, especially at night.

LOWER EAST SIDE

GRAND DAIRY RESTAURANT, 341 Grand St., corner of Ludlow St. Tel. 673-1904.
  Cuisine: KOSHER DAIRY. **Reservations:** Not accepted. **Subway:** J, M, Z, F to Delancey St.
$ **Prices:** All items under $9. No credit cards.
  Open: Sun–Fri 6am–4pm. **Closed:** Jewish holidays.

These days, students from the local Seward Park High School are as likely to be found here as are Jewish matrons stopping for coffee and blintzes after shopping. White Formica tables and orange chairs make for simple decor, with granite-speckled floors. The strictly kosher restaurant has a menu filled with hundreds of dairy items.

Try the cabbage soup or the borscht with sour cream to start. Dairy items include matzoh brei and kasha blintzes, and we've found the omelets and fish dishes here delicious. For dessert there's a wide variety of pastries, including homemade coffeecake and hamantaschen cakes.

KATZ'S, 205 E. Houston St., between First Ave. and Ave. A. Tel. 254-2246.
Cuisine: JEWISH DELI. **Reservations:** Not accepted. **Subway:** 6 to Astor Place; R to 8th St.
$ Prices: Sandwiches from $6.65. Credit card minimum $50. AE, MC, V.
Open: Sun–Thurs 8am–10:45pm; Fri–Sat 8am–12:45am.

Katz's is a haven for carnivores. Take a ticket at the door—you'll need it to pay your bill on the way out. The cavernous main dining room is decorated with a wall of salamis and jars of pickled products. Tables along the left-hand wall are reserved for waiter service. But it's more fun to approach the counter on the right, where meat is sliced, and the price is marked on your ticket. Katz's is famous for its deli sandwiches. Most cost $6, especially its pastrami and corned beef. Your sandwich maker will offer you a plate with a sample of meat. Eat the offering and leave a tip in its place. (Otherwise the quality of your sandwich may suffer.) See if you can spot the World War II–era sign that reads "Send a salami to your boy in the army."

RATNER'S, 138 Delancey St., between Norfolk and Suffolk sts. Tel. 677-5588.
Cuisine: JEWISH DAIRY. **Reservations:** Recommended on Sun. **Subway:** J, M, Z, F to Delancey St. **Bus:** M14 to Delancey St.
$ Prices: Appetizers $2.95–$4.95; main courses $7.95–11.95. AE, MC, V.
Open: Sun–Thurs 6am–midnight, Fri 6am–3pm, Sat sundown to 2am.

This huge, open dining room is reminiscent of a ballroom from the 1940s, with a pink scalloped ceiling and mirrored walls. There are a lot of old-timers on the staff, dressed in mustard-colored uniforms, who can tell you about the early days when the Harmatz and Zankel families first opened the restaurant. The bakery counter up front offers tempting treats, and the restaurant menu is world famous for its wide selection of Jewish specialties, like matzoh brei and kreplach.

To start, we suggest the cold borscht, with a generous helping of sour cream. Try the potato pancakes with applesauce, or the cheese, potato, or sour-cream blintzes. Splurge on the baked gelfilte fish with Créole sauce, vegetable, and potato, and for dessert, if you have room, try the strawberry cheesecake.

YONAH SCHIMMEL, at 137 Houston St., between Eldridge and Forsyth sts. Tel. 477-2858.
Cuisine: JEWISH DAIRY. **Reservations:** Not needed. **Subway:** F to Second Ave.
$ Prices: Knishes from $1.75. No credit cards.
Open: Daily 8am–6pm.

The knishes here are famous city-wide, and on Sunday morning it's not unusual to see limousines lined up outside this unpretentious eatery, buying knishes for fancy East Side brunches. Inside, a dumbwaiter on rope pulleys still delivers hot knishes and strudels from the kitchen. Lillian Berger, the present owner, is a descendant of Yonah Schimmel, who opened the restaurant in 1910.

While potato and kasha knishes are the star attractions, you can also get a homemade borscht with sour cream, cheese bagels, or apple strudel.

EAST VILLAGE

ANAR BAGH, 338 E. 6th St. Tel. 529-1937.
Cuisine: INDIAN. **Reservations:** Not needed. **Subway:** 6 to Astor Place.
$ Prices: Main courses $4.95–$10.95. AE, CB, DC, MC, V.
Open: Daily noon–midnight.

The Ahmed brothers' second enterprise (see Shah Bagh, below) features a similar menu and fancier decor than its cousin. A bright green, yellow, and red canopy hangs from the ceiling in the interior dining room, and there is an open garden for dining in back. The menu is translated into English, with explanations of traditional dishes. Try the poori (puffed Indian bread) as an appetizer, or the mulligatawny tomato soup. Korma dishes are cooked in a creamy sauce with mild spices, and there are curries available for braver palates, along with a wide selection of seafood dishes, including lobster. For dessert, try a roshgolla cheese ball or firni custard sprinkled with rose water.

AROUND THE CLOCK CAFÉ, 8 Stuyvesant St., east of Third Ave., at 9th St. Tel. 598-0402.

    Cuisine: AMERICAN/CONTINENTAL. **Reservations:** Not needed. **Subway:** 6 to Astor Place.

    $ Prices: Sandwiches $4–$6; main courses $5–$9. AE, MC, V. Credit card minimum $20.

    Open: Daily 24 hours. Breakfast served anytime.

This café draws a loyal following—especially for breakfast and lunch. Passersby who stop to admire the café's large centerpiece clock stay for the delicious food. The café's riverboat-era antique bar, imported from Missouri, adds to the timeless atmosphere. The menu includes a wide range of salads, burgers, omelets, and sandwiches. Sample the Mexican-style fajitas, the Oriental stir-fries, and pastas. Vegetarians enjoy black bean burritos or a fresh vegetable dinner, both featuring brown rice.

AVENUE A, 103 Ave. A, between 6th and 7th sts. Tel. 982-8109.

    Cuisine: JAPANESE. **Reservations:** Recommended. **Subway:** 6 to Astor Place.

    $ Prices: Appetizers and sushi rolls $5.50–$8.95. AE.

    Open: Mon–Sat 6pm–1am.

Only in New York would you find a place like this heady, trendy, New Wave sushi restaurant. Immerse yourself in A's funky interior, which is periodically revamped by local artists. There are two black-lacquered bars—one for sushi and one for drinks. In the back is more intimate seating with fresh flowers on the tables.

You might make a meal by sampling the appetizers and the sushi à la carte. If so, try the Avenue A specialties, prepared by Masa, a veteran sushi chef. These include the yado-kari—mushrooms, carrots, and bamboo shoots sautéed with crabmeat and baked in a clam shell with a white sauce. Or try the "Dynamite"—scallops, mushrooms, and smelt roe baked in white sauce with sesame seeds. Another favorite is the "Tiger's Eye"—salmon, spinach, and seaweed surrounded with squid to look like a tiger's eye. For bargain main dishes, try the katsu tama, a deep-fried pork cutlet and vegetables cooked with egg in a sukiyaki sauce, or the negimaki, beef stuffed with scallions, with teriyaki sauce.

BAMBOO HOUSE, 104 Second Ave., at East 6th St. Tel. 254-3502.

    Cuisine: CHINESE. **Reservations:** Recommended in winter months. **Subway:** 6 to Astor Place.

    $ Prices: Appetizers 90¢–$7.65; main courses $4.95–$9.50. No credit cards.

    Open: Daily 1–11:15pm.

Some local Chinese-food lovers won't eat anywhere but at Bamboo House. This small, unassuming restaurant is well known for its heaping portions and tasty Szechuan dishes. The vegetables here are crisp and the meats are carefully prepared. We started with the shrimp and sizzling rice soup for two and an order of tender honey spare ribs. Seafood lovers won't be able to resist the assorted hot pot with jumbo shrimp, cuttlefish, crabmeat, straw mushrooms, baby corn, snow peas, water chestnuts, and cabbage in an oyster sauce. The sesame chicken had just the right tangy kick.

The medium-sized square dining room features a modest decor, with Chinese prints and calendars and festive red Chinese trim. The candles on each table add a nice touch, but the food here is the main attraction.

BANDITO!, 153 Second Ave., between 9th and 10th sts. Tel. 777-4505.

    Cuisine: MEXICAN. **Reservations:** Not accepted. **Subway:** 6 to Astor Place.

$ Prices: Main courses $6.95–$10.95; specials $11.95–$12.95. AE, MC, V.
Open: Mon–Thurs 11am–2am; Fri–Sat 11am–4am.

A popular spot for indoor/outdoor drinking and dining, Bandito! offers a comfortable dining area, with complimentary hot tortilla chips and sauce on every table. For starters, the quesadilla (a soft tortilla with cheese, cilantro, and jalapeños) is plenty for two. But don't fill up on appetizers, because Bandito! believes in heaping platters (and large margaritas). We recommend the enchiladas suizas (two chicken enchiladas topped with cheese, salsa verde, and sour cream), or the avocado stuffed with chicken salad, made with a special cream-cheese and sour-cream dressing. Spice lovers will enjoy the chimichangas, topped with cheese and the secret salsa Bandito.

CHRISTINE'S, 208 First Ave., between 12th and 13th sts. Tel. 505-0376.
Cuisine: POLISH. **Reservations:** Not accepted. **Subway:** 6 to Astor Place.
$ Prices: Appetizers $2.50–$4.95; main courses $4.95–$7.95. No credit cards.
Open: Mon–Thurs 6am–10pm, Fri–Sat 6am–midnight, Sun 7am–10pm.

 Christine's is an ordinary-looking diner with extraordinary food. Try the home-made mushroom-barley soup with fresh challah bread, or the assorted pirogi platter, with your choice of eight stuffings for these Polish dumplings. Delicious breakfasts such as three-egg omelets, French toast, and blueberry pancakes are all under $5. And no matter how crowded the restaurant is (and it usually is crowded, as nearly everyone in the East Village knows about Christine's), the waitresses will always give you prompt service and a bright smile.

CLOISTER CAFÉ, 238 E. 9th St., between Second and Third aves. Tel. 777-9128.
Cuisine: AMERICAN/CONTINENTAL. **Reservations:** Not accepted. **Subway:** 6 to Astor Place.
$ Prices: Appetizers $4.95; main courses $5.95–$13.95. No credit cards.
Open: Sun–Thurs noon–12:30am; Fri–Sat noon–1:30am.

Retreat from the whirl of sightseeing at this outdoor garden patio with a small fountain and goldfish pond. Ivy-covered brick walls and festive night lighting add to the patio's charm. If it's raining or cold outside, move indoors to admire the Cloister Café's antique stained-glass windows. The Strauss salad, with chicken, crabmeat, spinach, garnishes, and fruit, is a meal in itself, and tortellini al pesto is another

---

Ⓕ FROMMER'S SMART TRAVELER: RESTAURANTS

1. Check to see if a restaurant participates in New York's "Tuesday Night Out" program—dozens of restaurants, bars, and nightclubs offer special deals to bring in business on this otherwise slow night.
2. Drinks can be expensive in New York, so keep an eye on your bar tab. If you want beer or wine with dinner, stick to BYOB spots—you'll save a bundle by bringing in your own six-pack or bottle of wine.
3. If your heart is set on a special splurge at a more expensive restaurant, go for lunch rather than dinner—you'll enjoy many of the same dishes at far cheaper prices.
4. Be adventurous and try some of the city's ethnic eateries. In Chinatown or Little India, for example, you can find cheap but authentic and delicious fare.
5. For lunch, rely on New York's street vendors for fabulous hot dogs, giant pretzels, knishes, falafel, or gyros. Pizza, bagels, and deli sandwiches, available from establishments on almost every block, are not only good budget bets, but favorite New York specialties.

favorite. You are invited to bring your own wine or beer. You can also linger over a café-au-lait, served French style in a large bowl, or sip on the other delicious teas and coffees. Don't come here if you're in a hurry, though. The help is as relaxed as the atmosphere.

CUCINA DI PESCE, 87 E. 4th St., west of Second Ave. Tel. 260-6800.
   Cuisine: ITALIAN. **Reservations:** Not accepted. **Subway:** 6 to Astor Place; R to 8th St.
$ Prices: Appetizers $2–$6; main courses $6–$10.95. No credit cards.
   Open: Dinner daily 5pm–midnight.

If you're prepared to put up with a long wait (often up to an hour) and crowded quarters, come here for one of the East Village's most interesting scenes. Descend the stairs from the street level and mingle with the crowds enjoying complimentary mussels marinara in the bar/waiting room. Once you're seated in the restaurant proper, choose from 13 different kinds of pasta and nearly as many varieties of fresh seafood. A complimentary salad is served. Try the asparagus and stringbeans with broiled mozzarella. A devoted following swears by the seafood fettuccine.

The blue dining room is lined with statues, maps, and mirrors (in which the predominantly young and sleek diners appraise each other).

DOJO, 24 St. Marks Place, between Second and Third aves. Tel. 674-9821.
   Cuisine: JAPANESE/AMERICAN. **Reservations:** Not accepted. **Subway:** 6 to Astor Place; R to 8th St.
$ Prices: Main courses $2.95–$7. No credit cards.
   Open: Sun–Thurs 11am–midnight; Fri–Sat 11am–2am.

Dojo offers a great mix of Japanese dishes, natural foods, and good old-fashioned American meals. Here you will find one of the widest selections and some of the best prices in the East Village. The highest-priced meal on the menu is the steamed seafood plate, with mussels, scallops, shrimp, and fish, served with salad and rice. The hamburger dinner, served with salad and home fries, and the salad plates are also bargains. For dessert we suggest the chocolate mud cake.

Situated in the heart of the East Village, Dojo's offers a great view of the East Village scene from its canopied sidewalk seating. Otherwise, enjoy yourself in any of the three inside rooms.

Breakfast is served until 5pm and after 11pm.

EAT, 11 St. Marks Place, between Second and Third aves. Tel. 477-5155.
   Cuisine: VEGETARIAN. **Reservations:** Not needed. **Subway:** 6 to Astor Place; R to 8th St.
$ Prices: Appetizers $3–$4; main courses $4–$8.95. No credit cards.
   Open: Sun–Thurs 10am–midnight; Fri–Sat 10am–1am.

If you think this name sounds like a rough, no-frills hash house, you're in for a pleasant surprise. This long, low-ceilinged restaurant offers a touch of class with its eye-catching art, wood trim, and fresh flowers on the tables. The menu is a mix of vegetarian dishes and pita sandwiches, with a few fish and chicken dishes thrown in for good measure. Try the cheese and chili-melt pita stuffer or the stir-fried vegetable pita stuffer. Pasta dishes are excellent—we suggest the broccoli fettuccine topped with mushroom sauce. Or ask about the fish selection of the day. Eat has an extensive imported beer and wine list.

GREAT JONES CAFÉ, 54 Great Jones St., just off the Bowery. Tel. 674-9304.
   Cuisine: CAJUN. **Reservations:** Not needed. **Subway:** 6 to Bleecker St.
$ Prices: Appetizers $2.95–$4.95; main courses $8.95–$13.95. No credit cards.
   Open: Brunch Sat–Sun 10am–4pm; dinner Sun–Thurs 5pm–midnight, Fri–Sat 5pm–1am.

When the Great Jones Café first opened, the owners planned a little neighborhood bar with food as a side attraction. But the word got out about some of New York's finest Cajun cooking. Now the crowds that usually fill up the bar are waiting for a table.

For a real treat, try the blackened fish (usually catfish), charred and crunchy on the outside, succulent and juicy inside, served with a vegetable and salad. Order up a piece of honey-sweetened, fresh-baked jalapeño cornbread on the side for 95¢. Another big favorite is the rich, thick Louisiana-style gumbo, with a slightly different version served every night; they average $9.75 and are served with salad and vegetable. Don't forget to check for daily specials. If you're waiting for a table, occupy your time with a chilled Cajun martini, a shot of straight vodka or gin flavored with jalapeño pepper ($3)—and you might need a beer chaser.

HARRY'S, 91 E. 7th St., near First Ave. Tel. 477-0773.
 Cuisine: MEXICAN. **Reservations:** Not needed. **Subway:** 6 to Astor Place; R to 8th St.
$ **Prices:** Appetizers $5.75; main courses $6–$7.95. No credit cards.
 Open: Sun–Thurs noon–midnight; Fri–Sat noon–1am.
Behind the steamed-up windows of its little storefront, Harry's serves up big helpings of California-style Mexican food to the appreciative young trendy types that crowd its five or six tables. The burritos and enchiladas are served with chicken, beef, or vegetables. If you like no-frills Mexican food in no-frills surroundings, a stop in Harry's will leave you sated.

KIEV INTERNATIONAL COFFEE HOUSE AND RESTAURANT, 117 Second Ave., at East 7th St. Tel. 674-4040.
 Cuisine: UKRAINIAN. **Reservations:** Not accepted. **Subway:** 6 to Astor Place; R to 8th St.
$ **Prices:** Main courses $6.75–$9.50. No credit cards.
 Open: Daily 24 hours.
Owner Michael Hrynenko has created a late-night hangout for the locals. The decor is diner style, with a take-out counter in front and Formica tables in the glassed-in dining room toward the back.

The menu includes breakfast items as well as Ukrainian specialties. Try the kielbasa and eggs, served with bread and home fries; the potato pancakes; pirogen; blintzes; or pita sandwiches, filled with falafel or liver—bargains all. A homemade babka with blueberries and ice cream will polish off your meal, or you might go for the apple cake. The challah is out-of-this-world.

KHYBER PASS, 34 St. Marks Place, between Second and Third aves. Tel. 473-0989.
 Cuisine: AFGHAN. **Reservations:** Recommended. **Subway:** 6 to Astor Place.
$ **Prices:** Appetizers $2.50–$3.50; main courses $6.50–$14.00. $5 minimum per person. AE.
 Open: Daily noon–midnight. **Closed:** Christmas and New Year's.

⭐ Making your way through the throngs of vendors along St. Marks Place is the East Village equivalent of wandering through a crowded Middle Eastern bazaar, so you'll be in the mood to enter this nondescript little place, decorated with imported rugs on the walls. Try to get seated at the low window table, where you'll nest on big Afghan pillows.

In the likely event that you've never had Afghan food before, your waiter or waitress will guide you through the menu. You might start with aushe, a hearty vegetable soup with homemade noodles and yogurt, or aushak, steamed scallion dumplings topped with a yogurt-mint sauce. But whatever you do, don't miss out on the incredible boulanne kadu, a turnover filled with perfectly spiced pumpkin. There's a wide selection of vegetarian dishes, but carnivores can choose a kabob, charcoal-grilled on a skewer and served with long-grain rice, salad, and home-baked Afghan bread. We tried the morgh kebab, boneless chicken marinated in yogurt and spices and served with grilled tomatoes, and found it tender and juicy. We also enjoyed the kabuk palow with lamb—browned basmati rice topped with shredded carrots, raisins, almonds, and chunks of lamb. Top off your meal with Turkish coffee or shir-chay, traditional Afghan tea brewed with milk, sugar, cardamon, and rose petals—we bet that this won't be the last time you try Afghan cuisine.

LA SPAGHETTERIA, 178 Second Ave., at East 12th St. Tel. 995-0900.
   Cuisine: ITALIAN. **Reservations:** Only needed for parties of 6 or more.
   Subway: 6 to Astor Place.
$ Prices: Appetizers $3.50–$5.25; main courses $7.25–$11.95. AE, MC, V.
   Open: Lunch Mon–Fri noon–3:30pm, Sat–Sun noon–4pm; dinner Sun–Thurs 5pm–midnight, Fri–Sat 5pm–1am.

La Spaghetteria is an unusually posh East Village restaurant. But don't be intimidated by the plush furnishings and subdued jazz music—jeans are still welcome here.

The lunch menu offers sandwiches, light pasta dishes, and salads. You might start a dinner here with the mozzarella e pomodori (mozzarella cheese and tomatoes with olive oil)—plenty for two. One of the house specialties is the fettuccine con salsice (fettuccine with sausage, mushrooms, and roasted red peppers). Finish your meal with a slice of double chocolate cake ($4.95).

THE LIFE CAFÉ, 343 E. 10th St., at Ave. B. Tel. 477-8791.
   Cuisine: INTERNATIONAL. **Reservations:** Not accepted. **Subway:** 6 to Astor Place. **Bus:** M13 to Avenue B.
$ Prices: All items $4.95–$7.95. AE, DC, MC, V.
   Open: Sun–Thurs 11am–1am; Fri–Sat 11am–2am.

The Life Café is a neighborhood hangout for artists, musicians, writers, and other assorted East Village types who enjoy the laid-back mood around the park from the sidewalk café. The café gets its name from the montage of pictures from old *Life* magazines pasted on its walls.

The international menu features cuisine from southern latitudes—exotic, fresh, and spicy, with a vegetarian/health food emphasis. If you've got an appetite, order the ever-popular megaburrito: two flour tortillas stuffed with brown rice, black beans, two cheeses, lettuce, tomato, onions, sour cream, and homemade salsa ($6.95). The assortment of burgers is eclectic—ranging from a regular deluxe served with yam fries (with the skins left on) to the Cajun burger.

Monthly art shows feature local artists with opening parties that are a happening scene. Live music is featured throughout the month.

MCSORLEY'S OLD ALE HOUSE, 15 E. 7th St., between Second and Third aves. Tel. 473-9148.
   Cuisine: PUB GRUB. **Reservations:** Not accepted. **Subway:** 6 to Astor Place; R to 8th St.
$ Prices: Sandwiches and main courses $4.25–$9.95. No credit cards.
   Open: Daily 11am–1am.

Every inch of McSorley's is covered with historical memorabilia. This bar dates from 1854, when members of General Custer's 69th Army Regiment convinced old McSorley, a blacksmith, to turn his blacksmith forge into an alehouse. The rest is history.

Only McSorley's special-recipe light or dark ale is served here. Many regulars swear by McSorley's corned-beef sandwiches, while others champion the daily special. Once you're settled with your beer and food, look around at the treasures covering the walls, including a pair of old shoes that the owner, Irishman Matt Maher, swears were worn by Joe Kennedy, father of President John F. Kennedy. Also hanging from the bar is the chair that President Abraham Lincoln reputedly sat in while he made his famous Emancipation Proclamation speech. Both students and old-timers fill McSorley's to the packing point, often smoking up a storm with McSorley's special-order cigars. But bear with the crowds, because you'll never forget your visit here.

MITALI, 334 E. 6th St. Tel. 533-2508.
   Cuisine: INDIAN. **Reservations:** Not needed. **Subway:** 6 to Astor Place.
$ Prices: Appetizers 90¢–$7.95; main courses $5.50–$14.95. AE, MC, V.

Open: Lunch Fri–Sun 11am–3:30pm; dinner daily 4:30pm–midnight.

While most of the restaurants on "Little India" row serve comparable food at comparable prices, Mitali is a bit more expensive and, in our opinion, serves the best food on the block. From your comfortable wooden table, you can watch the chef prepare your food behind a wall of plate glass. In addition to the usual curries, Mitali serves a complex and delicious assortment of tandoori dishes. Main dishes are reasonably priced. Mitali has a full-service bar and a good selection of wine and Indian beer.

MOGADOR, 101 St. Marks Place. Tel. 677-2226.

Cuisine: MIDDLE EASTERN. **Reservations:** Not needed. **Subway:** 6 to Astor Place; R to 8th St.

$ Prices: Appetizers $1.50; main courses $7.95–$9.95. No credit cards.

Open: Mon–Sat 10am–1am, Sun 10am–12:30am.

Mogador offers more authentic Middle Eastern cuisine than Yaffa Café. Your waiter will tempt you with a tray of a dozen different appetizers. The menu includes five varieties of couscous, ten different kinds of tahines (exotically seasoned lamb or chicken stew), and an enormous list of daily specials. Mogador patrons dodge the oscillating hips of belly dancers every Wednesday night.

ODESSA, 117 Ave. A, between East 7th St. and St. Marks Place. Tel. 473-8916.

Cuisine: UKRAINIAN. **Reservations:** Not accepted. **Subway:** 6 to Astor Place. **Bus:** M13 to Avenue A.

$ Prices: Appetizers $1.50–$2.45; main courses $4.45–$7.95. No credit cards.

Open: Daily 7am–midnight.

The informal decor here includes cheery red booths and bright white Formica tables. There's a sit-down counter in the center of this restaurant, and the menu boasts of fine home-cooking. The Odessa has become a regular hangout for black-clad East Villagers, who seem to feel quite at home in the traditional old-fashioned diner with its old-fashioned prices. The large menu offers everything from Ukrainian specialties (potato pancakes, pirogen, and homemade blintzes) to American hamburgers. Italian specialties, like veal parmigiana, are available, as are a broiled salmon steak and daily seafood specials. Try the homemade cheesecake, a bargain at $2.

SAPPORO, 245 E. 10th St., at 4th Ave. Tel. 260-1330.

Cuisine: JAPANESE. **Reservations:** Not needed. **Subway:** L to Third Ave.; N, R, 4, 5, 6 to Union Square.

$ Prices: A la carte sushi $1.40–$4. AE.

Open: Daily 5pm–1am.

With its wooden walls, paper screens, and claustrophobic tables, Sapporo feels very Japanese. People huddle over their tables and take their sushi very seriously here. A 15-minute wait is the norm, but it's worth it. Regulars insist that Sapporo serves the best sushi in the East Village. If you don't want to order à la carte, try the sushi dinner, with miso soup, a small salad, and ten varieties of sushi for less than $11. When you leave, the entire staff is likely to bow and shout "Thank you."

7A, 109 Ave. A, at East 7th St. Tel. 475-9001.

Cuisine: AMERICAN. **Reservations:** Not needed. **Bus:** M13 or M14 to Avenue A.

$ Prices: Appetizers $2.75–$5.75; main courses $5.50–$11. AE, CB, DC, MC, V.

Open: Daily 9:30am–3am.

This bright, airy café is decorated with pink-and-white walls, lots of wood and plants, and outdoor sidewalk seating. Try the bay scallops sautéed with herbs and wine over linguine, served with a vegetable and your choice of rice or potato. Or stay with simpler fare—the hearty half-pound burger is served on pita bread or an English muffin, with a garden salad or home fries. Desserts here are a local treasure. Treat yourself to the pecan pie or the irresistible chocolate cheesecake.

If you're getting a late start in the morning, try 7A's weekday breakfast special, which is served until 1pm. For less than $3.50, order your choice of three eggs any style, with home fries, toast or an English muffin, and coffee. For the same price you can also get blueberry pancakes with coffee.

SHAH BAGH, 320 E. 6th St., between First and Second aves. Tel. 677-8876.
   Cuisine: INDIAN. **Reservations:** Not needed. **Subway:** 6 to Astor Place.
$ **Prices:** Main courses $4.95–$10.95. AE, MC, V.
   Open: Daily noon–midnight.
The Ahmed brothers were the first to open their small basement restaurant on East 6th Street between First and Second avenues. Soon others followed suit, turning the block into an Indian-food lover's haven. Boasting that it was "the first on the block," Shah Bagh has an unpretentious interior with two dining rooms filled with small wood tables set with flowers and white cloth napkins. Tea is on the house.

To start your meal, try the coconut soup or the banana fritter. The à la carte menu features vegetable, chicken, beef, lamb, and crabmeat curries. There are also several kinds of biryani, dishes cooked with saffron rice, coconut, and spices. All main dishes are made mild, but you can request hot orders. For dessert, try the honey cake or the gulab jaman—a sweet fried cheese ball.

SHARAKU, 8 Stuyvesant Place, between Second and Third aves. Tel. 598-0403.
   Cuisine: JAPANESE. **Reservations:** Recommended on weekends. **Subway:** 6 to Astor Place; R to 8th St.
$ **Prices:** A la carte sushi $1.40–$4. AE, DC, MC, V.
   Open: Sun–Thurs 6pm–1am; Fri–Sat 6pm–4am.
Sushi fans will love this popular Japanese hangout. It serves a wide variety of sushi—we like the yellowtail or the giant clam. For those of you who prefer your fish cooked, we suggest the shrimp tempura. The medium-sized dining room is festive with Japanese prints and bamboo shades. The music is low-key and soothing.

SIDEWALK CAFÉ, 94 Ave. A, at Sixth St. Tel. 473-7373.
   Cuisine: AMERICAN. **Reservations:** Not accepted. **Subway:** F to Second Ave.
$ **Prices:** Main courses $5.95–$10.75. AE, DC, MC, V.
   Open: Daily 10am–4am.
The menu at Sidewalk features an ordinary and inexpensive roundup of burgers, salads, and sandwiches. But the endless parade of East Village oddballs strolling past its outdoor tables turns most meals into an unbeatable brand of offbeat dinner-theater. It's definitely one of the best people-watching perches in the city. Don't come for lunch—most of the local color will still be asleep.

SUGAR REEF, 93 Second Ave., between 5th and 6th sts. Tel. 477-8427.
   Cuisine: CARIBBEAN. **Reservations:** Accepted only for large parties. **Subway:** 6 to Astor Place.
$ **Prices:** Appetizers $3.75–$6.95; main courses $8.95–$13.95. No credit cards.
   Open: Sun–Thurs 5pm–12:30am; Fri–Sat 3pm–1:30am. Bar may be open later.
      Gaily decorated Sugar Reef is one of our all-time favorites. You'll feel as though you were suddenly transported from downtown Manhattan to the sunny tropics. The food is spicy, the portions are generous, and the atmosphere is a nonstop party.

You'll munch appreciatively on the baskets of warm, buttery bread continually replaced at your table. Do not under any circumstances miss the coconut shrimp—you'll thank us. It's a perfect combination, served with a fresh hearts of palm salad. Other favorites are the vegetable rôti—sautéed carrots, kale, cabbage, and potatoes, wrapped in fresh rôti pastry—and the Jamaican jerk chicken.

TWO BOOTS, 37 Avenue A, between 2nd and 3rd sts. Tel. 505-2276.
   Cuisine: ITALIAN/CRÉOLE. **Reservations:** Not accepted. **Subway:** F to Second Ave.

$ Prices: Appetizers $2.50–$6.95; pasta courses $5.95–$8.95; pizza $4.95–$19.50. No credit cards.
Open: Tues–Sun noon–midnight.

Anyplace where the jukebox plays old Louis Armstrong tunes is okay by us, but the attractions of Two Boots don't end there. It's as comfortable as the old broken-in boots scattered around the decor, with big red booths and red-checked tablecloths.

We came for lunch and enjoyed a special smoked mozzarella po' boy, served on fresh, crusty Italian bread with tortilla chips on the side, and sweet potato fries. Pizzas range from small individual selections to large creations a whole family could enjoy—and the toppings run the gamut from the mundane to calamari and BBQ shrimp. Your kids will be kept busy with coloring books and crayons while you down Anchor Steam beer or Woodpecker Cider served in a mug, boot, or pitcher. All ages will want to end their meal with the blueberry pie, the chocolate pecan pie, a black-and-white mousse cake, or peanut butter pie.

Brunch, served Saturday and Sunday from noon to 4pm, comes with coffee or tea and your choice of juice, a mimosa, or Cajun sangría. Whole-wheat waffles are topped with fresh fruit, toasted pecans, and maple syrup or sautéed apples, cinnamon, and sugar. Egg dishes come with an apple-walnut muffin or a buttermilk biscuit—you can choose the Atchafalaya omelet, with crawfish, jalapeños, and scallions, or baked eggs over polenta with andouille sausage, tomatoes, and mozzarella.

UKRAINIAN RESTAURANT, 140 Second Ave., between 8th and 9th sts. Tel. 529-5024.
Cuisine: UKRAINIAN. **Reservations:** Not accepted. **Subway:** 6 to Astor Place; R to 8th St.
$ Prices: All items under $7.50. No credit cards. **Open:** Daily 11am–11pm.

When a fire destroyed Ukrainian Restaurant's original home, its regulars couldn't wait for it to reopen. Entering the recently redecorated place is like stepping into a Ukrainian chalet. Ukrainian prints, traditional plates, and musical instruments called banduras decorate the stone walls. Ukrainian music is played, and the waiters and waitresses even wear traditional dress.

One thing that hasn't changed is the delicious food. Try the steak tartare, prepared to order with a basket of homemade challah bread, black, or rye. If you can't decide among all the tempting dishes, then choose the combination plate, with one stuffed cabbage, four varieties of pirogies, bigos, slices of kielbasa, tossed salad, and a basket of bread for less than $8.

YAFFA CAFÉ, 97 St. Marks Place. Tel. 674-9302.
Cuisine: MIDDLE EASTERN. **Reservations:** Not needed. **Subway:** 6 to Astor Place.
$ Prices: Appetizers and salads $3.75–$5.50; main courses $6.95–$11. AE.
Open: Mon–Thurs 10:30am–11:30pm; Fri–Sat 10:30am–12:30am.

On the north side of St. Marks Place, just east of First Avenue, you'll find a Middle Eastern oasis in the midst of the East Village's bohemian bustle. The Yaffa Café is a tranquil spot with sidewalk tables, an airy dining room, and an artsy clientele. A large shady garden is open in the summer.

Yaffa bills itself as an "international" restaurant. It nods to Middle Eastern cuisine with hummus, tahine, and baba ghanouj sandwiches on pita, but it also has a large menu of salads, pastas, and vegetarian specialties. Yaffa occasionally offers live music on weeknights.

7. CHELSEA/PENN STATION

BELLEVUE'S, 496 Ninth Ave. Tel. 967-7850.
Cuisine: CONTINENTAL. **Reservations:** Recommended. **Subway:** A, C, E to 42nd St.

$ Prices: Appetizers $4.25–$7.50; salads $4.25–$7.25; main courses $11.75–$17.50. CB, DC, MC, V.
Open: Lunch Mon–Fri 11:30am–3:30pm; brunch Sat–Sun 11am–3:30pm; dinner daily 6pm–midnight.

Brought to you by those same trendy folks who own Restaurant Florent, Bellevue's, with its friendly, crowded bar, is an unexpected oasis of casual chic in a rather run-down neighborhood. It's a dressed-up diner, offering simple yet elegant fare—lamb chops, mussels morellet, pâté, and duck mousse, and for the dessert strawberry gratinée with crème fraîche or profiteroles with hot chocolate sauce.

Bellevue's tongue-in-cheek "Recession Prix-Fixe," is $15.95 before 7pm and after 11pm, $17.95 the rest of the evening. You get an appetizer, soup, or salad; one of four main dishes, like steak frite or baked bluefish; crème brûlée or raspberry sorbet for dessert; and coffee or tea. Wine is available by the glass.

CENTRO VASCO, 208 W. 23rd St., between Seventh and Eighth aves. Tel. 741-1408.
Cuisine: SPANISH. **Reservations:** Necessary for parties of 4 or more.
Subway: 1, 9, C, E to 23rd St.
$ Prices: Main courses $7–$24. AE, CB, DC, MC, V.
Open: Mon–Fri 4pm–midnight, Sat–Sun 2pm–midnight.

From its blue-tiled exterior to its stucco walls, Centro Vasco has an authentic Spanish feel. Inside, the restaurant is decorated with original abstract art pieces painted by a Peruvian artist, in addition to more standard paintings of flamenco dancers. The setting is elegant, with candle-shaped wall sconces and chocolate-colored tablecloths draped over beige linen. Arched doorways and wooden beams complete the Mediterranean setting.

It's on the expensive side, but dinners, served in large portions, can be shared, with a $3 charge for an extra plate. To start, we suggest the black-bean soup or gazpacho. The seafood paella is big enough for two, and the lower-priced main dishes—veal parmigiana and shrimp in wine sauce—are also good. If you really want to go all-out, try the stuffed lobster dinner, perhaps topped off with flan or cheesecake.

CHINATOWN EXPRESS, 425 Seventh Ave., between 33rd and 34th sts. Tel. 563-3559.
Cuisine: CHINESE. **Reservations:** Not needed. **Subway:** 1, 2, 3, 9 to 34th St./Penn Station.
$ Prices: Appetizers $1–$4.95; main courses $4.95–$7.95. No credit cards.
Open: Mon–Fri 11am–9pm, Sat–Sun 11am–8pm. May be open later if there's a big event at nearby Madison Square Garden.

Chinatown Express is bright and clean, with green-and-white tiles at the front counter and behind the stove. Main dishes are temptingly displayed in a curved alcove covered by glass slats. Downstairs there are two dining rooms, decorated with plastic shields painted with Chinese characters. An upstairs dining room has a view of the avenue below.

You'll want to start with the wonton soup or an egg roll, of course, and then for you indecisive folks the menu features combination platters served in large portions, and a "Wok-In Chinese Buffet," priced by the pound.

J. J. APPLEBAUM'S DELI CO., 431 Seventh Ave., between 33rd and 34th sts. Tel. 563-6200.
Cuisine: JEWISH DELI. **Reservations:** Not needed. **Subway:** 1, 2, 3, 9, A, C, E to 34th St./Penn Station.
$ Prices: Appetizers $3.50–$10.75; sandwiches $4.75–$10.25; main courses $7.45–$17.50. AE.
Open: Mon–Fri 7:30am–8pm, Sat–Sun 8am–7pm.

Puns like the "star-shrimp enterprise" and the "central pork west" sandwiches abound on this restaurant's three-foot menu. The decor is modern and airy, with exposed-brick walls, black-and-white-checkered tile floors.

To start, try the Heart of Herring, marinated herring in cream sauce with onions. The huge "overstuffer" sandwiches are served with homemade coleslaw and your choice of four different condiments. You can have them "hot, cold, cut, uncut, or on your lap." The grilled Reuben is a mountain of hot pastrami covered with coleslaw, Russian dressing, and gobs of melting cheese. You can also get zucchini latkes, with sour cream or applesauce, and a steak sandwich with charcoal-broiled steak. For dessert, try the fresh pound cake or the carrot cake.

LOX AROUND THE CLOCK, 676 Sixth Ave., at 21st St. Tel. 691-3535.
   Cuisine: INTERNATIONAL. **Reservations:** Not accepted. **Subway:** R, 6 to 23rd St.
$ Prices: Appetizers $4.00–$5.50; main courses $6.95–$14.95; prix-fixe dinner $14.95. AE.
   Open: Sun–Wed 7:30–4am, Thurs–Sun 24 hours.
      The owners call Lox "an international Jewish cuisine restaurant" and it is that and more. Inside, sleek metal chairs and wooden tables fill the room, and an oversized Lox logo clock with moving fish caricatures hangs above the bar.
   Portions are huge, and for late risers, breakfast is served all day. Cheese blintzes, lox, and cream cheese on a bagel with garnish, and kasha varniskes with brisket gravy are some classic Jewish offerings. There are several big sandwiches, including a delicious curried chicken with salad on the side, and a tasty mozzarella, basil, and tomato sandwich served on garlic challah. Hot main dishes include stuffed cabbage and sautéed shell steak, grilled and served with steak fries and a vegetable. The prix-fixe dinner (served every night from 6pm on) includes coffee or tea and diners get a choice of one main dish plus any other two courses: appetizer, soup, or dessert. There are also five kinds of burgers, served with fries, omelets, and salads. If for some reason you still have room, Lox also offers fresh baked desserts like cheesecake and chocolate raspberry mousse cake, and a caloric treat called the "Here's the Guilt" banana split.
   Happy hour at Lox Around the Clock is from 4 to 8pm and features $1.25 draft beer plus different "international" drink specials every day.

MANGANARO'S GROSSERIA, 488 Ninth Ave., between 37th and 38th sts. Tel. 563-5331.
   Cuisine: ITALIAN. **Subway:** 1, 2, 3, 9, A, C, E to 34th St./Penn Station. **Bus:** M34 to Ninth Ave.
$ Prices: Antipasto bar $7.50–$15.50; sandwiches $2.75–$7.25; main courses $3–$16. AE, DC.
   Open: Mon–Sat 7am–7:30pm.
This colorful deli consists of a large specialty store (a gourmet cook's wildest fantasy) with a small luncheonette in the back. It's run by the five Manganaro sisters, who see to it that the biscotti and the delicious cheeses are all beautifully displayed. The sit-down deli is simply decorated, with a green floor and brown-wood Formica tables.
   Hot main dishes include three different types of fettuccini, tortellini, rigatoni, cannelloni, and, of course, spaghetti. The sandwiches are a treat—you can get a meatball hero or an eggplant parmigiana sandwich for a very reasonable price. If there are four of you, you might want to try Manganaro's Loaf Special. For dessert, the ricotta cheesecake made with rosewater is extraordinary.

MARY ANN'S, 116 Eighth Ave., at 16th St. Tel. 633-0877.
   Cuisine: MEXICAN. **Reservations:** Not accepted. **Subway:** 1, 2, 3, 9, A, C, E to 14th St.
$ Prices: Appetizers $3.95–$6.95; main courses $7–$12.95. No credit cards.
   Open: Lunch Mon–Fri noon–4pm; dinner daily 4–11pm; brunch Sat–Sun noon–4pm.
One of the most popular spots in Chelsea's burgeoning "Restaurant Row" on Eighth Avenue, Mary Ann's offers a nice variety of well-executed Mexican and Tex-Mex

dishes at very affordable prices. Stucco-and-brick walls, ceiling fans, south-of-the-border decorative crafts, and a tiny candle on each table are the simple but effective design touches that, along with the menu, attract a young neighborhood crowd.

After working your way through a bowl of tortilla chips and pungent dipping salsa, try a main dish like the chile relleno plate—two Monterey peppers stuffed with cheese and covered in a delightful sauce, served with rice and beans. Mole poblano, breast of chicken with a red-chile-and-chocolate sauce, comes with hot flour tortillas and is quite good. You can also get such daily specials as roast duck in a mole of green tomatoes and pumpkin seeds, served with rice and zucchini. From a limited but respectable wine list you can choose a bottle of a good French table white for under $10 (beer is also available). A cup of flan tops off the meal.

NICK'S PLACE, 550 Seventh Ave., between 39th and 40th sts. Tel. 221-3294.
> **Cuisine:** GREEK. **Reservations:** Not accepted. **Subway:** 1, 2, 3, 9 to 42nd St./Times Square.
> **$ Prices:** Main courses $4.95–$9.95. No credit cards.
> **Open:** Mon–Fri 11am–3pm.

Hidden away behind a freight entrance on 39th Street, this restaurant is a real find, with delicious homemade Greek specialties. There are only seven tables in the dining area, but the small room is cozily decorated, with dappled wallpaper and old-fashioned French posters.

Traditional Greek offerings include moussaka with vegetable or salad, spinach pie with salad, and stuffed grape leaves. There is also a wide variety of salads, including avocado vinaigrette and spinach varieties. For dessert, we like the fresh carrot cake or the homemade chocolate cake.

THE ROCKING HORSE MEXICAN CAFÉ, 182 Eighth Ave., between 19th and 20th sts. Tel. 463-9511.
> **Cuisine:** MEXICAN. **Reservations:** Accepted only for large parties. **Subway:** A, C, E to 14th St.; C, E to 23rd St.
> **$ Prices:** Main lunch courses $5.95–$8.95, main dinner courses $7.95–$14.95. AE, MC, V.
> **Open:** Lunch Mon–Sat 11:30am–4pm; dinner Sun–Thurs 4–11pm, Fri–Sat 4pm–midnight; brunch Sun noon–4pm.

⭐ This new and colorful café, owned by Marvin Beck and Roe DiBona (previously the owners of Buckwheat & Alfalfa, at the same location), is dedicated to serving its patrons "good, down home, quality fare." The menu, with a strong Mexican foundation and a southwest influence, has been carefully researched, and the owners claim it to be a "home away from home" for their regulars. You might want to try their fajitas, made the right way, with grilled strips of steak, chicken, or shrimp, sautéed with onions and peppers and served south-of-the border style—with guacamole, flour tortillas, and refried beans.

The food is authentic, and so is the decor, with red-and-yellow papier-mâché art decorating the ceilings, and photos of Mexico on the walls. The clientele is invited to join in the creativity with the monthly Frida Kahlo Drawing Contest. How to enter? Your table is lined with paper and you are supplied with enough crayons to keep your inner child amused for hours. The winner receives a certificate for dinner for two.

Happy hour is from 4pm to 6:30pm when the Rocking Horse serves "Two-For-One Margaritas," complimentary hors d'oeuvres, and a wide variety of Mexican beers.

SAM CHINITA, 176 Eighth Ave., corner of 19th St. Tel. 741-0240.
> **Cuisine:** SPANISH/CHINESE. **Reservations:** Not needed. **Subway:** 1, 9 to 18th St; A, C, E to 14th St.
> **$ Prices:** Appetizers $1.55–$6.25; main courses $5.15–$15.95. MC, V.
> **Open:** Daily noon–7pm.

Housed in an old shiny aluminum diner, this restaurant is decorated with a long Formica counter and blue Formica tables matched with aqua-colored linen curtains.

Two Chinese hanging lamps and a few other Chinese decorator items reflect the Asian half of the menu.

The menu, the top half listing Chinese food, the bottom, Spanish, offers a wide selection. The Chinese menu includes the standard wonton soup and egg roll, and also has roast pork and mushrooms, vegetable egg foo yung, and chicken with broccoli. From the Spanish menu you can choose peppersteak with rice and beans, beef steak with rice and beans, or roast chicken with bananas and salad.

SINGHA THAI CUISINE RESTAURANT, 240 Eighth Ave., between 22nd and 23rd sts. Tel. 741-1732.

Cuisine: THAI. **Reservations:** Not accepted. **Subway:** C, E to 23rd St; 1, 9 to 18th St. **Bus:** M23 to Eighth Ave.

$ Prices: Appetizers $4.15–$7.65; main courses $8.15–$15. AE, MC, V.

Open: Dinner Sun–Thurs 4–11:30pm, Fri–Sat 4pm–midnight.

If you're in the mood for something exotic, check out this casual and popular neighborhood restaurant. Thai silk paintings adorn the walls, and dominating the center of the restaurant is a large bronze sculpture of a singha ("lion" in Thai). Tasty multicolored shrimp chips are brought to the table for you to munch as you peruse the extensive, though simply priced, menu.

The menu offers a wide selection of Thai food from appetizers to desserts. The tom kha gai, chicken-coconut soup spiced with chile, lime juice, and galaga (a ginger-like spice), is excellent. Thai spring rolls make a nice light appetizer when shared. Most of the main dishes are sautéed with fresh vegetables, herbs, and spices; a specialty of the house is fried Rama chicken served with baby corn, carrots, and green beans, and topped with peanut sauce and fresh coriander. Of course, Singha beer is the beverage of choice to accompany the meal.

SUNG HO LO, 211 Seventh Ave., between 22nd and 23rd sts. Tel. 924-8580.

Cuisine: CHINESE. **Reservations:** Not needed. **Subway:** 1, 9 to 18th St.

$ Prices: Appetizers $1–$5.75; main courses $5.25–$9.50. MC, V.

Open: Mon–Thurs 11:30am–10:30pm, Fri 11:30am–11pm, Sat 5pm–11pm, Sun 5pm–10:30pm.

The food here is undeniably fresh; we once watched as the staff set steaming mountains of green beans at a back table. The informal, quiet restaurant is decorated with framed black calligraphy letters painted on rice paper, and Chinese watercolor prints.

Luncheon specials, ranging from $4 to $5, are the best deals of the day. Try the stir-fried Chinese vegetables for a light lunch, or if you're in the mood for something more substantial, try the beef with broccoli or the pepper steak. The à la carte menu, for both lunch and dinner, includes beef in hot garlic sauce and diced chicken in black bean sauce. For dessert, try the chilled lichee nuts. For a healthy twist, main dishes can be served with brown rice instead of white rice—just ask.

SUPREME MACARONI COMPANY, 511 Ninth Ave., between 38th and 39th sts. Tel. 502-4842.

Cuisine: ITALIAN. **Reservations:** Recommended. **Subway:** A, C, E to 42nd St.

$ Prices: Appetizers $5.25–$6.95; pasta courses $7.95–$12.25; main courses $11.95–$16.50. No credit cards.

Open: Dinner daily 5–11pm.

Supreme Macaroni is a family-run operation that's been around since 1947. You may think you're in the wrong place when you walk into a plain storefront selling homemade pasta—until you enter the charming, bustling back room, where rows of wine bottles hang from the skylight and ceiling fans whir overhead. Blue-and-white-checked tablecloths and exposed-brick walls create an old-world atmosphere that's enhanced by the fascinating black-and-white family photos on the wall. Service is brisk and cheery.

In an atmosphere like this, you'll want to go for the traditional favorites, and the kitchen does them well. We started with mussels marinara and zuppa di clams, before moving onto a perfectly spiced eggplant parmigiana and veal sorrentino. If you're feeling extravagant, go for the lobster Fra Diavola tails. Desserts are all priced at $3.75, and, of course, a cappuccino or espresso is de rigueur.

LA TAZA DE ORO, 96 Eighth Ave., between 14th and 15th sts. Tel. 243-9946.

Cuisine: PUERTO RICAN. **Reservations:** Not accepted. **Subway:** 1, 2, 3, 9, A, C, E to 14th St.

$ Prices: Appetizers $2.50–$5; main courses under $9. No credit cards.

Open: Daily 7am–11:15pm.

Located right outside the Village La Taza de Oro is a great place for some of the best Latin food around at bargain-basement prices. La Taza de Oro, or "cup of gold," is a simple luncheonette with Formica counters and Formica tables, where the music from the jukebox is Latin and almost everyone speaks Spanish. It's a neighborhood joint, and the menu, posted on two blackboards, is in English as well as Spanish. Many people come for the pork chops or the roast chicken, both of which are served with rice and salad. But the specialties are more exotic: tripe soup, pickled fish, and octopus salad are a few among many. We also recommend the mavi (an apple-cider drink) and tamarindo (a tropical fruit juice).

Breakfast is served until 11am daily. Sometimes the owners close on Sunday, so call first if you're planning on dropping by that day.

VERNON'S JERK PARADISE, 252 W. 29th St. Tel. 268-7020.

Cuisine: JAMAICAN. **Reservations:** Not needed. **Subway:** 1, 9 to 28th St.

$ Prices: Appetizers $1–$6; main courses $10–$12. AE, MC, V.

Open: Sun–Fri 11:30am–10 or 11pm; Sat 3–11pm or midnight.

If you've never been introduced to the wonders of Jamaican "jerk" cooking, this is a perfect place for your initiation. Service is extremely attentive and friendly, and your waiter will happily explain the menu. Vernon's is a lovely laid-back spot, with the perfect mix of background reggae and island insouciance.

We started off the proceedings with a tasting menu of appetizers, with vegetable and meat patties, codfish cakes, fried plaintains, and dumplings for dipping into a pot of jerk sauce. (Be prepared—it's spicy!) The main courses offer you the chance to try jerk-style beef, pork, lobster, or seafood—but we loved the perfectly seasoned chicken. The curried goat was also tender and spicy, and main dishes come with a side of rice and beans. Red Stripe beer is the drink of choice, but if you're going the nonalcoholic route, there's lots to choose from—ginger beer, carrot soda, and specialty drinks that go by names like the "Oh Lord," the "Knockdown," and the "Wah Dat." Check to see what's on the dessert menu for the evening. The mango ice cream is a delicately sweet treat, but if there's sweet potato pie, don't hesitate—it's so creamy and smooth it'll melt in your mouth. Save a couple of bucks to buy a jar of jerk sauce at the bar on your way out.

ZIGZAG BAR AND GRILL, 206 W. 23rd St., just west of Seventh Ave. Tel. 645-5060.

Cuisine: AMERICAN. **Reservations:** Accepted for parties of 5 or more. **Subway:** 1, 9 to 23rd St.

$ Prices: Soups and salads $1.95–$9.95; sandwiches $7.95–$9.95; burgers $5.25–$6.25; main courses $5.95–$11.95. AE, MC, V.

Open: Mon–Thurs 11:30am–1am, Fri–Sat 11:30am–2am, Sun 11:30am–midnight; brunch served Sat–Sun 11:30am–4pm.

After it's 1920s-style blue neon sign and framed-glass entrance, the first thing you notice about this upscale restaurant is that it's very long and thin. But once inside, the true size of the room is distorted by mirrors covering the walls; reflected in these mirrors is the jagged "zig zag" dropped ceiling of the bar.

The food is simple American bistro fare. You can get a chicken cheese steak sandwich with peppers, onions, and mozzarella, Black Forest ham and Brie, or a

"Health Sandwich" with guacamole, roasted red pepper, mixed vegetables, and sprouts. Of course, you can always get a hamburger with fries or onion rings. If you're in the mood for a bigger meal, you might want to try the sliced sirloin tips or the grilled filet of salmon with soy ginger sauce, both served with oven-roasted new potatoes and fresh vegetables. If that wasn't enough to fill you up, take a step into true decadence with Oreo cheesecake or chocolate truffle cake.

8. GRAMERCY PARK/MURRAY HILL

GRAMERCY PARK

Our favorite choice for sushi in the neighborhood is **East,** located at 366 Third Ave., between 26th and 27th streets (tel. 889-2326). See Section 9, "Midtown West," for a complete review of the branch in that neighborhood. Also check out Section 13, "Upper East Side/Yorkville," for a review of **Mumbles,** as there's another location in Gramercy Park, at 603 Second Ave., at 33rd Street (tel. 889-0750).

ALBUQUERQUE EATS, 375 Third Ave., at 27th St. Tel. 683-6500.
   Cuisine: MEXICAN. **Reservations:** Accepted only for large parties. **Subway:** 6 to 28th St.
$ Prices: Appetizers $4–$6.95; main courses $9.95–$16. AE, MC, V.
   Open: Daily 11:30am–1am; brunch served Sat–Sun 11:30am–4pm.

Towering over the handsome wood bar is a stuffed bison and at the top of a black metal staircase sits an authentic Sioux Indian water tank. While waiting for your meal, you can people-watch or create a masterpiece with crayons on your paper table covering.

For starters, we recommend the montaña de nachos azules, a "mountain" of blue-corn tortillas baked with three cheeses and served with salsa and guacamole. Also, try the guacamole cruda or the Mexican fish stew (sopa de pescada). Ensalada Albuquerque is a work of art: Plentiful slices of avocado and fruit are arrayed on a bed of spinach. (In warm weather, enjoy luscious melon, kiwi, and orange.) The obeja barbacoa—grilled lamb rubbed with garlic and herbs, and marinated with a Mexican barbecue sauce—is a highly recommended main course, and we enjoyed the ever-popular chimichangas. Dessert choices include flan almendrado and adobe mud cake.

If you visit Albuquerque Eats at night, be sure to check out the Rodeo Bar next door (formerly Albuquerque Drinks), with live country music every night until the wee hours of the morning.

AMERICA, 9–13 E. 18th St., between Fifth Ave. and Broadway. Tel. 505-2110.
   Cuisine: AMERICAN. **Reservations:** Recommended. **Subway:** 4, 5, 6, N, R, L to 14th St./Union Square.
$ Prices: Appetizers $4.95–$7.95; main courses $8–$20. AE, MC, V.
   Open: Daily 11am–3am.
America is big, big, big—the seating capacity is 400—so, unlike many New York establishments, the diner has ample elbow room. One of the hottest spots in town, America offers fun and a good meal at low prices. You'll find no sign outside, so look instead for the raised star standard out front. The dining area is lit by track lights that accentuate the high ceilings and the Art Deco murals on the walls. Strips of red-and-white neon tubes stream along the ceiling above a center walkway that separates the dining room into halves. Late-nighters lounge around the raised bar in the back that stretches nearly the width of the room.

The menu conjures up a taste of Americana, with a variety of dishes from all four corners of the country, including burgers, pasta dishes, and many varieties of pizza. Try the Tex-Mex fajitas with a generous portion of marinated beef grilled on charcoal, served with sour cream, salsa sauce, and tortillas for wrapping it all up. We couldn't resist the Cajun oyster po' boy sandwich, served with coleslaw and spuds. Move over a few states and partake of New Mexican pulled-chicken casserole with corn chiles, tomatoes, and three cheeses served with warm tortillas and salsa. A meal from a little farther north might be the grilled Jersey pork chops with onions, gravy, and sautéed apples. The good old all-American hamburger is also available, of course.

CEDARS OF LEBANON, 39 E. 30th St., between Park and Madison aves. Tel. 725-9251.
  Cuisine: MIDDLE EASTERN. **Reservations:** Recommended, especially Fri–Sat. **Subway:** 6 to 33rd St.
  $ Prices: Appetizers $3–$6; main courses $8–$13.95. AE, MC, V.
  Open: Mon–Tues and Thurs–Sun noon–11pm, Wed noon–2am, Fri–Sat noon–3am.
This Middle Eastern restaurant is named after the national symbol of Lebanon. Past the green awning, the bar is black and padded, and the walls are covered with textured wallpaper. The dining room is simple and spacious, with red-cushioned chairs, white linens, oil paintings, and gold-toned wallpaper with a tree motif.
  A weekday lunch special includes soup, a choice of main dish (such as shish kebab, lamb chops, and keftah kebab), baklava for dessert, and American coffee. With pita bread, a variety of appetizers can be a full meal—you can order hummus (mashed chickpeas with sesame), falafel (deep-fried vegetable burgers), and tabouli (chopped parsley, mint, and scallions). Main courses include grape leaves stuffed with minted lamb and a seafood kebab. On Fridays and Saturdays, entertainment (dancers and musicians) starts at 10pm.

CURRY IN A HURRY, 130 E. 29th St., between Lexington and Third aves. Tel. 889-1159.
  Cuisine: INDIAN/PAKISTANI/BANGLADESHI. **Reservations:** Not accepted. **Subway:** 6 to 28th St.
  $ Prices: Main courses $2.75–$5.75. AE, CB, DC, MC, V.
  Open: Mon–Sat 11:30am–9pm; Sun and hols 11:30am–8pm.
  This no-frills, fast-food place is decorated with mirrored walls, brown dinette chairs, and brown Formica tables. The linoleum floor is well worn, but everything is clean. You'll often see Indian families eating here. There's a small steam table, which fills the room with the smell of cumin, and you'll order from the overhead menu. A platter of beef or chicken curry, with one vegetable curry, pilaf rice with vegetables, bread, and salad makes a filling, fast meal. The special beef or chicken curry, pakora (a savory fritter) or a kebab, a vegetable curry, pilaf rice, bread, and salad can be yours for less than $8.

DENO'S PLACE, 155 E. 26th St., corner of Third Ave. Tel. 725-9386.
  Cuisine: GREEK. **Reservations:** Recommended. **Subway:** 6 to 23rd or 28th sts.
  $ Prices: Appetizers $4.95–$6.95; main courses $7.95–$14.95. AE, MC, V.
  Open: Mon–Fri 11:30am–midnight; Sat–Sun 4pm–midnight.
With its lovely brick and ironwork, Deno's Place is very Victorian. The glass-enclosed Corner Café is white and summery inside, with green cushions on white bentwood chairs, lots of flowers, a few small antique carousel horses in the corner window, white wrought iron, a terra-cotta tile floor, and white latticework and a stained-glass effect on the ceiling. For lunch, you might want to share an appetizer of mussels marinara, before moving onto fettuccine with meat sauce or red or white clam sauce. A classic Greek moussaka with eggplant, ground beef, and béchamel sauce is another especially good buy. Our favorite dinner main dish is beyond our budget but worth a splurge—frutta di mare includes shrimp, clams, mussels, calamari, scallops, and

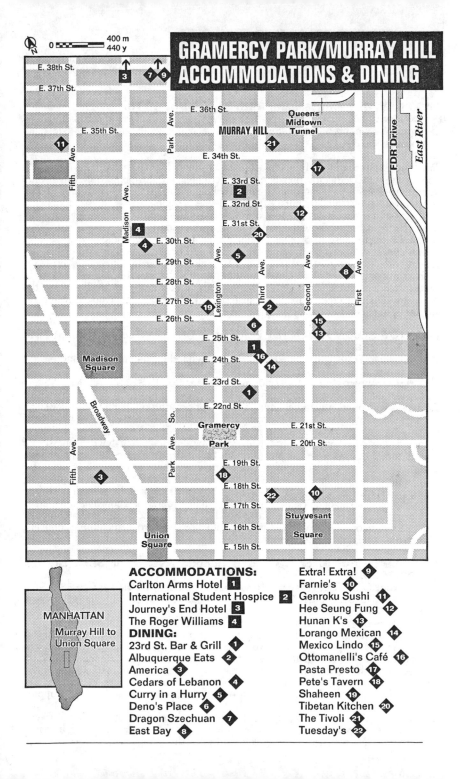

GRAMERCY PARK/MURRAY HILL ACCOMMODATIONS & DINING

0 400 m
440 y

E. 38th St.
E. 37th St.
E. 36th St.
E. 35th St.
E. 34th St.
E. 33rd St.
E. 32nd St.
E. 31st St.
E. 30th St.
E. 29th St.
E. 28th St.
E. 27th St.
E. 26th St.
E. 25th St.
E. 24th St.
E. 23rd St.
E. 22nd St.
E. 21st St.
E. 20th St.
E. 19th St.
E. 18th St.
E. 17th St.
E. 16th St.
E. 15th St.

MURRAY HILL
Queens Midtown Tunnel
FDR Drive
East River
Madison Square
Gramercy Park
Union Square
Stuyvesant Square

Fifth Ave.
Park Ave.
Madison Ave.
Lexington Ave.
Third Ave.
Second Ave.
First Ave.
Broadway
Park Ave. So.

MANHATTAN
Murray Hill to Union Square

ACCOMMODATIONS:
Carlton Arms Hotel **1**
International Student Hospice **2**
Journey's End Hotel **3**
The Roger Williams **4**

DINING:
23rd St. Bar & Grill **1**
Albuquerque Eats **2**
America **3**
Cedars of Lebanon **4**
Curry in a Hurry **5**
Deno's Place **6**
Dragon Szechuan **7**
East Bay **8**

Extra! Extra! **9**
Farnie's **10**
Genroku Sushi **11**
Hee Seung Fung **12**
Hunan K's **13**
Lorango Mexican **14**
Mexico Lindo **15**
Ottomanelli's Café **16**
Pasta Presto **17**
Pete's Tavern **18**
Shaheen **19**
Tibetan Kitchen **20**
The Tivoli **21**
Tuesday's **22**

octopus, served over a bed of lettuce. Other choices are tortellini and veal parmigiana. For dessert you shouldn't miss the chocolate-mousse cake, with a cappuccino or espresso on the side.

EAST BAY, 491 First Ave., at 29th St. Tel. 683-7770.

Cuisine: AMERICAN. **Reservations:** Not needed. **Subway:** 6 to 28th St.

$ Prices: Appetizers $1.60–$6.50; burgers and sandwiches $2.40–$7; main courses $5.75–$13.75. No credit cards.

Open: Daily 24 hours.

East Bay is clean and spiffy, with no worn corners. The spacious interior is Early American, with Delft-look tiles behind the counter, comfortable booths with blue seats, a brick floor, paneling, and a beamed ceiling with chandeliers. The dining room is often full of doctors and nurses from Bellevue Hospital across the street.

The menu is almost as big as the dining room—over 250 budget-priced items. It's a good bet for breakfast, with challah bread French toast, bagels served with Nova Scotia lox, and cheese or blueberry blintzes. There are dozens of sandwiches, from cream cheese and jelly to fried filet of flounder. The triple deckers are enormous, served with fries, pickles, and coleslaw. More elaborate main courses are available, such as a boneless breast of chicken with scampi sauce, a broiled halibut steak in butter sauce, or prime lamb chops in mint jelly. Cakes and pies are baked on the premises. The egg creams are made just right, or you can order up an ice-cream sundae. There is a full bar.

FARNIE'S SECOND AVENUE STEAK PARLOR, 311 Second Ave., at 18th St. Tel. 228-9280.

Cuisine: STEAK. **Reservations:** Recommended for parties of 3 or more only.

Subway: 4, 5, 6, N, R, L to Union Square.

$ Prices: Appetizers $6.25–$7.50; main courses $9.95–$22.95. AE, MC, V.

Open: Daily 11:30am–10:30pm.

Farnie's is well on its way to becoming a New York institution. For a thick juicy steak or barbecued ribs at reasonable prices, it's hard to beat. In the window is a beef chart—a sure sign of serious eating. Inside it's decorated for fun: the walls are carpeted, mirrored, and cluttered with memorabilia, including huge likenesses of Laurel and Hardy, Charlie Chaplin, and W. C. Fields, oversize coins, and authentic advertisements from the turn of the century. The whole atmosphere is old New York—bustling and a little offbeat. Dinner main dishes include chopped sirloin steak, barbecued spareribs, a junior sirloin, and charbroiled chicken. A lobster tail or shrimp scampi, plus a choice of chicken, ribs, or sole can be ordered as a combination platter. Dinner main courses come with a large bowl of salad, garlic bread, and a choice of french fries, onion rings, baked potato, vegetable, or spaghetti. Lunch brings omelets, ribs, steaks, sole, and hamburgers.

HEE SEUNG FUNG, or HSF, 578 Second Ave., near 32nd St. Tel. 689-6969.

Cuisine: CHINESE. **Reservations:** Recommended. **Subway:** 6 to 33rd St.

$ Prices: Appetizers $1–$4.95; main courses $6.95–$9.95; dim sum items $2–$2.75. AE, MC, V.

Open: Sun–Thurs 11:30am–11:30pm; Fri–Sat 11:30am–12:30am.

Dim sum is the venerable Hong Kong tradition of dining on many tidbits, and it literally means to point to what your heart wants most. Hee Seung Fung, the companion of a famed Chinatown restaurant, is civilized indeed. You pick from a cart, or order from the special menu (ask). HSF is very elegant, very hi-tech, with subdued browns and whites, thick linens, and columned walls. Set way back from the hurly-burly street (Hee Seung Fung is in one of the few suburban-looking shopping arcades in Manhattan), lunching here is a real respite. Dim sum morsels are not inexpensive—they can add up quickly—but keep in mind that three or four will satisfy most people. Among the delectables: beef shiu mai, stuffed crab claws, shredded chicken roll, crispy spring roll, and pork dumplings.

HUNAN K'S, 455 Second Ave., between 25th and 26th Sts. Tel. 689-3857.
Cuisine: CHINESE. **Reservations:** Required for large parties. **Subway:** 6 to 23rd St.
$ Prices: Appetizers $1.50–$7.95; main courses $7.50–$18. AE, CB, DC, MC, V.
Open: Mon–Thurs 11:30am–11pm; Fri–Sat 11:30am–midnight; Sun 1–11pm.
Hunan K's is a good place for lunch, when the weekday special is less than $7. You get a choice of 22 main dishes, including pork and broccoli with garlic sauce, spicy beef and Buddhist delight, a choice of white or fried rice, a choice of soup or an eggroll, and a pot of tea. A fortune cookie and a dish of delicious caramelized walnuts follow your meal. Another charming gesture: With new customers, owner Kent Huang sometimes brings over a complimentary cordial of plum wine and toasts you!

At dinner many main courses under $9 are available. But you can't beat the luncheon special. The service here is fast, attentive, and friendly. The restaurant itself is pleasantly decorated, with cane chairs, brown tablecloths, and fabric roses in bud vases on each table.

LORANGO MEXICAN RESTAURANT AND BAR, 321 Third Ave., at 24th St. Tel. 679-1122.
Cuisine: MEXICAN. **Reservations:** Not needed. **Subway:** 6 to 23rd St.
$ Prices: Appetizers $2.50–$4.95; main courses $6.50–$13.95. AE, CB, DC, MC, V.
Open: Lunch daily 11:30am–5pm; dinner daily 5pm–midnight; Sun brunch 11:30am–4pm.
This long room with large windows overlooking the street offers plenty of opportunity for young professionals to size up the competition. Lorango serves up authentic Mexican food—for starters try the quesadillas, and you get three soft flour tortillas filled with cheese. Single-main-dish dinners are best for the budget, but if you're feeling ravenous, double-main-dish combinations—from a choice of tacos, enchiladas, tostadas, or burritos, with rice and beans on the side—offer a ton of food. Wash it down with Dos Equis beer.

MEXICO LINDO, 459 Second Ave., at 26th St. Tel. 679-3665.
Cuisine: MEXICAN. **Reservations:** Not needed. **Subway:** 6 to 28th St.
$ Prices: Appetizers $3.99–$5.94; main courses $9.75–$32. $10 minimum per person. AE, MC, V.
Open: Mon–Thurs noon–11pm, Fri–Sat noon–midnight, Sun 3–11pm.
Fresh flowers, pink table linen, red brick, and a beamed ceiling create a convivial ambience at Mexico Lindo. Amber lamps, a terra-cotta tiled floor, and attractive oil paintings add to the south-of-the-border atmosphere. And the strolling guitarists who perform most nights will win your heart.

Menus are similar at lunch and dinner. There are almost 20 combination platters with favorites like tacos, chicken enchiladas with green sauce and sour cream, and tamales. There's seafood, too, including four spicy shrimp main dishes, and we recommend the flan for dessert.

OTTOMANELLI'S CAFÉ, 337 Third Ave., at 25th St. Tel. 532-2929.
Cuisine: AMERICAN/ITALIAN. **Reservations:** Not needed. **Subway:** 6 to 23rd St.
$ Prices: Appetizers $2.95–$4.50; main courses $6.75–$9.75. MC, V.
Open: Mon–Sat 11:30am–10:30pm; Sun noon–10pm.
This unpretentious neighborhood spot specializes in pasta (made from scratch each morning with recipes that Angelica Ottomanelli, the owners' mother, learned from her mother in Bari, Italy), burgers, and pan pizza. The decor is simple and homey, done up in green with lots of hanging plants.

The menu is limited, but the food is good and plentiful. Burgers are served with irresistible cross-hatch fries; the chicken parmigiana is cooked to perfection, and comes with spaghetti and garlic bread; or there's veal-sausage marinara and tortellini Alfredo. Finish your meal with fresh coffee and a slice of chocolate-mousse cake.

There are 13 other branches of Ottomanelli's scattered throughout Manhattan, including one at 119 E. 18th St., between Park Avenue South and Irving Place.

PASTA PRESTO, 513 Second Ave., between 33rd and 34th sts. Tel. 889-4131.
> **Cuisine:** ITALIAN. **Reservations:** Not accepted. **Subway:** 6 to 33rd St.
> **$ Prices:** Appetizers $2.50–$5.95; main courses $6.95–$12.95. AE, MC, V.
> **Open:** Daily noon–11:30pm.

This place is popular with the natives. Prices are reasonable, and the decor is cheerful and inviting. You step down into a room of white-brick walls, trimmed in red, with a white stucco ceiling and, in summer, old-fashioned ceiling fans.

Among the appetizers, we like the fresh mozzarella and sun-dried tomatoes or the fusilli and curried chicken breast. Try the whole-wheat linguine with spinach, mushrooms, and sun-dried tomato pesto, or the spaghetti bolognese. Another popular item is the fettuccine and Italian sausage in Dijon mustard. The dessert selection features a creamy cheesecake and Key lime pie.

PETE'S TAVERN, 129 E. 18th St., corner of Irving Place. Tel. 473-7676.
> **Cuisine:** PUB GRUB. **Reservations:** Recommended. **Subway:** 4, 5, 6, N, R, L to Union Square.
> **$ Prices:** Main courses $8.50–$22. AE, CB, DC, MC, V.
> **Open:** Lunch daily 11:30am–3pm; dinner Sun–Thurs 3–11:45pm, Fri–Sat 11:30am–12:45am; brunch Sat–Sun 11am–4pm.

Opened in 1864, Pete's Tavern is the oldest bar in New York City. Originally known as Healy's Bar, Pete's (bought in 1935 by Pete De Bella) was a Tammany Hall meeting place. During Prohibition it was one of New York's most notorious speakeasies, operating from behind a storefront florist's shop. Pete's also has a notable literary history—O. Henry penned "Gift of the Magi" while sitting in the very first booth after you enter the main doorway. Butch Cassidy and the Sundance Kid reputedly ate at Pete's, and President Kennedy dined here when he was staying in the Gramercy Park Hotel.

Although the original eating area has been expanded (the two back rooms used to be stables), Pete's has retained the feel of a real neighborhood tavern. Its authentic pub appearance—the original tin ceiling, tile floor, rosewood bar, and walls cluttered with photographs taken over the past 60 years—has made it a prime set location for TV commercials and films: the Miller Lite ads are filmed here; a scene from *Ragtime* (with James Cagney) was shot here. Today it's a melting pot for politicians, policemen, tourists, actors, sports figures . . . the list goes on.

Menu prices can go as high as $22 for a 16-ounce sirloin steak, so stick with the more reasonably priced burgers and pasta dishes. Pete's is famous for its 10-ounce burgers, served with fries, coleslaw, lettuce, and tomato. Main dishes—served with baked potato, a mixed green salad (ask for the house dressing, a creamy herb blend), or a side of spaghetti—include eggplant parmigiana, filet of sole broiled or fried, and London broil with mushroom sauce.

The most popular dessert, and we think deservedly so, is the Mississippi mud pie. There is also chocolate cheesecake, rum cake, and zabaglione, a mixture of eggs, sugar, and wine served hot.

A weekend brunch menu includes the drink of your choice, main dish (an omelet with fries and French toast with bacon are among the choices), and coffee or tea, all for $9.

SHAHEEN, 99 Lexington Ave., corner of 27th St. Tel. 683-2139.
> **Cuisine:** INDIAN. **Reservations:** Not accepted. **Subway:** 6 to 28th St.
> **$ Prices:** All items under $9. AE, MC, V.
> **Open:** Daily 11am–10:30pm.

Shaheen is a little Pakistani cafeteria, with piped-in Indian music overhead, but almost no decoration. The menu is on the wall—a half plate of lamb or chicken curry, rice, a piece of bread, and raita (yogurt) or dhal (lentil sauce) is a filling meal for well under $10. Niharee, a beef curry, with two pieces of nan (or naan) bread and dhal is $6.

Snacks and sweets are the real treats here: there are Pakistani doughnuts, jalabi (a sweet pretzel of sugar and flour), kheer mohan (deep-fried cottage cheese with cream on top), coconut and cheese balls, and several kinds of halvah, including pistachio, milk fudge, pink, almond fudge, and many more.

THE TIBETAN KITCHEN, 444 Third Ave., at 31st St. Tel. 679-6286.

Cuisine: TIBETAN. **Reservations:** Recommended. **Subway:** 6 to 33rd St.
$ Prices: Main courses $5.75–$8.50. No credit cards.
Open: Dinner daily 5:30–10:30pm.

There are only a few seats, but the servings are generous and the prices reasonable in The Tibetan Kitchen. Try the Himalayan khatsa—spicy hot cauliflower, fresh leeks, and bean curd, served cold on green leaf and hot bread. Or warm yourself up with a cup of thang soup, a delicious spinach-and-egg-drop concoction. Another traditional Tibetan beverage is bocha, a buttered and salted tea (served by the pot), which is a perfect dessert complement to deysee—a steamed sweet rice with raisins, served with cold yogurt.

TUESDAY'S, 190 Third Ave., 17th St. Tel. 533-7900.

Cuisine: AMERICAN. **Reservations:** Not needed. **Subway:** 4, 5, 6, N, R, L to Union Square.
$ Prices: Appetizers $3–$10; main courses $5.95–$15.95. AE, DC, MV, Transmedia, V.
Open: Daily 11:30am–midnight.

During the days of Prohibition, Tuesday's was a meeting place for showbiz types, and the restaurant still contains secret panels everywhere. The atmosphere is one of nostalgia for the racy days of yesteryear; black-and-white photographs of celebrities, inscribed to Joe "the Judge" King (who ran the speakeasy) line the walls.

The menu (encased in a black marble "tablet") is large and varied, and includes a special selection of vegetarian platters, ranging from a tossed salad to vegetable primavera. For a main dish, try the Oriental-style chicken, roasted in soy sauce, ginger, garlic, and sesame oil, or, if you're in the mood for something lighter, the shrimp-and-avocado salad. Most main dishes come with a large tossed salad, a delicious loaf of sesame bread, and potato or vegetable. For dessert we especially recommend the southern-style pecan pie, served warm and with a dollop of whipped cream.

For weekend brunch, you get a choice of omelet, eggs Benedict, or quiche, with French toast or fresh nut bread, potatoes, juice, and all the champagne you can drink. Guest jazz artists perform while you eat, though we're told the music can get a little loud.

Fat Tuesday's, located in the basement, serves up great jazz music every night (see Chapter 10, "New York City Nights").

THE 23RD STREET BAR AND GRILL, 158 E. 23rd St., between Third and Lexington aves. Tel. 533-8877.

Cuisine: AMERICAN. **Reservations:** Recommended. **Subway:** 6 to 23rd St.
$ Prices: Main courses $5.95–$16.95. AE, MC, V.
Open: Bar and restaurant daily noon–3am.

This lively meeting place attracts a young professional crowd after work. Turn-of-the-century molded-tin ceilings and the curved wooden bar and high stools create a Roaring '20s atmosphere. In fact, the bar was used in a scene in the movie *Cotton Club*.

The dining room, complete with green tables and Art Deco lamps, is located in the rear. The menu is the same for lunch and dinner. Burgers are large, and the smoked turkey with mozzarella, served with potato salad, is a particularly tasty sandwich. There are several salads on the menu—we like the pasta salad with Dijon dressing. Among the main dishes, served with vegetable and potato, the batter-fried chicken and broiled filet of sole are good choices.

Weekend brunch brings selections like omelets, eggs Benedict, and French toast with ham, sausage, or bacon, and maple syrup.

MURRAY HILL

DRAGON SZECHUAN, 338 Lexington Ave., between 39th and 40th sts. Tel. 370-9647.
   Cuisine: CHINESE. **Reservations:** Recommended. **Subway:** 4, 5, 6 to Grand Central.
   $ Prices: Appetizers $1–$6; main courses $6.95–$12.95. AE, CB, DC, MC, V.
   Open: Mon–Fri 11:30am–10pm, Sat–Sun 12:30–10pm.

Decorated in bright Oriental reds and greens, Dragon Szechuan sports flowers on the tables and traditional tasseled lamps hanging from the ceiling of the narrow room. We recommend going at lunchtime, when main courses are 50¢ to $1 less. For an appetizer, try sharing a dish of cold noodles with nutty-tasting sesame sauce. The menu also has two "king-size" main dishes that are easily shared: the Buddhist delight, a medley of sautéed vegetables, or the sweet-and-sour combination of pork, shrimp, and chicken.

EXTRA! EXTRA!, in the Daily News Building, 767 Second Ave., at 41st St. Tel. 490-2900.
   Cuisine: AMERICAN. **Reservations:** Not needed. **Subway:** 4, 5, 6 to 42nd St.
   $ Prices: Main courses $9.95–$14.95. AE, DC, MC, Transmedia, V.
   Open: Mon–Fri 11:30am–10:30pm; Sat 5pm–1am; Sun noon–4pm.

More than a cute theme restaurant with snippets of newsprint and headlines comprising the decor, Extra! Extra!, under new management, offers an astonishingly good menu, with a variety of pastas, pizzas, and seafood dishes. Watch for the nightly specials, ranging from special pasta offerings to a margarita night.

GENROKU SUSHI, 366 Fifth Ave., between 34th and 35th sts. Tel. 947-7940.
   Cuisine: JAPANESE. **Reservations:** Not accepted. **Subway:** B, D, N, R to 34th St.
   $ Prices: All items under $10. No credit cards.
   Open: Daily 11am–8pm.

Extraordinary is the only word for this completely automated and crowded Chinese/Japanese restaurant. The chain is the brainstorm of Taiwanese fast-food magnate Kin Syo Chin, who brings a modern efficiency to the old Hong Kong dim sum. You sit on backless stools at a Formica counter, as food travels by on an oval conveyor belt from the kitchen. What you like, you take, and at the end the waitress counts up your plates and gives you the tab.

   Among the many choices are Japanese miso soup (clear broth) and tempura, Chinese chop suey, fried rice, fried chicken, and lots of sushi—tuna, shrimp, salmon, octopus, egg, mackerel, squid, and so on. It's clanky and clattery, but great fun.

THE TIVOLI, 515 Third Ave., between 34th and 35th sts. Tel. 532-3300.
   Cuisine: AMERICAN. **Reservations:** Not needed. **Subway:** 6 to 33rd St.
   $ Prices: Burgers and sandwiches $3.50–$6.95; main courses $6.95–$14.95. AE, MC, V.
   Open: Daily 24 hours.

Tivoli is a first-rate coffee shop. In the heart of Murray Hill, it's worth a short walk from the 34th Street stores (Macy's, Herald Square Center, or A&S). The Tivoli is spotless and modern, with a long wooden counter up front and tile floors. The dining room in back seems almost private and is quite attractive—blond-wood tables, fresh flowers, brass, a mirrored back wall, and Ultrasuede-like seats. The food is excellent, and the Tivoli has nice touches, like a basket of pickles at each table.

   Sandwiches include everything from tuna or chicken salad to a turkey club or a burger with fries. Most main dishes—seafood, steaks, Italian pastas, chicken, and chops—cost under $11. Daily specials include the likes of moussaka with a vegetable and salad, or roast chicken. Our favorite seafood dish is stuffed filet of sole with crabmeat. Fresh fish is available every day.

9. MIDTOWN WEST

In the area encompassing the Broadway theater district and the "Diamond District" is an abundance of restaurant discoveries for the budget traveler. Midtown West is bounded roughly by 40th Street on the south, 57th Street on the north, Fifth Avenue on the east, and Ninth Avenue on the west. This is prime territory for sampling Thai or South American food.

ARRIBA ARRIBA!, 762 Ninth Ave., between 51st and 52nd sts. Tel. 489-0810.
   Cuisine: MEXICAN. **Reservations:** Not needed. **Subway:** A, C, E to 50th St.
$ **Prices:** Appetizers $2.95–$7.25; main courses $6.95–$12.45. AE, CB, DC, MC, Transmedia, V.
   Open: Daily noon–midnight; brunch served Sat–Sun noon–4pm.
Arriba Arriba!, sitting behind a bright yellow exterior, feeds young professionals and theater types who enjoy the socializing as much as the margaritas and the nachos.
   While dining at pink-linen-covered tables, surrounded by colorful Mexican murals, you can enjoy a combination platter, choosing from tacos, tostadas, burritos, enchiladas, or tamales, all with refried beans and rice on the side. If you still have room, finish with homemade flan—an authentic Mexican recipe of rich custard covered with brandy-caramel sauce—or buñuelos, deep-fried flour tortillas dusted in cinnamon and sugar, topped with chocolate or vanilla ice cream. Brunch features five different selections with a cocktail and coffee, and $5.95 lunch specials are served from noon to 4pm on weekdays. Happy hour is from 4 to 6:30pm, and Mondays bring "Margarita Madness," with half-price drink specials.

BANGKOK CUISINE, 885 Eighth Ave., between 52nd and 53rd sts. Tel. 664-8488.
   Cuisine: THAI. **Reservations:** Recommended. **Subway:** 1, 9 to 50th St.
$ **Prices:** Appetizers $3.75–$9.95; main courses $8.95–$17.95. AE, DC, MC, V
   Open: Mon–Sat 11:30am–11:30pm; Sun 5–11:30pm.
The first Thai restaurant to open in New York is still one of the most popular. Bangkok Cuisine sports metallic paintings on sleek black walls, Thai figurines, and huge fish tanks. (You can't help but feel you're in an opium den.) The center tables are close enough for eavesdropping.
   You might begin with Thai spring rolls or crispy squid tempura served with lime sauce. For an unusual spicy main course, try the generous portion of minced pork with lime juice and peanuts, served on a bed of iceberg lettuce. There's also Double Delight—chicken and shrimp in a mild chili paste sauce, with baby corn, straw mushrooms, and scallions. Slightly more expensive, but a real treat, is roast duck with the chef's special sauce. For vegetarians or those on a stricter budget, meatless dishes include sautéed mixed vegetables with hot curry and sautéed bean curd.

LA BONNE SOUPE, 48 W. 55th St., between Fifth and Sixth aves. Tel. 586-7650.
   Cuisine: FRENCH. **Reservations:** Accepted for parties of 6 or more. **Subway:** B, Q, N, R to 57th St.
$ **Prices:** Appetizers $3.25–$4.95; main courses $5.95–$15.75. $7 minimum per person; $10 credit card minimum. AE.
   Open: Daily 11am–midnight.
The charming second-floor terrace overlooking 55th Street is the prime dining area at La Bonne Soupe on a nice day. A quaint bistro ambience is created with low ceilings, subdued lighting, and red-and-white-checked tablecloths. You'll pass a small bar in back if you go upstairs to dine on the outdoor verandah or to view the restaurant's collection of Haitian primitive paintings on the upstairs walls.

There is one low-priced menu for lunch and dinner. Omelets come with such imaginative fillings as ratatouille or Gruyère cheese. Soups, served with bread, salad, dessert, and wine or coffee, make a complete meal—we loved the crème andalouse, a tomato-based cream of vegetable, and the traditional onion soup. Assorted pâté served with Brie, salad, and a glass of wine can satisfy light appetites. You can't go wrong with the poulet chasseur: chicken in a piquant sauce of mushrooms, tomatoes, shallots, and white wine. Finish by casting your calorie count to the winds with a fondue chocolat or crème caramel.

CABANA CARIOCA, 123 W. 45th St., between Sixth Ave. and Broadway. Tel. 581-8088.
   Cuisine: BRAZILIAN/PORTUGUESE. **Reservations:** Recommended. **Subway:** 1, 2, 3, 9 to Times Square.
   $ Prices: Appetizers $1.75–$6.95; main courses $5.95–$16.95; all-you-can-eat buffet special $8.95 adults, $5.95 children. CB, DC, MC, V.
   Open: Lunch Mon–Fri 11:45am–4pm; dinner Mon–Sat 4pm–midnight; brunch Sat–Sun 11am–4pm.

The highly recommended Cabana Carioca is one of the least expensive and certainly the most vibrant of midtown's Brazilian restaurants. The upstairs section, where the buffet specials are served, is almost as colorful as the tiles and brightly painted folkloric scenes at the entryway. A large window overlooking 45th Street is filled with plants, the walls are hung with oil paintings by a South American artist, and the tables are gaily covered with yellow linen cloths and brown napkins.

Start with a traditional appetizer—the linguica frita, hearts of palm salad, or canja de galinha (chicken soup). The main dish portions, testing the limits of human capacity, are served with rice, more black beans than you can eat, and a basket of fresh bread. The Brazilian national dish, feijoada completa, is a stew of black beans, pork, beef, and sausage; and there's a special fried chicken, galinha frita a canoca. All of this must of course be accompanied by a round of caipirinhas, a potent mix of sugarcane liquor over crushed limes and sugar.

CANCUN, 937 Eighth Ave., near 55th St. Tel. 307-7307.
   Cuisine: MEXICAN. **Reservations:** Recommended on weekends. **Subway:** 1, 9, A, C, D to 59th St.
   $ Prices: Appetizers $2.75–$4.50; main courses $7.95–$12.95. AE, DC, DISC, MC, V.
   Open: Sun–Thurs 11:30am–midnight; Fri–Sat 11:30am–1am.
Located across the street from Caramba! (below), Cancun offers tasty and reasonably priced—if not authentically Tex-Mex—food. While the owners/chefs are not Mexican, they come with experience from other New York Mexican restaurants.

Start out with nachos, topped with chorizo or jalapeño. Cancun has combo plates, with a choice of enchiladas, tacos, tamales, burritos, or tostadas—any two come with rice and beans for $7.95, any three for $9.95 if you're ravenous. There are also Mexican-flavored casseroles of eggplant and beef, vegetarian enchiladas, and seafood main dishes like shrimp with salsa verde. For "gringos" who don't like chili and cumin, there are burgers and California chicken, sautéed in wine. The bar offers margarita specials during happy hour.

CARAMBA!, 918 Eighth Ave., at 55th St. Tel. 245-7910.
   Cuisine: MEXICAN. **Reservations:** Not needed. **Subway:** 1, 9, A, C, D to 59th St.
   $ Prices: Appetizers $2.95–$6.95; main courses $5.95–$9.95; brunch $7.95. AE, CB, DC, MC, V.
   Open: Lunch Mon–Fri noon–4pm; dinner daily 4pm–midnight; brunch Sat–Sun noon–4pm.
Texans, Californians, and others "in the know" will complain that there is no real Mexican food in New York (Mexicans will agree), but Caramba! is among the city's best. Enjoy the festive, colorful decor of woven wall hangings, Indian masks, rustic

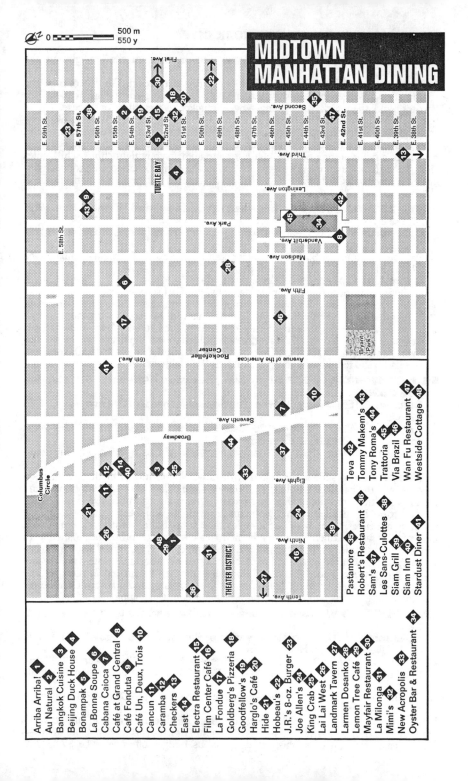

MIDTOWN MANHATTAN DINING

500 m
550 y

Arriba Arriba! 1
Au Natural 2
Bangkok Cuisine 3
Beijing Duck House 4
Bonampak 5
La Bonne Soupe 6
Cabana Caioca 7
Café at Grand Central 8
Café Fonduta 9
Café Un, Deux, Trois 10
Cancun 11
Caramba 12
Checkers 13
East 14
Electra Restaurant 15
Film Center Café 16
La Fondue 17
Goldberg's Pizzeria 18
Goodfellow's 19
Harglo's Café 20
Hide 21
Hobeau's 22
J.R.'s 8-oz. Burger 23
Joe Allen's 24
King Crab 25
Lai Lai West 26
Landmark Tavern 27
Larmen Dosanko 28
Lemon Tree Café 29
Mayfair Restaurant 30
La Milonga 31
Mimi's 32
New Acropolis 33
Oyster Bar & Restaurant 34

Pastamore 35
Robert's Restaurant 36
Sam's 37
Les Sans-Culottes 38
Siam Grill 39
Siam Inn 40
Stardust Diner 41

Teva 42
Tommy Makem's 43
Tony Roma's 44
Trattoria 45
Via Brazil 46
Wan Fu Restaurant 47
Westside Cottage 48

cement floors, and pink linen tablecloths. Or eat beneath the skylight on the patio-garden.

Forget about authenticity and fill up on truly tasty food. Go for one of the combination plates; first choose whether you'd like tacos, enchiladas, tostadas, or burritos, and then pick your filling—beef, chicken, vegetables, or cheese. Arrive hungry; with beans and rice on the side, you'll be leaving stuffed. We also liked the enchiladas de mariscos, two enchiladas with sautéed seafood in a cream sauce and topped with melted cheese and sour cream. The $7.95 brunch comes with a margarita, a mimosa, or a Bloody Mary; for a main dish you might choose chilaquiles chapultepec (chicken sautéed with onions and cilantro in green sauce and topped with melted cheese) or a Caramba omelet, made with chorizo, red pepper, onion, and fresh chilies.

EAST, 251 W. 55th St., between Broadway and Eighth Ave. Tel. 581-2240.

Cuisine: JAPANESE. **Reservations:** Recommended for dinner. **Subway:** 1, 9, A, C, D to 59th St.

$ Prices: Appetizers $3.50–$7; main courses $6.50–$10; sushi combinations $7.50–$11. Credit card minimum $10. AE, CB, DC, MC, V.

Open: Lunch daily noon–2:30pm; dinner daily 5–11pm.

Budget Japanese food is hard to come by, but East serves excellent selections at reasonable prices. We were refreshed by the traditional steaming hot towels handed to us when we sat down. Lunch main dishes come with soup, a small salad, and rice. We began with the exceptional negima, tender beef and scallions broiled in teriyaki sauce, and our favorite sushi selection was the negi hama maki, with yellowtail and scallion. The East Gourmet Box is a good deal—for $8.50, you'll get soup, salad, rice, tempura, chicken teriyaki, and a California roll.

FILM CENTER CAFÉ, 635 Ninth Ave., between 44th and 45th sts. Tel. 262-2525.

Cuisine: INTERNATIONAL. **Reservations:** Not needed. **Subway:** A, C, E to 42nd St.

$ Prices: Appetizers $4.50–$6.25; salads and sandwiches $6.50–$7.95; main courses $8.50–$13.95. No credit cards.

Open: Lunch Mon–Fri noon–5pm; dinner Sun–Fri 5pm–midnight, Sat 5pm–12:30am.

This very Art Deco spot is decorated with movie logos and mementos, with neon touches over the bar. The whole effect is clean, simple, and inviting, with booths and tables, a multicolored tile ceiling, and background tunes from the 1950s and '60s.

The food is imaginative and homemade, with a Thai beef salad offered as a tempting appetizer, along with classics like onion soup, buffalo wings, and crab cakes. One of our favorites here is a very French steak tartare of prime beef, filled with capers, onions, radishes, parsley, and a delicate mix of spices, served with fries. But you might also be lured by the Cajun chicken, a steamed vegetable plate with rice and peanut curry sauce, and the roasted Cornish game hen marinated in olive oil and cayenne pepper. Desserts include frozen chocolate mousse and a fantastic fruit salad that includes kiwi, banana, papaya, orange, grapes, and pineapple.

LA FONDUE, 43 W. 55th St., between Fifth and Sixth aves. Tel. 581-0820.

Cuisine: CONTINENTAL. **Reservations:** Recommended. **Subway:** B, D, F to Rockefeller Center; N, R to 57th St.

$ Prices: Appetizers $2.95–$4.75; lunch specials $7.45; "light repasts" $7.45–$7.95; "substantial repasts" $5.95–$8.45. $4.95 minimum per person. No credit cards.

Open: Mon–Thurs 11:45am–midnight; Fri–Sat 11:45am–12:30pm; Sun 11:45am–11pm.

"Delightfully Air-conditioned" boasts the sign outside La Fondue, and on this particularly hot day, that was all we needed to lure us inside. But what a find it was—a truly vast selection of sophisticated, delicious budget offerings. The $7.45 All-

American lunch special, enough to test the limits of any human's capacity, provided vegetable soup; a tuna, chicken salad, or turkey breast sandwich; crusty French sourdough bread; a homemade cake topped with chocolate whipped cream; and a beverage. The $7.75 continental cheese tour brings you Brie, Port-Salut, Cheddar, and Gouda, served with a basket of fresh fruit, sourdough bread, English cream crackers, and Danish pumpernickel. We were delighted with the pineapple crater, which the menu describes as "an explosion" of fruits and berries, "flowing" with cottage cheese, and topped with shredded coconut and toasted almonds.

Service was a bit brusque both times we visited, but it's a good bet all the same. Treat yourself to something special—you'll love the crab claws fondue at $12.95, with three dipping sauces for stuffed crab claws. The Swiss chocolate fondue provides assorted fruit and cubed banana fruitcake for dunking into a mixture of chocolate, honey, almonds, sweet cream, and brandy.

HIDE, 304 W. 56th St., between Eighth and Ninth aves. Tel. 582-0030.
    Cuisine: JAPANESE. **Reservations:** Not needed. **Subway:** 1, 9, A, C, D to 59th St.
$ **Prices:** Appetizers $1.50–$4.50; main courses $5.25–$9.95; sushi rolls $2.50; sushi combinations $9.95–$11.95. AE, MC, V.
    Open: Lunch Mon–Fri noon–2:30pm; dinner Mon–Sat 5:30–11pm.

Tucked away up a nondescript, dingy stairway, this excellent little restaurant is almost totally lacking in ambience. Hide (pronounced "hee-day") nevertheless draws a loyal crowd for its hospitality and delicious, moderately priced Japanese dishes. Favorites are chicken and beef teriyaki, shrimp and vegetable tempura, and kitsune soba (fried tofu in buckwheat noodle soup). Lunch specials, served Monday to Friday from noon to 2:40pm, include gyoza dumplings and sautéed vegetables with chicken, with all selections under $7.50.

KING CRAB, 871 Eighth Ave., corner of 52nd St. Tel. 765-4393.
    Cuisine: SEAFOOD. **Reservations:** Not accepted. **Subway:** 1, 9, C, E to 50th St.; A, D to 59th St.
$ **Prices:** Appetizers $2.95–$5.95; main courses $8.25–$26.95. AE.

 # FROMMER'S COOL FOR KIDS
RESTAURANTS

Tony Roma's (see p. 135) Small orders of ribs or a giant brick of onion rings can be had for less than $6. Booths and booster seats available for those who need them.

Peppermint Park (see p. 171) One of New York's best ice-cream parlors has more than enough flavors to satisfy the pickiest palates, with cones, floats, sundaes, egg creams, frozen yogurts, and pastries.

Hamburger Harry's (see p. 76) The burgers are mouthwatering, and children are heartily welcomed. Each table has paper tablecloths and a jar full of crayons. Kids will love the foot-long hot dogs, tacos, burgers, and grilled cheese sandwiches. Booster seats are available.

Two Boots (see pp. 112–113) Crayons and coloring books, beverages that come in boot-shaped mugs, pizzas with the toppings arranged in happy faces, high chairs, and special low-priced kids' offerings—what more could a parent ask?

Diane's Uptown (see p. 146) Burgers, fries, and all the foods kids love for a pittance. They'll get to top things off with gooey ice-cream creations from the Ben & Jerry's counter that shares the premises.

Open: Mon–Sat noon–midnight; Sun 4–11pm.

King Crab is a thoroughly classy restaurant with superb seafood at reasonable prices. The interior is exceptionally pretty, with a black marble bar, gilt-framed mirrors, oak floors, and Tiffany-style lamps.

Although the main dishes go up to $26.95 for Alaskan king crab legs, most offerings hover around the $12 mark. Start with an order of clams on the half shell before devouring the catch of the day—perhaps sea bass, cod, brook trout, flounder, and bluefish. Other offerings include shrimp scampi and scallops. Favorite desserts at King Crab are the carrot cake and pecan pie ($2.50). Expect a wait.

LAI LAI WEST, 859 Ninth Ave., at 56th St. Tel. 586-5083.

> **Cuisine:** CHINESE. **Reservations:** Not needed. **Subway:** 1, 9, A, C, D to 59th St.
> **$ Prices:** Appetizers $1–$6.95; main courses $5.25–$12.95. AE, MC, V. Credit card minimum $15.
> **Open:** Sun–Thurs 11:30am–11pm, Fri–Sat 11:30am–midnight.

Our favorite neighborhood Chinese restaurant has never been known to disappoint—from the sleek black-lacquer decor, which makes the place look more expensive than it is, to the artful presentation of the food and the fast, gracious service. The crisp spring rolls are always perfectly cooked, and we've always loved the shrimp toast. We swear by the crispy golden chicken, a fried chicken cutlet topped with a spicy soy sauce and scallions; the crispy prawns with honey-toasted walnuts, broccoli, and baby corn in a sweet-and-sour sauce; and the sesame duet, half beef and half chicken. Ask about the pretheater dinner menu, the weekend dim sum, and the low-cost lunch specials. Highly recommended.

LANDMARK TAVERN, 626 Eleventh Ave., at 46th St. Tel. 757-8595.

> **Cuisine:** IRISH/AMERICAN. **Reservations:** Required. **Subway:** A, C, E to 42nd St. **Bus:** M50 to Eleventh Ave.
> **$ Prices:** Sandwiches $6–$8.50; main courses $12–$25. AE, CB, DC, MC, V.
> **Open:** Lunch daily 11:30am–4:15pm; dinner Sun–Thurs 5pm–midnight, Fri–Sat 5pm–1am; Sun brunch noon–4:15pm.

The Landmark Tavern is a little out of the way (you might want to take a cab), but it's one of New York's most charming dining places. An innlike Irish tavern that dates back to 1868, the Landmark has an antique feel to it that few New York restaurants can match. There is dining on the second floor, in what served for a century as home to the Carly family, the Landmark's first owners. It is still the restaurant's homiest part; there are old floor rugs, antique furniture, brick fireplaces, and even a functioning grandfather clock. Downstairs in the main dining area is a gorgeous old Victorian bar with huge, beveled mirrors. Tables are covered with white linen and adorned with candles and fresh flowers.

The old mahogany bar at the Landmark offers 6 beers on tap, 34 single-malt scotches, and 17 varieties of brandy and cognac. For lunch there are shepherd's pie, fish and chips, sandwiches, and Irish potato soup with bacon. Dinner main dishes, served with potato, vegetable, and a relish dish, include lamb steak marinated in rosemary and red wine, grilled Mako shark with shallot butter, and a prime rib with Yorkshire pudding.

Sunday brunch at the Landmark offers four types of omelet, Irish oatmeal pancakes with Irish bacon, or mashed-potato pancakes—with a Bloody Mary, screwdriver, brandy-milk punch, fruit juice, or glass of champagne on the house.

LEMON TREE CAFÉ, 769 Ninth Ave., between 51st and 52nd sts. Tel. 245-0818.

> **Cuisine:** MIDDLE EASTERN. **Reservations:** Not accepted. **Subway:** 1, 9, C, E to 50th St.
> **$ Prices:** Appetizers $1.50–$3.25; main courses $2.50–$9.50. No credit cards.
> **Open:** Daily 11:30am–midnight.

This friendly little café with wood-latticed walls serves top-notch food at rock-bottom prices—you could dine on falafel or stuffed grape leaves for a mere $2.50.

There's an exceptional selection for vegetarians, like the babaganoush (baked eggplant ground with lemon and tehini) or the tabouli salad. Carnivores will be drawn to the thinly sliced, marinated flank of lamb or beef (schwarma), and the hummus with lamb. All grilled dishes are served with rice, hummus, or french fries and salad. There's an excellent, homemade baklava for dessert.

LA MILONGA, 742 Ninth Ave., at the corner of 50th St. Tel. 541-8382.
   Cuisine: ARGENTINIAN. **Reservations:** Recommended on weekend nights.
   Subway: 1, 9, C, E to 50th St.
$ **Prices:** Appetizers $1.95–$7.95; main courses $7.95–$24.95; $20 credit card minimum. AE, MC, V.
   Open: Daily noon–midnight.
This festive, Latin club–style restaurant is patronized by Argentinians, a sure sign of authenticity. The dining area is decorated with travel posters of Argentina and memorabilia of Argentinian tango singer Carlos Cardel.

Monday through Friday there are $6.95 lunch specials, but if you come for dinner, especially on weekends, you may be treated to live Argentinian folk or tango music. Begin with the empanadas or hearts of palm. Main course offerings include steaks, paella valenciana, and parillada, a sort of Argentinian mixed grill, with sweetbreads, kidneys, skirt steak, sausage, and short ribs. You can accompany your meal with sangría or Argentinian wine, and if you've still got room after indulging your carnivorous side, polish off the evening with flan or a filled crêpe.

NEW ACROPOLIS, 767 Eighth Ave., at 47th St. Tel. 581-2733.
   Cuisine: GREEK. **Reservations:** Recommended. **Subway:** 1, 9, C, E to 50th St.
$ **Prices:** Appetizers $3–$7.75; main courses $5.25–$19.50. AE, DC, MC, V.
   Open: Daily 11am–11pm.
The New Acropolis, decorated with simple white tablecloths, offers traditional Greek cooking. You won't go wrong by starting with the eggplant salad, the octopus, the sweetbread sauté, or the fried zucchini. Main dishes, most under $10, emphasize lamb dishes, such as our favorite, lamb with orzo, but you'll also find fried and broiled fish, stuffed vine leaves, moussaka, and varying daily specials. Finish off with fresh fruit or the requisite baklava.

ROBERT'S RESTAURANT, 736 Tenth Ave., between 50th and 51st sts. Tel. 581-4244.
   Cuisine: AMERICAN. **Reservations:** Recommended. **Subway:** C, E to 50th St. and walk west 2 avenues.
$ **Prices:** Appetizers $1.75–$7.25; salads and sandwiches $5–$8.75; main courses $10.50–$12.50. AE.
   Open: Daily noon–late. **Closed:** Kitchen closed Aug and hol weekends.
This friendly neighborhood hangout is a bit out of the way for most, but it's a comfortable place to drink and chat, with sports books and tourist brochures set out by the mahogany bar; in the summer there's a patio open in the rear. During lunch and early dinner a piano player undercuts the chatter with soothing melodies. The menu is limited but generally good; start with the warm Brie with apples or a tuna salad platter. The seafood linguine in red sauce is a good bet, as is Robert's Cajun meatloaf. There may also be soft-shell crabs in season.

SAM'S, 263 W. 45th St., between Broadway and Eighth Ave. Tel. 719-5416.
   Cuisine: AMERICAN/CONTINENTAL. **Reservations:** Recommended. **Subway:** A, C, E to 42nd St.
$ **Prices:** Appetizers $4–$9.25; main courses $4–$16.95; pretheater dinner $14.95. $20 credit card minimum. AE, CB, DC, MC, V.
   Open: Mon–Thurs noon–2am (kitchen closes at 12:45am); Fri–Sat noon–3am (kitchen closes at 1:45am); Sun 12:30–10pm (kitchen closes at 9pm).
Similar to Joe Allen's (see Section 15, "Worth the Extra Bucks"), Sam's has exposed-brick walls, a bar and dining room separated by brick archways, and

baby-blue tablecloths. While the ambience here is just as warm, Sam's blackboard menu has a wider selection of lower-priced items, with most appetizers under $6 and most main dishes under $10. Hummus with pita bread or duck liver mousse could precede such traditional offerings as London broil, burgers, fettuccine Alfredo, or a grilled Cajun chicken breast. Pastries with which to wreck your diet are baked right on the premises. There's a full bar for a quick cocktail before you dash off to catch a Broadway show.

SIAM GRILL, 586 Ninth Ave., between 42nd and 43rd sts. Tel. 307-1363.
    Cuisine: THAI. **Reservations:** Not needed. **Subway:** A, C, E to 42nd St.
$ **Prices:** Appetizers $2.50–$5.95; main courses $5.75–$15.95. AE, MC, V.
    Open: Mon–Thurs 11:30am–11pm; Fri 11:30am–11:30pm; Sat 4pm–11:30pm; Sun 4–10:30pm.
The Siam Grill is one of the few Thai places in the city that offers take-out and delivery service. House specialties include sautéed chicken with cashew nuts and chili paste sauce and nam sod, spicy ground pork seasoned with lime juice, ginger, and peanuts. Fish, such as red snapper or deep fried fish with sweet-and-sour sauce, are priced seasonally. Vegetarians will enjoy the highly spiced sautéed mixed vegetables with red curry sauce and coconut milk.

SIAM INN, 916 Eighth Ave., between 54th and 55th sts. Tel. 489-5237.
    Cuisine: THAI. **Reservations:** Not necessary. **Subway:** 1, 9 to 59th St. **Bus:** M50 to Eighth Ave.
$ **Prices:** Appetizers $3.45–$8.95; main courses $6.95–$15.95. AE, DC.
    Open: Lunch Mon–Fri noon–3pm; dinner Mon–Fri 5–11:30pm; Sat 4–11:30pm; Sun 5–11pm.
We think the Siam Inn serves the best Thai cuisine in Manhattan, hands down. It's a bit of a splurge—we each spent $30 here for a huge meal with drinks and a big tip—but it's worth every single penny. The decor is a bit cheesy, with doilies under glass, but that's okay, because it's clear that the Siam Inn spends its money, time, and energy on preparing a good meal. Service is quick and attentive, but not overly so. We began with an appetizer platter that let us sample several specialties. The spring rolls are exquisite, and there are not words to do justice to the dumplings, filled with ground beef and peanuts. Saté beef skewers were flamed at our table, and we dunked them in a perfectly blended peanut dressing. Our main courses—crispy noodles with pork and sautéed shrimp in garlic sauce—won similar raves. Don't miss it.

STARDUST DINER, 1377 Ave. of the Americas, corner of 56th St. Tel. 307-7575.
    Cuisine: AMERICAN. **Reservations:** Not accepted. **Subway:** B, N, R to 57th St.
$ **Prices:** Appetizers $3.95–$8.95; main courses $7.50–$13.95. Credit card minimum $20. AE, MC, V.
    Open: Mon–Thurs 7:30am–11:30pm; Fri–Sat 7:30am–12:30am; Sun 8am–11pm; weekend brunch served noon–4pm.
The "50's" are alive and well in the Stardust Diner—we spent most of our meal watching old Elvis performances on an ancient television and eyeing the gleefully campy memorabilia. (Look for the old posters touting the winners of the coveted "Miss New York Subways" title.) As befits a diner, the noise level is high and the service is breathless.

    Weekend brunch is an especially good deal at $9.95; it comes with a cocktail, coffee, or tea, and your choice of main dish. We liked the cinnamon-apple-raisin-swirl–French toast, or you might try a crisp Belgian waffle topped with fresh strawberries and kiwi slices and served with Iowa bacon.

    Burgers range from $6.25 up to the $8.75 Ed Norton Deluxe; sandwiches, like the New York cheese steak hero, run $4.75 to $8.95. If you're really ravenous, have a cup of Joe, "cow juice," or sarsparilla with Mom's chicken pot pie or baked meatloaf. But above all, save room for one of the fountain favorites ($1.95 to $4.25), like a lime rickey, a brownie mudslide, or a sundae that's "too scary for words." Other desserts worth blowing your diet for include a decadent chocolate-chip black-bottom cheesecake and Heath Bar crunch pie.

TONY ROMA'S, 1600 Broadway, corner of 48th St. Tel. 956-RIBS.

Cuisine: AMERICAN/RIBS. **Reservations:** Accepted only for parties of 8 or more, or for customers with special needs, like the disabled. **Subway:** 1, 9, C, E to 50th St.

$ Prices: Appetizers $2.50–$7.50; main courses $6.25–$12.95. MC, V.

Open: Lunch daily 11am–4pm; dinner Mon–Thurs 4pm–midnight, Fri–Sat 4pm–1am; Sun 4–11pm.

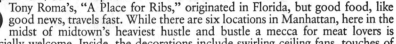 Tony Roma's, "A Place for Ribs," originated in Florida, but good food, like good news, travels fast. While there are six locations in Manhattan, here in the midst of midtown's heaviest hustle and bustle a mecca for meat lovers is especially welcome. Inside, the decorations include swirling ceiling fans, touches of brass and etched glass, bentwood chairs, and old-fashioned lamps.

At lunch a small order of tenderloin baby back pork ribs, St. Louis–style pork ribs, or truly bountiful beef ribs cost $8.95. Those with a hearty appetite can order the dinner-size portion for $12.95. The pork ribs have tender, ready-to-fall-off-the-bone meat; the enormous beef ribs are sturdier. All come with coleslaw and a choice of barbecued beans, baked potato, or french fries.

There are half-pound burgers with fries, as well as soups, salads, seafood platters, and chicken. If you haven't eaten in several days, try the Roma feast for two, which includes half a slab of baby back ribs, half a slab of pork ribs, three huge beef ribs, half a barbecued chicken, two ears of corn, two potatoes, and coleslaw for $25.95.

VIA BRAZIL, 34 W. 46th St., between Fifth and Sixth aves. Tel. 997-1158.

Cuisine: BRAZILIAN. **Reservations:** Recommended on weekends. **Subway:** 1, 2, 3, 9, N, R to Times Square; 4, 5, 6 to Grand Central.

$ Prices: Appetizers $1.50–$8.95; main courses $9.95–$16.95. AE, CB, DC, MC, V.

Open: Mon–Fri noon–11pm, Sat noon–midnight, Sun noon–10:30pm.

This sophisticated little bar and restaurant reflects modern Rio, with mahogany-stained wainscoting trimmed in jungle green, and watercolors of Brazilian scenes hung above on white walls. There is seating to the side in semiprivate cubicles, or at the front in a glassed-in patio. There's live music, often samba, Wednesday through Sunday.

The extensive menu includes paella, a truly special marinated rum steak, the traditional Brazilian feijoada, and moqueca de camarão—a shrimp stew with green herbs, onions, tomato, and coconut. Save a few dollars by ordering an extra plate for sharing for $2.50.

WESTSIDE COTTAGE CHINESE RESTAURANT, 788 Ninth Ave., between 52nd and 53rd sts. Tel. 957-8008.

Cuisine: CHINESE. **Reservations:** Recommended. **Subway:** 1, 9, C, E to 50th St. **Bus:** M50 to Ninth Ave.

$ Prices: Appetizers $1–$5.75; main courses $5.50–$9.95. AE.

Open: Mon–Thurs 11:15am–11pm; Fri 11:15am–11:30pm; Sat 11:30am–11:30pm; Sun 11:30am–11pm.

At this attractive little culinary find, the light-plum-colored walls are adorned with contemporary Oriental prints, and the unadorned butcher-block tables are set with plum napkins. There are a variety of inexpensive lunch specials served Monday through Friday until 4pm; for $5.50 or under you can get any of the 25 main dishes, accompanied with soup or eggroll and egg-fried or white rice. Brown rice is also available.

For dinner you might start with barbecued pineapple chicken or Szechuan dumplings in a spicy sauce. A full compliment of soups includes the house special for two, which is a tangy meat-and-seafood combination. Some of the more popular main dishes include eggplant with garlic sauce, sesame chicken, beef with orange flavor, and lamb with scallions. The hearty, ten-ingredients pan-fried noodles includes chicken, shrimp, and beef. The restaurant also provides unlimited glasses of house wine as well as a complimentary dessert of pineapple and orange chunks, and a fortune cookie.

There is also a Westside Cottage II at 689 Ninth Avenue, at 48th Street (tel. 245-0800).

10. MIDTOWN EAST

With its lunchtime hustle of businesspeople, U.N. diplomats, and elegant shoppers, Midtown East, located between 42nd and 60th streets east of Fifth Avenue, is a formidable challenge to budget-conscious diners. If possible, in fact, we'd recommend that you dine elsewhere, since we found the restaurants here rather expensive, but you can try the recommendations below if you're sightseeing in the neighborhood.

There's a **Jackson Hole** at Third Avenue and 35th Street (tel. 679-3264), which is one of the best bets in the neighborhood. See Section 13, "Upper East Side/Yorkville," for a review of the other branches.

AU NATURAL, 1043 Second Ave., at 55th St. Tel. 832-2922.
   Cuisine: HEALTH FOOD. **Reservations:** Not needed. **Subway:** 6 to 51st St.; 4, 5, 6 to 59th St.; or E, F to Lexington/Third aves.
   $ Prices: Appetizers $3.25–$7.50; sandwiches, burgers, and salads $7–$13.50; main courses $7.50–$16.50. AE, MC, V.
   Open: Mon–Fri 11am–11pm; Sat–Sun 10am–11pm.
Naturally beautiful people flock here. Like a designer's kitchen nook, the interior is filled with butcher-block tables, tiles, mirrors, and fresh flowers. Among the many main dishes are stir-fried sesame chicken, and pumpkin ravioli in a sun-dried tomato pesto sauce. Salads, organic omelets, and high-nutrition shakes round out the menu. Only the freshest organically grown grains, fruits, and vegetables are used, along with chemical-free chickens.

BEIJING DUCK HOUSE, 144 E. 52nd St., between Lexington and Third aves. Tel. 759-8260.
   Cuisine: CHINESE. **Reservations:** Not needed. **Subway:** 6 to 51st St.
   $ Prices: Appetizers $2.25–$8.95; main courses $10–$18; Peking duck for two $34. AE, CB, DC, MC, V.
   Open: Mon–Thurs noon–10pm; Fri–Sun noon–10:30pm.
True to its name, Beijing Duck House serves Peking duck throughout the day. There is no need for advance notice, but the limited supply goes on a first-come, first-served basis. The restaurant is small, with white tablecloths and fresh red carnations on every table.

The crisp-skinned duck is prepared with a sophisticated process that includes pumping air into the skin before roasting; it's served with thin pancakes. Try the sliced duck with green scallions and hoisin sauce, a kind of Peking duck without the skin. Other specialties include a spicy chicken with orange flavor or prawns with chili sauce.

BONAMPAK, 235 E. 53rd St., between Second and Third aves. Tel. 838-1433.
   Cuisine: MEXICAN. **Reservations:** Not needed. **Subway:** 6 to 51st St.; E, F to Lexington/Third aves.
   $ Prices: Appetizers $4–$4.25; main courses $8.25–$12.95. AE, CB, DC.
   Open: Mon–Fri noon–10pm, Sat 5pm–midnight.
Named for the Mayan Empire's sacred city of warriors, this place is authentically decorated with velvet paintings, desert plants in the window, Mexican pottery, and other curios. Pretty, multicolored blown-glass lamps create a warm atmosphere. (It's

easy to overlook, but head downstairs from street level—and be careful, as the stairs are a bit steep.)

Bonampak offers a mix of Tex-Mex and authentic Mexican dishes. Try the chicken in chocolate, almond, or lime sauce, or the beef-stuffed avocado. Combination platters with your choice of tacos, tostados, burritos, and tamales are available for lunch for under $5. The menu is in both Spanish and English, and the staff is quite friendly.

CAFÉ AT GRAND CENTRAL, West Balcony, Grand Central Terminal, West 42nd St. Tel. 883-0441.
   Cuisine: CONTINENTAL. **Reservations:** Not needed. **Subway:** 4, 5, 6 to Grand Central.
$ **Prices:** Salads and burgers under $10. AE, DC.
   Open: Lunch daily noon–4pm.
This café is located in one of New York's biggest attractions. Make sure you look up—the constellations on the huge domed ceiling shouldn't be missed; and from the vantage point of the café you can take in the whole main terminal. Lunch is the only meal served here, but the handsome bar attracts a good crowd of waiting commuters at 5pm every day. Our favorite sandwich is sopressata, salami, and imported Swiss on a baguette; the special changes daily and is always a good bargain. The niçoise and chicken salads are large, and steak tartare, when available, is custom-made to taste. For dessert, try the extra-chocolatey chocolate cake.

CAFÉ FONDUTA, 120 E. 57th St., near Lexington Ave. Tel. 935-5699.
   Cuisine: ITALIAN. **Reservations:** Not needed. **Subway:** 4, 5, 6 to 59th St.
$ **Prices:** Pasta courses $10–$14. AE.
   Open: Mon–Fri 11:30am–9:30pm; Sat 11:30am–4pm. **Closed:** Sat in summer.
You'll find light northern Italian fare and a pleasant atmosphere at Café Fonduta. Owner Luis Levero will usher you into the restaurant past a glass cabinet stocked with an excellent selection of wines. Be sure to taste the pasta dishes such as rigatti a quattro formaggio, with Cheddar, Swiss, Fontina da osta, and parmesan cheeses, mushrooms, and zucchini; tagliarini and chopped spinach in a light cream sauce; fettuccine Alfredo with vegetables and a cream sauce; and angel-hair fonduta, with tomatoes and basil.

CHECKERS, 201 E. 34th St., off Third Ave. Tel. 684-7803.
   Cuisine: AMERICAN/RIBS. **Reservations:** Not needed. **Subway:** 6 to 33rd St.
$ **Prices:** Lunch platters $3.45–$5.45; Mexican dishes $3.45–$7.95; chicken and rib selections $2.95–$13.95. AE.
   Open: Daily noon–10:30pm; lunch served noon–4pm.
This barbecue joint has lots of Manhattan pizzazz. Checkers promises healthy food at reasonable prices. The focus of the shop is the huge grill, with its lines of chicken and ribs in various stages of cooking. The aroma is wonderful. But Checkers is also decorated with imagination, so you won't feel that you're just chowing down in a take-out kitchen. The floor is black-and-white tile, and very clean in spite of the traffic. There are black tables set with red ashtrays, modern art on the walls, and salsa and rock music overhead.

You can order à la carte—3-pound chickens are available in quarter-, half-, or whole-bird sizes. The traditional red barbecue sauce has a salty kick, and there are also mustard-herb, soy-ginger, and salsa sauces. Side dishes round out your feast— baked potatoes with sour cream can be topped with cheese, chili, or guacamole, and the salads include country potato, crunchy raisin-carrot, and tangy cucumber-onion. Our favorite is the red cabbage coleslaw with white raisins and a sweet-sour dressing.

There's another Checkers at 867 Ninth Ave., between 56th and 57th streets (tel. 582-1888).

ELECTRA RESTAURANT, 949 Second Ave., at 53rd St. Tel. 421-8425.
   Cuisine: GREEK/AMERICAN. **Reservations:** Not needed. **Subway:** 6 to 51st St.

$ Prices: Appetizers $2.75–$5; main courses $5.95–$9.95. MC, V.
Open: Daily 6am–midnight.

A beautiful varnished blond-wood exterior is the first clue that this place is no ordinary Greek coffee shop. While the interior reverts to familiar Formica tables and brown booths, the wide variety of dishes is anything but "run of the mill."

Everything from breakfast dishes to hamburgers is served throughout the day. Try the special feta cheese with tomato omelet, or for a full meal, order the breaded veal cutlet. There are also Greek specialties like lamb shish kebab, along with hamburger specials. Try the homemade baklava or galaktoboureko for dessert.

GOLDBERG'S PIZZERIA, 966 Second Ave., at 52nd St. Tel. 593-2172.
Cuisine: PIZZA. **Reservations:** Not needed. **Subway:** 4, 5, 6 to 59th St.
$ Prices: Salads $3.95–$4.95; pizzas $5.75–$13.95. AE.
Open: Mon–Thurs noon–11pm, Fri noon–midnight, Sat noon–11:30pm, Sun 3–11pm.

For made-to-order deep-dish pizza, slide into one of the simple wooden booths at Goldberg's. If you're with your significant other, try the Sweetheart Pizza in the shape of a heart, or if you're counting calories, try the Diet Riot Pizza with no dough or crust. You pick the size and the toppings from a long list that includes "breathtaking garlic," "hog wild ham," and "satanic sausage." We fell in love with the Smog Pizza, with sausage, mushrooms, onions, and peppers. Picky Chicago purists will claim that it's not authentic, but we don't care—we still think it's terrific, and a great budget find.

GOODFELLOW'S, 1009 Second Ave., between 53rd and 54th sts. Tel. 759-8775.
Cuisine: AMERICAN. **Reservations:** Recommended. **Subway:** 6 to 51st St.
$ Prices: Main courses $9.95–$14.95. AE, DC, MC, V.
Open: Lunch daily 11:30am–4pm; dinner daily 5pm–midnight; late supper nightly midnight–2:30am.

"Come hungry," advises owner Joey Horn. His restaurant offers "a taste of old New York," which means excellent prime rib and filet mignon. Other house specialties include the veal scaloppine piccata, and the cold Irish smoked salmon platter with capers, onions, and tomato. Top off a hearty meal with the irresistible rum chocolate fudge cake. Like in the television show "Cheers," there is a downstairs bar—with piano music on Wednesday, Thursday, and Friday evenings.

HARGLO'S CAFÉ, 974 Second Ave., between 51st and 52nd sts. Tel. 759-9820.
Cuisine: AMERICAN/CAJUN. **Reservations:** Recommended. **Subway:** 6 to 51st St. **Bus:** M50.
$ Prices: Appetizers $3.25–$8.95; burgers $5.50–$6.75; main courses $6.95–$11.95. AE, MC, V.
Open: Daily 11:30am–11:45pm; brunch served Sat–Sun 10:30am–5pm. Bar open until 2am weeknights, 4am weekends.

An explosion of neon marks the exterior of Harglo's, and if you're in the mood for Dixie beer and some down-and-dirty Cajun cooking, you've come to the right place. We were in ecstasy over the French onion soup, a rich, hearty broth brimming with sweet onions and crowned with a thick layer of melted provolone cheese. The traditional jambalaya is hot and spicy, with smoked pork, sausage, ham, chicken, onions, peppers, and celery, seasoned and slow-cooked in a hearty stock and served over rice. The Cajun burger is a great buy at only $6.75—it's grilled in zesty creole spices, then topped with bacon, Cajun sauce, and melted Jack cheese. If you have any vestige of an appetite left, go for the chocolate cheesecake or the apple pie à la mode.

The weekend brunch, at $7.40, offers Cajun main dishes, like the fried Louisiana catfish or the Cajun popcorn and chips with a special dipping sauce. You can also create your own omelet or burger, choosing from a list of ingredients, or try the Texas-style brunch, with sirloin steak and eggs. And brunch should keep you happy all

afternoon—all this food comes with two rounds of Bloody Marys, s
mimosas, champagne, wine, or beer, or one frozen fruit colada, daiquiri, l
toasted almond, or orange blossom.

HOBEAU'S, 882 First Ave., between 49th and 50th sts. Tel. 421-288

Cuisine: SEAFOOD. **Reservations:** Recommended. **Subway:** 6 to 51st St.
and walk 3 avenues east. **Bus:** M50 to 1st Ave.
$ Prices: Appetizers $2.25–$6.95; main courses $5.95–$14.95. AE, CB, DC, MC, V.
Open: Lunch or brunch daily 11:30am–4pm; dinner daily 4pm–3am.

Boasting fresh fish caught right off Montauk Point, this place is a find, especially if you don't mind a packed house. With a typically nautical interior, Hobeau's is best for lunch, as dinner prices generally run $1 or $1.50 more for most dishes. The service is fast and no-nonsense. (You're even entitled to a free cocktail if your waiter forgets to take your drink order or doesn't tell you his or her name.) From fried shrimp stuffed with crabmeat to a mixed seafood platter, fish is the main attraction. There are also poultry and beef main dishes—from a hamburger platter to steak teriyaki and steak and Alaskan crab legs. We like to start with clam chowder, clams casino, or oysters Rockefeller. Lobsters are available at varying market prices (with a $5 charge for sharing twin lobsters), although they're pricier than our budget can afford. Brunch, which comes with a half carafe of Bloody Marys, screwdrivers, wine, or beer, costs $6.95 daily.

J. R.'S 8-OZ. BURGERS, 250 E. 58th St., between Second and Third aves. Tel. 980-1421.

Cuisine: AMERICAN/BURGERS. **Reservations:** Not needed. **Subway:** 4, 5, 6 to 59th St.; N, R to Lexington Ave.
$ Prices: Burgers and main courses $3.40–$8.95. No credit cards.
Open: Mon–Sat 6am–9:45pm, Sun 8am–9:45pm.

Serving great burgers as well as hearty breakfast and dinner basics, this place sports oak tables, an oak counter, tin ceilings, and tiled floors. The 8-ounce burger patties are made from lean meat and slowly grilled with just about any extras you can think of ordering—from a Texas burger with a fried egg to a Cowboy burger with baked beans. The house specialty is the East Side burger, with bacon, cheese, ham, mushrooms, and fried onions. Burgers can be ordered as platters with french fries, lettuce, and tomatoes for about $1 extra. There are daily blackboard specials, and hot platters, like the Romanian steak with fried onions or the breaded veal cutlet, are available. For breakfast, served till 11:30am, French toast with ham and two eggs ought to be enough to stuff you, or there's a lox and onion omelette.

LARMEN DOSANKO NOODLE SHOP, 423 Madison Ave., between 48th and 49th sts. Tel. 688-8575.

Cuisine: JAPANESE. **Reservations:** Not needed. **Subway:** 6 to 51st St.
$ Prices: Appetizers $3.50–$4.20; soups and main courses $4.80–$6.50. No credit cards.
Open: Mon–Fri 11am–10pm; Sat–Sun noon–8pm.

The Dosanko chain features huge steaming bowls of noodles mixed with a variety of meats and vegetables. The decor is informal, with seats at the counter up front or in orange booths toward the back. While it may strike you as the Japanese equivalent of "fast food," the noodles are good, inexpensive, and filling. We like to start with the chicken basket or gyoza dumplings; then there are six beef or pork larmen noodle dishes from which to choose, all accompanied by Kirin beer or saké.

There are several Larmen Dosankos elsewhere in the city, including 329 Fifth Ave., between 32nd and 33rd streets (tel. 686-9259).

MAYFAIR RESTAURANT, 964 First Ave., at 53rd St. Tel. 421-6216.

Cuisine: AMERICAN/CONTINENTAL. **Reservations:** Accepted only for parties of 4 or more. **Bus:** M15.
$ Prices: Main courses $11.25–$17.50. AE, MC, V.

midnight.

rior and regular patrons from the neighborhood, the Mayfair
ioned feel. There's a large bar at the front, decorated with a
d leather-covered wooden booths in the back. Green-checked
lit green lamps add the proper accent.

s change throughout the week, but all are hearty and filling.
roiled chicken are offered at all times. Try the Monday's beef
beef goulash with noodles. Desserts run $3.75 to $3.95; we're
Melba.

MIMI'S, 984 Second Ave., at 52nd St. Tel. 688-4692.

Cuisine: ITALIAN. **Reservations:** Recommended. **Subway:** 6 to 51st St.
$ Prices: Appetizers $4.75–$7.95; pasta courses $7.95–$9.95; main courses $8.95–$13.95. $7 minimum per person. AE, CB, DC, MC, V.
Open: Mon–Sat noon–4am; Sun 5pm–midnight.

Jazz up a pasta meal by going to this Italian piano bar, with a glassed-in terrace that looks out onto Second Avenue. Three stained-glass windows from an old temple serve as dividers between the terrace and main dining room. Tables are set with red-and-white-checked tablecloths and flowers in Perrier bottles. Mimi's has many loyal local patrons, who can often be found singing around the piano. Start off with cherrystone clams on the half-shell, Italian stuffed peppers, or a hot antipasto. We love the shrimp scampi, but your budget might favor the spaghetti with calamari sauce or the ziti à la siciliana with eggplant. Sample the house wine along with dinner; it comes by the glass, the carafe, or the half-carafe. Mimi's is a friendly neighborhood place with a growing reputation for good food, good music, good times, and reasonable prices.

PASTAMORE, 820 Second Ave., at 44th St. Tel. 983-4666.

Cuisine: ITALIAN. **Reservations:** Not needed. **Subway:** 4, 5, 6 to 42nd St.
$ Prices: Pizza and pasta selections $5.95–$9.95. AE, DC, MC, V.
Open: Mon–Fri 11am–11pm; Sat–Sun 4–11pm.

With its wide windows and eclectic decor, Pastamore is a pretty and cheerful spot to down a soul-enriching bowl of pasta. You'll be tempted by everything from angel hair primavera to fettuccine carbonara and linguine in clam sauce. Another good bet is an individual pizzamore or a 9-inch traditional pizza, and don't forget to save room for the tartufo.

LES SANS-CULOTTES, 1085 Second Ave., at 57th St. Tel. 838-6660.

Cuisine: FRENCH. **Reservations:** Recommended. **Subway:** 4, 5, 6 to 59th St.; N, R to Lexington Ave., then walk east.
$ Prices: Lunch main courses $9.25–$11.95; prix-fixe dinner $19.95. AE, DC, MC, V.
Open: Lunch daily noon–3pm; dinner daily 5–11:30pm.

It's hard to find a reasonably priced French restaurant in New York, but this place is a gem and the customers are just as likely to be French as American.

Lunch main dishes include entrecôte bordelaise; you can start with escargots or a green salad. Your best bet at dinner is the prix-fixe special (although you can order just a main dish for $14.95, just an appetizer for $9.95, or just a dessert for $3). Starters include a basket of vegetables, sausages, and the chef's pâté; or the traditional onion soup. Your main course choice might be grilled Cornish game hen or a crispy duck with orange sauce. The desserts, which are masterpieces, include a light chocolate mousse or crème caramel. Service is friendly and unpretentious, and the wine list is superb—the carafe of house wine is eminently reasonable.

TEVA, 122 E. 42nd St., between Park and Lexington aves. Tel. 599-1265.

Cuisine: MOROCCAN. **Reservations:** Not needed. **Subway:** 4, 5, 6 to 42nd St.
$ Prices: All items under $8. No credit cards.

Open: Mon–Fri 7am–5pm.

Taking up hardly more than a parking space in the basement of the Chanin Building, this hard-to-find place is a Moroccan take-out gem. The food is kosher, vegetarian, and great. Sandwiches in pita are very filling; there's also falafel and an excellent hummus. We recommend the couscous platter—if you like things spicy, ask for the harissa pepper sauce, and to cool fired-up taste buds, try the yogurt sesame sauce.

TOMMY MAKEM'S IRISH PAVILION, 130 E. 57th St., between Park and Lexington aves. Tel. 759-9040.

Cuisine: IRISH. **Reservations:** Recommended. **Subway:** 4, 5, 6 to 59th St.

$ Prices: Appetizers $4.50–$8.95; burgers and salads $7.95–$9.95; main courses $10.95–$17.95. AE, CB, DC, MC, Transmedia, V. Credit card minimum $15.

Open: Mon–Sat noon–2am.

Tommy Makem's offers a taste of Ireland. You'll enter under a three-leaf clover, and pass by an old-fashioned dark-wood bar into a cozy dining area with wooden beams and dark-green decor. The hearty traditional fare—lamb pot pie, bangers and mash, or fish and chips—is filling. We always order the ploughman's platter, available for lunch or dinner, with Cheddar, chutney, pickles, apple slices, and nutty brown bread. Folk musicians of international renown, including owner Tommy Makem, play here on a regular basis.

TRATTORIA, Pan Am Building, 45th St., between Vanderbilt and Lexington aves. Tel. 661-3090.

Cuisine: ITALIAN. **Reservations:** Recommended. **Subway:** 4, 5, 6 to 42nd St.

$ Prices: Salads and pasta courses $8.95–$13.95. AE, CB, DC, MC, V.

Open: Mon–Fri 7am–10pm.

"The Trat," as it's known by the regular business-lunch crowd, is a lively spot, with an interesting range of pasta and fish, as well as some house specialties like risotto with parmesan cheese and asparagus. The Caesar salad is a meal in itself, but you'll want to sample the carpaccio or an individual pizza with chicken and wild mushrooms. And save room for the tiramisu, ladyfingers soaked in espresso with a layer of Mascarpone mousse. There is a friendly bar inside and on the outdoor patio, which is open from May to October.

WAN FU RESTAURANT, 801 Second Ave., between 42nd and 43rd sts. Tel. 599-1231.

Cuisine: CHINESE. **Reservations:** Recommended for lunch. **Subway:** 4, 5, 6 to 42nd St.

$ Prices: Appetizers $1.75–$5.95; main courses $5.95–$11.95. AE, CB, DC, MC, V.

Open: Daily noon–10:30pm.

Located around the corner from the U.N., Wan Fu offers reasonable prices and a pleasant decor. The two dining rooms—one at ground level and one on an interior balcony—are decorated with red carpeting, Chinese paintings and murals, and silk flowers.

Lunch platters, served from noon to 3pm on weekdays, may include cold sunsee noodles with sesame sauce. Try the assorted-flavor soup or the combination platters. The house specialties are more expensive, but worth it. The chef will make dishes only as spicy as you want, and will skip the salt or MSG upon request. A small, full bar at the front of the restaurant gives the place a clubby feeling.

11. LINCOLN CENTER

The Lincoln Center neighborhood has changed radically since it inspired the Broadway musical *West Side Story*. The area has filled up with slick, expensive restaurants that can gobble up your budget in no time. When you've got tickets to a

Lincoln Center event, we suggest one of the reasonably priced restaurants and cafés listed here. All are within walking distance of Lincoln Center.

EMPIRE SZECHUAN, 193 Columbus Ave., between 68th and 69th sts. Tel. 496-8778.

Cuisine: CHINESE. **Reservations:** Not needed. **Subway:** 1, 9 to 66th St.
$ **Prices:** Appetizers $1.50–$5.95; main courses $6.25–$13.50. AE, MC, V.
Open: Sun–Tues 11am–1am; Wed–Sat 11am–2am.

Empire Szechuan serves some of the finest dishes from the southwestern Chinese province of Szechuan. There are two dining rooms separated by a short staircase. The first one has a mirrored wall, and the one in back is cozy and cheerful. There are many chef's specials every day, including Paradise Chicken, Empire Special Duck, and Hunan Flower Steak, and the regular menu has all the traditional Chinese favorites, with over 50 main dishes.

THE LINCOLN SQUARE COFFEE SHOP, 2 Lincoln Square, between 65th and 66th sts. Tel. 799-4000.

Cuisine: AMERICAN. **Reservations:** Not accepted. **Subway:** 1, 9 to 66th St.
$ **Prices:** Sandwiches $4.95–$6.95. Credit card minimum $20. AE, MC, V.
Open: Mon–Thurs 6:30am–midnight; Fri–Sat 6:30am–1am; Sun 8am–midnight.

This world-class coffee shop is located where Broadway meets Columbus. It has all the requisites, like Viennese coffee with lots of whipped cream, burgers, homemade pies and ice-cream sundaes, or "brownies all-the-way." Fresh-baked muffins and coffee tide over legions of local office workers rushing off to work, and French onion soup in a crock or a wide selection of sandwiches satisfy them at lunch. There are other special main dishes like eggplant milanese or Indian curried chicken.

THE OPERA ESPRESSO, 1928 Broadway, at 65th St. Tel. 799-3050.

Cuisine: AMERICAN/CONTINENTAL. **Reservations:** Accepted for large groups only. **Subway:** 1, 9 to 66th St.
$ **Prices:** Sandwiches, salads, and main courses $7.50–$10.95. No credit cards.
Open: Mon–Sat 7:30am–midnight; Sun 8:30am–midnight.

This elegant coffee shop is a perfect place for something simple before or after the show that doesn't cost more than your Lincoln Center tickets. The walls are adorned with framed copies of old Metropolitan Opera programs, and pictures of performers from Pavlova to Nureyev. Graceful brass chandeliers cast a soft glow. You can sit at the counter or in a booth, but the favored seats are outside, with a perfect view across Broadway to Lincoln Center.

Main dishes might include baked eggplant stuffed with ricotta and mozzarella, served with a salad, and chicken with biscuits, gravy, and salad. You can also get sandwiches, burgers, omelets with potato or salad, and—of course—a fresh cup of espresso with dessert.

LOS PANCHOS, 71 W. 71st St., between Columbus Ave. and Central Park West. Tel. 874-7336.

Cuisine: MEXICAN. **Reservations:** Accepted. **Subway:** 1, 2, 3, 9, C to 72nd St.
$ **Prices:** Main courses and combination platters $6.95–$10.95. AE, MC, V.
Open: Daily 11:30am–midnight; brunch served Sat–Sun 11:30am–4pm.

If you're in the mood for some south-of-the-border cuisine, start off your evening in the pleasant bar/lounge (known for its Cuervo margaritas) before heading into a dining room with white cloths and candles on the tables. The stucco walls are brightened, though not to garish excess, with sombreros, serapes, and Mexican paintings. When the weather is nice, you can also eat in the quiet back patio.

Lunch here is the best deal; most main dish prices increase by $3 to $4 for dinner. The menu includes typical taco, tostada, enchilada, and burrito combination plates with rice and beans. Other dishes include flautas—corn and flour tortillas stuffed with Munster cheese, deep-fried, and then covered with guacamole—served with tomato sauce, rice, and beans—and a bowl of hot and spicy chili, served with rice on the side. Guacamole dip is a popular appetizer, and flan is the perfect finish to a hot, spicy meal.

THE SALOON, 1920 Broadway, at 64th St. Tel. 874-1500.
> **Cuisine:** INTERNATIONAL. **Reservations:** Recommended. **Subway:** 1, 9 to 66th St.
> **$ Prices:** Appetizers $5.95–$7.95; sandwiches, burgers, and main courses $6.95–$16.95. AE, DC, MC, V.
> **Open:** Sun–Thurs 11:30am–midnight; Fri–Sat 11:30am–1am.

★ Located across from Lincoln Center, this outdoor café with roller-skating waiters is a high-ceilinged, exposed-brick gathering spot for West Siders. The menu is huge, in size and assortment, but appetizers and salads are exotic and affordable, as are sandwiches and other specialties. The blue-corn nachos chivera—with goat cheese, jalapeños, and guacamole—or the Cajun popcorn are almost enough for a full meal. Hot and cold salads are featured, including duckling and macadamia nuts, hot gulf shrimp salad, and a chef's salad. Pizzellas—wafer-thin pizzas—cost from $7 for a lighter meal.

URBAN GRILL, 330 W. 58th St., between Eighth and Ninth aves. Tel. 586-3300.
> **Cuisine:** AMERICAN. **Reservations:** Not needed. **Subway:** 1, 9, A, C, D to 59th St.
> **$ Prices:** Appetizers $2.95–$5.95; sandwiches and salads $5.50–$7.95; main courses $6.95–$13.95. AE, DISC, MC, V.
> **Open:** Mon–Fri 11am–11pm, Sat 4–11pm, Sun 11am–10pm. Sat–Sun brunch 11am–4:30pm.

The ambience is not much fancier than your average coffee shop, and the decor is kept simple, with light-wood tables and chairs, and the palest of pink tablecloths. The Urban Grill just concentrates on what's important—turning out consistently good, filling fare at low prices. The hearty among you might indulge in a half-pound burger for lunch, while daintier appetites may go for an individual pita pizza or a Caesar salad. Our favorite main course is the breast of chicken served in a Dijon mustard sauce. "Pastamania" dinner specials, offered from 4 to 10:30pm Monday through Saturday, till 10pm on Sunday, include choices like fettuccine with veal and wild mushrooms or angel hair with Norwegian salmon.

Brunch comes with a terrific assortment of warm muffins. You'll get champagne, a mimosa, or orange juice; coffee or tea; and your choice of main dish—perhaps eggs Benedict, French toast, or quiche and a garden salad.

WEST SIDE RESTAURANT, 2020 Broadway, at 69th St. Tel. 724-4000.
> **Cuisine:** AMERICAN/DINER. **Reservations:** Not needed. **Subway:** 1, 2, 3, 9 to 72nd St.
> **$ Prices:** Sandwiches and burgers $2.95–$5.95; main courses $6.95–$14.95. AE, DC, DISC, MC, V.
> **Open:** Daily 24 hours.

This nondescript family-style diner—with comfortable booths, wooden arches, and red swivel stools at the lunch counter—offers plenty of cheap, tasty food. A hot roast beef sandwich with potato and vegetable will leave you stuffed at lunch, or if you're being restrained, there's also a variety of diet delights—perhaps a chicken-salad platter on a bed of lettuce with tomato, scallions, cucumber, coleslaw, and sliced egg.

12. UPPER WEST SIDE

For a truly daunting burger experience, nothing tops **Jackson Hole,** 517 Columbus Ave., at 85th Street (tel. 362-5177). There's also a **Blue Moon Mexican Café** at 287 Columbus Ave., between 73rd and 74th streets (tel. 721-2701), and a West Side **J. G. Melon** at Amsterdam Avenue and 76th Street. The West Side **Sarabeth's Kitchen,** 423 Amsterdam Avenue, at 80th Street (tel. 496-6280), is a spacious, dressier restaurant with a slightly more extensive menu than its East Side counterpart. You'll have an incredibly long wait to be seated at brunch—bring your patience. See the reviews of the Upper East Side branches of these restaurants in Section 13, "Upper East Side/Yorkville."

Perhaps the best budget bet in the neighborhood is **Dallas B-B-Q,** 27 W. 72nd St., at Columbus Avenue (tel. 873-2004); see Section 5, "Greenwich Village," for a review of the downtown Dallas.

ALL STATE CAFÉ, 250 W. 72nd St., between Broadway and West End Ave. Tel. 874-1883.

    Cuisine: AMERICAN/CONTINENTAL. **Reservations:** Not accepted. **Subway:** 1, 2, 3, 9 to 72nd St.

$ **Prices:** Appetizers $6–$7; burgers and main courses $8.95–$14.95. No credit cards.

    Open: Daily 11:30am–1am.

Walk down the few front steps and you'll come upon the bar and a crowd of congenial yuppies guzzling beer, feeding the jukebox, and chatting with strangers. There's a cozy fireplace near the bar, and tables are in back, where you can order pasta, always a good bet; big, juicy burgers; or hot, rich chili.

AMSTERDAM'S BAR & ROTISSERIE, 428 Amsterdam Ave., between 80th and 81st sts. Tel. 874-1377.

    Cuisine: AMERICAN/CONTINENTAL. **Reservations:** Recommended. **Subway:** 1, 9 to 79th St.; C to 81st St.

$ **Prices:** Appetizers $5.95–$6.95; main courses $9.75–$16.50. AE, CB, DC, MC, V.

    Open: Daily noon–1am, with bar open later.

Amsterdam's is standing-room-only until it closes. Red homespun tablecloths, shiny black wood chairs, and freshly painted white brick walls create a cheery atmosphere. The kitchen is visible in the center of the restaurant. Whole chickens and cuts of beef roast dramatically on a spit while french fries sizzle in a fryer underneath.

Some prices are high, but the roast half chicken, with a fresh green herb sauce and a pile of crispy thin fries with their skins, is a good and savory buy. By all means try the spicy homemade catsup that sits on every table. Fresh Norwegian salmon is refreshing and delicious when served with a shot of frosty aquavit—a caraway-flavored Danish liqueur. Small salads (which come with the main dishes) are made with arugula, radicchio, and other flavorful greens, flavored with a balsamic vinegar dressing.

THE BURGER JOINT/THE PIZZA JOINT, 2175 Broadway, between 76th and 77th sts. Tel. 362-9238 or 724-2010.

    Cuisine: AMERICAN. **Reservations:** Not needed. **Subway:** 1, 9 to 79th St.

$ **Prices:** Appetizers $2–$4.65; burgers and sandwiches $2.85–$7.45; individual 10-inch pizzas $4.35–$8.25. No credit cards.

    Open: Daily 6am–5am.

These two "joints" have been Upper West Side institutions for almost 30 years, and have been featured on *Late Night with David Letterman.* Located right next door to each other between 76th and 77th streets, they are unpretentious eateries that offer wholesome, reasonably priced food. Since they are run under the same ownership, you can order from both menus at either "Joint."

The house specialties are, logically enough, burgers and pizzas—topped with everything from the conventional cheese to hearty chili con carne. The Big Nick hamburger, named for the Joints' owner, has a half pound of beef and should satisfy even the most ravenous traveler. Pizzas come in large pies, individual pies, and jumbo slices, including a whopping Sicilian combo with pepperoni, onion, green pepper, mushroom, sausage, and extra cheese. The Joints also serve breakfast, with a cheese omelet and pancakes among the offerings.

There's another Pizza Joint/Burger Joint on 71st Street at Columbus Avenue.

CAMELOT, 685 Amsterdam Ave., at 93rd St. Tel. 932-1950.

    Cuisine: AMERICAN. **Reservations:** Not necessary. **Subway:** 1, 9 to 96th St.

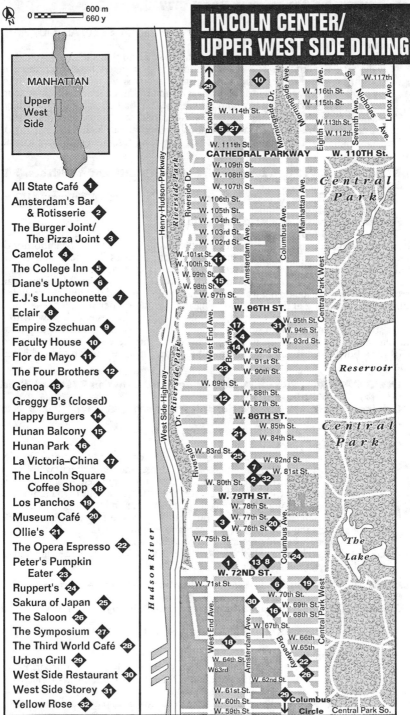

$ Prices: Lunch specials from $5.95; dinner specials from $8.50. AE, MC, V.
Open: Daily 6am–2am.

Marie Piccirilli's Camelot restaurant/diner is so clean that she says anyone can walk into her kitchen any time. Nothing is precooked here; everything is bought fresh and done, as she says, "almost in a wok way." No preservatives, no MSG; the only frozen food she uses is calamari. Lunch specials include soup or juice, a main dish, dessert, and a beverage. We had a turkey burger, which was not only delicious, but low in cholesterol. Steaks, chops, seafood, pastas, chicken, and veal dishes make for an enormously varied menu, including an array of low-fat, low-cholesterol specialties. One of our very favorites, and great value for the money.

THE COLLEGE INN, 2896 Broadway, between 112th and 113th sts. Tel. 663-0257.
    Cuisine: AMERICAN/GREEK. **Reservations:** Not needed. **Subway:** 1/9 to 110th St. **Bus:** M4 to 110th.
$ Prices: All items under $8. No credit cards.
    Open: Daily 24 hrs.

The College Inn is a longstanding tradition in the Columbia University neighborhood. The menu, which is almost too extensive to absorb, features American and Greek food. Customers sit on swivel stools at the counter or at wooden tables set with a bright-colored water jug. There are mirrors on three walls; above, Mediterranean street scenes are depicted on the wallpaper. You are likely to find this diner as crowded with students studying at 3am as it is during the evening dinner rush.

The daily specials feature family-style dinners, such as the Irish lamb stew, with a cup of soup, a green salad, and bread and butter; or the baked meatloaf, with potato and vegetable. The shish kebab is always a favorite. Soup here is 95¢ for a cup, and $1.10 for a bowl. And if you have any room left over, splurge with an old-fashioned banana split.

DIANE'S UPTOWN, 249–251 Columbus Ave., between 71st and 72nd sts. Tel. 799-6750.
    Cuisine: AMERICAN. **Reservations:** Not accepted. **Subway:** 1, 2, 3, 9, C to 72nd St.
$ Prices: Sandwiches and burgers $2.95–$6.95. No credit cards.
    Open: Daily 11am–2am.

Diane's Uptown is a great find. A stained-glass entry sets the mood. Inside, high-backed wooden booths, mahogany tables, and dark-green walls with judiciously placed mirrors create a relaxed, luxurious ambience. The menu is an even greater find, with bargains galore. You can create your own hamburger combinations with toppings ranging from mushroom and bacon to bleu cheese and onions. Each topping is 85¢. If you'd rather try something different, select a Virginia ham and cheese sandwich or a bacon-and-egg sandwich.

Devotees of Diane's heartily recommend rounding your meal off with dessert— the restaurant shares the premises with a Ben & Jerry's, making for a large selection of decadent milkshakes, malts, double dips, and sundaes.

ECLAIR, 141 W. 72nd St., between Columbus and Amsterdam aves. Tel. 873-7700.
    Cuisine: VIENNESE. **Reservations:** Accepted. **Subway:** 1, 2, 3, 9, C to 72nd St.
$ Prices: Main courses $7.95–$12.95; pastries under $4.50. MC, V. $20 credit card minimum.
    Open: Daily 8am–midnight.

A charming old neighborhood institution with a suitably old-fashioned decor, Eclair is nicely lit and airy; the terrazzo floors and white linen tablecloths speak of the proud Viennese heritage of owner Alexander M. Selinger.

As you might guess from the name, Eclair's specialty for 52 years has been pastries and cakes. You'll have a hard time choosing from over 200 varieties of scrumptious strudels, tortes, eclairs, fruit tarts, danishes, croissants—you name it. The perfect complement for one of these pastries is a cup of rich, smooth Viennese coffee with whipped cream.

But don't write Eclair off as just a coffee and pastry shop. It's a pleasant place for dinner before or after a concert, with such continental treats as Hungarian goulash and Viennese fried chicken—all served with creamed spinach or the vegetable du jour, potato, and your choice of cucumber, tossed salad, or applesauce. Add $4 to any of these dinners and you can get a soup (perhaps chilled borscht) or appetizer, dessert, and coffee or tea. Check the daily specials, which might include paprika chicken with nockerl and tossed salad or corned beef and cabbage.

If you're looking for lighter fare, try the quiche, served with a tossed salad, or one of a variety of sandwiches and burgers. We like to come in for brunch and indulge in the light-as-a-feather challah bread French toast. With a full soda fountain, wine, beer, and apéritifs, Eclair offers a huge variety of choices.

E. J.'S LUNCHEONETTE, 483 Amsterdam Ave., between 80th and 81st sts. Tel. 873-3444.

Cuisine: AMERICAN. **Reservations:** Not accepted. **Subway:** 1, 9 to 79th St.; C to 81st St.

$ Prices: Appetizers $3–$5; salads, sandwiches, and burgers $3–$10; breakfast items $1.50–$8. $2.50 sharing charge. No credit cards.

Open: Mon–Thurs 8am–11pm; Fri 8am–midnight; Sat 9am–midnight; Sun 9am–11pm.

We're big fans of diners, so we're overjoyed to see that the current fad for the art deco look is bringing them back into vogue. E. J.'s, decorated with shiny silver fixtures, ceiling fans, and a few sleek 1950s ads on the walls, has fast become a West Side yuppie favorite, especially among those who crave breakfast food at odd hours. Top your buttermilk or buckwheat flapjacks with various combinations of raisins, blueberries, apples, and other fruits. We couldn't polish off a Belgian waffle with strawberries and bananas. There's old-fashioned French toast, omelets, and cinnamon honey granola with yogurt.

For those of you in the mood for lunch or dinner, there's a good selection of grilled sandwiches, salads, and burgers—we're partial to the Canadian Mountie burger, with Canadian bacon, sautéed onions, Gruyère cheese, lettuce, and tomato on grilled challah bread. Save room for an egg cream, an ice-cream soda, or a root-beer float.

FACULTY HOUSE, 400 W. 117th St., near Amsterdam Ave. Tel. 854-1200.

Cuisine: CONTINENTAL. **Subway:** 1, 9 to 116th St.

$ Prices: Nonmember fixed-price buffet lunch $12; nonmember fixed-price buffet dinner $13.50 (plus $1.50 service charge).

Open: Lunch Mon–Fri noon–2pm; dinner Mon–Fri 6–8pm. **Closed:** Summer.

Tucked away behind a dormitory, Columbia University's gracious Faculty House is a little-known secret even among neighborhood residents. Delicious buffet lunches and dinners are open to nonmembers. Visitors can eat lunch in the cafeteria or lunch or dinner on the fourth floor, in a lovely large room with a great view of the city. Buffet lunches include two hot main dishes, cold selections, vegetables, a full salad bar, and a sumptuous dessert table. The soups are homemade and delicious, including delicate bisques, cream soups, and fresh vegetable creations. Waiters will bring coffee and tea to your table, and you may eat all you want from the buffet tables. Dinner often features delectable fish dishes with smooth sauces, coq au vin, and veal and lamb.

FLOR DE MAYO, 2651 Broadway, between 100th and 101th sts. Tel. 663-5530.

Cuisine: SPANISH/CHINESE. **Reservations:** Not needed. **Subway:** 1, 2, 3, 9 to 96th St.

$ Prices: Appetizers and soups $1–$7.45; main courses $6.15–$13.95. AE, MC, V.

Open: Daily 2pm–midnight.

The Chinese immigrant population in Latin America has made its cuisine as popular south of the border as it is in the U.S. Many Chinese restaurateurs went on to settle in New York and took along some of their newfound South American and Cuban recipes. Flor de Mayo is one such bi-national creation. It has absolutely no decor to speak of—its kitchen does all the talking. The Chinese half of the menu features standard fare like eggs rolls and fried rice interspersed with more imaginative creations, like the kung po gai ding, diced chicken and vegetables stir-fried with a special homemade sauce and peanuts.

We ordered the special Peruvian chicken, pollo a la brasa, and were completely won over. Lunch specials, served Monday to Saturday from 11:30am to 3:30pm, include dishes like Cuban pot roast or roast ham and crispy fried chicken for a mere pittance—$3.95. The chef also does a mean paella à la Valenciana.

THE FOUR BROTHERS, 2381 Broadway, at 87th St. Tel. 874-7532.
  Cuisine: AMERICAN/GREEK. **Reservations:** Not needed. **Subway:** 1, 9 to 86th St.
  $ Prices: All items under $10. DC, MC, V.
  Open: Daily 6am–midnight.
Run by four Greek brothers named Lolos, this is half coffee shop and half fancier dining room. There is a homey bar where locals sit and watch TV for hours. Behind the bar, decorations include a lamp made from a whiskey bottle with a sombrero perched on top and a balalaika next to a rope of seed beads hanging on the wall.

The diner offers one of the most reasonable breakfasts in town; less than $3 will bring you two eggs, home fries, toast, and coffee or tea; or a breakfast of juice, wheat cakes or French toast, and beverage. Lunches and dinners at this local hangout are also quite reasonable, with selections like Greek salad, omelets, and several roasts and fish and chicken dishes. There is a daily specials list every weekday and a wide variety of sandwiches. Drinks from the bar are quite inexpensive ($2 for a wine spritzer).

GENOA, 271 Amsterdam Ave., between 72nd and 73rd sts. Tel. 787-1094.
  Cuisine: ITALIAN. **Reservations:** Not accepted; expect a wait. **Subway:** 1, 2, 3, 9, C to 72nd St.
  $ Prices: Appetizers under $5; pasta courses $6.95–$8.95; main courses $9.95–$11.95. AE, MC, V.
  Open: Dinner Tues–Sat 5:45–10:30pm, Sun 5:30–9:30pm.

Owned by Robert Arena, who traces his lineage back to Sicily, Genoa consistently serves great Italian food at great prices, with the kind of romantic neighborhood feeling you'd find in Boston's North End. You'll feel the pride he takes in his restaurant as soon as you walk in and see the low beamed ceiling and amber lights overhead. Start with a heaping antipasto, cold or hot, and work your way into one of the wonderful homemade pastas or a veal or chicken main dish. Check out the daily specials, which are often the biggest bargains on the menu.

GREGGY B'S, 247 W. 72nd between Broadway and West End Ave. Tel. 799-0500.
  Cuisine: SOUTHERN. **Reservations:** Not necessary. **Subway:** 1, 2, 3, 9 to 72nd St.
  $ Prices: Appetizers $2.95–$8.95; main courses $6.25–$18.95. $10 credit card minimum. AE, DISC, MC, V.
  Open: Sun–Thurs 11:30am–11pm, Fri–Sat 11:30am–midnight.

Greggy B's claims to serve "country BBQ at its best," and it does. It's a brand-new restaurant, with a clean, simple decor. You can sit in the glassed-in front and people-watch while you eat, or sit inside near the fireplace and really feel at home. If you're familiar with Southern cooking, you'll enjoy seeing cheese grits, hush puppies, corn muffins, and fried okra on the menu. If you're not, and you're interested in knowing how it's done, go into the kitchen and the chef will teach you how to prepare your favorite dish.

We love the "Sometime Soup"—as they say, "sometime it's black bean & sometime it's split pea, sometime it's Mississippi Clam Chowder, and sometime it's chunky chicken noodle and sometime we ain't got any . . ." You can also get "salads and other fun thangs from the garden," like Aunt Mary's grilled chicken breast salad. If you're in the mood for some good ol' fashioned red meat, you might want to try Uncle George's Baby Back Ribs. If you're really hungry, go for the "Barnyard Git Together"—a combination of ribs and chicken, and, of course, there's always chicken-fried steak. Dig in!

HAPPY BURGERS, 2489 Broadway, between 92nd and 93rd sts. Tel. 799-7719.

Cuisine: AMERICAN. **Reservations:** Not accepted. **Subway:** 1, 2, 3, 9 to 96th St.

$ Prices: Burgers and main courses $5–$7.95. No credit cards.

Open: Daily 7am–11pm.

Unbeatable burgers with all kinds of toppings are served at this neighborhood favorite. The menu is varied, including such Greek specialties as moussaka and spinach pie, as well as more prosaic sandwiches, salads, and the like. The service is friendly and efficient, and you might escape with a bill under $7 if you're careful.

HUNAN BALCONY, 2596 Broadway, at 98th St. Tel. 865-0400.

Cuisine: CHINESE. **Reservations:** Recommended for parties of 5 or more. **Subway:** 1, 2, 3, 9 to 96th St.

$ Prices: Appetizers $1.50–$5; main courses $5.95–$13.95. AE, DC, MC, V.

Open: Sun–Tues noon–midnight; Wed–Sat noon–1:30am.

If you're looking for a fancier-than-average Chinese place, Hunan Balcony is the perfect choice. The comfortable two-story restaurant has a window view and some nice touches, such as fruit drinks served with colorful parasols. Service is fast, and the food is delicious and reasonable. Start with the fried dumplings or cold noodles with sesame sauce before moving on to such favorites as beef with four flavors; sliced beef and red pepper, garlic, green scallions, ginger, and watercress; or moo shu pork. Shredded pork with garlic sauce is also delicious.

HUNAN PARK, 235 Columbus Ave., between 70th and 71st sts. Tel. 724-4411.

Cuisine: CHINESE. **Reservations:** Not needed. **Subway:** 1, 2, 3, 9, C to 72nd St.

$ Prices: Appetizers $1–$6.95; main courses $5.95–$9.95. Credit card minimum $10. AE, MC, V.

Open: Sun–Tues 11:30am–midnight; Wed–Sat 11:30am–1am.

Declaring a Chinese restaurant "the best" in its neighborhood is a sure-fire way to start an argument, but we're going to go out on a limb here and state that this is it. We've eaten in this bustling place countless times, and have walked away from every meal satisfied and stuffed. It's always packed with West Siders, who know a good thing when they taste it. The cold noodles with sesame sauce have a spicy kick, and never has a dish better satisfied the munchies than the golden crispy chicken topped with brown sauce and scallions. As for the decor, it's a rather plain place. But you never know who might turn up—the owners boast that Alan Alda is a regular fan.

MUSEUM CAFÉ, 366 Columbus Ave., at 77th St. Tel. 799-0150.

Cuisine: AMERICAN. **Reservations:** Recommended. **Subway:** 1, 2, 3, 9, C to 72nd St.

$ Prices: Individual pizzas, salads, and burgers $6.95–$9.95. AE, DC, MC, V.

Open: Sun–Thurs noon–midnight; Fri–Sat 11:30am–1am.

Across Columbus Avenue from the Museum of Natural History, this place is a longtime neighborhood favorite for lunch, dinner, or late drinks. Its high ceilings and Mediterranean archways lend an elegant but casual feel to the place.

The menu features a wide range of dishes, with interesting twists on the fish-chicken-pasta triumvirate so popular currently. The omelets here are legendary; try one made with tasso, a Cajun spiced pork. The café serves individual pizzas with a variety of fillings, and a good selection of sandwiches and burgers.

OLLIE'S, 2315 Broadway, at 84th St. Tel. 362-3111.
   Cuisine: CHINESE. **Reservations:** Not accepted. **Subway:** 1, 9 to 86th St.
$ Prices: Appetizers $1–$4.50; soups $1–$5.50; main courses $5.95–$14.95. AE, MC, V.
   Open: Sun–Thurs 11:30am–midnight, Fri–Sat 11:30am–1am.

West Siders are insanely attached to Ollie's, a yupscale version of the traditional Chinese noodle shop—it's always packed. The decor isn't anything special, but the Cantonese wonton soups with roast meats and the Mandarin noodle soups are. If you stick to these and have a spring roll on the side, as we did, you'll have a filling meal for well under $10. We could hardly finish the "Little Bit of Everything" noodle soup and the wonton and roast duck soup (to which you can add cellophane noodles for an extra 50¢). The seafood main dishes get a bit pricy, but all the traditional Chinese beef, pork, chicken, and vegetable dishes are reasonable—the lemon chicken, beef with orange flavor, and baby ribs with black bean sauce come highly recommended.

There's another Ollie's that's home away from home for Columbia students, at 2957 Broadway, at 116th Street (tel. 932-3300), and delivery service is available.

PETER'S PUMPKIN EATER, 2452 Broadway, near 91st St. Tel. 877-0132.
   Cuisine: NATURAL FOODS. **Reservations:** Accepted only for large parties.
   Subway: 1, 2, 3, 9 to 96th St.
$ Prices: Appetizers $3.50–$4.95; main courses $10.95–$13.95. AE, MC, V.
   Open: Mon–Fri 9am–11pm; Sat–Sun 11am–11pm.

This place features "natural cuisine," an eclectic menu of macrobiotic, Middle Eastern, and Mexican fare. It is a quiet, peaceful restaurant, even at its busiest. Classical music plays in the background, small wooden tables are set with fresh flowers and candles, and plants hang near the front windows.

While there's no red meat on the menu, there's a varied selection of broiled fresh fish, and guacamole and hummus are popular appetizers. A hearty helping of coarsely cut vegetables—carrots, zucchini, broccoli, cabbage, and chickpeas on a bed of brown rice, smothered in an unusual sweet-and-spicy cashew sauce—is delicious. Mango lemonade is a refreshing beverage, or try a cool papaya smoothie that is both thirst-quenching and a reputed digestive aid.

You can start your day here with such breakfast fare as homemade scones, carrot-raisin muffins, and fresh-squeezed orange juice.

RUPPERT'S, 269 Columbus Ave., between 72nd and 73rd sts. Tel. 873-9400.
   Cuisine: AMERICAN. **Reservations:** Recommended. **Subway:** 1, 2, 3, 9, C to 72nd St.
$ Prices: Appetizers 95¢–$2.95; main courses $4.95–$10.95. AE, CB, DC, MC, Transmedia, V.
   Open: Lunch Mon–Fri 11:30am–4:30pm; dinner daily 5pm–12:30am; brunch Sat–Sun 11am–4pm.

Ruppert's is famous for its elegant decor, good food, and refreshing prices. The gray and maroon color scheme is highlighted with touches of brass at the bar rail and a beautiful glass atrium area that looks out onto Columbus Avenue.

Dinner offers a curried chicken salad with apples and chutney on a bed of greens, a build-your-own burger, and penne with eggplant, fresh mozzarella, and tomato sauce. Most items are under $7. Ruppert's is particularly lovely at brunch. Main dishes, served with a complimentary Bloody Mary, screwdriver, mimosa, or glass of wine, include eggs sardou (with creamed spinach, artichokes, and hollandaise).

SAKURA OF JAPAN, 2298 Broadway, at 83rd St. Tel. 769-1003.
    Cuisine: JAPANESE. **Reservations:** Recommended. **Subway:** 1, 9 to 86th St.
$ **Prices:** Main courses $9.95–$14.95; combination platters $13.95–$16.95; sushi from $1.25 a piece. AE, MC, V.
    Open: Lunch daily noon–2:45pm; dinner 5–11:45pm.
    Sakura is on the pricey side, but it does serve some of the best sushi in town. Entering this dark, atmospheric spot, you pass two large tanks full of tropical fish. Head for the sushi bar, where you can order a full range of freshly prepared items, either in combination on a platter with miso soup, or individually. There are also delicious main dishes like chicken teriyaki. Next door is the Loews's 84th Street movie theater, making this an excellent choice for a premovie bite.

THE SYMPOSIUM, 544 W. 113th St., between Broadway and Amsterdam Ave. Tel. 865-1011.
    Cuisine: GREEK. **Reservations:** Recommended. **Subway:** 1, 9 to 110th St.
$ **Prices:** Appetizers $3.25; main courses $6.25–$11.95. DC, MC, V.
    Open: Daily noon–11pm.
This Greek restaurant, downstairs on a quiet side street near Columbia University is an old favorite of ours. There are folk-art paintings on the ceiling, painted lightbulbs, Greek art on the walls, and drawings on the tables.
    Moussaka (eggplant and meat pie) and pastitsio (stuffed macaroni) are standouts, as is the "feta"ccini (Greek spinach noodles with feta cheese). A carafe of wine can accompany your meal, and a full array of Greek dessert delights is offered, including a fabulous baklava. If the weather permits, dine in the lovely rear garden decorated with strings of lights, hanging plants, and more paintings.

THE THIRD WORLD CAFÉ, 700 W. 125th St., between Twelfth Ave. and Riverside Drive. Tel. 749-8199.
    Cuisine: CARIBBEAN. **Reservations:** Not accepted. **Transportation:** Though the 1 train stops at 125th St. and Broadway, we recommend that you take a cab.
$ **Prices:** Appetizers $2.50–$3.95; burgers $3.95–$5.25; main courses $6.95–$12.95. No credit cards.
    Open: Dinner Tues–Thurs 5–11pm, Fri–Sat 5pm–midnight, Sun 4–10pm.
    This tiny place doesn't look like much from the outside—and the nervous among you may feel jittery in this rather desolate neighborhood. But if you're willing to take a cab ride north of Columbia and have an adventure, you're going to be treated to some fabulous, down-home cooking. Have some homemade lemonade, Red Stripe beer from Jamaica, or Club beer from Ghana while you enjoy the reggae music and study the blackboard specials. You can start with cornmeal fried fish fingers, served with sweet curry dipping sauce, or eggplant creole on a bed of greens with a dill vinaigrette. We opted for the hush puppies (some of the best to be had north of the Mason-Dixon line) with hot and sweet sauce and the creole mustard chicken wings.
    You can't do better than the Caribbean chicken breast, in a tangy sauce, with plantains and a salad. The spicy Brazilian shrimp and okra stew was to die for, but you might be tempted by the BBQ ribs with black beans and yellow rice or the jerk burger, with spicy Jamican black sauce.

LA VICTORIA-CHINA, 2536 Broadway, at 95th St. Tel. 865-1810.
    Cuisine: CUBAN/CHINESE. **Reservations:** Not accepted. **Subway:** 1, 2, 3, 9 to 96th St.
$ **Prices:** Appetizers $6.95; main courses $7.95–$14.50. AE, DC, MC, V.
    Open: Daily 11am–10:30pm.

This noisy neighborhood eatery is bright and busy, with Formica-and-vinyl booths, wall hangings, and bustling Chinese waiters. For a Cuban experience, try one of the generous combination plates such as chopped beef, with moros y cristianos (rice and beans) and salad. The savory sauce on the beef and the rice studded with black beans is delicious and hearty. Green or ripe plantains make an interesting and tasty dish. When you mix a meal with Chinese favorites like moo goo gai pan (chicken with mushrooms, bamboo shoots, and vegetables), a strange but satisfying blend can be yours.

WEST SIDE STOREY, 700A Columbus Ave., at 95th St. Tel. 749-1900.
   Cuisine: AMERICAN. **Reservations:** Not needed. **Subway:** 1, 2, 3, 9, B, C to 96th St.
$ Prices: Appetizers $2.95–$6; main courses $6.95–$11.95. MC, V.
   Open: Mon–Fri 7am–11pm, Sat–Sun 8am–11pm.
About ten blocks north of the chic Columbus Avenue strip, this restaurant offers a delightful meal to those customers who seek it out, and are often found waiting for the doors to open in the morning. They're probably eager for the special French toast: challah bread dipped in cream and served with real Vermont maple syrup. Three-egg omelets are also a treat, with fillings such as caviar, sour cream, and chives or mozzarella cheese and sausage.
   Lunch brings in another big crowd. The sandwich selection includes bacon, arugula, and tomato, served on your choice of bread, or fresh roast turkey. A dish of Moroccan chili comes with sour cream and a small salad, or you might go for the grilled hamburger on a seeded roll with fries. Dinners are quiet, but there is still a good selection that includes chicken gai yang with Thai hot sauce, and chicken livers sautéed in sherry with mushrooms. Meals may also be prepared for low-salt or low-calorie diets.
   The deli also has a take-out service.

YELLOW ROSE, 450 Amsterdam Ave., at 81st St. Tel. 595-8760.
   Cuisine: AMERICAN. **Reservations:** Not accepted. **Subway:** 1, 9 to 79th St.; C to 81st St.
$ Prices: Appetizers $2–$5; main courses $5.50–$16.95. $7 minimum per person after 6pm. AE, CB, DC, MC, V.
   Open: Mon–Thurs noon–11pm, Fri noon–midnight, Sat 10am–3:30pm and 4:30pm–midnight, Sun 10am–3:30pm and 4:30–11pm.
⭐ They do a mean chicken-fried steak at the Yellow Rose, and they know what goes well with it—a basket of warm fluffy biscuits and cornbread, and, of course, mashed potatoes smothered in gravy. All the best in Texan fare is here, from fried chicken to okra, and the menu boasts that the veggies are flown in from a garden in Fort Worth. The decor is campy and authentic too, with cowhide-covered chairs, and country tunes that just keep coming. The bar is hopping, especially when there are two-for-one margaritas from 5 to 7pm. We suggest that you polish off your meal with pecan or strawberry rhubarb pie.

13. UPPER EAST SIDE/YORKVILLE

See Section 12 above for a complete review of **Ruppert's;** the East Side branch is located at 1662 Third Ave., at 93rd Street (tel. 831-1900).

AFGHANISTAN KEBAB HOUSE, 1345 Second Ave., between 70th and 71st sts. Tel. 517-2776 or 517-2922.
   Cuisine: AFGHAN. **Reservations:** Recommended, especially on weekends.
   Subway: 6 to 68th St.
$ Prices: Afghan salad $2.50; main courses $6–$7. AE.
   Open: Mon–Thurs 11:30am–10pm; Fri–Sat 11:30am–10:30pm.

Ⓢ Charcoal-broiled meat and chicken dishes are the stars of the menu at this unpretentious spot. Try the half-chicken tandoori or the juicy lamb tikka kebab (chunks of lamb marinated in fresh grated spices, broiled over wood charcoal, and served with brown basmati rice and Afghan bread). And if you're not a carnivore, you needn't worry, as there are several vegetarian dishes offered; we favor the palau zucchini, cooked with onions, fresh tomatoes, herbs, and spices. Take-out and delivery services are available.

There's a West Side Afghan Kebab House at 764 Ninth Avenue (tel. 307-1612).

AGRA, 807 Lexington Ave., between 62nd and 63rd sts. Tel. 308-8281.
   Cuisine: INDIAN. **Reservations:** Recommended only for window tables.
   Subway: 4, 5, 6 to 59th St.
$ **Prices:** Appetizers $1.95–$3.50; main courses $8.50–$13.50. $7 minimum per person. AE, DC, MC, V.
   Open: Mon–Sat noon–midnight; Sun 4pm–midnight.
You'll find this charming retreat tucked away on the second floor of an otherwise nondescript building (go up the stairs and turn right). The Agra has Indian-print cloth on the walls and ceiling, and tables set in white linen and flowers. Ask for a seat by the windows, which are cut to look like Indian arches. Many regular patrons are Indian or have traveled in India—a good indication of this place's authenticity.

A special Tandoori dinner is offered for $14.50; two people can share for $28. You'll begin with shami kebab (a chopped meat patty) and puffy, slightly sweet poori bread. There's a choice of soup, then tandoori chicken with pillaw rice, dahl, a choice of dessert, and Indian tea or coffee. (Allow 20 minutes to prepare this extravaganza.) Other set dinners are available for $12.50 to $16.95, but if you'd rather order from the à la carte menu, the crab and lobster curry is tempting. Wine is available by the glass or the carafe, and King Fisher and other beers are offered.

BLUE MOON MEXICAN CAFÉ, 1444 First Ave., corner of 75th St. Tel. 288-9811.
   Cuisine: MEXICAN. **Reservations:** Not accepted. **Bus:** M30 crosstown or M15.
$ **Prices:** Appetizers $3.95–$6.95; main courses $9.95–$13.95. AE, MC, V.
   Open: Lunch daily 11:30am–4pm; dinner Sun–Thurs 5pm–midnight, Fri–Sat 5pm–1am.
Although the Blue Moon doesn't offer the most authentic south-of-the-border fare, the atmosphere is fun and prices are reasonable. Upper East Siders trickle in around 6:30pm, dressed in everything from dark suits to T-shirts and shorts. The decor is black and brass, with neon accents such as neon cacti mounted on the brick wall behind the bar.

Your table will be set with a dwarf cactus and a brimming bowl of chips with salsa. If the chips aren't appetizer enough, try the chicken taquitos, jalapeño cheese fries, or the special Blue Moon prime sirloin chili. The quarter-moon chili is mild, while the full moon is a hotter variety of the same. Dinner main dishes include chimichangas, enchiladas, fajitas, tostadas, and other Mexican specialties. All include refried beans and rice. There are even a couple of burger selections for those of you who refuse to get into the Mexican mode.

The Blue Moon also serves a $9.95 Saturday and Sunday brunch with unlimited champagne or one Bloody Mary, screwdriver, or margarita.

There are two other Blue Moons in Manhattan: at 150 Eighth Avenue, between 17th and 18th streets (tel. 463-0560); and 287 Columbus Avenue, between 73rd and 74th streets (tel. 721-2701).

BROTHER JIMMY'S, 1461 First Ave., at 76th St. Tel. 545-RIBS.
   Cuisine: BARBECUE. **Reservations:** Not accepted. **Bus:** M15 or M30.
$ **Prices:** Appetizers $2.95–$7.25; main courses sandwiches and Mexican dishes $5.95–$6.95; complete BBQ dinners $7.95–$11.95. $12 minimum per person. AE, CB, DC, MC, V.

Open: Dinner Mon–Thurs 5pm–midnight; Fri–Sat 5pm–1am; Sun 11am–3pm and 4pm–midnight.

From the outside, Brother Jimmy's looks like a bootlegger's shed; inside, a sign suggests that you "Put some South in yo' mouth." A corrugated tin awning decorated with melon-size plastic lights shades the entrance to this barbecue joint. And although the interior looks more like a garage than a restaurant, the food is excellent and the prices unbeatable. The whitewashed brick walls are lined with baseball caps, cowboy hats, and road signs from North Carolina and Texas. Up front in the bar, Skee Ball and a wide selection of beer keeps the crowd happy.

Back in the dining room, pull your silverware out from the wax-paper folders and dig into the terrific complimentary coleslaw. Start with the hush puppies or the BBQ chicken wings. For dinner, there's catfish, a few Mexican main dishes, or a whole slew of barbecued sandwiches. The specialties of the house are tender barbecued pork or chicken that have been smoked over hickory wood. Try the half chicken, or the southern-style ribs slathered in a spicy vinegar sauce. All complete dinners include cornbread and a choice of two side dishes (such as mashed potatoes or collard greens). Brother Jimmy's also offers a Li'l Tykes menu, with prices from $1.75 to $2.25 for a main dish served with potatoes (mashed or fried) and a green vegetable. For a cleaned plate, Brother Jimmy will give the li'l tyke a free bowl of ice cream. The bar stays open as long as there's a crowd, which is usually 2 or 3am. Check for specials—when we were there, kids under 12 ate free with an adult (limit two kids). There was a Sunday Rib Special, with all-you-can-eat ribs and all-you-can-drink beer with dinner, for $14.95—a true glutton's delight.

If you're downtown, check out Jimmy's cousin, **Brother's Bar-B-Q,** 228 West Houston St., between Sixth Avenue and Varick Street (tel. 727-2775).

CAFÉ AND RESTAURANT DIVINO, 1544/1556 Second Ave., between 80th and 81st sts. Tel. 517-9269 and 861-1096.

Cuisine: ITALIAN. **Reservations:** Not accepted. **Bus:** M79 crosstown or M15.

$ **Prices:** Appetizers $4.50–$6.95; half-orders of pasta $5.95; main courses $6.75–$15.25; pasta courses $10.75–$10.95. AE, CB, DC, MC, V.

Open: Lunch Mon–Thurs noon–4pm; brunch Sun noon–4pm; dinner Mon–Thurs 5pm–midnight, Fri–Sat 5pm–1am, Sun 5–11pm.

No need to go all the way downtown to Little Italy—this charming and intimate spot is *molto buono*. The small restaurant is decorated with green-and-white tablecloths, a green awning over the bar, green curtains, and posters of Italy on the white walls. The menu is the same at lunch and dinner. There are 12 different types of pasta, such as tortellini alla Panna and conchiglie ortolana. The six specials of the day might include chicken sorrentina or filet of sole in wine sauce. There's a varying dessert selection that usually features zuppa inglese and torta Divino, cannoli, and Italian ice creams.

The $9.95 brunch includes a complimentary bar drink and coffee, espresso, or cappuccino.

CAFÉ GEIGER, 206 E. 86th St., between Second and Third aves. Tel. 734-4428.

Cuisine: GERMAN. **Reservations:** Recommended. **Subway:** 4, 5, 6 to 86th St.

$ **Prices:** Appetizers $4–$7.50; salads and sandwiches $7–$12.50; main courses $8.75–$17.50. $5 minimum per person. AE, CB, DC, MC, V.

Open: Sat–Sun 9am–11pm.

This place will catch your eye with its exquisite front window display of enticing pastries. Inside there's a spacious, cheerful dining room with elegant touches like wood paneling and oil paintings. The staff is polite, and the Café Geiger has a loyal following.

There are many reasonably priced items on the menu. Main dish prices can go as high as $17.50, but most are under $14. House specials include potato pancakes with cranberries or applesauce, wiener wurstchen (Vienna-style frankfurter) with sauerkraut and potato, jaegernitzel, sauerbraten Bavarian style, and steak tartare. And

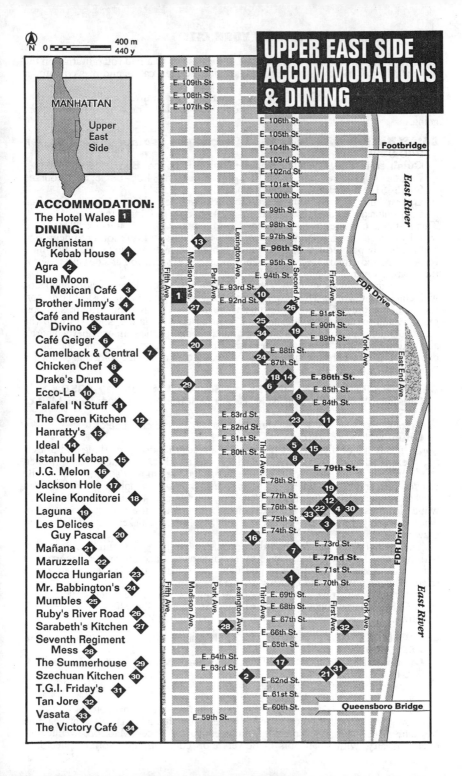

UPPER EAST SIDE ACCOMMODATIONS & DINING

ACCOMMODATION:
The Hotel Wales 1
DINING:
Afghanistan
  Kebab House 1
Agra 2
Blue Moon
  Mexican Café 3
Brother Jimmy's 4
Café and Restaurant
  Divino 5
Café Geiger 6
Camelback & Central 7
Chicken Chef 8
Drake's Drum 9
Ecco-La 10
Falafel 'N Stuff 11
The Green Kitchen 12
Hanratty's 13
Ideal 14
Istanbul Kebap 15
J.G. Melon 16
Jackson Hole 17
Kleine Konditorei 18
Laguna 19
Les Delices
  Guy Pascal 20
Mañana 21
Maruzzella 22
Mocca Hungarian 23
Mr. Babbington's 24
Mumbles 25
Ruby's River Road 26
Sarabeth's Kitchen 27
Seventh Regiment
  Mess 28
The Summerhouse 29
Szechuan Kitchen 30
T.G.I. Friday's 31
Tan Jore 32
Vasata 33
The Victory Café 34

need we remind you to save room for one of the pastries that had you salivating on the way in? Most of the fresh-baked tortes, strudels, waffles, cakes, and pies cost under $4.50.

Note: At press time, Café Geiger was open only on Saturday and Sunday as they were undergoing renovations, so you should call to check new open hours before going.

CAMELBACK & CENTRAL, 1403 Second Ave., corner of 73rd St. Tel. 249-8380.
    Cuisine: INTERNATIONAL. **Reservations:** Required. **Bus:** M15 or M30.
$ **Prices:** Appetizers $2.95–$7.50; salads and burgers $4.25–$8.95; main courses $8.95–$14.95. CB, DC, MC, Transmedia, V.
    Open: Lunch Mon–Fri 11:30am–3pm; dinner Mon–Fri 5–11:30pm, Sat–Sun 5pm–midnight; brunch Sat 11:30am–3:30pm, Sun 11:30am–4pm.

This restaurant, named for a crossroads in Phoenix, Arizona, offers excellent food, friendly service, and a minimalist decor. You can't miss it: Look for a red neon sign and a brightly painted red-brick exterior. There are huge windows, creamy white-brick walls, and an Art Deco bar. Trendy waiters will serve you at sidewalk tables if the weather's nice.

You might begin by splitting, as we did, a combination platter of hot appetizers, with chicken saté with a Thai peanut sauce, chicken wings, potato skins, and calamari fritti—all for only $7.50. The fettuccini Fra Diavola, with baby shrimp, scallops, mussels, and tomato sauce adorning a bed of pasta, is tempting, and we found the roast duck with a Grand Marnier sauce and apple and prune stuffing superb. There's also a down-to-earth meatloaf with mashed potatoes and gravy to make the choice difficult. Desserts here are rich—how can you go wrong with something called a "chocolate sin pie"?

CHICKEN CHEF, 301 E. 80th St., at Second Ave. Tel. 517-8350.
    Cuisine: AMERICAN/CHICKEN. **Reservations:** Not needed. **Bus:** M79 or M15.
$ **Prices:** Half chicken $4.49, whole chicken $8.79. No credit cards.
    Open: Daily 11am–11pm.

⑤ In this age of diversity it's nice to find a place that does one thing and does it extremely well. Chicken Chef does exactly that. Succulent flame-broiled chicken is the name of the game here, and we think it's at the top of the chicken-restaurant pecking order. The split-level interior is simple, with high-backed carved wooden chairs, butcher-block tables, marble counter tops, and black-and-white tile floors. The chicken is cooked on an open grill and the walls are covered with what can only be called "chicken arcana," obscure chicken-related facts and drawings.

The menu is even simpler than the decor. Broiled, juicy, flavorful chicken comes with pita bread and a choice of delectable homemade sauces, such as cranberry and hot Mexican salsa. Side orders of gourmet rice, spinach and rice, tabouleh, green salad, slaw, or potato salad cost less than $2.

Chicken Chef also has free delivery in 30 minutes. They have other locations, one at 1177 Second Ave., at the corner of 62nd Street (tel. 308-9400); and one at 21 Greenwich Ave., at the corner of 10th Street (tel. 929-1100).

LES DELICES GUY PASCAL, 1231 Madison Ave., at 89th St. Tel. 289-5300.
    Cuisine: FRENCH/CONTINENTAL. **Reservations:** Not needed. **Subway:** 4, 5, 6 to 86th St.
$ **Prices:** Breakfast $1.75–$6.25; salads and sandwiches $6.75–$8.25; main courses $7.25–$9.95. AE, DC.
    Open: Mon–Fri 7:30am–10pm; Sat 7:30am–9pm; Sun 8am–8pm.

This lovely tea room and pastry shop is a perfect stop after a hard day's sightseeing on Museum Mile—and it's surprisingly inexpensive for pricey Madison Avenue. It's open and airy, with small pots of flowers atop cool blue floral-print tablecloths.

Breakfast specials might feature a fresh croissant or egg dishes, and the desserts ($3.50 to $5.95) are enticing, perhaps with a cup of cappuccino or another hot beverage ($1.65 to $2.65). The sandwiches and fresh salads are complemented by a selection of more substantial main dishes, including a changing list of daily specials.

There's another, much smaller branch on the Upper West Side, on Columbus Avenue.

DRAKE'S DRUM, 1629 Second Ave., between 84th and 85th sts. Tel. 988-2826.

Cuisine: ENGLISH. **Reservations:** Recommended for dinner. **Subway:** 4, 5, 6 to 86th St. **Bus:** M18 or M15.

$ Prices: Appetizers $2.25–$5.95; main courses $7.50–$12.95; brunch selections $5.50 and $7.95. AE, CB, DC, MC, V.

Open: Lunch daily noon–4pm; dinner Sun–Thurs 5pm–1am, Fri–Sat 5pm–2am; brunch Sat–Sun noon–4:30pm. Open for drinks nightly until 4am.

We love this pub. It's favored by rugby players (one owner used to play and one still does), homesick Brits and other Europeans, and neighborhood fans. Drake's Drum is appropriately dim, with lanterns, dark wood, pillars wound with rope, red-and-white-checked tablecloths, sawdust on the floor, and huge, wonderful oil paintings, including one of the restaurant's interior. Regulars crowd the copper-topped bar to watch the latest world sports competition. In warm weather you can dine outdoors.

The dinner menu features main dishes like chicken parmigiana, pub-style fish and chips, southern fried chicken, broiled scrod, and even quiche. The "Draught and Steak" is a good deal with a 12-ounce sirloin, salad, and baked potato, and a choice of a 32-ounce pitcher of beer or a 16-ounce carafe of wine for $13.50. Also, check the menu for nightly low-priced specials; and on British holidays like St. George's Day (April 23), look for extra-specials like "toad in the hole," "bangers and mash," and roast beef with Yorkshire pudding.

Drake's Drum has two weekend brunch selections—the "Rugby," with a charcoal-broiled steak, two eggs, bacon, french fries, English muffin, and a 16-ounce pitcher of sangría or a Bloody Mary for $7.95; or there is the "Bicycle," with French toast, bacon, and sangría or a Bloody Mary for $5.50.

ECCO-LA, 1660 Third Ave., at 93rd St. Tel. 860-5609.

Cuisine: ITALIAN. **Reservations:** Not accepted. **Subway:** 6 to 96th St.

$ Prices: Appetizers $4.95; pizzas $6.95–$8.25; main courses $6.95–$10.95. No credit cards.

Open: Mon–Thurs noon–11:30pm, Fri–Sat noon–midnight, Sun noon–10:30pm.

★ It's a popular little spot (as the decibel level will certainly attest), but if you have a wait at Ecco-la, you can take a beer to one of the small benches outside the restaurant, as we did. Once seated, you'll be surrounded by vibrant primary colors, including brightly painted clocks on the wall, that highlight a black decor. It's all funky and modern, but the warm welcome and huge portions of well-presented Italian specialties impressed us even more than the trendy surroundings.

Standouts among the imaginative appetizers are the antipasto di mare—lobster with avocado, hearts of palm, chopped fresh tomatoes, and endive in a lobster mayonnaise—and the antipasto di campo, with grilled shiitaki mushrooms, hearts of palm, parmeggiano shavings, and asparagus. The individual pizzas are too much for one person to finish—just try to polish off the pizza verdura, with fresh mozzarella, broccoli, asparagus, spinach, artichoke hearts, and tomato sauce.

Ecco-la II is right next door, with a more traditional decor and a slightly different menu.

FALAFEL 'N STUFF, 1586 First Ave., between 82nd and 83rd sts. Tel. 879-7023.

Cuisine: MIDDLE EASTERN. **Reservations:** Recommended for parties of 3 or more. **Bus:** M18 or M15.

$ Prices: Appetizers $3–$6.50; vegetarian platters $7–$8.50; meat platters $10.50–$14.50. MC, V.

Open: Sun–Thurs noon–midnight; Fri–Sat noon–1am.
This Egyptian restaurant has more imagination than its name implies. Set in the narrowest of dining rooms, with salmon brick walls and white wall lamps, it is decorated with Egyptian art (and photos of the owner's son with famous customer Michael J. Fox). On the tables are fresh carnations with babies' breath.

On the menu are 14 filling and inexpensive vegetarian platters, each of which comes with salad, rice, vegetables, and pita bread. We think these maza dishes—falafel (crisp-fried chickpea balls), tabouli (crushed wheat salad), hummus (chickpeas and tahine)—are the best on the menu. The barbecued Pharaoh chicken is also a good deal at $10.50. Other meat dishes are similarly priced, but can go as high as $14.50 for baby lamb rib chops.

Jumbo sandwiches with maza fillings are another low-priced consideration, all under $5.50. An appetizer of stuffed grape leaves or stuffed zucchini is recommended. For dessert, try the magnificent bird's nest, a homemade concoction of phyllo, walnuts, and pistachios. A limited selection of beer and wine is available.

THE GREEN KITCHEN, 1477 First Ave., at 77th St. Tel. 988-4163.
  Cuisine: AMERICAN. **Reservations:** Not needed. **Bus:** M79 or M15.
  $ Prices: Appetizers $1.90–$8.40; breakfast items $4–$10.95, brunch $9.95; sandwiches, burgers, and salads $3–$9.25; main courses $8.75–$18.45. AE, CB, DC, MC, V.
  Open: Daily 24 hrs; brunch served Sat–Sun noon–4pm.
This fancy coffee shop has something for everyone. There's an oval-shaped area with booths, as well as a small bar, and an attractive porch with glass walls and nice tablecloths and fresh flowers on the tables.

The extensive menu offers breakfast items, including Belgian waffles; "Famous Salads"; sandwiches and 7-ounce burgers; and main dishes, most under $12. Look for specials, such as the pasta lover's menu, with pasta and salad available for $6.95. There's also a new low-calorie, low-cholesterol menu, although you may want to skip it and go straight for the homemade desserts, such as chocolate cheesecake and strawberry shortcake.

HANRATTY'S, 1410 Madison Ave., near 97th St. Tel. 369-3420.
  Cuisine: AMERICAN. **Reservations:** Recommended only for large parties.
  Subway: 6 to 96th St. **Bus:** M1, M2, M3, M4, or M18.
  $ Prices: Appetizers $3.25–$4.75; salads $6.75–$9.95; pasta courses $9.95–$10.95; main courses $9.95–$16. AE.
  Open: Lunch Mon–Fri 11:30am–4pm; dinner daily 5–11:30pm; brunch Sat–Sun 11:30am–4pm.
A friendly neighborhood spot, decorated with tasteful simplicity, Hanratty's has an attractive long wooden bar and a large blackboard with the daily specials. You can sit at a table by the window or in the more private dining area beyond the bar. There are candles on the table at dinner, and flowers in glass vases.

Dinner main dishes are served with a salad and a choice of side order. Among the offerings is veal lugano—a lightly breaded veal dish made with lemon, butter, and parmesan cheese. There are daily blackboard specials, and sandwiches available for $5.50 to $6.75. The rather decadent dessert selections include chocolate mud cake, "Holey Moses!" cheesecake, and pecan pie with Häagen-Dazs ice cream. The bar is open late, with waffles and dessert served nightly from 10:30pm.

IDEAL, 238 E. 86th St., between Second and Third aves. Tel. 535-0950.
  Cuisine: GERMAN. **Reservations:** Not needed. **Subway:** 4, 5, 6 to 86th St.
  $ Prices: Appetizers $1.75–$5; main courses $4.95–$7.75. No credit cards.
  Open: Daily 7am–11pm.
Ideal makes no pretensions to be anything but a straightforward luncheonette; it's been serving hearty food since 1932. There are a few tables, a long lunch counter stacked with reserves of beer, and fluorescent lighting overhead. Ideal has a character all its own, and it's a good place to eat for $10 or less.

Breakfast specials, served from 7 to 11am, are all under $5. The farmer's omelet, with bacon and onions, and the eggs with bratwurst are two of the most popular choices; both are served with pan-fried potatoes. You can make a meal of German pot roast with potatoes and red cabbage, schweinebraten (fresh ham with sauerkraut and potatoes), Hungarian goulash, lamb stew, or potato pancakes with applesauce. For the more adventurous, there are pigs' knuckles with sauerkraut and potatoes, or liver dumplings. A draft German beer is the beverage of choice.

ISTANBUL KEBAP, 303 E. 80th St., between First and Second aves. Tel. 517-6880.
   Cuisine: MIDDLE EASTERN. **Reservations:** Recommended. **Bus:** M79 or M15.
$ Prices: Appetizers $2.95–$3.50; main courses $8.95–$11.50. AE, CB, DC.
   Open: Daily 1pm–midnight.
Authentic Middle Eastern music sets the tone in this small, family-run spot, with Turkish rugs displayed on the walls. Lamb is the basis for many of the dishes here, and the yogurtta kebap is our favorite. It's a pita sautéed in butter and combined with sliced lamb kebap, then expertly seasoned—marinated in onion, parsley, and a special spiced sauce, then topped with yogurt, baked, and served with paprika sauce. We also enjoyed eit banya, cubes of tender lamb simmered in homemade tomato sauce with herb flavoring and served on a bed of rice. Desserts, at $3.25, include baklava and a special daily offering. No liquor is served.

J. G. MELON, 1291 Third Ave., at 74th St. Tel. 650-1310.
   Cuisine: AMERICAN. **Reservations:** Not needed. **Subway:** 6 to 77th St.
$ Prices: Soup $3; burgers, sandwiches, and salads $4.95–$14.95. No credit cards.
   Open: Mon–Sat 11:30am–4am; Sun noon–4am.
A few retired squash racquets and other objects hang on the brown walls, but J. G. Melon's interior is really made charming by its profusion of—what else?—melons: in painting, in neon, even in the real thing. J. G. simply stands for the owners, Jack and George. We think the restaurant (really more of a pub) is delightful. It's especially nice to get one of the four tables up front in the bar room, tucked on a platform under mullioned windows. Tables are covered with green-and-white-checked cloths, and the high ceiling is reddish tin.
   The tiny kitchen is smack in the middle, across from the bar. From it comes simple fare. Selections are written on the blackboard: hamburgers; bacon burgers; roast beef sandwiches; chef's, niçoise, or chicken salads. Most offerings are under $10, and for dessert, there are pies and cheesecake.

JACKSON HOLE, 232 E. 64th St., between Second and Third aves. Tel. 371-7187.
   Cuisine: AMERICAN. **Reservations:** Not needed. **Subway:** 6 to 59th St. or 68th St.
$ Prices: Appetizers $4.95; burgers $4–$8.10. $3 minimum per person. No credit cards.
   Open: Mon–Thurs 10:30am–1am; Fri–Sat 10:30am–4am; Sun noon–midnight.
There are Jackson Hole Hamburger Restaurants all over the Upper East Side, ranging from the very small original restaurant to the spacious, glass-walled one at 91st Street and Madison Avenue. They all have attractive if simple decor with posters of the Wyoming ski resort, and good, inexpensive hamburgers. And there's more: omelets; hot and cold sandwiches; honey-dipped fried chicken with salad and french fries; and salads, desserts, and beer and wine are available. Breakfast specials, under $3, are served daily.
   There is another Jackson Hole with the same hours at 1633 Second Ave., at 85th Street (tel. 737-8788). The Jackson Hole at the corner of Madison Avenue and 91st Street (tel. 427-2820) is open daily from 7am to 11pm.

KLEINE KONDITOREI, 234 E. 86th St., between Second and Third aves. Tel. 737-7130.
   Cuisine: GERMAN. **Reservations:** Recommended. **Subway:** 4, 5, 6 to 86th St. **Bus:** M18.

$ Prices: Appetizers $2.75; main courses $8.75–$18.75. $4 minimum per person. AE, DC.

Open: Sun–Thurs 11am–11pm, Fri–Sat 11am–midnight.

Founded in 1923, this elegant German restaurant tempts with a window display of exquisite pastries. The upstairs dining rooms are decorated with red carpeting and wallpaper, cherry paneling, burnished brass, and shaded sconces and chandeliers that are reminiscent of old Vienna. The tables have white linens and flowers.

You'll dine on filling fare—perhaps herring salad, chopped chicken liver, wiener wurstchen (German frankfurter), Hungarian goulash, or rainbow trout amandine. All main courses come with a choice of vegetable, salad, and potato. Cocktails are available, and desserts, such as vanilla pudding and homemade apple strudel, are around $2.75.

LAGUNA, 1748 Second Ave., near 90th St. Tel. 427-3106.

Cuisine: ITALIAN. **Reservations:** Recommended. **Subway:** 4, 5, 6 to 86th St.; 6 to 96th St. **Bus:** M18 or M15.

$ Prices: Salads and antipasti $3.50–$5.95; pizza $7.95–$8.95; main courses $5.95–$14.95. CB, DC, MC, V.

Open: Mon–Sat 5pm–midnight; Sun noon–midnight. Bar may be open later.

When we first walked by Laguna while researching this book, we didn't even bother to check the menu—the sleek decor just made it *look* too expensive to be included. But on closer look, we discovered that the prices are more than reasonable, and there's even a $10 fixed-price early-bird dinner, served Monday through Friday from 5 to 7pm, that includes your choice of antipasto, pasta dish, and coffee and dessert.

We give the pizza selections, made fresh in a wood-burning oven, a big thumbs up—especially the pizza quatro stagioni, with tomato, mozzarella, artichokes, prosciutto, olives, and mushrooms. Main courses, most under $10, include fusilli norcia, with hot and sweet sausage, tomatoes, and garlic, and grilled veal chops sautéed with sage and butter.

And the best part? Paper tablecloths, with crayons provided for doodling while you wait.

MAÑANA, 1136 First Ave., between 62nd and 63rd sts. Tel. 223-9623.

Cuisine: MEXICAN. **Reservations:** Not accepted. **Bus:** M103 or M15.

$ Prices: Appetizers $5.50–$6.75; soup $2.95–$5.75; main courses $10.95–$15.95; combination platters $10.50–$10.95. AE, DC, DISC, MC, V.

Open: Mon–Fri 11:30am–11:30pm, Sat–Sun 1–11:30pm.

Soft lights, white stucco walls, dark heavy woods, tapestry chairs, escutcheons, and candles create a graceful setting for Mañana's substantial and well-priced meals. Hearty combination platters include Mexican favorites with rice and beans; the vegetarian combination brings you cheese enchiladas, a bean burrito, and a guacamole tostada. A la carte items include chili con carne and a seafood chili relleno. Sangrita, a hot and spicy Bloody Mary, is served along with the usual margaritas and beers.

MARUZZELLA, 1479 First Ave., corner of 77th St. Tel. 988-8877.

Cuisine: ITALIAN. **Reservations:** Recommended **Bus:** M15 or M79.

$ Prices: Antipasti $7.25–$11.25; soups and salads $5.25–$6.50; pasta courses and pizzas $9.50–$14.75; main courses $12.75–$18. $15 minimum per person. AE, CB, DC, MC, V.

Open: Daily noon–1am.

Maruzzella is characterized by a huge yellow awning, white stucco walls, and—in summer—doors that swing out onto a sidewalk café. Once inside, the scent of a wood-burning pizza oven, fresh garlic, and olive oil will whet your appetite. The blond-wood tables and chairs and the red tile floor give this charming place a sunny personality. The waiters, in their blue workshirts and yellow aprons, chat in Italian as the pizza maestro tosses another thin-crusted pie in the open oven.

The food, like the atmosphere, is light and fresh. We split an antipasto for starters, but you might try the thinly sliced sun-dried beef with rucola also (known to New Yorkers as arugula), the homemade mozzarella with tomato lightly flavored with olive oil, or the fresh soups. The real specialties, though, are the pasta and pizza—and the pizza should not be missed. These thin, crisp, ten-inch delicacies are topped with a mellow tomato sauce and a carefully chosen selection of Italian specialties, including mozzarella, hot salami, anchovies, capers, olives, hot peppers, and/or artichoke hearts. Most can serve as a meal by themselves, although you might choose to top it all off with a cappuccino and a slice of the incredibly rich mocha-mousse cake or tiramisu.

Maruzzella offers a fixed-price weekday lunch for $10.95 and a weekend brunch for $11.95. There's a new party room and wine bar on the second floor.

MR. BABBINGTON'S RESTAURANT, 1568 Third Ave., corner of 88th St. Tel. 860-1980.

Cuisine: AMERICAN. **Reservations:** Not needed. **Subway:** 4, 5, 6 to 86th St.
$ Prices: Appetizers $1.95–$3.95; main courses $7.50–$13.95. MC, V.
Open: Lunch Mon–Sat 11:30am–4pm; dinner daily 5–10:30pm; brunch Sun 11:30am–4pm.

This place remains one of New York's true bargains. Most of its business comes from delivery, take-out, and catering, but the lucky few who visit the restaurant are in for a treat. The plant-filled windows, open kitchen, tile floors, and still-life murals combine to give the restaurant a rustic, homey feel.

But the real beauty here is the high quality and low prices. After starting with a bacon and scallion tart with Cheddar cheese or cream of split pea soup, you might try the pit-grilled half chicken with plum sauce or a marinated leg of lamb with spinach pecan leek stuffing in a peach nectar sauce. All dinner main dishes include a help-yourself salad bar and bread basket brimming with fresh-baked pumpernickel and corn muffins. If you still have room for dessert, order the deep-dish apple pie, the peach melba, or strawberry whipped cream cake, all at $1.95. BYOB.

MOCCA HUNGARIAN RESTAURANT, 1588 Second Ave., between 82nd and 83rd sts. Tel. 734-6470.

Cuisine: HUNGARIAN. **Reservations:** Recommended. **Bus:** M18 or M15.
$ Prices: Appetizers $1.25–$4.50; main courses $9.25–$13. No credit cards.
Open: Lunch daily 11:30am–3:45pm; dinner 3:45–11pm.

Crisp and cozy, Mocca sports a turn-of-the-century mosaic floor and marble accents. Brass wall lamps, mirrored panels, original pressed-tin ceilings, and lace curtains add to the charm.

The portions are generous; dinner main dishes come with potato, vegetable, and salad. You might start with a warming bowl of homemade noodle soup, with good broth, fine noodles, and sliced carrots. Main dishes include chicken paprikas (sautéed in creamed paprika sauce, with dumplings), veal goulash, a crisp breaded wiener-schnitzel, and stuffed cabbage. For dessert, consider the apple, cheese, or cherry strudel, or try the rich somloi galuska—if a cake soaked in rum, with nuts and chocolate sauce, and a smothering of whipped cream doesn't intimidate you!

MUMBLES, 1622 Third Ave., at 91st St. Tel. 427-4355.

Cuisine: AMERICAN/CONTINENTAL. **Reservations:** Not accepted. **Subway:** 4, 5, 6 to 86th St.
$ Prices: Appetizers $2.50–$5.75; main courses $8.50–$14.50. AE, MC, V.
Open: Daily noon–4am.

This place has been home-away-from-home for legions of East Side singles. Mumbles even looks homey, with wooden shingles inside and out, multipaned windows with lots of plants, a timbered ceiling, a well-trod wood floor, and small tables covered with green-and-white-checked cloths. Most of Mumbles' menu and all the specials are written on blackboards; the fare runs from hamburgers, salads, and sandwiches to veal marsala. When we were there, specials included a sunset dinner served from 5 to

7pm, with any main dish at $6.95, and a pick-your-own pasta-and-sauce combo for $8.95. Weekend brunch is offered until 4pm and comes with a Bloody Mary or a mimosa.

The newest **Mumbles,** 1491 Second Avenue, at 78th Street (tel. 772-8817), is all white and airy. You can dine inside near the bar or in a glass-enclosed terrace decorated with lush green plants. When the weather's warm, the sidewalk surrounding the restaurant becomes a lively outdoor café—an excellent spot to relax and people-watch. It's open daily from 11:30am to 4am.

RUBY'S RIVER ROAD CAFÉ AND BAR, 1754 Second Ave., at 92nd St. Tel. 348-2328.

Cuisine: CAJUN. **Reservations:** Recommended. **Bus:** M15 or M19.
$ Prices: Appetizers $3.50–$6.95; main courses $6.95–$15.95. AE.
Open: Daily 5pm–3am.

If you're hungry for authentic New Orleans fare, look no further. The theme here is Mississippi Delta. Up front in the bar, the casual, postcollege crowd taps their feet to the music of James Brown and Professor Longhair as they slug Delta Beer and gator shots beneath a ceiling covered with three-foot-long plastic alligators. Beyond the bar and the open jaws of two mammoth alligator skulls lies the dining room, where ceiling fans turn lazily above the mauve, gray, turquoise, and black faux-snakeskin tables and chairs.

For an appetizer, try the corn hushpuppies or the Cajun popcorn (lightly breaded crawfish tails served with spicy red sauce). For the main course, jambalaya with grilled sausage and chicken is one Louisiana specialty that's guaranteed to light your mouth on fire. On the cooler side, try the Texas-fried steak, the southern-fried chicken, the Delta catfish, or one of the daily specials. Watch for drink specials during the nightly happy hour from 5 to 7pm. Sunday is Ladies' Night, and on Mondays, Ruby's invites you to "relax with the Grateful Dead."

SARABETH'S KITCHEN, 1295 Madison Ave., near 92nd St. Tel. 410-7335.

Cuisine: AMERICAN. **Reservations:** Accepted for dinner only. **Bus:** M1, M2, M3, M4, or M19.
$ Prices: Breakfast items $2.75–$8.75; lunch courses $4–$11.50; dinner appetizers $4–$6.75; main dinner courses $14.50–$19. Lunch minimum $7.50 per person; dinner minimum $10 per person. AE, MC, V.
Open: Daily 9am–10:30pm.

Sarabeth's is a pastry-lover's dream. It's also a lovely, Laura Ashley–style place for a drink, tea, or a meal—morning, noon, or night, although the dinner prices are a bit out of our budget. The decor is early American, with parquet floors, gray marble tables, magnificent sprays of fresh flowers, crown moldings, and rosettes at the ceiling. If you're lucky, the gracious Sarabeth will be on hand to advise you about the daily specials.

You can have omelets with such fillings as apple butter or Cheddar cheese, any time of the day. Egg dishes come with your choice of muffin, scone, English muffin, or croissant and preserves. The menu is unrelentingly cute, listing "Baby Bear," "Mama Bear," "Papa Bear," and "Big Bad Wolf" variations on porridge. Perhaps the most delectable breakfast item is the pumpkin waffles, served with sour cream, raisins, pumpkin seeds, and honey, for $8. You might try the grilled smoked mozzarella sandwich with avocado and fresh tomato on seven-grain bread for lunch.

The pastries can't be missed—even if you have to take your sticky buns, elephant ears, and fabulous double-chocolate-chip cookies home with you! You may also be tempted to buy one of the delicious homemade preserves (even at $8 a jar).

SEVENTH REGIMENT MESS, The Armory, 643 Park Ave., at 66th St. Tel. 744-4107.

Cuisine: AMERICAN. **Subway:** 6 to 68th St.
$ Prices: Main courses $7.50–$19.95. AE, MC, V.
Open: Dinner Mon–Fri 5–9pm. **Closed:** Late June to Labor Day.

Exclusive Park Avenue has a neighborhood secret—a restaurant with good food at reasonable prices that's run by the U.S. Army! In spite of all the combat fatigues you'll see in the Armory, the public is welcome and the mood at ease. We think you'll agree that the Mess is a unique find!

You can't miss the Armory—this 19th-century red-brick building occupies the whole block. You enter through massive wooden doors studded with iron. Tell one of the soldiers inside the door that you'd like to go to the Mess, and he'll show you to the elevator to the left side of the Great Hall. Take time to look around. The Grand Staircase is grand indeed, and the Great Hall is full of antique cannons, military portraits, and flags that are black with age and so thin you can see through them. The Mess is on the fourth floor.

You can stop for a drink in the long lounge, where there are comfortable green tweed sofas, red leather chairs, and small metal plaques on the walls honoring members of the Seventh. The dining room, like the lounge, has a beamed ceiling, half-timbered walls, and mounted heads of long-dead moose and rams. The dining room also has a beautiful wood floor, tables covered with blue and white linen. Main dishes come with tomato juice, consommé, or the day's soup, as well as vegetable, potato, and coffee. You choices might include scrod or fried butterfly shrimp, baked manicotti, chicken à la Seventh au gratin, or a chef's salad.

THE SUMMERHOUSE, 50 E. 86th St., at Madison Ave. Tel. 249-6300.
   Cuisine: AMERICAN. **Reservations:** Accepted for dinner only. **Subway:** 4, 5, 6 to 86th St.
   $ Prices: Appetizers $4.75–$9.50; main courses $12–$18.50. AE, MC, V.
   Open: Mon–Fri 11:30am–11pm; Sat–Sun noon–11pm.

This airy café has a pleasing simplicity. Statuesque floral arrangements and an old carousel horse are in the windows. Tables are set with white linens, fresh flowers, and candles; chairs are turn-of-the-century oak with high backs. And a simulated screen-porch setting keeps things informal.

The menu is light and summery, perfect for lunch (when the prices are cheaper). You might enjoy a crab cake on an English muffin, curried chicken salad, an omelet filled with spinach and sour cream, or a large bowl of Texas chili and a house salad. There's a special brunch menu and a late-afternoon menu; both include fabulous desserts like fantastic fudge, coffee beautiful (coffee with Grand Marnier, Kahlúa, and whipped cream), Häagen-Dazs ice cream with chocolate sauce and whipped cream, fresh strawberries, and a lemon soufflé. A particularly nice touch with every meal is the strawberry butter served with a basket of warm biscuits.

SZECHUAN KITCHEN, 1460 First Ave., at 76th St. Tel. 249-4615.
   Cuisine: CHINESE. **Reservations:** Not accepted. **Bus:** M79 or M15.
   $ Prices: Appetizers and soup $1.10–$4.40; lo mein and rice $3.60–$5.90; main courses $5.90–$12.90. No credit cards.
   Open: Dinner Wed–Mon 5–10:30pm.

Szechuan Kitchen is one of those small favorites that New Yorkers try to keep to themselves. This simple, cozy restaurant with a bright red exterior is always packed, but everyone's friendly and the wait is worthwhile. The glass-topped tables are close together. In fact, when we were there, enthusiastic devoted customers were describing main dishes to newcomers at adjoining tables.

For starters, try the cold sesame noodles or the spring roll. All the main dishes are reasonably priced; try the diced chicken with hot peppers, the eggplant with hot spiced garlic sauce, or our favorite, the hot spiced ginger shrimp. BYOB.

TANJORE, 1229 First Ave., between 66th and 67th sts. Tel. 535-8718.
   Cuisine: INDIAN. **Reservations:** Recommended for weekend dinners and parties of 4 or more. **Bus:** M15 or M66.
   $ Prices: Appetizers $2.75–$5.95; soups, salads, and breads $1.95–$2.95; main courses $6.50–$16.95; fixed-price dinners $14.95–$18.95. AE, MC, V.
   Open: Lunch daily 11:30am–3pm; dinner 5:30–11pm.

This pleasant restaurant is decorated with mirrored walls, brick detailing, linen tablecloths, and ceiling fans. It first caught our eye with its lunch special, served Monday through Friday, with soup, rice, salad, nan bread, and a main dish for $5.95 to $8.95. Most main dishes on the regular dinner menu are priced under $12. A la carte, you might ask for an appetizer of chicken chat, which consists of crisp-fried pieces of chicken in a spicy lemon marinade. For dessert, there's mango sliced over ice cream, or fresh strawberries.

T. G. I. FRIDAY'S, 1152 First Ave., at 63rd St. Tel. 832-8512.
   Cuisine: AMERICAN. **Reservations:** Not needed. **Bus:** M66 or M15.
$ **Prices:** Appetizers $3.65–$6.95; salads and sandwiches $4.15–$7.95; main courses $7.50–$14.50. AE, CB, DC, MC, TR, V.
   Open: Daily 11:30am–1:30 or 3am; brunch served Sat–Sun 11:30am–3:30pm.
New York's first singles bar is still a landmark, in an outrageously blue corner building with red-and-white candy-striped awnings at every window. Friday's has mellowed with the years and the proliferation of other singles bars, but the small tables are still great for an intimate rendezvous. Friday's decor is a fun hodgepodge of Victoriana.

The eight-page, reasonably priced menu is full of suggestions for solid American fare. You can start with zucchini fries, baked Brie, or steak-on-a-stick. There are 11 ways to order a hamburger, including the "name your own." Salads are $7.25 and up. Main dishes include pasta selections, London broil, and barbecued shrimp, but you have to save room for the mocha mud pie or the hot deep-dish apple pie à la mode. A complete brunch for $10.95 to $13.95 comes with a Bloody Mary, screwdriver, mimosa, or all the champagne you can drink. And speaking of drinks, there's sure to be a special almost every night—for example, Tuesdays bring $3.75 margaritas, and on Wednesdays bottles of Budweiser are $2.

There's another branch at 94th Street and Second Avenue (tel. 410-3420).

VASATA, 339 E. 75th St., near First Ave. Tel. 988-7166.
   Cuisine: CZECH. **Reservations:** Recommended. **Bus:** M15, M30, or M79.
$ **Prices:** Appetizers $4.50–$5.75; main courses $11.50–$15.95. AE, MC, V.
   Open: Tues–Sat 5–11pm; Sun noon–10pm.
For more than 35 years Vasata has been a jewel of a restaurant with true European charm and simplicity. Soft light from coach lamps illuminates the wood-beamed ceilings and stucco walls of this long, cozy dining room. There is a highly polished wood bar tucked away near the entrance; tables, set simply with white linen and fresh flowers, are nestled farther back. Lovely old pieces of Czech pottery decorate the surrounding walls. The interior is as warm as the friendly people who run it. Mr. and Mrs. Vasata founded the restaurant, and their daughter, Linda Petlan, is the chef. A standout among the appetizers is the homemade duck liver pâté with pistachios, and there's a constantly changing menu of homemade soups, the best of which is the famous cream of mushroom. Main dishes come with a choice of two fresh vegetables; roast duckling Vasata, roast loin of pork, and chicken in paprika cream sauce are perhaps the most popular. But weinerschnitzel and Prague filet of beef in red wine sauce and crisp onions follow close behind. But don't let the regular menu distract you from the daily specials. If you're truly adventurous (and we admit we're not), there's fresh calf's brain with scrambled eggs, or pickled calf's brain on toast.

If you still have room for dessert, you're in luck. The traditional palacsinty, thin crêpes filled with apricot preserves or chocolate, can be flamed in brandy or Cointreau. There is a wide assortment of after-dinner liqueurs, or you can mix your tea with a little 160-proof Austrian rum.

THE VICTORY CAFÉ, 1604 Third Ave., at 90th St. Tel. 348-3650.
   Cuisine: AMERICAN. **Reservations:** Not accepted. **Subway:** 4, 5, 6 to 86th St.
$ **Prices:** Appetizers $1.50–$6.75; main courses $5.95–$13.50. AE, MC, V.
   Open: Daily 11:30am–midnight. Bar open most nights until 4am.
Long a neighborhood hangout, the casual yet stylish Victory Café is usually hopping on weekend nights. Start with an order of chicken wings, or our favorite, the baked Brie, before moving on to one of the traditional main courses. It's straightforward fare

here, with a few sophisticated touches. Try the grilled seafood brochette, the Yankee pot roast, or perhaps the grilled swordfish while you watch the young East Siders mingle. After the dinner crowd clears, the tables are pushed aside so that the optimum number of drinkers can crowd around the bar.

14. SPECIALTY DINING

A CULINARY EXCURSION TO BRIGHTON BEACH, BROOKLYN

If you're heading to Coney Island to visit the New York Aquarium or to spend the day at the beach, or if you simply have the time, take the Sixth Avenue D train all the way to the end of the line to Brighton Beach, where fantastic food, drink, and a full evening's worth of entertainment can be had for less than $10. The thousands of Russian Jews who have settled here in recent years call it "Little Odessa by the Sea." On the weekends they go all-out, partying and eating at dozens of local, authentic Russian restaurants. For the price of a subway token, and with the patience for the ride, you can join them.

The **Kavkas Restaurant,** 405 Brighton Beach Ave. (tel. 718/891-5400), serves authentic Armenian food, drawing in many Russian immigrants. It's the kind of place where friends and relatives wander in, pull up a chair, and reach without asking for one of the dishes of exotic food piled on the tables. Start with the red caviar served with pita bread; or with Ukrainian borscht, served hot and full of beef, cabbage, potatoes, and sour cream—it's one of the 11 different soups. Specialties of the house, ranging from about $5 to $12, include shaslik (grilled chunks of lamb that arrive on a skewer the size of a small sword), accompanied by a mountain of fried potatoes and raw onion; chicken Kiev; stuffed Ukrainian meat dumplings; and eggplant in walnut sauce. Things really heat up around 8pm, when a Russian band begins playing and the dance floor fills.

Kavkas serves food daily from 11am to midnight, but the music can go much later. There's entertainment nightly; reservations are a must on Saturday.

More of the same can be found at **Primorski,** 282B Brighton Beach Ave. (tel. 718/891-3111), a fancier place with tables covered in white linen. Try some of the cold appetizers, such as herring with onions, boiled potatoes, and vinaigrette. House specialties, around $6, include loolya kebab (ground meat with spices, grilled on skewers), roast lamb with potatoes, or chicken shaslik.

Georgian owner Buba Khotovli has also instituted a "party" menu ($27 a head for groups of four or more on Saturday, somewhat less on other nights) that features a bottle of domestic vodka or Lambrusco, every hors d'oeuvre on the menu, three or four main courses, and a basket of fruit. A daily lunch special offers soup, salad, one of the 16 main dishes, and coffee or tea.

Open daily from 11am to 2am, Primorski offers Russian, Georgian, and Israeli music nightly from around 9pm.

Other spots to try in the neighborhood are the **Zodiac Restaurant,** 309 Brighton Beach Ave. (tel. 718/891-2000); **Sadko,** 129 Brighton Beach Ave. (tel. 718/372-3088); and the **National Restaurant,** 273 Brighton Beach Ave. (tel. 718/646-1225). Each is a delight.

BAGELS

New Yorkers live and thrive on bagels; and for the budget traveler, they're a great standby. Many places will serve you bagels large enough to serve as a whole breakfast or lunch (usually topped with enough cream cheese to feed a starving village). And if you haven't tried them before, don't be afraid of lox. Putting fish on a bagel tastes a lot better than it sounds.

Jumbo Bagels and Bialys, 1070 Second Ave., between 56th and 57th streets (tel. 355-6185), is a reliable spot. It's open 24 hours a day, and sells bialys, muffins, and croissants, as well as whitefish or baked salmon salads. For only $5 you can get a lox, bagel, and cream-cheese sandwich. There are no tables, but late-night munchers often sit in the large bay window facing the street.

Our favorite, though, is **✪ H&H Bagels,** 2239 Broadway (tel. 595-8000). It, too, is open 24 hours, and no matter when you pop in, you'll get huge, fresh-baked bagels of all kinds (and they'll probably still be warm!). There are no tables, so buy a bag and take it along on a picnic or to keep your hotel room stocked with munchies. There's an **H&H Bagels East** at 1551 Second Ave., between 80th and 81st streets (tel. 734-7441).

DELIS

New York boasts the finest delis in the world, so get ready for the best pastrami, matzoh-ball soup, and egg creams you've ever had. Sandwich prices at some of the places listed below start at $7 or $8, and if that seems high, remember: they're colossal, perhaps enough to feed two.

One of the legendary spots is the **Stage Delicatessen,** 834 Seventh Ave., at 54th Street (tel. 245-7850), open daily from 6am to 2am. Even if you can get your mouth around the first half of your sandwich, you may need a doggy bag for the second. Bagels and lox, potato pancakes, and other deli favorites are served up in equally generous portions. Breakfast is served daily to 11am, with blintzes and French toast. This theater district hangout has been serving showbiz schmoozers and other colorful characters for more than 50 years.

The Stage's main competition is the **Carnegie Deli,** 854 Seventh Avenue, at 55th Street (tel. 757-2245), which was featured in Woody Allen's *Broadway Danny Rose.* Hats off to you if you can polish off the 4-inch-tall pastrami on rye. Open daily 6:30am to 3:30am.

Although Abe Lebewohl established his delicatessen late by Lower East Side standards (1954), meals at the **Second Avenue Deli,** 156 Second Avenue, at the corner of East 10th Street (tel. 677-0606), have become a tradition. With its flashy green stained-glass windows, the restaurant is easily spotted from a distance. Pickles are set at every table. Matzoh-ball soup, heaping hot pastrami sandwiches, traditional knishes and kugels, Hungarian goulash, and warm apple strudel are served up in abundance.

Another old favorite is **Fine and Schapiro,** 138 W. 72nd Street, between Broadway and Columbus Avenue (tel. 877-2721). Started in 1927, this place has a charmingly simple, old-fashioned decor with cedar walls and brown-painted wainscoting. Many regulars have been coming here for decades. You can get a pastrami, chicken salad, or chopped liver sandwich, or choose from a changing list of luncheon specials, such as stuffed cabbage, gefilte fish, or potted meatballs. A glass of Dr. Brown's Celery Tonic or a traditional cream soda is the proper accompaniment.

Sarge's, 548 Third Ave., between 36th and 37th streets (tel. 679-0442), is a true New York deli, with a counter full of roast meats and pies up front and a dining room with wood walls and wood captain's chairs. The food is delicious, the portions large, and the prices reasonable. Sandwiches are priced from $3.50 for cream cheese and jelly to $8.95 for a combination of turkey, pastrami, and Swiss cheese, and burgers are available. Main dishes range from corned-beef hash with poached egg and potato to a pricier prime shell steak with salad and baked potato. Weekend brunch, served from 11am to 3pm, includes a drink or fresh-squeezed orange juice, and coffee to accompany eggs Benedict, French toast stuffed with meat and cheese, or a lox, eggs, and onion omelet with a bagel and cream cheese. Open 24 hours.

PIZZA

New Yorkers have raised pizza-making to an art form. You'll run across a pizzeria on every other street corner, and almost all of them are high-quality. It's a budget traveler's dream—a slice, under $2, makes an authentic, filling meal.

If you're scouting around for pizza, you'll undoubtedly notice a bizarre New York phenomenon—the proliferation of establishments calling themselves Ray's Pizza. They're almost all unrelated (and almost none is owned by anyone named Ray). You'll see Ray's Pizza, Ray's Original Pizza, Ray's of Greenwich Village, Famous Ray's Pizza, Famous Original Ray's . . . well, you get the picture. The 1991 New York phone book listed around 35 variations on the name. No one seems to know which Ray's really started it all—and oddly enough, most of them are quite good.

Some New Yorkers think that the **Ray's Pizza** at the corner of 11th Street and Avenue of the Americas (tel. 243-2253) is the authentic one and worthy of its fame. The pizza here has a nearly perfect crust and gobs of mozzarella. On any given day—and seemingly at any hour—the line of people waiting for a slice snakes out the door and more are jammed around the stand-up counters and the restaurant's few tables. You can get a regular slice or a thick Sicilian slice for under $2, and the "famous" combo slice, at $3.50, is worth the extra few cents.

We also like the **Ray's Original Pizza** at 961 Second Ave., at 51st Street (tel. 752-2143). Thick Sicilian and thin Neapolitan pizzas are available with sausage, ricotta and mozzarella cheese, green peppers, eggplant, spinach, and other toppings. You can also get calzones—a small "pizza-hero" sandwich—for $3 and up.

Pizza Piazza, 785 Broadway, at the corner of East 10th Street (tel. 505-0977), is the place for deep-dish Sicilian-style pizza. The pizzas come in three sizes: Small ($5.95 to $7.95) is recommended for one person, medium ($11 to $14) for two, and large ($20 to $23) for four or more. The menu features a list of 12 types of pizza ranging from the "Basic," with tomato sauce and three kinds of cheese, to the "Californian," with tomato sauce and seasonal vegetables. The menu also offers pastas, burgers, chili, and salads. Cooking the pizzas takes 20 minutes, so you may want to while away the waiting time by trying an appetizer. Guacamole, and broccoli and shrimp vinaigrette, are both tasty. Open from 11:30am to 11:30pm Sunday through Thursday, to midnight on Friday and Saturday.

John's Pizzeria, 278 Bleecker St. (tel. 243-1680), is universally recognized as serving the best pizza in New York. See Section 5, "Greenwich Village," for a complete description.

DINING COMPLEXES

SOUTH STREET SEAPORT

Dining options at the South Street Seaport—a four-block complex that evokes the atmosphere of 19th-century New York—include a fantastic variety of fine restaurants (most regrettably too pricey for more than a brief mention here), cafés, and foodstalls. For gourmets and gourmands on a budget, the second floor of the Fulton Market building offers the next best thing to an around-the-world food cruise. You can munch on dim sum (Chinese dumplings), empanadas (Argentine meat turnovers), cheese steak sandwiches, burgers, chili, raw-fish bar goodies, Indian tandoori cooking, Greek barbecue, Japanese soup and noodle dishes, chicken and ribs, pizza, sushi, frozen-yogurt sundaes, fresh fruit, salads, sausages, New York delicatessen, and enough cake, candy, and ice-cream specialties to satisfy the most demanding sweet tooth.

At **Café Café,** 89 South St., Pier 17 (tel. 406-2870), you'll have a fine view of the harbor, and you can order draft beer with sandwiches, salads (including Caesar and seafood varieties), and desserts (try the chocolate mousse cake)—all under $10.

Gianni's, 15 Fulton St. (tel. 608-7300), is an Art Deco study in black and white; it's one of the Seaport's most attractive restaurants and offers one of the best views. Sit at the outdoor café, where you can order a Caesar salad, an arugula and endive salad, or a grilled-turkey sandwich. Open daily to 11:30pm.

Probably the most pervasive presence on the third floor of Pier 17 is the **Liberty Café,** 89 South St. (tel. 406-1111), sprawled across one end of the third floor, and offering a view of the harbor. Surrounded by an outdoor deck seating 200, Liberty is a blessed retreat from the hustle and bustle of the pier. Start off with the Fulton Market chowder, littleneck clams from the raw bar, or a jumbo shrimp cocktail. Main dishes like linguine with clam sauce or sautéed chicken with wild mushrooms are available for around $16, but we like the pizza, fresh from the wood-burning oven, for $10.50. Open till 1am on weeknights, till 3am on weekends; reservations are suggested.

The popular **North Star Pub,** 93 South St., at Fulton Street (tel. 509-6757), is a British ale house, so it's no wonder the menu has a British flavor. Among the choices are bangers and mash, a few variations on the ploughman's lunch, and, of course, fish and chips. Don't neglect to finish off your meal with the very deep-dish apple pie (perhaps with melted Cheddar or double Devon cream) or a raisin scone with raspberry jam. There's an enormous selection of beers and ales, and the longest list on single malt scotch whiskies we've ever seen (with several special tasting menus available).

Roebling's Bar and Grill, 11 Fulton St., in the Fulton Market Building (tel. 608-3980), offers a turn-of-the-century atmosphere, the perfect setting for hearty American fare: steaks, chops, blackened bluefish, grilled half chicken, oysters (raw or fried in beer), and smoked trout. Main dishes start around $12 and go way up. The place is often crammed with Wall Streeters at the day's end, and the bar stays open until 2am.

Sloppy Louie's, 92 South St. (tel. 952-9657), open daily until 10pm, is an old favorite that's been around for over 50 years, serving superb fresh seafood in a unpretentious setting. Main dishes start at about $12 and run way up, but you can easily avoid decimating your budget by ordering carefully—and remember, everything comes with potato and vegetable, so you'll be stuffed.

CITICORP CENTER

For relief from the bustle of midtown, the Citicorp Center, which covers the block from 53rd to 54th streets, bordered by Lexington and Third avenues, is a greenery-filled escape. The three-story skylit atrium below the shimmering steel office tower, is an arcade of shops and restaurants. Citicorp sponsors frequent concerts and exhibits in the central public space, and tables and chairs are scattered about, suited to brown-bagging and people-watching.

If you bring your own lunch, you can top it off with a freshly baked chocolate-chip cookie or muffin from the **Famous Chocolate Chip Cookie** on the second level. Cookies and pastries are also sold at the counter at **Café Buon Giorno** on the main level. Soups, sandwiches, quiche, frozen yogurt, and chili are also served, all under $5. The scents of freshly baked bread wafting across the main floor from **Au Bon Pain** (tel. 838-6996) are enough to send you heading for their take-out croissant sandwiches made with ham, turkey, salami, tuna, and french cheese. Breads, from rye to challah, are made fresh daily. No seating, only take-out. **Healthworks** (tel. 838-6221), brightly decorated with red chairs and green trim, offers daily specials like vegetarian lasagne, as well as many salads and quiches. Fresh baked goods can be purchased for dessert, along with frozen yogurt.

For less casual fare, there are several other restaurants inside the Citicorp Center. Some can be expensive, but most offer affordable weekly specials well worth the visit. With dark-green walls, copper lamps, brass-framed mirrors, white tablecloths, and etched glass, **Charley O's** (tel. 752-2102) has the feeling of an old pub. Checked-glass skylights brighten the restaurant in daytime. You can get large salads, omelets, burgers, and desserts while staying within our budget, and there's a happy hour after 5pm in the bar. **Alfredo's** (tel. 371-3367) is above our budget, but it makes a lovely stop for a drink or dessert, and there's a $12.95 Sunday brunch served from 12:30 to 4pm. Selections include soup, tomato juice or melon, Italian omelets, eggs Benedict, pastas, veal bocconcini, or sautéed chicken.

Our favorite spot in the Center is ✪ **Averignos** (tel. 688-8828), with sparkling white stucco walls, rounded arches, colorful Greek plates on the walls, and a kitchen open to full view. It serves authentic Greek food, with appetizers priced from $4.50 to $10.95. We like the spanakopita and the stuffed grape leaves. Some of the grilled main dishes, like the lamb souvlaki and the veal chops, should be saved for a splurge, but you can get by with moussaka for $11.95. Lunchtime here is sometimes frenetic, but always fun, with Greek music and waiters at your service.

LIGHT, CASUAL & FAST FOOD

Before you ever get to a restaurant, you'll be tempted by savory smells on nearly every streetcorner. You'll find pushcarts and peddlers hawking a tremendous variety of foods—hot dogs, soft pretzels, roasted chestnuts, knishes, empanadas, and little shish kebabs. For a few dollars, you can literally eat your way down the street.

Gray's Papaya, with locations at 402 Sixth Ave., at the corner of 8th Street (tel. 260-3532), and 2090 Broadway, at the corner of 72nd Street (tel. 799-0243), is one of New York's favorite round-the-clock fast-food stops. It's strictly stand and gobble—no seats. It's known for its 60¢ hot dogs, fast-moving lines, and wide variety of fruit shakes—papaya, coconut, pineapple, and fresh-squeezed orange juice.

For high-quality food on the run as you're sightseeing in midtown, try **Le Croissant Shop,** with speedy, cheerful service and fresh ingredients. You can watch the croissants and other specialties as they're baked on the premises. For a people-watching lunch on the marble steps of the New York Public Library (Fifth Avenue, between 40th and 42nd streets), try the Dijon chicken salad on a fresh-baked croissant, or ham and Brie on a French roll (prices average $3.95). The quiche is a fine pick, as are the hearty soups. For dessert, try one of the many fruit-filled turnovers or a chocolate croissant. You'll find branches of Le Croissant Shop at 459 Lexington Ave., at 45th Street; 918 Third Ave., between 55th and 56th streets; 1100 Ave. of the Americas, at 42nd Street; 8 W. 40th St., off Fifth Avenue; 200 W. 57th St., off Seventh Avenue; and 599 Lexington Ave., at 52nd Street. All are open from early in the morning until late afternoon.

DESSERTS, CAFÉS & COFFEEHOUSES

CHINATOWN

Don't fill up on fortune cookies; some of the most flavorful Chinese desserts are available at Chinatown's answer to Baskin-Robbins, the **Chinatown Ice Cream Factory,** 65 Bayward St., between Mott and Elizabeth streets (tel. 608-4170). Here you can try 36 homemade flavors as Chinese as chow mein or as exotic as the Orient, including almond cookie (our favorite), lichee, ginger, red bean, green tea, papaya, and mango. For the less adventurous, Occidental favorites from vanilla to Rocky Road are on the menu.

The five Seid Brothers—William, Henry, Eugene, Philip, and Otis—make all the flavors from all-natural ingredients in a huge freezer on the premises. Try the milkshakes, ice-cream sundaes, banana splits, and ice-cream cakes for a tasty alternative to the double-dip cone. Open daily till midnight.

LITTLE ITALY

There's no place for gracious old-world atmosphere like **Ferrara's,** 195 Grand St., between Mott and Mulberry streets (tel. 226-6150). Since 1892, it's been tempting New Yorkers with an outrageous variety of cakes and pastries. Just a peek at the long marble pastry counter laden with every imaginable confection and cake will have your mouth watering. The demand for Ferrara's goodies has made the café a nationally known business; Ferrara's ships its own brand of coffees, candies, and hundreds of other Italian delicacies all over the world.

The traditional Italian pastries include cannoli, eclairs, babas au rum, babas au ricotta, napoleons, cream puffs, and many others. Specialties of the house include Gianduja mousse cake, chocolate layer cake with praline paste; chocolate hazelnut mousse encased in a hazelnut chocolate; almond and cheese cakes; and a rustic peasant pie, filled with salami, fresh eggs, and smoked cheese. Espresso, cappuccino, and other Italian coffees cost between $1.50 and $3. Once you've made your choice, and if the weather is good, walk outside and sit under the white-and-red awning, while the rest of Little Italy strolls by. Ferrara's is open to midnight on weekdays, until 1am on weekends.

Another traditional and charming spot is **Caffè Roma,** 385 Broome St., at Mulberry Street (tel. 226-8413), authentically decorated with high ceilings, white tiled floors, and marble tables and counters. There are many paintings by the internationally renowned artist Frank Mason. The long gold pastry case is filled with some of the most delicious decadence in all of New York. Caffè Roma is known for its milk Sicilian cassatina, a special cake filled with ricotta and frosted with vanilla, and pieces of chocolate. Coffee costs from $1.25 to $3. Open daily 8am to midnight.

✪ **Im Bocca al Lupo** (In the Mouth of the Wolf), 113 Mulberry St., at Canal Street (tel. 431-9755), is a relatively new addition to Little Italy. Its sparkling-clean interior has an exposed-brick wall and floor-to-ceiling mirrors on the opposite wall, which give a feeling of depth to the tiny café. Sit by the working fireplace in fall or winter and enjoy an espresso with Sambuca or a mochaccino, a chocolate-flavored cappuccino. In the summer, sit outside in the fountain garden enclosed by brick walls. Large potted plants and twinkling lights on the tree branches add to the festive atmosphere.

Some of the delectable desserts to choose from are the Italian rum cake, chocolate cheesecake, and fruit-flavored Italian ices. For the truly decadent, there is coppa cha cha: hazelnut and cappuccino ice cream with tiny rum-soaked balls of cake, nuts, black cherries, and whipped cream. If you're hungrier, try the small pizzas and "paninis"—small Italian sandwiches made with provolone, salami, or prosciutto. Open daily till 2am.

SOHO

All over Manhattan, grocery shopping can be a dramatic undertaking, but only at **Dean & DeLuca,** 560 Broadway, at Prince Street (tel. 431-1691), does it become a spectator sport. For the price of a delicious cup of cappuccino ($1.50) or a looks-too-perfect-to-desecrate pastry (from $1 to $5), you can have a ringside seat. Housed in a block-long building that looks more like a gallery than a grocery, Dean & DeLuca is New York's premier gourmet food store. As you enter, work your way to the cappuccino/pastry bar on your left. There are no seats, but prop your elbows up on the elegant marble counters and enjoy the show. Is that Madonna outhustling Richard Gere for the last head of Belgian endive? Open daily till 7 or 8pm. The same hours are kept at Dean & DeLuca's other location at 121 Prince Street.

GREENWICH VILLAGE

Café society is alive and well in the Village—nowhere else in the world (except possibly in Paris) is it such a pleasure to sit at a sidewalk café nursing a cappuccino or a beer and just plain people-watch.

Smack in the heart of the Village, at the intersection of MacDougal and Bleecker streets, are four of our favorites; there's a cafe on every corner. At **Le Figaro Café, Café Borgia,** or **MacDougal's Café,** you can stake out a sidewalk table and enjoy the passing street scene to your heart's content. Reasonably priced sandwiches, burgers, and light fare are available at all of these. Our favorite place at this corner is **Carpo's Café,** where the cheesecake is light and creamy, the pecan pie is decadent, and the coffee selections run into the dozens. There's nothing like pulling up a chair here on a pleasant summer evening.

EAST VILLAGE

Since 1894 **Veniero's,** 342 E. 11th St., at the corner of First Avenue (tel. 674-7264), has been turning out wedding cakes and pastries. Settle into the noisy, old-fashioned, mirrored café area (where there's a $2.50 per person minimum) and order an iced coffee while you agonize over your selection—you'll be torn between the kiwi tart, an eclair, Sicilian cheesecake (topped with cherries and chocolate chips), chocolate mocha cake, and a chocolate-covered cannoli. All are under $3. We settled on the tiramisu and were rewarded with ecstasy. It's open Sunday to Thursday from 8am to midnight, Friday and Saturday from 8am to 1am.

MIDTOWN

Rumpelmayer's, in the St. Moritz Hotel, mid-block on glittering Central Park South, at 58th Street (tel. 755-5800), is a New York institution that's worth a peek if you're in the area. There are stuffed animals for sale; and there is an elegant marble soda fountain with pink padded stools. Beyond is the café, with mirrored arches, pink tables, and hanging ferns.

UPPER WEST SIDE

✪ **Café La Fortuna,** 69 W. 71st St., between Columbus Avenue and Central Park West (tel. 724-5846), is one of those delightful places where you should forget that calories exist. It's the perfect place to linger over an espresso and pastry after a Lincoln Center show. The walls are laden with old opera records and pictures of singing stars from Caruso to Pavarotti. One of the owner's favorite photos is the one of John Lennon, Yoko Ono, and their son, Sean—former regulars at the cafe—mugging it up in old-time costumes. During the summer you can enjoy the evening on the café's fenced-in patio.

Most of the pastries, including the sinfully rich cannoli, are Italian, although there are also some German delights, and most are under $3. A variety of cookies, cakes, homemade Italian ices, and gelati are also available. Open daily till 1 or 2am.

A civilized oasis for coffee and conversation is the sparkling **Café Lalo,** 201 W. 83rd St., at Amsterdam Avenue (tel. 496-6031). The twinkling lights decorating the trees outside the huge glass windows and the gracious classical or jazz music in the background make a romantic setting for your espresso.

The decor has to be seen to be believed at ✪ **Edgar's Café,** 224 W. 84th St., at Broadway (tel. 496-6126). The high ceilings sport an exotic design, with fans whirring overhead. It's a stunning setting, which can be yours for the price of dessert (all under $4.50) or coffee (all $2 to $3). Light fare is available, like the duck mousse pâté, but you won't be able to resist the likes of homemade tiramisu, blueberry crumb pie, hazelnut cheesecake, gelato, or dark-chocolate mousse pie. Open weeknights till 1am, weekends till 2am.

At the **Hungarian Pastry Shop,** 1030 Amsterdam Ave. (tel. 866-4230), you can enjoy some of the richest, lightest delicacies in New York with a cup of their special coffee or herbal tea. During the busiest hours, service can be slow—don't come here if you'll be in a rush. Open Monday through Friday from 8am to 11:30pm, Saturday from 9am to 11:30pm, and Sunday 9am to 10:30pm.

UPPER EAST SIDE

A favorite for young and old, **Peppermint Park,** 1225 First Ave., at the corner of 66th Street (tel. 288-5054), sports an old-fashioned candy and ice-cream counter up front with 40 delicious flavors of ice-creams, sherbets, and frozen yogurts. If you'd like to eat in the restaurant, well, the only word to describe the decor is green. The menu is rather amusing (sample offerings: crêpe gatsby, crêpe cod, the crêpe train robbery, crêpe canaveral, and crêpe expectations). Salads, chili, sandwiches, and main course specials are all under $8.50. When we were last there on a busy Saturday, the service was uninspiring, but never mind—you're here for dessert. You'll agonize over choosing a rich sundae, a mouthwatering Italian pastry, a banana boat, or a Belgian waffle with ice cream and fudge sauce. (All are under $3.50.) You can worry about that diet another day. Open Monday through Thursday from 10am to midnight, Friday from 10am to 1am, Saturday from 10am to 2am, and Sunday from 11am to midnight.

Another old-fashioned ice-cream parlor that's been around for generations is **Serendipity,** 225 E. 60th St. (tel. 838-3531). Burgers, shepherd's pie, and sandwiches are available, but hold out for an espresso or chocolaccino and the chocolate mousse or a decadent sundae.

PICNIC FARE & WHERE TO EAT IT

On a gorgeous day, there's nothing like escaping from the urban blight and spreading a picnic blanket in **Riverside Park** or **Central Park** (where Strawberry Fields is a beautiful spot). Pick up the fixings at **Zabar's,** 2245 Broadway, at 80th Street (tel. 787-2000), where the selection of breads, cheeses, deli meats, and gourmet groceries will leave you speechless.

For fresh fruit to add to your picnic basket, no place can match **Fairway,** just a few doors down at 2127 Broadway, at 74th Street (tel. 595-1888). It's packed with yuppies and celebrity-watchers, but the fruit selection makes it worth your while to fight through the crowds. The bakery counter sells a sinful Cheddar sourdough loaf.

LATE NIGHT/24-HOUR

New York never stops. When a craving for pastrami on rye, bagels and lox, a hamburger, or an honest-to-goodness breakfast strikes at 5am, chances are that a place right around the corner can satiate your yen for munchies. And for the ultimate in convenience, many of them deliver for free, so ask. We've listed below a selection of life-savers for night owls; see the neighborhood sections above for full reviews.

CHINATOWN

Hong Fat, 63 Mott St., between Bayard and Canal streets (tel. 962-9588). Open until 5am daily.

Sun Lok Kee, 13 Mott St., near Chatham Square (tel. 732-8295). Open until 4am daily.

Wo Hop, 15 and 17 Mott St., near Chatham Square (tel. 766-9160 and 406-3973, respectively). Open until 5am daily.

SOHO

Moondance Diner, 80 Sixth Ave., at Grand Street (tel. 226-1191). Open 24 hours on Friday and Saturday.

GREENWICH VILLAGE

Florent, 69 Gansevoort St., between Washington and Greenwich streets (tel. 989-5779). Open 24 hours daily.

The Pink Teacup, 42 Grove St., near Bleecker Street (tel. 807-6755). Open 24 hours on Friday and Saturday.

LOWER EAST SIDE/EAST VILLAGE

Around the Clock Café, 8 Stuyvesant Place, east of Third Avenue (tel. 598-0402). Open 24 hours daily.

Kiev International Restaurant, 117 Second Ave., at East 7th Street (tel. 674-4040). Open 24 hours daily.

CHELSEA

Empire Diner, 210 Tenth Ave., between 21st and 22nd streets (tel. 243-2736). Open 24 hours daily (but closed Monday from midnight to 4am).

Lox Around the Clock, 676 Sixth Ave., at 21st Street (tel. 691-3535). Open 24 hours daily.

GRAMERCY PARK/MURRAY HILL

East Bay, 491 First Ave., at 29th Street (tel. 683-7770). Open 24 hours daily.

Sarge's, 548 Third Ave., between 36th and 37th streets (tel. 679-0442). Open 24 hours daily.

Tivoli, 515 Third Ave., between 34th and 35th streets (tel. 532-3300). Open 24 hours daily.

MIDTOWN WEST

Carnegie Deli, 854 Seventh Ave., at 55th Street (tel. 757-2245). Open to 3:30am daily.

MIDTOWN EAST

Jumbo Bagels & Bialys, 1070 Second Ave., between 56th and 57th streets (tel. 355-6185). Open 24 hours daily.

UPPER WEST SIDE/LINCOLN CENTER

The Burger Joint/The Pizza Joint, 2175 Broadway, between 76th and 77th streets (tel. 362-9238 or 724-2010). Open from 6am to 5am daily.
   West Side Restaurant, 2020 Broadway, at 69th Street (tel. 724-4000). Open 24 hours daily.

UPPER EAST SIDE/YORKVILLE

The Green Kitchen, 1477 First Ave., at 77th Street (tel. 988-4163). Open 24 hours daily.

15. WORTH THE EXTRA BUCKS

DOWNTOWN/TRIBECA

BRIDGE CAFÉ, 279 Water St., at Dover St. Tel. 227-3344.
   Cuisine: AMERICAN/CONTINENTAL. **Reservations:** Recommended. **Subway:** 1, 9 to South Ferry; N, R to Cortland St.
$ Prices: Main courses $11.95–$18.95. AE, DC, MC, V.
   Open: Lunch Mon–Fri 11:45am–5pm; dinner Mon–Sat 6pm–midnight, Sun 6–11pm; brunch Sat–Sun noon–3:30pm.
Located two blocks from the South Street Seaport, the Bridge Café has a 19th-century Cape Cod charm that other landmark restaurants in the area have lost. From the outside, the red wood-frame building looks as if it's bowing before the towering Brooklyn Bridge above it. Inside, there are photos of the bridge on the café's cream-colored slat-board walls. There are potted flowers in the entry and front windows and red-checked cloths on the tables.
   The lunch menu changes weekly, but generally offers sandwiches, soups (such as clam chowder), a hot and a cold pasta dish, and fish, chicken, and meat main dishes, usually braised with a subtle sauce. Dinner main courses run higher, but there's usually an under-$15 choice, such as tortellini with sausage and tomatoes. Brunch features omelets (try the one with sour cream and chili), buckwheat pancakes, and pastas such as fettuccine primavera.

CAPSOUTO FRERES, 451 Washington St., at Watts St. Tel. 966-4900.
   Cuisine: FRENCH. **Reservations:** Recommended. **Subway:** 1, 9 to Canal St.
$ Prices: Main courses $14–$24. AE, CB, DC.
   Open: Lunch Tues–Fri noon–3:30pm; brunch Sat–Sun noon–4:30pm; dinner Sun–Thurs 6–11pm, Fri–Sat 6pm–midnight.
This place is by far the prettiest of TriBeCa's warehouse restaurants. The neo-Romanesque warehouse is housed in a landmark building dating to 1891, and the restaurant's owners have done wonders with its interior. From the high, exposed-beam ceiling hang gently turning antique ceiling fans and chandeliers of brass with fogged-glass tulip shades. Stately cast-iron columns appear to support the lofty ceiling. The floors are brightly polished hardwood; the walls are exposed brick with large, floor-to-ceiling windows framed by maroon velvet drapes. White linen cloths cover the tables, with fresh flowers on each.

Main courses are a bit too pricey for us, but there's a varied and more affordable selection of "petits plats" with delicious portions of coquilles St-Jacques, soufflés, and a vegetarian plate with wild rice. The dishes are à la carte, but servings are generous. The pastries and fruits are irresistibly pretty.

211 WEST BROADWAY, at Franklin St. Tel. 925-7202.
Cuisine: CONTINENTAL. **Reservations:** Recommended. **Subway:** 1, 9 to Franklin St.
$ Prices: Main courses $12–$22. AE, DC, MC, V.
Open: Daily 11:30am–11:30pm. Brunch served Sat–Sun 11:30am–4:30pm.
Less out-of-the-way than most of TriBeCa's warehouse restaurants, this place is cool gray and typically lofty, with a pressed-tin ceiling held high by Grecian-style columns and floor-to-ceiling windows screened with venetian blinds. Tables have marble tops on wrought-iron pedestals, graced by bud vases filled with fresh flowers.

The lunch menu offers a number of budget items. Try the breast of chicken with lime-herb marinade, tagliarini primavera, or the "Two-Eleven burger" with shoestring potatoes. The price goes up at dinnertime, but the juicy house burger is still affordable, as are the penne in spicy tomato sauce and the poached chicken salad.

The restaurant serves cocktail brunches on Saturday and Sunday. Once again, the house burger with shoestring potatoes is the best budget bet; among the other choices are eggs with smoked salmon and salmon caviar and a Spanish peasant omelet. All brunch main dishes are served with a mimosa, a Bloody Mary, or a screwdriver. Occasionally there is live music on Sunday.

MIDTOWN WEST

CAFÉ UN DEUX TROIS, 123 W. 44th St., between Sixth and Seventh aves. Tel. 354-4148.
Cuisine: FRENCH. **Reservations:** Needed for parties of 5 or more. **Subway:** 1, 2, 3, 9, A, C, E, N, R to 42nd St.
$ Prices: Appetizers $4.75–$6.50; main courses $11.50–$21.95. AE, MC, V.
Open: Daily noon–12:30am.
The main dishes are expensive here, but this restaurant's distinctive ambience is worth the price. Boisterous, bustling, brightly lit, and airy, it's the kind of place to go to when you don't want intimacy. In the heart of the theater district, the café is packed both before and after shows.

Butcher paper serves as tablecloths, and with crayons supplied by the café, your table becomes an adult playground, upon which the waiters reproduce the evening's menu. If it's your birthday, by all means request a serenade. The waiters' chorus sounds professional. Main dishes include roast duck, omelets, fresh seafood, and a large list of daily specials. Try the pâté de campagne ($5.75) as a before- or after-theater snack. For a big-splurge sweet, consider ordering profiteroles—three cream-puff pastries filled with vanilla ice cream and topped with bittersweet fudge sauce.

JOE ALLEN'S, 326 W. 46th St., between Eighth and Ninth aves. Tel. 581-6464.
Cuisine: AMERICAN/CONTINENTAL. **Reservations:** Recommended (accepted 1 week in advance). **Subway:** A, C, E to 42nd St.
$ Prices: Appetizers $3.50–$11.50; main courses $12–$19. MC, V.
Open: Sun–Tues noon–midnight; Wed and Sat 11:30am–midnight.
Joe Allen's is the place to go if you want to eat in unpretentious surroundings and still find yourself in the company of stars such as Al Pacino, Roy Scheider, and Angela Lansbury. The atmosphere is warm, if too noisy to be intimate. Exposed-brick walls bear framed theatrical posters, an inside joke—the shows are either flops or little known. Tables are covered with white linen tablecloths and plants hang in brick archways that separate the busy bar from the larger dining area. Out in back there's dining beneath a skylight.

The menu changes daily, but if it's available, we like the grilled lamb chops with ratatouille, or the sautéed filet of snapper. Order up a side of Buffalo wings or mashed potatoes and gravy, and for dessert, we've never been able to resist the likes of tollhouse cookies with vanilla ice cream or warm apple crumb pie.

MIDTOWN EAST

OYSTER BAR AND RESTAURANT, Grand Central Station, E. 42nd St., between Vanderbilt and Lexington aves. Tel. 490-6650.
   Cuisine: SEAFOOD. **Reservations:** Essential. **Subway:** 4, 5, 6 to Grand Central.
$ **Prices:** Main courses $8.95–$23.95. AE, DC, MC, V.
   Open: Mon–Fri 11:30am–10:30pm. Last seating at 9:30pm.

Located in the station's lower concourse, the Oyster Bar echoes the graceful arches of Grand Central Terminal. Here they are festooned with white lights, giving them an added elegance and sense of romance. The large restaurant has a main dining room, counter service for quick meals, a cocktail lounge, and a redwood-paneled saloon. Opened in 1913, the restaurant serves up seafood with style. There is a take-out booth modeled after a ship's deck.

The seafood is all fresh, and the menu changes daily to accommodate the current catch. Prices are high, but your budget will fare well with the oyster stew or the pan-roasted oysters. Main dishes like bouillabaisse and coquilles St-Jacques, however, top the $20 mark, and lobster is $18.95 to $21.95 per pound, depending on the season.

WHAT TO SEE & DO IN NEW YORK CITY

New York is viewed by many as the artistic and cultural capital of the country, if not the world. It would take years to exhaust the city's diverse treasures—museums, historical sites, neighborhoods, parks, and much more. But if you're here for only a short time, this chapter is your key to unlocking as much as you can. Don't be surprised if you find just walking around this on-the-go city a wonderful adventure.

Don't let stories about how expensive New York is intimidate you. Yes, it can be costly here, but the city is packed with loads of freebies, from street musicians (the good and the outlandish) to the U.N. General Assembly.

In fact, your biggest expense might be a sturdy pair of walking shoes. This chapter will take you on a tour from the venerable New York Stock Exchange on Wall Street, to swank midtown art galleries, to beautiful Central Park, and even farther, to Brooklyn and the Bronx.

SUGGESTED ITINERARIES

IF YOU HAVE 1 DAY

Only 24 hours to see New York? We feel sorry for you—but don't try to compensate by cramming too much into one day. Decide what most interests you, put on your walking shoes, and explore one aspect of the city at an enjoyable pace.

If you've never seen the city before, concentrate on downtown Manhattan—take the ferry out to the Statue of Liberty and Ellis Island and let the memorable view of the Manhattan skyline take your breath away. Head next for Battery Park City and the World Financial Center, one of New York's top visual attractions; perhaps you'll catch some free lunchtime entertainment. Spend the rest of your afternoon strolling around the South Street Seaport, or, if you're a financier at heart, tour the New York Stock Exchange. Take in a play in the evening (for information on where to get cheap tickets, see Chapter 10, "New York City Nights").

IF YOU HAVE 2 DAYS

Follow the suggestion for Day 1 above, then on Day 2, start out early at the Metropolitan Museum of Art; limit yourself to 2 or 3 hours (perhaps concentrating

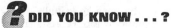**DID YOU KNOW . . . ?**

- Wall Street was once the site of a slave market.
- Between 1892 and 1954, Ellis Island processed 12 million immigrants—from whom at least 40% of today's U.S. population is descended.
- Over 25 million people visited New York in 1991.
- The Empire State Building was erected at a rate of four-and-a-half stories a week.
- Tchaikovsky conducted the opening concert at Carnegie Hall in 1891.
- Patriot Nathan Hale was hanged outside a tavern on Third Avenue.
- The triangular Flatiron Building measures only six feet across at 23rd Street.
- New York City has 6,400 miles of streets.
- The Convention and Visitors Bureau estimates that there are 11,787 licensed taxis in the city and over 17,000 restaurants.
- Mayor Fiorello La Guardia named the lions outside the New York Public Library "Patience" and "Fortitude," after the two qualities he thought were needed during the Depression.

on one specific wing, like the fabulous Egyptian collection or the American Wing). After a cup of tea in the landmark Plaza Hotel, continue down Fifth Avenue for window shopping at some of the most glamorous stores in the world. Wind up at the Empire State Building and take in that famous view from the Observation Deck; look for the Chrysler and Pan Am buildings. In the evening, head for dinner in Little Italy and a jazz club in Greenwich Village.

IF YOU HAVE 3 DAYS

If you're a real art enthusiast, you'll want to continue your museum-going on Day 3 with the Museum of Modern Art (MOMA), which boasts one of the world's premier collections of modern art. MOMA can easily be combined with another of midtown's famous sights, Rockefeller Center. If you're lucky enough to be here for the holidays, there's no more romantic sight than the giant Christmas tree and the ice-skating rink. Take a backstage tour of Radio City Music Hall, or head west toward the river and the *Intrepid* Air-Space Museum, which is perched on the edge of the Westside Highway in a berth on the Hudson River.

IF YOU HAVE 5 DAYS OR MORE

On Days 4 and 5, give yourself a break from all this structured sightseeing. Stroll through SoHo, poking into the galleries and offbeat shops that interest you. Everywhere you turn, you'll find a feast for the senses—from architectural wonders to street performers—and you'll make the city your own.

1. THE TOP ATTRACTIONS

CENTRAL PARK, extending from 59th to 110th sts. and from Fifth Ave. to Central Park West (Eighth Ave).

More than just a park, this 2½-mile expanse of greenery offers something for everyone—from culture to sports, nature to architecture. The park was planned and laid out between 1859 and 1870 by Frederick Law Olmsted and Calvert Vaux, whose "Greensward" plan won a park-design competition sponsored by the city of New York. Designed to give the illusion of being far removed from the crowded city streets, the park became a haven for urban dwellers: a place to relax and rejuvenate in a scenic, even rural, setting.

Designated a national landmark in 1965, Central Park reflects the diversity of New York City. It's a family park, a place where singles congregate on the grassy hills, couples stroll hand in hand, and city workers escape from their offices at lunchtime. It's a place where you can rent bikes and boats, ice skate in winter, swim in summer, and jog all year round. You might even spot a celebrity or two doing laps around the Reservoir, one of the most popular jogging tracks in New York.

During the spring and summer, the park hosts free performances of all kinds:

Shakespeare at the **Delacorte Theatre,** concerts by the New York Philharmonic and the Metropolitan Opera, as well as jazz and rock music by top recording artists, such as Paul Simon, on the **Great Lawn** and at the **Goldman Band Shell** in the Mall. For children, there are two zoos, playgrounds, model-boat sailing at **Conservatory Pond,** story-telling at the **Hans Christian Andersen statue,** an **Alice in Wonderland statue** to climb, and of course, the Carousel, with its hand-painted horses. (See Section 2, "More Attractions," for information on the **Central Park Zoo.**)

For one of the best views of the park, stand on the terrace of **Belvedere Castle,** inside the park at approximately 79th Street, a replica of a medieval castle that serves as a weather station and learning lab. For a prime example of Victorian architecture, don't miss the **Dairy,** inside the park at approximately 64th Street, one of Olmsted and Vaux's original park buildings. Recently renovated, the Dairy offers frequent exhibits, concerts, and a walk/talk series. For information about events at the Dairy, as well as park events in general, call 397-3156. A map and guide of all the paths and features of Central Park is available at the Castle and the Dairy for 50¢.

Those who remember John Lennon will want to pay a visit to **Strawberry Fields,** a living memorial to the singer just across Central Park West from the Dakota Apartments at 72nd Street, where Lennon lived and where he was shot on December 9, 1980. Countries from around the world have contributed gifts to this "International Garden of Peace," whose initial $1 million funding came from Lennon's widow, Yoko Ono.

We suggest several visits to Central Park if time permits, for it's not only a top sight, it's also a great place to relax when you're ready for a break from sightseeing.

A *final word:* Safety in Central Park is a matter of good judgment. Although the park is patrolled frequently by Parks Department staff and city police, stick to well-populated areas (in general, south of 96th Street), *don't frequent the park at night* unless attending a special event, and don't wear expensive jewelry. To keep track of your whereabouts in the park, check the numbers on any lamppost. The first two digits represent the nearest cross street; the second two digits represent east or west (west if odd, east if even).

Subway: Consult your subway map, as there are many entrances to the park on both the east and west sides. Take the following trains: 1, 9, A, D, C to 59th St.; C to 72nd, 81st, 86th, or 96th sts.; N, R to Fifth Ave. **Bus:** M10 on Central Park West, or M1, M2, M3, M4 on Fifth Ave.

DOWNTOWN

ELLIS ISLAND AND THE STATUE OF LIBERTY, in New York Harbor, with ferries leaving from Battery Park. Tel. 269-5755.

Millions of hopeful immigrants who pulled up their roots and headed for a new life in America passed through Ellis Island. And one of the first glimpses of their new homeland symbolized all their dreams—the Statue of Liberty, a gift from France, welcomes to America the world's "huddled masses yearning to breathe free."

Circle Line–Statue of Liberty ferries frequently depart from the Battery in Lower

---

IMPRESSIONS

If you should happen after dark
To find yourself in Central Park,
Ignore the paths that beckon you
And hurry, hurry to the zoo
And creep into the tiger's lair.
Frankly you'll be safer there.
—OGDEN NASH, *EVERYONE BUT THEE AND ME,* 1964

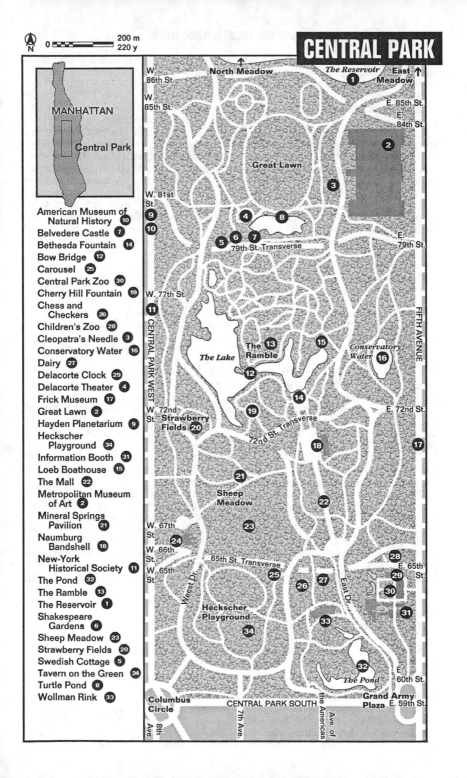

CENTRAL PARK

0 ━━━━━ 200 m
⎯⎯ 220 y

N

MANHATTAN

Central Park

American Museum of
  Natural History ⑩
Belvedere Castle ⑦
Bethesda Fountain ⑭
Bow Bridge ⑫
Carousel ㉕
Central Park Zoo ㉚
Cherry Hill Fountain ⑲
Chess and
  Checkers ㉖
Children's Zoo ㉘
Cleopatra's Needle ③
Conservatory Water ⑯
Dairy ㉗
Delacorte Clock ㉙
Delacorte Theater ④
Frick Museum ⑰
Great Lawn ②
Hayden Planetarium ⑨
Heckscher
  Playground ㉞
Information Booth ㉛
Loeb Boathouse ⑮
The Mall ㉒
Metropolitan Museum
  of Art ②
Mineral Springs
  Pavilion ㉑
Naumburg
  Bandshell ⑱
New-York
  Historical Society ⑪
The Pond ㉜
The Ramble ⑬
The Reservoir ①
Shakespeare
  Gardens ⑥
Sheep Meadow ㉓
Strawberry Fields ⑳
Swedish Cottage ⑤
Tavern on the Green ㉔
Turtle Pond ⑧
Wollman Rink ㉝

Manhattan and from Liberty State Park in New Jersey; you'll have a breathtaking view of the Manhattan skyline as you make your way out into the harbor. Shuttle service takes you from one monument to the other.

The immigration facility on tiny Ellis Island opened on January 1, 1892, and soon became a super-efficient operation, processing some 5,000 people on an average day. In its peak year, 1907, over 1 million people passed through immigration here (on April 17 of that year Ellis Island processed 12,000 people, its busiest day). After 62 years of service, the facility closed in 1962, after 12 million people from every corner of the world had passed through its doors, and the buildings gathered dust for years. The island began welcoming visitors again in 1990 after a $160-million restoration project, funded entirely by private donations—and the results are spectacular. Every American should go at least once for a greater understanding of our national heritage.

Don't miss the half-hour film *Island of Hopes, Island of Tears,* with rare footage of turn-of-the-century immigrants making the arduous journey to America. The Great Hall, where new arrivals were processed, has been restored to its 1918–24 appearance; videotaped interviews give a sense of the terror and hope these new Americans felt. One of the most moving displays, "Treasures from Home," contains actual immigrant artifacts brought from the Old World—dolls, clothing, books, and family heirlooms. Multimedia exhibits throughout the galleries illustrate the arrival of various ethnic groups—where they settled, how they contributed to American language, how they adapted to their new country, and the suspicion and racism that sometimes greeted them. The American Immigrant Wall of Honor includes the names of 200,000 immigrants who have been commemorated by their descendants; there's also a computer registry for those names.

The museum also features an oral history studio, open by appointment only (write to: Museum Services Division, The Statue of Liberty National Monument, Liberty Island, NY 10004), and the Ellis Island Learning Center, which uses interactive video technology to make history come alive. You also have to make an appointment to see the learning center; contact the Chief of Interpretation at the same address.

Just a short distance away in the harbor, the Statue of Liberty stands 152 feet tall. She weighs 450,000 pounds, and has a 35-foot waist and a 4½-foot nose. Since she was shipped to the United States in 214 crates and erected in 1886, she has stood in New York's lower harbor as a symbol of freedom.

Closed for renovation in 1984, the statue was reopened to the public in a gala Centennial celebration on July 4, 1986. Now cleaned and strengthened, Miss Liberty holds a new, handcrafted torch with a gold-plated flame.

For a spectacular view of New York Harbor, take the new, glass-walled elevator to the top of the pedestal. From there, you can climb the spiral staircase to the statue's crown, if the prospect of climbing 168 steps doesn't dampen your enthusiasm.

In the pedestal, be sure to visit the museum exhibits on the second- and third-floor levels. The Statue of Liberty exhibit, featuring displays on the history, restoration, and symbolism of the statue, includes the original torch and flame plus a full-scale copper replica of the statue's face. Another exhibit offers a portrait of America's immigrants, both famous and obscure, through artifacts, slides, and evocative black-and-white photographs.

The Ellis Island Museum and the exhibit at the base of the statue are fully accessible to the disabled.

Admission (including both monuments): $6 adults, $5 seniors, $3 children ages 3–17, children under 3 free.

Open: Winter daily 9:30am–5pm; summer daily 9:30am–5:30pm. **Subway:** 4, 5 to Bowling Green; or 1, 9 to South Ferry. **Bus:** M15 from the East Side; M6 from the West Side.

BATTERY PARK CITY, near the World Trade Center.

Across the street from the twin monoliths that are the World Trade Center (see "Panoramas," in Section 2, "More Attractions," below) lies Battery Park City, a masterwork of urban planning. Although it was completed as recently as 1988, it's destined to become another treasured New York cityscape. This brand-new neighborhood was constructed literally from the ground up—built on a 92-acre landfill from construction of the World Trade Center. The project displays an eloquent respect for the city's architectural history with breathtaking anticipation of things to come.

At the heart of Battery Park City is the ✪ **World Financial Center**—architect Cesar Pelli's complex of office towers, restaurants, shops, a yacht harbor, outdoor plazas, and indoor gardens.

We last stopped by on a summer evening when the Count Basie orchestra was keeping swing dancers busy with a free concert on the harborside plaza—you'll find some of New York's best summer entertainment here, all absolutely free. Wall Streeters rub elbows with just plain folks who come from all over the city to have a cocktail and watch the sunset over the water.

Perhaps the center's most stunning feature is its sparkling centerpiece, the **Winter Garden** (tel. 945-0505). The crystal atrium arches 80 feet into the air, enclosing a marble plaza where, no matter what the temperature outside, strollers can enjoy the sun inside. Palm trees tower 45 feet overhead, and if you look up through the glass ceiling, you'll see the World Trade Center soaring above you—a gorgeous view at night when all its lights are twinkling.

Like the outdoor plaza, this atrium has become one of Manhattan's most popular and beautiful informal settings for music, dance, and other live performances. Among the amazing array of free evening and afternoon entertainment offered recently at the Winter Garden was a dance performance by the world-renowned Paul Taylor Company, and musical performances by Hank Jones (jazz pianist) and Tommy Flannigan (bebop artist). There are usually several performances each week, either at 12:15pm or sometime between 6 and 8pm.

Even if there are no performances scheduled, a stroll through Battery Park City can be a relaxing retreat from urban blight. The shaded walkways south of the Winter Garden through the residential developments offer radiant gardens, some of which are designed to give the impression of untouched nature. On the west side of Battery Park City, the landscaped esplanade along the Hudson River is a romantic waterfront park that recalls the Hudson's shoreline as it was during the 18th and 19th centuries. You can't miss the ferry landing, protected by huge white circus-style tents—they're gorgeous against the water, almost reminiscent of a sultan's lair.

Directions: 1, 9, N, or R to Cortlandt St.; or A, C, or E to Chambers St.–World Trade Center, and then walk west. In front of the World Trade Center, a pedestrian bridge at Vesey St. and another at Liberty St. can take you over the traffic on West St. and into Battery Park City.

SOUTH STREET SEAPORT AND THE SOUTH STREET SEAPORT MUSE-UMS, at the southern tip of Manhattan. Tel. 406-3434 (for information on special events).

In these days of telecommunication and air travel, it's easy to forget that New York rose to its present greatness from its original role as the nation's greatest seaport. At the restored South Street Seaport, located on 11 square blocks of downtown Manhattan, along Fulton and Water streets and on piers 15, 16, and 17 on the East River, that heritage is preserved in a revitalized area that contains one of the city's most exciting educational and recreational attractions. As you explore the Seaport's all-pedestrian cobblestone streets, restaurants, specialty stores, public terraces with waterfront views, and restored 19th-century rowhouses, you'll be caught up in the whole new spirit of enterprise and imagination that has magically brought the old port back to life, recalling the days when China clippers, transatlantic packets, Caribbean schooners, grain barges, and Long Island Sound steamboats crowded its teeming wharves.

Your tour should begin at the **Pilot House** on Pier 16, where you can purchase an admission ticket to the **South Street Seaport Museum** that includes a guided walking tour of the historic district and antique ships, and admission to the Seaport Gallery ($4 for adults, $3 for senior citizens, and $2 for children 12 and under).

FROMMER'S FAVORITE
NEW YORK EXPERIENCES

A Stroll Through Greenwich Village Manhattan's most colorful neighborhood is the perfect place for bar-hopping, café-sitting, and people-watching.

A Night Out at the Theater Naysayers may insist that Broadway's lights have dimmed, but there's still nothing like a glitzy, glamorous production on the Great White Way.

A Summer Afternoon in Central Park Pack a picnic from Zabar's—cheeses, deli meats, breads, and your favorite beverage—and head into the park. Rent a rowboat from Loeb Boathouse for a romantic trip around the lake, or try your hand at rollerblading. You'll no doubt be treated to the sounds of street performers—perhaps a classical violinist, a folk group, or a percussion ensemble—all absolutely free.

An Evening in Little Italy Almost any restaurant you choose in Little Italy will serve up heaping helpings of pasta and lots of Old World charm. Top off your evening with cappuccino and a decadent pastry at the legendary Ferrara's.

A Ride on the Staten Island Ferry For a mere 50¢, a view of the most romantic skyline in the world can be yours.

Visit the **Seaport Gallery,** 215 Water Street, for a schematic indoor tour of the area's historic buildings. See Chapter 9, "New York City Shopping," for a full description of the shops in the Museum Block, along **Cannon's Walk**—a charming interior courtyard tucked away in the center of the block—and along Fulton Street, named for Robert Fulton, inventor of the steamboat who inaugurated the Fulton Ferry to Brooklyn at the foot of the street. Also on Fulton Street is **Schermerhorn Row,** an architectural treasure of a red-brick blockfront dating back to 1811.

The festive-looking three-story brick-and-granite building occupying the block bordered by Fulton, Front, Beekman, and South streets is the fourth **Fulton Market Building** on this site since 1822. Colored with the vitality and rich confusion of traditional market activity, the new Fulton Market incorporates the stalls of honest-to-goodness fresh fish and seafood merchants (along South Street) as well as an extraordinary variety of restaurants, outdoor cafés, and food shops. Just like the good old days, only better.

The tang of salty air will lead you across South Street to the piers where the old ships are moored: the four-masted steel bark *Peking* and the U.S. Coast Guard lightship *Ambrose.* You can also take a 90-minute excursion on the *Andrew Fletcher,* a sidewheel paddle ship modeled after 19th-century paddlewheel steamers. (Andrew Fletcher was the name of both a father and a son who were leading builders of sidewheel engines in the latter half of the 19th century.) From the deck of the boat, you'll get a closeup view of the Statue of Liberty as well as the spectacular sights of the lower Manhattan skyline. The boat departs from Pier 16 three times daily, and the price is $10 for adults, $6 for children 12 and under. Call 385-0791 for information.

Finally, you might cap off your trip to the Seaport with a visit to the **Pier 17 Pavilion,** a three-story glass-and-steel structure on the water's edge. Inside are more than 100 shops and restaurants; each floor has an outdoor promenade, and the top floor offers spectacular views of the Statue of Liberty, Brooklyn Bridge, and waterborne traffic on the East River.

Most Seaport attractions are open from 10am to 5pm daily, except Thanksgiving,

Christmas, and New Year's days, with ship hours shorter during the winter. On Memorial Day weekend, July 4th weekend, Labor Day weekend, and New Year's Eve, the Seaport comes alive with spectacular fireworks presentations, live indoor and outdoor concerts, and other entertainment.

Subway: 2, 3, 4, 5 to Fulton St. and walk east toward the waterfront.

MIDTOWN

ROCKEFELLER CENTER, between 47th and 50th sts. from Fifth to Sixth aves. Tel. 698-8500.

To see Rockefeller Center is to see a microcosm of New York, with 19 buildings occupying a space of 22 acres. Skyscrapers, plazas, stores, and theaters all come together in this magnificent complex—America's first and foremost urban mall. A promenade lined with stores and offices leads to Rockefeller Center's famous sunken ice-skating rink, marked by an immense gold-colored statue of Prometheus, and during the Christmas season, by an enormous, brightly lit tree. (This winter playground becomes a festive outdoor café in the summer.) At the center of the mall is a cluster of skyscrapers capped with rooftop cafés and gardens that offer spectacular views of Manhattan. One of the most noteworthy structures is the **RCA Building,** which has a magnificent black granite lobby lined with murals by José María Sert. But most impressive is the celebrated **Radio City Music Hall.** It has a 6,000-seat theater and 60-foot-high lobby. On one wall is Ezra Winter's rich gold-and-bronze painting *Fountain of Youth,* and on the staircase is a perfectly patterned Art Deco rug. Taken as a whole, the building is empowered with all the grandeur of the decade in which it was built—the 1930s.

The theater's productions are as grandiose as its architecture. There are concerts, ice extravaganzas, circuses, and special 90-minute Christmas and Easter spectaculars.

No view of New York is complete without seeing this mall. And unlike many of the city's attractions, Rockefeller Center can be enjoyed inexpensively. You can enjoy a film and exhibit on the center's history at 30 Rockefeller Plaza Monday through Friday from 9am to 5pm. Be sure to pick up the free brochures at the information desk. Tickets for performances at Radio City start around $18, but for only $7 there's a guided tour of the theater that might prove just as entertaining. For information, call 632-4041.

Subway: B, D, F, Q to Rockefeller Center.

EMPIRE STATE BUILDING, Fifth Ave. between 33rd and 34th sts. Tel. 736-3100.

The Empire State Building will always be New Yorkers' favorite skyscraper. When it opened its doors in 1931, this creation of architects Shreve, Lamb & Harmon was the tallest structure in the world, and it ushered in a new age of daring urban architecture. Depression-struck New Yorkers scrimped for weeks to save the then-$1 admission fee to "The Eighth Wonder of the World," "The Everest on Fifth Avenue," or "The Miracle on 34th Street."

At 102 stories and 1,250 feet, it's no longer the tallest building in the world (it was eclipsed by two Chicago skyscrapers and the twin-towered World Trade Center downtown), but it remains one of the most beloved of the city's buildings.

It's difficult to imagine New York's skyline without the profile of the 1,250-foot tower and familiar silver spire (conceived as a mooring mast for zeppelins, though that scheme never worked). Each year more than two million tourists flock to the building's observation decks on the 86th and 102nd floors, where on a clear day the view is a spectacular one of 60 miles or more. You'll be right in the middle of a concrete forest of skyscrapers, looking down on them. The viewing area on the 86th floor has a raised walkway platform backed by mirrors, and those without a fear of heights can venture outside to the promenade. On the 102nd floor, viewing is from the inside only, through round porthole windows. Take one of the building's elevators to the observation deck.

If you've got children along, stop in at the **Guinness World Records Exhibit**

Hall, on the concourse level (open daily from 9am to 9pm with extended hours during peak season; $4 for adults, $2.75 for children 11 and under). See Section 4, "Cool for Kids," below, for more information.

Admission: $3.50 adults, $2.75 students with identification, $1.75 children under 12 and senior citizens.

Open: Daily 9:30am–midnight (tickets sold until 11:30pm), except on Christmas and New Year's Eve, when the deck closes at 7pm. Summer days and weekends all year long are especially crowded, so you might want to try a weekday, or better still, a star-studded evening. **Subway:** B, D, F, N, Q, R to 34th and Sixth Ave.; 6 to 33rd and Lexington Ave.

MUSEUM OF MODERN ART, 11 W. 53rd St., between Fifth Ave. and Ave. of the Americas. Tel. 708-9500, or 708-9480 for information on current exhibitions.

✪ The MOMA is one of the world's great museums. Founded in 1929, it offers an unrivaled survey of the modern arts from 1880 to the present. Its collection includes over 100,000 paintings, sculptures, drawings, prints, photographs, architectural models and plans, and superbly designed objects, as well as 8,000 films, four million film stills, and a library containing some 80,000 books and periodicals. The museum's changing exhibitions focus on specific artists' works, styles, and modern art movements. You can explore the development of modern art—from the masterpieces of post-Impressionists like van Gogh and Cézanne to works by modern masters Rauschenberg and Stella—in more than 20 galleries. And—against a soothing backdrop of weeping birch and beech trees, reflecting pools, and fountains—you can enjoy the sculpture of Picasso, Rodin, and many others in MOMA's Abby Aldrich Rockefeller Sculpture Garden. Recent exhibitions have included "Surrealist Drawings," "Seven Master Print Makers," and Lee Friedlander's "Nudes."

Films—mainly by international and American independent filmmakers—are shown daily in the museum's two theaters, and video exhibitions are screened in the Video Gallery. Both are free with admission. For information on film showings, call 708-9490.

Admission: $7 adults, $4 students with ID and senior citizens; children under 16 accompanied by an adult and over 65s are admitted free; Thurs 5–9pm, pay as you wish.

Open: Thurs 11am–8:45pm and Fri–Tues 11am–5:45pm. **Closed:** Dec 25. **Subway:** E, F to Fifth Ave.; 1 to 50th St.; B, D to Rockefeller Center.

UNITED NATIONS, First Ave. at 46th St. Tel. 963-7713.

Like a sea-green monolith, the Secretariat building at the United Nations towers over a white marble plaza with the grandeur befitting its international status. Built on land that is internationally owned, it's the meeting place for delegates from over 150 nations, who discuss everything from disarmament to fishing rights.

General Assembly meetings are sometimes open to the public, and admission is free. Check the *New York Times* or call 963-7558 for information about meetings. Tickets are issued on a first-come, first-served basis, and meetings are sometimes cancelled on short notice.

The U.N. also offers guided tours of its huge assembly halls, decorated with donations from Scandinavian countries. Your tour guide will probably speak more than one language, and will describe the U.N.'s history from its inception. Some tours even include a briefing with one of the delegates. Tours last approximately an hour.

The U.N. also shows free films about its history and about different U.N. projects, for ninth-graders and above. Call the day before you plan to visit and tell them which subjects you would like to see on film.

Admission: General Assembly meeting free when open to the public; tours $5.50 adults, $4.50 seniors, $3.50 students. Children under 5 not admitted.

Open: Tours given every half hour daily 9:15am–4:45pm. **Bus:** M27, M25, or M50 to First Ave.

ROCKEFELLER CENTER

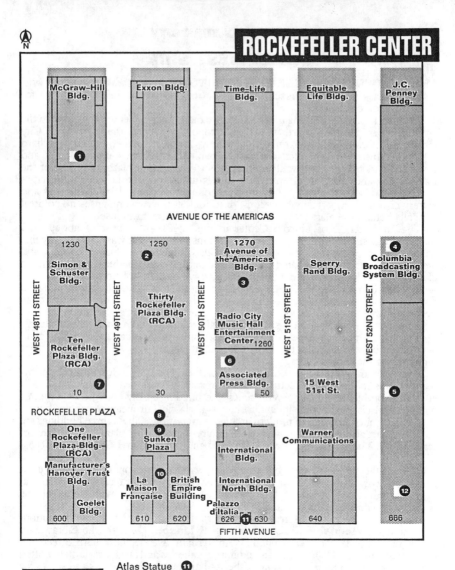

McGraw-Hill Bldg. ❶

Exxon Bldg.

Time-Life Bldg.

Equitable Life Bldg.

J.C. Penney Bldg.

AVENUE OF THE AMERICAS

1230
Simon & Schuster Bldg. ❷

1250
Thirty Rockefeller Plaza Bldg. (RCA) ❷
30

1270 Avenue of the-Americas Bldg. ❸

Radio City Music Hall Entertainment Center 1260 ❻

Associated Press Bldg. 50

Sperry Rand Bldg.

Columbia Broadcasting System Bldg. ❹

15 West 51st St.

Warner Communications

❺

WEST 48TH STREET
WEST 49TH STREET
WEST 50TH STREET
WEST 51ST STREET
WEST 52ND STREET

Ten Rockefeller Plaza Bldg. (RCA) 10 ❼

ROCKEFELLER PLAZA

❽
❾
Sunken Plaza

One Rockefeller Plaza-Bldg.- (RCA)
Manufacturer's Hanover Trust Bldg.
Goelet Bldg. 600

La Maison Française 610 ❿ **British Empire Building** 620

International Bldg.
International North Bldg.
Palazzo d'Italia 626 ⓫ 630

640

666 ⓬

FIFTH AVENUE

MANHATTAN
Rockefeller Center

Atlas Statue ⓫
CBS TV Studios ❹
Channel Gardens ❿
Guild Theater ❻
NBC TV Studios ❷
New York Experience Theater ❶
Prometheus Fountain ❽
Radio City Music Hall ❸
Rainbow Room ❼
Skating Rink ❾
Top of the Sixes ⓬
Twenty-One Club ❺

UPPER WEST SIDE

LINCOLN CENTER FOR THE PERFORMING ARTS, between W. 62nd and W. 66th sts. from Amsterdam to Columbus aves. Tel. 875-5000 for information on tours.

New York City has nothing more impressive than Lincoln Center. It's home to the city's premier performing artists—the Metropolitan Opera, the New York City Opera, the New York Philharmonic, the New York City Ballet, and the Juilliard School of Music. It's a complex of theaters separated artfully by fountains, cafés, and tree-filled parks. When you walk up the steps to the central plaza, the noise of the traffic fades and there is a sense that this is an island untouched by the city's commotion. It's worth a visit just to sit on the fountain's edge and watch the sleek and glittery crowds during the intermissions, or to look at the two immense and colorful Chagalls behind the glass facade of the Metropolitan Opera House.

The construction of Lincoln Center in the 1960s—at a cost of about $165 million—was surrounded by controversy. It transformed what was once a sprawling ghetto into a prime real estate area, but also increased traffic. Architects and architectural critics alike debated endlessly and angrily over whether to build it in the classical or modern style. What finally emerged was a blend of both.

The 2,800-seat **New York State Theater** (at the left side of the plaza), designed for ballet and musical theater, is the most clearly classical building. It has a lobby decorated lavishly in the baroque style, and above that there's a grand foyer with decorative metal balcony railings, colored chain drapery, and a gold velvet ceiling.

The **Metropolitan Opera House,** also built in classical style, has a grand auditorium of red and gold, but most noteworthy here are the Chagalls in the front lobby facing the central plaza.

Avery Fisher Hall (on the right side of the plaza), built for musical performances, was the most architecturally controversial because of its widely publicized acoustical problems. Rebuilt several times, the building finally emerged as a mix of modern and classical styles. Its auditorium is a classic European rectangle, but its simple flat planes derive from modern architectural notions. These three buildings are separated by an open plaza with a fountain. Behind the plaza is the **Vivian Beaumont Theater,** and **Alice Tully Hall** and the **Julliard School** are across 65th Street.

Performances are expensive, but anyone can wander in and out of the buildings, or for the price of a drink, sit in one of the outdoor cafés or indoor restaurants. A special program, Meet the Artists, offers visitors a chance to talk with some of the performers. For information, call 875-5000.

Nestled between the Metropolitan Opera House and the Vivian Beaumont Theater is the **New York Public Library at Lincoln Center** (the Library and Museum of the Performing Arts), 111 Amsterdam Avenue, near 65th Street (tel. 870-1630). On the "A" floor are four exhibition galleries and an auditorium that often offers free performances. The first floor shelves hold hundreds of books and scores for drama, dance, and music. The second floor has a projection room for films and an extensive children's library, and the third, a gallery collection of old clippings, photos, playbills, and costumes. There are research libraries with large and varied collections of material on dance, music, and theater. It also has records, earphones, and turntables available for public use. Open Monday through Saturday; hours vary, so call for the daily schedule.

Tours: 1-hour tours daily for $7.50 adults, $6.50 students and seniors, $4.25 children 12 and under.

Subway: 1, 9 to 66th St. **Bus:** M66 to Broadway or Columbus Ave.

AMERICAN MUSEUM OF NATURAL HISTORY, Central Park West and 79th St. Tel. 769-5100.

We love this museum and recommend it especially to visitors with children. Focusing on all forms of animal and human life, with more than 30 million artifacts and specimens, the museum offers the visitor an incredible range of

natural wonders, from a miniscule chromosome to a 94-foot replica
whale—the largest mammal that ever lived. But don't try to see all the exh
you'll quickly become overwhelmed.

Among the many excellent exhibits are the Gardner D. Stout Hall o
Peoples, which features over 3,000 artifacts and artworks; the Hall of Mexic
Central America, which has an impressive collection of pre-Columbian jade
carved stone pieces; the Hall of African Peoples; and the recently opened Hall
South American Peoples. You'll marvel at the dazzling Star of India sapphire, and th
largest meteorite ever retrieved. Also on display are dioramas of many preserved
animals shown in every type of habitat from the savannah to the tundra. Every native
New Yorker has fond memories of taking a school field trip to see the huge dinosaurs
on display—they're sure to be one of the highlights of your child's visit.

The museum's Naturemax Film Theater offers features sure to delight anyone with
a sense of adventure. The Naturemax motion-picture format uses a film frame ten
times the size of a standard 35-mm frame, resulting in a display of breathtaking images
unsurpassed in resolution and detail. Tickets—$5 for adults, $3.75 seniors and
students, $2.50 for children ($7 adults, $5.50 seniors and students, $3.50 children for
double features)—can be purchased at the box office in the main lobby. Call
769-5650 for shows and times.

The museum also has a pleasant gift shop, a reference library, a cafeteria, and a
restaurant. See also the Hayden Planetarium listing, below, and Section 4, "Cool for
Kids," for information on children's favorite features in the museum.

Suggested admission: $5 adults, $2.50 students and children.

Open: Sun–Thurs 10am–5:45pm; Fri–Sat 10am–8:45pm. **Subway:** 1, 9 to 79th
St.; B or C to 81st St. **Bus:** M79 to Columbus Ave.

THE HAYDEN PLANETARIUM, Central Park West and 81st St. Tel. 769-5920.

The closest thing to stargazing you're likely to get in Manhattan is a Sky Show
at the Hayden Planetarium. When the lights go out and the quarter-million-
dollar Zeiss VI projector splashes a star-studded sky on the 75-foot dome
ceiling, you'd almost believe you were sitting on a mountaintop. The shows, which
vary from season to season, trace man's fascination with the stars and the planets, the
mythical and scientific explanations for cosmic phenomena, and the possibilities for
future exploration. Shows take place weekdays at 1:30 and 3:30pm, on Saturday and
Sunday at 1, 2, 3, 4, and 5pm (an 11am Saturday show is added October through June).

The planetarium also contains exhibits explaining such things as orbital patterns,
gamma rays, rainbows, and why the sky is blue. Its Hall of the Sun is the largest
exhibit in the world devoted entirely to our nearest star. And if you're curious to
know what you'd weigh on Mars, Jupiter, Venus, the sun, or the moon, jump onto a
scale in "Your Weight on Other Worlds." Twenty-two projection screens in the
Guggenheim Space Theater exhibit multi-image presentations on space science (be
sure to notice the large moving model of the solar system on the ceiling and the
colorful Aztec calendar at the center of the room).

Most popular with the young crowd is the **Laser Show**—a dazzling show that
combines laser images with rock music to create a vibrant kaleidoscopic effect. Shows
are Friday and Saturday at 7, 8:30, and 10pm. Tickets cost $6 and at times sell out, so
you should plan to arrive early (the box office opens at 6pm) or to buy tickets in
advance at Ticketron. For Laser Show information, call 769-5921.

Admission: $5 adults, $3.50 students with ID and senior citizens, $2.50 ages
2–12.

Open: Mon–Fri 12:30–4:45pm, Sat–Sun noon–4:45pm. Laser Light Show
Fri–Sat shows 7, 8:30, 10pm. **Subway:** C or B to 81st St., or 1, 9 to 79th St. and walk
east from Broadway.

NATIONAL MUSEUM OF THE AMERICAN INDIAN—SMITHSONIAN INSTITUTION, 3753 Broadway, at 155th St. Tel. 283-2420.

This museum contains the world's largest and finest collection of artifacts made by
the Indians of the Western Hemisphere. Arranged in three floors of exhibits, these

ceremonies and daily activities of Indian cultures. The first
the different North American Indian societies. Here you
quois silver jewelry and beadwork, Sitting Bull's war club
by Crazy Horse, Hopi kachina dolls, Geronimo's warrior
baskets, and Inuit (Eskimo) fur parkas. On the third floor
life in South and Central America, Amazonian Indian
xtiles, ancient Peruvian ceramics, and Taíno and wood

upies one of the imposing and elegant buildings that
errace complex. At the beginning of 1993 the museum will
storic landmark building, the old U.S. Customs House, in lower
attan.

Admission: $3 adults, $2 students and senior citizens, free for children under 7.
Open: Tues–Sat 10am–5pm; Sun 1–5pm. **Closed:** Holidays. **Subway:** 1, 9 to
157th St. **Bus:** M4 or M5 to 155th St.

UPPER EAST SIDE

METROPOLITAN MUSEUM OF ART, Fifth Ave. and 82nd St. Tel. 535-7710.

⭐ This grande dame of American museums has something to interest almost
everyone. Its collection, the largest in the Western Hemisphere, comprises
everything from ancient Greek vases and Renaissance paintings to Native
American masks and a room designed by Frank Lloyd Wright. In addition to its
permanent collection, the Met offers several special exhibitions of works on loan from
around the world each year. The museum's Costume Institute, which preserves
clothing from as far back as the 1600s, organizes some gorgeous exhibitions of period
or regional clothing; and the exquisite period rooms offer a glimpse of life in ages past.
The American Wing gives a comprehensive picture of three centuries of American life
and art, and its glassed-in sculpture garden is a lovely place to relax. At one side of the
garden you'll find some breathtaking stained-glass windows created in the much-
acclaimed Tiffany Studios.

In June 1983 the final 13 galleries of the Met's Egyptian collection opened,
concluding a 25-year project and marking the first time that the entire collection has
been on public view. With an estimated 40,000 objects spanning over 500,000 years
of Egyptian history, the collection is, in fact, so large that it requires 32 galleries to
accommodate it! In the 25th gallery, visitors will find the Temple of Dendur, circa 15
B.C. from Lower Nubia. As part of a project to preserve Egypt's treasures from
destruction during the building of the Aswan High Dam, this temple was excavated,
sent piece by piece to the Met, and painstakingly rebuilt for public viewing. Visitors
are invited to walk around the temple to experience its beauty firsthand.

Reopened after a $10 million renovation, the Pierpont Morgan wing shows the
museum's collection of arms and armor. Also of note is the Michael C. Rockefeller
Wing, which exhibits a fascinating array of native art from Africa, the Americas, and
the Pacific Islands. In addition, visitors can relax in the Iris and B. Gerald Cantor Roof
Garden—a 10,000-square-foot open-air garden with an installation of 20th-century
sculpture. The garden affords a spectacular view of the New York City skyline and
Central Park, and is open May through October. Or if you'd rather rest indoors, you
can visit the Lila Acheson Wing for 20th-century art and the Japanese Galleries. The
mood in these galleries—which display ceramics, kimonos, armor, and woodblock
prints—is enhanced by traditional Japanese architecture and by an indoor garden that
replicates a contemporary Japanese garden.

If you get hungry, visit the museum's restaurant. If you just want to relax, sit on the
steps outside the front entrance and join other museum-goers munching hot dogs and
watching the antics of street performers. A bit more tranquil are the tree-shaded park
benches off to the side, where the splashing of the fountains drowns out the noise of
the traffic.

Floor plans are available from any of the information booths at the entrance.

There are daily tours given in English and weekly tours given in Spanish. (French tours can be arranged by appointment, and German-speaking visitors can rent an audio tour for a nominal fee.) Also, visitors can rent audio tours of the permanent collections.

The Met's Uris Center for Education offers a variety of student- and family-oriented programs (see Section 4, "Cool for Kids,"). For information on museum facilities for the physically disabled, call 879-0421 or 570-3828.

Suggested contribution: $6 adults, $3 students and senior citizens, members and children under 12 free.

Open: Sun and Tues–Thurs 9:30am–5:15pm, Fri–Sat 9:30am–8:45pm. **Subway:** 4, 5, 6 to 86th St.; walk west. **Bus:** M79 crosstown to Fifth Ave; M1, M2, M3, M4 on Fifth Ave./Madison Ave.

THE CLOISTERS, Fort Tryon Park. Tel. 923-3700.

Isolated at the upper tip of the island, this uptown branch of the Metropolitan Museum of Art resembles a medieval monastery in location and appearance. Built in the 1930s by Charles Collens, the architect of Riverside Church, this stone complex combines parts of five medieval monasteries—a 12th-century chapter house, a Romanesque chapel, and a 12th-century Spanish apse—into one. The Cloisters contains the Met's vast collection of medieval art, including the famous *Unicorn Tapestries* (seven 16th-century tapestries that depict the hunting of the mythical one-horned creature). Among other spectacular pieces on view is the famous *Altarpiece of the Annunciation,* as well as important illuminated manuscripts and striking stained-glass windows. You may want to take a free guided tour, which is given Tuesday through Saturday at 3pm. After looking at the collection, sit in the herb garden and soak in the tranquility of this serene oasis.

This unusual museum is well worth the half-hour trip from downtown.

Suggested admission: $6 adults, $3 students and senior citizens, free for children under 12 accompanied by an adult.

Open: Tues–Sun 9:30am–5:15pm. **Subway:** A train to 190th St.–Overlook Terrace. Then take no. 4 bus or walk through Fort Tryon Park to museum. **Bus:** Madison Ave. no. 4 to Fort Tryon Park.

FRICK COLLECTION, 1 E. 70th St., at the corner of Fifth Ave. Tel. 288-0700.

The Frick Museum is a jewel, although it is not as well known as other New York museums. Its collection belonged to Pittsburgh coal-and-steel magnate Henry Clay Frick, and the museum was once his home. It's much like visiting a very rich—and hospitable—friend who just happens to have Gainsboroughs in the dining room, a drawing room full of Fragonards, Titians in the living room, and an El Greco over the fireplace. The Fricks collected art for 40 years, and arranged to leave their house to the public as a museum. Though the magnificent house has been expanded to almost double its original size, it still looks like a home, complete with books and easy chairs among the grander antiques. Two of the more notable additions made since the Frick opened in 1935 are the garden court with a splashing fountain and a lovely garden designed by the late British landscape artist Russell Paige. There is also a museum shop.

No children under 10 are allowed in, and those under 16 must be with an adult. Call or write for information on lectures and weekly concerts (tickets must be arranged in advance).

Admission: $3 adults, $1.50 students and senior citizens.

Open: Tues–Sat 10am–6pm; Sun and hols 1–6pm. **Subway:** 6 to 68th St. **Bus:** M66 crosstown to Fifth Ave.

GUGGENHEIM MUSEUM, 1071 Fifth Ave., at 89th St. Tel. 727-6200.

✪ The Solomon R. Guggenheim Museum is housed in a spectacular spiral building designed by the architect Frank Lloyd Wright. Visitors generally take the elevator to the top floor, then walk downhill in wide circles viewing artworks along the curved walls.

The museum's landmarked building has been closed for over a year while being restored to its original pristine condition. An addition will double the original exhibition space, and the bookstore and restaurant have been expanded as well. It is scheduled to reopen in spring of 1992.

Displayed on the ramp will be works by new artists, as well as rotating exhibits of art by modern masters. On permanent display are such modern masterpieces as Picasso's *Mandolin and Guitar,* Bracque's *The Buffet,* and Chagall's *The Green Violinist.* The museum also has 20 other Picassos and one of the largest collections of works by Vasily Kandinsky in the world. In the permanently installed Justin K. Thannhauser Collection, off the main building, hang paintings by Manet, Renoir, Cézanne, Gauguin, and van Gogh.

Note: As of press time, new admission prices and open hours were not available, so call before going.

Subway: 4, 5, 6 to 86th St. **Bus:** M2, M3, or M4 to Madison Ave.

BROOKLYN

THE BROOKLYN MUSEUM, Eastern Parkway and Washington Ave. Tel. 718/638-5000.

One of the nation's premier art institutions, the Brooklyn Museum contains approximately 1½ million works of art, ranging from ancient Egyptian artifacts to American painting and sculpture. There are 28 American period rooms, and an outdoor sculpture garden consisting of architectural sections from demolished New York buildings. In the gift shop you can purchase original folk art from around the world. The museum has an art reference library, with more than 100,000 volumes, and the Wilbur Library of Egyptology that has more than 25,000 books on the subject.

Suggested admission: $4 adults, $2 students, $1.50 senior citizens; children under 12 free.

Open: Wed–Sun 10am–5pm. **Subway:** 2, 3, 4 to Eastern Parkway–Brooklyn Museum stop.

2. MORE ATTRACTIONS

ARCHITECTURAL HIGHLIGHTS

TRIBECA

WOOLWORTH BUILDING, 233 Broadway, near Park Place.

Cass Gilbert designed the 792-foot-tall Woolworth Building in 1913, and it stood as the world's tallest skyscraper until 1930. Frank Woolworth paid $13.5 million for it (in cash), and it remains one of New York's landmark buildings today, with its Gothic detailing and ornate lobby. If you enter the building from the Broadway entrance, look closely at the first archway to your left and you'll see representations of Mr. Woolworth and his architect in each corner. In the rear of the lobby, a plaque details the history of the building.

Subway: 2, 3 to Park Place; N, R to City Hall.

EAST VILLAGE/GRAMERCY PARK

COOPER UNION FOR THE ADVANCEMENT OF SCIENCE AND ART, 41 Cooper Square, at Third Ave. and East 7th St. Tel. 353-4100.

A tuition-free school of art, architecture, and engineering, the Foundation was established by Peter Cooper, an industrialist and philanthropist whose early poverty prevented him from gaining an education, and spurred him in later years to begin the first privately endowed, tuition-free college in the country.

The building, which opened in 1859 and is a national historic landmark, is technologically interesting—it was among the first anywhere to use rolled-iron beams in construction, which earned it the designation as a forerunner to the modern skyscraper. It is also of political and historical interest. It provided New York City with its first free reading room, and the building's "Great Hall" (which seats about 950) was once the largest public auditorium in the city. That hall was the site of the first free public lecture series in the nation, and it has been a mecca for debate. It drew Abraham Lincoln arguing against the extension of slavery, Susan B. Anthony calling for women's suffrage, Mark Twain, Ulysses S. Grant, Theodore Roosevelt, and Margaret Mead, among many others. It was here that the campaign to overthrow the New York Tweed Ring was launched and here that a meeting leading to the establishment of the National Association for the Advancement of Colored People was held.

The music, poetry, and lecture series—with a roster of notable speakers—is held from October through April. Call for scheduled events.

Subway: 6 to Astor Place; N or R to Greenwich Ave.

THE FLATIRON BUILDING, Broadway and Fifth Ave., at 23rd St.

Wedge-shaped to fit into a triangular piece of property, the building got its nickname for its obvious resemblance to the old-fashioned iron for clothes. It's a fine example of how architects have used every available space in the city to create unusual structures.

Subway: N, R to 23rd St.

MIDTOWN

CHRYSLER BUILDING, 405 Lexington Ave., between 42nd and 43rd sts.

The distinctive Art Deco spire atop the sleek Chrysler building brought it to a height of 1,048 feet; it reigned as the world's tallest building until the Empire State Building came along. For some, it's the most romantic building in the city.

Subway: 4, 5, 6 to Grand Central. **Bus:** M42 or M104.

DAILY NEWS BUILDING, 220 E. 42nd St., at Second Ave.

The Art Deco home of the city's largest-circulation newspaper is worth a peek. The main lobby contains a huge globe that turns, and sometimes there's a show of newspaper photographs taken over the years.

Open: Main lobby open 24 hrs. **Bus:** M15 or M104.

FORD FOUNDATION, 320 E. 42nd St., between First and Second aves.

The garden of the Ford Foundation is its focal point, with light streaming in overhead from a skylight. A small, fern-lined pool of water keeps the air moist for a jungle of plants. **Open:** Garden Mon–Fri 9am–5pm. **Bus:** M15 or M104.

GRAND CENTRAL TERMINAL, Park Ave. and 42nd St.

This is no mere train station: It has been New York City's great hall for more than 75 years, a place consummately public yet able to provide a private nook. It is a distillate of the city itself, a collision of the rich with the destitute, an intermingling of a glamorous past with a less romantic and more commercial present.

The Beaux-Arts building, completed in 1913, has often been called "a city within the city," and aptly so. It was once the largest enclosed space in the world, and today houses more than 60 stores and banks. Within its corridors you can buy French pastries or potted plants, books, bric-a-brac, booze, or a basketball. You can place a bet, fill a prescription, have a pair of shoes or a watch repaired, dine on a fine meal or a variety of fast food.

It throbs at rush hour. On a normal weekday one million people stride through its corridors, concourse, and waiting room, plunging into or out of the tubes and tunnels. In their wake they leave six or seven tons of litter daily—enough to require a 55-person cleanup crew. Yet for all its swirling hubbub, there are quiet eddies too. The lower level is nearly always tranquil, and one can sit peacefully on the long wooden benches of the waiting room, underneath the ornate brass chandeliers and carved ceiling beams. Upstairs, take time to behold the wonderful ceiling mural of the

Mediterranean winter sky, with 2,500 stars painted in gold, vaulting over the concourse. The subdued marble-and-stone elegance of both that room and the waiting room evoke an earlier era, when your train might be the Twentieth Century to Chicago, instead of a commuter to Connecticut. Or stop off at the "kissing room" on the main concourse level near Track 41. This waiting room for incoming trains has been renovated to the smallest detail of how it looked in 1913.

Subway: 4, 5, 6, 7 or the shuttle to Grand Central/42nd St.

TRUMP TOWER, Fifth Ave. between 56th and 57th sts.
One of the newer buildings in the city, and certainly one of the most glamorous, is Trump Tower, owned by the dealmaker New Yorkers love to hate. The tall glass-sided building is primarily a residence for tenants capable of shelling out upward of $1 million for an apartment. But the best part, or worst, depending on your taste, is a gorgeous pink marble lobby and atrium where browsers can stop in at expensive shops and just look around. There is something so New York about Trump Tower that we definitely recommend a visit.

Subway: E, F to 53rd St.

CHURCHES/HOUSES OF WORSHIP

Many of New York's religious institutions are among the city's architectural gems. They are fascinating museums of religious art, and their tree-shaded churchyards are pleasant sanctuaries from the city's tumult. The budget-conscious traveler can also look to many of these houses of worship for inexpensive, high-quality entertainment. New York's churches and synagogues have become increasingly alive with the sound of contemporary music, especially jazz, and they host first-rate concerts, dance recitals, and plays. Many of these events are free, and others can be attended at little cost.

DOWNTOWN

ST. PAUL'S CHAPEL, Broadway and Fulton St. Tel. 602-0874.
This Episcopal church is the oldest public building in continuous use in Manhattan, dating from 1766, and one of the city's best examples of Georgian-Revival-style architecture. Much of the chapel's interior, including a hand-carved altar and a handsome winding stair, was designed by Pierre L'Enfant, who also designed the city of Washington, D.C. George Washington worshiped here from 1789 to 1791 (a replica of his original pew is intact), and the chapel was also visited by the Marquis de Lafayette, Lord Cornwallis, Benjamin Harrison, and Grover Cleveland. St. Paul's now serves as a parish chapel for Trinity Church. Call to check out the free noonday concerts.

Subway: J, M, Z, 2, 3, 4, 5 to Fulton St.

TRINITY CHURCH, corner of Broadway and Wall St. Tel. 602-0800.
This famous Episcopal church, consecrated in 1846, is the third Trinity to stand at this corner (a corner valued, by the way, at more than $25 million). The first, dating back to 1698, was destroyed in the Great Fire of 1839, and the second was torn down because of structural defects. Trinity may well be the city's premier Gothic-Revival

---

IMPRESSIONS

In New York the earth seems to spin more quickly round its axis.
—HERBERT BEERBOHM TREE, "IMPRESSIONS OF AMERICA," 1916

It is altogether an extraordinary growing, swarming, glittering, pushing, chattering, good-natured, cosmopolitan place, and perhaps in some ways the best imitation of Paris that can be found (yet with a greater originality of its own).
—HENRY JAMES, LETTER TO GEORGE DU MAURIER, APRIL 1883

church; in the mid-19th century its spire was the highest structure on the New York skyline. Alexander Hamilton, Robert Fulton, Capt. James ("Don't give up the ship") Lawrence, and other historic figures are buried in a cemetery surrounding the church. The museum has exhibits relating to Trinity's history.

Open: Church Mon–Fri 7am–6pm, Sat–Sun 8am–4pm; museum Mon–Fri 9–11:45am and 1–3:45pm, Sat 10am–3:45pm, Sun 1–3:45pm. **Subway:** 4, 5 to Wall St.; 1, 9 to Rector St.

EAST VILLAGE

FRIENDS MEETING HOUSE, 15 Rutherford Place, off E. 15th St. between Second and Third aves. Tel. 777-8866.

Built in 1860, this typical Quaker meeting house is understated, especially for structures in the Gothic-Revival style. In its southeast corner is a granite hitching post from William Penn's Philadelphia home.

Subway: L, N, R, 4, 5, or 6 to 14th St.

ST. MARKS-IN-THE-BOWERIE, St. Marks Place, E. 10th St. and Second Ave. Tel. 674-6377.

Dating from 1799, this church stands on the site of the Peter Stuyvesant family chapel. A blend of disparate styles, it has an Italianate cast-iron portico, a Georgian chapel, and a Greek-Revival-style steeple. Stuyvesant is buried in a crypt beneath the church along with 70 of his descendants, and a bust of him (donated by Queen Wilhelmina of the Netherlands in 1915) stands in the tree-shaded courtyard. Heavily damaged by fire in 1978, the building is now almost fully restored. St. Marks is extremely active in the cultural and artistic life of the East Village, hosting dance performances, concerts, writing workshops, and poetry readings, though not during July or August. The readings, with a suggested contribution of $2, are particularly noteworthy; they've been going on for more than 20 years and often feature such well-known poets as Allen Ginsberg and Anne Waldman. Call for exact times and performer information.

Subway: 6 to Astor Place.

MURRAY HILL

CHURCH OF THE TRANSFIGURATION, 1 E. 29th St., near Fifth Ave. Tel. 684-6770.

Legend has it that this picturesque Episcopal church, built in 1849, has seen more weddings than any other its size, and there's a "bride's altar" (in the Holy Family Chapel) built with funds donated by the thousands of people who were married here. Among the church's many famous parishioners were writers Stephen Vincent Benét and William Sydney Porter (O. Henry). The church can be visited daily, and there's usually a tour after the Sunday morning service.

Subway: N, R, 6 to 28th St.

MARBLE COLLEGIATE CHURCH, corner of W. 29th St. and Fifth Ave. Tel. 686-2770.

Marble Collegiate is the city's oldest Dutch Reformed church. Its elegant facade was constructed entirely of marble, hence the church's name. The church boasts a number of firsts: It was the first to be built with hanging balconies, the first to install an electronically operated pipe organ, the first to be air-conditioned, and the first to use closed-circuit television for overflow congregations. For years Dr. Norman Vincent Peale, world-renowned author and theologian, gave his spirited sermons here.

Subway: N, R, 6 to 28th St.

MIDTOWN

CENTRAL SYNAGOGUE, E. 55th St. and Lexington Ave. Tel. 838-5122.

It's been called the finest example of Moorish-Revivial-style architecture in the city. This Reformed Jewish synagogue was erected in 1872 and has been designated a national landmark. Although the sanctuary is open to the public only during Friday-evening and Saturday-morning worship services, you can arrange for a tour by writing the synagogue office at 123 East 55th Street.

Subway: 6 to 51st St.; E, F to Lexington/Third aves.

ST. BARTHOLOMEW'S CHURCH, Park Ave. between 50th and 51st sts. Tel. 751-1616.

This 155-year-old Episcopal church was originally located downtown on Lafayette Street. In 1918 the church moved to its current home, which is distinguished by an Italian Romanesque portal and dome.

Subway: 6 to 51st St.; E, F to Lexington/Third aves.

ST. PATRICK'S CATHEDRAL, 50th St. and Fifth Ave. Tel. 753-2261.

⭐ St. Patrick's is the city's major Roman Catholic cathedral. Everything about the church (the second largest in Manhattan) is majestic. Its twin spires (modeled after the Cathedral of Cologne) rise to 330 feet above street level, and its great Rose Window measures 26 feet in diameter. Dedicated in 1879, the cathedral took 21 years to build. Inside, there's an impressive array of altars and shrines, including those of Elizabeth Ann Seton and John Neumann—the first American-born saints.

Subway: E, F to Fifth Ave.; B, D, F, Q to Rockefeller Center.

ST. PETER'S LUTHERAN CHURCH, 54th St. and Lexington Ave. Tel. 935-2200.

Nestled in a corner near the Citicorp skyscraper, this modern church built in 1977 provides visitors with a sense of simplicity, dignity, and strength. In contrast to the bank's sleek, 900-foot aluminum-clad tower, the granite outer walls of the church reach humbly into the sky like two hands in prayer. The feeling is continued in the main sanctuary—an immense angular tent with butcher-block pews, and a beautiful, tiny white chapel designed by world-renowned artist Louise Nevelson. (The walls of the chapel are lined with three of Nevelson's enigmatic wood assemblages.)

St. Peter's is particularly well known for its commitment to the performing arts. Many of the greatest names in jazz have performed at Jazz Vespers. The service is conducted by the Rev. John Garcia Gensel, who serves as pastor to New York's jazz community and for whom Duke Ellington wrote "The Shepherd Who Watches Over the Night Flock." A more traditional Lutheran service takes place here as well. This is a good place to see in combination with a trip to the Citicorp complex, right next door, which features a fabulous collection of shops and restaurants.

Subway: 6 to 51st St.; E, F to Lexington/Third aves.

UPPER WEST SIDE

CATHEDRAL CHURCH OF ST. JOHN THE DIVINE, W. 112th St. and Amsterdam Ave. Tel. 316-7400.

St. John the Divine is the city's major Episcopal church and the largest Gothic cathedral on earth. (In fact, among all the world's churches, only St. Peter's Basilica in Rome is larger.) Its immense nave stretches more than 600 feet, the length of two football fields, and has a seating capacity of 5,000. Though its first ground-breaking ceremony took place in 1892, the building is still only two-thirds completed. Currently, in a building program evocative of the Middle Ages, a dozen young apprentices are putting chisel to stone to raise two 323-foot towers on the cathedral's west front. You can relax in the church's "Biblical Garden," which is planted with a variety of herbs and flowers mentioned in the Bible. The church offers frequent and often avant garde performances of music and theater.

Subway: 1, 9 to 110th St. **Bus:** M4 to Amsterdam.

CONGREGATION SHEARITH ISRAEL, Central Park West and 70th St. Tel. 873-0300.

Almost directly across the park from Temple Emanu-El (below) is the Orthodox Spanish and Portuguese synagogue. Founded in 1654, this Sephardic congregation is the oldest Jewish congregation in America. (Its first members were descendants of Jews who fled Spain and Portugal during the Inquisition and made their way to New York via Brazil.) The windows of this landmark, neoclassical structure were designed by Louis Comfort Tiffany in simple yet elegant patterns. Services are held daily—mornings and evenings. You can arrange for a tour by contacting the synagogue office, 8 W. 70th Street.

Subway: C to 72nd St.

THE RIVERSIDE CHURCH, Riverside Drive, between 120th and 122nd sts. Tel. 222-5900.

The best way to see this famous church is in conjunction with a trip to Grant's Tomb. As befits its status as one of the city's most active churches, Riverside's 392-foot tower looms high above the Upper West Side. Built in 1930, the Gothic-style church was funded by John D. Rockefeller, Jr., and modeled on the Cathedral of Chartres. Its main chapel features heroic statues of six Christian preachers, and one of the largest church organs (13,000 pipes) in the world.

Be sure to take an elevator to Riverside's 20th floor, where an antique practice clavier can be seen. From there, a narrow staircase winds through a 74-bell carillon (the largest in the world) to an observation platform, 355 feet above ground. For $1 you can purchase platform tickets in the lobby and get an unobstructed bird's-eye view of Manhattan and its environs. Carillon recitals are given before and after the Sunday service as well as at many other times throughout the week. In addition, Riverside often sponsors special music, dance, and theater events.

Subway: 1, 9 to 125th St. **Bus:** M15 to Riverside Drive.

UPPER EAST SIDE

TEMPLE EMANU-EL, Fifth Ave. and E. 65th St. Tel. 744-1400.

The world's largest Reformed Jewish synagogue is also the third-largest house of worship in New York City, after the Cathedral of St. John the Divine and St. Patrick's. Built in 1929, this gray limestone structure is a lofty mix of Romanesque, Byzantine, and Gothic architecture, with occasional flourishes of Art Deco. Its stately, awe-inspiring main sanctuary is 77 feet wide, 147 feet long, and 103 feet high, with seating for 2,500. A tour is available by appointment only.

Subway: 6 to 68th St. **Bus:** M66 to Fifth Ave.

HARLEM

THE ABYSSINIAN BAPTIST CHURCH, 132 W. 138th St., near Lenox Ave. Tel. 862-7474.

Built in 1808, New York's oldest and largest African-American church is an intriguing mix of Gothic and Tudor architecture. In the 1950s and 1960s it was best known as the parish of Harlem's renowned congressman and preacher, the Rev. Adam Clayton Powell, Jr. Now the church is famous for its 75-member choir, which has sung with the New York Philharmonic and Boston Pops orchestras.

Subway: 2, 3 to 135th St.

HISTORIC BUILDINGS

Beneath that famed Manhattan skyline you can still find old New York, in buildings and homes preserved by concerned citizens and the city government. Here are a few of our favorites, arranged by geographical location.

DOWNTOWN

FEDERAL HALL NATIONAL MEMORIAL, corner of Wall and Nassau sts. Tel. 264-8711.

A few blocks north of Fraunces Tavern is the Federal Hall National Memorial—the site of George Washington's inauguration as our country's first president. John Quincy Adams Ward's famous statue of Washington stands in front of the building.

Completed in 1842, the building is considered one of the city's finest examples of Greek Revival architecture. A reconstruction of the original Federal Hall—the nation's first capitol building—it served as a U.S. Customs House and as a subtreasury before being converted into a national memorial. Inside, there's a museum with Washington's inaugural suit as well as several exhibitions commemorating the inauguration. There's also a colonial folksinger who re-creates, through song, the history of Colonial New York.

Admission: Free.
Open: Mon–Fri 9am–5pm. **Subway:** 2, 3, 4, 5 to Wall St.

FRAUNCES TAVERN, corner of Broad and Pearl sts. Tel. 425-1778.

Built in 1719, this landmark building is a rare vestige of colonial America—an America of old Dutch homes, cobblestone streets, and trading ships. The building takes its name from Samuel Fraunces, the West Indian innkeeper who converted it into a tavern in 1762. It was here, in a long banquet room on the second floor, that George Washington bade an emotional farewell to his officers in 1783. (Later, when Washington became president, Fraunces became his chief steward.) Restored in 1904, the tavern now houses a restaurant on the first floor (open weekdays from 7:30am to 9pm) and a museum of early Americana (see "Museums," below). Its collection of Revolutionary War memorabilia—flags, musketry, colonial maps, and paintings—is particularly noteworthy. The tavern also holds exhibitions of paintings throughout the year.

Admission: $2.50 adults; $1 seniors, students, and children under 12.
Open: Mon–Fri, and occasionally Sun, 10am–4pm. **Closed:** Holidays (except for Washington's Birthday and July 4th). **Subway:** N, R to Whitehall St. and walk to Pearl St.

NOHO

OLD MERCHANT'S HOUSE, 29 E. 4th St., between Lafayette St. and the Bowery. Tel. 777-1089.

Now a museum, the Old Merchant's House is a perfectly furnished period house in an area that has been largely taken over by trucking companies. That the building survived is not surprising once you know its story. The five-story Georgian brick house was built in 1832 and bought 3 years later by Seabury Tredwell—a prosperous hardware merchant. Three of his six daughters lived there all their lives, keeping the house just as it had always been, and refusing to depart when the fashionable area of town moved north. When the youngest of those daughters died in 1933 at the age of 93, hardly anything had changed. The house still lacked plumbing and electricity; its original furnishings, linens, china, and family memorabilia were all intact. Closets and cabinets were filled with old clothes, much of it dating from the 1800s, remarkably preserved and apparently not touched for nearly a century: A playbill from an 1860s theatrical production was found in the pocket of one dress. More than most such museums, the house has the haunting quality of time's having stopped, and the visitor cannot help but wonder at the lives of the reclusive spinster sisters who lived there. It has classic Greek-Revival parlors with the original mahogany furniture, fine decorative plaster molding, and handsome hand-carved columns. Call for special group tours or lectures. Three of the house's five stories are open to the public.

Admission: $3 adults, $2 students and senior citizens.
Open: Sun 1–4pm. **Closed:** Aug. **Subway:** 6 to Astor Place and walk south on Lafayette to 4th St.

GRAMERCY PARK

THEODORE ROOSEVELT HOUSE, 28 E. 20th St., between Broadway and Park Ave. South. Tel. 260-1616.

This landmark house is the birthplace of Teddy Roosevelt, the gutsy "Rough

Rider" who first led the charge up San Juan Hill and later became the nation's 26th president. The house is actually a reconstruction of the original, which was torn down in 1916, but it has much of the original's Victorian furnishings and 19th-century relics. Free chamber-music concerts are presented September through June on Saturday from 2 to 3:30pm on the fourth floor.

Admission: $1 adults; senior citizens and children under 17 free.
Open: Wed–Sun 9am–5pm. **Subway:** 6, N, R to 23rd St.

UPPER EAST SIDE

ABIGAIL ADAMS SMITH MUSEUM, 421 E. 61st St., between York and First aves. Tel. 838-6878.

A beautiful residential home, perched on a raised grassy site, the Abigail Adams Smith Museum is one of the few 18th-century buildings left in Manhattan. It was built in 1799 as the carriage house on the estate of Abigail Adams Smith, the daughter of President John Adams. Made of schist, a stone quarried in colonial Manhattan, the house is furnished throughout with museum-quality antiques from the Federal period. Outside there's a path leading to a quiet garden and sitting area—a mainstay of homes of this era.

Admission: $2 adults, $1 senior citizens; children under 12 free.
Open: Mon–Fri noon–4pm, Sun 1–5pm. June–July Tues hours 5:30–8pm.
Closed: Aug; Sun in summer. **Subway:** 4, 5, 6 to 59th St., then walk four blocks east to First Ave. **Bus:** M15 or M66.

GRACIE MANSION, E. 88th St. and East End Ave. Tel. 570-4751.

Ironically, the leader of our most urban of urban areas lives in a pastoral sanctuary overlooking the East River. The mansion was in fact originally built as a country estate by Archibald Gracie, a New York merchant, in 1799. After years of disrepair, Gracie Mansion became the first home of the Museum of the City of New York, and was then restored as a home and reception site for civic events. It's been home to New York mayors since 1942. The peaceful grounds of Carl Schurz Park surrounding the house are open to the public. Tours of the house are available on Wednesday by phone appointment.

Suggested donation: $3 adults and children, $2 senior citizens.
Bus: M18 to East End Ave.; M15 to 88th St.

MORNINGSIDE HEIGHTS

GRANT'S TOMB, Riverside Drive and 122nd St.

Ulysses S. Grant, U.S. president from 1868 to 1876, was laid to rest in this marble-and-granite tomb. Set on a hill overlooking the river, the mausoleum was paid for by donations from over 90,000 people.

Subway: 1, 9 to 125th St. **Bus:** M15 to Riverside Drive.

HARLEM

MORRIS-JUMEL MANSION, corner of Edgecombe Ave. and 161st St. Tel. 923-8008.

This white-columned Georgian-Federal mansion is a remnant of a time when Upper Manhattan was predominantly rural: the summering place of New York's aristocracy. Built by Col. Roger Morris in 1765, it sits atop a grassy hill in the middle of a park filled with lilac and magnolia trees. Outside, there's a colonial herb garden. This peaceful setting served first as Washington's headquarters and then as British headquarters during the Revolutionary War; later the widow of Stephen Jumel lived there with Aaron Burr, her second husband. The house recently became an accredited museum and there's a special exhibitions gallery on the third floor.

Admission: $2 adults; $1 students and senior citizens; children under 12 accompanied by an adult free.
Open: Tues–Sun 10am–4pm. **Subway:** A, B to 163rd St. **Bus:** M2 or M3 to 158th St.

WASHINGTON HEIGHTS

THE DYCKMAN HOUSE, 4881 Broadway at 204th St. Tel. 304-9422.
A surprise to find on upper Broadway, this 18th-century Dutch Colonial farmhouse was built of brick, wood, and stone to replace one that was destroyed by the British. Occupied by both the Continental and the British armies during the Revolutionary War, the house is now a museum containing Dutch and English period furniture and possessions of the Dyckman family.
Admission: $1.
Open: Tues–Sun 11am–noon and 1–4pm. **Subway:** A to 207th St.

THE BRONX & STATEN ISLAND

RICHMONDTOWN RESTORATION, Visitor Center, Court Place. Tel. 718/351-1617.
Located on Staten Island, this recently completed restoration shows the development of a Staten Island village through the 17th, 18th, and 19th centuries. It includes a Dutch schoolhouse, general store, carriage house, and historical museum.
Admission: $4 adults, $2.50 seniors and children.
Open: Mon–Fri 10am–5pm; Sat–Sun 1–5pm. **Directions:** Take Staten Island Ferry (1 to South Ferry); when you reach the other side, pick up a no. 113 bus to Court Place, then walk up Court Place to visitor center.

MUSEUMS

DOWNTOWN

FRAUNCES TAVERN MUSEUM, corner of Broad and Pearl sts. Tel. 425-1778.
This fascinating museum of early American history and culture is housed in the site of Fraunces Tavern—a landmark 18th-century building (see "Historic Buildings," above). The museum's permanent collections include Early Americana, Revolutionary War memorabilia, and portraits of President George Washington, who is the tavern's most famous guest. A recent three-part exhibition included "Capitol City: New York After the Revolution," "To Inspire and Inform: Selections From the Fraunces Tavern Museum Collection," and "George Washington at Fraunces Tavern." The museum also boasts two fully furnished period rooms: the Long Room, site of Washington's emotional farewell to his officers in 1783, and the 19th-century Clinton Dining Room. The museum hosts lectures, workshops, concerts, and theatrical performances, as well as special exhibitions on such topics as "Education in the Early Republic." Group tours are available by appointment.
Suggested admission: $2.50 adults; $1 students, senior citizens, and children under 12. Free on Thurs.
Open: Mon–Fri 10am–4pm. **Subway:** N, R to Whitehall St.; 2, 3 to Wall St.; J, M, Z to Broad St.

SOHO

MUSEUM OF HOLOGRAPHY, 11 Mercer St., in SoHo, half a block north of Canal St. and one block west of Broadway. Tel. 925-0581.
The Museum of Holography is devoted to the display of holograms—the three-dimensional images made by exposing photographic film to laser beams. The result is images that never stop moving and often trick the eye. For example, in one display, miniature holographic images of celebrities, such as the artist Andy Warhol and the opera singer Beverly Sills, seem to move and vibrate as though alive. This is a fascinating museum for anyone curious about light, science, or new directions in art

made possible by technology. The museum store sells books, jewelry, pendants, and fine art by holographic artists. For example, you can buy a holographic recording of a human eye, or the inside of a clock. Also, the museum offers workshops.

Admission: $3.50 adults; $2.50 students, seniors, and members of AAA; $2 children under 12.

Open: Daily 10:30am–6pm. Groups scheduled in advance can begin their visit at 10am Mon–Fri. **Subway:** A, C, E, N, R, J, M, Z, 6 to Canal St.

THE NEW MUSEUM, 583 Broadway in SoHo, between Houston and Prince sts. Tel. 219-1222.

This contemporary art museum differentiates itself from more traditional institutions by supporting new and unrecognized artists. The museum has no permanent collection, but shows all kinds of artworks, from painting and sculpture to conceptual art. The works, never more than 10 years old, are often experimental, innovative, and radically different.

Suggested admission: $2.50 adults; $1.50 students, artists, and senior citizens.

Open: Wed–Sun noon–6pm; Fri–Sat noon–8pm. **Subway:** A, B, C, D, E, F, Q to West 4th St.

GREENWICH VILLAGE

FORBES MAGAZINE GALLERIES, 62 Fifth Ave., at 12th St. Tel. 620-2389.

Here you'll find a permanent exhibit of the world's largest collection of Fabergé Imperial Easter Eggs and special exhibits, such as "The Constitution: Two Centuries of America."

Admission: Free.

Open: Tues–Wed and Fri–Sat 10am–4pm. **Subway:** N, R, 4, 5, 6 to Union Square.

EAST VILLAGE

UKRAINIAN MUSEUM, 203 Second Ave., between 12th and 13th sts. Tel. 228-0110.

Tucked away in a small building, this museum features Ukrainian folk art from the 19th and 20th centuries: textiles, ceramics, metalwork, and woodwork. Because of the museum's limited space, only a few of its 5,000 craft items can be displayed at any one time. Highlights of the collection include festive folk costumes on permanent display and the museum's annual Easter exhibition of pysanky (colored Easter eggs). Pieces from the permanent collection are shown throughout the year in rotating exhibits.

Admission: $1 adults, 50¢ students and senior citizens; children under 6 free.

Open: Wed–Sun 1–5pm. **Subway:** 6 to Astor Place.

MIDTOWN WEST

AMERICAN CRAFT MUSEUM, 40 W. 53rd St., between Fifth and Sixth aves. Tel. 956-3535.

If your impression of crafts is limited to potholders, let this museum introduce you to the latest trends in clay, wood, fiber, glass, and metal crafts. The museum mounts thematic and group exhibitions and single-artist shows; it also houses a permanent collection whose objects represent high points in the 20th-century American craft movement. You might want to make a stop in the museum shop before heading to your next sightseeing destination.

Admission: $4.50 adults, $2 students and senior citizens; children under 12 free.

Open: Tues 10am–8pm; Wed–Sun 10am–5pm. **Subway:** B, D, F, Q to Rockefeller Center.

THE NEW YORK PUBLIC LIBRARY, Fifth Ave. between 40th and 42nd sts. Tel. 340-0849.

★ If you sit on the front steps, between the lions Patience and Fortitude, you'll see street musicians, vendors, and undiscovered comedians vie for the attention of the bustling crowds. Inside the library, at table after table, in room after room, people pore intently over books. But there is more to do here than read. The library, one of the centers of New York's artistic and cultural life, also has exhibition rooms, art galleries, and permanent displays of 19th-century American paintings. To find out about special events, check the library's publication, *Events*, available at all branches. Call for information about the library's other branches.

Admission: Free.
Open: Main Reading Room Mon–Wed 10am–9pm, Thurs–Sat 10am–6pm.
Subway: B, D, F, Q to 42nd St. **Bus:** M1, M2, M3, M4, M5.

MIDTOWN EAST

THE GROLIER CLUB, 47 E. 60th St., between Park and Madison aves. Tel. 838-6690.

This private club for bibliophiles and book collectors, which recently celebrated its centennial, runs changing exhibits on anything to do with books, from the 19th-century British Gothic Revival, to the art of stencil, to Ezra Pound. The library at the club is open to scholars and members only.

Admission: Free.
Open: Mon–Sat 10am–5pm. **Closed:** Sat in summer. **Subway:** 6 to 68th St.

IBM GALLERY OF SCIENCE AND ART, Madison Ave. and 56th St. Tel. 745-3500.

Located in the IBM Building, the city's largest "lobby" gallery offers a wide variety of exhibits. In the past, these have included "Sorolla: The Painter of Light," "The Flag Paintings of Childe Hassam," and "Frontier America: Works from the Buffalo Bill Historical Center." The gallery, which has 13,000 square feet of exhibition space, usually offers two shows at a time. Be sure to visit the adjacent botanical garden tended by the New York Botanical Garden. In the midst of Manhattan's concrete hustle and bustle, it's a soothing oasis of horticultural beauty.

Admission: Free.
Open: Tues–Sat 11am–6pm. **Subway:** 4, 5, 6 to 59th St.

MUSEUM OF TELEVISION AND RADIO, 25 W. 52nd St. Tel. 752-7684.

★ With more than 40,000 videotaped programs, the collection covers over 70 years of television and radio history, from news to children's shows. Opened in 1976, the museum collects, preserves, and interprets radio and TV programs. Having just moved to a new $50-million, 17-story building that better accommodates its growth, the museum is a mecca for fans of popular culture.

All tapes can be screened by the public. At 96 broadcasting consoles, you can listen to Edward R. Murrow's London broadcasts or FDR's fireside chats. You can also view TV programs of all kinds, from Sid Caesar's comic routines to shots of the moon or serious documentaries. Exhibitions at presstime included "Jack Benny: The Radio and Television Work," and "A Half Century of Public Service: A Retrospective of Advertising Council Campaigns."

Suggested admission: $4 adults, $3 students, $2 senior citizens and children under 13.
Open: Tues noon–8pm; Wed–Sat noon–5pm. **Subway:** C, E to 50th St.; 1, 9 to 50th St.

PIERPONT MORGAN LIBRARY, 29 E. 36th St., at Madison Ave. Tel. 685-0008.

Designed by Charles McKim, this Renaissance palazzo contains a collection of 15th-century and earlier books, illuminated manuscripts, and drawings. Almost always on exhibit are selections from Morgan's collection, including Erasmus's *Defense of Folly* and one of the Gutenberg Bibles—both on display with other rare books in the ornate East Room library. Also part of the Library Complex is the palatial residence of J. P. Morgan, Jr. (the ground floor is open to the public) and the

new glass-enclosed Garden Court. *Note:* Be forewarned, this is not a place for children; they will get restless.
Suggested admission: $5 adults; senior citizens, students, and children asked to donate as they can.
Open: Tues–Sat 10:30am–5pm; Sun 1–5pm. **Closed:** Hols, Sun–Mon in July, and second half of Aug. **Subway:** 6 to 33rd St. **Bus:** M16 or M34 to Madison Ave.

LINCOLN CENTER/UPPER WEST SIDE

THE HISPANIC SOCIETY OF AMERICA, Broadway and 155th St. Tel. 690-0743.

The society owns an impressive collection of paintings, sculpture, and decorative arts that represent Hispanic culture from prehistoric days to the present century. Though the society specializes in the art, literature, and cultural history of Spain and Portugal, it also features a good selection of Latin American pieces. Included in the collection are paintings by El Greco, Velazquez, and Goya, plus Mexican ceramics and Spanish earthenware.

With its rich terra-cotta floors, Valencia tapestries, and high ceilings, the museum's interior has the feel of a majestic cathedral. The air of solemnity is accented by the sculptured effigies of Spanish nobility lined up against one wall. The society's library, filled with books about Hispanic culture, conveys a similar air of hushed grandeur.
Admission: Free.
Open: Tues–Sat 10am–4:30pm; Sun 1–4pm. **Subway:** 1, 9 to 157th St. **Bus:** Madison Ave. M3, M4; Sixth Ave. M5 to 155th St. and Broadway.

MUSEUM OF AMERICAN FOLK ART, Eva and Morris Feld Gallery, 2 Lincoln Square, Columbus Ave., between 65th and 66th sts. Tel. 595-9585.

Although still in the process of completing its new facilities on West 53rd Street, the museum is rotating exhibits at this address. Visitors can see works drawn from all the American folk arts, such as painting, sculpture, needlepoint, quilts, woodcarvings, decoys, painted and decorative furniture, and decorative arts in the folk tradition. Since the museum is immediately adjacent to the Lincoln Center for the Performing Arts, and on the west side of Central Park, theater-goers and Sunday strollers can take advantage of the gallery's flexible hours.

If you're more in the mood to browse, take a stroll through the museum's crafts shop. Enthusiasts might also want to visit the museum's other gift shop, at 62 West 50th Street, between Fifth and Sixth avenues, open Monday through Saturday from 10:30am to 5:30pm.
Admission: Free.
Open: Museum daily (including most holidays) 9am–9pm. Crafts shop Mon–Tues and Sat 11am–6pm; Wed–Fri 11am–7:30pm; Sun noon–6pm. **Subway:** 1, 9 to 66th St. **Bus:** M66 to Lincoln Center.

NEW-YORK HISTORICAL SOCIETY, 170 Central Park West, at 77th St. Tel. 873-3400.

The library and museum of the New-York Historical Society specializes in American history and art (with a special emphasis on New York and the early nation). It was founded in 1804 and is still one of the city's most important cultural institutions. The Society houses New York's oldest museum and a renowned research library. The museum rotates exhibits from its collection of Hudson River landscape paintings, early American portraits, furniture, New York silver, and early American toys. The museum has a wonderful Tiffany glass gallery and a continuing exhibition of American historical documents. A selection of their 433 John James Audubon watercolors, *Birds of America,* is always on view. In addition, there is a print and photographic department.
Suggested admission: $4.50 adults, $3 senior citizens, $1 children under 12. Pay as you wish Tues.

Open: Tues–Sun 10am–5pm. **Subway:** C to 81st St. **Bus:** M79 to Central Park West.

UPPER EAST SIDE

ASIA SOCIETY GALLERIES, 725 Park Ave., at 70th St. Tel. 288-6400.
Located in the society's earth-toned headquarters, the galleries provide a permanent home for the Mr. and Mrs. John D. Rockefeller III Collection of Asian Art. Included in this prodigious collection of art from China, Japan, India, and Southeast Asia are dancing Krishna statues, Ming porcelain, and delicate Japanese folding screens. The first floor is devoted to changing exhibits on specific themes in Asian art.
Admission: $2 adults, $1 students and senior citizens; children under 12 free.
Open: Tues–Sat 11am–6pm; Sun noon–5pm. **Subway:** 6 to 68th St.

THE COOPER-HEWITT MUSEUM, National Museum of Design, 2 E. 91st St., at Fifth Ave. Tel. 860-6868.
The Smithsonian Institution established its National Museum of Design in the former Andrew Carnegie mansion. The museum's name honors its founders: Peter Cooper, a 19th-century philanthropist, and his three granddaughters; and the Hewitts, who envisioned a museum for the designer, the artisan, and the student. Since the Hewitt sisters started the museum in 1897, the collection has grown into one of the foremost collections of decorative arts and design in the world, including objects from every historical period over a span of 3,000 years: drawings, prints, wallpapers, textiles, porcelain, glass, furniture, woodwork, metalwork, jewelry, and woven and printed fabrics. The museum's collection of original architecture and design drawings is the largest in the United States.
The permanent collections are not always on view, but the regularly changing exhibitions always relate to some aspect of design—from the dash and style of engraved and sculpted cane handles to the skyscrapers built in Manhattan in the 1920s and 1930s. Watch for coming exhibitions on a variety of design themes. Don't miss the peaceful garden, lined with shaded benches, on the southern side of the museum.
Admission: $3 adults, $1.50 students and senior citizens; children under 12 free; free Tues after 5pm.
Open: Wed–Sat 10am–5pm; Sun noon–5pm; Tues 10am–9pm. **Closed:** Major hols. **Subway:** 4, 5, 6 to 86th St.; walk west. **Bus:** M19 to Fifth Ave.

INTERNATIONAL CENTER OF PHOTOGRAPHY, 1130 Fifth Ave., at 94th St. Tel. 860-1777.
One of the museums on Fifth Avenue's "Museum Mile," the ICP is in an elegant landmark building. Its exhibitions, under the stewardship of Cornell Capa, show the sophistication and diversity of contemporary photography and the techniques and styles of the past. Changing exhibits sometimes focus on one photographer or on one genre, such as still lifes, photo essays, or portraits. In the permanent collection are works by such famous photographers as Henri Cartier-Bresson, W. Eugene Smith, and Andreas Feininger. For those striving to become famous, the museum offers photography classes throughout the year for every level of experience. A large selection of photography books, postcards, and posters are sold in the first-floor shop.
ICP Midtown is at 1133 Avenue of the Americas (tel. 768-4680).
Admission: $3 adults, $2 students and seniors.
Open: Tues 11am–8pm; Wed–Sun 11am–6pm. **Subway:** 6 to 96th St. **Bus:** M19, M1, M2, M3, or M4.

THE JEWISH MUSEUM, at the New-York Historical Society, 170 Central Park West, at 77th St. Tel. 399-3430.
This museum, usually housed in the former Warburg mansion, contains the most comprehensive collection of Judaica in the United States, and one of the largest in the world. The museum addresses the entire Jewish experience, from biblical times to the present. The permanent collection includes ceremonial objects, antiquities, paintings,

prints, drawings, sculpture, photographs, textiles, decorative arts, broadcast material, and coins and medals from around the world. Once known as a forum for any type of avant-garde art, the museum now displays modern art with Jewish content or by Jewish artists. Concerts, lectures, films, and children's programs are scheduled regularly, along with art courses and music programs.

Note: The museum will return to its former address (1109 Fifth Avenue) in late 1992.

Admission: $4.50 adults, $3 students and senior citizens, $1 children under 12. **Open:** Sun and Tues–Thurs 10am–5pm, Fri 10am–3pm. **Closed:** Major Jewish and legal hols. **Subway:** 1, 9 to 79th St.; C to 81st St.

EL MUSEO DEL BARRIO, 1230 Fifth Ave., between 104th and 105th sts. Tel. 831-7272.

The vivid culture of Puerto Rico and Latin America is explored here through sculpture, paintings, graphics, and photography. Recently, the museum has featured major exhibitions of pre-Columbian artifacts and Puerto Rican santos (wood-carved figures of saints). All extended shows are supplemented with changing exhibits that focus on Puerto Rican culture on the island, in New York City, and in the Americas.

Suggested admission: $2 adults, $1 students and senior citizens; members and children under 12 free.

Open: Wed–Sun 11am–5pm. **Subway:** 6 to 103rd St. **Bus:** M1, M2, M3, or M4.

MUSEUM OF THE CITY OF NEW YORK, Fifth Ave. and 103rd St. Tel. 534-1672.

This beautiful old Georgian building contains an informative and entertaining collection of New York City memorabilia. Even if you yawn at the thought of history, this museum will spark your interest. Through slide shows, colorful dioramas, and detailed exhibits, the museum guides you through the "Big Apple's" history from the time when the city was the Dutch colony of Nieuw Amsterdam to the present. Permanent exhibits capture the mood of Wall Street and the activity of New York Harbor with slide shows, taped sounds, and enlarged photographs. The museum has an excellent collection of American silver and some fine portraits of early American patriots and statesmen. Rooms filled with models, photographs, old fire engines, maps, and toys, plus period recreations of furniture and dress, provide a sense of the city's rich social and cultural past.

Suggested admission: $4 adults; $3 students, seniors, and children; $6 for families.

Open: Wed–Sat 10am–5pm; Sun 1–5pm. **Subway:** 6 to 103rd St.; walk west. **Bus:** M1, M2, M3, M4, or M19.

THE NATIONAL ACADEMY OF DESIGN, 1083 Fifth Ave., at 89th St. Tel. 369-4880.

Founded in 1825 as an art school and exhibition space, the National Academy of Design houses a permanent collection of 19th- and 20th-century fine arts. It also houses an eclectic array of exhibitions that are meant to introduce the viewer to new subjects. Recent exhibits have focused on the work of little-known European masters and neglected American 19th-century talents.

Admission: $2.50 adults, $2 students and seniors; friends of the Academy free; free Tues 5–8pm.

Open: Tues noon–8pm; Wed–Sun noon–5pm. **Subway:** 4, 5, 6 to 86th St. **Bus:** M18 to Fifth Ave.

WHITNEY MUSEUM OF AMERICAN ART, 945 Madison Ave., at 75th St. Tel. 570-3676.

In the heart of the gallery district, the Whitney concentrates on 20th-century American art. Even the building is a piece of modern art. Designed by Marcel Breuer (the creator of the tubular-steel chair that bears his name), the Whitney is made out of rich gray granite and looks like an inverted pyramid.

Here you'll see paintings that reflect all the historical trends in American art from

John Sloan to Julian Schnabel: naturalism, Impressionism, pop art, throwaways, and abstractionism through the stylistic pluralism of the present. Don't miss the whimsical *Circus* by Alexander Calder on the first floor. Made out of steel, metal, felt, and fiber, this circus is a delightful creation of cavorting animals and swinging acrobats. On the upper floors, the Whitney displays pieces from its renowned permanent collection and highlights changing exhibits. Every two years the Whitney presents a show that features the work of both new and accomplished artists, and provides a revealing look at new trends in American art. Sarabeth's at the Whitney offers lunch and an afternoon tea service daily, and brunch on weekends.

The Whitney operates the **New American Film and Video Series,** which provides a showcase for the work of independent film producers. Call 570-0537 for a schedule. (Admission to the films is included in the general admission fee.)

Admission: $5 adults, $3 senior citizens 62 and older and students; children under 12 accompanied by an adult free; free Tues 6–8pm.

Open: Tues 1–8pm; Wed–Sat 11am–5pm; Sun 11am–6pm. **Subway:** 6 to 77th St. **Bus:** M1, M2, M3, or M4 to 76th St.

HARLEM

BLACK FASHION MUSEUM, 126th St. between Lenox Ave. and Adam Clayton Powell, Jr., Blvd. Tel. 666-1320.

Visitors can view the country's largest collection of African-American fashion design and memorabilia here. The oldest pieces date from the late 1600s and the more recent from such Broadway plays as *The Wiz* and *Bubblin' Brown Sugar.*

Admission: Free, but donations accepted.

Open: By appointment only. **Subway:** 2, 3 to 125th St. **Bus:** M101 to Lenox Ave.

STUDIO MUSEUM IN HARLEM, 144 W. 125th St., near Lenox Ave. Tel. 864-4500.

The Studio Museum highlights the work of prominent and emerging African-American, African, and Caribbean artists. Changing exhibits present the work of such artists as Romare Bearden, James Van Der Zee, and Beauford Delaney. The museum's permanent collection includes paintings, prints, sculpture, and photographs. Its gift shop has arts and crafts from all over the world.

Admission: $2 adults, $1 students and children under 12, $1 seniors.

Open: Wed–Fri 10am–5pm; Sat–Sun 1–6pm. **Subway:** 2, 3 to 125th St.

YESHIVA UNIVERSITY MUSEUM, 2520 Amsterdam Ave., at 185th St. Tel. 960-5390.

Paintings, photographs, and ceremonial objects that record the Jewish historical experience are all featured in this university collection. The detailed architectural models of ten famous synagogues are especially interesting.

Admission: $3 adults, $1.50 children under 16 and senior citizens.

Open: Tues–Thurs 10:30am–5pm; Sun noon–6pm. **Subway:** 1, 9 to 181st St.

NEIGHBORHOODS

In addition to the neighborhoods mentioned here, see the walking tours in Chapter 8 for tours of the Financial District; Chinatown and Little Italy; SoHo; Greenwich Village; Times Square—42nd Street; Midtown—Fifth Avenue; the Upper West Side; and the Upper East Side Historic District.

TRIBECA

An artistic community named for its location—the *Tri*-angle *Be*-low *Ca*-nal Street—TriBeCa extends (loosely) south to the World Trade Center, and west of Broadway to the Hudson River. It can be reached by the 4, 5, or 6 trains to the Brooklyn Bridge stop. You'll emerge from the subway near **City Hall Park,** the scene of one of the first public readings of the Declaration of Independence, an event witnessed by George Washington and his troops. Several blocks south of the park, on Broadway at Vesey Street, is **St. Paul's Chapel.** Built in 1766, it's the oldest church building in Manhattan. Walk one block north from St. Paul's, along Broadway, and you'll encounter the **Woolworth Building.** This magnificent example of Gothic architecture was built in 1913 and for 18 years held the title of the world's tallest building. This "Cathedral of Commerce" possesses one of the most beautiful lobbies we've ever seen, with marble walls and floors, bronze wall decorations, and a mosaic ceiling. (See also Chapter 8 "Walking Tour 1—Downtown and the Financial District" for these sites.)

Continue up Broadway to Warren Street and turn west toward the Hudson. This street is a bargain hunter's mecca, so do indulge if you'd like to buy a $30 man's shirt for $5 or a $27 book for $4.

North on Greenwich Street from Warren Street you'll see many factory buildings that have been born again as lofts. Despite fears of high-rent development, the loft-dwellers coexist peacefully with the olive oil/nut/coffee/produce businesses in the neighborhood. Continue up Greenwich Street to Harrison Street and you'll see a row of original Federal town houses, saved from the wrecker and sold, by lottery, 25 years ago to lucky bidders.

Hudson Street, which runs parallel to and is one block east of Greenwich Street, is the main street of TriBeCa. The shops, galleries, and cafés in TriBeCa will give you a feeling of what SoHo was like before commercialization.

THE LOWER EAST SIDE

For 50 years the Lower East Side was the home of tens of thousands of immigrant Jews from Eastern Europe, who soon proceeded to provide the city with important leaders in the labor movement, politics, education, industry, science, and the entertainment world. Today most of the old tenement buildings still stand, but mixed among them on the narrow streets are modern housing projects. And side by side in what was once an exclusively Jewish neighborhood live Asians, Italians, Puerto Ricans, Ukrainians, African Americans, and young free-'n-easy types, as well as a few of the older Jewish residents who originally gave the area its flavor.

A trip to the Lower East Side will appeal not only to the sociologist, but to the bargain hunter as well. The streets abound in tiny stores of every variety, selling merchandise at prices a good 20% to 30% lower than in any other neighborhood in New York. Wear comfortable shoes, for after a subway ride down to Delancey Street, it's by foot all the way.

Don't drive here, especially on a Sunday when it is crowded and impossible to park. Take the Sixth Avenue F train downtown to Delancey Street. When you leave the Delancey Street station, walk west to Essex Street, turn left down Essex Street, and on the east side of the street, between Broome and Delancey streets, you'll come to the first of the four city markets that stretch up to Stanton Street (three blocks across Delancey). It's fun to browse through the **Essex Street Markets.**

The cavernous indoor markets are crammed with stands and stalls (each rented from the city by private shopkeepers) displaying an enormous variety of food and delicacies, dry goods, hardware, clothing—even home furnishings. The markets cater almost equally to the Jewish and Spanish residents of the neighborhood, and you can buy cabrito (goat meat) or queso blanco (soft, white milk cheese), as well as kosher pickles to munch on as you walk, or slabs of creamy halvah (ground sesame-seed candy).

As you leave the markets, look to your left toward East Broadway. East Broadway was once the Fleet Street of the Lower East Side, but now the last of the famous Yiddish newspapers, the *Forward,* has moved. At Rivington Street (north of Delancey Street), head west, passing shops housing barrels of smoked fish, bins of unusual candies, jars of dried fruits, bags of lentils, and similar exotica. The clothing and toy stores display their wares right on the sidewalk, each owner carrying on his business from the doorway. Many of these stores are owned by Orthodox Jews and are therefore closed on Saturday, but all are open on Sunday, when they do a thriving business. Cross Allen Street, turn left, and you'll be in the center of one of the busiest antiques sections in the city, specializing in copper and brass items. Narrow, dusty stores sell copper candlesticks, crystal chandeliers, antique gift frames, brass headboards, and decorative antique accessories for the home—but no furniture. Now walk down to Grand Street, turn right, and you'll soon pass rows of bridal shops selling budget-priced wedding apparel. Then turn back and cross Allen Street again. Remain on Grand Street as it becomes a linen and fabric section. You can stock up here on sheets and towels at bargain prices, or have draperies or bedspreads made for much less than you'd be charged anywhere else in the city. Grand Street intersects Orchard Street, the heart of the shopping scene, with many discount stores for men's and women's apparel. From Grand Street, return to Essex. Turn left at Essex and continue walking two blocks to Delancey Street, where you'll come to the subway station.

See Chapter 9, "New York City Shopping," for specific shopping recommendations in this area.

CHELSEA

Like so many once rundown areas of Manhattan, Chelsea is enjoying a renaissance. The area, which is loosely defined as bounded by Fifth Avenue on the east and the Hudson River on the west, runs from 14th Street to 34th Street. Chelsea was the center of the city from the mid- to late 19th century and is rich with historical interest. Before funding for the erection of the Statue of Liberty was completed, her hand (complete with torch) rested in Madison Square Park (Madison Avenue at 23rd Street). Madison Square Park, by the way, was the location of the original Madison Square Garden, which encompassed the entire city block, Fourth Avenue (now Park Avenue South) to Madison Avenue and 26th to 27th streets.

Don't miss the **Flatiron Building,** a unique structure at the triangle formed by Broadway and Fifth Avenue at 23rd Street.

Walk west on 23rd Street, once the heart of New York's theater district, dominated by the long-gone Grand Opera House on the corner of 23rd Street and Eighth Avenue. The **Chelsea Hotel** at 222 West 23rd Street, between Seventh and Eighth avenues, has been home to noted show business, musical, and literary figures, including Sherwood Anderson, O. Henry, Isadora Duncan, Virgil Thompson, and Dylan Thomas. Today many rock stars enjoy the relative privacy of the Chelsea. Continue west on 23rd Street to Ninth Avenue, once the site of the home of Clement Clark Moore, who wrote "The Night Before Christmas." Chelsea owes its name to Moore's father-in-law, a sea captain, who named his estate after a home for retired seamen (not the famous London district). When Moore died, he willed the land between 20th and 21st streets between Ninth and Tenth avenues to the General Theological Seminary. The seminary's beautiful gardens are open to the public during daylight hours.

The segment of Sixth Avenue in Chelsea from about 18th to 23rd streets was known as Ladies Mile during the mid-19th century—the street was lined with exclusive shops and stores. Ladies Mile continues to the east, on Broadway, from 20th Street south to 10th Street. The building on the southwest corner of Broadway and 20th Street, for example, was an early location of Lord & Taylor's department store.

Farther uptown, on Sixth Avenue, is the **wholesale flower district** between 26th and 29th streets. Buy yourself a bargain posy or stroll along West 28th Street between Fifth Avenue and Broadway and imagine it 100 years ago when it was the world's Tin Pan Alley.

THE GARMENT CENTER

Save a lunchtime for the Garment Center, heart of New York's, and perhaps the world's, fashion industry. The bulk of the activity takes place on Broadway or Seventh

Avenue from 34th Street to around 42nd Street. The streets are crowded with carts of women's clothes pushed recklessly by boys and men of every nationality who look-up only to admire the models, whose trademarks—the makeup bags—give them away. You'll see salesmen, executives, and workers, all gathered in front of buildings, often spilling over into the busy streets, gesturing with their hands, talking, wheeling, dealing—all in the name of fashion.

HARLEM

Many guidebooks—and even natives—give the impression that sightseeing in northern Manhattan stops with the Upper West Side. This is an unfortunate misapprehension, and we would like to set the record straight! Manhattan continues to fascinate . . . even beyond 200th Street.

But before proceeding, it *is* wise to note that while this area is not dangerous if explored wisely, Harlem, more than anywhere else in Manhattan, demands street-smarts. Unless you are traveling with someone who lives in or is familiar with the neighborhood, visit during the day. You can map out the stops you want to make and take the most direct routes via several public transportation lines. MTA buses go uptown on Broadway and on Riverside Drive; the subway lines also serve the area. Consult subway and bus maps or call MTA route information (tel. 718/330-1234) for specifics. There are many organized tours that go through Harlem; for information, call the **Uptown Chamber of Commerce** (tel. 427-7200) and consult Section 6, "Organized Tours."

YORKVILLE

Yorkville is one of our favorite neighborhoods. Its center is East 86th Street, one of New York's liveliest crosstown streets. Bustling during the day with shoppers, it becomes even more alive at night with pleasure seekers who frequent its cafés and restaurants, beer halls, and dance palaces. Although some of the restaurants tend to get expensive, there are several German and Viennese restaurants where you can stop in for coffee and delicate pastries. Our favorite is the **Kleine Konditorei** (no. 234).

At the eastern end of 86th Street, past the commercial section, lies East End Avenue, one of the city's most expensive and quietest residential areas. There, also, between the East River and East End Avenue is a broad expanse of greenery called **Carl Schurz Park,** a place peopled with joggers, skateboarders, youngsters, and older people who sit on the benches in good weather and watch the world go by. At the north end of the park is **Gracie Mansion,** the beautiful 18th-century house that is home to New York's mayor. You can walk around the park near the mansion, and if you're lucky, you'll get a glimpse of the local and international notables who pop in and out of the house for meetings and receptions.

Across East End Avenue between 86th and 87th streets is a block of Queen Anne 19th-century town houses that has been designated a historic landmark area. The back side of these red-brick buildings is on a tiny street called Henderson Place, which you can enter from 86th Street. It has the flavor of a turn-of-the-century village—unless you look to one side, where a massive apartment house looms to dwarf the tiny houses underneath it.

For suggestions about restaurants in the neighborhood, see Chapter 6, "Where to Eat in New York City."

NEW YORK STOCK EXCHANGE

At the heart of Wall Street—so named because in 1653 the Dutch governor, Peter Stuyvesant, ordered that a wall of thick planks be constructed to protect the city from Native American tribes marauding from the north—lies the New York Stock Exchange. The forerunner of the present-day Exchange was founded in 1792 by 24 brokers who sealed the bargains with a mere handshake. Times have indeed changed, as any visitor to the Exchange will see firsthand. From the gallery overlooking the floor of the Exchange you can watch the frenetic and seemingly chaotic trading from

9:15am (when the floor opens) to 4pm Monday through Friday. Tickets are free, but a limited number are handed out beginning at 9am, so arrive early to guarantee yourself a spot. There is a taped explanation of the floor activities, and audiovisual exhibits and a short film presentation of the Exchange's history and present-day operations.

The Exchange is located at 20 Broad Street, off Wall Street, on the third floor. For groups of more than ten, reservations are recommended: phone 656-5168. You can get there on the 4 or 5 trains; get off at the Wall Street station.

PANORAMAS

DOWNTOWN

THE BROOKLYN BRIDGE, Park Row.

"All modern New York, heroic New York, started with the Brooklyn Bridge," said the British art historian Kenneth Clark. The bridge, which celebrated its centennial on May 24, 1983, was the first link over the East River between what were then the separate cities of New York and Brooklyn. But it was—and is—much more than that. It was the first great bridge, the longest suspension bridge in the world at the time, a brilliant feat of engineering. It took 16 years to build, piece by piece, by hand. In its time it was as daring an event as a space shot. And it is an architectural triumph: its roadway and great stone gateways on either end make the cables look more like delicate cobwebs than the heavy steel strands they are. And the bridge provided New York City, which then had buildings of only five and six stories, with its first skyscrapers: the two huge granite towers, each 276 feet above high water, were the tallest and grandest man-made things in the city. The roadway itself provided a spectacular panorama of Manhattan.

Today the panorama is far different, but no less stunning. Daily, some 5,000 pedestrians and bicyclists walk, jog, or wheel across the bridge's mile-long wooden promenade; and if you have time, you should consider becoming one of them. A walk across the bridge, in either direction, is an experience unlike anything else New York offers: the view of the Manhattan skyline is spectacular, and strolling underneath the crisscross of cables, with the tumult of the traffic below, makes the crossing a kind of ceremony.

If you feel like continuing your jaunt after crossing the bridge, you can journey a short distance to the East River promenade in Brooklyn Heights, where benches provide a perfect place to rest.

Subway: 4, 5, 6 to Brooklyn Bridge–City Hall; A, C to High St.–Brooklyn Bridge in Brooklyn; return on foot to Manhattan over the bridge.

STATEN ISLAND FERRY, leaving from South Ferry in downtown Manhattan. Tel. 806-6940.

The ferry is probably the best deal in town, and certainly one of the most restful things any tour-weary visitor can do. For a mere 50¢ you can take a five-mile, 25-minute voyage and watch tugs nosing tankers and sun sparkling off the water, gaze on the shadowy silhouette of the Verrazano-Narrows Bridge, glide past the Statue of Liberty and Governor's Island, and listen to the cry of gulls. Day or night, the view of the Manhattan skyline from the ferry is superb.

The ferry runs every half hour from 6:30am to 11:30pm weekdays, then every hour until the next morning; weekend rides are on a similar schedule.

Subway: 1, 9 to South Ferry; 4, 5 to Bowling Green; N, R to Whitehall St.–South Ferry.

WORLD TRADE CENTER, Church and Vesey sts. Tel. 466-7377.

Although these soaring buildings have none of the Empire State Building's romance, the twin towers of the World Trade Center—each 110 stories and 1,350 feet tall—do have a vista. On any given day nearly 130,000 people pass through the center's revolving doors—50,000 to work and another 80,000 as tourists. Many of the latter come to marvel at the breathtaking panorama from the observation deck on the 107th floor in the No. 2 World Trade Center building—a quarter of a mile in the air—and from the rooftop platform just above it (open only when the weather permits). On a crystal-clear day you can see 60 miles in every direction. Diagrams on the floor-to-ceiling windows identify buildings and other points of interest. The ride up is swift (at 20 miles per hour, it takes just under a minute) and silent. In addition to the view there's a display on the history of trade, a souvenir shop, and a classy fast-food snack bar with a stupendous view.

Down below the concourse, underneath the buildings, there's a complete city in itself, with restaurants and shops. There's also a pleasant, if windy, outdoor plaza with benches and plants centered around a large fountain and a huge bronze sculpted globe. It's a pleasant place to picnic.

Admission: $3.50 adults, $1.75 children ages 6–12 and seniors over 62; children under 6 free.

Open: Summer daily 9:30am–9:30pm. Hours may vary in other seasons. **Subway:** 1, 9, N, R to Cortlandt St.; A, C, E to Chambers St.–World Trade Center.

PARKS & GARDENS

BROOKLYN BOTANIC GARDEN, just east of Prospect Park. Tel. 718/622-4433.

Though outsized by the Bronx Gardens (below), the Brooklyn Botanic Garden is nevertheless among the nation's leading botanical gardens. Reclaimed from a waste dump in 1910, the garden's 52 acres are densely planted with more than 12,000 types of vegetation. Most famous is the Japanese Hill-and-Pond Garden. In April and May the spectacle of masses of flowering cherry trees and fragrant magnolias is a sight to behold. The Rose Garden, at its peak in June *and* September, is the third-largest public collection of roses on display in the U.S., boasting over 1,000 varieties. There is also a herb garden, a fragrance garden for the blind, a fresh fruit and vegetable garden grown by children, and a Shakespeare garden—carpeted with the violets, rosemary, chamomile, and other plants from the Bard's plays and sonnets.

The Garden's three-pavilion conservatory features desert, tropical, and temperate houses, as well as exotic bonsai, orchid, and aquatic houses. The complex also houses a restaurant and gift shop. Guided tours leave every Sunday from the administration building at 1pm.

Admission: Conservatory $2; Sat–Sun and holidays greenhouses and Japanese Garden 25¢.

Open: Tues–Fri 8am–6pm; Sat–Sun and all holidays 10am–6pm. **Subway:** 2, 3, or 4 to Eastern Parkway station.

NEW YORK BOTANICAL GARDEN, 200th St. and Southern Blvd., Bronx Park. Tel. 220-8700.

✪ This 250-acre horticulture oasis, just 25 minutes from downtown Manhattan, is one of the most extraordinary sights New York has to offer. A short distance from its neighbor, the Bronx Zoo, the New York Botanical Garden is a preserve of woods, waterways, carefully tended lawns, lovely gardens, and a spectacular glass conservatory. In every season there is something else to see: strolls through the rhododendrons and azaleas in mid- to late May; visits to the rock garden

IMPRESSIONS

Far below and around lay the city like a ragged purple dream, the wonderful, cruel, enchanting, bewildering, fatal, great city.
—O. HENRY, *STRICTLY BUSINESS: THE DUEL*, 1910

and the native plant area; walking tours through the many special gardens; the Peggy Rockefeller Rose Garden, the Louise Loeb Vegetable Garden, the Jane Watson Irwin Perennial Garden, the Mae L. Wien Summer Flower Garden, a 40-acre hemlock forest (the only uncut woodland in New York City), a restored 19th-century mill, a plant shop, and a beautiful, airy, well-stocked gift shop. And there's also a not-to-be-missed gorgeous crystal palace, inspired by the 1844 Palm House of the Royal Gardens at Kew, England. The beautiful Enid A. Haupt Conservatory, renovated through the largesse of benefactress Haupt, contains under its glass roof an acre of gardens, ferns, orchids, and an array of flowering plants not to be believed. The Library at the Garden has one of the world's largest collections of horticultural books. Guided tours are available.

Suggested donation: $3 adults; $2 children, students, and seniors over 65; members and children under six, free. Policy says "Pay as much as you wish, but you must pay something."

Open: Apr 1–Oct 31 Tues–Fri 10am–4pm, Sat–Mon and holidays 10am–6pm. Nov 1–Mar 31 daily 10am–4pm. **Guided tours:** Conservatory Sat–Sun 11am–3pm, Mon and holidays 1:30–3:30pm, Thurs 1:30–2:30pm. Gardens & grounds Sat–Mon and holidays 1 and 3pm, Thurs 3pm. Forest Tours, Sat–Mon and holidays 1:30–3:30pm, Thurs 2pm. **Subway:** 4 to 200th St. and Jerome Ave.; D to Bedford Park Blvd. **Train:** Metro North Harlem local from Grand Central Terminal to Botanical Garden Station.

QUEENS BOTANICAL GARDENS, 43–50 Main St., Flushing. Tel. 718/ 886-3800.

Popular as a pastoral respite for local residents, and worth a visit if you're in the borough, these gardens were built upon land recovered from use as a garbage dump. The 38 acres are planted with rose gardens (more than 8,000 bushes), a Victorian "wedding garden" (available by appointment for the big event), a crab apple grove, and an "all-American" display of native North American plants. Year round there are lectures and workshops open to the public. The garden boasts the largest display of European-style annuals in the U.S. Especially great for kids are the bird garden and the beer garden with an observatory hive. A plant shop on the grounds offers indoor and outdoor flora and gardening items.

Open: Daily 9am–dusk. **Directions:** Take 7 train to last station, Main St.; take Q44 bus south—or walk 10 minutes—down Main St. to Botanical Gardens on right.

WAVE HILL, West 249th St. and Independence Ave., the Bronx. Tel. 549-2055.

This estate and public garden is located high on the banks of the Hudson River, in the hilly, tranquil Riverdale section of the Bronx. Once home to the likes of Mark Twain, Theodore Roosevelt, and Arturo Toscanini, the 28-acre estate is now a public garden and cultural center with programs in education, garden history, and the visual and performing arts. For aspirants to the country-estate "good life" or just city-weary travelers, a visit to Wave Hill—with its manicured grounds, historic houses, and sweeping view of the Hudson River and the Palisades—is well worth the 45-minute bus and subway ride (30 minutes by car) it takes to get there. Built in 1843, the estate served for more than a century as home to various eminent Americans and foreign dignitaries. It was presented to the City of New York in 1960 by its last owners.

Today visitors can explore its four greenhouses, nature trails, formal and wild gardens, herb and aquatic gardens, and the only public alpine house east of the Rockies. In summer and fall Wave Hill hosts concerts and outdoor theater; year round

---

IMPRESSIONS

There is no greenery: it is enough to make a stone sad.
—NIKITA KRUSCHCHEV, REMARK DURING VISIT, OCTOBER 1960

New York City isn't a melting pot, it's a boiling pot.
—THOMAS E. DEWEY, IN CONVERSATION WITH JOHN GUNTHER, *INSIDE U.S.A.*, 1947

there are lectures, and garden and bird walks; on Sunday at 2:15pm there are guided greenhouse and garden tours. Wave Hill also boasts an archive of rare commercial recordings by Toscanini, as well as memorabilia from the maestro. Call for special events. Indoor and outdoor concerts and dance performances, scheduled intermittently, are frequently on Saturday and Sunday afternoons, with admissions running from $4 to $9.

Admission: Free Mon–Fri; Sat–Sun $1 adults, 50¢ seniors and students; free for children under 14.

Open: Memorial Day–Labor Day Thurs–Sat and Mon–Tues 10am–5:30pm, Wed 10am–sunset, Sun 10am–7pm. Other seasons daily 10am–4:30pm. **Bus:** Express service by Liberty Lines from mid-Manhattan from East and West Sides. Have the exact $3.50 fare ready. Call 652-8400 for Liberty's Manhattan Riverdale Express bus schedule.

ZOOS

Note: Both the **Queens Zoo,** in Flushing Meadows (tel. 718/699-7239), and the **Brooklyn Zoo,** in Prospect Park (tel. 718/965-6560), are closed for renovations.

BRONX ZOO, Fordham Rd. and the Bronx River Pkwy. Tel. 220-5188.

The world-famous Bronx Zoo serves as both a fascinating educational and a recreational center for animal lovers of all ages, and as one of the world's most successful repository/breeding centers for the earth's diminishing wildlife. With 265 acres, it's the largest urban zoo in the U.S. and is home to 4,500 wild animals. Among them are 75 species considered endangered and 4 species officially extinct in nature (look for them: Père David's deer, Mongolian wild horses, Formosan Sika deer, and the European bison). Each year there are more than 1,000 births among the zoo's animal population; other zoos throughout the country—and even the world—look to the Bronx Zoo for new acquisitions.

One of the zoo's most popular features is Wild Asia, an exciting 38 acres in which 19 species of Asian animals roam an open expanse of land cultivated to simulate their natural environment. The area, open May through October, is accessible only by monorail, with a 22-minute tour narrated by a knowledgeable guide. Wild Asia hosts Siberian tigers, Asian elephants, gaur (the world's largest wild cattle), and axis deer, all of which pass before the windows of the monorail. One of the zoo's most ambitious projects is the award-winning Jungle World, a one-acre wood- and glass-enclosed habitat in which animals wander more or less freely through a re-created volcanic scrub forest, a mangrove swamp, a lowland evergreen rain forest, and a mountain rain forest. It uses an artful combination of real and artificial elements to simulate the natural habitats of the species it contains. Jungle World is open year round.

The zoo's newest feature is the Keith W. Johnson Zoo Center, home to Asian elephants and rhinoceroses. The Himalayan Highland Habitat is a 2½-acre haven for the endangered snow leopard, considered by many to be the most beautiful of the big cats. The habitat is built to resemble the mountainous terrain of northern India, Nepal, and Tibet, and is also home to red pandas, white-naped cranes, and pheasants.

One of the zoo's unique attractions is its participatory Children's Zoo, which is open from March through October. Here, youngsters can don giant fox ears and turtle shells, climb a giant rope spider web, and crawl through a prairie dog tunnel to see what it's like to be an animal. For an overview of the zoo, take the Safari train (closed in winter); to get from one end of the zoo to the other quickly, board the Skyfari tramway (also closed in winter). But for real excitement, climb atop a camel for the ride of your life.

You can easily spend an entire day at the zoo; and for those who do, there's a reasonably priced cafeteria, snack bars throughout the park, and picnic tables.

Admission: Tues–Thurs donation days; Fri–Mon $5.75 adults, $2 children 2–12 and seniors; children under 2 free.

Open: Winter daily 10am–4:30pm; other seasons Mon–Fri 10am–5pm, Sat–Sun and hols 10am–5:30pm; **Subway:** 2, 5 to Pelham Parkway; proceed west to Bronxdale entrance. **Bus:** Liberty Lines provides express bus service from stops in

Manhattan on Madison Ave. (call 652-8400 for schedule and stops); have exact $3.50 fare.

CENTRAL PARK ZOO, 64th St., off Fifth Ave. Tel. 360-8111.

★ The New York Zoological Society (creators of the wonderful Bronx Zoo) have turned the old Central Park Zoo into a state-of-the-art delight for young and old. Stop to watch the playful seals swimming around the tank just past the entrance before wandering through three "biomes" under a glass-covered colonnade. Everyone's favorite spot is in the polar zone—a pool with windows to give visitors an underwater view of swimming polar bears. In the tropic zone, toucans and other birds fly freely in a giant aviary. In the temperate zone, Japanese snow monkeys live on an island habitat re-created expressly for them. The zoo has a cafeteria with indoor and outdoor seating, and a gift shop.

While you're at the Central Park Zoo, you might want to take your kids to the **Lehman's Children's Zoo** as well. (See Section 4, "Cool for Kids," below.)

Admission: $1 adults, 50¢ senior citizens, 25¢ children aged 3–12; free for children under 3.

Open: May–Sept Wed–Mon 10am–4pm, Tues 10am–7:30pm; Oct–Apr Mon–Fri 10am–4:30pm, Sat–Sun and holidays 10am–5pm. **Subway:** 6 to 68th St. and walk west. **Bus:** M1, M2, M3, M4.

3. GALLERIES, EXHIBITION SPACES & AUCTION HOUSES

GALLERIES

For artists, dealers, collectors, and art lovers around the world, New York is an irresistible magnet, drawing the newest, the finest, the most prestigious in the visual arts. Dozens of art galleries are continually setting new trends and making new reputations. Whatever you want to see, it's here: from the paintings of old masters to works on the cutting edge. Remember, don't expect to cover all of New York's galleries in a day or two, so take your time and enjoy yourself.

Galleries don't charge admission—they're businesses with art to sell. The prices are posted, usually near the front desk. Sometimes the prices are more interesting and usually more shocking to the public than the artworks, so if you're interested, go ahead and ask for them.

Below, we've listed many of the galleries that the art world takes seriously, as well as the type of work and artists each gallery features. For those who want the most current listings (galleries generally change shows monthly), the gallery-goer's bible is *Gallery Guide,* a monthly glossy paperback that lists virtually every gallery's shows, plus maps. It's available free in most galleries. You can also pick up a copy of *Art in America* ($4.75) at a magazine stand, for gallery listings and maps, slick photos, and reviews with the latest, but not last, word on the ever-changing art scene.

Galleries are generally open Tuesday through Saturday 10am to 6pm; they may have special summer hours. Note that some galleries close during August.

MADISON AVENUE/UPTOWN

Prestigious Madison Avenue is lined with art galleries and expensive stores, and each block abounds with architectural and historic landmarks. Window-shop, browse, and join the well-heeled residents of the brownstones, town houses, mansions, and apartment houses that line the side streets off Madison Avenue.

At the **Forum Gallery,** 1018 Madison Avenue, between 78th and 79th streets (tel. 772-7666), you can enjoy your art al fresco, because the gallery exhibits its contemporary sculpture in a charming penthouse roof garden. Inside, admire the works of American figurative painters and sculptors.

The **Rachel Adler Gallery** (tel. 308-0511) houses European art of the teens, 20s, and 30s, and specializes in the early abstract movements, Russian avant-garde, and Italian futurists.

The **Graham Gallery,** 1014 Madison Avenue, at 78th Street (tel. 535-5767), features three floors of eye-pleasing art. The first two floors show 19th- and 20th-century American paintings and sculpture, plus British pottery. The third floor, **Graham Modern,** shows contemporary paintings and sculpture.

The focus at the **David Findlay Gallery,** 984 Madison Avenue, at 77th Street (tel. 249-2909), is 19th- and 20th-century French art. The ambience is appropriately intimate and chic, and you can view old French favorites like Dufy and Vuillard.

On the second floor of 851 Madison Avenue, between 70th and 71st streets, are three top-notch galleries. The **Barbara Mathes Gallery** (tel. 249-3600) shows Americans of the early 20th century such as Calder and Arthur Dove, works on paper by such Europeans as Matisse and Picasso, as well as contemporary artists. **Hirschl and Adler Modern** (tel. 744-6700) features contemporary paintings and sculptures, including works by Joseph Beuys, and paintings by Joan Snyder and Philip Pearlstein. And **Hirschl and Adler Folk** (tel. 988-FOLK) specializes in American folk art, mostly of the 18th and 19th centuries. You might see anything from calligraphy to Navaho weavings here.

Occupying a historic landmark building at 21 East 70th Street, off Madison Avenue, is **Hirschl and Adler Galleries, Inc.** (tel. 535-8810). On the first two floors you will find museum-quality shows of art from the 18th to the 20th century. The range is dazzling, from American paintings, watercolors, drawings, prints, and sculpture to 19th- and 20th-century American decorative arts, European Impressionist painting and modern art.

M. Knoedler & Co., 19 East 70th Street, near the Frick Museum (tel. 794-0550), has an old-masters department, but much of its focus is on modern masters like Robert Motherwell, Frank Stella, Richard Diebenkorn, David Smith, and Adolph Gottlieb.

If you are interested in contemporary sculpture, go to **The Sculpture Center,** which is a nonprofit alternative gallery specializing in emerging and mid-career sculptors. Located in an old carriage house at 167 East 69th Street, between Lexington and Third avenues (tel. 879-3500), the center also houses a school that teaches the traditional methods of sculpture—carving, clay modeling, and casting.

The **Richard York Gallery,** 21 East 65th Street, between Fifth and Madison avenues (tel. 772-9155), is the place to see important American art dating from 1800 to 1950. Featured are works by members of the Hudson River School, American Impressionists like William Merritt Chase, modernist works by Georgia O'Keeffe and Joseph Stella, and still lifes and marine paintings.

At the **Wildenstein Company Gallery,** 19 East 64th Street, between Fifth and Madison avenues (tel. 879-0500), you can lose yourself in the dreamy colors of master French Impressionists Monet, Manet, and Renoir.

57TH STREET/MIDTOWN

Busy, bustling midtown is the heart of the city. It moves to the beat of the well-dressed people moving in and out of its tall office buildings and upscale department stores. This area has long been home to many of the more established, blue-chip galleries that should be a part of any serious exploration of the city's art treasures. Most of the galleries aren't at street level; you'll find these hushed, pleasant spaces an elevator's ride above the noisy midtown crowds.

It's difficult to choose which galleries you should visit out of the many that are housed in the beautiful **Fuller Building,** 41 East 57th Street, at the corner of Madison Avenue. The structure itself is an architectural knockout that's considered one of the best examples of Art Deco design in the city. Look at the bronze doors, wall decorations, marble fixtures, and mosaic walls—and plan to spend some time investigating the many galleries within.

The **Robert Miller Gallery** (tel. 980-5454) features 20th-century and contemporary art by such artists as sculptor Louise Bourgeois, painter Joan Mitchell, and photographer Robert Mapplethorpe.

André Emmerich (tel. 752-0124) has two specialties. This gallery shows works by contemporary American and European artists like David Hockney, Helen Frankenthaler, Anthony Caro, and Hans Hofmann. But it also features ancient art. The lineup at the **James Goodman Gallery** (tel. 593-3737) includes Picasso, Matisse, Botero, Calder, and Klee, as well as contemporary masters like Rauschenberg and Rosenquist.

If you have time to visit only a few galleries while you're in New York, be sure to include the bustling **Pace Gallery**, 32 East 57th Street, between Fifth and Madison avenues (tel. 421-3292). This famous gallery shows an impressive array of modern and contemporary artists, from Picasso and Calder to Chuck Close and maverick painter Julian Schnabel. Other modern greats on the gallery roster are Chamberlain, Martin, Oldenburg, Serra, and Dine. In the same building, **Pace Editions** (tel. 421-3237) shows contemporary and old-master prints, and **Pace Primitive** (tel. 421-3237) features turn-of-the-century African sculpture.

The **Pace/MacGill Gallery**, 11 East 57th Street, between Fifth and Madison avenues (tel. 759-7999), is a good place to see contemporary photography—from the classic works of Walker Evans to the avant-garde images of Joel-Peter Witkin.

The work at the **Holly Solomon Gallery**, 724 Fifth Avenue, near 57th Street (tel. 757-7777), defies easy classification but should not be missed. Solomon is something of a legend in the art world for showing provocative work. You never know what you may see here—rows of television sets by Nam June Paik, videotapes of the artist William Wegman's dog, or the wild and colorful installations of Judy Pfaff.

In the same building are two other galleries you might want to visit. The **Merrin Gallery** (tel. 757-2884) shows only ancient art—classical Greek and Roman, Etruscan, Near Eastern, and Egyptian—from bronze figures to polished stone sculptures. The **Grace Borgenicht Gallery** (tel. 247-2111) hosts an unpredictable and eclectic mix of works by old masters, established modern artists, and emerging younger artists.

A few doors down at **Blum Helman,** 20 West 57th Street, between Fifth and Sixth avenues (tel. 245-2888), the focus is on American and European postwar and contemporary painting and sculpture, with works by heavyweights like Ellsworth Kelly, the contemporary landscape painter David Deutsch, and sculptor Bryan Hunt.

At the **New York Gallery Building,** 24 West 57th Street, between Fifth and Sixth avenues, several galleries are worth a visit. Among them are the **Marian Goodman Gallery** (tel. 977-7160), which shows contemporary art in all media, with an emphasis on well-known Europeans like German artist Anselm Kiefer, and French artist Christian Boltanski. Two floors up, at **Arnold Herstand & Co.** (tel. 664-1379), you'll find African art and modern and contemporary art by such masters as Jean Dubuffet and Roberto Matta.

Modern art aficionados should not miss the **Marlborough Gallery.** Located in a skyscraper office building at 40 West 57th Street, between Fifth and Sixth avenues (tel. 541-4900), this prestigious gallery exhibits the gurus and greats of modern art, such as Moore, Calder, Sutherland, Botero, Feininger, and Arp.

In the same building, stop in at the **Kennedy Galleries** (tel. 541-9600), where the walls are lined with collector-quality 18th-, 19th-, and 20th-century American paintings, drawings, and prints. Savor especially the works of John Marin, John Copley, Georgia O'Keeffe, and Charles Prendergast.

There are ten galleries at 50 West 57th Street, between Fifth and Sixth avenues. One of the best is the **Frumkin/Adams Gallery** (tel. 757-6655), which specializes in works by such well-known contemporary artists as James Surls, Jack Beal, and Roy De Forest, many of whom hail from Texas and California.

The **Sidney Janis Gallery,** 110 West 57th Street, between Sixth and Seventh avenues (tel. 586-0110), shows a wide range of modern and contemporary art—from legends like Mondrian, Brancusi, Leger, and Segal to aspiring legends like Crash (John Matos) and Maya Lin, the sculptor who designed the controversial Vietnam War Memorial in Washington, D.C.

SOHO

When rents in nearby Chelsea and Greenwich Village soared in the early 1960s, artists moved into the airy lofts and commercial buildings in SoHo (which stands for *so*-uth of *Ho*-uston Street). Today SoHo is a chic neighborhood of restaurants, bookstores, antique shops, and boutiques. And rents in the area have risen so high that most artists can no longer afford to work here. Still, SoHo remains one of the commercial centers of the art world. You'll find more than 200 art galleries in just five square blocks of SoHo, many of them housed in 19th-century cast-iron buildings. Visually, SoHo is one of the most stimulating neighborhoods in the city. So as you wander from gallery to gallery, be sure to check out the trendy shops and shoppers.

You might begin your tour at the **Leo Castelli Gallery,** 420 West Broadway, between Prince and Spring streets (tel. 941-9855). Castelli's unerring knack of spotting ground-breaking modern artists is legendary. At this, one of his three galleries in the city, you'll see works by "old" greats (Warhol, Johns, Stella, Lichtenstein, and Oldenburg), by newer greats (Dan Flavin, Donald Judd, and Ed Ruscha), and by rising stars like Charles Simonds, whose miniature clay sculptures are reminiscent of lost cities.

At the same address you'll find the highly regarded **Sonnabend Gallery** (tel. 966-6160), which features the works of such contemporary artists as sculptor Jannis Kounellis, photographer John Baldessari, and artist Jeff Koons. **Germans Van Eck Gallery** (tel. 219-0717) is also there, with an eclectic mix of contemporary American and European art.

The **Mary Boone Gallery,** across the street at 417 West Broadway (tel. 431-1818), has become one of SoHo's institutions, with an impressive roster of contemporary artists like Eric Fischl, Sigmar Polke, Sherrie Levine, Barbara Kruger, Ross Bleckner, and A. R. Penke.

The **Heller Gallery,** 71 Greene Street (tel. 966-5948), shows the work of artists of the Studio Crafts Movement, including such sculptors in glass as William Carlson and Harvey Littleton.

At the **Barbara Gladstone Gallery,** 99 Greene St., between Prince and Spring streets (tel. 431-3334), the work is hard to classify. But many artists who show here are the talk of the town. They include Jenny Holzer, whose work incorporates moving electric message signs, and Leon Golub, who is known for his sociopolitical paintings.

The **John Weber Gallery,** 142 Greene Street, between Houston and Prince streets (tel. 966-6115), established in 1971, represents conceptual, minimal, and sociopolitical artists such as Sol Lewitt, Robert Smithson, Hans Haacke, and Allan McCollum.

In the same building, visit the **Sperone Westwater Gallery** (tel. 431-3685), which shows important contemporary artists such as the Italian neo-expressionists Chia and Clement; Cy Twombly, who is known for his elegant scribble-like drawings; and painter Susan Rothenberg.

Down the street, at **Barbara Toll,** 146 Greene Street (tel. 431-1788), you might find anything from a Garden of Eden, complete with flora, fauna, and a working fountain, to photographs of famous figures in the art world. And at **Metro Pictures,** 150 Greene Street (tel. 925-8335), you might see Cindy Sherman's provocative photographic portraits (in which she herself stars); Robert Longo's hefty, large-scale sculptures; or Louise Lawler's controversial photographs of other artists' artwork.

The **Paula Cooper Gallery,** 155 Wooster Street, just south of Houston Street (tel. 674-0766), shows a mixed bag of well-known contemporary artists. They include painters Jennifer Bartlett and Elizabeth Murray, and sculptors Carl André, Jonathan Borofsky, and Joel Shapiro.

On Broadway, in the first two blocks below Houston, several recently renovated buildings now house a variety of galleries specializing in contemporary art. While some of these galleries are brand new, others have moved here from elsewhere in SoHo and from the fast-fading art scene of the East Village.

You might begin this leg of your art tour in the two adjoining buildings at 578 and 568 Broadway. On the first floor, the **Marcus Pfeifer Gallery Ltd.** (tel. 226-2251) is a great place to see photography. As the sign on the front desk says, there are "works on hand from Atgee to Weegee."

On the third floor, two more Castelli galleries—**Leo Castelli** and **Castelli Graphics** (tel. 941-9855)—exhibit more works from the impresario's stable of illustrious artists. The **Phoenix Gallery,** on the fifth floor (tel. 226-8711), is the oldest cooperative gallery in the city, with over 200 artists from around the country as members. The art may not be well known, but it may be the most affordable art in SoHo (we saw a few small paintings going for as little as $200). The gallery also hosts musical events, but it is closed in the summer.

It is worth making the trip up to the **Lorence Monk Gallery,** on the 11th floor (tel. 431-3555). The gallery features works in all media, for example, prints by Johns and Rauchenberg and monumental wood sculptures by Ursula von Rydingsvard, or drawings by young artist Carole Seborovski.

The building at 560 Broadway, near the corner of Prince Street, houses another newly renovated cluster of art galleries. We've picke out just a few; but if you have time, we'd urge you to ride the elevator and explore other galleries in the building as well.

On the second floor, the **Max Protech Gallery** (tel. 966-5454) specializes in American and European art and architecture. And the **Wolff Gallery** (tel. 431-7833) shows works by younger artists and has some interesting theme shows. For example, a recent exhibit of performance art featured Chris Burden's photographs of himself crawling through broken glass and getting shot in the arm.

TRIBECA/DOWNTOWN

Just a few blocks south of SoHo is another old loft district turned trendy—TriBeCa. It was once the center of the city's produce industry, but in the late 1960s developers relocated much of that industry to make way for the construction of the World Trade Center. In the 1970s artists fleeing the rents and trendiness of SoHo moved into TriBeCa and revitalized the area. In many ways today's TriBeCa resembles the SoHo of 15 years ago, but this relatively quiet neighborhood—where five-story buildings predominate and iron canopies, like sidewalk rooftops, still run along whole blocks—has its own personality. The following list includes the key art attractions.

Artists Space, 223 West Broadway, between White and Franklin streets (tel. 226-3970), is one of New York City's most active alternative spaces. It focuses on emerging artists; for instance, a recent show featured paintings and sculptures by young artists from Eastern Europe who had never before shown in the West.

The **Alternative Museum,** 17 White Street (tel. 966-4444), also exhibits works in a variety of media by unknown or underrecognized artists. Much of the work has a sociopolitical content.

The **Clocktower,** 108 Leonard Street, on the 13th floor (tel. 233-1096), is one of two exhibition spaces run by the Institute for Art and Urban Resources. Housed inside one of Manhattan's few existing clocktowers, it features provocative contemporary art—for example, the entries in an architectural competition to unite the two islands in the Bering Strait. The Clocktower also features concert programs and performances, and offers low-rent studios to artists from the U.S. and abroad.

Hal Bromm, 90 West Broadway, at Chambers Street (tel. 732-6196), is a well-lit second-floor gallery that features interesting and thought-provoking art in a variety of media. A recent exhibit included works by Jody Pinto, Mike Bidlo, Rosemarie Castoro, Russell Sharon, Luis Frangella, Macyn Bolt, Krusztof Wodicxko, David Wojnarowicz, and Julian Opie.

THE EAST VILLAGE

Time was when this area between Third Avenue and Avenue C, and from East 1st to East 13th streets, wasn't even a blip on the cultural map. Then, overnight, the East Village became home to a funky genre of art that swept through the New York art world and drew packs of young collectors and yuppies to the area. Today the East

Village gallery scene is in a state of near-oblivion. The successful galleries have either moved or plan to move to SoHo. And the less successful ones have succumbed to rising rents. But a few galleries remain, and if you're exploring the East Village, you may want to check them out. Both galleries listed below have rather laid-back hours. They're open Wednesday through Sunday from 1 to 6pm.

Kenkeleba Gallery, 214 East 2nd Street, between avenues B and C (tel. 674-3939), shows a wide range of known and unknown contemporary artists. **P.S. 122,** at 409 East 9th Street (tel. 228-4249), is a nonprofit gallery housed in a 100-year-old public school. It is run by Painting Space 122 Inc., a collective of 18 artists who have low-cost studio space in the building, which is shared by other organizations such as Performance Space 122. Closed during August.

OTHER EXHIBITION SPACES

The **Dia Art Foundation,** 548 West 22nd Street, between Tenth and Eleventh avenues (tel. 431-9232), is a nonprofit arts organization that has come up with an unusual way to give contemporary artists a chance to create and exhibit their work. Each of the four floors of its West 22nd Street exhibition space is devoted to the work of one artist, who works and shows in the space for a year. One such artist, Jenny Holzer, created an installation of granite tombstones and her trademark electronic-message boards on her floor.

The Dia Art Foundation also has two exhibition spaces in SoHo, and each houses a single installation piece by Walter De Maria. At 393 West Broadway, between Spring and Broome streets (tel. 925-9397), you can see De Maria's *The Broken Kilometer,* a piece that consists of 500 solid brass rods, weighs 37,000 pounds, and spans a kilometer (six-tenths of a mile). At 141 Wooster Street, between Houston and Prince streets, on the second floor (tel. 473-8072), you can see *The New York Earth Room,* an earth sculpture that consists of 250 cubic yards of earth covering 300 square feet of floor space.

Like the Clocktower in TriBeCa, **P.S. 1,** at 46-01 21st Street, in Long Island City, Queens (tel. 718/784-2084), is run by the Institute for Art and Urban Resources and features high-caliber one-person and group shows, and also houses low-rent studios. As the name suggests, P.S. 1 is in the city's first public school, a Romanesque Revival building of the 1890s. The exhibition space is open Wednesday through Sunday from noon to 6pm. Admission is $2. To get there, take the Eighth Avenue E train or Sixth Avenue F train to 23rd Street–Ely Avenue, or the Flushing 7 train to 45th Avenue–Courthouse Square.

So that more people can see art on a daily basis, several corporations have helped make it possible for the Whitney Museum of American Art to curate special shows of American art in three locations around the city. As reflected in the titles of some recent exhibits—"Straphangers" (the local term for the city's subway riders), "Urban Figures," and "Suburban Homelife: Tracking the American Dream"—these shows can be quite interesting, and they tend to be about topics close to the lives of the people viewing them. What's more, the museum-quality shows at the following three locations are free.

The **Whitney Museum of American Art at Equitable Center,** 181 Seventh Avenue, at 52nd Street (tel. 554-1000), is open Monday through Friday from 11am to 6pm (on Thursday to 7:30pm), and on Saturday from noon to 5pm.

The **Whitney Museum of American Art at Philip Morris,** 120 Park Avenue, at 42nd Street (tel. 878-2453), is actually two spaces. The first is a regular gallery open Monday through Saturday from 11am to 6pm (on Thursday to 7:30pm). The other, called the Sculpture Court, is a sun-drenched, indoor sculpture garden, open Monday and Friday and Saturday from 11am to 6pm and on Sunday from 11am to 7pm.

In lower Manhattan, the **Whitney Museum of American Art,** downtown at Federal Reserve Plaza, 33 Maiden Lane, at Nassau Street (tel. 943-5655), is open Monday through Friday from 11am to 6pm.

If you are in downtown Brooklyn, visit the **Rotunda Gallery,** in the Brooklyn War Memorial, on Cadman Plaza West near Orange Street (tel. 718/875-4031). This nonprofit gallery has helped spark the careers of several Brooklyn artists who have earned national and international recognition.

AUCTION HOUSES

The quality of a new piece of work can often be measured by the amount one is willing to bid for it. Artistic movements are made or forgotten at the city's great auction houses. Although you may have to pay a "bidding paddle" fee in order to buy something—one doesn't bid here by raising a hand—there are pre-auction exhibits open for public inspection at no charge.

Mention "art auction" and people think of **Sotheby's,** at 1334 York Avenue, between 71st and 72nd streets (tel. 606-7000). The million-dollar art sales will have you holding your breath, but don't forget to check out the less pricey, more down-to-earth auctions of quilts, furniture, antique clothes, and autographs.

Christie's Galleries, 502 Park Avenue, at the corner of 59th Street (tel. 546-1000), auctions paintings and sculpture fit for a millionaire or a museum. At **Christie's East,** 219 East 67th Street, between Second and Third avenues (tel. 606-0400), you can pick up an entire collection of mounted hunting trophies, or if you have no room in your home for those, settle for perhaps a few prints, some antique clothing, dolls, or Victoriana.

William Doyle, 175 East 87th Street, between Third and Lexington avenues (tel. 427-2730), is another major-league gallery; sales are held every other Wednesday. You can view the items Saturday through Tuesday.

Swann Galleries, 104 East 25th Street, between Park Avenue South and Lexington Avenue (tel. 254-4710), is for you if you're interested in books, autographs, photographs, and the like. Fans of folk art, puppets, country furniture, and other upscale, down-home items may want to check out **Greenwich Auction Room Ltd.,** at 110 East 13th Street, between Third and Fourth avenues (tel. 533-5550).

4. COOL FOR KIDS

Besides the many suggestions and listings that follow here, check the sports and recreation sections and the Calendar of Events for more festivals and frolics.

Look under Section 1, "The Top Attractions," and Section 2, "More Attractions," both above, for full descriptions of the following city attractions that have major appeal to kids of all ages, since they're only summarized here. Be sure to see the Central Park listing, for example. There's the **Carousel Ride,** a nice stroll in from either side of 65th Street—a ride on one of the gaily painted horses is 75¢. And if your children still want more, rustle them over to the **Alice in Wonderland statue** next to the model boat pond near the East 77th Street entrance to the park, and let them climb to their heart's content.

ATTRACTIONS
LOWER MANHATTAN

CON EDISON ENERGY MUSEUM, 145 E. 14th St., just west of Third Ave. Tel. 460-6244.

Most children will enjoy this museum devoted to one of America's best-known homespun geniuses, inventor Thomas Edison. The museum focuses on the development of electricity, from Edison's invention of the electric lightbulb to the present, and includes some hands-on exhibits.

Admission: Free.

Open: Tues–Sat 10am–4pm. **Subway:** N, R, 4, 5, 6 to Union Square.

FEDERAL HALL NATIONAL MEMORIAL, corner of Wall and Nassau sts. Tel. 264-8701.

Take your kids back two centuries into the nation's past. The memorial is housed in an 1842 building on the site where the Declaration of Independence was read in July of 1776, where the first Congress met to count the electoral votes of the first presidential election, and where George Washington was inaugurated in 1789 as the nation's first president. Anyone interested in this country's past will appreciate the museum's extended and temporary exhibits displaying art, architectural models, dioramas of the first inauguration, an 8-minute video on the history of the site, and a newly installed, hands-on computer exhibition called "A Celebration of the 200th Anniversary of the Constitution." The memorial itself is self-guiding, so children can explore as they wish. In addition, each Wednesday, year round, concerts are performed at 12:30pm in the memorial's rotunda; admission is free.

Admission: Free.

Open: Museum Mon–Fri 9am–5pm; bookstore Mon–Fri 10am–4:30pm. **Subway:** 4 or 5 to Wall St.; 1, 9, N, R to Rector St.

FIRE DEPARTMENT MUSEUM, 278 Spring St., between Hudson and Varick sts. Tel. 691-1303.

Nearly two centuries of fire-fighting history are stored away in this museum. The oldest engine here dates back to 1820 and was hand-pulled by a team of volunteer firemen to the scene of a New York fire. Also on display are leather fire hoses, steam engines, Brooklyn's first fire bell, and pictures and drawings (including a Currier & Ives) of famous fires. There's even a stuffed dog named Chief, who earned his stripes by saving kittens from burning buildings.

Admission: Donation suggested.

Open: Tues–Sat 10am–4pm. **Closed:** Hols. **Subway:** C, E to Spring St. **Bus:** M21 to Sixth Ave.

FORBES MAGAZINE GALLERIES, 62 Fifth Ave., at 12th St. Tel. 620-2389.

Children don't have to hunt far for the world's largest collection of Fabergé Imperial Easter Eggs. The *Forbes* Galleries offer a permanent exhibit of these masterpieces. Also sure to delight children are exhibits of presidential autographs and memorabilia, the toy boats, toy soldiers, and trophies on display.

Admission: Free.

Open: Tues–Wed and Fri–Sat 10am–4pm. **Subway:** N, R, 4, 5, 6 to Union Square.

MUSEUM OF HOLOGRAPHY, 11 Mercer St., half a block north of Canal St. and one block west of Broadway. Tel. 925-0526 or 925-0581.

Children and adults will enjoy being confounded at the Museum of Holography, where 3-D images seem to be alive and kicking. This museum features extensive educational displays, including a selection of the earliest and state-of-the-art holograms.

Admission: $3.50 adults; $2.50 students, members of AAA, and senior citizens; $2 children under 12.

Open: Tues–Sun 11am–6pm, Wed 10:30am–6pm. **Subway:** A, C, N, R to Canal St.

SOUTH STREET SEAPORT MUSEUM, 207 Front St. Tel. 669-9416.

The museum offers maritime exhibits and films, in addition to a number of family activities and children's workshops that deal mainly with the early social history of New York's maritime district. Some past exhibits displayed artifacts from archeological digs under Wall Street, and an extensive exhibition of antique and reconstructed model ships. The museum's Children's Center, open year round, offers weekend activities, hands-on workshops, mock archeological digs, arts and crafts, and 19th-century games. Each activity is coordinated with subjects in the main gallery. All materials are provided.

The museum also coordinates tours of the historic ships, docked at the Seaport (30 to 45 minutes), and walking tours of the Seaport's backstreet area (50 minutes). Both explain the history of the area's focus on commerce in the 1800s. Each tour is included in the price of the museum admission. For a combination charge, museum visitors can also experience life on the water in a replica of an 1800s paddlewheeler. The boat ride runs from April through October and travels for 90 minutes around lower Manhattan and out to the Statue of Liberty (the boat does not dock at the statue). During April and the first part of May the boat usually runs only on weekends; from mid-May through October the boat runs on weekdays and weekends at noon, 2pm, and 4pm. Those who are interested in taking only the boat ride can do so. Prices are $12 for adults, and $8 for students, children, and senior citizens.

Admission: $6 adults, $5 senior citizens, $4 students with valid ID, $3 children ages 4–12.

Open: Daily 10am–5pm. **Subway:** 2, 3, 4, 5 to Fulton St.

GRAMERCY PARK

POLICE ACADEMY MUSEUM, 235 E. 20th St., between Second and Third aves. Tel. 477-9753.

If anyone in your family is interested in the men and women in blue, try a visit to the Police Academy Museum. It boasts one of the world's largest collections of police memorabilia—from weapons to handcuffs—plus exhibits on current police procedures and uniforms.

Admission: Free.

Open: Mon–Fri 9am–3pm (but call to make sure). **Subway:** 6 to 23rd St.

MIDTOWN WEST

CHILDREN'S MUSEUM OF MANHATTAN, at the Tisch Building, 212 W. 83rd St., between Broadway and Amsterdam. Tel. 721-1234.

⭐ The borough's only participatory museum for children ages 2 through 10, this is a strictly hands-on place, where children have fun and learn by doing. The media center includes a "hands-on" television production and editing studio where visitors become newscasters, camera operators, actors, and animators while making their own videos. There's also a 150-seat theater where guest artists, dancers, puppeteers, and storytellers perform on weekends and holidays. In the Art Studio, children and teens make their own creations while they learn painting, sculpture, calligraphy, printmaking, drawing, and bookmaking with artists-in-residence. The museum shop stocks art supplies, toys, games, and gifts from around the world.

Admission: $4 children and adults. Additional $1 for workshops.

Open: Mon, Wed, and Fri 1–5pm; Sat–Sun 10am–5pm. **Subway:** 1, 9 to 79th St.; B, C to 81st St.

INTREPID SEA-AIR-SPACE MUSEUM, Hudson River, foot of West 46th St. and Twelfth Ave., at Pier 86. Tel. 245-2533.

This fascinating museum of technology is housed on an old aircraft carrier. There are four theme halls—each devoted to a particular aspect of our country's recent achievements on the seas, in the air, and beyond. Each hall offers a related film.

Admission: $7 adults, $4 children under 12, $6 senior citizens.

Open: Daily 10am–5pm. **Bus:** M27, M42, or M50.

MUSEUM OF MODERN ART, 11 W. 53rd St., between Fifth and Sixth aves. Tel. 708-9480.

MOMA has plenty of powerfully communicative art children can appreciate. Monet's _Water Lilies,_ Chagall's _I in the Village,_ Calder's _Mobile,_ Jackson Pollock's _No. 1,_ and Picasso's _Goat_ (in the sculpture garden) are just a few of the works popular with children. On Saturday mornings during the school year, Family Gallery Programs and Family Film Series are offered for $5 per family; call the Department of Education at 708-9745 for schedule.

Admission: $7 adults, $4 students with ID, $3 senior citizens; free for children under 16 accompanied by an adult; Thurs 5–9pm donations welcome.

Open: Fri–Tues 11am–5:45pm, Thurs 11am–8:45pm. **Subway:** B, D, F, Q to Rockefeller Center.

MIDTOWN EAST

AT&T INFOQUEST CENTER, 550 Madison Ave., at 56th St. Tel. 605-5555.
For those who suffer from technophobia, a visit to the fascinating AT&T InfoQuest Center may be just the cure. The center is a permanent exhibit at AT&T World Headquarters, featuring 40 interactive exhibits on photonics and microelectronics. Meet Gordon, the robot, who explains computer software.
Admission: Free.
Open: Tues 10am–9pm; Wed–Sun 10am–6pm. **Closed:** Holidays. **Subway:** 4, 5, 6 to 59th St.

MUSEUM OF RADIO AND TELEVISION, 1 E. 53rd St., just off Fifth Ave. Tel. 752-7684.
More than 40,000 videotapes and radio programs show the younger generation that, yes, there was life before MTV. Visitors select tapes from the museum's holdings, and view them at individual consoles on a first-come, first-served basis. Pick out a few of your own favorite kids' shows—"Howdy Doody" and "Kukla, Fran, and Ollie" are here—or let your kids choose reruns of their own favorites.
Suggested contribution: $4.50 adults, $3.50 students, $2.50 senior citizens and children under 13.
Open: Tues noon–8pm, Wed–Sat noon–5pm. **Subway:** 6 to 51st St.; E, F to Fifth Ave.

NEW YORK DOLL HOSPITAL, 787 Lexington Ave., between 61st and 62nd sts. Tel. 838-7527.
This is the place to bring grandmother's wax doll for a facelift, an injured Cabbage Patch kid for a specialist's care, your teddy bear for restuffing, and your talking dolls and animals for a throat exam. The Doll Hospital began almost 90 years ago as a concession to a hairdressing salon—children could get their doll's hair done just like their mother's. Although there aren't any ambulances here, you're welcome to observe any of the "operations" and view the collections of bisque, foreign, and celebrity dolls. To get there, ring the bell at the sidewalk door and then go up one flight of crooked old stairs after you're buzzed in.
Open: Mon–Sat 10am–6pm. **Subway:** N, R to Lexington Ave.; 4, 5, 6 to 59th St.

UPPER WEST SIDE

AMERICAN MUSEUM OF NATURAL HISTORY, Central Park West at 79th St. Tel. 769-5100.
Most native New Yorkers have fond childhood memories of the Museum of Natural History. The dinosaur room, filled with huge skeletons of our prehistoric predecessors, is a kids' favorite. Also visit the People Center, which offers lectures, poetry readings, and educational activities for children of all ages in the fall and spring. Other highlights are the Natural Science Center and the Discovery Room, which give kids a chance to learn about plants, animals, and the geology of New York City. And don't miss the popular science films that are shown in the Naturemax Film Theater—the screen is 40 feet high and 66 feet wide and projects images that have proven to be a delight for both children and adults alike. Our favorite recent showing was *Beavers: The Biggest Dam Movie You Ever Saw.* Call to find out the schedule of activities (tel. 769-5650).
Suggested contribution: $5 adults, $2.50 children. Naturemax tickets $5 per adult, $3.75 seniors and students, $2.50 children ($7, $5.50, and $3.50 for double features).
Open: Sun–Thurs 10am–5:45pm, Fri–Sat 10am–8:45pm. **Subway:** B, C to 81st St.; 1, 9 to 79th St.

HAYDEN PLANETARIUM, Central Park West and 81st St. Tel. 769-5920.

★ For a dramatic journey in time and space, travel right next door from the Museum of Natural History to the Hayden Planetarium. For more than 50 years the planetarium has been taking viewers of all ages out of this world with glittering sky shows on its huge domed ceiling. There's also a 14-ton meteorite, an exhibit exclusively devoted to the sun, and scales where you can find out what you would weigh on different planets (for show times, call 769-5920).

Due to popular demand, the Planetarium has begun Saturday programs featuring shows especially for children under 10—for example, "Robots in Space," or a storyteller explaining myths and legends of the stars. There's a "Sky Show" included in your admission (one recent offering was "UFOs: Searching for Life Among the Stars"). Parents should call for show times and schedules. On Friday and Saturday nights the Planetarium presents Laser Rock Shows at 7, 8:30, and 10pm. Dazzling laser visuals dance to contemporary rock sounds ($7 per person, per show). Call 769-5921 for current program.

Admission (including Sky Show): $5 adults, $3.75 students and senior citizens with ID cards, and $2.50 children 2–12. Laser Rock Show tickets $7.

Open: Mon–Fri 12:30–4:45pm, Sat 10am–4:45pm, Sun noon–4:45pm. **Closed:** Thanksgiving and Christmas. **Subway:** B, C to 81st St.; 1, 9 to 79th St.

NEW-YORK HISTORICAL SOCIETY, 170 Central Park West, between 76th and 77th sts. Tel. 873-3400.

Children over 10 may be interested in the exhibitions at the historical society. The fine collections include Early American tin and cast-iron toys, Tiffany lamps, and (although the entire collection is not always on view) the complete set of John James Audubon's Birds of America original watercolors.

Admission: $4 adults, $2 senior citizens and children under 12; Tues donations accepted.

Open: Tues–Sun 10am–5pm. **Subway:** B, C to 81st St. **Bus:** M10.

UPPER EAST SIDE

COOPER-HEWITT NATIONAL MUSEUM OF DESIGN, 2 E. 91st St., at Fifth Ave. Tel. 860-6868.

The Cooper-Hewitt is a must visit for aspiring designers and artists. As the Smithsonian Institution's National Museum of Design, it has an immense collection of historical and modern objects and designs (nearly 700 items) from all over the world. While the permanent collection is not on view, the changing exhibits focus on various aspects of design, from hairstyles to skyscrapers.

Admission: $3 adults, $1.50 senior citizens and students; children under 12 free; free Tues 5–9pm.

Open: Tues 10am–9pm, Wed–Sat 10am–5pm, Sun noon–5pm. **Closed:** Holidays. **Subway:** 4, 5, 6 to 86th St.

EL MUSEO DEL BARRIO, 1230 Fifth Ave., at 104th St. Tel. 831-7272.

For children interested in learning more about a vibrant but little-known culture shared by more than five million U.S. citizens, this museum is a must.

Suggested contribution: $2 adults, $1 students and senior citizens; members, and children under 12 accompanied by an adult free.

Open: Wed–Sun 11am–5pm. **Subway:** 6 to 103rd St. **Bus:** M2, M3, or M4 to Madison Ave.

GUGGENHEIM MUSEUM, Fifth Ave. at 89th St. Tel. 860-1300.

Although the Guggenheim doesn't have special children's programs, it is housed in a spectacular spiral building designed by Frank Lloyd Wright. Visitors generally take the elevator to the top floor, then walk downhill in wide circles, viewing artworks along the curved walls. While parents view the museum's collection of avant-garde art dating back to the late 19th century, kids can get a kick out of the building's playful design. No strollers are allowed on the ramp, but there is a place to check them.

Note: At press time, new admission prices and open hours were not yet set as the

museum has been closed for renovation, although it will be open sometime in the spring of 1992. Call for current information.
Subway: 4, 5, 6 to 86th St.

THE JEWISH MUSEUM, at the New-York Historical Society, 170 Central Park West, at 77th St. Tel. 399-3430.
Housing the world's largest collection of Jewish ceremonial art and historical objects, the museum offers some special family programs, usually for children 5 to 12, that focus on current exhibitions or upcoming Jewish holidays. Advance reservations are required, so call ahead to the education department (tel. 860-1863) for schedules and reservations.
Note: The museum will return to its former address (1109 Fifth Avenue) in late 1992.
Admission: $4.50 adults, $3 senior citizens and students, $1 children under 12.
Open: Sun and Tues–Thurs 10am–5pm, Fri 10am–3pm. **Closed:** Major Jewish holidays. **Subway:** 1, 9 to 79th St.; B, C to 81st St.

METROPOLITAN MUSEUM OF ART, Fifth Ave. at 82nd St. Tel. 879-5500 or 535-7710 for recording.
The Met displays, to the eye-opening delight of children, mummies, knights in armor, and a real Egyptian temple, as well as famous paintings. What's more, some of New York's finest street performers use the sidewalk in front of the museum as their stage.
Throughout the year the Met's Uris Center for Education offers family- and child-oriented workshops, gallery talks, discussions, and films. The events are usually an hour long and are presented on Tuesday evenings and weekends January through June, and weekdays only in July and August. Places are given on a first-come, first-served basis, and are free with museum admission. All materials are provided. Also, since family-program schedules vary, we suggest that you call ahead for details (tel. 879-5500; ask for Educational Services, ext. 3308).
Suggested contribution (including workshops): $6 adults, $3 students and senior citizens; members and children under 12 free.
Open: Sun and Tues–Thurs 9:30am–5:15pm, Fri–Sat 9:30am–8:45pm. **Subway:** 4, 5, 6 to 86th St. and walk west. **Bus:** M79 crosstown to Fifth Ave.

MUSEUM OF THE CITY OF NEW YORK, 571 Fifth Ave. at 103rd St. Tel. 534-1672.
To give your children a glimpse of New York City before the invasion of skyscrapers and high-rise apartments, visit the Museum of the City of New York, where slide shows, dioramas, and other exhibits trace the city's history from its founding as a Dutch colony in 1625. While older children may find the historical information here interesting, younger children can take a look at the museum's wonderful doll and dollhouse collection, the largest of its kind in the city. Displays of old fire engines, maps, and toys will also appeal to youngsters.
Suggested admission: $4 adults; $3 children, students, and senior citizens; $6 families.
Open: Wed–Sat 10am–5pm, Sun 1–5pm. **Subway:** 6 to 103rd St. **Bus:** M1, M2, M3, or M4.

HARLEM

MUSEUM OF THE AMERICAN INDIAN, Smithsonian Institution, Broadway at 155th St. Tel. 283-2420.
This museum contains the world's largest and finest collection of artifacts made by the Indians of the Western Hemisphere. Three floors display artifacts that vividly catalog the ceremonies and daily activities of Indian culture. The first and second floors focus on the different North American Indian societies. Children will love seeing the wampum belts, Iroquois silver jewelry and beadwork, Sitting Bull's war club, the feather bonnet worn by Crazy Horse, Hopi kachina dolls, Geronimo's warrior cap and cane, Pomo feather baskets, and Inuit (Eskimo) fur parkas. On the

third floor children will learn about Indian life in South and Central America, Amazonian Indian featherwork, archaeological textiles, ancient Peruvian ceramics, and Taino and wood objects.

Note: At the beginning of 1993, the museum will move to a historic landmark building, the Old U.S. Customs House, located at the lower end of Manhattan. The new facility will be known as the George Gustav Heye Center of the National Museum of the American Indian.

Admission: $3 adults, $2 students and senior citizens; free to members and children under 7.

Open: Tues–Sat 10am–5pm, Sun 1–5pm. **Subway:** B, C to 81st St.; 1, 9 to 79th St.

THE STUDIO MUSEUM IN HARLEM, 144 W. 125th St., between Lenox and Seventh aves. Tel. 864-4500.

This is an elegant museum dedicated to African-American culture and Harlem's vibrant local art. Programs for children—for example, weekend classes in batik, collage, silkscreening, and African masks—are offered throughout the year. Other frequently scheduled events include films and puppet shows about events in African-American history (for example, Rosa Parks and the bus boycott), and concerts, lectures, and readings by nationally known artists and scholars. Activities may cost extra; call for more information.

Admission: $2 adults, $1 children under 12, students, and seniors.

Open: Wed–Fri 10am–5pm, Sat–Sun 1–6pm. **Subway:** A, B, C, D to 125th St.

BROOKLYN, QUEENS & STATEN ISLAND

BROOKLYN CHILDREN'S MUSEUM, 145 Brooklyn Ave., at St. Mark's Ave. in Crown Heights, Brooklyn. Tel. 718/735-4400.

Kids and parents alike will have a ball. The museum—the first and oldest of its kind in the world—is housed in a remarkable $5-million multitiered structure and is a playground of participatory fun. Children enter by crossing a steel-mesh bridge and popping through the museum's entrance—an old-fashioned trolley-car kiosk. Inside they find themselves skittering down the People's Tube—a huge, simulated river with locks, dams, waterwheels, and a turbine that can be worked to make the water level rise or fall. The museum has a greenhouse, where children mix soil and gather seeds to grind into flour in a gristmill. On the more traditional side, the museum rotates exhibits from its collection of more than 20,000 artifacts from ancient China, Egypt, Europe, and colonial America, along with a collection of more than 2,500 rare dolls. New to the museum is the Early Learners Arena, which is a section of activities for children under 5. In addition, the museum offers a number of daily workshops, classes, and films for children; call to find out daily and weekly schedules.

Suggested contribution: $3.

Open: Summer Wed–Mon noon–5pm. Hours may vary in other seasons. **Subway:** 3 or 4 to Kingston Ave. Walk one block west to Brooklyn Ave. and then six short blocks up to Kingston Ave. and St. Mark's Ave. (you'll see Brower Park on the corner).

BROOKLYN MUSEUM, Eastern Parkway and Washington Ave., Brooklyn. Tel. 718/638-5000.

The Brooklyn Museum offers year-round weekend workshops and activities for children and families. "Arty Facts," for children 4 to 12 accompanied by an adult, takes place on Saturday. This workshop's main focus is to get kids involved with the creation of art. All materials are provided free of charge. If you would like your child to learn more about the museum's exhibits while you go off on your own, inquire about the new program called "What's Up?" for children ages 6 to 12. Each Saturday and Sunday the What's Up? group goes through certain galleries of the museum and discusses various aspects and bits of history about art. Both of these programs are free with museum admission. Call for information.

Suggested contribution: $4 adults, $2 students, $1.50 seniors; children under 12 free.
Open: Wed–Sun 10am–5pm. **Subway:** 2, 3, 4 to Eastern Parkway/Brooklyn Museum.

CHASE MANHATTAN DISCOVERY CENTER, 1000 Washington Ave., off Eastern Parkway in Prospect Heights, Brooklyn. Tel. 718/622-4433.

To teach urban youngsters how plants grow in the wild or on farms, the Brooklyn Botanic Garden has opened the Chase Manhattan Discovery Center, with exhibits, games, and self-guided demonstrations. Among the exhibits is a walk-through model of an oak tree with stuffed squirrels, chipmunks, owls, and rabbits nestling in its trunk. The tiny doors in the bark reveal insects and acorns, and the leaves change with the seasons.

Kids can grind wheat into flour, and a picture game will give them a chance to move various vegetables around a supermarket—into the produce section and then onto the shelves. Helping children learn the relationship between plants and food—tomatoes to ketchup, celery to cream of celery soup, corn to microwave popcorn—is one of the main goals of this program. Call the Brooklyn Botanic Garden (tel. 718/622-4433) for more information.
Admission: Free.
Open: Tues–Fri 10am–4pm, Sat–Sun 11am–4pm. **Subway:** 2, 3, 4 to Eastern Parkway/Brooklyn Museum.

NEW YORK AQUARIUM, Coney Island, Brooklyn. Tel. 718/265-FISH.

Sharks! Big ones, and plenty of them . . . dazzling little butterfly fish . . . a colony of comical penguins . . . white whales from the arctic and fearsome piranhas from the tropics. These and nearly 22,000 marine creatures are on display at the New York Aquarium practically on the ocean at Coney Island. Included in the price of admission is a whale- and dolphin-training show, an electric eel demonstration, and various special exhibits and demonstrations. For the kids there is a "Touch-It" exhibit, where you are invited to pick up sea stars and pet the fish. At the new Discovery Cove exhibit, visitors will encounter everything from the world's smallest invertebrates to its largest mammals through dioramas, graphic and photographic displays, push-button demonstrations, and participatory exhibits. For a view of a continuous rocky coastal habitat, bringing together animals from the tips of both poles, visit the new Sea Cliffs exhibit, scheduled to open in 1992. Call for more information on exhibit activities.

Feeding times for the penguins, sharks, seals, and walruses vary, so call 718/265-3400 to catch the feedings.
Admission: $5.75 adults; $2 children 2–12 and seniors; children under 2 free; free Mon–Fri after 2pm.
Open: Mon–Fri 10am–4:45pm; Sat–Sun and summer holidays 10am–5:45pm.
Subway: D, F to West 8th St.; walk down the ramp to Surf Ave.

STATEN ISLAND CHILDREN'S MUSEUM, Snug Harbor Cultural Center, 1000 Richmond Terrace. Tel. 718/448-6557.

This museum occupies a four-story building and offers exhibitions based on themes from the arts, sciences, and humanities; workshops for young children; theater performances; and an activity center, where children can be found learning anything from basket weaving with straws to printmaking on egg cartons. If you happen to be visiting in the spring, don't miss the famed Meadowfair—Snug Harbor's annual spring arts fair. Reservations are required for all workshops and can be made by simply calling the museum.
Admission: $2; children under 2 free.
Open: Tues–Sun 11am–5pm. **Directions:** Take ferry and a free ride on a motorized trolley.

NEW YORK HALL OF SCIENCE, 48th Ave. and 111th St., in Flushing Meadows, Queens. Tel. 718/699-0675.

The museum features over 150 interactive science/technology exhibitions and demonstrations, a planetarium, and an amateur radio station. A recent exhibition was titled "Thrill of the Atom." There is also a giant maze, and keep an eye out for Science Detective Workshops.

Admission: $3.50 adults, $2.50 children and senior citizens; free Wed–Thurs 2–5pm.

Open: Wed–Sun 10am–5pm. **Subway:** 7 to 111th St.–Roosevelt Ave. station, then walk 4 blocks south to the museum.

FOR OLDER CHILDREN

AMERICAN NUMISMATIC SOCIETY, Broadway and 155th St. Tel. 234-3130.

Coin collectors will appreciate this place. It features "The World of Coins," which is a comprehensive exhibit surveying the history of the world's coinage and paper money. Kids will delight in seeing coins made of salt, shells, and beads—and in learning how and why money has made "the world go round" for millennia. There's a computer on hand to provide detailed information on any coin or object in the show.

Admission: Free.

Open: Exhibition room and library Tues–Sat 9am–4:30pm; exhibition room only Sun 1–4pm. **Subway:** 1 to 157th St.

THE CLOISTERS, Fort Tryon Park, Washington Heights. Tel. 923-3700.

The Cloisters offer a welcome respite from the hustle and bustle of midtown Manhattan. This uptown branch of the Metropolitan Museum resembles a medieval monastery in location and appearance—and the park itself is the perfect place for a family picnic.

Suggested contribution: $6 adults, $3.50 students and senior citizens; children under 12 accompanied by an adult free.

Open: Tues–Sun 9:30am–5:15pm. **Subway:** A to 190th St.–Overlook Terrace, then take no. 4 bus or walk through Fort Tryon Park to museum. **Bus:** M4 to Fort Tryon Park–The Cloisters stop.

HISPANIC SOCIETY OF AMERICA, American Indian–Heye Foundation, Broadway at 155th St. Tel. 690-0743.

This place has a small yet lively collection of paintings by El Greco, Velazquez, Goya, and other Hispanic artists. With its terra-cotta floors and high ceilings, the building replicates a small Spanish villa. Walk through the Sorrolla Room, where there is a vivid series of murals painted by Joaquin Sorrolla y Bastida in 1911; the walls burst with scenes of fiesta life in regional Spain.

Admission: Free, but donations accepted.

Open: Tues–Sat 10am–4:30pm, Sun 1–4pm. **Subway:** 1 to 157th St.

OTHER ATTRACTIONS

In addition to the better-known museums, there are smaller, offbeat sights that will appeal to children as well.

BELVEDERE CASTLE, Central Park, 79th St. just south of the Great Lawn. Tel. 772-0210.

You'll see one of the best views of the city from the top of this majestic stone castle. Inside is a National Weather Service station. Kids can make puppets and learn about the park through activities like leaf pressing in the participatory Discovery Chamber. Special Saturday workshops in science and art for children ages 5 to 11 run from 1 to 2:30pm. All workshops are free, although you must make a reservation.

Admission: Free.

Open: Tues–Thurs and Sat–Sun 11am–5pm, Mon and Fri 1–5pm. **Subway:** B, C to 81st St.

FEDERAL RESERVE BANK, 33 Liberty St., between Nassau and William sts. Tel. 720-6130.

For a glimpse of the world of finance, young entrepreneurs will enjoy a visit to the gold vault, the currency-processing department, and an exhibit hall that explains the Federal Reserve's role in the economy. Tour reservations must be made at least 1 week in advance by phone or by mail. To assure yourself a spot, we advise that you call 2 weeks ahead.

Open: Tours by reservation only. **Subway:** 2, 3, 4, 5 to Wall St.

GUINNESS WORLD RECORDS EXHIBIT HALL, Empire State Building, Fifth Ave. and 34th St. Tel. 947-2335.

★ Located in the concourse of the Empire State Building, which gets honorable mention here as the third-tallest building in the world, this exhibit hall holds great appeal for children. Most of the displays are replicas of record holders, including a statue of the world's tallest man (8 feet 11 inches) and a model of the hand with the longest fingernails (uncut from 1952 to 1987).

Admission: $4 adults, $2.75 children 11 and under.

Open: Daily 9am–9pm, with extended hours during peak season. **Subway:** 6 to 33rd St.; B, D, F, N, Q, R to 34th St.

JAMES A. FARLEY POST OFFICE, Eighth Ave. and 33rd St. (across from Penn Station). Tel. 330-3604.

Kids 14 and older can see the U.S. mail at work in the huge Farley Building. One of the nicer buildings in the city, the post office has a two-block-long lobby with a magnificent ceiling. You must make tour arrangements at least 2 weeks in advance. Write to the Communications Department, Room 3023, James A. Farley Building, New York, NY 10199-9461. Tours of nonmechanized facilities also are available for younger children. The post office will send you a letter confirming your reservation—be sure to bring it on the day of the tour. Tours take about 45 minutes.

Admission: Free.

Subway: 1, 2, 3 to 34th St.

ZOOS

BRONX ZOO, Fordham Rd. and Southern Blvd. Tel. 220-5188.

Aside from the myriad animals in imaginative settings, the Bronx Zoo offers a special children's zoo. Conceived as a "participatory" zoo, it's a place where children can assume the behavior, live in the environments, and even don the body parts (fox's "ears," turtle shells) of wild animals, to find out just what it's like to be an animal. There's a prairie dog tunnel that is child-size and a giant rope spiderweb for climbing.

Also not to be missed is the camel ride, and a monorail ride through Wild Asia, where tigers, rhinos, and wild Asian deer roam relatively unconfined in a 38-acre area designed to simulate their natural environment. The zoo's most ambitious project is Jungle World, a one-acre wood- and glass-enclosed habitat in which animals wander more or less freely through a re-created volcanic scrub forest, a mangrove swamp, a lowland evergreen rain forest, and a mountain rain forest.

Admission: Tues–Thurs donation days; Fri–Mon $5.75 adults, $2 children 2–12 and seniors; children under 2 free.

Open: Winter daily 10am–4:30pm; other seasons Mon–Fri 10am–5pm, Sat–Sun and holidays 10am–5:30pm; **Subway:** 2, 5 to Pelham Parkway and proceed west to Bronxdale entrance. **Bus:** Liberty Lines provides express bus service from stops in Manhattan on Madison Ave. (call 652-8400 for schedule and stops); have exact $3.50 fare.

LEHMAN'S CHILDREN'S ZOO, Central Park, off East 66th St. and Fifth Ave. Tel. 408-0271.

This fantasyland features a miniature bridge, a red barn, Noah's Ark, and a sculpted gray whale. The zoo's inhabitants are winsome ducks, rabbits, cows, and goats, plus more exotic critters like ferrets and African Pigmy goats. Call the above number or park information (tel. 360-8111) for special events.

Admission: 10¢.

Open: Daily 10am–4:30pm. **Bus:** M1, M2, M3, or M4.

STATEN ISLAND ZOOLOGICAL PARK AND CHILDREN'S ZOO, 614 Broadway, Staten Island. Tel. 718/442-3100.

An internationally renowned collection of reptiles—including most species of the U.S. rattlesnake—can be found here. The zoo also features a pond, and feedable animals such as goats and sheep.

Admission: $3 adults and children over 12; $2 children 3–11; free to handicapped people and children under 3. Wed 2–4:45pm free.

Open: Daily 10am–4:45pm. **Directions:** Take Verrazano-Narrows Bridge to Staten Island Expressway, to Slosson Ave. exit. Follow Slosson to zoo parking lot at Clove Road. **Bus:** From Staten Island Ferry depot at St. George, take bus 107 to Forest Ave. at Broadway, then walk three blocks up Broadway.

ENTERTAINMENT

Stage lights and grease paint hold a special thrill for children, and New York theaters put on a wide variety of shows throughout the year that are appropriate for young people of all ages. Many productions are participatory, so your children may get a chance to step into the limelight.

For the most current and complete listings, check the *New York Times,* the *New Yorker, New York* magazine, and the *Village Voice.* Below are a few playhouses and other entertainment establishments that regularly feature children's shows.

THE BIG APPLE CIRCUS, Lincoln Center, Broadway between 62nd and 63rd sts. Tel. 391-0760.

The Big Apple Circus is a delightful one-ring circus that performs from October through January, then travels from borough to borough during the spring and summer. Call for schedule.

Admission: $8–$30.

COTTAGE MARIONETTE THEATER, Central Park, near West 81st St. Tel. 988-9093.

If puppets are your child's passion, a visit to the Cottage Marionette Theater is just the thing. Established in 1947, the playhouse presents puppet renditions of many children's classics including *Cinderella, The Magic Flute,* and *Rumpelstiltskin,* from October to May.

Admission: $2.

FOURTH WALL THEATER, 79 E. 4th St., between Second and Third aves. Tel. 254-5060.

This company presents rock-and-roll musicals for kids ages 3 to 13.

Admission: $6 children, $10 adults.

Shows: Sat–Sun 3:30pm. **Closed:** Mid-June to mid-Sept.

THE JAN HUS PLAYHOUSE, 351 E. 74th St., between First and Second aves. Tel. 772-9180.

The Jan Hus Playhouse presents musical comedies for children age 3 and up. *Jack and His Rock 'N' Roll Beanstalk, Pinocchio,* and *Peter Pan Meets the Wicked Wizard* are a few of the musicals offered from September through April. From April through June, the **Funzapoppin Magic Show** takes over. Performances last about an hour.

Admission: $4.50.

Shows: Sun 1 and 2:30pm.

THE LITTLE PEOPLE'S THEATER, Courtyard Playhouse, 39 Grove St., near Seventh Ave. South. Tel. 765-9540.

The Little People's Theater is one of the city's longest-running children's theater groups. From Labor Day till the end of June, it offers *Cinderella* and seven other participatory and comic adaptations of children's classics geared for kids between the ages of 3 and 8. Reservations are a must.

Admission: $6 adults and children.

Shows: Sat–Sun 1:30 and 3pm.

THE MARKET AT CITICORP CENTER, East 53rd St. at Lexington Ave. Tel. 559-2330.

The Market presents a wide range of entertainment for children. Call for schedule.
Admission: Free.
Shows: Sat 11am–noon.

ON STAGE PRODUCTIONS, Hartley House, 413 W. 46th St., near Ninth Ave. Tel. 666-1716.

This company offers, from October to early May, six plays for family audiences. Half the plays are for ages 3 to 12, the rest are for ages 12 and up. Most are original musicals.
Admission: $5 ages 3–12, $8 ages 12 and older, $3 students and seniors.
Shows: Sat 1 and 3:30pm, Sun 3:30pm.

THE PAPER BAG PLAYERS, Symphony Space, 2537 Broadway, at 95th St. Tel. 362-0431.

The Paper Bag Players are a much-praised, award-winning theater group that uses costumes made out of commonplace household items in an hour-long show of madcap musical skits and sketches.
Admission: $11.
Open: Jan–early Mar Sat–Sun 2pm.

THEATER WORKS, Promenade Theatre, at Broadway and 76th St. Tel. 677-5959.

Theater Works has been producing a variety of original, and often topical, plays for children. Offerings such as a musical celebration of the space program, *Footprints on the Moon,* and a musical introduction to Shakespeare, *The Play's the Thing,* have made this company one of the hottest tickets in New York children's theater.
Admission: $9–$15.
Shows: Sept–May Sat–Sun 12:30pm.

13TH STREET REPERTORY COMPANY, 50 W. 13th St., between Fifth and Sixth aves. Tel. 675-6677.

Audience participation is part of the charm here. The company performs *Wiseacre Farms,* a one-hour musical. Reservations are recommended. If you'd like to hold your child's birthday party here, call ahead and the company will set up a special table (cost: $10; you provide the food and decorations).
Admission: $4 adults and children.
Shows: Sat–Sun 1–3pm.

EXCURSIONS

The **Staten Island Ferry** is still the best deal in town, at 50¢ a ride. See "Panoramas," in Section 2, "More Attractions," for details. The **Statue of Liberty Ferry** to Liberty Island leaves from Battery Park (see Section 1, "The Top Attractions"). And last but not least, skip ahead to Section 6, "Organized Tours" to learn about **Circle Line** tour boats that sail completely around Manhattan from Pier 83 at the foot of West 43rd Street.

Glide along a steel tightrope high above the East River for a breathtaking 5 minutes on the **Roosevelt Island Tramway.** For $1.25 each way, you can rise high above it all and arrive almost instantly in Manhattan's newest and nearest commuter community (formerly Welfare Island, once a hospital and prison center), where garbage is collected by vacuum tubes and electric buses replace cars. The tramway departs from 60th Street and Second Avenue, and runs every quarter hour on the quarter hour until after midnight, every 7½ minutes during rush hour. Once on the island, have a stroll around and enjoy the green parks and clean streets.

AN AMUSEMENT PARK

If you feel like getting out of the city for a short day trip, you can go on a safari to the wilds of New Jersey at **Great Adventure,** Jackson, N.J. (tel. 201/928-3500). The

500-acre park has lions, bears, and giraffes that run freely in a natural setting. You can drive your own car through the safari route (windows and doors must be locked) or take a guided bus tour. There's also a big amusement park here, with all the expected rides and attractions.

The safari park is open from 9am to 5pm, but the schedule varies so call ahead. A combined ticket for the safari and amusement park is $23 for adults, and $15 for children 54 inches and under. Admission to the safari park alone is $9. Children under 3 are admitted free.

Great Adventure is about an hour's drive out of the city. By car, take the Jersey Turnpike to Exit 7A and follow signs to I-95 East. Exit at Mount Holly and turn south onto N.J. 537, which takes you to the park.

PARADES, STREET FAIRS, FESTIVALS & EVENTS

Each year New York hosts parades and festivals on a grand scale. The color and hoopla make them great events for kids, so we've sketched out a few time-tested favorites to watch for.

Topping the parade list is the **Macy's Thanksgiving Day Parade**—a must-see pageant of cartoon creatures, decked-out high school bands, mounted horsemen and -women, wonderous flower-bedecked mechanical floats, gigantic helium balloons, and marching celebrities. The parade usually begins around 9am at Central Park West and 72nd Street, and travels down Broadway to Macy's at Herald Square (West 34th Street).

St. Patrick's Day (March 17) is the occasion for the granddaddy of all New York's parades. You'll be surprised by how many Irish accents you hear, but then, everyone's a little bit Irish on St. Paddy's Day. Be prepared for the revelry to get pretty wild. The parade travels up Fifth Avenue from 38th to 86th streets.

Chinatown and Little Italy both have raucous celebrations of their own. The **Chinese New Year,** on the first day of the full moon between January 21 and February 19, is ushered in with a dragon parade and fireworks throughout Chinatown. And right next door to Chinatown is Little Italy, scene of the **Feast of San Gennaro,** in mid-September on Mulberry Street between Spring and Park streets. The feast is like a half-mile-long church fair, with game booths and stalls selling all kinds of Italian food.

Keep in mind that both Chinatown and Little Italy are among the oldest sections of New York, with narrow streets that are usually mobbed by nightfall of the respective celebration days. Those with small children in tow should come early (in the afternoon, if possible) to beat the thickest crowds. Hang onto your wallets and have fun!

Come Easter, the Parks Department holds its annual **Easter Egg Rolling Contest** in Central Park. Check the newspaper for the time and location (other groups hold egg hunts as well, some of which are free).

You Gotta Have Park is another natural classic that Central Park offers kids. For one weekend in mid-May, races, concerts, and games are arranged to support the theme of Central Park as an urban oasis. Throughout the year, call the Parks Department at 360-3444 or 360-1333 for a recording of weekly events.

Staten Island greets ferry riders and other visitors with its annual **Children's Day Fair,** held the first Sunday in June on the museum grounds at 75 Stuyvesant Place, Staten Island (a 5-minute walk from the ferry). A mini-zoo and other exhibits help celebrate such themes as "The World According to Puppets."

Readers of all ages shouldn't miss the biggest merchandizing day in the publishing industry, **New York Is Book Country,** featuring the largest concentration of bookstores in the nation. From bookbinding to book signing, authors, entertainers, and lovers of the printed word fill Fifth Avenue between 48th and 57th streets the third Sunday in September from 11am to 5pm.

A good number to call for information on just about anything happening in the city is the New York Visitors and Convention Bureau (tel. 397-8222).

Christmas is a special time in New York. The stores and streets are as pretty—and busy—as the songs say. The following stores usually have special windows for the holidays, with mechanized puppets and trains that tell a story or theme. Dress warmly, because chances are you'll have to stand in line. And call first to make sure the windows are up.

Lord & Taylor, 425 Fifth Ave., at 38th Street (tel. 391-3344).

Saks, 611 Fifth Ave., at 50th Street (tel. 753-4000).

Macy's, Broadway at 34th Street (tel. 736-5151).

You might also want to stop by the **Metropolitan Museum of Art,** the **Museum of the City of New York,** and **The Cloisters** for their special decorations.

Of course, you shouldn't miss seeing the Christmas tree at **Rockefeller Center** either.

5. SPECIAL-INTEREST SIGHTSEEING

WOODY ALLEN'S NEW YORK

Woody Allen *is* New York for thousands of film-goers, and we can think of no better introduction to the Big Apple than to watch for some of the following locations in his movies and then scout them out on your own.

Manhattan: Allen's picture-postcard opening shots of New York capture all its grime and glamour. That's the Art Deco **Empire Diner** (Tenth Avenue, between 21st and 22nd streets) and the **Washington Square arch** juxtaposed against scenes of Garment District bustle and street construction. The action opens in **Elaine's** (1703 Second Avenue, between 88th and 89th streets), where Allen has been known to drop by for drinks himself. Watch Woody romance Mariel Hemingway with a **carriage ride in Central Park,** and fall in love with Diane Keaton while walking through a moonscape in the **Hayden Planetarium.**

Annie Hall: This time out, Woody's neuroses were caused by his childhood home—under the roller coaster at **Coney Island**—and he keeps dragging poor Diane Keaton to see *The Sorrow and the Pity* at the **Beekman Theatre** (65th Street and Second Avenue). They say their bittersweet good-byes at **Lincoln Center** (Broadway and 65th Street).

Broadway Danny Rose: Have a pastrami on rye in the **Carnegie Deli,** where Woody gathered with his aging Jewish show-biz friends.

And last but not least, you might see Allen in person if you drop into **Michael's Pub,** 211 E. 55th St., between Second and Third avenues, where he sometimes plays clarinet with a Dixieland band on Monday nights.

LITERARY NEW YORK

POE COTTAGE, Grand Concourse, East Kingsbridge Rd. Tel. 881-8900.

The last home of author Edgar Allan Poe was a wood-frame cottage in the Bronx where he wrote "Annabel Lee," "The Bells," and "Eureka." Built in 1812 and opened

IMPRESSIONS

"Chapter One. He adored New York City. He idolized it all out of proportion. . . . To him, no matter what the season was, this was still a town that existed in black and white and pulsated to the great tunes of George Gershwin."
—WOODY ALLEN, MANHATTAN

as a museum in 1917, it is a memorial to Poe. Group tours are available by appointment.

Admission: $1 adults; children under 12 free.

Open: Wed–Fri 9am–5pm; Sat 10am–4pm; Sun 1–5pm. **Subway:** 4 to Kingsbridge station.

WASHINGTON SQUARE, Greenwich Village.

Henry James was born at 21 Washington Place, just east of the park. You may remember that his heroine Catherine Sloper lived in one of the town houses on the square.

Subway: A, B, C, D, E, F, Q to West 4th St./Washington Square.

MILLAY HOUSE, 75 Bedford St.

Edna St. Vincent Millay lived in this tiny town house briefly before moving to upstate New York. She caused a sensation in the Village literary and social circuit, and for many, she symbolizes this neighborhood's old bohemian spirit.

Subway: 1, 9 to Sheridan Sq.

THE WHITE HORSE TAVERN, at the corner of Hudson and 11th sts. Tel. 243-9260.

The White Horse will be forever known as the place where Dylan Thomas literally drank himself to death (although he actually expired at nearby St. Vincent's Hospital).

Subway: 1, 9 to Sheridan Sq.

THE ALGONQUIN HOTEL, 50 W. 44th St. Tel. 840-6800.

Stop in at the Oak Room for a drink and you'll be treading in the footsteps of the legendary Round Table members—James Thurber, George Kaufman, Robert Benchley, and of course the inimitable and formidable Dorothy Parker. The Algonquin still has a clubby, literary atmosphere.

Subway: 1, 2, 3, 9, D, E, F, N, R to 42nd St.

THE CHELSEA HOTEL, 222 W. 23rd St. Tel. 243-3700.

Tennessee Williams, Dylan Thomas, Mark Twain (and Sid and Nancy)—they've all been here. Several notable books have been penned here, from Thomas Wolfe's *You Can't Go Home Again* to Arthur Clarke's *2001*.

Subway: 1, 9 to 23rd St.

6. ORGANIZED TOURS

BY BOAT

THE CIRCLE LINE

One of the best ways to view New York's famous skyline, bridges, and other architectural marvels is via a rivergoing trip on one of the **Circle Line** boats. The 3-hour, 35-mile trip takes you on a cruise down the Hudson River, past the Statue of Liberty, across the lower harbor of Manhattan, under the Brooklyn Bridge, then up the East River past the U.N., across the Harlem River, under the George Washington Bridge, and back down the Hudson again. Along the way, a trained guide comments over a loudspeaker on the sights you pass.

Circle Line boats leave from Pier 83, at the foot of West 43rd Street (on the Hudson River). Boats begin operating in mid-March and continue through November. From mid-June to the first week of September boats depart about once an hour, beginning at 9:30am. Call first to check the exact schedule and to inquire about Harbor Lights Evening Cruises at 563-3200. Fare is $16 adults, $8 for children under 12.

THE TNT EXPR

If you're pressed for time and want a quicker rive
TNT Express. This 82-foot Catamaran glides thro
up to 29 knots and offers a 1-hour narrated tour o
Express departs from Pier 11, two blocks south of
Wall Street. It travels north up the East River to
around, heads back down the river, and glides pas
World Financial Center, and Governor's Island be

The TNT Express departs Monday through Sat
$15 for adults, $13 for senior citizens, $8 for child
under 5. For more information, call 201/CAT-RI

and give you far more in
from other tours. Yo
Bronx, Queens, a
Manhattan. The
hoods and ex
groups all
prices an
Tal
Ne
F

BY TROLLE

One of the newest and most innovative tours starts
and goes to Battery Park, the World Trade Center, the World Financial District, City
Hall, Chinatown, Little Italy, and to various spots on the Lower East Side. The
Manhattan Neighborhood Trolley seats 35 and is designed to look like the
trolleys used in Manhattan in the 19th century. Because you're allowed to get out
wherever you want, wander around, and get back on later, you can turn this into a
full-day excursion.

You can buy a full-day pass ($4) in front of Pier 17, at the corner of South and
Fulton streets. Trolleys leave every hour on the hour from noon to 4pm on weekends
and holidays, and the last one returns to the Seaport at 5pm. When you purchase your
pass, pick up a map and guide of the neighborhoods you'll be visiting. For more
information, call 677-7268.

BY HELICOPTER

New York Helicopter can provide you with the sightseeing experience of a lifetime,
if you're willing to make a big splurge, with thrilling closeup views of major
skyscrapers. All sightseeing flights originate from the Heliport at the foot of East 34th
Street on the East River. Call 683-4575 for information.

ARCHITECTURAL & OTHER TOURS

For students of architecture, New York is a wonderland. From the very old to the very
latest, it offers more variety of styles, forms, and types than probably any other New
World city. From the fanciful New York Yacht Club at 37 West 44th Street, off Fifth
Avenue, and the Italian Renaissance Villard Houses on Madison Avenue between
50th and 51st streets, to the cast-iron warehouses of SoHo, you'll find treasures
throughout the city. Find out what's happening in architecture in the city by reading
Paul Goldberger's frequent columns in the *New York Times,* or consult his *The City
Observed,* which is a guide to the architecture of New York. For the best walking tour
of cast-iron buildings in SoHo and TriBeCa, pick up the book by Friends of Cast-Iron
Architecture, available at the Okay Harris Gallery on West Broadway near Grand
Street.

The real story of the buildings and neighborhoods you'll see is the lives of the
people who've lived there. For that, you might want to turn to Jeff Kisseloff's book
*You Must Remember This: An Oral History of Manhattan from the 1890s to
World War II*—a fascinating neighborhood-by-neighborhood portrait of the city by
the people who lived in the first half of this century.

The **Municipal Art Society** (tel. 935-3960) offers a tour series that includes
weekend walks through architectural areas of the city. Recent tours included
"Tompkins Square Park," "Chinatown," and "Gardens of the Upper West Side."
Guided walks are $12 for nonmembers and take place on Saturday and Sunday every
week. Every Wednesday there's a free tour of Grand Central Terminal at 12:30pm.

Our favorite guided tours of New York are offered by the Graduate Department of
Urban Planning at Hunter College. **Planners' New York Tours** take you to the
more unlikely areas for tourists—New York's neighborhoods and outer boroughs—

...sight into the social reality of the city than you're likely to get ...will be taken by bus to such places as East Harlem, the South ...Brooklyn, as well as the more frequented neighborhoods of ...guides will tell you the urban-planning histories of various neighbor- ...plain the challenges they are facing in the 1990s. Tours are given to ...ear round and last from 2 to 6 hours. Call 772-5605 for the most recent ...scheduling assistance.

...a "historywalk" with **Joyce Gold,** who teaches Manhattan history at the ...School for Social Research and New York University, and gives tours of the ...nancial District, Greenwich Village, Chelsea, the Lower East Side, and the East Village most Sundays each spring, summer, and fall for $10. She is also available to give private tours to individuals or groups, and for $6.20 will mail you one of her books, which offer self-guided tours to Greenwich Village or the Financial District. Call or write to Joyce Gold, 141 W. 17th St., New York, NY 10011 (tel. 242-5762).

The **Museum of the City of New York** offers walking tours in all five boroughs with an emphasis on the architectural wonders of the city and the personal-interest stories of the people who made the Big Apple what it is today. Tours run in the spring and fall on Sunday and cost $15 for nonmembers. For details, call 534-1672.

The guides from the **92nd Street Y** tours are experts in their fields and offer everything from walking tours of gourmet eating places, artists' studios, or the political history of New York, to a Valentine's Day tour that takes you to the house where Marilyn Monroe lived and the residence where Valentino began his womanizing career. The Y specializes in "theme tours," and they do everything imaginable in this city that offers the most unimaginable things. Celebrate Independence Day by taking an all-night tour, including an escort by a fife-and-drum band and a visit to the mayor's office, or take a tour on roller skates or a bicycle. Tours are given most Sundays and often midweek, and are well worth the $15 to $20 fee. For more information, write or call The 92nd Street Y, 1395 Lexington Avenue, New York, NY 10128 (tel. 427-6000, ext. 599).

Twenty-one special tours, lasting anywhere from 2 to 9 hours, are offered by **Gray Line** (tel. 397-2600). We once enjoyed a terrific Discovery Tour of Brooklyn, which went through Russian, Middle Eastern, Italian, and Caribbean neighborhoods, with stops at such famous sites as the Brooklyn Promenade, the Brooklyn Museum, and the Williamsburg Bank Tower. Most major hotels have brochures available from Gray Line outlining their complete range of offerings (and there's a morning courtesy pick-up bus from many hotels). Reservations are not needed for most tours; you can just show up 30 minutes before departure at one of the two terminals: 166 W. 46th St., near Seventh Avenue, or 900 Eighth Avenue, between 53rd and 54th streets. Prices begin at $14.75 for adults, with reduced rates available for children.

Additional special-interest tours are offered by **Sidewalks of New York**— ranging from Famous Murder Sites, a tour of "haunted" sites in the Village, and an organized visit to old-time Village taverns. Prices begin at $10, and you can check *New York* magazine for current offerings. Call 517-0201 for more information.

GUIDED TOURS OF HARLEM

Call 722-9534 for information on **Harlem Renaissance Tours,** departing from Gray Line's Eighth Avenue terminal (see above). The Sunday gospel tour, at $31, is especially popular.

Harlem Spirituals, Inc., 1697 Broadway (tel. 302-2594), offers several packages to introduce you to the neighborhood, from the $27 "Harlem on Sunday" tour to the $65 "Soul Food and Jazz Tour."

NATURE WALKS

You may not have come to the city to find nature, but the **Urban Park Rangers** offer interesting tours in all five boroughs of the more than 500 parks in the area. For instance, in Manhattan's Central Park the rangers might take you on an early-morning wildlife walk with sightings of rabbits, raccoons, and all kinds of native birds.

Occasionally they also have a geology tour of glacial periods and rocks, history tours, and landscape design tours. In Brooklyn, the rangers have fashioned a nature trail at Marine Park, a chance to see the salt marshes and wetlands of an undeveloped area. They also give a "mounted tour" of Prospect Park—on horseback—which requires reservations up to 2 weeks in advance. All the rangers' tours are offered year round, usually on weekends; best yet, most are free. Phone the ranger office for more information at 427-4040.

Pick your own wild food with **"Wildman" Steve Brill,** who is an expert on the identification, collection, and use of the hundreds of vegetables, berries, fruits, nuts, herbs, seeds, and mushrooms that you can find—where you least expect them—in the city's parks. Mr. Brill offers leisurely 4-hour walks, with a stop for lunch, on Saturday and Sunday, March to December, and you can stuff yourself with such delights as black raspberries, cherries, and mulberries, or take home a load of gourmet mushrooms and wild spinach. These charming and educational walks will enchant anyone who has looked at a field of greenery and seen only grass. Call or write to "Wildman" Steve Brill, 143-25 84th Drive, no. 6C, Jamaica, NY 11435 (tel. 718/291-6825). Mr. Brill, a Parks Department naturalist, is also available for private groups.

BEHIND-THE-SCENES TOURS

"Exploring the world within our reach . . . within our means" is the motto of **Adventure on a Shoestring,** a 26-year-old organization that arranges near-daily group visits to the unique places and people that make New York the exciting city it is. The group has some 2,000 members who share a desire to explore the city's more offbeat and least-explored treasures. In recent years shoestringers have toured a factory that manufactures models of Rudolph ("the Red-nosed Reindeer") and the Easter Bunny, gone backstage at the Metropolitan Opera House, and visited a subway training school. They have met with a vampire researcher, a Broadway playwright, a famous New York novelist, a lie-detection expert, an acclaimed watercolor artist, and a professional hypnotist who trained Mike Tyson.

For a free brochure describing the dozens of novel, low-cost adventures, write Shoestring at 300 W. 53rd St., New York, NY 10019 (tel. 265-2663).

Theater lovers can take a unique, 1-hour backstage tour of a Broadway theater through the graces of a group called **Backstage on Broadway.** The tours are led by Broadway stage managers, directors, lighting designers, and even leading actors and actresses, depending on availability. You'll see how a show is put together, from the hanging of the scenery to the blocking of the stage. Tours are usually scheduled for Monday through Saturday at 10:30am, and advance reservations by phone only are essential—tours fill fast. For reservations, call 575-8065. For information, write Backstage on Broadway, Suite 344, 228 W. 47th St., New York, NY 10036.

7. SPORTS & RECREATION

SPECTATOR SPORTS
BASEBALL

Baseball took over from horseracing as New York's most popular spectator sport in 1986 when the **New York Mets** won the World Series. You can see the Mets at Shea Stadium in Queens, where they play from April to October. Tickets start at $6, and the box office opens two hours before game time. Call 718/507-8499 for ticket information. You can reach Shea Stadium by taking the no. 7 IRT-Flushing train to the Shea Stadium stop.

American League fans can catch the **New York Yankees** at Yankee Stadium in the Bronx (tel. 293-6000). The Bronx Bombers are guaranteed to entertain the fans. Tickets start at $4.50 for bleacher seats and go on sale 2 hours before the game. Box seats are on sale at the stadium ticket office. To reach Yankee Stadium, take the Sixth Avenue D train or the Lexington Avenue 4 train (marked "Woodlawn") to the Yankee Stadium stop.

BASKETBALL

For basketball fans, New York is a great town. Professionally, the **New York Knickerbockers** (the Knicks) play at Madison Square Garden from November through April (tel. 465-6741). Patrick Ewing and company have established themselves as a force to be reckoned with in the 1990s. Tickets, which are hard to come by, start at $15. Reach the Garden by taking the IRT Seventh Avenue no. 1, 2, or 3 train to the 34th Street–Pennsylvania Station stop.

The **New Jersey Nets** play at the Brendan Byrne Arena at the Meadowlands Sports Complex, East Rutherford, N.J. (tel. 201/935-8888). Ticket prices start at $6. The arena is only a short bus trip from the Port Authority Bus Terminal (at Eighth Avenue and 42nd Street), and special buses run regularly on game nights.

On the college level, Madison Square Garden is also the home of the famous postseason **N.I.T.** collegiate tournaments. The tournaments are held in November and March and attract top college teams from around the nation. Call the Garden for ticket information.

BOXING

Madison Square Garden stages pro boxing bouts twice a month on Thursday nights and occasionally a championship fight. The Felt Forum, a part of the Garden sports complex, also hosts the annual Golden Gloves amateur tournament, held in March or April. Phone 465-6741 for details on upcoming matches.

FOOTBALL

The **New York Jets** are still nominally New York's home team even though they've left (some say deserted) Shea Stadium for the newer Giants Stadium in the Meadowlands Sports Complex across the river in New Jersey (tel. 201/935-8222). The Jets, who play from September to December, have plenty of company, as the **New York Giants** also play there. Tickets for the Jets start at $22.50, and those for the Giants at $23, but they're hard to come by in the former case and nearly impossible in the latter, because of all the season-ticket holders. Tickets for preseason games in August are easier to get.

HOCKEY

The competition between the **Islanders** and the **Rangers** makes New York a great place for rabid hockey fans. See the Rangers at Madison Square Garden (tel. 465-6741), with tickets starting at $11. The Islanders skate at the Nassau Coliseum, Hempstead Turnpike, Uniondale, N.Y. (tel. 516/587-9222), where tickets start at $10. To reach the Coliseum, take the Long Island Rail Road from Penn Station to Hempstead, and then take a bus from there (ask at the Hempstead station for directions to the bus), or take the train to Westbury and a taxi to the Coliseum.

HORSERACING

New York's second most popular spectator sport is available year round. **Belmont Park,** Hempstead Turnpike and Plainfield Avenue, Elmont, N.Y. (tel. 718/641-4700), races thoroughbreds from May through July and September through mid-October. The Long Island Rail Road goes to Belmont from Penn Station.

Aqueduct Racetrack, Rockaway Boulevard at 108th Street, Jamaica, Queens (tel. 718/641-4700), presents thoroughbred racing from mid-October through May.

The **Meadowlands Racetrack,** in East Rutherford, N.J. (tel. 201/935-8500), also races thoroughbreds from September through mid-December and presents trotters late December through August, plus simulcasts from other tracks year round.

Yonkers Raceway, in Yonkers, N.Y. (tel. 914/968-4200), races trotters year round, plus carries the simulcast from the various New York tracks during the day.

Most of the tracks have special bus service from the Port Authority Bus Terminal, 42nd Street and Eighth Avenue in Manhattan. For Aqueduct, take the Eighth Avenue A train to the Aqueduct station.

TENNIS

The annual **U.S. Open Championship** is played at the National Tennis Center at Flushing Meadow Park every fall during early September. The center can be reached by taking the IRT Flushing line (no. 7 train) to the Shea Stadium stop. For ticket information, call 718/271-5100.

WRESTLING

You can catch Hulk Hogan and "Rowdy" Roddy Piper in action at **Madison Square Garden** (tel. 465-6741). Ticket prices start at $9.

RECREATION

BEACHES

World-famous **Coney Island** on Brooklyn's Atlantic coast has a sandy beach more than seven miles long and a welter of other attractions: roller coasters, carnival attractions, Ferris wheels, and loop-the-loops. On a fine summer Sunday the air is overburdened with cries, laughter, and music while the smell of hot dogs and sticky cotton candy pervades the air, and rows of bodies are stretched out on the sand. Yet for all its continued popularity, Coney Island is in a rundown area, certainly safe by day because of the enormous crowds in season, but best avoided by night.

The beaches at Coney Island are free. To get there, take the Sixth Avenue B, D, or F train, or the BMT N line, to the last stop in Brooklyn, Stillwell Avenue.

If you are taking a day at the beach, be sure to stop in at **Astroland Amusement Park,** which towers above the boardwalk and the beach. The **New York Aquarium** is nearby (see Section 4, "Cool for Kids," above, for details).

Just east of Coney Island is **Brighton Beach.** The beach is the same but the atmosphere is a little less frenetic and the crowds a little smaller. Also, thanks to the recent wave of Soviet immigrants, you will hear more Russian and see more Russian eateries in a few blocks of Brighton than just about anywhere outside of Russia (see Chapter 6, Section 14, "Specialty Dining"). Take the Sixth Avenue D or Q train to the Brighton Beach stop.

Beyond the city limits, but worth a visit, is **Jones Beach State Park.** In addition to a beautiful series of beaches, there are tennis courts, heated pools, outdoor roller-skating rinks, and fishing. You can get there on the Long Island Rail Road, which leaves from Pennsylvania Station and connects with a shuttle bus at the Freeport, Long Island, station. The railroad offers a special day-trip ticket for $8.50 for adults, and $5 for children. The ticket covers round-trip rail and bus transportation. For details, call 718/454-5477.

BICYCLING

Central Park's roadways are closed to cars on weekends throughout the year so that pedalers can make their way through the park unhindered. Biking hours are 8pm Friday to 6am Monday. The park is also closed to cars on weekdays from early April to early November, from 10am to 3pm and 7 to 10pm.

You can rent a bike at the **Loeb Boathouse,** Park Drive North at 72nd Street (tel. 861-4137), for $7.50 per hour or $30 for the whole day. If you go a few blocks away from the park, you can rent a bike for about $6 an hour ($7.50 an hour for a 10-speed) at **West Side Bicycle Store,** 231 West 96th Street, at Broadway (tel. 663-7531); **Metro Bicycles,** 1311 Lexington Avenue, at 88th Street (tel. 427-4450); or **Gene's Bicycles,** 242 East 79th Street, at Second Avenue (tel. 249-9218), where after the first 3½ hours, the rest of the day is free. All the above businesses require identification and/or a substantial deposit. Call for details.

From early spring until well into the fall, **American Youth Hostels,** 75 Spring Street, between Broadway and Lafayette Street (tel. 431-7100), organizes weekly bicycle tours of the city and outlying areas. The tours are led by an experienced leader and are a great way to see the city. Call AYH for details and a schedule.

BILLIARDS & POOL

We like **Chelsea Billiards,** 54 W. 21st St. (tel. 989-0096), and the **Amsterdam Billiard Club,** 344 Amsterdam Ave., near 76th Street (tel. 496-8180). **Society Billiards,** 10 E. 21st St. (tel. 529-8600), is an especially elegant spot, located below glamorous Café Society.

BOATING

Rent a rowboat at Central Park's **Loeb Boathouse,** Park Drive North at 72nd Street (tel. 517-4723). From April until winter, you can drift along the lake and enjoy the beauty of Central Park from the water. It's only $6 an hour, but you must leave a $20 deposit. Open 7 days a week beginning in April (and until the weather becomes prohibitive) daily from 11:30am to 6pm.

If you prefer sailing on a 70-foot yawl, the **Petrel,** which is the fastest sailboat in New York Harbor, sails from the southeast corner of Battery Park (tel. 825-1977), near the Statue of Liberty excursion lines. Prices range from $8 for 45 minutes to $20 for 2 hours. It is open from April through October.

BOWLING

New York used to have more than 30 bowling lanes but now just a few remain. **Bowlmor Lanes,** 110 University Place, between 12th and 13th streets (tel. 255-8188), has 44 lanes and is open Sunday through Thursday from 10am to 1am and on Friday and Saturday until 4am. A game costs $3 and shoe rental is $1.

CHESS

Have a grandmaster in your family? The **Manhattan Chess Club,** on the tenth floor of Carnegie Hall, 154 West 57th Street, at Seventh Avenue (tel. 333-5888), was established in 1877 and is one of the oldest chess clubs in the world. Bobby Fischer, among other chess stars, has played here. Your child can play chess all day for $5. Open daily from noon to 10pm.

If you want to while away an afternoon over a chess game, you can play for $1.50 an hour at the **Chess Shop,** 230 Thompson Street, at West 3rd Street (tel. 475-9580). They're open daily from noon to midnight.

HORSEBACK RIDING

The **Claremont Riding Academy,** 175 West 89th Street, between Columbus and Amsterdam avenues (tel. 724-5100), will provide you with a horse for cantering on the nearby Central Park bridle path. The cost is $30 an hour and you must be experienced riding in an English saddle. They also give riding lessons. Private lessons are $32 a half hour; group lessons, $32 an hour. It's open 7 days a week: from 6:30am to 10pm weekdays and from 8am to 5pm on weekends. Reservations are recommended for weekend rides.

ICE SKATING

A winter tradition is a whirl around the ice at the **Rockefeller Center Ice-Skating Rink** (tel. 757-5731). Few things are as enjoyable as skating around the giant

Rockefeller Center Christmas tree on a brisk winter's evening. Sessions cost from $7 to $9, plus $4 for skate rental. The rink is open from October through April.

Indoor ice skating is available year round at the **Sky Rink**—billed as the world's highest rink—located on the 16th floor at 450 W. 33rd St., between Ninth and Tenth avenues (tel. 695-6555). The rink has afternoon and evening sessions for children and adults; call for the exact schedule. Admission is $7.50, plus $2.50 for skate rental.

The newly renovated **Wollman Rink** at 63rd Street and East Drive in Central Park is open from November to early April. Admission is $5 for adults and $2 for children, plus $2.50 for skate rental. The rink is open daily. Call 517-4800 for hours.

The Lasker Memorial Rink, also in Central Park at 107th street near Lenox Avenue (tel. 996-1184), is an outdoor rink that doubles as a swimming pool in the summer. The winter season is from mid-November through early March. Admission is $1 for children, $2 for adults on weekdays; $2.50 for skate rental. Open Sunday and Tuesday through Thursday from 11am to 9:30pm, on Monday until 5pm, and on Friday and Saturday until 11pm.

KITE FLYING

The best place in Central Park to fly kites is in the **Sheep Meadow,** opposite the West 67th Street entrance to the park (also a good place to spread a blanket and relax).

For an unusual kite, try **Big City Kite Company,** at 1201 Lexington Avenue, between 81st and 82nd streets (tel. 472-2623). Prices start at $5 and fly all the way up to $550.

MODEL BOAT SAILING

Conservatory Lake, in Central Park at 72nd Street and Fifth Avenue, is the place to launch your model boat. You'll see some serious sailors and sailboats here, and as many adults as children. Races are held every Saturday beginning March 21 from 10am on.

PICNICS

On a warm, sunny day, a picnic is a special delight in the city, and it's as easy as picking up sandwiches and spreading a blanket. Central Park, of course, is just about the best place to go to stretch out, sunbathe, and let your kids run. In addition to the hot-dog vendors and orange-juice squeezers on most street corners, there are summertime kiosks at the **Bethesda Fountain** in Central Park at 72nd Street, where you can buy franks, sausages, drinks, and other snacks. More expensive are the special picnics-to-go that you can pick up at the **Tavern on the Green Restaurant,** 67th Street and Central Park West (tel. 873-3200), and other elegant eateries on the Upper East and West sides.

On the West Side, you'll find a nice little park for lunch or a rest stop on **West 50th Street** between the Avenue of the Americas and Seventh Avenue, not far from Radio City Music Hall. The park has white patio chairs and tables, a fountain, and a bronze life-like sculpture of a teenage boy reading a book on fishing. It's so realistic that you can read about angling over his right shoulder, but don't ask him to share the hamburger he also holds!

Another serene haven in the heart of the city is **Paley Park.** Located a few steps east of Fifth Avenue on 53rd Street, it is a tiny oasis about the size of a tennis court. High brick walls on three sides, vaulting honey locust trees, ivy, and pots of begonias shield you from the city's bustle. You can dine al fresco at patio tables, and there's a refreshment stand for light snacks. The park is open from 8am to 8pm Monday through Saturday.

There are numerous **city-sponsored playgrounds,** but one of the roomiest and most pleasant is on First Avenue between 67th and 68th streets. It has safety swings, mini-theaters, and a log mountain with a giant slide. There's also a toddler area with a smaller slide and sand to play in. There are lots of tall trees and shaded benches. The park closes at dusk.

RUNNING

Contact the **New York Road Runners Club,** 9 East 89th Street, between Fifth and Madison avenues (tel. 860-4455), for information concerning evening group runs in Central Park and races ranging from short runs through Central Park to full-fledged marathons. (The Road Runners sponsor the annual New York City Marathon in November.)

SKIING

If it's the middle of winter, and you're longing to be outside cross-country skiing, there are a number of ski areas within a few hours of the city. The **Fairview Lake Touring Center** in Newton, N.J., has 12 miles of groomed trails. Trail fee is $5 for adults and $3 for children. Rental equipment is available. Call 201/383-9282 for information and directions.

The **White Memorial Foundation** in Litchfield, Connecticut, is a 4,000-acre wildlife sanctuary with 30 miles of old carriage roads and nature trails running through it. The skiing is free, but there are no rentals on site. However, you can rent skis in the city at Eastern Mountain Sport, 611 Broadway at Houston Street (tel. 505-9860).

SWIMMING

If you're willing to pay to leave the crowds behind, swim at the **Sheraton City Squire Hotel,** 790 Seventh Avenue, between 51st and 52nd streets (tel. 581-3300). The pool, located on the fifth floor, is open to nonguests Monday through Friday from 6:30am to 7:45pm and on weekends from 7:30am to 7:45pm. Fees run upward from $15, with children under 12 half price. Towels and comfortable locker facilities are included, and you can stay all day if you wish. The pool is moderate-sized, with glass walls on three sides.

Otherwise, the city has several public pools. Fees are minimal and they open generally from the first week in July until Labor Day.

At the **West 59th Street Pool,** 533 West 59th Street (tel. 397-3159), facilities include an indoor pool open during the winter, a gymnasium with weight room, a handball court, and a small basketball court. It is open from 11am to 7pm. Admission is free, but you must bring a padlock and towel. Take the Broadway/Seventh Avenue 1 or 9 train, the Sixth Avenue B or D, or the Eighth Avenue A or C train to Columbus Circle.

John Jay Pool, East 77th Street and Cherokee Place, one block east of York Avenue (tel. 397-3177), is usually the busiest pool in Manhattan, with a view of the East River for sunbathers. Open from 11am to 7pm 7 days a week. Admission is free. Take the Lexington Avenue 6 train to 77th Street and Lexington Avenue. Transfer to the crosstown bus on 79th Street going east.

East 54th Street Pool, 54th Street between First and Second avenues (tel. 397-3148), is an indoor pool, open year round, Monday through Friday from 3pm to 10pm and on Saturday from 10am to 5pm. Bring a lock and a towel. There is a $2 yearly fee.

CHAPTER 8

STROLLING AROUND NEW YORK CITY

1. DOWNTOWN & THE FINANCIAL DISTRICT

2. CHINATOWN & LITTLE ITALY

3. SOHO & THE CAST-IRON DISTRICT

4. GREENWICH VILLAGE

5. TIMES SQUARE & 42ND STREET, EAST & WEST

6. MIDTOWN & FIFTH AVENUE

7. UPPER WEST SIDE

8. UPPER EAST SIDE HISTORIC DISTRICT

To us, the most fascinating free activity in New York is to walk through some of Manhattan's interesting areas.

Walking is one of the very best ways to get to know the city—to see the famous sights, enjoy architecture, explore unusual shops, observe the people, and simply to soak up the ambience of such fabled neighborhoods as Greenwich Village, SoHo, the refurbished Columbus Avenue area on the Upper West Side, and, of course, Chinatown and Little Italy downtown.

The walking tours below cover all these areas as well as the downtown section where New York's history began, the elegant midtown shopping area, the East Side, and last, but not least, Times Square and the theater district.

Put on a pair of comfortable shoes and let's begin.

WALKING TOUR 1 — Downtown & the Financial District

Start: Broadway and Chambers Street (half the subways in Manhattan must stop within a block or so of this intersection)
Finish: Bowling Green (adjacent to the Lexington Avenue IRT station)
Time: About 1¼ hours.

Start at Broadway and Chambers Street, the upper corner of which is:

1. **City Hall Park,** a 250-year-old greensward surrounded by landmark buildings. Before you go anywhere, look east on Chambers Street toward the **Municipal Building.** It's that slightly Stalinesque wedding cake straddling Chambers Street on the other side of the park. This is really the best vantage point for admiring McKim, Mead, and White's monumental city office complex built in 1914. It cleverly utilizes an awkward site and combines functionalism with beauty in a manner too often forgotten by modern architects. The statue at the very pinnacle

of the thing represents *Civic Fame,* whatever that might be. Certainly she (he?) is high enough to overlook the corruption that has historically plagued this region of Manhattan.

Those interested in Beaux Arts architecture should walk east on Chambers Street to the end of the block. At 31 Chambers St., at the corner of Park Row and just across the street from the Municipal Building, is:

2. **New York's Surrogates Court,** a Frenchified palace built in 1911. The stupendous marble lobby of this place is surely worth a look. Here is a public building built to impress, not merely to drag along with the drab duties of civic life.

Now turn around and retrace your steps along Chambers Street back in the direction of Broadway. Just inside City Hall Park on your left is the:

3. **Tweed Courthouse,** that dull-gray and capacious old 1872 Italianate building. Actually, it is officially called the New York City Courthouse. But William Marcy ("Boss") Tweed, during whose tenure on the Board of Supervisors it was built, stole so much of its construction funds that it has evermore borne his name. When the cornerstone was laid in 1861, the city had budgeted $250,000 for its construction. By the time it was finished 10 years later, the total cost had approached $14 million. Tweed and his cronies induced every subcontractor to present padded bills. For example, one Andrew Garvey, subsequently known in the press as the "Prince of Plasterers," was paid $45,966.89 by the city for a single day's work. An estimated $10 million went into the pockets of Tweed and his pals. The ensuing scandal would eventually end Tweed's career. He died in jail 4 years later, without a penny to his name.

When you reach Broadway again, turn left and continue south for two blocks to Murray Street. Now we're going to enter City Hall Park and head for the front door of:

4. **City Hall,** which faces the parking area in the middle of the park, about on the line of Murray Street. In what historian T. A. Janvier termed a "shrewd thrust of prophetic sarcasm," New York City originally housed both convicted felons and city officials in the same building down on Wall Street. The present City Hall is a rather fragile-looking gem, considering the hardball that's been played here since 1811. The design is clearly 18th century, an amalgam of French and British antecedents cooked up as part of a city-sponsored contest. The winning architects were Joseph Mangin, a Frenchman who had worked in Paris on the Place de la Concorde, and a Scot by the name of John McComb. When completed in 1811, this was practically the northernmost structure in town. As a result the rear wall was faced with brownstone (cheaper than the limestone used on the rest of the place) on the theory that since hardly anybody would see it, why not save the money? In subsequent years the brownstone was replaced. Parts of City Hall are open to the public on weekdays from 10am to 4pm. It's a beautiful place, but one constantly wonders how such a big city can be managed from such a small city hall.

Before leaving City Hall, stop for a moment on the steps to admire the:

5. **Brooklyn Bridge,** built in 1883. Looming impressively in the east, it was the world's first steel suspension bridge. It's possible, if you are so inclined, to walk all the way across it to Brooklyn. The walkway is free, and the views are truly superb. Let's leave it for another day's excursion, however, and continue with our tour.

Return now to Broadway at Murray Street, noting the:

6. **Statue of Nathan Hale,** by Frederick MacMonnie, located just inside the park opposite Murray Street. Noble, isn't it? (Guess who designed the base? Stanford White.) Turn left on Broadway and continue south for one block to Park Place. On the west side of Broadway, occupying the block between Park Place and Barclay Street, is the:

7. **Woolworth Building.** Five-and-dime czar Frank W. Woolworth ponied up $13.5 million in cash back in 1913 to pay for his new headquarters. During the opening ceremonies President Woodrow Wilson himself pressed a button in

Washington that illuminated 80,000 bulbs in the tower. The Rev. S. Parkes Cadman, witnessing the scene, declared the building to be a "Cathedral of Commerce," the sight of which provoked "feelings too deep even for tears." For 17 years this architectural marriage of Gothic Europe and the American skyscraper was the tallest building in the world. It still ranks as one of New York's handsomest. By all means, go inside the lobby. With its marble walls and domed ceiling it's certainly as ornate as most cathedrals.

Leave the Woolworth Building and pause for a moment on the sidewalk outside. The other side of City Hall Park is bounded by a street called:

 8. Park Row, which, in the early years of this century, contained the offices of 12 New York City newspapers. In those days the area now containing the approaches to the Brooklyn Bridge was known as Printing House Square. Today the entire industry has scattered to various other parts of town.

Go another block down Broadway from the Woolworth Building, past Barclay Street, to Vesey Street. On your right, occupying the western blockfront of Broadway between Vesey and Fulton streets, is:

 9. St. Paul's Chapel. This delicious old Georgian church dates from 1766, although the steeple wasn't added until 1794, after the Revolution. George Washington worshiped here; Pierre L'Enfant, the planner of Washington, D.C., designed the gilded sunburst above the altar; the graveyard outside contains the picturesque tombs of now-forgotten city squires and their ladies. The building is an incredible contrast to the huge towers of the World Trade Center scraping the sky behind it. You're free to wander inside for a look. And if the interior layout seems confusing, bear in mind that St. Paul's was originally designed to face the river. That's the side with the steeple. But as Broadway grew to become the town's most important thoroughfare, it was decided to erect a new portico here instead of on the original front.

Leave St. Paul's, turn right, and continue south again on Broadway. Across Fulton Street on the next block, you'll see the:

 10. AT&T Building, occupying a site that extends from Fulton south to Dey Street. If you're in the mood for another taste of the majesty of capitalism, have a look at the lobby. It's a perfect forest of immense columns. Indeed, the exterior of this building has more columns than any other stone structure in the world. Built in 1917, it was recently abandoned by AT&T for a new headquarters up on Madison and 56th.

When you've marveled sufficiently at what long-distance rates hath wrought, exit and turn right (south) to the corner of Dey and Broadway. Turn right again onto Dey Street and continue west to the corner of Church Street. Before you is the:

 11. World Trade Center, a $700-million building. If you wish, you can detour to the Observation Deck on the 110th floor of Two World Trade Center, the tower to your left as you face the complex from the other side of Church Street. You might also venture a block west of the World Trade Center to the:

 12. World Financial Center at Battery Park City, whose four soaring granite-and-glass towers house corporate headquarters for many international financial firms. Cross the North Pedestrian Bridge that connects the World Trade Center to the World Financial Center and you'll find yourself in the splendid indoor **Winter Garden,** a crystal palace atrium with a 120-foot vaulted glass ceiling, a magnificent marble-and-granite staircase, live palm trees, changing art exhibits, and glorious views out to the Hudson, the Statue of Liberty, and lower New York Harbor. It's one of New York's great indoor spaces. There are lots of shops, services, and restaurants here, as well as an outdoor plaza where there is always some sort of free entertainment going on in good weather.

To continue on with our tour, retrace your steps back up Dey Street to Broadway. Now cross Broadway and continue east on:

 13. John Street (which is just Dey Street with a name change). This canyon-like thoroughfare is so narrow that it's closed to traffic at lunch hour. Note the

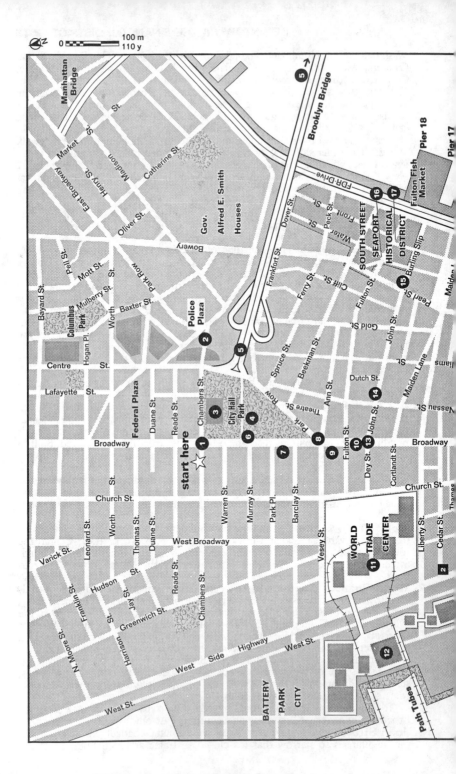

WALKING TOUR — DOWNTOWN & THE FINANCIAL DISTRICT

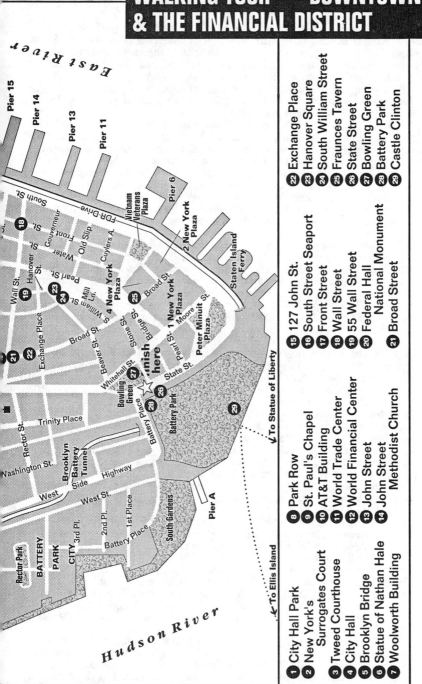

1. City Hall Park
2. New York's Surrogates Court
3. Tweed Courthouse
4. City Hall
5. Brooklyn Bridge
6. Statue of Nathan Hale
7. Woolworth Building
8. Park Row
9. St. Paul's Chapel
10. AT&T Building
11. World Trade Center
12. World Financial Center
13. John Street
14. John Street Methodist Church
15. 127 John St.
16. South Street Seaport
17. Front Street
18. Wall Street
19. 55 Wall Street
20. Federal Hall National Monument
21. Broad Street
22. Exchange Place
23. Hanover Square
24. South William Street
25. Fraunces Tavern
26. State Street
27. Bowling Green
28. Battery Park
29. Castle Clinton

modern skyscraper castle, complete with crenelated turrets, at the corner of John and Nassau.

Cross Nassau, keeping on John, and continue east. Here you'll find the:

14. John Street Methodist Church, simple and steepleless. At 44 John St. (in the shadow of the huge new tower) the present building was erected in 1841, but the congregation has owned and worshiped at this address since 1768, making it the oldest Methodist society in America.

Keep going east on John Street for 4½ more blocks. It's a short walk, down an 18th-century street lined with towering 20th-century buildings. On the last of these blocks, between Pearl and Water streets, is:

15. 127 John St., a 1969 office building with a street-level concourse filled with 1960s nonsense. There are an astonishingly complicated digital clock, blue neon-lined tubes leading to the elevators, and all manner of whimsical constructs for seating and shelter. Not beautiful, but very evocative of the 1960s.

Pearl Street, by the way, was originally called Mother-of-Pearl Street, because it was once the beach that ran along the shore of the East River. Water Street, a block farther east, was built on landfill, as was everything beyond it.

Turn left off John onto Water Street, skirting the perimeter of 127 John, and continue north for one block to Fulton Street. The corner of Fulton and Water marks the entrance to the:

16. South Street Seaport. From this point to the East River, Fulton Street has been transformed into a cobbled pedestrian mall. Between Water Street and South Street it's lined with restored buildings, Seaport Museum galleries, pricey shops, and a variety of restaurants. The seaport is definitely worth a day unto itself. For now, you might stroll the two short blocks down Fulton to South and admire the sailing ships at berth in the river, after which you might get a snack at one of the restaurants or food stalls in Pier 17. Then return one block up Fulton to Front Street and turn left (south).

Keep south on:

17. Front Street for six short blocks. Until recently this area was filled with ancient brick buildings similar to those in the seaport. Their sudden disappearance and replacement by the modern behemoths that line the street today was a principal factor leading to the founding of the Seaport Museum.

The sixth intersection you'll come to is that of Front Street and:

18. Wall Street, and here you'll turn right. As you may already have heard, Wall Street follows the line of a crude palisade erected in the 17th century by the Dutch to deter Indian attacks. It was never put to a test, even though the Indians did almost as much mischief as the Dutch in other regions of Manhattan. Start walking west on Wall Street, past Water and Pearl streets. Ahead you'll see the slender spire of **Trinity Church,** located at Broadway and Wall. It's hard to believe that this tiny antique, cringing at the bottom of a Grand Canyon of concrete, was once the tallest structure on Manhattan, a landmark visible from far out in the harbor.

On the left side of the next block, just past Hanover Street, is the entrance to:

19. 55 Wall Street. This was the site of a Merchants' Exchange destroyed in the great New York fire of 1835. The exchange was rebuilt in 1836, and the first three floors of it still exist right here in 55 Wall. In 1907 the place was remodeled for National City Bank, and its size was doubled in the process. The building now belongs to Citibank, and its banking floor is well worth a look. This interior resembles nothing so much as an imperial Roman bath. Beneath the soaring marble walls and columns are perfectly ridiculous-looking modern banking islands. We should be glad, however, that nobody has tried to tear the place down.

Exit 55 Wall, turn left (west), and continue in the direction we've been heading. Stay on Wall past the intersection of William Street until you see on your right the statue of George Washington standing above the steps to:

20. Federal Hall National Memorial. This museum, located at the corner of Wall and Nassau streets, occupies a very fine Greek Revival building erected in

1842. New York's City Hall, before being relocated to the present City Hall Park, formerly stood at this site. In 1789 the father of our country took the oath of office on the balcony of the old building, which at that point had been remodeled by Major L'Enfant and rechristened Federal Hall. There's a free museum inside the present Federal Hall, with exhibits pertaining to the building, the Revolution, Washington, and so forth.

Federal Hall stands at the head of:

21. **Broad Street,** down which we're now going to turn. Just south of Wall, on the right (west) side of Broad Street, is the gratifyingly magnificent columned facade of the **New York Stock Exchange,** at 3 Broad Street. There's been a stock exchange in New York since 1792, when a group of brokers started meeting under a buttonwood tree near Wall and William streets. The initial purpose of the exchange was to sell government bonds to pay off the debt left over from the Revolutionary War. The market grew in power and importance throughout the 19th century. In 1903 it moved to the present building, which can be visited free.

The next intersection to the south is that of Broad and:

22. **Exchange Place.** Turn left (east) onto Exchange and behold the popular image of "Wall Street" before your very eyes. This street is so narrow you want to turn sideways to walk down it. And the buildings along its sides are so tall that direct sunlight probably hasn't hit the pavement since 1917. Continue to the end of the block and cross William Street. Then continue on Exchange to the end of the next block (these are very short blocks, by the way) and turn right onto **Hanover Street.** It's only about 30 feet to the corner of **Beaver Street,** where you'll turn right again for another 30 or 40 feet until you arrive at the corner of **William Street.** And here, with Delmonico's Restaurant facing you across the street, you'll turn left onto William for another 50-odd feet until you arrive at:

23. **Hanover Square,** quite a historic corner of old New York. Like so many other districts, Hanover Square had its day in the sun as an elite residential enclave. The premier householder was none other than Captain Kidd, a notorious pirate abroad (the English caught him and hanged him in 1701) but a respected citizen of New York City and a contributor to Trinity Church. The first newspaper in town, the *New-York Gazette,* was also printed in Hanover Square, in 1725 by William Bradford. The great fire of 1835 started with a gas explosion in Hanover Square. The ensuing conflagration engulfed 20 acres and destroyed 650 buildings, including everything that had survived until then from the Dutch period. **India House,** that charming old brownstone building on the south side of William at the corner of Pearl, was built in 1854 as the Hanover Bank. It is today a private club.

Now turn around and go back on William Street to Delmonico's. When you reach the corner of William and Beaver, take a sharp left onto:

24. **South William Street.** The wall of Delmonico's will be on your right as you walk down South William. There are wonderful opportunities hereabouts for pictures of twisting narrow streets and huge soaring skyscrapers. South William continues for one block only, until it joins Broad Street. When you get to the corner, turn left (south) onto Broad for two blocks to Bridge Street and pause for a moment on the corner.

At Broad and Pearl is:

25. **Fraunces Tavern,** that old brick building just ahead of you. Samuel Fraunces was a black man whose "Queen's Head Tavern," as the place was originally called, figured in several passages of American history. The New York Chamber of Commerce was founded here in 1768. In 1783 the tavern was the scene of DeWitt Clinton's gala celebration of the British evacuation of occupied New York. It was here, also in 1783, that George Washington (Fraunces was his chief steward) bade farewell to his officers and announced his retirement to Mount Vernon. The building had fallen pretty low by the end of the 19th century. In 1904 it was lovingly restored by the Sons of the Revolution, although the authenticity of its present appearance is questionable. Today it is again a restaurant with a small museum attached.

Turn right off Broad Street onto Bridge Street and walk one block to the corner of Whitehall Street. Cross Whitehall and continue another short block to:

26. State Street, where you'll turn right. The huge building to your right was, until 1973, the **U.S. Customs House.** It's a shame Customs moved to the World Trade Center. Nothing could match the magnificence of this 1907 Beaux-Arts masterpiece, which has stood vacant ever since.

The main entrance to the Customs House is at the head of State Street facing:

27. Bowling Green, a little park that was once a Dutch cattle market, and later a green for bowls. The iron fence around it has been there since 1771, and was erected originally to protect an equestrian statue of King George III. On July 9, 1776, a rowdy crowd, excited by a reading of the Declaration of Independence, descended upon Bowling Green, tore the statue down, and broke it into pieces. Legend has it the lead was melted down and made into bullets that subsequently felled 400 British soldiers.

The greensward that faces the side wall of the Customs House on the other side of State Street is:

28. Battery Park, named after a gun emplacement that once stood along the line of present State Street. Usually just called the Battery, this very pleasant park is constructed entirely on landfill. It's an ideal place for strolling and admiring unobstructed views of New York Harbor.

At the northern end of the Battery, located directly on the waterfront, is:

29. Castle Clinton, an old fortress that started life in 1807 as another gun emplacement. Before the waterfront was filled in, it sat about 300 feet offshore on a pile of rocks. In the 1820s the federal government ceded it to the city, which converted it to a civic reception hall. Lafayette, President Jackson, and the Prince of Wales were all officially greeted here by the City of New York. By 1850 it was called Castle Garden and operated as a concert hall. This is where P. T. Barnum first presented Jenny Lind, "The Swedish Nightingale," to an adoring American audience. Five years after that the building was converted to the Immigrant Landing Depot. Almost eight million future Americans were processed at Castle Garden before Ellis Island was completed in 1892. After its immigrant era it became the New York Aquarium, which it remained until that institution moved to Coney Island in 1941. Vacant and threatened with demolition in the years thereafter, it was eventually rescued and restored in 1976 by the National Park Service to its present somewhat dry appearance.

And with that, we come to the end of the tour.

WALKING TOUR 2 — Chinatown & Little Italy

Start: New York County Courthouse
Finish: Old Police Headquarters
Best Times: If you don't mind the crowds, mid-September, early June, or late January to early February, for the street festivals

Chinatown and Little Italy are all about street life, sometimes strident and overwhelming, but always vibrating with an energy unmistakably their own. Although there are few architectural landmarks and most housing is tenement-style, these tiny neighborhoods offer a real glimpse of New York's cultural diversity at its lively best. Begin at the:

1. New York County Courthouse (1912), 60 Centre Street, Foley Square. Architect Guy Lowell won the competition for his design, a Corinthian-colonnaded temple in a "hexagon" shape that foreshadowed the "Pentagon" of 30 years later. The New York Supreme Court occupies the building. Until the mid-19th century, when Foley Square was completed, this area was known as

Five Points, one of the worst slums in the country, an infamous, crime-ridden hellhole of filth and squalor centered around an old brewery whose lane was called "Murderers' Alley." Here lived over a thousand unfortunate men, women, and children in an area so dangerous that even the police wouldn't go near it.
   Cross Worth Street and turn right to:

2. **Mulberry Street,** farther north, the main street of Little Italy, here Chinatown's southern boundary. Turn left on Mulberry along the border of the park, past the rows of brick tenements, many of which are now Chinese funeral homes. At Bayard Street turn right. Notice as you pass Mott Street a skyscraper straight ahead, incongruous and intrusive.

REFUELING STOP   3. At the **Original Chinatown Ice Cream Factory,** 65 Bayard Street, no less than 32 flavors tempt you—among them, exotic lychee, almond cookie, ginger, and mango. A single scoop costs $1.70, a double is $3.

   Backtrack and turn right on:

4. **Mott Street.** It rhymes with "what street" in a famous lyric from the tune "I'll Take Manhattan" of some years back. This is Chinatown's colorful main artery, wider than most, and dotted with terrific shops and restaurants, notably:

5. **Hong Fat,** no. 63. The lines are long, the atmosphere grates, the waiters are rude, and they rush you. But the food is first-rate and the prices cheap. There's also an uptown branch at 1799 Lexington Avenue.

6. **New Lung Fung Bakery,** no. 41. If the aroma doesn't get you, the abundance of pastry will. Where else can you find a black bean doughnut? Or coconut bread? The pastries are 40¢ and 50¢, a real bargain. The:

7. **Oriental Dress Co.,** no. 38, sells gorgeous embroidered silk fabrics by the yard.
   Amid all this cacophony there's an oasis, the Georgian-Gothic:

8. **Church of the Transfiguration,** 25 Mott Street, near Mosco Street, reconstructed in 1853 from a structure built in 1801 with the same stone used for St. Paul's Chapel. The pitched gables and rich entablature are characteristic of the English Gothic style.
   Continue toward:

9. **The Chinatown Fair Game Arcade,** 8 Mott Street. What distinguishes this maze of pinball machines and video games from the 42nd Street arcades are two live chickens, one named "Birdbrain," who plays tic-tac-toe with the customers for a sack of fortune cookies (he wins), and another that dances on request.
   At the end of Mott Street cross Chatham Square, noticing the:

10. **American Legion Chinese Memorial** (1962), a simple archway honoring Chinese-American soldiers killed in battle.

REFUELING STOP   Dim sum is a Chinese tradition of grazing from a selection of bite-size hors d'oeuvres, mostly dumplings of one sort or another, wheeled on a trolley to your table. There's no better place to try dim sum than the: **11. Golden Unicorn Restaurant,** at 18 E. Broadway near Catherine Street. This sleek and stylish restaurant on the second floor of a sterile office building attracts a well-heeled local crowd. Besides dim sum, offered daily from 8am to 3:30pm, there are lunch and dinner menus that feature standard Cantonese cuisine. Highly recommended.

   Returning to Chatham Square, turn right until you come to the tiny:

12. **Confucius Square,** with its bronze likeness of the great philosopher mounted on a marble base.
   At Pell Street cross Bowery and notice the restored red-brick house from the Revolutionary period, one of the few remaining historic buildings in the area.

Walk down Pell to Mott Street and if you haven't already done so, have tea and a sweet at New Lung Fung Bakery.

Head north on Mott to Canal Street. Gilt statues of Buddha decorate the windows of the:

13. **Eastern States Buddhist Temple of America,** 64 Mott Street, where the aroma of incense permeates the air, and the illuminated altar inside contains three statues of Buddha. You can read your fortune for a $1 donation.

Nestled in among the restaurants and food shops are stores offering a mind-boggling variety of wares, from satin slippers, kimonos, and kites, to paper lanterns, fans, chopsticks, and medicinal herbs. Spend some time browsing.

14. **Canal Street** was once the dividing line between Chinatown and Little Italy, but Chinatown has been spilling north in recent years. Many of the buildings above Canal are now in Chinese hands, with the curious result that storefronts with Chinese names share space cheek to jowl with Italian fraternities.

Turn left and enter:

15. **Kam Man Food, Inc.,** 200 Canal Street, an emporium that dazzles with such exotic items as dried ginseng and deer antler, enormous jars of dried seafood, cellophane-wrapped whole fish, unusual spices and sauces, teas, and much more.

Cross Mulberry Street and enter:

16. **Little Italy.** From Houston to Canal streets, and the Bowery to Lafayette, this is an ethnic stronghold where traditions are tenaciously preserved by the older generation of Italians. The area crackles with life on holy days and family occasions, and for the Feast of San Gennaro, when Mulberry Street closes to traffic and improvised food stalls compete for their fair share of business. It's great fun, and the calzone, sausages of every description, and cannoli taste vastly better al fresco.

Set back from the street is the rectory of the:

17. **Franciscan Fathers Most Precious Blood Church** (circa 1890), 109 Mulberry Street, a dignified element in the string of cafés and restaurants. The church entrance is around the corner on Baxter Street.

The gift shop at:

18. **No. 119** Mulberry St. has an interesting tile mosaic out front that depicts gondolas and harlequins in Venice.

19. **Il Cortile Restaurant** (1975), 125 Mulberry Street, a handsome brick structure with dark oak trim and plenty of glass, was designed by neighborhood architects Donato Savoie and Antonio Morello, who convinced the owner that architecture could be both contemporary *and* Italian. The interior dining room is under a skylight, so even in gloomy weather, the space is cheerful and light.

Another Savoie/Morello design is the:

20. **Café Biondo,** 141 Mulberry Street, a successful balance of old—the existing cast-iron exterior columns, and new—a sheer glass front and black-and-white marble, brass, and Formica interior.

In the block between Hester and Grand streets, on one side of a warehouse wall, is a witty:

21. **Trompe l'oeil mural,** by Richard Haas, that resembles a group of storefronts. And on the same block is:

22. **Paolucci's Restaurant,** 149 Mulberry Street, a historic 1816 two-story Federal brick house originally built for Stephen Renssalaer, hero of the War of 1812 (and later a New York State congressman). The restaurant has been called "Le Pavilion" of Little Italy, though it's not nearly as expensive.

Cross Mulberry Street, turn the corner, and stop for a sweet and cappuccino at:

23. **Ferrara's,** 195 Grand Street, a New York landmark bakery that's a hundred years old and still going strong.

Turn left at Grand Street and notice the architectural dichotomy between the brand-new La Grande condominiums on one side, and the diminutive four-story brick Victorian, with its ornate arched and carved windows, on the other. Turn right at Centre Street. The entire block is occupied by the:

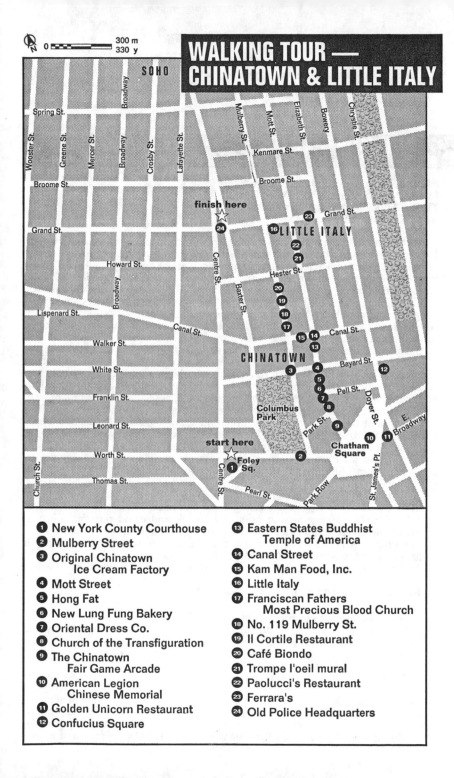

WALKING TOUR —
CHINATOWN & LITTLE ITALY

1 New York County Courthouse

2 Mulberry Street

3 Original Chinatown
Ice Cream Factory

4 Mott Street

5 Hong Fat

6 New Lung Fung Bakery

7 Oriental Dress Co.

8 Church of the Transfiguration

9 The Chinatown
Fair Game Arcade

10 American Legion
Chinese Memorial

11 Golden Unicorn Restaurant

12 Confucius Square

13 Eastern States Buddhist
Temple of America

14 Canal Street

15 Kam Man Food, Inc.

16 Little Italy

17 Franciscan Fathers
Most Precious Blood Church

18 No. 119 Mulberry St.

19 Il Cortile Restaurant

20 Café Biondo

21 Trompe l'oeil mural

22 Paolucci's Restaurant

23 Ferrara's

24 Old Police Headquarters

24. Old Police Headquarters (1909), 240 Centre Street, a richly embellished French Renaissance–Revival "hotel de ville" (city hall), palatial and grand, symbolic of the drama of police work. In 1988 the building was converted to cooperative apartments.

WALKING TOUR 3 — SoHo & the Cast-Iron District

Start: West Broadway and Houston Street
Finish: Sixth Avenue and Houston Street
Time: About 1 hour and 25 minutes
Best Times: Anytime

Until the late 1840s, what we now call SoHo (a fractured acronym for South of Houston Street) was a quiet residential quarter of the northern edge of town. Starting in about 1850 a commercial building boom (petering out finally in the 1890s) totally transformed the place into a neighborhood of swank retail stores and loft buildings for light manufacturing. All this activity coincided with the development of cast iron as a building material. Columns, arches, pediments, brackets, keystones, and everything else that once had to be carved in stone could now be mass-produced at lower cost in iron. The result was a commercial building spree that gave free rein to the opulent architectural styles of the day.

But after the spree came long generations of neglect. By the late 1960s the area was dismissed as too dismal for words. And for that precise reason it began attracting impoverished artists. Back then you could rent huge spaces in SoHo's former sweatshops (considerable exploitation went on behind these handsome facades) for next to nothing. But restless fashion was not about to ignore a developing new brew of art and historic architecture. By the early 1970s the land boom was on. Today West Broadway is literally lined with rarified boutiques, avant-garde galleries, and trendy restaurants. SoHo lofts now appear in the pages of *Architectural Digest* and they're more likely to be inhabited by art patrons than artists.

Yet one cannot dismiss SoHo as a travesty of art sold out to commerce. Its concentration of galleries soon made it a major force in world art markets, and as such, a major force in the very shape of today's art. The intellectual and artistic ferment in SoHo had strong parallels to what was happening in Paris and Berlin between the wars or in Greenwich Village at the turn of the century. The rediscovery of the old buildings is somewhat ironic (no pun intended), as they are about as spiritually distant from modern art as it is possible for buildings to be.

Admittedly, SoHo doesn't look too promising from our departure point at Houston and West Broadway. Back in the 1920s Houston was widened when the IND subway line was constructed. It seems somehow or other never to have healed.

To begin, proceed south from Houston down:

1. West Broadway in the direction of the World Trade Center towers that loom so picturesquely in the distance. Although this street is the center of the gallery world and SoHo's most famous thoroughfare, it does not by a long shot contain the best cast-iron buildings. Top honors in that category probably belong to Broome Street, which we'll visit farther on.

What makes West Broadway so famous, besides lots of places to shop for chic clothes, is its concentration of galleries. You don't need an appointment to go in and look. And what you'll see could be anything from the highly representational to the intensely personal, from Neo-Impressionist landscapes to sculpture to constructions that challenge your entire definition of "art." In between galleries bearing names like Leo Castelli, Sonnabend, Access, O. K. Harris, and Nancy

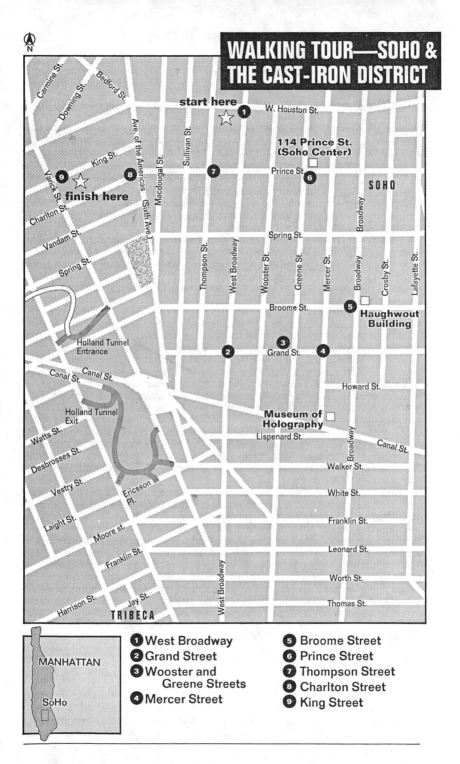

WALKING TOUR—SOHO & THE CAST-IRON DISTRICT

start here

W. Houston St.

114 Prince St. (Soho Center)

Prince St.

SOHO

Carmine St.

Bedford St.

Downing St.

Ave. of the Americas (Sixth Ave.)

Sullivan St.

Macdougal St.

King St.

Varick St.

finish here

Charlton St.

Vandam St.

Spring St.

Broadway

Spring St.

Thompson St.

West Broadway

Wooster St.

Greene St.

Mercer St.

Broadway

Crosby St.

Lafayette St.

Broome St.

Haughwout Building

Holland Tunnel Entrance

Grand St.

Canal St.

Canal St.

Holland Tunnel Exit

Howard St.

Museum of Holography

Lispenard St.

Broadway

Canal St.

Watts St.

Desbrosses St.

Walker St.

Vestry St.

Ericsson Pl.

White St.

Laight St.

Franklin St.

Moore st.

Leonard St.

Franklin St.

West Broadway

Worth St.

Harrison St.

Jay St.

Thomas St.

TRIBECA

MANHATTAN

SoHo

❶ West Broadway
❷ Grand Street
❸ Wooster and Greene Streets
❹ Mercer Street
❺ Broome Street
❻ Prince Street
❼ Thompson Street
❽ Charlton Street
❾ King Street

Hoffman are shops like If, Red Bird, Giraudou, Rizzoli, and Think Big!, selling everything from books to clothing designed in Milan. The streetside atmosphere is exciting and cosmopolitan in a very particular way: SoHo is a local lifestyle, and a stylish one at that.

When you reach the end of the fourth block south of Houston Street you'll be at the intersection of West Broadway and:

2. Grand Street. Turn left on Grand and head east. Now we're really getting into cast-iron country. Note the newly renovated building at the end of this block, on the corner of Grand and Wooster streets. This marvelous Victorian facade is typical of what's been rediscovered down here. Structurally speaking, cast-iron buildings were not particularly innovative. They were usually supported by the same brick walls and timber floors as the buildings they replaced. The cast iron was merely mounted on the facades as a substitute for carved stone. Nor did it necessarily cover an entire facade. But it did have a definite "look."

The next block of Grand, between:

3. Wooster and Greene streets, shows this look to best advantage. Iron pillars seem to line the street into infinity. A century ago these sidewalks were crowded with shoppers. The ground floors of the buildings contained all manner of dry-goods emporia, while the upper levels were jammed with immigrants crouched over sewing machines for 12 hours a day. The building at the southwest corner of Greene and Grand (the one that says 1873 on top) sums up the commercial aesthetic of those times. It is a real iron palace, lifted direct from the Italian Renaissance as interpreted by some 19th-century architect. The cast-iron building at the southeast corner of the same intersection sums up the SoHo of today: innovative, visually arresting, and expensive. Before we move on, glance up Greene Street for more cast-iron vistas. Historical footnote: During the cast-iron heyday of SoHo, Greene Street was one of New York's premier red-light districts.

Continue another block east on Grand to the corner of:

4. Mercer Street. The old Empire Safe Company Building on the south side of the street shows how cast iron was combined with other building materials. In this case, it's been confined to the first floor facade, which doesn't look as if it's changed one bit in the last century. Turn right and continue one block south to the corner of Mercer Street and **Howard Street.** Overlooking the intersection at 11 Mercer Street is the **Museum of Holography** (described in Section 2 of Chapter 7, "What to See and Do in New York City"), worth a look for those interested in laser imaging.

From the Museum of Holography, proceed east on Howard Street (it's the only direction you can go, since Howard begins at Mercer Street) and go one block to the corner of Broadway.

Continue north up Broadway for another block to:

5. Broome Street. At 488 Broadway, on the northeast corner of Broadway and Broome, is the many-pillared Haughwout Building. Among other things, this building is noted for its original 1857 Otis elevator, still in service. The street-level showrooms of 488 Broadway were once filled with the silver, chandeliers, and crystal goods of one Eder Haughwout. While the original cream-colored paint job is a distant memory, the structure remains essentially unaltered, an evocative reminder of Broadway's former commercial glory.

Turn left onto Broome Street and continue two blocks west to the intersection of Broome and Greene streets. Much of SoHo, as you can see, remains pretty gritty and industrial, notwithstanding its historic buildings and trendy new art culture. And yet a critical mass has definitely been achieved. Today the dirtiest SoHo street corner manages somehow manages to look "fashionable," at least in the eyes of a downtown New Yorker.

Turn right onto Greene Street and proceed two blocks north to the corner of:

6. Prince Street. Before you reach Prince you'll see examples of just about everything that's happening in SoHo these days. There are cast-iron buildings (some gloriously renovated, some still grotty), another clutch of galleries, a new condominium (in a renovated iron building at 97 Greene that's clearly not being marketed to starving artists), various unglamorous old-time tool and rag businesses, and a nightclub called Greene Street.

Pause for a moment at Prince and Greene and look up at the eastern wall of **114 Prince Street,** also called the SoHo Center. This cleverly painted blank brick wall re-creates the cast-iron street facade, complete to the painted cat in the painted open window.

Turn left off Greene onto Prince Street and walk west for two blocks to West Broadway. Chic shops and restaurants proliferate the closer you draw to that celebrated thoroughfare.

Cross West Broadway, keeping on Prince, and continue for another block to:

7. Thompson Street. The cast-iron district is behind you now; this is tenement country. The next street you'll cross is Sullivan Street, shortly after which you'll see **203 Prince Street** on your right, a perfectly beautiful restored Federal house. The next street that crosses Prince is MacDougal, and a few steps farther is the great swath of widened Sixth Avenue hurtling south from Greenwich Village.

Directly across Sixth Avenue, angling a little to the south of the course of Spring Street, is:

8. Charlton Street. That's where you want to go, although crossing Sixth Avenue can be daunting. Charlton Street is the center of a small historic district notable for its concentration of intact Federal-period houses. The site was originally a country estate located midway between New York and Greenwich. The mansion, built in 1767 and named Richmond Hill, surveyed the surrounding countryside from the top of a sizable hill, leveled in 1817, when John Jacob Astor developed the property into building lots. Illustrious inhabitants of Richmond Hill have included Vice-President John Adams, whose wife, Abigail, described the view south to New York as "delicious," and Aaron Burr, who lived here at the time of his fateful duel with Alexander Hamilton.

After its hilltop was sliced from beneath it, the Richmond Hill mansion was moved to a new site on the southeast corner of Varick and Charlton. It became a theater, then a tavern, and was finally torn down in 1849. Despite the towering loft buildings standing in the background, the block of Charlton between Sixth Avenue and Varick Street retains much of the flavor of early 19th-century New York. It gives you a good idea, too, of what SoHo looked like before the cast-iron invasion.

When you reach Varick Street, turn right for one block to:

9. King Street and turn right again, noticing the fancy ironwork balconies and fire escapes on the red-brick and gray buildings from here to Sixth Avenue.

At the end of King Street you'll be back on Sixth Avenue (a major uptown bus route), one block south of Houston Street.

WALKING TOUR 4 —— Greenwich Village

Start: Sixth Avenue and Waverly Place near the West 4th Street subway station
Finish: Same as start
Time: Approximately 1 hour and 10 minutes

It's erroneously believed, even by many New Yorkers, that Greenwich Village centers around Washington Square and two honky-tonk strips on Bleecker and West 3rd Street between Sixth Avenue and LaGuardia Place. Actually, this is not at all the case.

The original Greenwich Village, the separate town that once lay beyond the boundaries of New York, is located someplace else. Today people sometimes refer to that area as the "West Village"; it occupies the region between Greenwich Avenue and the Hudson River, bounded on the south by West Houston Street. Greenwich Village was one of the earliest settlements on Manhattan. It remained a bucolic hamlet during and after the Revolution, then experienced explosive growth in the 1820s. Its sudden prosperity was largely a function of the poor quality of the drinking water in the neighboring city of New York. In those days epidemics of typhoid and smallpox were almost annual affairs. As soon as the new season's plague struck New York, everyone who could afford to decamped immediately to healthful, semi-rural Greenwich.

Greenwich possessed its own network of built-up streets well before burgeoning New York City engulfed it. They still exist, radiating at bewildering angles from the grid plan that dominates the rest of Manhattan. The old Village surveyors must have been a little weak when it came to right angles. Original Village blocks are almost, but not quite, square. Many are parallelograms. The block plan is further complicated by subsequent swaths slashed through it for the construction of Seventh and Eighth avenues. On top of all this, some of the old named streets have been given numbers supposedly corresponding to adjacent numbered streets. The results are baffling intersections, such as that point where West 4th Street, West 12th Street, and Eighth Avenue all converge. Even native New Yorkers get lost in the Village, at least without a map.

Our tour starts at Sixth Avenue and Waverly Place, an intersection located one block south of 8th Street and quite near the uptown exits from the Washington Square–West 4th Street subway stop. Proceed east from Sixth Avenue toward Washington Square Park to:

1. **Waverly Place,** a typical Village street lined with well-used brick town houses from the early 19th century, as well as buildings of more recent vintage. At the end of one block you arrive at:
2. **MacDougal Street** and **Washington Square Park.** In 1789 the park you see before you was designated a pauper's burial ground. It was an unprepossessing patch of land then, not terribly close to New York, not wanted by anyone else. But by 1826 fashion was on the march. The paupers were unceremoniously removed and the former graveyard became a parade ground. Soon fine Greek Revival houses began to appear along the southern boundary. Every one of these has disappeared, victims of time and the encroaching building programs of New York University's campus.

   Known collectively as:
3. **The Row,** the brick houses that still stand on the park's northern boundary give a vivid idea of what the whole square once looked like. They enjoyed their day (in the 1830s) as the home of New York's elite. Like good neighborhoods everywhere they were eventually abandoned for palmier addresses, this time farther up Fifth Avenue. Henry James and Edith Wharton, incidentally, both lived and worked at 1 Washington Square North. Today many of these old mansions are only facades masking new apartments inside. But a few have survived almost intact.

   Now let's make a short detour. Turn to your left (north) and head away from Washington Square Park up MacDougal Street. After a few steps you'll see:
4. **MacDougal Alley** on your right. This little street, lined with former carriage houses, is typical of the sort of small enclave that makes the Village such an appealing place to live. You might stroll up to the end of MacDougal Street (the Alley is private) and have a look at:
5. **West 8th Street** while you're here. It's a wilderness of shoe stores, clothing stores, poster shops, and copy centers. It's hard to believe that its mutilated

---

IMPRESSIONS

Greenwich Village is the Coney Island of the soul.
MAXWELL BODENHEIM, QUOTED IN ALLEN CHURCHILL,
THE IMPROPER BOHEMIANS, 1959

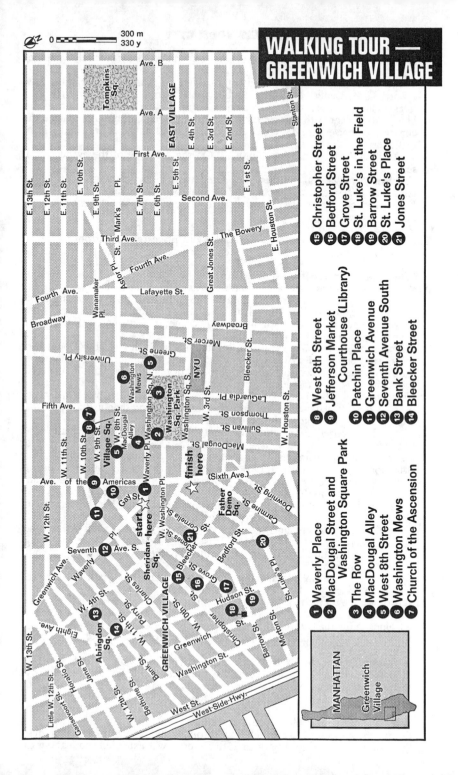

① Waverly Place
② MacDougal Street and Washington Square Park
③ The Row
④ MacDougal Alley
⑤ West 8th Street
⑥ Washington Mews
⑦ Church of the Ascension

⑧ West 8th Street
⑨ Jefferson Market Courthouse (Library)
⑩ Patchin Place
⑪ Greenwich Avenue
⑫ Seventh Avenue South
⑬ Bank Street
⑭ Bleecker Street

⑮ Christopher Street
⑯ Bedford Street
⑰ Grove Street
⑱ St. Luke's in the Field
⑲ Barrow Street
⑳ St. Luke's Place
㉑ Jones Street

0 300 m / 330 y

EAST VILLAGE

Ave. B
Ave. A
First Ave.
Second Ave.
Third Ave.
Fourth Ave.
Lafayette St.
Broadway
The Bowery

E. 13th St.
E. 12th St.
E. 11th St.
E. 10th St.
E. 9th St. Pl.
St. Mark's Pl.
E. 7th St.
E. 6th St.
E. 5th St.
E. 4th St.
E. 3rd St.
E. 2nd St.
E. 1st St.
E. Houston St.
Great Jones St.
Stanton St.
Astor Pl.
Wanamaker Pl.

Tompkins Sq.

Fourth Ave.
Fifth Ave.
Broadway
University Pl.
Greene St.
Mercer St.
Bleecker St.

NYU
Washington Sq. Park
Washington Sq. N.
Washington Sq. S.
Washington Mews
Village Sq.
MacDougal Alley

W. 11th St.
W. 10th St.
W. 9th St.
W. 8th St.
Waverly Pl.
Washington Pl.
W. 3rd St.
LaGuardia Pl.
Thompson St.
Sullivan St.
MacDougal St.
W. Houston St.

Fifth Ave.
Ave. of the Americas (Sixth Ave.)

start here
finish here
Sheridan Sq.
Gay St.
Christopher St.
Father Demo Sq.
Carmine St.
Downing St.
Bedford St.
Bleecker St.
Grove St.
Hudson St.
Morton St.
Barrow St.
St. Luke's Pl.

W. 12th St.
W. 11th St.
Seventh Ave. S.
Waverly
Greenwich Ave.
Cornelia St.
W. Washington Pl.

GREENWICH VILLAGE
Greenwich
Charles St.
Perry St.
W. 4th St.
W. 11th St.
Abingdon Sq.
Bank St.
Bethune St.
Jane St.
Horatio St.
Gansevoort St.
Little W. 12th St.
W. 12th St.
W. 13th St.
Eighth Ave.
Washington St.
West St.
West-Side-Hwy.

MANHATTAN
Greenwich Village

buildings were ever aristocratic private houses. And yet that is precisely what they were.

Now return to Washington Square, turn left (east) and walk along the Row toward Fifth Avenue. Note the double house at no. 20, built in 1828 as a freestanding suburban mansion for one George P. Rogers. The very air on this block is redolent with the gentility of the past. One can almost imagine the clip-clop of horses and the creak of carriage springs as the ladies climb out to make their calls.

At Fifth Avenue, turn left (uptown). On the east side of the avenue you'll see:

6. **Washington Mews,** another alley lined with former carriage houses now converted to residences. Although the original town houses along this stretch of Fifth were long ago replaced with apartment buildings, the street preserves a dignified residential air.

Three blocks north of Washington Square at 10th Street is the:

7. **Church of the Ascension,** a pleasant old place set back from the street behind an antique iron fence. It's been here since 1841, although the interior dates from a renovation in the 1880s by the celebrated McKim, Mead, and White. Turn left off Fifth Avenue onto:

8. **West 10th Street,** one of the nicest blocks in the Village, lined with fine city houses. Note no. 12, a particularly capacious old manse once owned by Bruce Price, the architect of Tuxedo Park and the father of etiquette expert Emily Post.

At the end of the block you'll reach the corner of Sixth Avenue. Here you'll have a fine view of the:

9. **Jefferson Market Courthouse,** located across Sixth and now a branch of the **New York Public Library.** This exuberant Victorian castle, dating from the 1870s, was once considered one of the half dozen most beautiful buildings in the United States. Subsequent generations considered it a horror. Concerned Villagers saved it from demolition in the late 1960s after it had stood vacant for over 20 years. When built, it was part of an innovative multiple-use complex that included a jail, a market, a courthouse, and a prison.

Cross Sixth Avenue for a closer look at it. Note how 10th Street now angles off to the south, following old Village road lines. The lovely garden (lovely except for a perfectly awful chain-link fence that surrounds it) occupying the rest of the courthouse block replaces a 1931 House of Detention for Women. Until its demolition in 1974, evenings on this block were characterized by husbands and boyfriends down on the street howling up to their womenfolk behind bars.

Across 10th Street from the Jefferson Courthouse is another little enclave of the sort that so typifies Greenwich Village. Called:

10. **Patchin Place,** it contains but ten modest brick houses facing one another across a leafy cul-de-sac. Theodore Dreiser, Jane Bowles, and e. e. cummings were among Patchin Place's illustrious residents in the days when the Village was America's "bohemia."

Now continue walking west on 10th Street away from Sixth Avenue. The corner ahead is:

11. **Greenwich Avenue,** a busy local shopping street. Originally it was called Monument Lane after a pre-Revolutionary obelisk that stood at its northern terminus. Note the bathroom-brick behemoth at 33 Greenwich Avenue. This is the sort of building that won't be built anymore (thank goodness!) in landmark Greenwich Village.

Cross Greenwich Avenue and keep walking west on 10th Street. The modest-looking tenements that line the street contain apartments as pricey as those on the elegant block between Fifth and Sixth. Why? Because they're on West 10th Street, a premium New York address.

Continue straight across the intersection of 10th Street and Waverly Place. After one more short block you'll come to:

12. **Seventh Avenue South,** cutting through the venerable Village blocks. Seventh Avenue used to stop up at 11th Street. It was extended south about the

time of World War I, over the protests of the entire Village. Before we move on, glance downtown (to your left) and you'll see the gleaming twin towers of the World Trade Center down on Vesey Street.

Crossing Seventh Avenue is something of a hazard. You want to get over to where West 10th Street picks up on the other side. When you regain West 10th, go just a few steps to the intersection of West 10th and West 4th streets, one of those conceptually bizarre intersections for which the Village is famous. Now turn right and start walking northwest up West 4th. Now we're getting into the real historical Village. The next couple of intersecting streets—Charles, Perry, West 11th, and Bank—are filled with old brick houses, shady trees, a smattering of better shops and galleries, and a great feeling of calm. Note the brick house at the corner of West 11th and West 4th. It must have looked just as it does now for over 100 years, which is no mean feat in New York.

Turn left (west) when you reach:

13. Bank Street, where during the smallpox epidemic in the 1820s so many New York banking institutions set up temporary offices on this street that the village of Greenwich named it after them. Note the ancient wisteria growing on no. 60. This is the sort of tenement house that invaded the Village as it became less fashionable in the latter part of the 19th century. Today even the tenements have an appealing patina of age. Many fine old Greek Revival houses remain on this block of Bank, making it one of the Village's nicest.

At the end of the block, Bank intersects:

14. Bleecker Street adjacent to Abingdon Square. Turn left (south) and continue down Bleecker. This is a street of antiques shops whose windows display Dutch chests and French chandeliers. There are occasional boutiques, interesting bookstores, cracked sidewalks, and some pretty blowsy looking modernish buildings. The narrow tree-lined side streets, however, are absolutely delightful.

Continue south on Bleecker for five blocks to:

15. Christopher Street and turn right (west toward the Hudson). Ahead in the distance you can see New Jersey across the river. On the street around you you'll see gay New York in full flower, as Christopher Street is more or less its spiritual center.

REFUELING STOPS   There are restaurants on every Village street, and most of them are quite good. For the real flavor of old Greenwich Village, try **The Grand Ticino** at 228 Thompson Street, serving classic Italian food, **Sabor,** 20 Cornelia Street, is for those who like Cuban food, hot and wonderful. **Mexican Village,** 224 Thompson Street, is a good place for a south-of-the-border dinner. And **Rio Mar,** all the way west in the meat-packing district at 7 Ninth Avenue at Little West 12th Street, is a Village find, with the atmosphere of old Spain.

Stay on Christopher one short block to:

16. Bedford Street and turn left (south). At the end of the block, on the corner of Grove Street, is a nest of particularly picturesque wooden houses. No. 17 Grove Street, on the corner of Bedford and Grove, was built by a Village sash-maker in the 1820s. It sags wonderfully and evokes the past quite vividly. No. 100 Bedford Street, located midblock between Grove and Christopher, is a Grimm's fairy-tale concoction of stucco, timbers, and crazy angles. This individualistic renovation was paid for in 1925 by financier Otto Kahn. Called **Twin Peaks,** it is the design of Clifford Daily, who thought the Village was becoming too dull, architecturally anyway, for the proper stimulation of its artistic population. During a wild housewarming party in 1926, Princess Anna Troubetzsky climbed atop one peak to make an offering of burnt acorns to the gods, while screen star Mabel Normand climbed atop the other and smashed a bottle of champagne on the ridgepole. Kahn's daughter lived in the house for many years, hence her father's willingness to foot the bill.

Make a right on Grove Street in the direction of the Hudson. The road makes a dogleg turn just a few steps from Bedford. Right at the angle of the turn you'll see a little gate set into a brick wall. Although it's private beyond, you can step up to the gate and look over it into:

17. Grove Court. Built for blue-collar tenants about 1830, and originally called Mixed Ale Alley, this tree-shaded enclave of little brick houses is the sort of Village spot many New Yorkers would kill to live in.

After you've admired the Federal houses in Grove Court, continue another half block to the end of Grove at Hudson Street. The old church across Hudson is:

18. St. Luke's in the Fields, also built in the 1820s when so much of this part of the Village was going up. The original St. Luke's was destroyed by fire, but the restoration preserves its rural look, despite the enormous Victorian-era warehouses looming behind it.

As you leave Grove Street, turn left (south) on Hudson for one block to:

19. Barrow Street, and turn left again. The first corner you'll come to is called **Commerce Street.** The intersection sports an interesting pair of identical houses, no. 39 and no. 41 Commerce Street, which were built in the 1830s and "modernized" in the 1870s with matching mansard roofs. Turn right off Barrow into tiny Commerce Street. This crooked little thoroughfare used to be called Cherry Lane until the big smallpox scare of 1822 sent so many businesses up here from New York that the name was changed.

When you reach the end of the block, you'll be back on Bedford Street. Turn right (south) again, and then look to your right for **75½ Bedford Street.** This 9½-foot-wide house holds the distinction of being the narrowest house in Greenwich Village, as well as the one-time residence of poet Edna St. Vincent Millay.

Keep walking south on Bedford. In another block you'll come to one of the intersections violently wrought so many years ago by the extension of Seventh Avenue. Immediately on your right is Morton Street. Don't turn here, but continue another block south on Seventh Avenue to:

20. St. Luke's Place, where you should turn right. Although the south side of St. Luke's Place is occupied by a modern playground, the north side preserves a terrific old row of houses from the 1850s. No. 6 St. Luke's Place was the residence of a former mayor of New York, the popular James J. ("Gentleman Jimmy") Walker. Although a crook and a scoundrel, Walker managed to epitomize the glamour of the 1920s. Incredibly enough, he is remembered quite fondly to this day.

After you've admired Jimmy Walker's digs, return to Seventh Avenue and continue straight across it on the line of St. Luke's Place. Once across Seventh you'll note that St. Luke's becomes **Leroy Street.** Stay on Leroy, past the continuation of Bedford Street for one block to the corner of Bleecker Street. Just before this intersection, note no. 7 Leroy Street, a nearly perfect circa 1810 house, complete with alley entrance and original dormers.

When you get to Bleecker, you'll find a Rocco's Pastry Shop, a local shopping area with enterprises such as the Bleecker Street Fish Market ("If It Swims, We Have It"), a record shop called Discorama, and assorted souvenir shops. Turn left on Bleecker for two very short blocks to:

21. Jones Street. Turn right onto Jones and take a quick look at no. 17 to see what usually happens to old houses like the one at no. 7 Leroy. A pity, no? At the end of the block, you'll be back on West 4th Street. Turn right for another short block and presto, here you are again back on Sixth Avenue, a mere two blocks south of Waverly Place, where our tour began.

WALKING TOUR 5 — Times Square & 42nd Street, East & West

Start: 42nd Street and Seventh Avenue

Finish: 42nd Street and First Avenue
Time: About 1 hour and 30 minutes

An advertising man by the name of O. J. Gude is credited as being the first to call **Times Square** the "Great White Way." This was back in 1901, when the golden age of electrically lit billboards had its start. These billboards, whose successors still dominate the intersection of Seventh Avenue and Broadway, reached their apogee in the 1940s and 1950s. There was once an immense sign for Camel cigarettes over Times Square that blew real smoke rings (as long as the wind obliged), another for Gilbey's gin that featured a 40-foot simulated waterfall of hootch, and yet another consisting of a monumentally scaled image of Little Lulu clutching a Kleenex.

The days of fabulous signs on this strip of honky-tonk, running roughly from 42nd Street to 47th Street, are hardly over. Instead of smoke rings we have computer-run extravaganzas that present mesmerizing and ever-changing advertisements on huge boards of multicolored lights. And we have the old familiars, like Coca-Cola and Castro Convertibles, glaring benignly over Broadway, day in and day out. It's bright enough to read a newspaper here at midnight, a state of affairs that seems unlikely to change any time soon.

Occupying a small triangular block on the north side of 42nd Street—Broadway is on one side of it, Seventh Avenue is on the other—is the first attraction on our tour:

1. ***Times* Tower.** Unfortunately, it's a really hideous building, made ugly by an uncomfortable-looking white marble skin affixed to it in 1966. The *Times* Tower was once headquarters of the world-famous *New York Times*. At the turn of the century *Times* publisher Adolph Ochs had set a daring precedent by moving his paper out of Printing House Square, adjacent to City Hall, downtown, and up to what was then called Longacre Square, a backwater dominated by harness and carriage shops. However, Longacre Square lay directly on the route of the new IRT subway. And Ochs, in a stroke of public relations genius, got the Longacre station renamed Times Square.

   Times Square has always had a slightly seedy/voluptuous reputation, as if some combination of artistic exaltation, luxury, and human degradation was endemic to the very locale. People will tell you about the "lobster palaces" that once thrived here, places with names like Shanley's and Rector's where swells like Lillian Russell and Diamond Jim Brady laughed and drank and spent freely. But at the same time the sporting set was quaffing champagne at the Café de Paris or in the roof garden of the old Astor Hotel, people routinely were being mugged a few blocks south in the heart of the Tenderloin.

   Even with the arrival of the *Times,* together with a coincident influx of legitimate theaters (most were converted to movie palaces in the 1920s), the area never really lost its slightly dicey air. The proliferation of pornography in the 1970s was nothing new for Times Square. During the 19th century, but a few blocks away, prostitutes openly displayed themselves in windows overlooking the tracks of the Sixth Avenue Elevated Railway. The present drive to "Clean Up Times Square" is nothing new either. It's just the latest round in an ongoing battle between vice and virtue that some unseen deity has seen fit to stage at the intersection of Broadway and Seventh Avenue.

   Anyway, let's get moving (always a prudent idea on Times Square). Head north (uptown) for two blocks from 42nd Street to 44th Street. Now turn back and look at the old *Times* Tower. From here you'll see:

2. **The Spectragraph,** a quite fantastic computer-driven sign that dominates the narrow uptown prow of the old joint. If you want, you can buy space on that sign and have a personal message displayed for a loved one (who'd better be there for the expensive moment it appears). Every New Year's Eve at midnight, the famous electrically lit ball (in more recent years an apple) descends a mast attached to the

top of this same building, launching the sea of people below into a frenzy of excitement.

At 44th Street you're right in the epicenter of Times Square. Actually, the north end of the place, up at 47th Street, is called:

3. **Father Duffy Square** after the "Fighting Chaplain" who accompanied New York's 69th Regiment into World War I. Up there at 47th Street is the day-of-performance outlet for half-price theater tickets, known as **TKTS** (see details in Chapter 10, "New York City Nights"). On the west side of Broadway between 43rd and 44th streets is the **Paramount Building,** at 1501 Broadway. The famous Paramount Theater, one of New York's premier movie palaces, once occupied the south side of this place until it was gutted and replaced with offices.

Walk up to:

4. **45th Street** and turn left (west). Before you, occupying the blockfront from 45th to 46th streets, is the new **Marriott Marquis Hotel,** a pricey behemoth catering mostly to the convention trade. One hesitates to call the Marriott beautiful, but the 37-story interior atrium is certainly amazing to behold. To take a look, find the hotel's midblock vehicular entrance on 45th Street, go inside, and take the glass-walled elevator to the eighth-floor lobby. Stroll around, look up, and when you've had enough, check out the Broadway Lounge, a lobby-level bar overlooking Times Square. There's an excellent view from here, especially at night when all the signs are lit.

Leave the Marriott via the 45th Street exit, cross 45th Street, and find:

5. **Shubert Alley,** the little lane that connects 45th and 44th streets. This is pretty much the heart of New York's legitimate **Theater District,** which since the 1920s has been located on the side streets flanking Broadway. On your left, as you proceed down Shubert Alley toward 44th Street, is the back wall of **One Astor Plaza.** This huge and curious-looking modern skyscraper has a roofline reminiscent of the tail fins on a 1959 Plymouth. It occupies the site of the old Astor Hotel, spiritual forebear of today's Marriott.

On the right (west) side of Shubert Alley look for the:

6. **Shubert Theater,** one of the district's approximately 40 theaters, on 44th Street. The Shubert brothers and their many theaters became such a powerful force on Broadway, and indeed throughout the country, that the federal government brought an antitrust suit against them. A decree in 1956 compelled them to sell off 12 theaters in six cities. They still remain a major theatrical power.

When you reach 44th Street, turn left (east) and return to Times Square. Then turn right and proceed two blocks south to the northwest corner of Seventh Avenue and 42nd Street. To your right, according to the big sign across the street, is the:

7. **"Greatest Movie Street in the World,"** where the lineup of movie marquees stretching from Seventh to Eighth avenues on 42nd Street certainly gives credence to the claim. All of these theaters were built originally for legitimate stage shows. Many, especially the New Amsterdam, are incredibly opulent inside, despite the ravages attendant on decades of Viking movies and porno flicks. All sorts of sharpies make this block their home, so be careful.

Turn left on 42nd Street, cross Seventh Avenue, and then continue on across Broadway. On the south side of the street, at 142 West 42nd Street on the corner of Broadway, is the:

8. **Knickerbocker Hotel,** built in 1902 for John Jacob Astor IV. Now an office building, the Knickerbocker has the same sort of Astorian brick-and-limestone elegance that characterized the now-vanished Hotel Astor. Maxfield Parrish's famous mural of King Cole once hung in the bar of this hotel.

Keep walking east toward Sixth Avenue. This part of 42nd Street has been considerably sanitized of late. Perhaps by the time you read this there won't be an X-rated bookstore left. This seems hard for some of us to believe, but change, they say, is inevitable. The **New York Telephone Building,** a black-glass and white-marble high-rise box at the southwest corner of Sixth Avenue and 42nd Street, is presumably a harbinger of things to come.

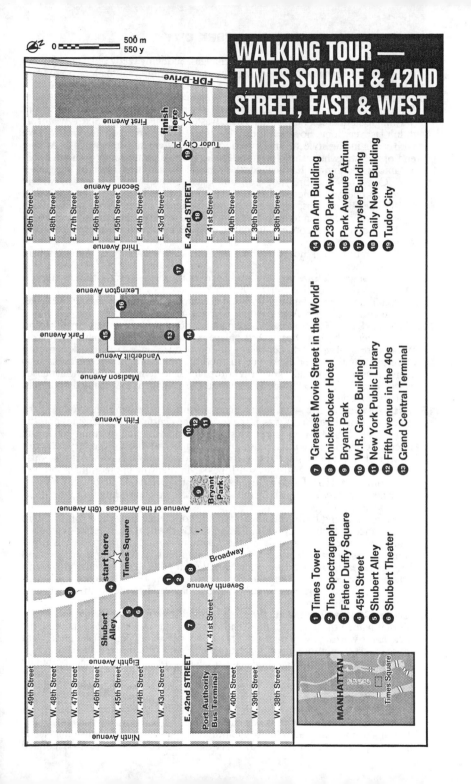

WALKING TOUR — TIMES SQUARE & 42ND STREET, EAST & WEST

1 Times Tower
2 The Spectragraph
3 Father Duffy Square
4 45th Street
5 Shubert Alley
6 Shubert Theater
7 "Greatest Movie Street in the World"
8 Knickerbocker Hotel
9 Bryant Park
10 W.R. Grace Building
11 New York Public Library
12 Fifth Avenue in the 40s
13 Grand Central Terminal
14 Pan Am Building
15 230 Park Ave.
16 Park Avenue Atrium
17 Chrysler Building
18 Daily News Building
19 Tudor City

Cross Sixth Avenue and everything changes. Suddenly seedy old Times Square is gone and fashionable Midtown surrounds you. Running south along Sixth from 42nd to 40th streets is:

9. **Bryant Park,** a lush patch of greenery named in 1884 after the famous poet William Cullen Bryant. In 1822, after the city removed the buried paupers from Washington Square, a new potter's field was established here on Sixth Avenue. It didn't last very long, however, for by 1842 the Croton Reservoir (a four-acre lake with walls in the style of an Egyptian tomb) was erected on the Fifth Avenue end of the site (where the New York Public Library stands today). And in 1853, a famous exhibition hall called the Crystal Palace was built at the other end. Constructed entirely of iron and glass, the Crystal Palace was widely touted as being completely fireproof, at least until it burned to the ground in 1858. The Bryant Park we see today was designed in the 1930s. Renovations have recently been made here, and some of the park is open again. The TKTS both for dance and concert discounted tickets is located on the park's north side.

Now return to 42nd Street and continue east toward Fifth Avenue where you'll see the:

10. **W. R. Grace Building,** a slope-sided black-glass tower. It's an atypical skyscraper design of the mid-1970s.

You'll notice that the neighborhood gets more solid with every step you take. At the corner of Fifth Avenue you'll be right alongside the:

11. **New York Public Library,** whose main entrance faces Fifth between 40th and 42nd streets. This 1911 Beaux-Arts palace is one of the finest buildings in New York, a fitting place for the repository of knowledge. Make a one-block detour to the right (south) on Fifth Avenue to the library's main entrance. The famous stone lions out front make good backdrops for snapshots. The building's interior is worth exploring too. "Imperial" is about the only word that really describes it. Continue along:

12. **Fifth Avenue in the 40s,** which bears absolutely no resemblance today to the quiet residential quarter it was at the turn of the century. The mansions and the clubs have all been swept away, victims of a runaway tide of rising real estate prices. At one time the intersection of Fifth and 42nd marked the very center of New York domestic fashion, being located midway between Mrs. Astor's house at Fifth and 34th and Mary Mason Jones's Marble Row in the "hinterlands" at Fifth and 57th. How hard it is even to imagine those days, surrounded now by the roar of traffic, the crush of the sidewalk crowds, and the giddy heights of today's tall buildings.

Before crossing Fifth, you might note the good view uptown to your right. In the distance at 50th Street is **St. Patrick's Cathedral,** silhouetted fetchingly against the brown-glass wall of the Olympic Tower. Now cross Fifth and continue east toward Madison Avenue. Cross Madison when you get there and keep going east. The handsome office building at 60 E. 42nd Street, on the south side of the street, is the **Lincoln Building,** built in 1939. In another moment you'll be at Vanderbilt Avenue, a short street that starts on the north side of 42nd Street. Here you'll find:

13. **Grand Central Terminal,** the great railroad station. Commodore Vanderbilt himself named the place "Grand Central" in the late 1860s, notwithstanding the fact that it was then way out in the boondocks. The original station underwent more or less continuous alterations until the present structure replaced it in 1913. Besides being visually magnificent, it's an engineering tour de force, combining subways, surface streets, pedestrian malls, vehicular viaducts, underground shopping concourses, and 48 pairs of railroad tracks together with attendant platforms and concourses into one smoothly functioning organism.

Turn left on Vanderbilt Avenue and go one block north to the 43rd Street entrance to Grand Central. Inside these doors is a perfectly breathtaking sight. The main concourse of Grand Central is one of America's most impressive interior spaces—125 feet high, 375 feet long, and 120 feet wide. It's decorated with fine stone carvings, gleaming marble floors, sweeping staircases, and a blue vaulted ceiling decorated with the constellations. In 1960 the owners proposed that this space be divided into four levels, but it was saved from this destructive renovation and has been a city landmark since 1965. Today much of it is being restored as part of a deal worked out with developer Donald Trump for bonuses on an adjacent site.

Descend the cascading staircase to the main concourse. Then cut diagonally to your left across the floor toward the bank of escalators on the north wall. Ride the escalators up, admiring the wonders of the old terminal as you go. Note the chandeliers (how do they change those bulbs?). The escalator will deposit you at the south end of the:

14. Pan Am Building, also known as 200 Park Avenue. Just keep walking north, away from Grand Central, and you'll eventually emerge on 45th Street between Vanderbilt and Lexington Avenues.

REFUELING STOP **Tropica Bar and Seafood House,** in the Pan Am Building, serves seafood with a Caribbean flair and is immensely popular with an upscale business lunch crowd. If you haven't made reservations (tel. 867-6767) stop in at the lounge, where light food and daily specials are served on a first-come, first-served basis.

Walk directly across 45th Street and into the ornate doorway of:

15. 230 Park Avenue, a handsome structure now known as the Helmsley Building, after its current owner, real estate magnate Harry Helmsley. Built in 1929 as the New York Central Building, it is a triumph of the business-palatial style. When the fortunes of the railroad began to falter, the place was sold and the sign on the wall was changed to the New York General Building. The Helmsley interests have changed the name again and decorated the facade with a considerable amount of gold leaf. Walk straight through the lobby, notable for its sumptuous marble and bronze work. At the far end you'll emerge on 46th Street, right in the middle of Park Avenue.

Turn right, cross over the northbound roadway of Park Avenue, and head toward Lexington Avenue. Don't go all the way to Lexington, but look instead on your right for the doorway to the:

16. Park Avenue Atrium. This new building is worth a detour for a look at its handsome multistory atrium, furnished with plush burgundy carpeting, polished granite benches, chromium walls, and silent exterior-mounted elevators that whoosh up and down past an immense and dramatic hanging sculpture made of golden metal bands. A pretty restaurant surrounded by potted ficus trees occupies the area adjacent to the soaring central space. It looks like a nice place for a glass of wine and a refined lunch. Next to it is a more informal bar called Charley O's that serves sandwiches and big drinks.

Take the Lexington Avenue exit from the Park Avenue Atrium and turn right (south). Three blocks ahead, on the east side of Lexington Avenue between 42nd and 43rd streets, is the:

17. Chrysler Building, once the tallest building in the world, until eclipsed by the Empire State Building. The exterior demonstrates all that's right about old-time skyscrapers. It's an ornament to the skyline. Notice the huge winged radiator caps that mark the base of the tower. The lobby inside has lots of brown-veined marble and a signature Art Deco angularity. It's so glamorous you almost expect Jean Harlow to whiz around the corner in a satin dress.

Exit the Chrysler Building via the 42nd Street door, turn left, and continue east on 42nd toward Third Avenue. At 220 E. 42nd Sreet., between Third and Second avenues, is the:

18. *Daily News* Building. This modern brick tower, built in 1930, was the inspiration for the *Daily Planet* Building, where Clark Kent worked when he wasn't being Superman. The exterior was ahead of its time for 1930. Even today it hardly looks 59 years old. The lobby contains a huge revolving globe sunk in the floor and surrounded with little plaques bearing messages like: "If the sun were the size of this globe and placed here, then comparatively the moon would be one-third inch in diameter and placed at the main entrance to Grand Central Terminal." Elsewhere in the lobby are gauges disclosing wind direction, humidity, temperature, and so on, plus such things as blowups of news photos and famous front pages.

When you're done with the News Building, return to 42nd Street and turn right. Continue east across Second Avenue, then cross 42nd Street to the north side of the block. That slablike building beyond the big Tudor City sign is the **United Nations Secretariat Building** (described in Section 1, Chapter 7, "What to See and Do in New York City"). Midway between Second and First avenues, on the north side of the street, is the brownish granite fortress of the **Ford Foundation Building.** Built in 1967, it contains an early atrium that has yet to be surpassed in terms of beauty. There's a little pool with water gurgling into it, brick paths wandering through terraces of greenery, and a great sense of calm.

Return to 42nd Street and, if the mood seizes you, walk up the brick stairs flanking 42nd Street to:

19. **Tudor City,** a very large apartment complex dating from the 1920s. It is done entirely in the sort-of-Tudor style so popular after World War I. When built, it was surrounded by slums and slaughterhouses so that by necessity the project included its own park, shops, restaurants, and post office, as well as some heart-stoppingly beautiful apartments, many of which rent today for absurdly low controlled prices. Gaze up at those walls of double-height leaded windows on the upper floors. It looks almost as if a series of English country mansions had been grafted onto the top of a row of apartment towers.

When you've had enough of Tudor City, return to 42nd Street. The crosstown bus stops at the corner of First Avenue. Don't forget to ask the driver for a free transfer if you're eventually heading north or south of 42nd.

WALKING TOUR 6 —— Midtown & Fifth Avenue

Start: Grand Army Plaza, Fifth Avenue and 59th Street
Finish: Seventh Avenue and Central Park South
Time: Approximately 1½ hours

Start at:

1. **Grand Army Plaza,** or simply "The Plaza," one of New York's most handsome outdoor spaces. Its centerpiece is a fountain atop stacked reflecting pools, donated to the city in 1916 by publishing czar Joseph Pulitzer. At its summit is a graceful statue of Pomona, Roman goddess of bounteous gardens. Some of the finest private mansions in New York once overlooked this square, notably the 138-room chateau of Cornelius Vanderbilt, grandson of the original Commodore Vanderbilt. This lamentably long-demolished house once occupied the entire Fifth Avenue blockfront from 57th to 58th streets. The site has been occupied since 1928 by:

2. **Bergdorf Goodman,** one of the most elegant stores in New York. The facial expressions and body language of its display mannequins are a ready barometer of fashionable attitudes.

Also overlooking the Plaza is the august:

3. **Metropolitan Club,** designed in 1893 by McKim, Mead, and White and located on the corner of 60th Street and Fifth Avenue. Supposedly, this club was organized by J. P. Morgan to accommodate friends who couldn't get into the nearby University Club on Fifth and 54th. Whatever its origins, it is about as magnificent a building as one can imagine.

If you're interested in magnificence, you should take a quick look at the gilt and marble lobbies of:

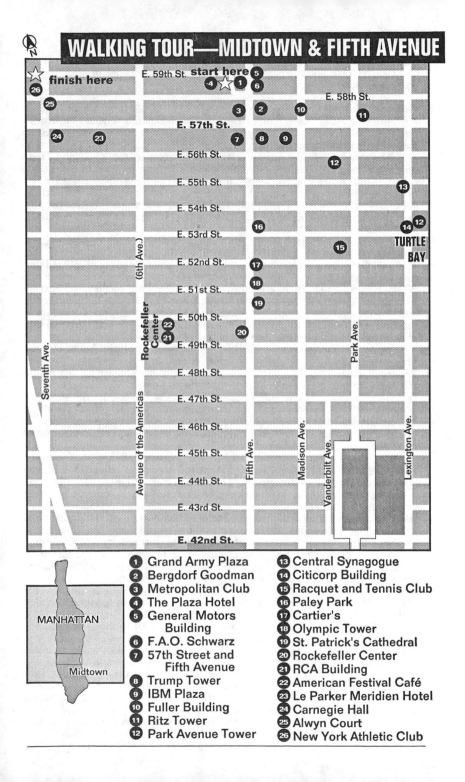

WALKING TOUR—MIDTOWN & FIFTH AVENUE

1. Grand Army Plaza
2. Bergdorf Goodman
3. Metropolitan Club
4. The Plaza Hotel
5. General Motors Building
6. F.A.O. Schwarz
7. 57th Street and Fifth Avenue
8. Trump Tower
9. IBM Plaza
10. Fuller Building
11. Ritz Tower
12. Park Avenue Tower
13. Central Synagogue
14. Citicorp Building
15. Racquet and Tennis Club
16. Paley Park
17. Cartier's
18. Olympic Tower
19. St. Patrick's Cathedral
20. Rockefeller Center
21. RCA Building
22. American Festival Café
23. Le Parker Meridien Hotel
24. Carnegie Hall
25. Alwyn Court
26. New York Athletic Club

4. **The Plaza Hotel,** on the western boundary of the Plaza between 58th Street and Central Park South. Designed by Henry J. Hardenbergh in 1907, it is a gorgeous place.

Also worth a look inside is the:

5. **General Motors Building,** which is the white marble tower directly across Fifth from the Plaza Hotel. Built in 1968 the G. M. Building provides showroom floors full of brand-new cars so that carless New Yorkers can see what the rest of the country is driving around in.

The Plaza is a divider between business districts to the south and fancy residential areas to the north. Northward from this spot Fifth Avenue was once called **"Millionaires' Mile."** It was literally lined with the ornate chateaux and brownstone palaces of the merchant elite. Today, most are gone (others like them survive along the side streets), replaced by swank apartment houses. But I'm saving the upper-crust East Side until later. For now we're heading south down Fifth Avenue.

Between 58th and 59th streets, on the same side of the street as the G. M. Building, is:

6. **F. A. O. Schwarz,** the famous luxury toy store. You may not have realized that toys could be so opulent. When you're done browsing, walk to the corner of:

7. **57th Street and Fifth Avenue,** perhaps the best retailing address in Manhattan. **Tiffany & Co.** and **Van Cleef & Arpels** overlook this intersection and provide nuclearproof-looking windows full of amazing gems. Glance up at the **Crown Building,** too, on the southwest corner of 57th and Fifth. All that glittery yellow stuff on the stonework is real gold leaf.

Stay on the Tiffany side of Fifth for another half a block. About midway between 56th and 57th streets is the entrance to:

8. **Trump Tower.** This glittery mixed-use cooperative has commercial tenants on the lower floors and million-dollar-plus apartments upstairs. Real estate developer Donald Trump was New York's *wunderkind* in the 1980s. Push the huge gold T's mounted on the doors and you'll enter a posh shopping atrium with an 80-foot waterfall and more pink marble than you would have supposed was in all of Italy. Shops here sell antiques, Paris fashions, jewels, and all sorts of other good stuff.

After a few exhilarating breaths of Mr. Trump's world, follow the sign to the left of the escalator that says "To IBM Plaza and Madison Avenue." You'll cross through a little bit of **Lafayette Galleries,** a Paris-based specialty shop adjoining Trump Tower, before emerging in yet another dramatic enclosed atrium. You are now in:

9. **IBM Plaza,** nothing less than a glass-enclosed bamboo forest. It's a great place to sit and have a light snack from the refreshment kiosk (crowded, however, at lunchtime). There are tables and chairs, fascinating aromatic floral plantings that change with the seasons, and an impressive sense of space. If you're fortunate, there may even be a little concert (chamber music or some such) in progress beneath the bamboos. IBM deserves high marks for this one.

Leave IBM Plaza by the 57th Street door, then cross Madison Avenue. That good-looking Art Deco office tower on the northeast corner of Madison and 57th is the:

10. **Fuller Building,** built in 1929. If you stand at the foot of the Fuller Building and look south down Madison, you'll get a fine view of Philip Johnson's new **AT&T Building.** It's the big granite number that looks like a Queen Anne highboy standing on the east side of Madison down at 55th and 56th.

Continue walking on 57th Street now, eastbound in the direction of Park Avenue. This is one of the most splendid and cosmopolitan shopping districts on earth. The shop windows are filled with museum-quality antiques, precious crystal and jewels, and the latest fashions.

When you reach Park Avenue, pause for a moment. That slender and elegant building across the avenue on the northeast corner of Park and 57th is the:

11. **Ritz Tower.** Built in 1925, it is best known as the former home of Le Pavillon,

once the most famous French restaurant in New York. Now look to the south down Park Avenue. Straddling the roadway is the gilded **Helmsley Building,** formerly the New York Central Building. Its famous silhouette was severely injured in 1963 when the egg-crate-like Pan Am Building was built right behind it.

Stroll down the west side of Park to 56th Street, then glance down 56th toward Madison Avenue. The new:

12. **Park Avenue Tower,** which isn't on Park Avenue at all but rather on the south side of 56th Street, gives the appearance of twisting at the strangest angle. Now continue down Park to 55th and cross to the east side of the street. The green-roofed tower down the road, by the way, belongs to **The Waldorf-Astoria** hotel at Park and 50th Street.

Continue eastbound on 55th Street for one block to the corner of Lexington Avenue. The block from Park to Lexington, with its dignified town houses, gives a good idea of what this neighborhood looked like before the era of the mighty glass office building. The onion-domed structure at the southwest corner of Lexington and 55th looks like a little bit of old Moscow. Actually it's the:

13. **Central Synagogue,** the oldest synagogue building in continuous use in New York City. The structure, erected in 1871, was designed by Henry Fernbach, New York's first practicing Jewish architect.

Continue south one block on Lexington to 54th Street. The huge complex on the east side of Lexington between 53rd and 54th is the:

14. **Citicorp Building.** Inside is yet another atrium, this one called the Market. It contains the obligatory incredible interior space, plus lots of places (many of them quite reasonable) to eat. Most sell food that you can carry out with you to one of the many tables and chairs beneath a very lofty skylight.

If you've temporarily had enough of atriums, turn right (west) on 54th Street back in the direction of Park Avenue. You might note 11 E. 54th Street as you pass. This former private home was built in the architectural style fashionable just before this neighborhood turned commercial.

At Park Avenue and 54th Street, look downtown at that low building on the west side of Park between 52nd and 53rd streets. This is the:

15. **Racquet and Tennis Club,** a patrician stronghold containing one of the handful of court tennis courts in the country. (Court tennis, by the way, is more difficult and complicated than regular tennis and was played by Henry VIII at Hampton Court Palace on a 90′ × 30′ court still in use there.) Several years ago the Racquet Club assured its future finances by selling valuable air rights to the developer of the glass office tower that now looms behind it.

Stay on 54th Street, cross Park Avenue, and continue one block west to Madison Avenue. Now cross to the west side of Madison Avenue and go one block south to 53rd Street. While you're here, you might do a bit of window-shopping in the chic shops at the foot of the angular **Continental Illinois Building.**

Turn right on 53rd Street and head west one block toward Fifth Avenue. The East 50s were once New York's most exclusive and opulent mansion district. A survivor is 12 E. 53rd Street, no longer a residence but still complete with battlements, balconies, and leaded windows. On the north (right-hand) side of this block, just before Fifth Avenue, is:

16. **Paley Park,** a delectable little cobbled enclave furnished with lacy locust trees, climbing ivy, metal chairs and tables, and a wall of falling water at its far end. Built in 1967 on the site of the famous Stork Club, it's a wonderful place to sit and meditate on life, or maybe have a sandwich.

Leave Paley Park and go to the corner of Fifth Avenue. To your right, up at the northwest corner of Fifth Avenue and 54th Street, is the **University Club,** McKim, Mead, and White's 1899 homage to the Italian Renaissance. We're going the other direction, however. One block south to 52nd Street is:

17. **Cartier's,** housed in a former private palace on the southeast corner of Fifth and 52nd. A now-forgotten millionaire named Morton Plant was induced by the

Vanderbilt family to build this house in 1904. The Vanderbilts, many of whom had houses on Fifth in the 50s, were trying desperately to keep the area residential. They failed, and all their houses are gone. Mr. Plant's remains. It has been occupied by the jewelry firm of Cartier since 1917.

Continue south on Fifth Avenue for another block to 51st Street. The big brown glass tower on the northeast corner of Fifth and 51st is the:

18. **Olympic Tower,** another fashionable multiple-use building.
19. **St. Patrick's Cathedral,** seat of the Archdiocese of New York, occupies the east side of Fifth between 51st and 50th, a magnificent Gothic style structure. Its interior is well worth a look.

Continue south to 50th Street and cross Fifth Avenue. Now you're in the region of:

20. **Rockefeller Center,** one of the most handsome urban complexes in New York, perhaps in the nation. Facing the famous **Promenade,** which leads off Fifth, and occupying the entire eastern blockfront from 49th to 50th Streets is **Saks Fifth Avenue,** one of New York's great department stores. Save Saks for a later browse and turn right (west) into the Promenade, also located midway between 49th and 50th streets.

As you turn off Fifth into the Promenade, you'll see the slender tower of the:

21. **RCA Building** (known also by its address, 30 Rockefeller Plaza), looking like something out of H. G. Wells. At Christmastime the Rockefeller Center tree stands before it. Walk around the sunken plaza and have a look inside. The lobby is the epitome of high style à la 1933 (the building's completion date). Above the black marble floors and walls are monumental sepia-toned murals depicting the unending labors of Michelangelo-esque men and women; they were painted by José María Sert. Originally, a highly political mural by Diego Rivera faced the building's front door. Rather than remove an image of Lenin hovering over a tableau of rich people playing cards, Rivera insisted the mural be destroyed. The Rockefellers willingly obliged.

Stroll down the Promenade and admire the beautiful plantings. Here's where you'll find our next:

REFUELING STOP   22. The American Festival Café is an exuberant celebration of American regional cooking, in a colorful setting overlooking the skating rink in winter and the garden in summer.

Walk all the way down the lobby of the RCA Building to the exit on Sixth Avenue. Now turn right (north) and start walking back uptown. There used to be an elevated train on Sixth Avenue, which for most of the neighborhood's history exercised a fairly depressing influence. A building boom in the 1960s and 1970s transformed the dreary blockfronts into an astonishing canyon of 50-story glass skyscrapers. Although this is just another Manhattan business district and the buildings individually aren't of great note, taken together they form an urban environment of considerable grandeur.

At 56th Street, turn left (west) toward Seventh Avenue, and go a few steps to the entrance to:

23. **Le Parker Meridien Hotel,** located on the north side of the street. Enter the lobby doors and walk straight across the reception area toward the big hanging tapestry on the wall ahead. Bear to the right into the atrium court. This is a public area, not restricted to guests. And the atrium, with its columns and balustrades and palette of pale peach, coral, and cream, is quite beautiful. Exit the atrium via the door market "57e Rue." You'll pass through another spectacular interior space with marble floors and an immensely high polychrome ceiling. Its sole purpose is to serve as a passageway to 57th Street.

Outside on 57th, turn left (west) toward Seventh Avenue. At the end of the block, on the southeast corner of 57th and Seventh, is:

24. Carnegie Hall, built in 1891 and saved from demolition by a hairsbreadth in the early 1960s. It recently underwent a total restoration.

Now cross 57th Street and continue north (uptown) on Seventh Avenue. This neighborhood is really an extension of the apartment-house district along Central Park South. Most of the buildings hereabouts are anonymous enough, with the blinding exception of:

25. Alwyn Court. Built in 1909 on the southeast corner of Seventh and 58th Street, its facade is a frenzied tour de force in terra-cotta ornamentation. Descriptions cannot do it justice; it must be seen to be believed.

The next block of Seventh, between 58th and Central Park South, contains the:

26. New York Athletic Club, famous for its prosperous ambience. And the corner ahead, that of Seventh Avenue and Central Park South, marks the end of our tour.

WALKING TOUR 7 — Upper West Side

Start: Lincoln Center for the Performing Arts
Finish: The Dorilton, Broadway at 71st Street
Time: 2 to 6 hours, depending on stops
Best Times: Tuesday to Sunday, when museums are open

Begin at:

1. Lincoln Center for the Performing Arts, Broadway to Amsterdam Avenue, from 62nd to 66th streets. An energetic revitalization of the Upper West Side really began full force with the completion of the city's multicultural facility at Lincoln Center. This controversial—some criticize the architecture as too conservative, others fault it for being too daring—complex includes: Avery Fisher Hall, formerly Philharmonic Hall, 1962; New York State Theater, 1964; Vivian Beaumont Theater, 1965; New York Public Library and Museum of the Performing Arts, 1965; Metropolitan Opera House, 1966; Alice Tully Hall and Juilliard School of Music, 1968. Three of the buildings face the central plaza—the Metropolitan Opera House in the middle, Avery Fisher Hall to the right, and the New York State Theater to the left. The plaza itself is dominated by a handsome fountain and, on summer evenings, by café tables that spill out from Avery Fisher Hall. (See Section 1, "The Top Attractions," in Chapter 7, "What to See and Do in New York City," for a full description.)

Tours are given between 10am and 5pm daily, last an hour, and cost $7.50 for adults, $6.50 for seniors and students, and $4.25 for children 12 and under. To reserve, or for further information, call 877-1800, ext. 512. Looking east across the plaza, notice the rooftop replica of:

2. The Statue of Liberty, 43 West 64th Street. Her torch is gone, and her spiral staircase is now closed permanently, but this 1902 lady is an exact duplicate of her larger, more famous counterpart.

In front of the plaza is the tiny:

3. Dante Park. The bronze statue of the Italian poet Dante Alighieri was erected here in 1921 to commemorate the 600th anniversary of his death. He holds a copy of *The Divine Comedy,* in good company with the artistic offerings of Lincoln Center.

Cross Broadway and walk north to the:

4. Museum of American Folk Art, 2 Lincoln Square (tel. 977-7298). (See Chapter 7, "What to See and Do in New York City," for details.) The museum also has a charming shop filled with such treasures as ceramics, mobiles, toys, doll houses, and miniature Pennsylvania Dutch blanket chests—all handmade, naturally. The shop's hours are Monday, Tuesday, and Saturday 11am to 6pm; Wednesday through Friday, 11am to 7:30pm, Sunday noon to 6pm.

Crossing west on Broadway at 66th Street, you pass:

5. Tucker Park. A bronze bust honors Richard Tucker, the operatic tenor who, during his 21-year career with the Metropolitan Opera, sang almost 500 performances.

A branch of:

6. Tower Records, 1965 Broadway at 66th Street (tel. 799-2500), contains two neon-lit floors of CDs, tapes, and videos, both domestic and imported, at discount prices.

Cross Broadway again and head east on 67th Street toward Central Park. The block between Columbus Avenue and the park is a delightful enclave of older buildings designed originally as artists' studios. Concealed behind the facades are double-height studio spaces.

7. The Atelier, no. 33, dates from 1902 and has a handsome stone-arched facade.

8. No. 15 is notable for its Gothic-Revival lobby resembling a chapel. And finally, the:

9. Hotel des Artistes, no. 1, is one of New York's treasures. Completed in 1918, this splendid building actually shows balconied artists' spaces behind its buoyant Elizabethan facade. A list of past residents reads like a Who's Who of entertainment and the arts: Noel Coward, Norman Rockwell, Isadora Duncan, and Edna Ferber, among others. An early occupant, Howard Chandler Christy, decorated the prestigious ground-floor *Café des Artistes* with his painting of a pin-up girl.

Just across Central Park West and slightly into the park, trees strung with tiny lights identify:

10. Tavern-on-the-Green, at 67th Street near Central Park West (tel. 873-3200), one of the most romantic dining/dancing spots in town. Though expensive, this is a must-visit, if only to stroll the grounds behind the glorious Crystal Room.

11. Central Park, 59th to 110th streets, Fifth Avenue to Central Park West, is a tribute to the foresight of the city fathers, and especially to poet William Cullen Bryant (1794–1878), who pleaded the case for an urban recreation area and public park. The city bought the land in 1856, sponsored a competition for the best development plan, and awarded the prize to landscape architects Frederick Law Olmsted and Calvert Vaux, who subsequently spent 20 years supervising their 840-acre virtuoso masterpiece of landscaped lakes, hills, meadows, footpaths, bridges, bridle paths, secluded glens, a bird sanctuary, two skating rinks, a first-rate zoo, multiple recreational facilities, and an impressive collection of sculpture. The park was designated a National Historic Landmark in 1965. It remains one of the most successful landscaped areas anywhere.

At the southwest corner of Central Park West and 70th Street is:

12. The Spanish and Portuguese Synagogue, Congregation Shearith Israel, 8 W. 70th Street. This is the third home of the oldest Jewish congregation in the United States—Spanish and Portuguese refugees from the Inquisition in Brazil, who built their first house of worship in 1730. After three successive moves uptown, this classic Revival building was erected in 1897. A connecting "Little Synagogue" at the rear of the building is an accurate reconstruction of the 1730 Mill Street temple, with many of the original artifacts and furnishings.

Continuing north you reach the:

13. Majestic Apartments, 115 Central Park West from 71st to 72nd streets. Built in 1930, this is a fine example of the art deco style that was all the rage during the late 1920s and 1930s. One of four twin-towered apartment houses that enliven the Central Park skyline, the attractive, much-imitated brickwork was designed by the French sculptor René Chanbellan.

14. The Dakota Apartments, northwest corner of Central Park West and 72nd Street. Legend has it that this building got its name for its location in what was, in 1884, the boondocks of Manhattan, so remote from the city center that it might

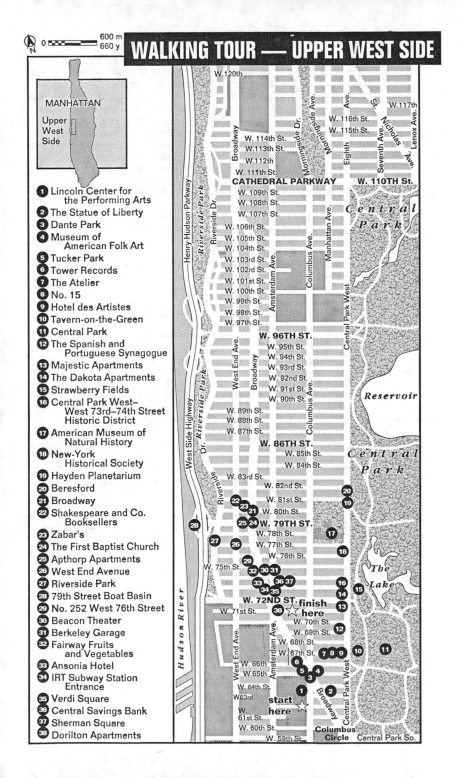

WALKING TOUR — UPPER WEST SIDE

MANHATTAN
Upper West Side

1 Lincoln Center for the Performing Arts
2 The Statue of Liberty
3 Dante Park
4 Museum of American Folk Art
5 Tucker Park
6 Tower Records
7 The Atelier
8 No. 15
9 Hotel des Artistes
10 Tavern-on-the-Green
11 Central Park
12 The Spanish and Portuguese Synagogue
13 Majestic Apartments
14 The Dakota Apartments
15 Strawberry Fields
16 Central Park West–West 73rd–74th Street Historic District
17 American Museum of Natural History
18 New-York Historical Society
19 Hayden Planetarium
20 Beresford
21 Broadway
22 Shakespeare and Co. Booksellers
23 Zabar's
24 The First Baptist Church
25 Apthorp Apartments
26 West End Avenue
27 Riverside Park
28 79th Street Boat Basin
29 No. 252 West 76th Street
30 Beacon Theater
31 Berkeley Garage
32 Fairway Fruits and Vegetables
33 Ansonia Hotel
34 IRT Subway Station Entrance
35 Verdi Square
36 Central Savings Bank
37 Sherman Square
38 Dorilton Apartments

as well have been in Dakota. Built by Singer Sewing Machine heir Edward S. Clark on a hunch that the Upper West Side had potential as a residential area, it was designed by Henry J. Hardenbergh (architect also of the Plaza Hotel) in German Renaissance style, part fortress (it's surrounded by a dry moat), part chateau, with dormers, gables, arches, balconies, finials, and ornate stonework. Its status then and now as one of New York's most exclusive multiple dwellings notwithstanding, the Dakota has a moody atmosphere, and was the setting for the film *Rosemary's Baby*, and for Jack Finney's science-fiction novel *Time and Again*. In December 1980 it was also the site of the tragic murder of former rock star and Beatle John Lennon, in whose memory his widow, Yoko Ono, has created the touching memorial directly across the street:

15. **Strawberry Fields,** in Central Park at 72nd Street (see Chapter 7, "What to See and Do in New York City," for details).

Cross Central Park West, walk to 73rd Street, and turn left, noticing the ornamental iron gate and dry moat of the Dakota. Clark and Hardenbergh joined forces in another project after the Dakota, the development of what is now the

16. **Central Park West—West 73rd—74th Street Historic District,** animated by a series of rental row houses in polychrome, a departure from the relentless rows of brownstones that lined the city streets during the 1870s and '80s. One of the houses was occupied by Edward Clark, and it is thought to be connected to the Dakota by an underground passageway. Note especially nos. 15A–19 and 41–65, built between 1882 and 1885.

REFUELING STOPS Columbus Avenue from 72nd to 81st streets is dotted with good eating places in a range of prices. **Rupert's** (72nd–73rd streets) and the **Museum Café** (77th Street) are well-established and popular bets for leisurely lunches and dinners (they can get crowded, so best arrive at off hours.) More casual and less pricey is an attractive branch of **Pizzeria Uno** at 81st Street.

As a diversion from sightseeing, explore some of the shops along Columbus Avenue. A selection of hand-made products is available at Craft Galleria (no. 290). Kenar (no. 303), French Connection (no. 304), and Express (no. 321) sell women's fashions. The jewelry at Ylang-Ylang (no. 324) is funky and off-beat. Putamayo (no. 339) specializes in interesting ethnic clothing and accessories. At Mythology (no. 370) you'll find everything from art supplies to antique toys. The Hero's Journey (no. 489, between 83rd and 84th streets, necessitating a short detour). It's a serene emporium oriented to inner development, with a wide selection of metaphysical books, New Age music, natural crystals, crystal jewelry, and the like.

Along Columbus Avenue to Central Park West, from 77th to 81st streets, is the spectacular:

17. **American Museum of Natural History** (tel. 769-5100), which houses one of the world's most important scientific collections, and is among the most frequently visited museums in town. The original entrance is at the 77th Street side, a massive Romanesque Revival edifice in pink Vermont granite built from 1892 to 1899, with a carriage entrance, arcaded porch, towers and turrets, and a grand staircase. The Central Park West facade is dominated by an equestrian statue of Theodore Roosevelt sculpted by J. E. Frazer in 1939. (See Chapter 7, "What to See and Do in New York City," for details.)

Though overshadowed by the Natural History Museum, the:

18. **New York Historical Society,** on the southwest corner of 77th Street (tel. 873-3400), is a pleasing, understated classical palace begun in 1908, with wings added in 1938; it's a major research venue for students of American history. (See Chapter 7, "What to See and Do in New York City.")

Walk north, rounding the corner at 81st Street to the:

19. **Hayden Planetarium,** at 81st Street and Central Park West (tel. 769-5920),

wherein "cosmic laser concerts" are featured along with other heavenly explorations. The building is a 1935 adjunct to the American Museum of Natural History.

Before heading west, glance at the:

20. Beresford, northwest corner of 81st and Central Park West, an eminent cousin to the San Remo and built in 1929 during Central Park West's glory days, a luxury apartment house crowned by a baroque tower that gives it a decidedly romantic aura, not easy for a structure as large as this.

Walking west to Broadway you pass the typical turn-of-the-century residential brownstones that characterize the side streets of the Upper West Side. At Broadway the foot-weary can hop a no. 7 or no. 104 bus north to visit the **Cathedral of St. John the Divine** (Amsterdam Avenue and 112th Street) and/or **The Riverside Church** (Riverside Drive and 122nd Street)

The hardy can continue south along:

21. Broadway, the main thoroughfare of the Upper West Side, and the only major artery that runs on the diagonal in New York's grid system of streets. Seedy though it may be in parts, it's a monumental avenue edged by monumental buildings and centered by wide grassy malls.

22. Shakespeare and Co. Booksellers, on the southwest corner of Broadway and 81st Street, is a great place to browse. And just south is:

23. Zabar's, at Broadway and 81st Street. New York would be unimaginable without the gourmet food emporium whose variety of temptations defies categorizing. Known throughout the city, frequented by the cognoscenti in all boroughs, Zabar's is a landmark, an institution, an absolute must for anyone interested in the New York state of mind. Continue south to:

24. The First Baptist Church, at Broadway at 79th Street, is an austere Romanesque Revival structure dating from 1891, with curious asymmetrical twin towers.

The entire block, Broadway to West End Avenue, and West 79th to West 78th streets, is taken up by the:

25. Apthorp Apartments, a dignified luxury building that still retains its old-world elegance. Built for William Waldorf Astor in 1908, the limestone structure surrounds a central courtyard with a fountain beyond high vaulted passageways. Except for ground-floor shops on Broadway, the building remains intact and original. It is named for Charles Apthorpe, who bought the land in 1763. It remained in the family until 1879, when Astor purchased it.

Walk west on 77th Street to:

26. West End Avenue, until the early 20th century, a "millionaire's row" of stylish town houses. The wealthy moved a block west when Riverside Drive opened, but after World War I, a plethora of apartment houses were built to lure tenants back.

Continue west down the hill to:

27. Riverside Park, designed in 1875 by Central Park architect Frederick Law Olmsted and completed 15 years later.

A flight of steps to the left lead to a tunnel that in turn takes you down more steps, along a path, and through a rotunda to the:

28. 79th Street Boat Basin, an unexpected and delightful marina where many New Yorkers tie up or live permanently in their house-boats.

Return to Riverside Park and relax on a bench for a few minutes before taking the curved stairway at the basketball court up to Riverside Drive. Head east on 76th Street to:

29. No. 252 West 76th Street; view it from the opposite side to appreciate the eclectic classical facade, recently restored, and quite splendid.

Turn right at Broadway. On the east side, near 75th Street is the:

30. Beacon Theater. No matter what's playing, don't miss the magnificent art deco interior, a designated city landmark.

Walk around the theater to the:

31. Berkeley Garage, at 201 West 75th Street, a wonderful 1890 Romanesque Revival building that once housed the stables of the New York Cab Company.

The three arches provided a broad entrance for horses and carriages in the 1880s and '90s. Return to the west side of Broadway and continue south past:

32. Fairway Fruits and Vegetables, Broadway near 74th Street, popular with neighborhood types and connoisseurs, who flock there in droves to take advantage of fresh high-quality produce at bargain prices. Another Upper West Side institution.

One of New York's architectural masterpieces is the:

33. Ansonia Hotel, on Broadway, at the northwest corner of 73rd Street. Now a bit frayed (a restoration is in progress), the Ansonia was a grande dame among apartment hotels when it opened in 1904. Opulent and richly ornamental, it meant to imitate the French resort hotels along the Riviera. In its heyday it featured a roof garden, two swimming pools, and basement shops. Over the years the Ansonia became the bastion of the music profession, much the same as the Chelsea was popular with the literary set. Among its illustrious tenants were Enrico Caruso, Ezio Pinza, Lily Pons, Igor Stravinsky, Arturo Toscanini, and Yehudi Menuhin. It was also a favorite at one time or another of Florenz Ziegfeld, Billie Burke, and Theodore Dreiser. The building is striking for its mansard roof and rounded towers.

REFUELING STOP **Genoa Restaurant,** 271 Amsterdam Avenue, near 73rd Street (tel. 787-1094), is a tiny neighborhood hangout that serves very good modestly priced southern Italian cuisine in casual surroundings. Open for dinner only, 5 to 10:30pm, Tuesday through Saturday.

At the intersection of Broadway and West 72nd Street, the:

34. IRT Subway Station Entrance is one of the few remaining Art Nouveau structures of its kind, dating from 1904, when the underground railway was first built.

The intersection is divided into Verdi Square to the north and Sherman Square to the south.

35. Verdi Square honors the Italian composer, whose statue in marble stands on a granite pedestal above life-size figures of four of his characters—from *Aida, Falstaff, Otello,* and *La Forza del Destino.*

Dominating the north side of Verdi Square is the:

36. Central Savings Bank Building (now the Apple Bank), on the northeast corner of 73rd Street and Broadway. This massive Palladian palace gives an impression of financial security—obviously its builders' intention. The wrought-iron window grilles and lanterns (by Samuel Yellin) embellish the facade, while two lions flanking a large clock decorate the 73rd Street entrance.

37. Sherman Square is the southern part of the intersection where Broadway crosses Amsterdam Avenue. The:

38. Dorilton Apartments on the northeast corner of Broadway and 71st Street, for all its overblown embellishment, is a fascinating 1902 example of French Second Empire architecture. Controversial, it was harshly criticized at the time by the *Architectural Record* for its "gross excess of scale throughout, the wild yell with which the fronts exclaim 'Look at me,' as if somebody were going to miss seeing a building of this area twelve stories high! . . . How everything shrieks to drown out everything else!"

WALKING TOUR 8 — Upper East Side Historic District

Start: Grand Army Plaza, Fifth Avenue at 60th Street
Finish: Madison Avenue and East 91st Street

Time: Approximately 1 hour and 20 minutes

It was predicted over a century ago that fashion would settle permanently along the verges of Central Park. And that prediction has turned out to be true. Fifth Avenue north of Grand Army Plaza was called the **"Millionaires' Mile"** in the era of private palaces. Judging from old pictures, it was something to behold. Today it's lined with apartment houses interspersed with the occasional remaining mansion. But let's not believe for an instant that the age of imperial living is over. Some of the buildings on Fifth (as well as on Park and elsewhere on the East Side) contain apartments that are every bit as palatial as the now-vanished mansions. Even New Yorkers are surprised to hear of apartments with 20, 30, or even 40 rooms. But they do exist, and probably in no fewer numbers than the great houses they replaced.

Before we start you might take a look at Augustus Saint-Gaudens' **equestrian statue of General William Tecumseh Sherman,** which stands at the northern end of the Plaza between the lines of 59th and 60th streets. It was Sherman, of course, whose Civil War "March to the Sea" dealt the Confederacy such a staggering blow. The Plaza is officially called Grand Army Plaza in honor of the Grand Army of the Republic, or the Union Army. Saint-Gaudens' statue was shown in Paris in 1900 and erected here in 1903. It's more in tune with the area's residential past than the traffic and tumult that surround it today. But it remains a welcome aesthetic touch, and is very much in the spirit of the "City Beautiful" movement of the early 20th century.

To begin we're going to go north (uptown) on Fifth Avenue. Cross the extension of 60th Street that doglegs into the corner of Central Park and stay on the park side of Fifth. If the weather is good check out the:

1. **Bookstalls** lining the sidewalk near 60th Street. This is a bit of a self-conscious touch of Paris, but it's still rather nice. After browsing through a few old books, glance back at the gaggle of deluxe hotels crowding around the Plaza. They serve as a sort of conceptual buffer between midtown businesses to the south and uptown residences to the north.

    Also in the immediate vicinity are several of Manhattan's classiest clubs. On the corner of Fifth Avenue and 60th Street is the:

2. **Metropolitan Club,** a painted-stone Italian palace designed by the celebrated (and ubiquitous) McKim, Mead, and White. If you like this sort of thing, you might detour across the street for a look at the main entrance on 60th Street. At 4 E. 60th Street, right across from the Metropolitan, is the **Harmonie Club,** an elite Jewish social club also designed by McKim, Mead, and White in 1905, a little over ten years after the Metropolitan. These two fine buildings purposely complement one another.

    Go back to Fifth and keep walking uptown. At the corner of 62nd Street is the:

3. **Knickerbocker Club,** which looks a lot like the big private houses that once characterized the avenue. The Georgian brick Knickerbocker, built in 1914, was the work of a firm called Delano and Aldrich, a favorite of society in the early years of this century. It retains a very pedigreed image.

    The next block up is 63rd Street and on the corner you'll see:

4. **820 Fifth Avenue,** one of the earliest apartment houses hereabouts, and also one of the best. Built in 1916, there is but one apartment on each floor, with five fireplaces and seven bathrooms in each.

    Go back to Fifth and continue northward to 64th Street. Just inside Central Park, facing 64th, is the:

5. **Arsenal,** built in 1848 as an arms depot when this neighborhood was distant and deserted. The **Central Park Zoo** is right behind it. Across Fifth Avenue on the southeast corner of 64th Street is the former **mansion of** coal magnate **Edward Berwind.** If you've seen the mansions at Newport, Rhode Island, you've probably already seen Mr. Berwind's summer house, "The Elms" on

Bellevue Avenue. His New York residence dates from 1896 and has been preserved as cooperative apartments.

Turn right (east) off Fifth Avenue onto 64th Street and proceed toward Madison Avenue. This is a particularly handsome East Side block, lined with architectural extravaganzas of the sort that formerly stood on Fifth Avenue. Note in particular:

6. **3 E. 64th Street,** an opulent beaux arts mansion built in 1903 for the daughter of Mrs. William B. Astor. The house was designed by Warren and Wetmore, the firm responsible for Grand Central Terminal. Also worthy of admiration on this block are nos. 11, 19, and 20. No. 19, which looks more antique than its 1932 construction date, was built not as a house but as the art gallery it is today.

At the corner of:

7. **Madison Avenue** and 64th Street, turn left and proceed two blocks north to 66th Street. Madison is lined with fashionable shops and boutiques catering to the carriage trade. Note the rather fantastical apartment house built in 1900 on the northeast corner of 66th and Madison, then turn left (west) off Madison onto 66th Street, heading back in the direction of Fifth Avenue. Among the many notable houses on the block is 5 E. 66th Street, now the **Lotos Club,** but built in 1900 as the city residence of William J. Schiefflin. The architect was Richard Howland Hunt, and the style is Manhattan Magnificent, courtesy of the French Second Empire.

Now return to Madison Avenue and continue northward for two more blocks to 68th Street. At 68th Street, turn right (east) toward Park Avenue. Now you're on a block with lots of private houses, even though most people don't quite realize it. One of the best of these houses is:

8. **58 E. 68th Street,** on the south corner of the block at Park Avenue. Now occupied by the Council on Foreign Relations, the house was originally built in 1920 for Harold I. Pratt, son of Rockefeller partner Charles Pratt. Its construction signaled a major departure for this member of the famously close-knit Pratts. His three brothers all built mansions in Brooklyn opposite their father's. Virtually the entire family summered together in a complex of adjoining estates at Dosoris near Glen Cove, Long Island. But 58 E. 68th Street is in Manhattan, with no other Pratts in sight.

Look across 68th Street from the Pratt house to:

9. **680 Park Avenue,** a fine brick-and-marble mansion built in 1909 for banker Percy Pyne. The house once belonged to the Soviet Delegation to the United Nations. Khrushchev waved to curious crowds from its Park Avenue balcony during his famous shoe-banging visit to the U.N. many years ago. In 1965 this house was saved from demolition at the 11th hour by the Marquesa de Cuevas (born a Rockefeller), who bought it and donated it to the present occupant, the Center for InterAmerican Relations. The entire west side of Park Avenue from 68th to 69th streets is lined with refined brick-and-marble Georgian Revival houses like that of Percy Pyne. It's a surprise they're all still here!

Go north on Park to 69th Street, then turn right and cross Park Avenue, and continue eastbound on 69th Street toward Lexington Avenue. On the corner of Park and East 69th Street is the:

10. **Union Club,** designed in 1932 to house New York's oldest club. On the other side of 69th Street, and occupying the entire block from 68th to 69th and Park to Lexington, is **Hunter College.** Continue toward Lexington, soaking up the East Side atmosphere. Note 117 E. 69th Street, a prototypical not-so-small private East Side house.

When you arrive at:

11. **Lexington Avenue,** turn left (north) and go one block to 70th Street. Then turn left again (to the west) and continue down 70th back in the direction of Park Avenue. Note **125 E. 70th Street,** a post–World War II mansion built for Paul Mellon in a sort of French Provincial style. **East 70th Street** presents a succession of elegant houses, one more beautiful than the other. Some consider this the finest street in New York.

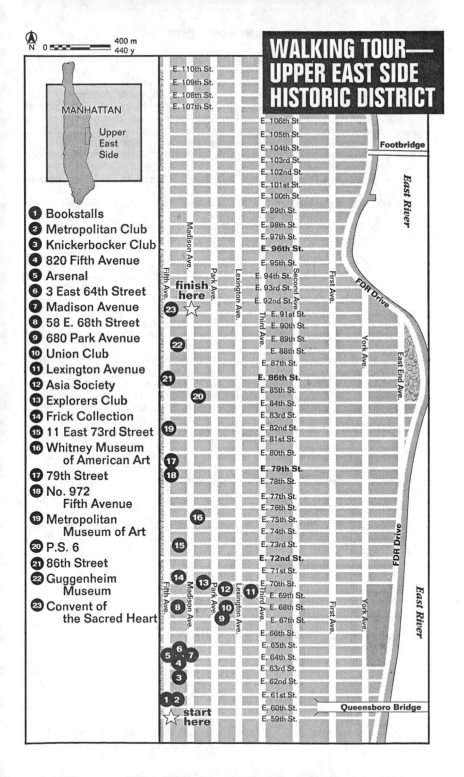

When you arrive at the Park Avenue end of the block, note the modern building housing the:

12. **Asia Society,** with its changing exhibits as well as its Asian-focused bookstore and gift shop. Then look across the street at **720 Park Avenue,** on the northwest corner of the intersection. This is a premier example of the sort of swanky Park Avenue building that lured former mansion dwellers away from their private houses. The complex upper floors of buildings like no. 720 often contain apartments with three or four floors and dozens of rooms.

Cross Park Avenue and continue west toward Fifth Avenue on 70th Street. Here you'll see the famous:

13. **Explorers Club** in the mansion at 46 East 70th Street, hard to beat for pure East Side class.

At the end of this block, cross Madison Avenue and continue on 70th toward Fifth Avenue. At the corner of Fifth is the:

14. **Frick Collection,** housed in the 1914 mansion of coke and steel magnate Henry Clay Frick. The beautiful classic garden overlooking 70th Street was built in 1977 and landscaped by Russel Page. It's a good fake; it looks definitely like something from the gilded age. Inside the Frick is a notable collection of paintings, as well as many original furnishings. Frick intended that the house, an 18th-century palace occupying a full blockfront on Fifth Avenue, be converted to a museum after his death. Huge as it is, this is not the biggest house still standing on Fifth. (Otto Kahn's is, farther up Fifth.)

Turn right at the corner of Fifth and 70th and continue three blocks north to the corner of Fifth and 73rd Street. Now turn right onto 73rd in the direction of Madison Avenue. Note:

15. **11 E. 73rd Street,** a particularly sumptuous house built in 1903 by (who else?) McKim, Mead, and White for Joseph Pulitzer, publisher of a once-famous but long-vanished newspaper called the *New York World.* Pulitzer rarely lived in this house because of an extreme sensitivity to sound. At one time it contained a special soundproofed room (mounted on ball bearings, no less) to prevent vibrations. The house today contains cooperative apartments.

Continue to the end of the block at Madison Avenue and turn left (north). Now stroll up Madison for six blocks to 79th Street. This is the heart of Madison Avenue Gallery Country. It's presided over by the **Hotel Carlyle** at 76th Street. On the southeast corner of Madison and 75th, by the way, is the:

16. **Whitney Museum of American Art,** that weird-looking box designed in 1966 by Marcel Breuer in the appropriately named "brutalist" style of architecture. Inside is a superb collection of modern art, and a cute restaurant called "Sarabeth's at the Whitney." At:

17. **79th Street,** turn left (west) and return to Fifth Avenue. The south side of 79th is a landmark block, designated too late, alas, to prevent the senseless demolition of the house on the Madison Avenue corner. More than enough remains, however, to provide a pretty good idea of how Fifth Avenue looked in its heyday. There's everything here, from Loire Valley chateaux to Neo-Georgian town houses.

When you reach the corner of Fifth, turn left for a look at:

18. **No. 972 Fifth Avenue,** the block between 78th and 79th. It is now the French Embassy's Cultural Services Office, but it was built in 1906 as a wedding present for one Payne Whitney by his doting (and childless) rich uncle, Col. Oliver Hazard Payne. This McKim, Mead, and White opus cost $1 million and was the talk of the town in its day. Next door, on the corner of 78th Street, is the classic French-style mansion of tobacco millionaire James B. Duke. His daughter, Doris, occupied the house intermittently until 1957, when she donated it to New York University. NYU now operates it as a fine arts institute.

Now turn around and walk north on Fifth until you reach 82nd Street. On your left is the:

19. **Metropolitan Museum of Art,** one of New York's greatest cultural resources, with its imperial-scale entrance. The block of 82nd Street that faces

the museum's mammoth staircase almost acts as a sort of formal court. The sumptuous brick-and-limestone mansion at 1009 Fifth Avenue is another old house preserved as a cooperative apartment building.

REFUELING STOPS Retreat to **Le Refuge,** an enchanting French bistro not far from the Metropolitan, at 166 E. 82nd Street, for omelets, salads, and other light lunch fare. Or visit **Kalinka,** 1067 Madison Avenue at 81st Street, a charming Russian café, for blinis, borscht, and an admirable chicken Kiev.

Turn right off Fifth Avenue onto 82nd Street and head toward Madison Avenue again. This is another fine East Side block, lined with elegant old town houses. Across Madison between 81st and 82nd streets is:

20. **P.S. 6,** a Manhattan public school whose excellent reputation is a major reason for the high rents hereabouts. Walk two blocks north on Madison to 84th Street and then turn left (west) toward Fifth Avenue.

When you reach Fifth, turn right (north) and continue uptown for two more blocks to:

21. **86th Street.** This is a big dividing line on the East Side, a fact which may not be apparent to visitors. It's a measure of the snobbery of some East Siders that they won't even go north of 86th Street. The big brick-and-limestone mansion on the southern corner of Fifth and 86th was built in 1914 for William Star Miller. It was to this house in 1944 that Mrs. Cornelius Vanderbilt retreated when her famous 640 Fifth Avenue house was sold. No. 640 Fifth was located down on 51st Street; by 1944 Mrs. V. was pretty much alone down there, surrounded by ghosts of the Vanderbilt past and lots of noisy traffic and new office buildings. No. 640 Fifth was the first of a concentration of Vanderbilt family houses that at one time caused Fifth in the 50s to be called "Vanderbilt Alley." The exile to 86th Street appears, at least from the look of this house, to have been comfortable, anyway. Today the building houses the Yivo Institute.

Two blocks farther up Fifth is the:

22. **Guggenheim Museum,** between 88th and 89th streets. Designed by Frank Lloyd Wright in 1959 (it's his only building in New York), it's as architecturally controversial today as it was when built. One block past the Guggenheim, between 90th and 91st streets, are the enormous enclosed grounds of the former **Andrew Carnegie Mansion,** now occupied by the Cooper-Hewitt Museum of Design and Decorative Arts. Built in 1901, this Georgian-esque palace originally shared the neighborhood with squatters' shanties and roaming pigs. By the time the squatters were gone and the streets were built up with fine houses, Carnegie was dead. His widow lived on in the house until 1949.

Across 91st Street from the Carnegie Mansion is the:

23. **Convent of the Sacred Heart,** occupying the largest private house ever built in Manhattan. Constructed in 1918 for financier Otto Kahn, it survives in pretty much its original condition. Other houses on this 91st Street block, notably nos. 7 and 9, are almost as grand. By now, Madison Avenue is approaching in the near distance, and that's the end of our tour. No subways are around here, but you can easily catch a downtown bus on Fifth Avenue, or a crosstown bus to the West Side down on 86th Street.

CHAPTER 9

NEW YORK CITY SHOPPING

1. CLOTHING
2. SHOPPING A TO Z
3. FOOD

There is one point that all visitors—and all New Yorkers too—seem to agree on: New York is the shopping capital of the United States. Nowhere else is there such a wealth of goods—made right here or imported from all over the world—to tempt the purchaser. Mexican wedding shirts, chic French jeans (even for pregnant women), African fabrics, Japanese kimonos, Berber capes, the latest imports from the People's Republic of China, Ukrainian decorated Easter eggs, Indian saris—you'll find it all here, in great profusion. Indeed, shopping is one of the city's finest entertainments.

But the thrill of shopping in New York goes even beyond the seemingly infinite variety of merchandise. For whether you're looking for a new camera, a Parsons table, or a Dior original, you can find it for less in the Big Apple. The purpose of this chapter, then, is to steer both the visitor and the resident to the most exciting bargains in town. We'll begin with clothing, then proceed alphabetically, listing everything from antiques to umbrellas. And we'll wind up with a gastronomical buying tour— everything from eggroll wrappers to homemade mozzarella cheese.

Most shops stay open Monday through Saturday from about 10am to 6pm. In the Village and SoHo, hours may be later. Many shops are open on Sunday afternoons; many on the Lower East Side, run by Orthodox Jews, are always closed on Saturday and open on Sunday; some stores close on summer weekends, some on Mondays. Best advice: If you're going out of your way to visit a shop, always call in advance to check the hours. Special shop hours are noted in the shop descriptions.

1. CLOTHING

The fashion industry is at the very heart of New York life. New York's Garment Center—an area that runs along Seventh Avenue ("Fashion Avenue") from 20th to 40th streets—produces nearly half the dresses and suits worn in the United States. Accordingly, it's no wonder that there are many good buys in retail clothing. Of course, nothing is as cheap as it used to be, but inveterate New York bargain hunters have a system. They use the major department and specialty stores—such as Macy's, Bloomingdale's, Lord & Taylor, Saks Fifth Avenue, and the like—for browsing, learning, and buying on sale; most of their purchases are made at designer discount stores and little shops off the beaten path where values are high and the strain on the pocketbook is manageable.

WOMEN'S CLOTHING & ACCESSORIES

ALEXANDER'S, Lexington Ave. and 58th St. Tel. 593-0880.
A diversified department store selling items that range from perfumes to video cassettes, toys, and appliances, Alexander's manages to maintain both a high-fashion policy and a low-price profile. It's filled with merchandise from all parts of the world. For across-the-board bargains, it is outstanding. There are usually great buys in cashmere sweaters and knitwear. If you're touring downtown New York, stop in at the Alexander's at the World Trade Center.

RICHARD'S ARMY-NAVY, 233 W. 42nd St. Tel. 947-5018.

Richard's Army-Navy, located between Seventh and Eighth avenues, is one of the country's largest repositories of Jacques Cousteau skin- and scuba-diving equipment. It also has one of the largest swim shops, with year-round selections of men's and women's professional and fashion swimsuits, goggles, and accessories. An oddball among the city's inexpensive clothing shops, Richard's was once a typical warehouse-type outlet for military surplus, and indeed the store's major stock in trade remains such items as regulation navy pea jackets, of which they sell several thousand a year. But Richard's is also well known to designers of high-camp styles, and even to Yves St. Laurent, whose visits a few seasons back resulted in a line of military-looking clothes designed specifically for women, as well as sporting wear modeled after military fashions. Richard's has all these (at a much lower price than anywhere else), plus Levi's denim jeans, Schott, and much more—everything from Adidas footwear to basketballs, leather flight jackets, and new camouflage fatigues. Newest rage for European tourists: their Dunham boots and shoes.

DESIGNER & OTHER DISCOUNT SHOPS

We know how you feel—you love clothes by Norma Kamali and Givenchy; Oscar de la Renta and Calvin Klein do wonders for your spirits; and Perry Ellis, Harvé Benard, Cathy Hardwick, and the like design the outfits you really want to wear. If you can't afford the top designers at boutique prices, don't despair: New York has many off-price stores where the price is right.

AARON'S, 627 Fifth Ave., between 17th and 18th sts., Brooklyn. Tel. 718/768-5400.

Aaron's is a marvelous store that specializes in high-fashion women's wear at discount prices. Current merchandise is sold at 25% to 30% off regular prices. Famous-brand, expensive knit dresses that go for $125 to $500 elsewhere cost $88 to $333 at the most here. Designer clothes of every type—coats, sportswear, cashmere sweaters—are all sold here. There's a large community dressing room, but the sales staff is courteous and helpful. Aaron's own parking field is across the street. Subway: Take BMT R local train to Prospect Ave. Walk one block to Fifth Ave.

BOLTON'S, 1180 Madison Ave., at 86th St. Tel. 722-4454.

Wherever you go in Manhattan, it seems, you'll find a Bolton's. And no wonder: Bolton's is Manhattan's largest women's discount chain. It offers current contemporary merchandise at 20% to 50% off major department and specialty-store prices. Bolton's prides itself on buying key fashion merchandise made of top-quality fabrics and workmanship; there's no junk to weed through here, just lots of good buys in coats, dresses, suits, sportswear, loungewear, sleepwear, and accessories. Dresses range from about $50 to over $100. We've had good luck here with handbags many times.

Fresh selections arrive three times a week, so it's not uncommon for people to stop in often. There are many other Bolton's locations around the city, including 685 Third Ave., at 43rd St. (tel. 682-5661); 4 E. 34th St., just off Fifth Ave. (tel. 684-3750); and 27 W. 57th St., between Fifth and Sixth avenues (tel. 935-4431). Check the local phone book for other addresses.

CANAL JEAN CO., 504 Broadway. Tel. 226-1130.

Canal Jean is a tremendous favorite with young people. Located a few blocks south of Houston Street, a short walk from Chinatown, Little Italy, or the heart of SoHo, it offers a wide selection of colorful merchandise, from antique clothing and military surplus to better sportswear for men and women to accessories and lingerie—and all at super-low discount prices. Start in front of the store, where bins always offer plenty of good values for inveterate bargain hunters. We once saw antique tweed coats and jackets for $1 and antique sweaters at three for $5. Inside, look for such popular basics as 100% cotton dyed T-shirts (five styles, ten colors at any given time at $5 each, or three for $12), or their own 100% cotton mock turtlenecks (available in 23 colors) for $17. Or expect the unexpected. Perhaps a Hawaiian aloha shirt at $9, brand-new American military trenchcoats at $30, a 100% cotton Canal Jean beach towel for under $5, or seasonal designer closeouts at 50% to 75% off regular retail prices. Canal Jean, which covers 12,000 square feet of space, also claims to be New York's, possibly the world's, largest retailer of Levi's jeans.

CENTURY 21, 12 Cortlandt St., between Church St. and Broadway. Tel. 227-9092.

Century 21 is a smart shopper's paradise. First-quality, current-season, moderately priced to expensive designer clothes are offered at good and sometimes huge discounts. Merchandise includes children's clothes, men's clothes, ladies' undergarments and sleepwear, beautiful shoes, linens, giftware, appliances, and much, much more. No try-ons allowed, but they do offer full refunds on all purchases. They're also in Brooklyn at 472 86th St.

DAFFY'S, 11 Fifth Ave., at 18th St. Tel. 529-4477.

Savvy New York shoppers have been celebrating—and buying—like crazy ever since Daffy's opened its first retail store in Manhattan a few years back. For years, New Yorkers either had to drive to Daffy's suburban New Jersey stores or just dream about those incredible, in-depth bargains their New Jersey friends always raved about. Daffy's first New York store, 35,000 square feet of merchandising space over three floors, is nothing if not dramatic, with vivid colors, glass staircases, and twin glass elevators. And the values on the racks are even more dramatic. Daffy's buyers buy "opportunistically" from the best designers on Seventh Avenue and in Europe and offer their finds for anywhere from 40% to 80% off regular retail prices every day of the week. When there's a special sale going on, they practically give the goods away. Here's what you might find on a typical shopping day: 100% silk dresses, regularly $158, $70 here; hand-knit wool sweaters that would be $118 elsewhere, $20 here; silk crepe-de-chine printed blouses, $48 in other stores, $17 to $20 here; flannel pants, $62 to $68 elsewhere, $30 here. There are also faux furs from France, leathers from Italy, cashmere sweaters from Scotland, lingerie, handbags, hats, and jewelry. Sizes range from 2 to 14, with some petites, and some fashions for larger women too. Children's and men's clothing are also featured at great savings. Daffy's has another, smaller store at Madison Avenue at 43rd Street (335 Madison Avenue, tel. 557-4422).

FILENE'S BASEMENT OF BOSTON, 187-04 Horace Harding Expressway, Fresh Meadows Shopping Mall, Queens. Tel. 718/479-7711.

No need to go all the way to Boston to enjoy the legendary shopping buys of Filene's Basement. In nearby Flushing you can sample the wares of the world's original "bargain basement." While this new version lacks the size and frenzied atmosphere of the original, the bargains are similar, if on a smaller scale; and there is even an improvement: dressing rooms, which somehow they never thought of in Boston. Filene's buys up huge lots of perfect and "nearly perfect" merchandise from leading manufacturers, and also from famous stores that need to dispose of unsold goods or are going out of business. Many of the original store labels—Neiman Marcus, Saks Fifth Avenue, I. Magnin, Sakowitz—are right on the garments. And the prices are always fractions—small fractions—of the originals. We've seen Neiman-Marcus sports coats for $98, Maggy London dresses for $60, handbags from Stone Mountain at $20, Buxton all-leather clutches at $5. Designer names show up frequently among the name-brand merchandise. Buys in lingerie and loungewear are outstanding. There's also a shoe department and a downstairs store for the men. New merchandise arrives daily, so if you don't find anything you need one day, come back the next. Yes, they do give refunds. Filene's is a bit of a trip by subway, but it's easy driving. There are other Filene's Basements on Long Island: in Manhasset at the Miracle Mile, 1400 Northern Boulevard; in Huntington on Rte. 110, adjacent to Walt Whitman Mall; in Copiague at 1101 Sunrise Highway; in Carle Place, across the street from Roosevelt Field Shopping Mall; as well as in Scarsdale, N.Y., and Paramus, N.J. Subway: For Fresh Meadows Shopping Mall take the Eighth Ave. E train to 169th

St., then take the Q17A bus. By Car: For Fresh Meadows Shopping Mall take the Long Island Expressway to Exit 25.

FISHKIN'S, 314 Grand St., at Allen St., and at 63 Orchard St., near Grand St. Tel. 226-6538.

There are hefty discounts on designer sportswear at this store. Merchandise includes sweaters, separates, bathing suits, cruisewear, shoes, handbags, and so on. Closed: Sun in July; Sat all year.

THE FORGOTTEN WOMAN, 888 Lexington Ave. Tel. 535-8848; 60 W. 49th St. at Rockefeller Center. Tel. 247-8888.

The Forgotten Woman caters to the larger-size woman who has difficulty finding stylish, upscale clothing. The store stocks both items that are currently in fashion and good basics that can be considered "investment dressing." The clothes are definitely good value (prices start at $25).

THE GAP, 22 W. 34th St., west of Fifth Ave. Tel. 695-2521.

The Gap is a phenomenally successful chain of stores selling jeans, sweat clothes, shirts, blouses, and other casual sports clothes for men, women, and children at moderate prices. Styles are sophisticated, merchandise all top-quality. Nifty polo shirts cost from $25 up. With some 24 stores in Manhattan, you'll find The Gap, it seems, every few blocks. Some central locations are Pier 17 at the South Street Seaport (tel. 374-1051); and 734 Lexington Ave., at 59th Street (tel. 751-1543). The Gap has an outlet store at 34th and Broadway (tel. 643-8960).

THE GREATER N.Y. WOMAN, 215 E. 23rd St., between Second and Third aves. Tel. 725-0505.

Downtown, the fashion-conscious larger woman has an ally in Carol Lefkowitz of the Greater N.Y. Woman, who has a great eye for high style at decent prices. There's a large collection of sportswear, daytime dresses, and executive clothing, and knowledgeable salespeople to help the customer put it all together.

KAISER-ROTH PERSONNEL, 1211 Sixth Ave., between 47th and 48th sts. Tel. 730-0924.

On the lower concourse level of the Celanese Building, this place is 18,000 square feet of bargains. All we can say is, "Come on down!" It is a factory outlet for many famous-brand items, and discounts run as high as 40% below wholesale. They have ladies' sportswear, lingerie, childrenswear, handbags, accessories (e.g., belts, gloves, hosiery, and so on), and socks for men, women, and children. They carry men's sportswear, and recently added a full complement of men's suits, sports coats, dress shirts, and ties.

LABELS FOR LESS, 186 Amsterdam Ave., between 68th and 69th sts. Tel. 787-0850.

If you're in the Lincoln Center area, you may want to walk a few blocks to check out the neighborhood branch of Labels for Less, which sells designer fashions at good discounts. There are thirteen other locations throughout Manhattan. Check the local phone book.

LOEHMANN'S, 236th Street and Broadway, Bronx. Tel. 543-6420.

A leader of the designer discount chains, Loehmann's offers an enormous selection of women's coats, suits, dresses, evening wear, sportswear, and accessories, often in styles that are simultaneously being sold in Manhattan for twice the price, and occasionally more. You'll have to plow persistently through dozens of racks. Veteran Loehmann's shoppers love to exchange "war stories" about their experiences. Shopping there, say, on the Saturday before New Year's Eve is not unlike charging into battle, armed, of course, with a credit card. The fruit of your valor can be a superb outfit at a wonderfully low price.

Other Loehmann's branches are located at 19 Duryea Place at Beverly Rd., in Brooklyn, off Flatbush Avenue (tel. 718/469-8900); and in Rego Park, Queens, in

Lefrak City (tel. 718/271-4000). **Directions:** For Bronx location, take Broadway/ Seventh Avenue 1 train to 238th St. and walk two blocks back to 236th St., or call Liberty Lines (tel. 652-8400) for the schedule of their express bus, which leaves from stops all over Manhattan, and, for $3.00, will whisk you in coach comfort to a spot several blocks' walk from the Bronx store. To reach the Brooklyn location, take the Sixth Avenue D train to Beverly Road; Loehmann's is located 3½ blocks west of the station. Phone each store for exact hours.

REMINISCENCE, 74 Fifth Ave., near 13th St. Tel. 243-2292.

Big sellers in Europe and Japan, the clothing creations of Reminiscence are a favorite with the under-30 international set. This anchor store is at the top of Greenwich Village. Green-and-pink walls, neon signs, and spotlights set the scene for Stewart Richer's award-winning designs that are a redefinition of the 1950s with a New Wave accent. Richer designs clothes, mostly in natural fabrics, that are fun, comfortable, and exciting—a blend of antique and ultracontemporary. They also carry reproductions of antique and nostalgic clothing such as their own "Hawaiian" shirts, which are exact duplicates of the patterns and styles sold during the 50s. There are jewelry, housewares, and bath departments. In the back of the store is a selection of reasonably priced genuine antique clothes. They also carry some light suits, army-surplus pants, coveralls, and jackets that are dyed unusual and brilliant colors.

ROYAL SILK, 820 Third Ave., between 50th and 51st sts. Tel. 644-7455.

Every kind of silk you can imagine—crepe de chine, silk charmeuse, silk chiffon, crushed silk, knitted silk, silk batiste (silk and cotton), and much more—is found here. Best of all, silk shirts, blouses, pants, skirts, sweaters, lingerie, and so on, are at much less than regular retail prices—we saw silk sweaters for $29, basic shirts for $31, and a dinner skirt for $52. Even better bargains are found in the clearance section. Incidentally, most of the garments are washable; after all, silkworms were doing their thing long before the invention of dry cleaners! Any woman who loves silk—does that exclude anybody?—should check this one out.

S&W FAMOUS DESIGNER APPAREL, corner of 26th St. and Seventh Ave. Tel. 924-6656.

S&W's four stores are located in a small cluster of designer discount stores a stone's throw from New York's prestigious Fashion Institute of Technology. Weekends are a big shopping time here, and all stores stay open on Sunday. With incredible buys in top-designer clothing, S&W is very "in" with fashion-conscious New York women. The shop at 165–167 W. 26th St., which has a clearance center on the ground level, offers designer suits, dresses, sportswear, and lingerie; 283 Seventh Ave. carries designer handbags, shoes, and accessories; 287 Seventh Ave. has designer coats, including petite coats and raincoats, and also carries moderate-priced sportswear; and 171 W. 26th St. is the outlet store for the best buys of all. Closed on Saturday.

SAM'S KNITWEAR, 93 Orchard St., between Delancey and Broome sts. Tel. 966-0390.

While you're perusing Lower East Side shops, don't miss Sam's Knitwear where discounts of 50% and more are offered on name-brand and designer clothes. Sales are held year round. We bought a dress here for $30 that we had seen (but only coveted) at $80 elsewhere.

SYMS, 42 Trinity Place, between Rector St. and Battery Park, four blocks south of the World Trade Center. Tel. 794-1199.

Located in the downtown Financial District, Sym's is another treasure trove of designer clothing at discount prices. Everything has the nationally advertised price on it. Syms marks down ladies' dresses every 10 days: for example, a $100 outfit goes on the racks at $59; after 10 days it goes down to $48; 10 more days, to $38; after 30 days, when the price becomes final, it's $29. The dates of markdowns are on the ticket, so you might want to trust your luck and wait for the lowest prices. We've also found excellent bargains here in fine leather bags, shoes,

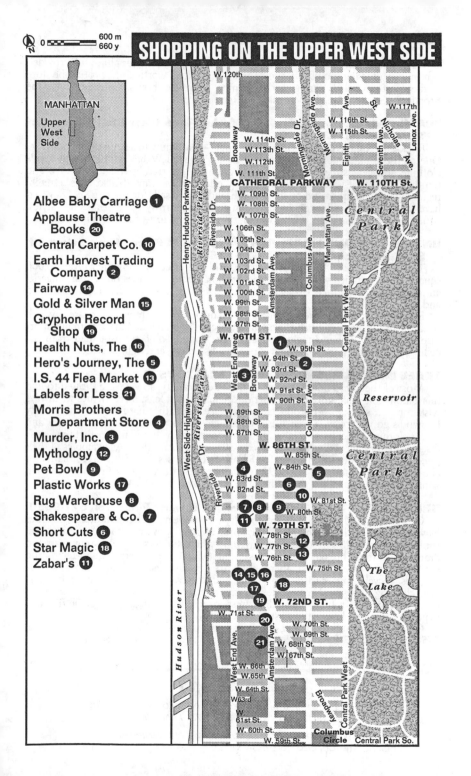

SHOPPING ON THE UPPER WEST SIDE

0 600 m
   660 y

MANHATTAN
Upper
West
Side

Albee Baby Carriage ❶
Applause Theatre
  Books ❷⓿
Central Carpet Co. ❿
Earth Harvest Trading
  Company ❷
Fairway ⓮
Gold & Silver Man ⓯
Gryphon Record
  Shop ⓳
Health Nuts, The ⓰
Hero's Journey, The ❺
I.S. 44 Flea Market ⓭
Labels for Less ㉑
Morris Brothers
  Department Store ❹
Murder, Inc. ❸
Mythology ⓬
Pet Bowl ❾
Plastic Works ⓱
Rug Warehouse ❽
Shakespeare & Co. ❼
Short Cuts ❻
Star Magic ⓲
Zabar's ⓫

gloves and scarves, lingerie, and linens. This is pipe-rack shopping and crowded community dressing rooms, but the bargains make it all worthwhile. *Note:* The store is the least crowded during early-morning shopping hours. Subway: Take the Broadway/Seventh Ave. 1 or 9 trains to Rector Street.

TRASH AND VAUDEVILLE, 4 St. Marks Place (East 8th St.), east of Third Ave. Tel. 982-3590.

Rock-and-roll fun clothes for the young set—that's how this store defines its style. One of the funkier stores in the funky East Village, TAV has women's and men's clothing and accessories that are both expensive and trendy and inexpensive and trendy. This place is known for its huge collection of jeans (black, blue, stretch, regular, you-name-it), including their own brand, which sells for $48 to $72. They also have an enormous collection of shoes, in sporty to dressy to "outrageous" styles. Motorcycle and bike wear; weird, way-out jewelry; and lots of London imports, too.

UNIQUE CLOTHING WAREHOUSE, 718 and 726 Broadway, below 8th St., Greenwich Village. Tel. 674-1767.

The atmosphere at Unique is exciting, and the prices are inviting. Over 30,000 square feet is jammed with avant-garde clothing, which includes outerwear, lingerie, antique garments, and accessories. They also have toys, do-it-yourself T-shirt painting, and men's clothing.

Recently, Unique opened a small (500 square feet) cafeteria-club area, which occasionally features live bands and variety acts. Also included are a permanent art display entitled "Urban Jungle," an array of "found" objects suspended from the ceiling, and a refreshment bar serving sodas, hot dogs, and light snacks.

THREE WISHES, 355 W. Broadway. Tel. 226-7570.

Most of the SoHo boutiques are of the pricey variety, so we were thrilled to find this genuine off-price store in this part of town. It has at least three virtues we always wish for in a shop: good products, good prices, and that hard-to-find commodity known as good service. Three Wishes manufactures a good deal of sportswear and career clothing under its own label, and also carries many brand names that they can't disclose in print, all at discounts of at least 30% off regular prices. As examples of their price range, consider silk blouses for $34 to $46, dresses for $59 to $118, pants for about $30 to $40, and suits for $79 to $89. They also do a lot of knits, carry coats in winter, and are expanding their line of petites. Sizes run 4 to 14.

URBAN OUTFITTERS, 374 Sixth Ave., at Waverly Place. Tel. 677-9350.

Geared to city dwellers who are country folk at heart, Urban Outfitters describes its wares as "lifestyle merchandise" for young adults. Derivative of its Woodstock-era roots, the store is 90's in spirit (gone are days when students slept on straw mats and drank wine from broken coffee cups), and 60's at heart (retro, quasi-retro, and semi-retro are the bywords). In addition to candlesticks, kitchen gadgets, school supplies, recycled paper cards, glassware, and kooky, kitschy "toys" and gifts, they have clothing, shoes, and accessories for men and women that could include a pair of over-dyed oxfords, a funky baby-doll dress, or a hat that might just be the ticket to bypassing the long line at the East Village club of the moment.

Other Urban Outfitters are at 628 Broadway, between Houston and Bleecker (tel. 475-0009), and 127 East 59th St., between Park and Lexington aves.

IMPRESSIONS

I think this city is full of people wanting inconceivable things.
—JOHN DOS PASSOS, *MANHATTAN TRANSFER*, 1925

New York's like a disco, but without the music.
—ELAINE STRITCH, *OBSERVER*, SAYINGS OF THE WEEK, FEBRUARY 17, 1980

WHAT'S NEW, 166 Madison Ave., between 32nd and 33rd sts. Tel. 532-9226.

Juniors can have a field day shopping for name-brand sportswear at What's New, where we spotted $90 rayon dresses for $35 and $40 skirt sets for $14. The store is tiny so it's best avoided during the lunch hour, when nearby office workers are out in full force. There's another What's New store at 122 E. 42nd St., on the subway level (tel. 867-0574). Closed on weekends.

MATERNITY

REBORN MATERNITY, 1449 Third Ave., between 81st and 82nd sts. Tel. 737-8818.

Reborn Maternity, which also has a shop at 564 Columbus Ave. (between 87th and 88th streets), carries exclusive designer and contemporary fashions for mothers-to-be. They see their mission as translating the very latest styles into sophisticated and comfortable maternity clothing. Shoppers can select an entire wardrobe, from career and evening wear to weekend fashions and lingerie.

BRIDAL GOWNS, WHOLESALE & RETAIL

Bridal gowns are far from inexpensive these days, so every prospective bride should know about the buildings at **1385 Broadway** and **499 Seventh Ave.** in the Garment Center; they house some of the leading bridal manufacturers and designers in the country. On Saturday mornings, between 10am and noon, 1385 Broadway is open to brides, bridesmaids, mothers of the bride, and flower girls. To shop efficiently here, shop elsewhere first: Know your merchandise and prices before you set foot in the door. Then you'll have a guide for comparison-shopping; and in some—but not every—case the savings can be enormous. For the best bargains, check the discontinued and sample racks.

Gaining access to the showrooms at 499 Seventh Ave. may sometimes be difficult, but worth a try; ask the elevator starters what floors will be open. Good bets are floors 15 and 21. Again, this one is for Saturday.

It will be well worth your while to take a trip to Brooklyn to shop for wedding clothes at **Kleinfeld and Son,** Fifth Ave. and 82nd St., Bay Ridge (tel. 718/833-1100). Kleinfeld is known for one of the largest selections of designer bridal gowns, bridesmaid's dresses, mother-of-the-bride clothes, designer evening wear, and special-occasion clothes in the country. Discounts range from 20% to 40%. There are many imports from England, France, and Italy in misses and junior sizes.

You must telephone in advance for an appointment. Closed Saturday, Sunday, and Monday in July and August. Call for directions.

SPECIAL-OCCASION DRESSES

If you're looking for party, prom, mother-of-the-bride, and other special-occasion dresses, make note of the wholesale building at **498 Seventh Ave.** Call designer Annemarie Gardin at 736-2895 to make an appointment: She has beautiful dresses, long and short, in chiffon, lace, linen, and silk, and many mother-of-the-bride outfits. Prices run from $200 to $500 wholesale.

RESALE SHOPS

Some of the best-dressed women in New York—glamorous types who look as if they've just stepped off the pages of *Vogue* or *Town and Country*—are actually wearing secondhand clothes that they purchased at chic Madison Avenue resale shops! These are the places where society women, actresses, models, and fashion editors often take dresses, gowns, suits, and coats that they've worn only a few times. The castoffs are then resold to customers like you, in excellent condition (they've received a thorough cleaning), and at a fraction of their original prices.

ENCORE RESALE DRESS SHOP, 1132 Madison Ave., at 84th St. Tel. 879-2850.

Encore stocks an enormous supply of women's outer apparel at prices averaging a third what the original owners paid. In addition to terrific buys on designer clothing, you'll also find incredible values in fine furs. Many of the famous have unloaded whole wardrobes here. Note, too, a large supply of new clothing, and a great selection of accessories, including designer handbags, shoes, jewelry, scarves, belts, and so on. There are two floors to browse through. Closed on Sunday, July to mid-August.

MICHAEL'S, 1041 Madison Ave. (second floor), at 79th St. Tel. 737-7273.

After exhausting the possibilities at Encore, you'll do well to walk five blocks south to Michael's. The resale shop with the highest fashion styles, Michael's resembles Bergdorf Goodman more than it does a secondhand store. The clothing here comes from some of the wealthiest and best-dressed women in the world; when they empty their closets, they fill Michael's with the very best collection of designer names you're apt to find under one roof anywhere: Valentino, Calvin Klein, Yves St. Laurent, Armani, Ungaro, Blass, and so on. We've seen $500 coats priced at $125 (and you'd never know they weren't new).

BUTTONS & BUCKLES

TENDER BUTTONS, at 143 E. 62nd St., between Lexington and Third aves. Tel. 758-7004.

And now, after scouring the resale shops for bargains, you may decide all your new dress needs is some elegant buttons.

This charming shop carries every kind of antique and modern button, plus exquisite antique buckles. It also has the largest collection of men's blazer buttons (antique and new) in the world, as well as antique men's cufflinks, dress sets, studs, and stickpins.

If you are interested in the history behind some of the pieces in the shop, ask proprietors Diana Epstein and Millicent Safro. The two just authored *Buttons,* a chronicle of buttons from pre-historic times through the 20th century. It has 206 color illustrations and is sold at the shop for $49.50. Closed on Saturday in July and August.

LINGERIE

A. W. KAUFMAN, 73 Orchard St., between Grand and Broome sts. Tel. 226-1629.

A. W. Kaufman has vast selections of designer lingerie at greatly discounted prices: loungewear, sleepwear, camisole sets, ensemble sets, hostess gowns, cashmere and wool robes, bedjackets, slippers, and so on, in silks, satins, and cottons. Closed on Friday and Saturday.

CHAS. WEISS FASHIONS, 331 Grand St. Tel. 966-1143.

Chas. Weiss Fashions claims the city's largest bra and foundation department, and largest brand diversity. They also sell sleepwear, slips with camisoles, Danskin, and bathing suits—all at typical Orchard Street discount prices. Closed on Saturdays.

GOLDMAN & COHEN, INC., 55 Orchard St., between Hester and Grand sts. Tel. 966-0737.

Another huge selection of the top names in ladies' lingerie can be found here. Discounts start at about 20%. Closed after 3:30pm Friday and Saturday.

ULTRA SMART, 15 E. 30th St., between Fifth and Madison aves. Tel. 686-1564.

Ultra Smart buys up stockings from the big mills and puts them out under their own label. These are the exact stockings you'd pay up to five times as much for under a designer label.

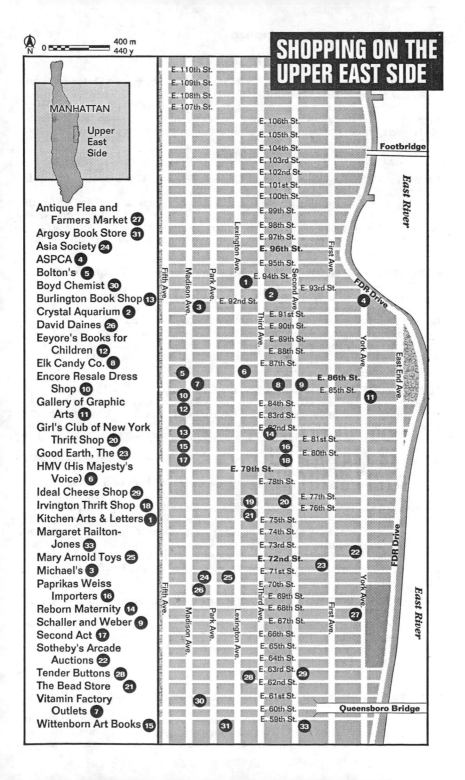

SHOPPING ON THE UPPER EAST SIDE

MANHATTAN
Upper East Side

0   400 m
    440 y

East River

Footbridge

FDR Drive

East End Ave.

Queensboro Bridge

Fifth Ave.
Madison Ave.
Park Ave.
Lexington Ave.
Third Ave.
Second Ave.
First Ave.
York Ave.

E. 110th St.
E. 109th St.
E. 108th St.
E. 107th St.
E. 106th St.
E. 105th St.
E. 104th St.
E. 103rd St.
E. 102nd St.
E. 101st St.
E. 100th St.
E. 99th St.
E. 98th St.
E. 97th St.
E. 96th St.
E. 95th St.
E. 94th St.
E. 93rd St.
E. 92nd St.
E. 91st St.
E. 90th St.
E. 89th St.
E. 88th St.
E. 87th St.
E. 86th St.
E. 85th St.
E. 84th St.
E. 83rd St.
E. 82nd St.
E. 81st St.
E. 80th St.
E. 79th St.
E. 78th St.
E. 77th St.
E. 76th St.
E. 75th St.
E. 74th St.
E. 73rd St.
E. 72nd St.
E. 71st St.
E. 70th St.
E. 69th St.
E. 68th St.
E. 67th St.
E. 66th St.
E. 65th St.
E. 64th St.
E. 63rd St.
E. 62nd St.
E. 61st St.
E. 60th St.
E. 59th St.

HANDBAGS

FINE AND KLEIN HANDBAGS, 119 Orchard St., between Delancey and Rivington sts. Tel. 674-6720.
For the best values in better handbags, head for this Lower East Side store. Their huge selection of name and designer bags spans three floors and offers such names as Jay Herbert, Varon, Sharif, and Susan Gail, at discounts of 35%. Closed on Saturday.

SHOES

ANBAR, 93 Reade St., between Church St. and West Broadway. Tel. 227-0253.
Try Anbar for good prices on high-fashion women's shoes. They don't have all sizes, but if you're lucky, you'll get a bargain on designer names. Under the same ownership, **Shoe Steal,** around the corner from Anbar at 116 Duane St. (tel. 964-4017), has shoes at even lower prices ($15 to $40 a pair). Closed Saturday in July and August and on Sunday.

LACE UP SHOE SHOP, 110 Orchard St., corner of Delancey St. Tel. 475-8040.
Lace Up Shoe Shop, another Orchard Street special, has quite an array of designer footwear, including names like Charles Jourdan, Bruno Magli, Anne Klein, Luc Berjen, Yves St. Laurent, Margaret Jerrold, Joan & David, and Calvin Klein. Styles and colors are current, and the store carries a wide range of sizes and widths. Lace Up also carries men's and women's Mephisto walking, biking, golfing, and casual footwear, of which they claim to have the largest selection in the Northeast. Telephone orders are accepted. Closed on Saturday.

LESLIE BOOTERY, 319 Grand St., off Orchard St. Tel. 431-9196.
This Lower East Side standby has a new location, which features men's, ladies', and designer shoes. You'll see such names as André Assous, Bally, Cole-Haan, Perry Ellis, Esprit, Enzo, Frye, Calvin Klein, 9 West, Perry Ellis, Prevato, Reebok, Rockport, Timberland, Unisa, and Via Spiga, all at a minimum of 20% off. Closed on Saturday.

M. & M. SHOE CENTER, 302 Grand St. Tel. 966-2702; and MAXIMUM, 91 Orchard St. Tel. 966-4622.
These two stores are under the same management, and both offer a wide range of top name-brand sandals, shoes, and boots at discounts of 20% to 25%. They stock everything from high-style designer shoes to comfortable everyday styles, and it's all first-quality, all-leather, current stock. Among the brands represented, we spotted Amalfi, Dennis Cameau, Rangoni of Florence, Sesto Menucci of Florence, Newton Elkin, Barefoot Originals, and Rockport (Rockports that sell for $70 to $80 uptown are $54 to $64 here). Check the big clearance sales in July and the end of December. In Brooklyn, the same management runs M. & M. Classics, 45-26 13th Ave. (tel. 718/972-2737).

ORCHARD BOOTERY, 75 Orchard St., between Broome and Grand sts. Tel. 966-0688.
Orchard Bootery has many designer shoes—Jacques Levine, Bandolino, Bruno Melli, Versani, Charles David, Peter Kaiser, Martinez Valero, Palizzio, d'Rossana, Dennis Cameau, and so on—discounted 30% or more. Closed on Saturday.

FURS

RITZ THRIFT SHOP, 107 W. 57th St., between Sixth and Seventh aves. Tel. 265-4559.
Some of the best bargains in New York on gently used furs can be found at the Ritz Thrift Shop. This is where New York's society women shed their furs, sometimes after only a few months' wear. All the coats, stoles, and jackets are in excellent

condition. Mink coats currently sell for between $500 and $3,500. Other popular furs are raccoon, fox, beaver, and other long-haired furs, which start at about $500 and can go up to as much as $2,500. Not readily available, but very popular, are sable, lynx, and fisher, which sell for between $2,000 and $20,000. All garments are altered at no charge. The Ritz encourages inquiries by those who have furs to sell.

MEN'S CLOTHING & ACCESSORIES

Before launching into our listings for menswear, we refer you back to Richard's Army-Navy, Unique Clothing Warehouse, and the downtown wholesale shoe district, all of which carry goods for men also and are described in the "Women's Clothing and Accessories" section above.

SUITS, PANTS, JACKETS & COATS

ARNIE'S PLACE, 37 Orchard St., at Hester St. Tel. 925-0513.

Arnie's Place is a good bet for designer jeans—good discounts on Calvin Klein, Lee, and Levi's 501 jeans, among others. Closed on Saturday.

BORISLAW CUSTOM CLOTHIER, 2 E. 17th St., just off Fifth Ave. Tel. 242-8134.

Values are also good at Borislaw, which sells ready-to-wear brand names, including suits, leather jackets, and pants, at varying discounts. They also do custom clothing and sell and rent wedding tuxedos. A recent sale advertised quality wool or wool-blend men's suits for $49 to $165. Closed on weekends.

BUYER'S FACTORY OUTLET [BFO], 149 Fifth Ave., at 21st St. Tel. 254-0059.

Located here on two floors is another big outfit where prices can sometimes be discounted as much as 50% off regular retail. There's a large selection of Italian suits and sports coats, famous-brand shirts, ties, and sweaters. We've seen suits for $175 and up, sports coats for $105 and up, and many designer and big-name brands. Alterations are available while you wait.

DAFFY'S, 111 Fifth Ave., at 18th St. Tel. 529-4477.

Although Daffy's is known primarily for women's fashions, husbands need not sit idly by while the wives get all the bargains. We spotted designer cotton sweaters that would sell for $80 to $150 elsewhere that cost from $24 to $40 here; Italian wool gabardine trousers were $50 here and $100 in other stores; cotton sport shirts that were selling uptown for $40 to $62 were $14 to $20 here—just to give you an idea.

FENWICK CLOTHES, 22 W. 19th St. (fifth floor), west of Fifth Ave. Tel. 243-1100.

Fenwick Clothes is a manufacturer of quality men's clothing that has opened its doors to the public. As a result you get to buy at wholesale prices and can purchase suits, overcoats, topcoats, jackets, slacks, and so on, for about 40% to 50% off retail price. Suits that would retail for $550 to $775 are $279 to $409 here; sports jackets that cost $425 in the retail stores are $259 to $289; and slacks retailing for $145 are from $79 to $110. Quality is excellent. Alterations are extra.

G&G INTERNATIONAL, 53 Orchard St. Tel. 431-4530.

You'll find Adolpho and Geoffrey Beene suits, clothing by San Remo, Lubiam, Bill Blass, Harvé Benard, and much more. Hathaway and Christian Dior shirts are discounted from 20% to 30%. Alterations are free. Closed Friday an hour before sundown and on Saturday.

L. S. MEN'S CLOTHING, 18 W. 45th St. (Suite 403), between Fifth and Sixth aves. Tel. 575-0933.

A good midtown resource for traditional executive wear at discount prices is L. S. Men's Clothing. Designer suits, natural-shoulder suits, jackets, and coats are all American made and sold at 45% to 65% off their typical retail prices of $375 to $650. They also have a large selection of silk ties and slacks. There's a tailor on the premises.

PAN AM MEN'S WEAR, 50 Orchard St., between Grand and Hester sts. Tel. 925-7032.

A tradition of quality and service keep the customers coming back to Pan Am Men's Wear. They carry coats, jackets, suits, shirts, and sportswear by such top designers as Perry Ellis, Polo by Ralph Lauren, Alexander Julian, Charles Jourdan, Tallia, Lubiam, Marzotto of Italy, and a full line of Italian designers. Discounts are sizable and expert tailoring is free. Closed Friday after 3pm and on Saturday.

ROTHMAN'S, 200 Park Ave. South, 17th St. at Union Square. Tel. 777-7400.

Harry Rothman was the first discounter of men's quality clothing in New York. When the original store lost its lease several years ago, his grandson, Ken Giddon, relocated to handsome new quarters and kept the same philosophy, discounting the high end of the menswear lines—the best-tailored clothes in the country—for 20% to 50% off regular retail prices. Everything is under the Rothman label—the top manufacturers who supply the store will not allow their labels to be used or advertised—but savvy shoppers who know their top designers can find them, sans labels, greatly discounted here: A suit we spotted uptown for $875 was going for $485 here; a $750 suit was $395. We also saw top designer suits for $299; $40 pinpoint (tightly woven) cotton shirts sell for $20; braces (suspenders) go for $15 to $50; ties, $15 to $30—all discounted 20% to 25%. They recently began selling better Italian suits, such as Canali and Lubiam, which they claim are not carried elsewhere. Canali suits, usually $1,100, are $699 here. Lubiams, sold elsewhere for $800, are $545 at Rothman's. With prices like these, it's no wonder that some of New York's best-dressed men do their scouting at prestigious emporiums like Saks Fifth Avenue or Barney's, then come to Rothman's for the savings.

SYMS, 42 Trinity Place, between Rector St. and Battery Park. Tel. 791-1199.

Located two blocks south of the World Trade Center, Syms has three entire floors of men's apparel and accessories, including shoes. Many designer labels are in every department, and the savings can be incredible. Men will find everything at Syms, from designer coats and suits, to jeans, shirts, warmup suits, and pajamas. Women's and children's clothing are also available (see above). Closed on Monday.

SHIRTS

PENN GARDEN SHIRT COMPANY, 63 Orchard St., between Grand and Hester sts. Tel. 431-8464.

Penn Garden has designer and famous-name men's shirts at incredibly low prices—20% to 30% less than you'd pay elsewhere, from $15 to $90.

THE SHIRT STORE, 51 E. 44th St., at Vanderbilt Ave. Tel. 557-8040.

For excellent values in men's and women's shirts in the midtown area, stop in at the Shirt Store. All shirts are 100% cotton and are made by the owner in Pennsylvania, which assures affordable prices. Selections are wide and service is excellent: If you can't fit into their wide range of sizes (men's neck sizes 14 through 18½, sleeve lengths 32 through 37), they will alter stock garments for a reasonable fee and have your shirt ready within the week. Stock shirts for men range in price from $37.50 to $80. They also do made-to-measure garments for both men and women. Varying sales promotions—when we were last there they were giving away free ties with every shirt purchased—add to the fun.

VICTORY, THE SHIRT EXPERTS, 96 Orchard St., between Delancey and Broome sts. Tel. 677-2020 or 800/841-3424.

The Victory Shirt Company is our favorite among the many stores on the Lower East Side that sell discounted men's shirts on Orchard Street. They make all their own shirts, and specialize in top-of-the-line cotton fabrics—oxford cloths, pima broadcloth, Pinpoint, Egyptian and Sea Island—and since you are, in effect, buying from the manufacturer, savings are great. Stock size shirts range from 14 to 32 through 18½ to 36, and usually range in price from $42.50 to $95. Handmade ties go for $15 to $50. Suspenders and accessories are available. Victory also whips up made-to-measure shirts from a full paper pattern, practically a lost art. They also carry handmade ties, which may run from $15 to $50. While you're there, you can pick up a catalog, and order by phone once you're back home. Closed on Sunday.

SHOES

For sneakers—Puma, Adidas, Nike, and so on—head to one of these stores, all under the same ownership: **Jules Harvey,** 132 Orchard St. (tel. 475-4875); **H & J Shoes,** 131 Orchard St. (tel. 982-0840); (these are between Rivington and Delancey streets); and **Peck & Chase Shoes,** 163 Orchard St., between Rivington and Stanton sts. (tel. 674-8860). These also carry many name-brand and designer shoes, boots, dress shoes, and work shoes, including Timberland. Closed on Saturday.

LESLIE BOOTERY, 319 Grand St., off Orchard St. Tel. 431-9696.

Leslie Bootery offers discounts of at least 20% on designer and name-brand men's and women's shoes. Brand names for men include Bally, Cole-Haan, Rockport, Timberland, Kenneth Cole, and Bostonian.

J. SHERMAN SHOES, 121 Division St., at the south end of Orchard St., one block south of Canal St. Tel. 233-7898.

This place is a find for men looking for discounts of 20% to 70% on high-quality designer shoes. You'll find top brands from Switzerland, Italy, the U.S., and England, and casual and dress shoes in contemporary styles. Closed on Saturday.

TIES

Ties are discounted at almost all the men's stores mentioned above. In addition, **Tie City,** at Grand Central Terminal, East 42nd St. (tel. 599-1121), offers a large assortment of patterns and materials for as little as $4 a tie; maximum price is $10 for a pure silk, handmade tie.

On the Lower East Side, **Allen Street** is tie street, with about ten stores located between Delancey and Houston sts. All offer the low prices you'd expect in this area.

CHILDREN'S CLOTHING

A & G INFANTS & CHILDREN'S WEAR, 261 Broome St., between Orchard and Allen sts. Tel. 966-3775.

A & G sells name-brand (Tickle Me & Tackle Me, Nane Bashe, Choozie, Ruth Scharf, Youngland, Carters, and so on) children's clothes at discounts of at least 25%. You can get clothes here for infants to preteens. Closed on Friday an hour before sundown and on Saturday.

DAFFY'S, 111 Fifth Ave., at 18th St. Tel. 529-4477.

Don't plan on getting the children's basic duds here, but do try Daffy's when you want to outfit your little darlings in the finest designer sportswear, including European imports. Designer and European samples go for 50% off regular prices, as do designer dresses for girls. Leather clothing for boys and girls is discounted 40% to 50%, as are cotton terry robes for both boys and girls. Especially nice is the 100% cotton layettewear at 50% off regular prices.

M. KREINEN & CO., INC., 301 Grand St., between Allen and Eldridge sts. Tel. 925-0239.

This place also offers the types of children's clothes you can expect to find at A & G (see above).

MORRIS BROTHERS DEPARTMENT STORE, 2322 Broadway, at 84th St. Tel. 724-9000.

West Side mothers watch for the twice-yearly sales (July–August and January–February) at Morris Brothers when the pickings are good in name-brand children's

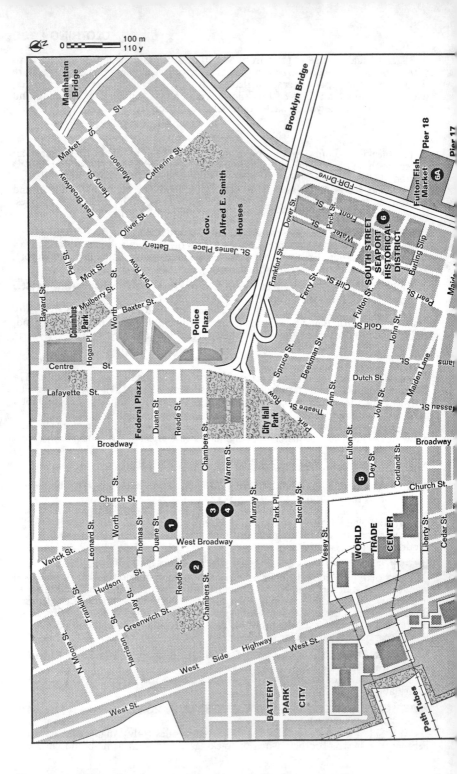

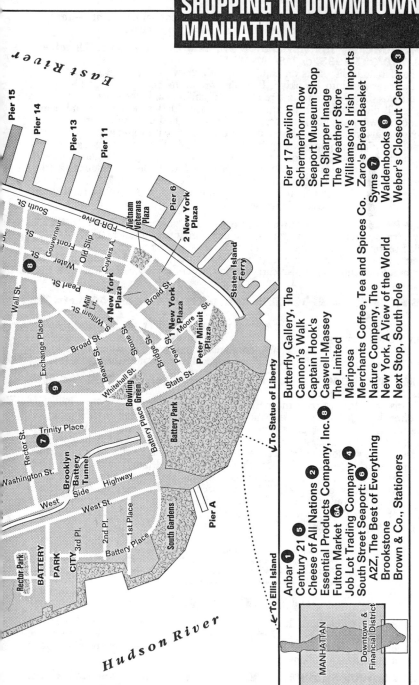

SHOPPING IN DOWNTOWN MANHATTAN

East River

Pier 15
Pier 14
Pier 13
Pier 11
Pier 6
2 New York Plaza

Vietnam Veterans Plaza

Staten Island Ferry

South St.
FDR Drive
Front St.
Water St.
Old Slip
Cuyler's A.
Pearl St.
Gouverneur St.
Wall St.
William St.
Mill Ln.
Broad St.
Exchange Place
Beaver St.
Stone St.
Bridge St.
Whitehall St.
Bowling Green
State St.
Pearl St.
Moore St.
Peter Minuit Plaza
New York Plaza
4 New York Plaza
Broad St.

Trinity Place
Rector St.
Washington St.
West Side Highway
West St.
West St.
Battery Place
Battery Park
South Gardens
Battery Place
1st Place
2nd Pl.
3rd Pl.
1st Place
Battery Place
Rector Park

Brooklyn Battery Tunnel

BATTERY PARK CITY

Pier A

↙To Ellis Island

↓To Statue of Liberty

Hudson River

MANHATTAN
Downtown & Financial District

Anbar **1**
Century 21 **5**
Cheese of All Nations **2**
Essential Products Company, Inc. **8**
Fulton Market **6A**
Job Lot Trading Company **4**
South Street Seaport: **6**
A2Z, The Best of Everything
Brookstone
Brown & Co., Stationers
Butterfly Gallery, The
Cannon's Walk
Captain Hook's
Caswell-Massey
The Limited
Mariposa
Merchants Coffee, Tea and Spices Co.
Nature Company, The
New York, A View of the World
Next Stop, South Pole
Pier 17 Pavilion
Schermerhorn Row
Seaport Museum Shop
The Sharper Image
The Weather Store
Williamson's Irish Imports
Zaro's Bread Basket
Syms **7**
Waldenbooks **9**
Weber's Closeout Centers **3**

clothing. The store has a large and varied selection and specializes in jeans—many of them for mothers and fathers as well as kids. Closed on Sunday.

NATAN BORLAM, 157 Havemeyer St., near South 2nd St., Brooklyn. Tel. 718/387-2983, or 718/782-0108.

S For fabulous discounts on children's clothing, we suggest you venture across the river and into Brooklyn. If you're willing to brave the largest shopping crowds you've ever encountered (leave the children at home when you visit this store), you'll discover superb discounts on better children's clothing (brand names every mother will recognize) at Natan Borlam. You'll find underwear, dresses, suits, snowsuits, coats, tights, polo shirts, and so on—many with top-name labels still in them and most at discounts ranging from 25% to 50%. They also carry teenage and ladies' clothing. If Borlam's doesn't have what you want (which is highly unlikely), then browse around Havemeyer Street; it's dotted with discount shops offering children's furniture and clothing. Subway: Take the Lexington Ave. 4, 5, or 6 train to Brooklyn Bridge, then change to the BMT J train to Marcy Ave. Walk four blocks down South 2nd Street to 157 Havemeyer St.

RICE & BRESKIN, 323 Grand St., corner of Orchard St. Tel. 925-5515.

If you're after real bargains in kids' clothing—infants to toddlers to size 14—try Rice & Breskin. This store has three floors of just about everything for kids, with all the better-known American brands, including Carter's, Healthtex, Dorissa Dress, Renzo, and Rothschild. They also carry layettes, and offer a 20% discount on already low prices.

SAKS FIFTH AVENUE, 611 Fifth Ave., between 49th and 50th sts. Tel. 753-4000.

As for New York department stores, nothing can beat the twice-yearly sales (usually around January and June) at Saks when crowds of mothers from everywhere swoop down on the children's department to realize savings of anywhere from 30% to 50% on beautiful merchandise. (Savings are huge all over the store during these sales.)

SECOND ACT, 1046 Madison Ave. (upstairs), between 79th and 80th sts. Tel. 988-2440.

The discount houses offer the best value in new children's clothing; the resale shops offer the biggest bargains in hand-me-downs, some of them quite elegant and bearing name tags from high-fashion stores like Saks Fifth Avenue and Bergdorf Goodman. One of the oldest and best of these in town is Second Act, where you can purchase outgrown clothing in excellent condition, often items that have been worn only a few times, at prices 50% less than the original. Many French and English imports, as well as American-made coats, toddlers' snowsuits, girls' skirts, boys' slacks, Levi's, jackets, and so on. We've even seen ski and riding gear. Every item is freshly cleaned and only the latest styles are sold. In addition, Second Act has a large selection of children's books (from $1.50 to $12, and used ice skates. Closed Saturday, Sunday, and July and August.

2. SHOPPING A TO Z

ANTIQUES

In addition to the following shops, you can explore Hudson Street in Greenwich Village, Amsterdam Avenue from 79th to 86th streets on the Upper West Side, or the cross streets from 72nd to 86th streets on the Upper East Side—all are areas with a concentration of antique shops.

BRASS ANTIQUE SHOPPE, 32 Allen St., between Canal and Hester sts. Tel. 925-6660.

Connoisseurs of brass will want to peruse the merchandise at this store, which specializes in small items such as candlesticks and andirons at good prices. This Lower East Side shop also has vases, old Russian samovars, antique drawer pulls, kiddush cups, and much more. Closed on Friday and Saturday, other days after 4:40pm.

EARLY HALLOWEEN, 130 W. 25th St., between Sixth and Seventh aves. Tel. 691-2933.

You'll need to make an appointment to see the collection of props and vintage clothing for men, women, and children. You could find a slinky satin nightie, a poplin print housedress, or woolen jodhpurs. Shoes, ties and hats, jackets and coats, accessories in excellent condition—many never-worn items—are available at reasonable prices. Open by appointment only, Monday to Friday, noon to 6pm.

APPLIANCES

We'd never buy a stereo, radio, TV, camera, toaster, hairdryer, watch, sewing machine, blender, washing machine—or any other major or minor household appliance—without first comparison-shopping along Canal and Essex streets on the Lower East Side. The stores listed below all stock a wide variety of brand-new, major-brand household appliances, in perfect condition, with the usual warranties—at prices up to 50% less than those in major department stores! Unless you know exactly what brand and model appliance you want, however, it's a good idea first to stop in at one of the city's better department stores and discuss pros and cons of every make and model with a knowledgeable salesperson. Then simply check out these Lower East Side shops (where gracious service is almost unheard of), and buy where the price is best: They won't give prices on the phone. Ask about refund and exchange policies when you buy, as some of these stores have neither. One last warning—you don't know the meaning of the word "mobbed" if you haven't seen one of these shops on a Sunday; it's best to go during the week, and preferably in the morning.

Along Essex Street, between Hester and Canal streets, try Dembitzer Bros. Domestic & Export Company, 5 Essex St. (tel. 254-1310); Lewi Supply Company, 15 Essex St. (tel. 777-6910); Essex Camera & Electronic Discount Center, 17 Essex St. (tel. 677-6420); Foto Electric Supply Company, 31 Essex St. (tel. 673-5222); and Central Electronics, 37 Essex St. (tel. 673-3220).

On Canal Street, between Essex and Orchard streets, try ABC Trading Company, 31 Canal St. (tel. 228-5080). Another, Bondy Export Corporation, sells photo equipment and luggage, as well as appliances and electronics at low discount prices. Also try Kunst Sales Corporation, 45 Canal St. (tel. 966-1909), and a bit uptown, Electrical Appliances Rental and Sales Company, 40 W. 29th St., near Broadway (tel. 686-8884). Both Kunst Sales and Electrical Appliances Rental and Sales are open only on weekends.

ART SUPPLIES

CHARRETTE, 215 Lexington Ave., at 33rd St. Tel. 683-8822.

Formerly known as Eastern Artists, this store has a huge selection (they stock 35,000 different items!) of art, architectural, and drafting supplies. Everything is available at discounts of 20% to 70%. Closed on Sunday.

PEARL PAINT COMPANY, 308 Canal St., between Broadway and Church St. Tel. 431-7932.

Pearl Paint Company is a bargain-hunter's store, and everyone—from famous-name artists to household painters—comes to Pearl's to stock up. Everything is sold at 20% to 50% off list price. Items are available by mail.

AUCTIONS

The Friday "Weekend" section of the *New York Times* is a good source for times and dates of estate and antique auctions. On Sunday, these announcements can be found either in the "Arts and Leisure" section, or at the tail end of "Help Wanted," part 9. For other types of auctions, check each day's paper.

Here is a rundown of those worth checking out.

GENERAL POST OFFICE AUCTION. Tel. 330-2931 or 967-8585.
The Post Office holds sales every 4 to 6 weeks. Phone for information, or check the classified sections of the local papers.

LUBIN GALLERIES, 30 W. 26th St., between Fifth and Sixth aves. Tel. 924-3777.
Lubin Galleries is another place to pick up excellent values in antique and used furniture at auction every other Saturday, year round. Antique and traditional furniture, pianos, silver, bronzes, Oriental rugs and tapestries, porcelain, china, and so on, are offered. You can see the items on display the Thursday (10am to 7pm) and Friday (9am to 3pm) before the sale. If you can't make the auction, you can leave your bid with a 25% deposit.

POLICE DEPARTMENT AUCTIONS OF VEHICLES AND GENERAL PROPERTY. Tel. 406-1369.
Call the above number for a complete recording of current police auction information—days, times, locations, and so on. As with all of the following auction listings, you might pick up anything and everything here, from an unclaimed sofa to a box of hankies, all at extraordinary bargain prices. If you have more questions, call 374-5905.

SOTHEBY'S ARCADE AUCTIONS, 1334 York Ave., at 72nd St. Tel. 606-7409.
The best place to find major antique pieces at sensible prices is at auction houses, and our favorite is the "budget" gallery of the wildly expensive Sotheby's. You might be lucky enough to pick up a room-size Persian carpet for under $1,000 at their 10:15am Tuesday auctions. Items are on exhibit the preceding Thursday, Friday, Saturday, and Monday from 10am to 5pm. While you're there, don't hesitate to go up to Sotheby's main galleries on the second floor to ogle, perhaps, the likes of Egyptian carvings, Monet watercolors, or ice-cube-size diamond rings.

U.S. CUSTOMS SERVICE.
Auctions on behalf of the U.S. Customs Service are now held by EG&G Dynatrend. Those closest to the New York metropolitan area take place in Jersey City, N.J., just across the river from Manhattan. They advertise for the three Sundays preceding the auction in the classified section of the *New York Times*.

BABY CARRIAGES, TOYS & FURNITURE

ALBEE BABY CARRIAGE, 715 Amsterdam Ave., corner of 95th St. Tel. 662-5740.
Albee Baby Carriages carries what may be the city's largest selection of carriages: everything from a lightweight aluminum umbrella stroller to custom-made English-style prams. In addition, they carry a full line of juvenile furniture and furnishings, as well as a marvelous selection of cribs, beds, toys, and infant wear by leading manufacturers. Everything is sold at considerable discounts, which vary according to the item. Closed on Sunday.

BEN'S BABYLAND, 81 Ave. A, near East 6th St. Tel. 674-1353.
In business since 1911, Ben's Babyland emphasizes customer service and very low prices. It is a large store with a wide selection of children's furniture, carriages, layettes, and all related items. Aprica strollers are priced from $140.

SCHNEIDER'S, 20 Ave. A, corner of East 2nd St. Tel. 228-3540.
Located in the heart of the East Village, Schneider's has a good selection of strollers and carriages, including top-of-the-line brands such as McClaren and Chicco-Combi-Perego. There are soft-bodied and lightweight folding units. Schneider's also carries discount-priced baby furniture, as well as a full line of children's toys and accessories for the nursery.

BOOKS

New York is a legendary mecca for book retailing. Nationwide chains—B. Dalton and Waldenbooks—are well represented as well as the city's own Doubleday stores.

It is impossible to list all the interesting stores. We, therefore, give you only a small sampling of the diversity and list only some of the specialty stores. Many are open into the evening (you must call ahead to check), because, in New York, perusing books is still an activity that is somewhere between a pastime and a passion.

GENERAL

BARNES & NOBLE ANNEX, Fifth Ave. between 17th and 18th sts. Tel. 633-3500.

Occupying half a city block, this annex is the bookstore for bargain-hunters. It's the only bookstore we've ever seen that provides supermarket baskets, but that's what you'll need to carry out your finds. Every book in the store (and there are hundreds of thousands) is discounted: *New York Times* hardcover bestsellers at 30% off; discounts on children's books, remainders, reviewers' copies, and scholarly books vary. It also houses one of the largest classical record departments in New York City, as well as a video department with over 1,300 titles to choose from, many of which are at discount prices.

Just across the street is the main (original) Barnes & Noble (105 Fifth Ave., at 18th St.), which stocks nearly three million hardcovers, paperbacks, and new and used textbooks.

In the busy midtown area, budget-conscious booklovers head for the Barnes & Noble Bookstore at 600 Fifth Ave., at 48th St. (tel. 765-0590), where every single book is discounted every single day. Ditto for the eleven other Barnes & Nobles that are sprinkled all over Manhattan.

BOOK FRIENDS CAFÉ, 16 W. 18th St., between Fifth and Sixth aves. Tel. 255-7407.

Book Friends Café, the descendant of a store called Book Friends, specializes in books published between 1890 and 1940, and books that highlight that era. What this means is that if you are interested in Edwardians, Bloomsbury, Paris in the 1920s, and Old New York, this is the place for you. Although most of the books are out-of-print, there are some new titles whose subject matter is pertinent, such as Louis Auchincloss titles that are set in the Vanderbilt era. They have a weekly lecture series, and serve food and drink, including afternoon tea, 7 days a week.

BRENTANO'S BOOKSTORE, 597 Fifth Ave., between 48th and 49th sts. Tel. 826-2450.

A division of Waldenbooks, Brentano's occupies the landmark location that had previously housed the famous Scribner Bookstore. The store opened in late 1989 and is worth a visit to see the 30-foot-high vaulted sales room and the central staircase and balcony with cast-iron railings. The Landmarks Preservation Commission describes it as "among the finest interiors in New York City." Brentano's is a general bookstore that features over 33,000 titles in hardcover and paperback, with specialization in biography, travel, arts, literature, and culture. It has one of the largest history book sections in the city.

BURLINGTON BOOK SHOP, 1082 Madison Ave., between 81st and 82nd sts. Tel. 288-7420.

Neighborhood people, many authors, and other influentials consider this place a treasure trove, as much for the fact that its compact quarters hold 30,000 different titles (give or take), as that the staff, especially owner Jane Trichter, are knowledgeable, helpful, and patient. They will special-order any book (even a paperback), and regularly undertake searches for out-of-print volumes. The collection of books is handpicked, with a mind-boggling selection of literature, poetry, biography, books on fine and decorative arts, and gardening books, to cite a few categories. They are especially strong on backlist paperbacks. New releases of merit are always on hand. Burlington Antique Toys, also on the premises, but under separate management, offers lead soldiers and other antique collectibles. Steve Balkin will answer questions on these. Call him at 861-9708.

GOTHAM BOOK MART, 41 W. 47th St., between Fifth and Sixth aves. Tel. 719-4448.
New York's most famous literary bookstore is the Gotham Book Mart, which has been in business since 1920. Its founder, Frances Steloff, who passed away at the age of 101, was an early champion of such modern writers as Henry Miller, Ernest Hemingway, and James Joyce; the James Joyce Society still meets here four times a year. The current owners carry on her dedication to modern literature—novels, poetry, film and theater books, with many first editions, hard-to-find and out-of-print literature, and a vast collection of literary magazines. Their Christmas tree is famous, laden with antique ornaments, some of which are for sale. The store is an authentic, old-fashioned piece of New York City, and a literary browser's idea of paradise.

SHAKESPEARE & CO., 2259 Broadway, corner of 81st St. Tel. 580-7800.
One of the best bookstores on the Upper West Side, Shakespeare & Co. can always be counted on for excellent, carefully chosen selections. They pride themselves on having a "deep selection of the classics and modern literature," as well as an array of books on personal growth (including dream analysis), drug and alcohol abuse primers, drama books, and an extensive gay studies section. Their cookbook selection is also excellent.

A second Shakespeare & Co. can be found downtown, at 716 Broadway, between East 4th Street and Astor Place (tel. 529-1330). This one has an especially large stock of theater titles.

STRAND, 828 Broadway, corner of 12th St. Tel. 473-1452.
The once-famous secondhand book area of New York, between Fourth Avenue and Broadway, from 8th to 14th streets, is declining, but a few stores are still doing business in the old neighborhood. The biggest of these is Strand, which has been at this location for over 60 years. Here, 37,500 feet of selling floor hold over 2½ million books on 8 miles of shelves, making the Strand the largest used-book store in the country. It's a browser's paradise—it stays open 7 days a week until 9:30pm, and has an extensive collection of books on history, art, the humanities, and literature. Prices range from 50¢ to $35,000. There are plenty of publisher's remainders (published anywhere from 1 to 20 years ago) at bargain prices. The newest reviewer's copies, including new paperbacks and bestsellers, are sold for half the publisher's list price. No trip to the Strand is complete without a visit to the Rare Book Rooms, where you will find a large selection of art books, modern first editions, and collector's copies in fine bindings. There is a second Strand located at 159 John Street in the South Street Seaport, where the best of the Strand specials are conveniently arranged on bookshelves. In the summer, you can visit Strand kiosks at Central Park, 59th at Fifth Avenue, and at Tramway Plaza, Second Avenue at 60th Street, just below the Roosevelt Island Tram. Kiosks are open in fair weather, and close up at dusk.

ART

ACADEMY BOOKSTORE, 10 W. 18th St., between Fifth and Sixth aves. Tel. 242-4848.
Academy specializes in books on art, architecture, photography, design, and graphic and decorative arts. Their collection of used, out-of-print, and rare books is considered one of the most extensive in the city, and they also carry new releases. Because proprietor Alan Weiner, who is very quality-conscious in his selections, buys from estates, and scoops up warehouse stocks and remainders, he is able to pass the savings along to his customers. Prices are quite good.

Academy also carries on a brisk and impressive trade in used and out-of-print classical records, and is one of the few places in the city (if not the country) to sell used CDs. These are popular and classical.

HACKER ART BOOKS, 45 W. 57th St., between Fifth and Sixth aves. Tel. 688-7600.

Hacker's has been a gem for art-lovers for years, and it's now moved across the street from its old location. It still boasts the largest selection of art books in the city, covering topics from ancient art to contemporary Post-Modernist, in both hardcover and quality paperbacks. Closed Saturday in July and August and on Sunday.

RIZZOLI BOOKSTORE, 31 W. 57th St., between Fifth and Sixth aves. Tel. 759-2424.

Give yourself lots of time to browse through Rizzoli, which boasts one of New York's most exhaustive and sophisticated collections of art books, classical and jazz recordings, and European magazines. There are two Rizzoli outposts, one in the Wall Street area and another in SoHo. The shop at 200 Vesey St., in the Winter Garden at the World Financial Center (tel. 385-1400), specializes in books on art, architecture, and design, and also has a selection of business and computer books. The SoHo store, at 254 W. Broadway, between Prince and West Houston streets, has, in addition to many of the usual array of Rizzoli books, a particularly good selection of books on architecture. All Rizzoli stores are open daily, have extended hours, and some stay open 'til midnight on certain days. Call for details.

WITTENBORN ART BOOKS, 1018 Madison Ave. (second floor), between 76th and 79th sts. Tel. 288-1558.

George Wittenborn, a German refugee bookseller, opened this store back in 1937. Wittenborn was able to secure the confidence of significant artists, including a coterie of German refugee artists in New York, most of whom were Abstract Expressionists. The spirit and passion with which Wittenborn collected books prevails. Now in the hands of Gabrielle Austin, it carries both new and out-of-print books, many in Italian and German, some in French, and a few Danish titles. The stock of books in English is sparse. But no matter, most are exquisite to behold. You can prevail upon them to special-order from Europe, choosing from among the titles offered through eight or nine different catalogs, each devoted to a different subject—19th-century art, 20th-century art, decorative art, sculpture, and so on. Catalogs will also be sent in response to telephone requests. This place is not for the dabbler. Only serious art bookophiles are encouraged.

BUSINESS

MCGRAW-HILL BOOKSTORE, 1221 Ave. of the Americas. Tel. 512-4100.

Tucked away in the basement of the McGraw-Hill building at Rockefeller Center, this store carries books from all publishers, with a special emphasis on business publications and computer books.

WALDENBOOKS, 57 Broadway at Exchange Place. Tel. 269-1139.

This store is the largest Waldenbooks of all in the national chain. It stocks all of the titles you'd expect to see at any Waldenbooks in the country. It accommodates the nearby Wall Streeters who spend lunch hours in its aisles, by stocking an "unusually strong" list of business publications.

CHILDREN'S BOOKS

BOOKS OF WONDER, 132 Seventh Ave. at 18th St. Tel. 989-3270.

Books of Wonder is New York's largest children's bookstore, and one of its most imaginative. Books are carefully selected to stimulate a love of reading in children, beginning with books for reading aloud to infants, all the way up to novels for those ages 10 to 17. Kids are encouraged to browse, sit on the floor, and handle the books; and you'll often find parents here reading aloud to their youngsters. Wide aisles and double doors accommodate strollers. In addition to a large selection of classic and modern books, the store also deals in collectible children's books, first editions, and out-of-print books, including the world's largest collection of Oz books. Knowledgeable staff members can advise parents on selections. The other store, which is smaller and has fewer antiquarian and Oz books, is located at 464 Hudson St., at Barrow St. (tel. 645-8006). Write for free catalogs to the Seventh Avenue address.

EEYORE'S BOOKS FOR CHILDREN, 25 E. 83rd St., between Fifth and Madison aves. Tel. 988-3404.

⭐ The granddaddy of New York's children's bookstores has a huge selection through which youngsters are invited to browse, and a friendly staff to advise parents. Look here for hard-to-find classics as well as current children's books, fiction and nonfiction; Eeyore's has them all. As if that were not enough, they also have a free story hour every Sunday from September to May. Interactive events include baseball storytelling, face-painting, and origami workshops. You might catch Madeleine L'Engle reciting from *A Wrinkle in Time,* or Chris Van Allsberg holding forth from *The Polar Express.* You could see a magic show, maybe a slide show on the wonderful world of sharks. For a schedule of events, write to the above address, or to the other branch of Eeyore's, at 2212 Broadway, between 78th and 79th streets (tel. 362-0634). As a special accommodation for working moms, the Broadway Eeyore's is open until 8pm on Mondays and Thursdays. Closed on Sunday in July and August.

DRAMA & THEATER

APPLAUSE THEATRE BOOKS, 211 W. 71st St., between Broadway and West End Ave. Tel. 496-7511.

Applause offers plays, musical librettos, screenplays, criticism, biographies, and books catering to actors and performers. They also publish an exclusive selection of books and videos, most unavailable elsewhere. Anyone interested in theater or film could easily spend a day here.

DRAMA BOOKSHOP, INC., 723 Seventh Ave. (second floor), at 48th St. Tel. 944-0595.

Drama Bookshop was established in 1923. It is a performing arts specialty store and stocks plays, textbooks, criticism, and anthologies relating to theater, dance, and film. Open until 8pm on Wednesday, for those who would like to sweep in after a matinee.

SAMUEL FRENCH, INC., 45 W. 45th St. (second floor), between Sixth and Seventh aves. Tel. 206-8990.

Samuel French, Inc., has been publishing plays for 160 years. The business was started in the early part of the 19th century, and has been flourishing ever since. This location (there are others in Los Angeles, Canada, and London, but all are now independently run and do not necessarily have similar merchandise) keeps 5,000 current titles, and has original manuscripts dating back to the 1800s. Especially in the fall, drama students, acting teachers, and others throng the place looking for material that appears on class reading lists. All Samuel French titles are dispensed through a service window. You simply make your request, or locate what you want in one of their catalogs (available for $1.25 and $1.50), and one of the helpful people behind the counter will fetch it for you. Other titles, published elsewhere, are on display in the main part of the store, and you could pick up an interesting out-of-print piece here—because Samuel French is off the beaten path, it may have something that has long been sold out at another store. Despite all that is for sale, they like to think of themselves more as a reading room than a bookstore. A table and chairs are available for serious browsing, and you can sit all day if you like. An informed salesperson (an aspiring librarian, no doubt) will pop out and answer your questions as traffic allows.

GAY & LESBIAN

A DIFFERENT LIGHT BOOKSTORE, 548 Hudson St., between Charles and Perry sts. Tel. 989-4850.

This store offers a huge selection of books that are of interest to the gay and lesbian community. Aside from novels and nonfiction titles concerning gay issues, they stock a wide variety of magazines from around the country and around the world.

OSCAR WILDE MEMORIAL BOOKSHOP, 15 Christopher St., across from Gay St. Tel. 255-8097.

This bookshop, in existence for 25 years, was the first bookstore to cater to the gay and lesbian community. It offers a small but fascinating range of titles, covering subjects that range anywhere from AIDS to baseball to bodybuilding. All books with a list price of at least $7.95 are discounted.

JUDITH'S ROOM, 681 Washington St., between 10th and Charles sts. Tel. 727-7330.

Judith's Room carries fiction by female authors, nonfiction titles about women's issues, and a variety of buttons, cards, and posters. There are extended hours Tuesdays through Saturdays. Call for details.

METAPHYSICAL & NEW AGE

EAST WEST BOOKS, 78 Fifth Ave., at 14th St. Tel. 243-5994.

This outstanding bookstore dealing in matters esoteric is an affiliate of the Himalayan Institute. There's a serene atmosphere here, and an excellent collection of titles in religion, philosophy, New Age, health and nutrition, psychology, and so on. Cassettes and CDs of New Age music are available, as are some jewelry and crystals.

Uptown, there's a smaller branch at 568 Columbus Ave., between 87th and 88th streets (tel. 787-7552). Classes in hatha yoga, meditation, and cooking are available at both locations.

OPEN CENTER, 83 Spring St., between Broadway and Lafayette St. Tel. 219-2527.

In the SoHo area, anyone interested in spiritual, holistic, and metaphysical studies should check the bookstore at this nonprofit holistic learning center. The shop carries a selection of quality titles, music, calendars, crystals, cards, and jewelry. The shop stays open 'til 10pm weekdays. Call for weekend hours and more specifics.

QUEST BOOKSHOP, 240 E. 53rd St., between Second and Third aves. Tel. 758-5521.

Located in the midtown area, the Quest Bookshop is part of the New York Theosophical Society. It specializes in books on Theosophy, the mysticism of the great religions, mind science, health and healing, meditation, and the like. Tapes, incense, cards, and some videos round out a collection of some 5,000 carefully chosen titles.

THE HERO'S JOURNEY, 489 Columbus Ave., between 83rd and 84th sts. Tel. 874-4630.

At this serene emporium oriented to inner development, you'll find a wide selection of metaphysical books (everything from Tibetan Buddhism to shamanism to healing), New Age music, natural crystals and crystal jewelry, chimes and bells, sculpture from India, Tiber, and Egypt, and some very affordable gift items, as well.

SAMUEL WEISER, 132 E. 24th St., between Lexington Ave. and Park Ave. South. Tel. 777-6363.

In business since 1927, Samuel Weiser has been characterized as the finest bookstore stocking books on metaphysics in the world. Its quarter-of-a-million volumes, including many rare and out-of-print works, cover a wide range of philosophical, occult, metaphysical, and New Age persuasions. They have many hard-to-find titles published in India. After you've browsed the books (people have been known to stay here for hours), check out the jewelry, crystals, crystal balls, and the very large selection of Tarot cards.

MYSTERY & SCIENCE FICTION

MYSTERIOUS BOOKSHOP, 129 W. 56th St., between Sixth and Seventh aves. Tel. 765-0900.
This shop stocks an extensive array of new, used, and rare mystery and detective books. Closed on Sundays.

MURDER, INC., 2486 Broadway, between 92nd and 93rd sts. Tel. 362-8905.
If it's a mystery or detective novel, you'll find it here. They also carry espionage, true crime, and Sherlockiana, along with rare and out-of-print mysteries. Frequent autographing parties are held.

FORBIDDEN PLANET, 821 Broadway, between 11th and 12th sts. Tel. 473-1576.
The original downtown store (and its uptown branch) features science-fiction books, old and new comic books, original art from comic books, space and science-fiction-oriented toys and games, and sci-fi film memorabilia. They call themselves the largest of their kind, and we believe it. The newer store is located at 227 E. 59th St., between Second and Third aves. (tel. 751-4386).

SCIENCE FICTION SHOP, 168 Bleecker St., between Sullivan and Thompson sts. Tel. 473-3010.
"Small but mighty" is the way the owners characterize their Greenwich Village store. In business for over 18 years, it is well known to readers worldwide, from Japan to Sweden to Sri Lanka. It deals exclusively in the literature of science fiction and fantasy, with a large backstock of titles in print in the United States, supplemented with books from England. Recently, they've added a stock of horror books, too.

You may find yourself running into an autographing party or special event for such famous writers as Arthur C. Clarke, Isaac Asimov, Anne McCaffrey, and many others.

OTHER SPECIAL-INTEREST BOOKSTORES

ASIA SOCIETY, 725 Park Ave., at 70th St. Tel. 288-4600.
The bookstore at the Asia Society is a superb resource for books on Asia, including Australia and the islands of the South Pacific, with titles in art, architecture, history, fiction, travel, philosophy, and religion. It's often a first stop for people about to move to or travel in Asian countries. Tapes of music are available, as are many imported titles and catalogs from exhibitions at the Asia Society. Adjoining it is a tasteful gift shop with such items as posters, jewelry, pottery, cards, maps, and wall decorations.

IRISH BOOKS AND GRAPHICS, 580 Broadway, between Prince and Houston sts, in SoHo, Room 1103. Tel. 274-1923.
Proprietor Angela Carter couples genuine Irish warmth and charm with a depth of knowledge and enthusiasm. She is pleased to guide the novice through the store's treasure trove of new and out-of-print Irish books, in both English and Gaelic. Miss Carter, a member of the New York Irish Roundtable, speaks fluent Gaelic, and is well equipped to provide useful assistance to those of scholarly bent. The store's collection of Irish language learning materials, and fiction and nonfiction books in the language is one of the best outside Ireland.

Do browse. You might come upon a signed, limited edition of the poetry of Seamus Heaney, considered Ireland's best living poet. You might find a photo or a sketch of Joyce or Yeats, or pick up a tape or CD of Irish instrumental music (especially harp), songs, or readings. The shop is also a clearing house for information about Irish cultural events. Miss Carter will be happy to consult her folder of programs and announcements, and offer advice on the best of the lot.

KITCHEN ARTS AND LETTERS, 1435 Lexington Ave., between 93rd and 94th sts. Tel. 876-5550.

Kitchen Arts and Letters offers a huge array of books on cooking, food, and wine, organized both by type of food and by region. An excellent source for the serious cook.

CAMERAS & COMPUTERS

See also "Appliances" in this chapter.

BROTHERS, 466 Lexington Ave., corner of 45th St. Tel. 986-3323.
Brothers is a big name in New York for good buys in cameras, electronics, and video. There is another East Side store at 599 Lexington Ave., at 52nd Street (tel. 888-2090).

CAMERA BARN, 1272 Broadway, near 32nd St. Tel. 947-3510.
When New York's professional photographers need new equipment or film, chances are they'll head for a branch of Camera Barn. Whether you're interested in a simple Polaroid camera or a sophisticated 35-mm system, you'll find the right prices and a helpful staff.

47TH STREET PHOTO, 67 W. 47th St., between Fifth and Sixth aves. Tel. 260-4410 or 608-6934, or toll free 800/221-7774.
The buys are often spectacular in cameras, electronics, computers, typewriters, copiers, dictation equipment, fax and telephone answering machines, watches, fine jewelry, and much more at 47th Street Photo. Huge ads in the *New York Times*, *Newsday*, and the *Wall Street Journal* list bargains almost daily. The store is often crowded, but the staff is knowledgeable and the bargains just great. We've seen portable cassette players with earphones selling for almost half the regular department store price. Their prices on film can't be beat either! Their catalog is available free for the asking. Other branches include the store at 115 W. 45th St. between Sixth and Seventh aves.; 116 Nassau St.; and 35 E. 18th St. between Fifth Ave. and Broadway (the last called the "Professional Photography Store"). Closed on Saturday.

WILLOUGHBY CAMERA STORES, 110 W. 32nd St., near Herald Square. Tel. 564-1600.
A dizzying display of photographic paraphernalia meets your eyes when you enter this place. In business for 90 years, it's still growing! You can get just about anything in the photographic line here, from a Kodak pocket camera for around $20 to a Nikon that goes up into the hundreds. There are projectors, film photo albums, and a complete line of developing and darkroom gear. In addition to all that, Willoughby is also a leader in the computer, video equipment, audio, and electronic lines as well. They have one of the largest selections of personal computers and advanced video equipment in the metropolitan area, and even carry a complete line of multisystem video (e.g., PAL and PALSECAM) for overseas use. Bargains are great! You can also come in from 7:30am on for early developing and printing services.

CARPETS

ABC CARPET & HOME COMPANY, 881 and 888 Broadway, at E. 19th St. Tel. 677-6970.
ABC is perhaps New York's best-known name for rug and carpet values, with thousands of rolls of rugs at very good prices: A recent trip turned up all-wool imported Berber broadlooms, valued at $40 per square yard, selling for $10 here. Along with the carpet collection, the rug assortments are huge, encompassing everything from fine handmade Orientals selling for thousands, to handcrafted Indian and other rugs imported from around the world that might go for as little as $100 for a 9' × 12'. There's also an enormous selection of area rugs. New departments include a huge antique furniture department and a bed, bath, and linen shop; prices in these areas are high, but the merchandise is first-rate.

CENTRAL CARPET CO., 426 Columbus Ave., between 80th and 81st sts. Tel. 787-8813.

Central Carpet, well known on the Upper West Side, has been in this spot for 47 years. Its stock of 8,000 rugs includes antique, semi-antique, and new: Persian, kilim, needlepoint, hook, machine-made Oriental, dhurrie, and Indo-Persian and Pakistani rugs. Prices here are up to 50% off the tab at department stores! You could pick up a machine-made Oriental for $119, or spring for a 9'×12' antique Persian for $12,000 to $13,000. Shipping is available.

THE RUG WAREHOUSE, 220 W. 80th St., at Broadway. Tel. 787-6665.

Another favorite on the Upper West Side, the Rug Warehouse draws those with a keen eye for values. Owner Larry Feldman carries almost 3,000 new and used Oriental carpets of the finest quality and at some of the lowest prices you'll find anywhere in this country. Prices begin at less than $200 for a 9'×12' Oriental-style carpet.

CHINA, POTTERY, CRYSTAL & GLASSWARE

EAST SIDE GIFTS AND DINNERWARE, 351 Grand St., near Essex St. Tel. 982-7200 or 529-6328.

This place offers discounts of from 35% to 60% on all major brands of china, crystal, and flatware, and ships anywhere. Closed on Saturday.

FISH'S EDDY, 889 Broadway, at 19th St. Tel. 420-9020.

You won't find fish of any kind at Fish's Eddy, just fabulous vintage china from now-defunct restaurants, hotels, and occasionally, ocean liners. It's all heavy, kitschy, and monogrammed—and evocative of bygone grace and splendor. There are bins of 50¢, 75¢, and 95¢ cups and saucers to mix and match (you're on your own in this endeavor; the staff does *not* pitch in). With the exception of a line of re-issue Fiestaware (like the old Fiestaware, but made *without* lead), everything else is overstock, or was plucked from its original larder.

Fish's Eddy was named for a small fishing town (eddy, as in stream) in upstate New York—the owner's favorite retreat from civilization. Another store is at 551 Hudson St., between Perry and 11th sts. (tel. 627-2956).

GRAND STERLING COMPANY, INC., 345 Grand St. Tel. 674-6450.

On the Lower East Side, check out Grand Sterling, which offers sterling silver bargains in hollowware, flatware, centerpieces, candelabras, and gift items, all at about 60% off retail. They will ship anywhere.

GREATER NEW YORK TRADING COMPANY, 81 Canal St. Tel. 226-2808.

On the Lower East Side are at least half a dozen shops offering excellent buys in china, crystal, and usually sterling silver. One of the best is the Greater New York Trading Company, which has been in business for 60 years; it regularly offers discounts of 25% to 60% on china, dinnerware, sterling silver, silver-plated and stainless flatware, as well as crystal. Frequent sales can bring the discounts up to as much as 70% off regular prices. Closed on Saturday.

LANAC SALES COMPANY, 73 Canal St., corner of Allen St. Tel. 925-6422.

Similar wares and discounts are found at Lanac, on the Lower East Side. Closed on Saturday.

POTTERY BARN/WILLIAMS-SONOMA, 231 Tenth Ave., between 23rd and 24th sts. Tel. 206-8118.

This 15,000-square-foot store, which housed the original Pottery Barn (and later the fabulous Pottery Barn Outlet), now serves as an outlet not only for Pottery Barn, but also for Williams-Sonoma, Hold Everything, Chambers, and Gardener's Eden. It is under the imaginative management of William Sonoma, who, through mass purchasing and low overhead, manages to sell stunning, imported, modernistic designs, most of which are manufactured according to his own specifications, at low, low prices. You'll find kitchenware, dishes, glassware, mugs, vases, baskets, picture frames, rugs, storage systems, and casual furniture. A recent visit turned up excellent buys in frames, white porcelain dinnerware, and 11-ounce wineglasses. All these great buys (often on discontinued items) can be found here at 30% to 70% off their original low retail prices. Pottery Barn/Williams-Sonoma will ship anywhere in the country, and many items may be ordered via a catalog (Chambers and Gardener's Eden products are available only through the catalog). Write to: Mail Order Department, Pottery Barn/Williams-Sonoma, P.O. Box 7044, San Francisco, CA 94120 to request a catalog.

If you wish to find newer stock on these lines, visit one of the 12 Pottery Barns, three Williams-Sonomas, and two Hold Everything stores in Manhattan. Most of these, including the Tenth Avenue outlet, are open 7 days a week. Check a local directory for locations, and telephone ahead to verify hours.

ROBIN IMPORTERS, 510 Madison Ave., between 52nd and 53rd sts. Tel. 753-6475 or 752-5605.

A high-rent, prime midtown location does not deter Robin Importers from offering generous discounts—30% to 60% on most items—on china, stainless flatware, stoneware, giftware, and table linens by major manufacturers. They show over 1,000 patterns in stainless and china, and also carry crystal and glassware. They ship anywhere in the United States via UPS. Closed on Sunday.

CIGARS

J-R TOBACCO, 11 E. 45th St., just off Fifth Ave. Tel. 869-8777.

Cigar lovers should run, not walk, to J-R Tobacco, where cigars are sold at 30% to 40% off retail. Another J-R is downtown at 219 Broadway, between Vesey and Barclay sts. (tel. 233-6620). Both are closed on Sundays.

COSMETICS

BOYD CHEMIST, 655 Madison Ave., between 60th and 61st sts. Tel. 838-6558.

Boyd's is the place to go for unusual and imported cosmetics and beauty supplies. The cosmeticians will gladly give you a demonstration of any product you buy, such as eye shadow, for a glamorous professional look. They also carry designer fashion jewelry, as well as a great selection of hair accessories. Closed on Saturday in July and August.

CASWELL-MASSEY CO., LTD., 518 Lexington Ave., at 48th St. Tel. 755-2254.

Caswell-Massey is still formulating and selling the same cologne that George Washington used. Try some if you're feeling presidential, or if you're in a lighter mood, buy a cake of any of their aromatic hand-milled soaps. Caswell-Massey is the

---

IMPRESSIONS

*In New York beautiful girls can become more beautiful
by going to Elizabeth Arden
And getting stuff put on their faces and waiting
for it to harden,
And poor girls with nothing to their names but a letter
or two can get rich and joyous
From a brief trip to their Ioyous
So I can say with impunity
That New York is a city of opportunity. . . .*
—OGDEN NASH, "A BRIEF GUIDE TO NEW YORK," 1945

oldest chemist and perfumer in America, founded in 1752, with a superb line of toiletries and personal-care items, many from Great Britain and Europe. There are branches at 21 Fulton St., at the South Street Seaport (tel. 608-5401); and in the World Financial Center (tel. 945-2630). Closed on Sunday.

CHRISTINE VALMY INTERNATIONAL SCHOOL, 260 Fifth Ave., at 28th St. Tel. 581-1520.

If you'd like to relax with a facial while you're in New York, call the Christine Valmy. The beauty school from this famous Fifth Avenue salon will cream, massage, and pamper you for the bargain rate of $20. Your facial will be completely supervised by an instructor. Other services available are makeup lesson and applications, waxing, and nail art. Appointments should be scheduled 2 to 3 days in advance. Closed on weekends.

CLAIROL CONSUMER RESEARCH FORUM, 345 Park Ave., between 51st and 52nd sts. Tel. 546-2707.

Clairol is always seeking consumer responses to their new and existing hair- and skin-care products. Women and men are invited to make an appointment to come in to test products—using them as they would at home. You might be asked to test a hair-color, hair-care, or skin-care product. Each consumer who qualifies and participates is given a complimentary gift bag of products. Call the above number to arrange an appointment. To be absolutely sure of getting a convenient appointment, write or phone several weeks before your visit.

MAKE-UP CENTER, 150 W. 55th St., between Sixth and Seventh aves. Tel. 977-9494.

For fantastic buys in top-quality cosmetics, head for the Make-Up Center, where models and actresses have been shopping for years. The center sells its own line of products for half of what regular name brands cost. Available treatments are eyebrow shaping and tweezing, makeup consultations, facials, manicures, and pedicures. Because so many models have their makeup applied here, you must make an appointment for the consultation. Best of all, there's no pressure to buy the products. They recently opened a satellite store at 1013 Third Avenue, between 60th and 61st streets (tel. 751-2001), where cosmetics are sold and makeup consultations are available by appointment.

DISCOUNT HOUSES

BURLINGTON COAT FACTORY WAREHOUSE, 45 Park Place. Tel. 571-2631.

They call themselves the "financial district's greatest savings institution," and that's not a bad way to describe the new New York branch of the largest retailer of coats in the United States, a company with 175 warehouse-stores from coast to coast. Burlington sells first-quality brand-name and designer merchandise at prices that are considerably lower—from 20% to 60%—than you'd find in department stores. They have woolens, cashmere, leather coats and jackets, fake furs, and real furs, too. In addition to something like 15,000 coats for men and women, they also have a complete men's department (4,000 suits, even a big men's section), a good women's section (sportswear, suits, career clothing), and a children's department, outfitting youngsters from kindergarten to college. They also carry linens and bath accessories. The store is two blocks from the World Trade Center, and a short walk from the Park Row station of the Broadway/Seventh Ave. Line.

CONWAY, 1333 Broadway, at Herald Square. Tel. 967-5300.

If you've ever been to an old-time bargain basement where everything is piled high on tables and you have to fight your way through mobs to get to the goodies, you'll have an idea of what shopping is like at Conway. Except that Conway stores are at street level and not in basements, and that there appears to be a Conway every few doors on West 34th Street, between Seventh and Eighth avenues, as well as the one at Herald Square. At last count, New York had ten Conways. This is not designer shopping by a long shot, but standard items are deeply discounted. Most Conways sell men's, ladies', and children's clothing; a few sell plus sizes for women; baby carriages and cribs; children's and ladies' shoes; health and beauty aids; and towels and linens as well. You'll even find imported and domestic designer name fragrances here. On West 34th Street, there are Conways at nos. 11, 225, 243, 245, 247, and 251; at 450 Seventh Ave. at 34th St.; as well as the one at 1333 Broadway. Branches are also at 201 East 42nd St., at Third Ave. and 45 Broad St.

DOLLAR BILL'S, 90 E. 42nd St. Tel. 867-0212.

 This storefront in Grand Central Terminal has a bargain-basement appearance, but there are treasures within. On a recent visit we saw scads of well-tailored gentlemen milling about a rack of Italian designer men's suits that were selling for $399. Since Dollar Bill's is not allowed to advertise or publicize designer's names, we won't spoil their secret, but the labels are there, and we will tell you that suits by this Italian designer normally sell for $800 to $1,000 elsewhere. A salesman let us in on the secret: the owner goes to Italy and buys directly from the designers, in huge quantities, and passes the extraordinary bargains on to the customer. Women's Italian knits are another specialty, none of them inexpensive, but of fine quality. The bargains go on and on, and there's simply no telling what you will turn up here.

JOB LOT TRADING COMPANY, INC., 140 Church St., between Chambers and Warren sts. Tel. 962-4142.

Depending on what they have in stock on the day you visit, a stop at this downtown store, also known as "The Puschcart," could be one of the memorable shopping experiences of New York. You'll find everything and anything from famous-name children's toys to fishing rods, from toothpaste to knapsacks, to boxes of candy—all discounted at least 50%. Especially around holidays, the crowds are thick. There are stores at 1633 Broadway, at 50th St. (tel. 245-0921), and at 80 Nassau St., near Fulton St. (tel. 619-6868). Check for individual store hours.

ODD JOB TRADING, 7 E. 40th St., just off Fifth Ave. Tel. 686-6825.

Odd Job Trading sells brand-name close-out toiletries, linens, stationery, glassware and china, tools, toys, and just about anything else you could think of at low, low prices. Occasionally, you may luck into designer clothing and shoes; we once saw Joan and David shoes, which go from $120 to $220 uptown, here for only $25! Other branches are located at 149 W. 32nd St., between Sixth and Seventh aves. (tel. 564-7370); 66 W. 48th St., between Fifth and Sixth aves. (tel. 575-0477); and 10-12 Cortlandt St., a few doors from Century 21 (tel. 571-0959).

WEBER'S CLOSEOUT CENTERS, 138 Church St. Tel. 571-3283.

Again, you never know what you're likely to find at another popular group of job-lot merchants. We've spotted $50 Italian designer summer sandals for $12, $20 straw hats for $4, and sweaters, jeans, housewares, tools, china, all for way-below-wholesale prices. In all there are four branches of Weber's. The others are in midtown at 475 Fifth Avenue (tel. 251-0613) and at 45 W. 45th Street, between Fifth and Sixth aves. (tel. 819-9780); and on the Upper West Side at 2064 Broadway, at 72nd Street (tel. 787-1644). The Upper West Side store is open every day. Most have extended hours. Call for details.

DRUGS & VITAMINS

DRUG LOFT, 1103 Lexington Ave., at 77th St. Tel. 879-0910.

For a complete line of drugstore items, as well as prescriptions, try the Drug Loft. Ordinary drugstore products are sold at a discount of at least 20%. Most prescriptions are 20% to 50% lower than at regular drugstores. Vaporizers, hairdryers, surgical stockings, thermoses, electric heating pads, hot-water bottles, and everything else are all at low, low prices. Cosmetics, too, are discounted. Closed Sunday.

DUANE READE, 350 Fifth Ave., near 33rd St. Tel. 714-2417.

Since they have 34 stores in Manhattan, it's not hard to find a branch of Duane

Reade. It's been in business for 30 years and is the largest independently owned drugstore chain on the East Coast. Prices are amazing—and the bargains extend all the way from prescriptions (averaging 50% off regular prices) to health and beauty aids, tobacco, cosmetics, fragrances, photo developing, hosiery, candies and cookies, convenience foods, and lots more. Vitamins are also sold at incredibly low prices; they carry all the major national brands, many of the organic and natural brands, and their own generic vitamins. Check the phone book for a complete list of Duane Reade stores, but for starters, in the most popular midtown areas, you'll find Duane Reade: at 215 W. 34th St., between Seventh and Eighth aves., near Macy's (tel. 714-9410); and at 51 W. 51st St., near Radio City Music Hall (tel. 582-8525). Hours vary.

VITAMIN FACTORY OUTLETS, located in Prescriptions Limited Pharmacy, 1151 Madison Ave., at 85th St. Tel. 628-3210.

The Vitamin Factory Outlet offers a huge selection and very low prices on all-natural and organic vitamins: they are hypo-allergenic, with no sugar, starch, artificial colors, flavoring, salt, or preservatives, and most have no yeast, corn, wheat, rye, barley, milk, or salt. You can get a free vitamin consultation and a free catalog, which enables you to order from home via a toll-free number.

VITAMIN SHOPPES, 139 E. 57th St., at Lexington Ave. Tel. 371-3850.

For the leading brands of natural and organic vitamins and supplements, it's hard to beat the values at Vitamin Shoppes. Discounts are at least 20%, and often go up to 40% or more on special sales. Popular brands here include Schiff, Solgar, and Twin Labs. If you don't see what you want, inquire. The stock is voluminous, and if it is not available at one location, it may be at another. They will be happy to have it brought over for you, either within a few hours, or by the next day. Among the nine Manhattan locations, a few of the most centrally located are the Vitamin Shoppes at 2086 Broadway, at 72nd Street (tel. 580-7620); 375 Ave. of the Americas, at Waverly Place, in Greenwich Village (tel. 929-6553); and 120 W. 57th St. at Sixth Ave. (tel. 664-0048). Most are open Sunday. Check your directory for additional locations, and call for hours.

DRY GOODS

EZRA COHEN, 305 Grand St., at Allen St., Lower East Side. Tel. 925-7800.

For towels, linens, curtains, bedspreads, comforters with matching sheets, decorative pillows, and draperies, Ezra Cohen is a bargain shop that offers name brands at prices at least 25% lower than comparable uptown shops.

Continuing along Grand Street, between Allen and Forsyth streets, you'll find over ten more dry goods stores stocking similar wares.

WHOLESALE HOUSE, 2960 Ave. U, off Nostrand Ave., Brooklyn. Tel. 718/891-5800.

Wholesale House is worth a trip on the BMT to buy designer bedroom and bathroom linens and accessories at tremendous discounts. All the major brands are sold at below "White Sale" prices. They can custom-design your bedroom using sheet fabrics of your choice. They ship all over the country. Subway: 6 to Bleecker St., change to D train to Ave. U; take Ave. U bus to Nostrand Ave.

AN ECOLOGICAL DEPARTMENT STORE

TERRA VERDE TRADING COMPANY, 72 Spring Street, between Lafayette and Crosby sts. Tel. 925-4533.

New York's first—and only—all-ecological department store opened in SoHo about a year ago, and for ecology-minded folks, it's a joy to behold, bright and sunny beneath a big skylight. The bywords here are beautiful, useful, durable—good for you and good for the planet. The stock is varied, and much of it is organic. There are natural cotton blankets; organic cotton mattresses, pillows, and futons; and unbleached and untreated towels and sheets (some paisley-patterned, all beautiful). Why organic cotton? Sadly, most of the cotton in use today is grown and processed in a way that "causes environmental havoc": employing pesticides, defoliants (which make the cotton easier to pick), chlorine or dyes, and formaldehide.

Most unusual are the handsome sweaters (around $200) made from cotton that is genetically bred according to principles developed by the Aztecs centuries ago, so that it actually grows in colors—green, brown, and camel—and needs no dyes, not even vegetable ones. Very popular here are nontoxic house paints, made with all-natural plant and mineral-based pigments, as well as nontoxic detergents and bathroom cleaners. Recycled glasses, every bit as beautiful as the ones found in any contemporary housewares store, are made in Spain and Mexico. There is a huge selection of recycled paper products, everything from elegant stationery to fax paper, Filofax fillers, and computer paper. A paper-making kit for kids enables them to make paper out of junk mail (at last, a use for the stuff!). A wonderful place.

ELECTROLYSIS

MARGARET RAILTON-JONES, at Helio De Souza, 1107 Second Ave., between 58th and 59th sts. Tel. 644-6366.
Electrolysis tends to be expensive in New York, but good prices and expert professional care are available here. Ms. Railton-Jones, who will use either sterilized or disposable needles, claims that she can get as much done in a quarter hour—for which she charges $20—as others can in a much longer period of time. She also offers very good rates on waxing, facials, nail care, and eyebrow styling, which is a particular specialty. Please mention this book for special rates.

EYEGLASSES

COHEN'S OPTICAL, 117 Orchard St., corner of Delancey St. Tel. 674-1986.
The very best choice for huge discounts is Cohen's Optical, where the choices, including all top-designer frames—Givenchy, Dior, Pierre Cardin, Yves St. Laurent, and so on—number into the thousands! Prices begin at $15. They also have contact lenses. Another advantage at Cohen's is 2 hours of free parking (they reimburse you) at the Municipal Garage on Essex Street between Rivington and Delancey streets. Open 7 days a week.

EMPIRE OPTICAL, 70-10 141st St., one block off Main St. and Jewel Ave., in Flushing, Queens. Tel. 718/268-7411.
At Empire Optical, you can choose from hundreds of first-quality frames—many by top designers. Discounts on frames and lenses are in the 30% to 50% range. Bring your prescription or a correct pair of glasses. For relatively simple prescriptions, costs can be as low as $29.95. Call for details, hours, and directions.

FABRICS

The Lower East Side of New York is the place to find fabrics at the cheapest prices in America. The streets here are jammed with little stores that are themselves jammed with bolts of cloth, scraps of cloth, bits of fur, and suit materials.

Also, be sure to shop West 40th Street between Seventh and Eighth avenues for an exciting array of high-fashion fabrics at reasonable prices.

ART MAX, 250 W. 40th St., between Seventh and Eighth aves. Tel. 398-0755.
A good place to buy fabrics at near-wholesale prices is Art Max. The store is jammed with bolts of imported and domestic fabrics of all types and patterns. Bridal fabrics—such as imported French laces, Swiss embroidered organza—are specialties here, as are "mother-of-the-bride" fabrics—such as imported beaded silk chiffons,

chantilly, and metallic laces. Salespeople are highly knowledgeable and are fluent in many languages. There are lots of bargains downstairs.

FABRIC WAREHOUSE, 406 Broadway, at Canal St. Tel. 431-9510.
This place sells fabrics, trimmings, patterns, and anything else you might ever need for home sewing at amazing discount prices.

BECKENSTEIN'S HOME FABRICS, 130 Orchard St. (second floor), between Rivington and Delancey sts. Tel. 475-4887.
Slipcovers, upholstery goods, and draperies made to order are the specialties here.

BECKENSTEIN'S LADIES' FABRICS, 125 Orchard St., between Rivington and Delancey sts. Tel. 475-7575.
This shop carries laces, embroideries, imported wools and silk couturier fabrics, as well as patterns and notions all at excellent prices. Closed on Saturday.

BECKENSTEINS's MEN'S FABRICS, 121 Orchard St., between Rivington and Delancey sts. Tel. 475-6666.
This shop features suiting fabrics, many from England and Italy, in pure worsteds and blends, for a fraction of the price charged in midtown textile marts. Closed on Saturday.

HARRY SNYDER, 70 Hester St., between Allen and Orchard sts. Tel. 925-0855.
Pay a visit to Harry Snyder, which has lovely imports and designer fabrics—wollens, silks, cottons, novelty fabrics, and soon at about one-third the cost elsewhere. Closed on Saturday.

SUTTER TEXTILES CO., 257 West 39th St., between Seventh and Eighth aves. Tel. 398-0248.
Spanning 12,500 square feet, Sutter Textiles (also known as Equity Fabrics) is the largest retail fabric store in midtown, and certainly one of the most reasonably-priced. Most fabrics are garment quality, but there are also some upholstery fabrics. The store specializes in closeouts, and always passes the savings along to the customers, which means that an identical silk velvet may be $12 a yard one week and $6 the next. The trick is to buy it when you see it, because once a closeout is sold, it's gone forever. If, however, you are looking for something special—50 yards of green damask, for example—Richard Sutter will keep an eye out for it and let you know when it comes in. And the store ships anywhere.

Designers, design students, and home sewing enthusiasts love this place. Fabric could be as low as 79¢ a yard. A pure silk or pure linen (*not* a blend) could go for $5, and tapestries selling for $20 to $50 a yard elsewhere could be $4.50 to $5.50 a yard here. Sutter discounts top-quality designer fabrics as well as those from major textile manufacturers, and has a wide selection of American woolens, gabardines, and printed velours. Their prices on German challis and tissue lamés are the lowest in town. Trimmings start at 10¢ a yard, and they have an array of French bridal laces.

If you want guidance, ask for Richard Sutter. He will not let you leave the store with a fabric unsuited to your purpose. If a fabric is too heavy for a garment, or too flimsy for a slipcover, he'll tell you so, and work with you until you find something you like which *is* suitable.

FLEA MARKETS

Flea markets come and go with some rapidity in New York and the vendors who work the fleas can often be found in the streets—particularly around Sheridan Square in Greenwich Village and in the Lincoln Center area. Goods vary from junk to gems, from fine crafts to factory overruns, seconds, and just plain bargains, all of which may include hand-knit sweaters, copies of designer bags, jeans, cosmetics, jewelry, and more. A few of the more durable flea markets include the following.

ANNEX ANTIQUES AND FLEA MARKET, Ave. of the Americas and 25th St. Tel. 243-5343.

This is the town's biggest outdoor flea market, and it's prime hunting ground for antique lovers—everything from wicker furniture to old clocks and cameras to Art Deco pieces to stained glass to antique kitchenware turns up here. Admission is $1 for adults, and free for children. They run another market, across the street, open only on Sundays, where admission is free. Open weekends from 9am to 9pm.

ANTIQUE FLEA AND FARMERS MARKET, P.S. 183, at East 67th St. and York Ave.
This market is the East Side equivalent of the I.S. 44 "Green Flea" (see below). Art, antiques, clothing, crafts, manufacturer's closeouts, and so forth, are sold inside the school building; outdoors is popular farmers' market. Open year round on Saturday from 6am to 6pm.

CANAL WEST FLEA MARKET, 370 Canal St.
Down on Canal Street, crowds throng the Canal West Flea Market, where used tools, hardware, electronic items, and clothing are more in evidence than antiques and crafts. Open on weekends.

GREENWICH VILLAGE FLEA MARKET, P.S. 41, Greenwich Ave., at Charles St.
Many local artists and craftspeople can be found at this schoolyard flea market. Open year round on Saturday from noon to 7pm.

P.S. 44 FLEA MARKET, "GREEN FLEA," W. 77th St. and Columbus Ave. Tel. 678-2817.

Going strong since 1984, this flea market is the brainchild of the Parents Association of several local schools, and all proceeds go to fund after-school programs for children. Vendors crowd the schoolyard and the indoor cafeteria, selling collectibles, antiques, secondhand clothes, plus lots of new items like sweaters and knits from South America, hats, gloves, T-shirts, scads of jewelry, and books. Combined with the flea market is Greenmarket, a popular farmers' market that brings in fresh produce, freshly baked goods, ciders, jams, honeys, and other goodies from New York state and Pennsylvania farms. No wonder this one is such a delight! Open year round on Sunday from 10am to 6pm.

TOWER MARKET, Broadway between West 4th and Great Jones sts.
This enjoyable Greenwich Village market offers work by many local craftspeople. Open in warm weather on weekends.

WALTER'S WORLD-FAMOUS UNION SQUARE SHOPPES, 15 E. 18th St., Tel. 255-0175.
You don't need to wait for the weekend to visit Walter's. Old magazines and periodicals, comic books, antique clothing and furniture, and costume jewelry are all popular sellers here. Closed on Sunday.

FLOWERS & PLANTS

The wholesale flower district of New York is located on Sixth Avenue around 28th Street—it's a tourist attraction in itself—and many of the wholesale distributors will sell to individuals at prices that are much lower than your corner florist would charge. If you're looking for something in particular—window-box plants, cacti, and so forth—check out all the stores and comparison-shop.

One of the best stores in the area is **Bill's Flower Market,** 816 Sixth Ave., at 28th Street (tel. 889-8154), where top-quality fresh flowers are sold at very reasonable prices. Bill's also has dried flowers, seeds, and lovely silk flowers. They offer all florist services, too—FTD, Interflora, and so on.

FUTONS/FOAM

Economy Foam Futon Platform Bed Center, 173 E. Houston St., at First Ave. Tel. 473-4462.
This futon store cuts foam to size, custom covers cushions in vinyl or fabric, sells

materials, pillows, and mattresses, all at discounted prices. Herculon upholstery fabric costs $7.50 here; it's normally $12.50 a yard or more elsewhere. They claim to have the lowest prices on futons, frames, platform beds, and covers in the city, and the selection is large.

FURNITURE

In addition to the places listed below, you may want to shop the Bowery, between Hester and Delancey streets, where many restaurant supply stores also sell to the public at far below list prices. The wide range of goods includes everything from bar stools to tables, commercial dishes and cooking equipment, cabinets, tables, chairs, and so on.

BON MARCHÉ, Bon Marché Building, 55 W. 13th St., between Fifth and Sixth aves. Tel. 620-5550.

 Perhaps the most imaginative budget-priced furniture stores in town are the Bon Marché shops. They have literally cornered the market on young couples who want to decorate their apartments inexpensively in Scandinavian-modern style. They are best known for their prices and range on all kinds of drawer units and bookcases (we've seen big teakwood bookcases selling for $90 to $100 each), Danish teak extension tables, and quality Italian chrome goods.

A recent trip turned up marble tops from Taiwan and Portugal selling at one-third to one-quarter off the going price. Prices are considerably lower than comparable merchandise elsewhere. And, rare for New York, almost everything that's on the floor is in stock—which means instant delivery. Customers can pick up from the 13th Street store or pay for delivery. Just browsing here is a pleasure. The other store is located at 1060 Third Ave., at 63rd St. (tel. 620-5592). Closed on Sunday.

CASTRO CONVERTIBLE SHOWROOM & CLEARANCE CENTER, 43 W. 23rd St., between Fifth and Sixth aves. Tel. 255-7000.

This store has many floors (plus a mezzanine) jampacked with convertible sofas, modular groups, recliners, tables, wall units, lamps, and much more. Convertibles can be custom-covered to your order; dozens of floor samples are ready for immediate delivery. They ship anywhere. There's free parking on the premises at all times.

PLEXI-CRAFT QUALITY PRODUCTS CORPORATION, 514 W. 24th St., between Tenth and Eleventh aves. Tel. 924-3244.

This factory sells to the public at net prices—about 50% less than retail! They have Plexiglas and Lucite tables, chairs, magazine racks, telephone stands, cubes, shelving, television stands, you name it. Shipping is possible. A catalog is available for $2.

SALVATION ARMY STORE, 536 W. 46th St., between Tenth and Eleventh aves. Tel. 757-2311.

This place is the largest of the Salvation Army stores, some of which are large warehouses full of furniture, books, toys, clothing, and bedding. The furniture is old, some of it antique, some even stylish, but it costs peanuts, and can often be used for those staple furniture items (beds, for instance) whose appearance you may not care about. Speaking of beds, this Salvation Army store has nearly an entire floor of them, assembled or disassembled into mattresses, frames, and bedsteads. A double bed with frame, box spring, headboard, and mattress recently went for $100. Delivery service is available. There are six other Salvation Army stores in Manhattan. Call for additional information and the locations of the other stores. All are closed on Sunday.

GIFTS/MISCELLANEOUS

See also "China, Pottery, Crystal, and Glassware" in this chapter.

AZUMA, 666 Lexington Ave., near 56th St. Tel. 752-0599.

New York's many Japanese shops are good places for inexpensive gifts. There's always an exciting selection of wares at Azuma—wicker furnishings, basketry, bedspreads, clothing, paper lampshades, toys, baskets, stationery, mugs, saké sets, tea services, jewelry, posters, paper flowers, papier-mâché boxes, you name it! You'll feel as if you're at an exotic fair. See the phone book for other Azuma locations.

HOFFRITZ FOR CUTLERY, Grand Central Terminal. Tel. 682-7808.
Try Hoffritz stores for pocket knives, scissors, kitchen gadgets, unique shaving equipment, and imaginative gift items. They periodically hold 50%-off sales on their high-quality cutlery, so you can really get an excellent buy at those times. Other stores are located at Penn Station (tel. 736-2443); 331 Madison Ave., at 43rd St. (tel. 697-7344); 203 W. 57th St., between Seventh and Eighth aves. (tel. 757-3431); 30 Rockefeller Plaza (tel. 757-3497); 324 World Trade Center Concourse (tel. 938-1936); 805 Third Ave., at 50th St. (tel. 421-3326); and at the South Street Seaport (tel. 732-1945). Check with each individual store for hours.

PLASTIC WORKS, 2107 Broadway, between 73rd and 74th sts. Tel. 362-1000.
Plastic Works has a lot more than plastic, although you *will* find the proverbial Lucite coffee tables and TV stands, and they are handsome. They also carry throw pillows, very lifelike silk potted plants, practical and pretty things for shower and bath, and an extensive selection of closet organizers. Their tasteful array of picture frames is well priced, starting at just $1.99. Gilt-framed, reproduction antique mirrors go from $16 to $50. Wares here are eclectic, fairly priced, nicely displayed. You may pick up the perfect gift for someone, even if that someone is you.

HAIRDRESSERS & BARBERS

Hair care is very expensive in New York, but many women—and men too—have learned to beat the high costs by patronizing beauty schools or training sessions at some of the city's finest beauty salons. You'll be worked on by qualified students who need some live heads to practice on. No need to be alarmed—you can choose the style, the results are usually excellent, and the prices will certainly make you feel beautiful.

ATLAS BARBER SCHOOL, 32 Third Ave., at the corner of 9th St. Tel. 475-1360.
Atlas charges $6 for ladies', men's, and children's haircuts—any style. A shampoo, haircut, and blow dry is $12. No appointment necessary. Closed on Saturday; call for details.

DAVID DAINES, 833 Madison Ave., between 69th and 70th sts. Tel. 535-1563.
The nicest thing about the training sessions at the fine beauty salons is that you can get your hair done absolutely free! Service is on a first-come, first-served basis at Daines' training sessions on Tuesdays (no appointments necessary). You must arrive at 6pm exactly to get your free shampoo, complete restyling (their choice of hairdo), and blow dry. David Daines specializes in a natural look.

CHILDREN

ASTOR HAIR DESIGNERS, 2 Astor Place, just off the corner of Astor Place and Broadway, near 8th St. Tel. 475-9854.
Older children may prefer going to Astor Place—the hippest haircutters downtown. The barbers here can cut your hair in any odd shape and color you can imagine—or stick to more conventional looks. Go early to avoid the crowds. It opens about 8am, but by noon, particularly in summer, customers are lined up outside, creating a festive atmosphere as they wait their turns under the scissors. Haircuts are $10, $2 extra if you want your hair washed.

MICHAEL'S, 1263 Madison Ave., at 91st St. Tel. 289-9612.

Michael's specializes in haircuts for children. They charge $20 per haircut. No appointment is necessary. Open 7 days a week.

SHOOTING STAR, F. A. O. Schwarz, 767 Fifth Ave., corner of 58th St. Tel. 758-4344.

Shooting Star is a full-service children's salon. Haircuts cost between $20 and $30. Appointments are not necessary. Closed on Mondays, except during July and August, when the salon is closed on Sunday and open on Monday.

SHORT CUTS, 104 W. 83rd St., between Amsterdam and Columbus aves. Tel. 877-2277.

At Short Cuts, a haircut costs $18.50 and up. It is worth the trip—kids can get their hair cut and shop for toys and clothes. There's also a parent-child special (both can have haircuts for $34.50). Closed on Sunday and Monday.

HARDWARE

Come to Canal Street and rummage for bargains (job-lot and closeout merchandise, for the most part) in the bins that line both street and stores in this area. **Canal Hardware,** 305 Canal St., at the corner of Mercer Street (tel. 226-0825), specializes in hardware for hobbyists and professionals alike.

JEWELRY

ASTRO MINERAL GALLERY, 155 E. 34th St., between Lexington and Third aves. Tel. 889-9000.

If you like crystals or geodes, amber, or semiprecious jewelry, check out Astro Mineral Gallery. They offer an extensive, well-priced collection of rocks, petrified wood, sculpture, and jewelry, in a relaxed and beautiful gallery setting (with fountains and ponds). Their selection of crystals is outstanding. Admire precious rocks selling for thousands of dollars or purchase a string of beggar beads for under $10. There's a large selection of jewelry including tiger eye, garnet, carnelian, malachite, and rose quartz in the $10- to $20-per-strand price range. You may luck into a 50%-off sale.

THE BEAD STORE, 1065 Lexington Ave., at 75th St. Tel. 628-5383.

If you love beads and/or would like to learn to string them, this exotic addition to Manhattan is a must. Imported baubles travel here from Austria (crystal), Venice, Czechoslovakia (glass), Peru (clay), and Africa (trade beads). Silver, cloisonné, porcelain, and silver beads are no less beautiful than onyx, garnet, cornelian, and rose quartz varieties. Stock is both new and antique: prices start at 10¢ a bead, and could go as high as $150. If you've never worked with beads before, take one of their two-hour, $25 classes, offered very frequently. Each student goes home with a necklace, barrette, and a pair of earrings. Pearl knotting, Indian bead weaving, and other special techniques are also taught. Lost beads can be matched. For those who wish to concoct their own designs, The Bead Store provides tools, glue, a table to work on, and friendly assistance, all at no extra charge.

By the time you read this, there may be a satellite store in SoHo. Call for exact address.

GOLD AND SILVER MAN, 2124 Broadway, between 74th and 75th sts. Tel. 724-6393.

⭐ For that special piece of jewelry you can't find anywhere else, take a little trip to the Upper West Side to Gold and Silver Man, where two talented craftsmen (one of them a tenth-generation jeweler to the King of Nepal), can create, copy, and repair any type of jewelry, from costume to museum pieces. Everything is made right in the store, so no need to worry that you'll see the same piece everywhere; and prices are reasonable for the quality and interest of the work. Earrings are a specialty (if you don't have pierced ears, they will pierce them for you or put the earring on a clip), starting around $10 and averaging about $50; and so are a wide variety of unusual pendants ranging from $25 to $200—we saw silver unicorns, OMs, Chais, stars, winged Pegasus horses, crosses, all of which can be matched to a large collection of silver chains or transformed into pins. There are wonderful beads made of lapis, black onyx, sterling silver, crystals, and rose quartz; a collection of natural crystals; for men, cufflinks, tie pins, money clips, and rings. Nobody but an expert would know that the four-karat "diamond" ring set in sterling silver is really a cubic zircon, a most entertaining gift to yourself for $45.

KITCHENWARE

See also "China, Pottery, Crystal, and Glassware" in this section.

THE BRIDGE, 214 E. 52nd St., between Second and Third aves. Tel. 688-4220.

For pepping up your kitchen, this very French-looking but budget-priced store carries the most extensive and interesting housewares selection in town, and at substantially reduced prices—we've comparison-shopped. Prices start at 95¢ for wooden-handled spatulas (hard to find elsewhere), and go way up for gigantic copper pans that would cost much more anywhere else. This is where Julia Child buys the tiny French paring knife she used constantly on her television show "The French Chef." They also carry French white porcelainware, a full line of stainless-steel items, and the Zester, to make vegetable strips, twists, and so on.

CONRAN'S, Citicorp Building, 160 E. 54th St., at Third Ave. Tel. 371-2225.

This American branch of the well-known London-based Habitat chain has some fabulous buys in pottery, kitchenware, china, glass, linen, bath accessories, home office supplies, seasonal garden products, and lots of other things (including furniture). Marvelous browsing here, even if you don't buy. Another store is located at 2–8 Astor Place, near Broadway and 8th St. (tel. 505-1515); a third is at 2248 Broadway, at 81st St. (tel. 873-9250).

ZABAR'S, 2245 Broadway, at 80th St. Tel. 787-2000.

⭐ Believe it or not, Zabar's world-famous home of appetizers, delicacies, fresh coffee, everything, has among the best prices in town on all kitchen equipment, including Cuisinarts, pressure cookers, copperware, coffee pots and espresso machines, and much more. It's a marvelous shopping adventure.

LAMPS & LIGHTING FIXTURES

NEW YORK GAS LIGHTING CO., INC., 145–149 Bowery, between Broome and Grand sts. Tel. 226-2840.

Located on the Bowery, this store offers vast selections of lamps, ceiling fans, and lighting fixtures at substantial discounts.

LUGGAGE

You simply can't beat the prices at **Bettinger's Luggage Shop,** 80 Rivington St., off Allen Street (tel. 674-9411). They offer discounts of 25% to 40% on first-quality brand-name luggage—Andiamo, American Tourister, Samsonite, and so on—plus exact replicas of the extremely popular nylon Sportsacs for 25% less, a full line of business and attaché cases, wallets, and much more. They also stock a complete line of trunks. Closed on Saturday.

MALLS/SHOPPING CENTERS

A&S PLAZA, 33rd St. and Ave. of the Americas.

A&S Plaza, a super, urban-based mall, offers shoppers 60 stores on nine floors. Its dramatic atrium, the focal point of the complex, is reminiscent of those found in elegant shopping meccas in downtown Hong Kong. There are well-known national and local chains (A&S is the anchor tenant), and small entrepreneurial merchants. There are 200,000 square feet of shopping floors, including four levels of The Childrenswear Center, and 16 international and American eateries. If you can think of it, it's here. Among the chains represented here are Barnes & Noble, The Body Shop, Oak Tree menswear, Lady Footlocker, Lechter's, L'Express, Hallmark, 9 West, Plymouth, Wilson's House of Suede, Strawberries, and more. Interesting others include Bathique Plus, Sun Coast Motion Pictures (a video store), Jungle Fever (they sell jungle clothing and gear—well, they do say New York is a jungle), Canary and the Elephant (they sell jewelry—you could've stumped us), Sun Gear (a menagerie of sunglasses and accessories), and, in perfect company, Mousin' Around, where Mickey and Minnie appear on everything from nightshirts to toothbrushes. If your credit card is burning a hole in your pocket, head over.

THE SOUTH STREET SEAPORT

The South Street Seaport and its marketplace have a bevy of exciting shops—enough to make it a one-stop center for gift shopping. While many of the stores here are pricey (such as Laura Ashley, Abercrombie & Fitch, Pavo Real, Banana Republic), there are still dozens of shops where quality is high and prices are competitive. The intriguing selection of goods and the crowds of people having a good time out shopping while enjoying the waterfront breezes and vistas add up to a delightful outing.

The main shopping action here is at the **Pier 17 Pavilion,** which offers some of the most scenic shopping in New York: public promenades of the steel-and-glass pavilion, set on a pier that extends out into the East River, open to vistas of the Brooklyn Bridge to the north and New York Harbor to the south. One of our favorite stores here is **The Sharper Image,** the ultimate catalog store, where people wait in line to try out state-of-the-art gadgetry like do-it-yourself acupressure massage tables or scales that speak. Then there's **A2Z, The Best of Everything,** with another array of marvelous gadgets, like "The World's First Waterproof Massager and Back Scrubber" ($15), a neon telephone ($49), or an electronic organizer ($13). We like the philosophy espoused by the people at **The Weather Store,** who say "you can do something about the weather—enjoy it." A good selection of raincoats, boots, umbrellas, water-repellant bags, and other waterproof items make that possible.

If you can't get enough of penguins, you can get them on tote bags, on ties, emblazoned on T-shirts, and immortalized in "Penguin People," from a penguin bathtub stopper ($5.50) to giant stuffed penguins for $80, at **Next Stop, South Pole.** Another specialty store at Pier 17 is **New York, A View of the World,** where views of the city with whimsical geography appear on such things as posters, cards, and T-shirts. You've probably seen local versions of this store in other cities around the country. Besides beautiful displays of mounted butterflies treated as works of art, **Mariposa, The Butterfly Gallery,** also has hand-worked paua-shell jewelry from New Zealand; small pieces begin around $20.

The most exciting clothing shopping at Pier 17 has to be at **The Limited.** You may have seen these shops elsewhere—there are over 800 around the country, and 2 in New York (the other is at 62nd Street and Madison Avenue). Women can find fashionable, wonderfully priced, up-to-the-minute clothing here, for work into play, or just play. A recent look around turned up cashmere blazers at $129, and angora sweaters at $39. And should you change your mind when you get back to your hotel, no problem; their motto is "No Sale Is Ever Final"—even up to a year after the time of purchase! (Bring your receipt.)

After you've shopped your heart out, you can pick up some food from the stalls at Pier 17, take it out to the decks, and usually watch some sort of free entertainment or the jaunty harbor craft chugging along the East River.

The **Fulton Market,** which was the Seaport's first shopping area, has considerably fewer stores, although it does boast, on the first floor, the marvelous **Zaro's Bread Basket,** which gives you a chance to sample traditional New York Jewish-style baking. Wonderful strawberry and blueberry cheesecakes, hearty breads like raisin pumpernickel, delicious pastries, and goodies galore are here.

Also on the first floor of this building is **Merchant's Coffee, Tea and Spices Co.,** whose huge sacks of fragrant coffee beans perfume the air. This store may well have the largest selection of coffees and pure-water-process decaffeinated coffees in the country. Consider, for example, decaffeinated amaretto, Irish cream, Swiss mocha almond, espresso roast, and so on, for about $9 a pound. Luscious flavored coffees like Dutch mocha mint, cinnamon mocha royale, and chocolate cherry are about $7. Coffees from Africa, South and Central America, the Caribbean, and the Pacific are featured, and all are sold fresh and ground on the premises. They also offer coffee makers and mugs, cappuccino machines, loose and packaged teas, and more.

Across from the Fulton Market is **Schermerhorn Row,** where there are a number of very entertaining shops. Outstanding here is **The Nature Company,** a branch of the national chain headquartered in Berkeley, California. Everything here is designed to provide products that will help people observe, understand, appreciate, and conserve the natural world. Nature lovers of all ages will find plenty here to keep them occupied, from "Moo Boxes" at $3, all the way to books, recordings, crystal clusters and crystal balls, fossil specimens, Native American jewelry, and magnificent animal sculptures that go up into the hundreds of dollars. Sierra Club posters and guides are sold here. The Nature Company also sponsors occasional children's story hours; phone the store (tel. 422-8510) for information and reservations.

Also good fun to explore at Schermerhorn Row is **Williamson's Irish Imports,** which sports green ties, ties with shamrocks on them, handmade sweaters, Waterford crystal, lovely knitted caps and shawls, tweed hats and berets, and lots more. A poster of Irish writers was just $9.

Gadget lovers should not miss **Brookstone,** which, like its mail-order catalog, offers unusual hardware and gadgets. As soon as we win the lottery, we're going to get their Oriental Shiatsu massage chair for a mere $2,000. Kids have a good time here trying out the tabletop games. **Captain Hook's,** next door, is laden port to stern with marine antiques, brass fittings, seashells, and seashell jewelry. The **Seaport Museum Shop** in this block has nice T-shirts, tote bags, posters, cards, mugs, and the like.

The other Seaport Museum Shop at nearby **Cannon's Walk** is larger and shows lovely hand-painted pottery, books, prints, and home accessories in its Curiosity Shop. Cannon's Walk also has a branch of **Caswell-Massey,** America's oldest apothecary shop, which began importing goods from Europe 200 years ago on these very docks. Try something traditional, such as the Williamsburg Potpourri.

Bowne & Co., Stationers, north of the Titanic Tower in the Seaport district, is a recreation of a printing office typical of those found in mid-19th-century New York. It is named for a real firm established in 1775. The shop is located at 211 Water St., on the first floor of a Greek Revival building dating back to 1835. Here you will find daily letterpress printing demonstrations; letterpress classes and workshops are available by preregistration. Bowne & Co. sells stationery items that are set by hand from its large collection of lead and wooden types and printed on antique presses. Orders for personal stationery, invitations, announcements, and holiday cards are accepted.

MAGIC

TANNEN'S MAGIC, 6 W. 32nd St., between Broadway and Fifth Ave. Tel. 239-8383.

Kids (and adults too!) will love visiting the world's largest magic store. On the fourth floor, you will find over 5,000 magic tricks for sale. The store also runs frequent magic shows.

MILLINERY & NOTIONS

West 38th Street between Fifth Avenue and Avenue of the Americas is where New Yorkers go for ribbons, veils, buttons, feathers, hats, stones, and jewelry-making items. Wander in and out of the various shops, making sure to stop at the following addresses.

M&J TRIMMINGS, 1008 Ave. of the Americas, between 37th and 38th sts. Tel. 391-6968.

M&J sells both retail and wholesale, with excellent prices for bridal headpieces, veils, and accessories, as well as trimmings of every kind. In addition to the main store, M&J has two other stores on the same block. Call for information.

MANNY'S MILLINERY SUPPLY COMPANY, 63 W. 38th St. Tel. 840-2235.
At Manny's, combs are only $3 a dozen and flowers to decorate them start at 50¢ each.

SHERU BEAD, CURTAIN, & JEWELRY DESIGNERS, 49 W. 38th St. Tel. 730-0766.
This place is the spot for hobby supplies, buttons, flowers, millinery, ribbons, cloisonné, appliqués, beads, and so on.

MUSICAL INSTRUMENTS

For great buys (40% or more off) in new and secondhand musical instruments, particularly violins, call the **Ardsley Musical Instrument Service** in Westchester County (tel. 914/639-6639 or 1-800-VIBRATO). They have an exclusive contract with a violin factory in Florence that makes half and quarter-size violins for children. They also carry a line of violins made in Bulgaria. And they have a Virtuoso Rental Plan for high-quality instruments. We also found new and used band instruments of every type. The store is open Monday through Saturday by appointment only.

PERFUME

Why spend a small fortune for expensive French perfumes when you can buy quality interpretations of the famous fragrances at a fraction of the price? Here's where to do it:

ESSENTIAL PRODUCTS COMPANY, INC., 90 Water St., between Wall St. and Hanover Square. Tel. 344-4288.
Essential Products sells all its perfumes for a mere $19 an ounce, and $10 for four ounces of men's colognes. They offer 45 perfumes, including highly popular new versions of Coco, Obsession, Poison, and Beautiful. Also available are 18 men's colognes: the newest versions of Antaeus, Giorgio, Drakkar Noir, and Paul Sebastian. Mail orders are shipped promptly. Essential will send you free five fragrance cards, a fragrance list, and an order form if you call or write (90 Water Street, New York, NY 10005) for information.

TULI-LATUS PERFUMES Ltd., 146-36 Thirteenth Ave., Whitestone, NY. Tel. 718/746-9337.

Tuli-Latus does a marvelous job of replicating such scents as Joy, L'Air du Temps, Lauren, Madame Rochas, Bal à Versailles, Opium, Obsession, Coco, and so on, as well as Cuir de Russie and other men's perfumes. Their version of Chanel No. 5 (Tuli-Latus No. 6) has long been a personal favorite. Prices range between $20 and $30 an ounce. They also have an excellent line of skin-care products. Call or write (P.O. Box 422, Whitestone, NY 11357) for a catalog.

PETS & PET SUPPLIES

ASPCA, 441 E. 92nd St., corner of York Ave. Tel. 876-7711.
Want to adopt a poor deserving little dog? Then go to the ASPCA, where you can adopt a dog for $55 and a cat for $45. In addition, you can pick up more unusual animals (which occasionally include parakeets, hamsters, and so forth); the ASPCA will examine the animal, inoculate it, and give it an optional free medical examination for up to 2 weeks after adoption, free vaccination, spaying or neutering, and free feline leukemia testing. To adopt, you must be at least 18 years old and have two forms of ID. The ASPCA also proudly presents the "Purina Pets for People" program for senior

citizens aged 60 years and over who can adopt free of charge. For further information on this program, call the above number Monday through Friday from 11am to 7pm.

BIDE-A-WEE HOME, 410 E. 38th St., east of First Ave. Tel. 532-4455.
Another worthy animal-adoption agency is the smaller Bide-a-Wee Home. They place dogs and cats and ask a $30 to $55 donation, depending on the animal's age. All animals here have been inoculated, neutered if they are 6 months or older, and in perfect health. You must be at least 21 to adopt and have two forms of certifiable ID.

BIRD JUNGLE, 401 Bleecker St., near W. 11th St. Tel. 242-1757.
⭐ This 500-square-foot wonder has macaws, cockatoos, Amazons, lories, finches, love birds, doves, and pigeons, and that isn't the half of it. The store carries 50 species of finches, 15 species of Amazon parrots. If you have questions, ask owner Ford Fernandez—he knows everything there is to know about birds, including their needs and preferences.

The store does medical consults over the phone, and even makes housecalls (or should we call them cage calls?) to trim claws and beaks. Movie studios rent Bird Jungle's inhabitants, and customers, some of whom are famous, come from as far away as Japan and Saudi Arabia. They ship birds anywhere, so if you find the cockatoo of your dreams, rest assured. They'll send it back home to Kansas. The store has cages imported from France, Spain, Italy, Japan, and Taiwan, in addition to stocking domestic wares, and 75 different types of birdseed. Oh, and how could we forget to mention this—you can visit the store and experience the joy of having a friendly cockatoo sit on your shoulder. It's very crowded on Saturdays and Sundays, so try to visit during the week.

CRYSTAL AQUARIUM, 1659 Third Ave., at 93rd St. Tel. 534-9003.
Although it carries standard pet-store items, the main attraction at Crystal Aquarium is row after row of glass aquariums and their seemingly endless varieties of fish. In fact, local biology teachers often visit the store with their classes because it carries such a large stock of exotic aquatic creatures.

JBJ DISCOUNT PET SHOP, 151 E. Houston St., between First and Second aves. Tel. 982-5310.
When you enter JBJ, the call of the wild really *will* be audible (with tropical fish, reptiles, rabbits, guinea pigs, hamsters, mice, and birds on hand, what did you expect it to sound like, the library?). The prices are great here. We once popped in and found an array of small tropical fish sale-priced at between 85¢ and $1.50 each. Bait and tackle are also available.

PET BOWL, 440 Amsterdam Ave., at 81st St. Tel. 595-4200.
Everything you'll need to keep your new pet comfy and contented can be found—often at a discount—at Pet Bowl. In addition to dog and cat food, they carry a large stock of accessories and furniture, including beds, toys, collars, leashes, and so on. Stop in to put your name on their mailing list; you'll receive their catalog and be notified of special sales.

WHISKERS HEALTH FOOD AND PRODUCTS FOR PETS, 235 E. 9th St., between Second and Third aves. Tel. 979-2532.
Although most items are geared to dogs and cats, there is a supply of birdseed, and if it happens to be your red-letter day, you might find a snack for your pet piranha. Orangutan and reptile owners, as well as those who keep guinea pigs, bunnies, turtles, and tigers, are out of luck, and could end up shuffling home feeling pretty hangdog.

The staff and management take a holistic approach to the health of animals and are knowledgeable in that area—and helpful. If Fluffy or Rex feels itchy or has an upset stomach, stop in, or telephone, for advice. They'll ask some pertinent questions and suggest a natural remedy, usually nutritional or herbal, and available on the premises. If a homeopathic agent is required, they will explain what to get and how to administer it, and send you over to **Angelica Herb & Spice** (147 Third Ave., tel. 677-1549), where there is a wider array of things homeopathic (Whiskers has some), to pick it up.

PRINTS & POSTERS

ARGOSY BOOK STORE, 116 E. 59th St., between Park and Lexington aves. Tel. 753-4455.

Argosy places enormous bins of old maps, prints, and books out in front of the store (prints begin here at $1; inside, they begin at $1 and go way up). They also have catalogs of Americana, medicine, rare books, autographs, modern 20th-century first editions, and so on.

ASSOCIATED AMERICAN ARTISTS, 20 W. 57th St., off Fifth Ave. Tel. 399-5510.

Original graphics, etchings, lithographs, serigraphs, and woodcuts bearing the artists' signature are for sale, beginning at $40. Closed on Saturday, June through August, and Sunday.

GALLERY OF GRAPHIC ARTS, 1601 York Ave., between 84th and 85th sts. Tel. 988-4731.

This gallery has been presenting top-notch graphic art in an intimate, neighborhood setting for many years. Owner Ellie Seibold is an avid collector (and seller) of contemporary American, European, and Japanese lithographs, etchings, woodcuts, and authentic Mexican and New England tombstone rubbings. She's always on the lookout for works by young artists, and delights in selling quality work at prices people can afford. Small prints begin at around $50. She also does some very special framing work (some of the leading museums are her clients) and takes pride in framing the hard-to-frame—full-size quilts, tapestries, antique textiles, Indian beadwork, or whatever. If you need such work done, drop in to see Ellie or call and discuss it with her: Send her the object, and she'll frame it superbly and mail it back to you. Her motto: "If there's any way to get it on the wall, we do it."

UNTITLED, 159 Prince St., SoHo. Tel. 982-2088.

Untitled is a postcard store the likes of which you've never seen. Subjects run the gamut from cave paintings to the very latest in New Wave art cards. This is the place to finally start a postcard collection for yourself, or invest in a starter set for a friend as a remembrance of New York. The other store is located at 680 Broadway, at 3rd St. (tel. 254-1360).

RECORDINGS

See the listing on Academy Art Books, which has a great selection of rare and out-of-print classical records and used CDs—pop and classical.

FOOTLIGHT RECORDS, 113 E. 12th St., between Third and Fourth aves. Tel. 533-1572.

Footlight specializes in out-of-print and hard-to-find records, and has Broadway musical recordings, film soundtracks, vocalists, jazz and big band anthologies, as well as rock and country recordings. They carry CDs, buy record and CD collections, and accept mail orders.

GRYPHON RECORD SHOP, 251 W. 72nd St., between Broadway and West End aves. Tel. 874-1588.

Gryphon, which also specializes in out-of-print and rare recordings, has an impressive collection of classical, jazz, Broadway, soundtracks, and audiophile material. There is another Gryphon at 2246 Broadway, between 80th and 81st sts. (tel. 262-0706), which has shelf stock on classical, jazz, and pop recordings. The Gryphon at 246 West 80th St., between Broadway and West End Ave. (tel. 724-1541), specializes in theater, film, soundtrack, and spoken word recordings. They also have a small stock of international titles.

HMV (HIS MASTER'S VOICE), Lexington Ave. at 86th St. Tel. 348-0800.

This giant British-based company just arrived in the New World (i.e., NYC) a couple of years ago, and they made a dramatic entrance with this East Side store, which, at 14,000 square feet, is rumored to be the largest store of its kind in the country. They have a stage for live performances, listening booths where you can sample before buying, and an absolutely mind-boggling selection of every kind of music you can conjure up. There is even an extensive collection of international pop music. Classical recordings are segregated from other types, to allow different types of customers to coexist peacefully, which can be a problem at some record stores. Prices are competitive, salespeople know a great deal, stock is carefully indexed and displayed, and they will order what is not on hand. Another HMV is located at 72nd and Broadway (tel. 721-5900). It's smaller, but not diminished in scope or stature.

SAM GOODY'S, 51 W. 51st St., at Sixth Ave. Tel. 246-8730.
Big music selections at great prices? You'll find them at Sam Goody's here on the West Side and at other New York locations. Goody's is one of the world's largest dealers in recorded classical and popular music; they also handle a full line of compact discs, portable radios, and all associated accessories. Each branch carries a complete line of these products, all selling at reasonable prices. Watch the newspapers for special sales. Other stores are located on the East Side at 666 Third Ave., at 43rd St. (tel. 986-8480), and 1101 Third Ave., at 60th St. (tel. 751-5809). Hours vary, so call each store for specifics.

TOWER RECORDS, 692 Broadway, at East 4th St. Tel. 505-1500.
Tower Records is as much a downtown "happening" as a record store, with its three floors of records, CDs, and tapes throbbing with excitement 365 days a year. The *New York Post* once called it "the hottest place to meet a member of the opposite sex," and that it is, as the crowds watch videos, attend special events, listen to music, and get to know one another. Well, even if you're just looking to buy records or tapes at good prices, Tower Records is good to know about. The largest eastern outpost of the well-known western chain, Tower has one of the world's largest collections, in all categories, from classical to rock to rhythm-and-blues and international pop. Records are often sold for as little as $7. There's another gigantic Tower Records uptown in the Lincoln Center area at 1967 Broadway, at 66th St. (tel. 799-2500), and a block north of that, at 1977 Broadway (tel. 496-2500), is Tower Video.

SPACE-AGE GIFTS

STAR MAGIC, 275 Amsterdam Ave., at 73rd St. Tel. 769-2020.
Something like 2,000 products that show that "science and spirit are not incompatible" can be found here. This is a unique and magical store that should be experienced by those into either inner or outer space. Celestial music, flashing lights, and hi-tech design set a futuristic scene in which you can find anything from telescopes, globes, robots, prism, holograms, and space shuttle models to healing crystals, gemstone pendants, pyramids, books on higher consciousness, and statues of the Buddha. Tapes, albums, and CDs run the gamut from New Age and synthesized space music to Tibetan gongs. The price range is wide, from 25¢ for a sticker to $6,000 for a home planetarium. Rose quartz spheres can go from $100 to $500.
There's another large and exciting Star Magic downtown at 743 Broadway, near 8th St. (tel. 228-7770), and a smaller one on the Upper East Side at 1256 Lexington Ave., between 85th and 86th sts. (tel. 988-0300).

SPORTING GOODS

HERMAN'S WORLD OF SPORTING GOODS, 135 W. 42nd St., between Broadway and Ave. of the Americas. Tel. 730-7400.
Herman's carries a full line of equipment and supplies for golf, racquet sports, hunting, fishing, camping, exercising, skiing, and team sports. It also has a large selection of active sportswear and athletic apparel, athletic shoes, ski wear, and rugged outerwear for men, women, and children. Value is outstanding. And everything is geared to the novice as well as the serious amateur athlete. Other stores are located at 845 Third Ave., at 51st St. (tel. 688-4603), and 39 W. 34th St., off Fifth Avenue (tel.

279-8900). Stores are closed on Sunday except for the 34th Street branch (noon to 5pm).

PARAGON, 867 Broadway, between 17th and 18th sts. Tel. 255-8036.

Paragon is a well-known source for camping equipment. They carry all kinds of backpacking and climbing gear, tents, and camping clothing, not to mention a wide variety of sporting goods and sports clothing.

THRIFT SHOPS

Along Second and Third avenues in the 70s and 80s is a string of thrift shops that feature used merchandise—of every sort—sold in "as is" condition, and that donate their proceeds to hospitals, nursing homes, and other charitable institutions. Some of the merchandise, admittedly, is hand-me-down, but very often you turn up excellent buys here. Many smart shoppers regularly canvas these shops for real finds.

GIRLS' CLUB OF NEW YORK THRIFT SHOP, 202 E. 77th St., between Second and Third aves. Tel. 535-8570.

Top choice of these shops is the Girls' Club, which is almost elegant in appearance compared to many others of the genre. They feature men's, women's, and children's clothing in "mint condition," some of it new. Prices go from $1 up. They sell designer clothing and fine furs at reasonable prices. Also, furniture, bric-a-brac in excellent condition, many antiques in all categories, and books from 25¢ up.

IRVINGTON THRIFT SHOP, 1534 Second Ave., at 80th St. Tel. 879-4555.

This thrift shop sells women's and men's clothing, from dollar items to designer numbers. They also have furs, linen, furniture, rugs, decorative accessories, paintings, porcelains, books, silver, and glassware.

ST. GEORGE'S THRIFT SHOP, 61 Gramercy Park North, near 21st St. and Park Ave. South. Tel. 260-0350.

Thrift-shop fans downtown swear by St. George's, which sells gently used clothing and accessories for men, women, and children, as well as bric-a-brac, books, records, linens, sometimes furniture, and lots more.

TOYS

ACE HOBBIES, INC., 35 W. 31st St., between Fifth and Sixth aves. Tel. 268-4151.

Ace is the place to go for military and car models from around the world. In the back is a case of painstakingly completed models with magnificent detailing, and a jumbled work area where staffers work on models in their free time. It's a fascinating shop.

B. SHACKMAN & CO., 85 Fifth Ave., near 16th St. Tel. 989-5162.

B. Shackman sells wonderful reproductions of antique toys, picture books, and dolls. Here you'll find the kind of Victorian greeting cards and teddy bears that are sold in museum gift shops. Cat lovers will enjoy the Kitty Cucumber® items.

THE DOLL HOUSE, 176 Ninth Ave., at 21st St. Tel. 989-5520.

For new and antique dollhouses, miniatures, and dolls, a good bet is the Doll House. The selection is overwhelming for such a little place.

ENCHANTED FOREST, 85 Mercer St., between Spring and Broome sts., SoHo. Tel. 925-6677.

While the Enchanted Forest celebrates "the spirit of the animals, the old stories, and the child within," it is not exclusively a children's store. Many of the stuffed, carved, and painted animal figures are unique collector's items with price tags up to $1,500. See the *Coyote in Dapper Clothing* upstairs, for instance, and the glittering wizard dressed in antique clothing. But the shop does stock plenty of less costly items for children, and it's worth a trip to see the shop's rainbow-colored rooms, waterfall, and tree-house-like second floor. Unusual, one-of-a-kind stuffed animals range in price from $5 to $25, and animal trinkets, notecards, coloring books, and wind-up toys are available from $2 to $10. Fine handmade kaleidoscopes run $2.50 to $150.

F. A. O. SCHWARZ, 767 Fifth Ave., corner of 58th St. Tel. 644-9400.
A 28-foot animated Clock Tower welcomes you to the World of Toys as you enter F. A. O. Schwarz. The two-story wonderland of toys features a Plush Animal Zoo, Little Madison Avenue, magnificent doll collection, and many other boutiques to delight the young and young-at-heart. There is even a children's hair salon.

KIDDIE CITY, 35 W. 34th St., between Fifth and Sixth aves. Tel. 629-3070.
Kiddie City carries 18,000 discounted, name-brand toys.

MACY'S, 151 W. 34th St., at Herald Square. Tel. 563-3894.
Macy's has a great, if higher-priced, children's section on the fifth and sixth floors.

MARY ARNOLD TOYS, 962 Lexington Ave., between 70th and 71st sts. Tel. 744-8510.
Mary Arnold Toys has a nice selection of toys and classic family games that could be just what a desperate parent needs. Harried hotel-bound parents might also consider story tapes and cassettes, from $6.95 to $12. Summertime hours vary.

MYTHOLOGY, 370 Columbus Ave., at 78th St. Tel. 874-0774.
The new and collectible toys at Mythology seem as popular with grown-ups as with kids: There's always a flock of people ogling the antique windup toys, the posters, the unusual rubber stamps, earrings, architectural toys and kits, inflatable rafts and floats, Mexican masks, Burmese puppets, crazy salt and pepper shakers, just to give you an idea. If you can leave this little store without buying something, you have more sales resistance than we do! Unusual flip books, all kinds of tiny toys at tiny prices, and much, much more are available. Open late on weekends; call to check hours.

PENNY WHISTLE TOYS, 132 Spring St., between Wooster and Greene sts. Tel. 925-2088.
At all three Penny Whistle stores you'll be greeted at the door by a bubble-blowing, life-size stuffed bear, and the treats just begin there. There are age-appropriate and educational games, from soap bubbles to speak-aloud spelling games. Prices range from $2.50 into the thousands (for a jungle gym complete with swings, rope ladder, and a large tent for a backyard campout). Other branches are located at 448 Columbus Ave., between 81st and 82nd sts. (tel. 873-9090); and at 1283 Madison Ave., at 91st St. (tel. 369-3868).

TOYS 'R' US, 1293 Broadway, at 33rd St. Tel. 594-8697.
The world's biggest toy store—with over 500 branches in the United States alone—opened its first Manhattan store about a year ago, right near Macy's and A&S Plaza, and it's a huge success. The three-floor store carries something like 18,000 different items that run the gamut from diapers for infants to electronic games for older children. The store stays open late most days (call for exact hours), and always offers "everyday low prices." Right above them is a sister establishment, Kids 'R' Us, with a vast selection of children's clothing at excellent prices.

TYPEWRITERS

LEXINGTON TYPEWRITER AND BUSINESS SYSTEMS, 300 Park Ave. South (tel. 674-8584).
This is one of the nicest places in New York to buy a typewriter. Discounts range from 15% to 20%, and typewriters are set up at tables with comfortable chairs so you can really try them out. In marked contrast to the frenzied

atmosphere at other typewriter discount marts, the staff here is really helpful with advice on which machine is best for your needs, and they will teach you how it works. Lexington, in business for over 47 years, is an authorized dealer for Smith Corona, IBM, Brother, and Sharpe, with a wide range of electronic typewriters and word processors for home or office use. Owner Jeff Riggio advises that you can usually get a better price on a typewriter in Manhattan, where so many dealers must compete by offering good deals, than in a small town, where there may be only one dealer who will charge list prices. The Smith Corona XL 1500 electronic typewriter here was $129, as against a list price of $229; the sophisticated Smith Corona PWP1200 was $350 here, and cost $475 elsewhere. And for those of you who simply refuse to move ahead with progress, we even found a tiny manual typewriter—an Olivetti—for all of $69.

UMBRELLAS

If you've never been able to find the perfect umbrella in your local stores, **Gloria Umbrellas,** 39 Essex St., on the Lower East Side (tel. 475-7388), should have one in stock to suit your fancy—and at a 30% discount! Whether you're looking for an oversize, folding, or windproof umbrella, we're sure you won't be disappointed here. They are also experts at repairing all types of umbrellas.

3. FOOD

Food, food, beautiful food. In New York, everyone's a gourmet. For the best prices on the essentials—plus the frills from Spanish saffron to Hungarian prune whip— consult the following:

CHEESE

BEN'S, 181 E. Houston St., between Allen and Orchard sts. Tel. 254-8290.
Ben's features homemade baked flavored farmer and cream cheese—strawberry, pepper, walnut, raisin—that are irresistible and relatively inexpensive. And we can't forget to mention the fresh tub butter, and hundreds of varieties of domestic and imported cheeses.

CHEESE OF ALL NATIONS, 153 Chambers St., between Hudson and Greenwich sts. Tel. 732-0752.
New York abounds with cheese stores, but it's hard to beat the prices at Cheese of All Nations. Almost a thousand varieties are in stock, all modestly priced. A trip down here is well worthwhile since the neighborhood abounds in bargain stores.

EAST VILLAGE CHEESE STORE, 34 Third Ave., near E. 9th St. Tel. 477-2601.
Low, low prices for a wide variety of cheeses, cold cuts, pâtés, coffees, and many other luxury foods are found in this small but compact old-fashioned neighborhood store. The prices are possibly the lowest in New York since owner/manager Steve Kaufman specializes in finding super-special bargains for his loyal customers. The shop has won many accolades; people come here from all over the city. Perfect for stocking up for that picnic, since getting these foods in a restaurant would cost multiples of the prices.

FAIRWAY, 2127 Broadway, at 74th St. Tel. 595-1888.
Fairway has a marvelous cheese section, at some of the best prices anywhere. Up front are acres of super-fresh fruits and vegetables, which, along with the cheeses and pastas and breads and other goodies, bring the customers from far and wide.

IDEAL CHEESE SHOP, 1205 Second Ave., at 63rd St. Tel. 688-7579.
Ideal Cheese is one of the best cheese stores in New York, with the best of

everything, including the largest selection of goat and sheep cheese in the country, many of which are American made. They also claim to have the largest selection of low-fat, low-cholesterol cheeses in the country. Depending on the season you can usually find between 250 and 300 cheeses here. They also sell gift baskets, gourmet coffees, and pâtés. A free catalog is available upon request.

MURRAY'S CHEESE SHOP, 257 Bleecker St., between Sixth and Seventh aves. Tel. 243-3289.
Murray's has hundreds of varieties of imported cheeses at unbeatable prices. The quality is excellent, and there are frequent specials.

COFFEES & TEAS

MCNULTY'S, 109 Christopher St., between Hudson and Bleecker sts. Tel. 242-5351.
McNulty's has been serving coffee- and tea-loving New Yorkers since 1895. They sell about 100 varieties of choice coffees and rare, hard-to-obtain teas.

GOURMET GROCERIES

DEAN & DELUCA, 560 Broadway, corner of Prince St., SoHo. Tel. 431-1691.
Dean & deLuca has every type of cheese, great loaves of black bread, sweet ham, savory pies, pastries, pastas, condiments, magnificent fresh produce, coffees, and croissants to name a few categories. Everything is fabulous, but be warned: Prices are high.

BASIOR-SCHWARTZ, 421 W. 14th St. Tel. 929-5368.
Located in the bustling wholesale meat market district, Basior-Schwartz is an enormous cooler that is also a large wholesale supplier to stores and restaurants. It services the retail customer as well, selling cheeses, pâtés, smoked fish, crackers, and biscuits at very big discounts, and much, much more. Olive oil, spices (1 lb. minimum), and tuna fish are available at great savings too. Open early morning hours, Monday to Friday from 5 to 10:30am.

ELK CANDY CO., 240 E. 86th St., between Second and Third aves. Tel. 650-1177.
Elk Candy offers every kind of sweet imaginable, but specializes in wonderful-tasting and whimsical-looking marzipan.

PAPRIKAS WEISS IMPORTERS, 1546 Second Ave., between 80th and 81st sts., Yorkville. Tel. 288-6117.
This store specializes in Middle European foods, as well as unusual kitchen utensils from all over the world. Hard-to-find spices are available here in bulk. Coffees and teas, ready-to-use strudel dough sheets, Hungarian salamis, nuts, cheeses, homemade jams and syrups, every kind of canned good imaginable, a huge selection of French pâtés, foie gras, and fresh goose livers, plus continental candies, make this place an international food bazaar par excellence. They also sell gift items from Hungary: hand-embroidered peasant blouses, kerchiefs, and shawls, for example. Send $1 to subscribe to their mail-order catalog.

SCHALLER AND WEBER, 1654 Second Ave., corner of 86th St. Tel. 879-3047.
While you're in the neighborhood, stop in at Schaller and Weber for "gold medal award-winning" cold cuts and gourmet products.

ZABAR'S, 2245 Broadway, at 80th St. Tel. 787-2000.
A gigantic, mind-boggling emporium that attracts patrons from far and wide, day and night, is what we have in Zabar's. Here is your classic New York "appetizing" store—and that means salty smoked fish and pickled herring, lusty breads, fragrant coffee beans, delicate cheeses, imported candies, virgin olive oils, and much, much more—not to mention superb prepared gourmet foods to go.

There's a coffee and pastry shop on the premises, and upstairs, a mezzanine full of housewares and kitchen gadgets at the best prices in town (Zabar's frequent price wars with Macy's on name-brand equipment is usually highlighted in the window).

GREENMARKETS

You wouldn't expect to find farmers' markets in the asphalt jungle, but New York does have them, and New Yorkers adore them. If you're in the neighborhood of the biggest and most popular of the Greenmarkets—the one held at **Union Square** (17th Street and Broadway) every Wednesday and Saturday, year round, do take a stroll around. Whether or not you're cooking in, it's worth a visit to see and sample the wonderful produce, freshly baked breads and pastries, ciders, honeys, and so forth, that are grown by farmers in New York state and Pennsylvania, brought to the city and sold by the growers themselves. Prices are very reasonable and everything is the freshest and finest. On a recent summer visit, we spotted a variety of pies—shoofly, cherry, peach, and apple—baked by farm women from Pennsylvania's Amish country for around $5 each; they were also selling their own butter and cheese. Fishermen from Montauk on the tip of Long Island were selling freshly caught fish. New York state farms were selling wild mountain strawberries, fresh sweet corn, raspberry preserves, fresh apple cider, and hydroponically grown tomatoes, lettuce, and cucumbers. Pennsylvania Dutch farmers were selling organically produced meats and handmade pretzels. There were goat cheeses, free-range chickens, and raspberry preserves and New York state wines, and scads of stands selling plants and fresh country flowers. In cold weather, you can often pick up a steaming bowl of potato chowder from one of the stands.

Other popular Greenmarkets that you may want to visit are the ones in **Greenwich Village,** at Gansevoort and Hudson streets, in the heart of the meat market area, open on Saturday from June 3 to November 18; in the **East Village** at St. Marks Church, 10th Street and Second Avenue, on Tuesday from May 30 to November 21; **West 57th Street** and Ninth Avenue, on Wednesday and Saturday, year round; downtown at the **World Trade Center,** on Thursday year round and also on Tuesday from June 6 to December 19. The Greenmarket at **Columbus Avenue** and W. 77th Street, in the schoolyard of I.S. 44, shares space with one of the city's most engaging flea markets, making it doubly delightful. It's known as "Green Flea."

Most Greenmarkets are open from 8am to 5 or 6pm, or until they sell out. The earlier you come, the fresher and better are the pickings.

For more information on Greenmarkets, phone or write the Council on the Environment of New York City, 51 Chambers St., New York, NY 10017 (tel. 566-0990).

HEALTH & NATURAL FOODS

It sometimes seems that half the people in New York are on a health and fitness kick. As a result, there are health-food specialty stores every few blocks, plus huge natural-food emporiums here and there. Some of the best:

BROWNIES, 91 Fifth Ave., between 16th and 17th sts. Tel. 242-2199.
Natural nutrition may be the "in" thing these days, but at Brownies, healthful eating has been the vogue for over 50 years. Brownies purveys vitamins, grains, beans, seeds, herbal teas—a full line of natural food items. They also have sandwiches, salads, and a full line of baked goods that use only whole-grain flours, honey, and other natural ingredients.

COMMODITIES, 117 Hudson St., corner of North Moore St., TriBeCa. Tel. 334-8330.
Commodities is a macrobiotic superstore, with what they call perhaps the largest selection in the world of macrobiotic products. But there's also plenty in this huge store for those who are not into macrobiotics. Where almost 95% of the goods are organically grown—and that includes fresh fruits and vegetables, grains,

beans, seaweeds, unusual flours (chestnut, chickpea, and so on), even the very pleasant Altura coffee from Mexico, which has half the usual amount of caffeine. Rows of bins house staple items; homeopathic and herbal remedies (including Dragon Eggs, a line of Chinese herbal medicines) comprise a natural pharmacy. There are sections of cookwares and natural cosmetics, too. And prices on these hard-to-find items are all discounted from 7% to 20%. Many people from out of the neighborhood come here on weekends to stack their cars with the good buys. Closed only on Thanksgiving and Christmas days.

DOWN TO EARTH, 337 Seventh Ave., between 12th and 13th sts. Tel. 924-2711.

⭐ The best source for natural produce in the Village is Down to Earth. This bustling, crowded emporium also has good supplies of macrobiotic staples, herbs, an excellent frozen-food section, and a counter for fresh juices and healthy snack items.

EARTH HARVEST TRADING COMPANY, 700 Columbus Ave., at 94th St. Tel. 864-1376.

This place is an uptown mecca for organic fruits and vegetables, meat, fish, and poultry, as well as a wide variety of natural-food products, vitamins, and herbal preparations. Their slogan is "Your Whole Week's Shopping Naturally," and they live up to their word.

THE GOOD EARTH, 1334 First Ave., between 71st and 72nd sts. Tel. 472-9055.

The Good Earth carries a wide array of organic and natural foods—fruits, vegetables, meats, dairy products, breads, cakes—natural cosmetics, natural vitamins, and so on. Its other store at 182 Amsterdam Ave., at 68th St. (tel. 496-1616), is just 2 minutes from Lincoln Center.

THE HEALTH NUTS, 2141 Broadway, at 75th St. Tel. 724-1972.

The Health Nuts is another outstanding source for natural foods, including produce. They stock herbs, macrobiotic products, and natural foods from quality companies. Other branches of The Health Nuts are at 2611 Broadway, at 99th St. (tel. 678-0054); and on the East Side at 852 Second Ave., between 44th and 45th sts. (tel. 490-2979), and 1208 Second Ave., at 63rd St. (tel. 593-0016).

PERELANDRA, 175 Remsen St., between Clinton and Court sts., in Brooklyn Heights. Tel. 718/855-6068.

⭐ If natural foods presented with panache strike your fancy, make the short subway trip (call for directions) to Perelandra, and while you're there, have a little something to eat—they have scrumptious organic salads, vegetarian main dishes and sandwiches; the selection often includes things like tabouli and organic pad Thai. You can take your selection out to the Esplanade and have a picnic. This health food store is unusual: a glass-doored freezer and refrigerator run the length of the store, stocked with frozen organic vegetables, frozen main dishes, and an assortment of dairy and nondairy frozen desserts. There is also a full range of fresh organic produce. An entire wall is devoted to environment-friendly cleaning products, and another to all natural pet foods. The selection of natural cosmetics and hair and skin care products is impressive. An entire department is set aside for vitamins and supplements, staffed by people who really know their amino acids from their trace elements. Perelandra also has a glass-enclosed, temperature-controlled room, self-service, that houses nuts, grains, flours, and the like, all of which maintain better freshness under refrigeration. This is the only health food store in the city that has such a room—and it may be the only one in the country.

NATURAL BAKERIES

BLACK HOUND, 149 First Ave., between 9th and 10th sts. Tel. 979-9505.

From the plain looks of this low-profile East Village shop, you'd never imagine the goodies inside! Three Israelis, Erez, Ami, and Dror (Erez was a principal dancer with the Israel Ballet) opened this little shop 3 years ago, and named it after the hound dogs that dig for truffles in the French countryside. Their cookies, cakes, truffles, and pies are made with unbleached flour, and without artificial ingredients, including colors and preservatives. Only fresh flowers and fruits are used to decorate the cakes; for example, they do a chocolate birthday cake adorned with pink blossoms that is a work of art. And their bittersweet chocolate truffles won an award at New York's competitive and highly regarded Fancy Food Show. All packaging materials are environment-friendly—and they can include Shaker boxes, tin containers, terra-cotta receptacles, as well as a special line of signed, handblown glass. A second shop may be opening soon on 59th Street between Park and Madison avenues; call for exact details.

WHOLE EARTH BAKERY, 60 Spring St., between Broadway and Lafayette. Tel. 226-8280.

If you're browsing SoHo, stop into this place for some natural munchies. All the ingredients used in baking are organic, unprocessed and grown without the use of pesticides of any kind. The only sweeteners used are apple juice and rice syrup and, on rare occasions, honey. Flavorful muffins come in gingerbread, rice bran, wheat bran, oat bran, blueberry, corn with sunflower seeds and raisins, and more. Scones, baked with organic whole-wheat pastry flour and apple juice, may be munched in cranberry or blueberry versions. And you could even get a sugar-free, wheat-free, egg-free, dairy-free, four-grain muffin, sweetened with apple juice.

This is a family business, and run with all the care that connotes. Peter Sylvestri took it over from his mother, who opened the bakery 15 years ago.

HERBS & SPICES

APHRODISIA, 264 Bleecker St., between Sixth and Seventh aves. Tel. 989-6440.

In Greenwich Village, Aphrodisia is the place to go for exotic herbs and spices. You can also purchase flower oils to make your own perfume or potpourri, fo-ti (an Oriental herb reputed to have healthful qualities), and dandelion root (a healthful coffee substitute); they even carry crystallized roses (a perfect cake decoration), which are hard to find. There are lots of books here on nature's own medicines, health foods, recipes, aphrodisiacs, and magical herbs.

PETE'S SPICE AND EVERYTHING NICE, 174 First Ave., between 10th and 11th sts. Tel. 254-8773.

Pete's is considered a prime source among the city's serious cooks and professional caterers. Almost everything here is sold in bulk (from an ounce to 100 pounds), and that includes herbs and spices, teas, grains, flours, dried beans, dried fruit, shelled and unshelled nuts, plus various gourmet items—all at budget prices. Try the coffee beans—mocha java was going for a reasonable $5.25 a pound when last we looked in.

PRODUCE

The cheapest produce—as well as groceries, meat, and other items—in town is sold in the **City Markets,** which are warehouse-type buildings in which pushcart peddlers and other small food entrepreneurs place their carts, stalls, and bins. The food is more exotic than you'd find in the commercial groceries, very little of it is canned, and the prices are rock bottom. Several such markets exist, but our favorites are the ones located on **Essex Street** on the Lower East Side, between Stanton and Broome streets and between Delancey and Rivington streets (tel. 254-6655). The markets are closed on Sunday.

SWEETS & DRIED FRUITS

WOLSK'S CONFECTIONS, 81 Ludlow St., between Broome and Delancey sts. Tel. 475-7946.

Best buys in this category are on the Lower East Side. Wolsk's Confections has been here since 1939, both wholesaling and retailing dried fruits, nuts, candies, chocolates, halvah, and more. They have 50 varieties of nuts for eating or baking, and 30 varieties of domestic and imported dried fruits. Nuts are roasted fresh daily on the premises. Hand-dipped chocolates, made of only the finest and purest ingredients, are made weekly. In lots of 100 or more, one can buy imported and domestic hard candies, licorice, gummies, boxed chocolates, and so on at 20% to 50% below regular retail prices. Mail order is available, and they ship UPS.

WINES & SPIRITS

Offering one of the city's most comprehensive and inexpensive selections of domestic and imported wines is **Astor Wines and Spirits,** 12 Astor Place, between Broadway and Lafayette Street, just below 8th Street (tel. 674-7500). You can get a very nice imported French table wine for around $5, and prices on all their stock—especially their own Astor label—are most reasonable. In addition, a wide choice of liquors and liqueurs is sold at competitive prices.

NEIGHBORHOOD MARKET AREAS

CHINATOWN

KAM MAN FOOD PRODUCTS, INC., 200 Canal St., between Mott and Mulberry sts. Tel. 571-0330.
Don't miss this fascinating, vast emporium that offers everything from fish, meat, and housewares, to furniture and exotic Chinese remedies. Not only is the food of excellent quality and relatively inexpensive, but the drug products come in intriguing little metal boxes and wonderful wrappings. The line in the front is generally for the barbecued duck hanging in the window. This place is wonderful for gift shopping or just browsing.

UNITED SUPER MARKET, 84 Mulberry St., between Bayard and Canal sts. Tel. 962-6440.
United Super Market specializes in Chinese meats—pork and liver sausages, dried duck, and so on.

LITTLE ITALY

The neighborhood people who live in Little Italy, a section that runs the length of Mulberry Street from East Houston Street to Canal Street, swear by the quality and low prices at the many food shops in the area.

ALLEVA DAIRY, 188 Grand St., at Mulberry St. Tel. 226-7990.
In business even longer than Di Palo's (see below), Alleva Dairy has been offering fresh ricotta and mozzarella (try the smoked mozzarella) since 1892. In 1992 they celebrate their 100th birthday! They are the oldest makers of these products in America. Closed on Sunday.

CARUSO'S FRUIT MARKET, 152 Mott St., between Broome and Grand sts. Tel. 226-2978.
We get our Italian vegetables at Caruso's, which supplies some of the finest restaurants in Little Italy. All the hot and sweet peppers you may desire, as well as a good selection of the freshest fruits and a wide variety of other vegetables. Closed on Sunday.

DI PALO'S, 206 Grand St., at the corner of Mott and Grand sts. Tel. 226-1033.
We like Di Palo's, which has been selling cheese at this address since 1925. The

store features cheese that is made on the premises—fresh mozzarella and ricotta made with whole milk—plus a good selection of imported cheeses. Provolone is available in weights from 2½ to 100 pounds. Closed on Sunday.

FRETTA BROTHERS FAMOUS ITALIAN SAUSAGES, 116 Mott St., at Hester St. Tel. 226-0232.

A good bet for sausages—they've been making them at the same location since 1890—is Fretta Brothers. They call their products "the Rolls-Royce of sausages." Closed on Monday.

ITALIAN FOOD CENTER, 186 Grand St. at Mulberry St. Tel. 925-2954.

For specialty breads, Italian sausages, quality imported cheeses, fresh homemade mozzarella, salads, and award-winning hero sandwiches, visit the Italian Food Center, across the street from Alleva.

PARISI BAKERY, 198 Mott St., between Kenmare and Spring sts. Tel. 226-6378.

This little bakery is the biggest supplier of bread in the area. Large and crusty loaves of bread sell for 95¢ to $1 each. You can also buy "lard and pepper" cookies and butter biscuits for $2.75 a pound. Closed on Sunday.

PIEMONTE RAVIOLI COMPANY, 190 Grand St., between Mott and Mulberry sts. Tel. 226-0475.

For excellent homemade pasta, try Piemonte Ravioli Company, where owner Mario Bertorelli turns out ravioli, manicotti, cannelloni, gnocchi, cavatelle, spinach noodles, spinach lasagne, egg lasagne, and a host of other pastas. Closed on Monday.

RAFFETTO'S, 144 W. Houston St., between MacDougal and Sullivan sts. Tel. 777-1261.

At this location since 1906, Raffetto's is the oldest fresh pasta-maker in the city. This family-owned and -operated (third generation) business still makes homemade pasta the "Old World" way, using machines dating back to 1916. Yet Raffetto's offers a wide variety of fresh noodles and filled pastas, all made daily and cut to order, at extraordinarily reasonable prices, from their famous noodles ($1.60/lb) to more exotic fare like black ink squid pasta ($3.80/lb).

NINTH AVENUE

The city's most colorful market area, where prices are exceptionally low, is Ninth Avenue from 37th to 42nd streets. Everywhere you look here, the eye is attracted by vivid color, the nose by tantalizing smells. Up and down the street, bins are overflowing with fresh seafood (crabs, shrimp, squid, mussels), fruits, and vegetables; bakery windows are crowded with still-warm French and Italian loaves and flaky pastries; huge cheeses, ripe enough to burst, beckon invitingly from inside dark groceries; butchers proudly advertise their rock-bottom prices, and announce via window posters fresh game, baby lamb, and other delicacies. Excellent homemade pastas and sauces are available at very reasonable prices.

INTERNATIONAL GROCERIES AND MEAT MARKET, 529 Ninth Ave. Tel. 279-5514.

The block between 39th and 40th streets is where you'll find fresh fruit and spices. At **International Groceries and Meat Market,** boxes of imported spices line the sidewalk, and inside are row upon row of burlap sacks filled with more spices (over 50 kinds in all), beans, and grains. You'll also find Middle Eastern and European delicacies here—everything from stuffed grape leaves to Spanish saffron. They also have a wide selection of olive oils and cheeses, a wide variety of dried fruits and nuts, plus freshly made pasta and Greek feta cheese, as well as fresh pita bread daily. Closed on Sunday.

MANGANARO'S HERO-BOY RESTAURANT, 492 Ninth Ave., between 37th and 38th sts. Tel. 947-7325.

Stop in at Manganaro's and order a "mile-high special," made of heaping big portions of meat and cheese: prosciutto, salami, mortadella (Italian baloney), capicola (cold shoulder loin of pork), cooked salami, provolone, fried peppers, tomato, lettuce, and spices. If you simply want to rest your feet and have some dessert, this is a good place to get delicious cappuccino, espresso, cheesecake, cannoli, and the like. Next door at 488 Ninth Ave. (tel. 563-5331) is its retail store, where you can buy the ingredients for the sandwich just described. Great cheeses and salamis are suspended from the ceiling, along with giant bags of Italian candy and pasta. Closed on Sunday.

POSEIDON CONFECTIONERY, 629 Ninth Ave., between 44th and 45th sts. Tel. 757-6173.

This especially hospitable, family-owned pastry shop is a personal favorite—a guaranteed hit if you're a fan of honey-rich delicacies made with the purest ingredients. Look toward the back of the spotless store and you'll see one of the owner's sons spreading out the 16-square-foot sheets of paper-thin phyllo dough, used to make exotic pastries and strudels. Buy it and freeze it. Pistachio-filled honey rolls, rich baklava, and innumerable other exotic delights are also for sale. Delicious cheese, spinach, meat, and vegetable pies are available in both cocktail and regular sizes. Everything can be frozen. Closed on Monday.

WASHINGTON BEEF COMPANY, 573 Ninth Ave., between 41st and 42nd sts. Tel. 563-0200.

The Washington Beef Company's very reasonably priced beef, pork, poultry, lamb, and other meats draw New York's most knowledgeable shoppers.

THE BRONX'S ARTHUR AVENUE

One of the city's most unusual shopping areas is not in Manhattan but in the Bronx. The **Arthur Avenue** section is predominantly Italian, with lots of food shops and bakeries as well as a smattering of retail shops selling clothing and household items. But food is first on Arthur Avenue, and a walk along the avenue is a must for every gourmet who enjoys eating and cooking Italian food. Shoppers will be glad to learn that prices are considerably lower here than in most parts of Manhattan.

Our favorite stretch of the avenue is between 184th and 187th streets, where a number of the best shops are located. To reach the Arthur Avenue section by subway, take the Sixth Avenue D train uptown to Fordham Road in the Bronx. Then take the no. 12 bus from Fordham Road to Hoffman Street, and walk one block to Arthur Avenue. The shopping area is three blocks away.

ARTHUR AVENUE RETAIL MARKET, 2344 Arthur Ave.

This big market is chock-full of privately operated stalls, each of which offers vegetables and fruit at competing prices. You can walk through and buy what you want after checking the price and quality of the various vendors. Meats and poultry, cheeses and sausages, espressos, coffees, pastries, all Italian specialties, housewares, and candies—spices, too—are all sold here under one roof and the atmosphere is very European. This is a good place to do your budget shopping. Closed on Sunday.

DE LILLO PASTRY, 606 E. 187th St. Tel. 367-8198.

This pastry shop is located on 187th Street, which intersects Arthur Avenue, and is a continuation of the Italian food shopping in this area. De Lillo offers all types of Italian goodies baked right on the premises.

DANNY'S PORK STORE, 626 E. 187th St. Tel. 933-1690.

Danny's sells every cut of pork imaginable, and specializes in homemade Italian pork sausage, made fresh every day. Dry-cured sweet and hot sausage (pepperoni), made daily from September through May, is another specialty.

MADONIA BROTHERS BAKERY, 2348 Arthur Ave. Tel. 295-5573.

In business since 1918, this family-run establishment still uses the recipes created years ago. No additives are used. Fifteen different kinds of bread, typical of the varied regions of Italy, are baked in the old-fashioned ovens with painstaking care. And their cookies are excellent, too.

RANDAZZO'S, 2327 Arthur Ave. Tel. 367-4139.

For fish, got to Randazzo's. On the sidewalk in front of the store a raised bench full of ice shavings holds an interesting array of mussels, clams, and unusual small fish. Inside you can buy anything from porgies to lobster, and the fish is always fresh and well priced. Occasionally the owners themselves have caught the fish they sell.

CHAPTER 10

NEW YORK CITY NIGHTS

1. THE PERFORMING ARTS

- **THE MAJOR CONCERT/ PERFORMANCE HALLS**

2. THE CLUB & MUSIC SCENE

3. THE BAR SCENE

4. MORE ENTERTAINMENT

After dusk falls, New York City's frantic daytime scurry reemerges—in the cafés, clubs, bars, and cabarets. Quiet or closed during the day, they are transformed into glittery, swirling havens for night owls. There are piano bars, cabarets, and elegant watering holes for sophisticated fun. And there are jazz and dance clubs for hot, sensual nights.

A night on the town can be expensive—sometimes over $100—and we've listed some places for special splurges. But we'll also tell you where, for the price of a moderate cover charge, or even just a drink, you can find lively and interesting entertainment.

For the latest information on music, theater, dance, and film offerings, check the Friday "Weekend" or Sunday "Arts and Leisure" sections of the *New York Times*, or the latest editions of *New York* magazine, the *New Yorker*, and the *Village Voice*.

DISCOUNTS

CONCERTS & DANCE PERFORMANCES

Before you call a box office, consider these money-saving tips: Some companies have "rush" tickets, sold at discount the day of performance to senior citizens and students with identification. Not all box offices offer this, but if you qualify, ask! Both the New York City Opera and the New York Ballet give group discounts on tickets sold in blocks of 20 or more to some performances, but this must be established in advance.

Finally, try the **Bryant Park Music and Dance Tickets Booth,** at 42nd Street just east of the Avenue of the Americas, at the edge of Bryant Park, for low-priced ballet and concert tickets to events at such places as Lincoln Center, Carnegie Hall, and the 92nd Street YMHA. Tickets are sold for cash only on the day of performance at half price, with a small service charge. The booth is open on Tuesday, Thursday, and Friday from noon to 1:45pm and 3 to 7pm, on Wednesday and Saturday from 11am to 2pm and 3 to 7pm, and on Sunday from noon to 6pm. Call 382-2323 after 12:30pm for information on ticket availability.

THEATER

Many visitors shun the New York theater scene because they consider it too expensive. But with a little imagination and persistence, almost anyone can see even the glossiest productions at reasonable prices.

For those with hearts set on the expensive, glittery **Broadway** shows, there are services that can help you beat the price. We have listed several of them below. For those willing to venture beyond the mainstream, a vast array of small **Off** and **Off Off Broadway** theaters and companies produce highly competent work at lower cost. They produce experimental and original shows, and because of that, have gained a luster of their own in recent years. Many theater-goers prefer Off and Off Off Broadway to their more conventional Broadway counterparts. With the increased patronage, these shows have also become more expensive, though they still undercut

Broadway prices. Off Broadway tickets cost between $15 and $35. Seats for Off Off Broadway performances, which may be even more experimental and unusual, usually cost between $8 and $20.

Tickets for most orchestra seats run between $35 and $100, and even second-balcony tickets seldom start at less than $20. Inexpensive seats are more accessible during the slower, summer months. Finding good, low-priced seats is always difficult on short notice.

One solution is to attend **previews**—performances given before opening night, when the critics attend. You get to see the show at prices reduced by as much as a third. You also risk spending money on an unsuccessful performance. However, most New York theater-goers consider previews a good bet. They're listed in the *New York Times,* the *Village Voice,* and other local publications.

Using **twofers** is another way to beat the system. These coupons buy two tickets for the price of one. When a production is nearing the end of its run or when the audience is sparse, producers distribute twofers to fill up empty seats. Less popular Broadway shows distribute the coupons prodigiously to hotels, drugstores, and barbershops. More successful productions keep circulation low to protect sales of full-price tickets at the box office. Producers send the coupons out through mailing lists and to clubs, organizations, colleges, labor unions, and doctors' offices, which makes obtaining them without an insider's knowledge difficult.

One reliable source of twofers is **Hit Shows.** Send a self-addressed, stamped envelope to their office at 630 Ninth Ave., New York, NY 10036, and ask to be placed on their mailing list. You can also call them at 212/581-4211, and after requesting their schedule, pick up the coupons at their office, located between 44th and 45th streets. The service is open Monday through Friday between 9:15am and 3:45pm. Another good source for twofers is the **New York Convention and Visitors Bureau** at 2 Columbus Circle and 158 W. 42nd St.

TKTS, the Times Square Theater Center, at Broadway and 47th Street (tel. 354-5800), is a nonprofit service that sells half-price tickets to Broadway and Off Broadway shows on the day of the performance (with a $2-per-ticket service charge). It's open Monday through Saturday from 3 to 8pm, and on Sunday from noon to closing. Wednesday and Saturday matinee tickets are sold on the day of performance from 10am to 2pm. TKTS has a second office at 2 World Trade Center in the Financial District, which is open Monday through Friday from 11am to 5:30pm, and on Saturday from 11:30am to 1pm. Tickets may be paid for with cash or traveler's checks only. The group that sponsors TKTS, the Theatre Development Fund, also offers a package of five OFF OFF Broadway vouchers to foreign students for only $15.

RESTAURANTS, CLUBS & BARS

Hundred of businesses, from restaurants and nightclubs to museums and parking garages, offer special discounts to patrons on Tuesday night. Contact the New York Convention and Visitors Bureau for a complete list of establishments participating in **Tuesday Night Out.**

FREE BUT FIRST-CLASS ENTERTAINMENT

Aside from appearances at Lincoln Center, the **New York Philharmonic** sounds off during the summer on Central Park's Great Lawn and in other parks in all five boroughs; some of the concerts are accompanied by fireworks. Call the Philharmonic parks hotline (tel. 877-5709 from early summer through mid-August) for details.

The **Metropolitan Opera** company offers free "Met in the Parks" concerts each June, which are noted in local newspapers and feature such offerings as Verdi's *Don Giovanni* and *Un Ballo in Maschera.*

Central Park also hosts **Summerstage** (tel. 360-2777 for events information). Los Lobos, the Gipsy Kings, Marshall Crenshaw, and the New York Grand Opera have been among the recent musical performers, and the program also includes readings by literary greats like Ken Kesey and Oscar Hijuelos.

Many of the student recitals and concerts at the **Juilliard School** are free if you

IMPRESSIONS

When you are away from old Broadway you are only camping out.
—GEORGE M. COHAN, quoted in FRED. J. RINGEL (ed),
AMERICA AS AMERICANS SEE IT, 1932

If Paris is the setting for a romance, New York is the perfect city in which to get over one, to get over anything here. Here the lost douceur de vivre is forgotten and the intoxication of living takes its place.
—CRYIL CONNOLLY, "AMERICAN INDECTION," 1947

---

reserve tickets in advance. Call 874-7515 for details. Another source of free or low-cost entertainment in the complex is the **New York Library for the Performing Arts** (tel. 870-1630). Tickets are given out several hours in advance on the day of performance for the concerts, workshops, and competitions held in Bruno Walter Auditorium.

One of the best free deals is the summertime **New York Shakespeare Festival.** Tuesday through Sunday from late June to early September, some 2,000 people fill the outdoor Delacorte Theatre in Central Park (tel. 598-7100 or 861-7277). Against a backdrop of thick, green summer trees, the audience watches big-name stars like Morgan Freeman, Meryl Streep, Raul Julia, Christopher Walken, or Mary Beth Hurt in Shakespeare plays. It's no surprise that there are long lines in front of the Delacorte, which distributes one ticket per person, at 6:15pm each night before the 8pm show. (If the line gets long enough, they'll issue vouchers for you and one other person, so that you can come back and claim your place in line just before showtime. Both of you have to appear in person to claim the actual tickets.) The theater is accessible by the 79th Street entrance on the East Side and 81st Street entrance on the West, and the line forms along the Great Lawn. Get there several hours in advance—the tickets run out fast.

The Wall Street area features free lunchtime concerts in some of the city's oldest landmarks. Try **Trinity Church,** on Broadway and Wall Street, on Tuesday, or **St. Paul's Chapel,** at Broadway and Fulton Street, on Monday and Thursday. On Wednesday, take your pastrami on rye over to the **Federal Hall National Memorial,** 26 Wall St. (tel. 264-8711), and enjoy the sunshine and sounds.

The **World Financial Center** (see Section 1, "The Top Attractions" in Chapter 7, "What to See and Do in New York City") presents a wide variety of free entertainment, attracting the likes of the Paul Taylor Dance Company, Dizzy Gillespie, the Count Basie Orchestra, and the Preservation Hall Jazz Band. Other, more offbeat programs in the summer of 1991 included Indonesian dance and flamenco. Call 945-0505 for information.

Many of the major midtown skyscrapers, such as the **IBM Building,** 590 Madison Ave., at 55th Street (tel. 407-6390), and the **Citicorp Center,** 153 E. 53rd St., at Lexington Avenue (tel. 559-2330), offer free concerts in their atriums, especially during lunchtime.

1. THE PERFORMING ARTS

Just to clarify things, Lincoln Center is a complex that is home to such major performing arts companies as the Metropolitan Opera, the New York City Opera, the New York Philharmonic, and the New York City Ballet. It encompasses several theaters and venues, including the New York State Theater, the Metropolitan Opera House, Avery Fisher Hall, Alice Tully Hall, the Vivian Beaumont Theater, the Mitzi Newhouse Theater, and the New York Public Library and Museum of the Performing

Arts. Tours of the entire complex are discussed in Chapter 7, "What to See and Do in New York City"; below we'll introduce you to each of these groups and auditoriums separately, according to the type of entertainment offered.

PERFORMING ARTS COMPANIES
OPERA
The Top Companies

METROPOLITAN OPERA, Metropolitan Opera House, Lincoln Center, 64th St. and Broadway. Tel. 362-6000.

★ In its modern and quite awesomely huge theater, this world-renowned opera company performs classics (Mozart's *Don Giovanni* or Verdi's *Un Ballo in Mashera* or *Aida,* for example) with an occasional foray into modern pieces. James Levine is music director and principal conductor. Performers include such internationally acclaimed stars as Luciano Pavarotti, Placido Domingo, Samuel Ramey, Mirella Freni, Kathleen Battle, and Marilyn Horne. The opera season runs from the last week in September through the last week in April.

The summer of 1991 the Met hosted the Bolshoi Opera's world premiere production of Tchaikovsky's *Eugene Onegin* and the staging of Rimsky-Korsakov's *Mlada.*

A trip to the opera is an expensive evening, but there are bargains to be found. Standing-room tickets go on sale at 10am the Saturday before the performance. We recommend arriving hours before the box office opens—lines are long and tickets sell fast. Reservations can be made by phone for a $3.50 handling charge per ticket. The box office is open Monday through Saturday between 10am and 8pm, and on Sunday from noon to 6pm.

Prices: Tickets $19–$125; $9–$12 standing room.

NEW YORK CITY OPERA, New York State Theater, Lincoln Center, 64th St. and Broadway. Tel. 870-5570.

Christopher Keene has replaced Beverly Sills as director of the popular and critically acclaimed New York City Opera. Recent productions have ranged from Bizet's *Les Pêcheurs de Perles* and Verdi's *La Traviata* to Loesser's *The Most Happy Fella,* to several avant-garde productions of modern operas.

Prices: Tickets $8–$62.

Additional Offerings

AMATO OPERA THEATER, 319 Bowery, near East 2nd St. Tel. 228-8200.

The Amato features young performers and a popular repertoire. *La Traviata* was one recent offering; another performance featured zarazuela excerpts and classic Hispanic music.

Prices: Tickets $15.

BROOKLYN ACADEMY OF MUSIC [BAM], 30 Lafayette St., Brooklyn. Tel. 718/636-4100.

BAM, where Caruso once graced the stage, features contemporary opera, unfamiliar and neglected works from the past, and new, fresh musical interpretations of more familiar operas.

BAM staged its first opera in 1861, more than 20 years before the heralded Metropolitan Opera was founded. The innovation and excitement generated by the new BAM productions in the last several years has reverberated throughout New York's opera community. The season runs from February to June. Call the BAM ticket office for details.

Prices: Tickets $15–$35.

BROOKLYN LYRIC OPERA, Hirsch Hall, Temple Ansche Chesed, 100th St. and West End Ave. Tel. 718/837-1176.

THE MAJOR CONCERT/PERFORMANCE HALLS

Avery Fisher Hall, Lincoln Center, Tel. 875-5030
Brooklyn Academy of Music (BAM), 30 Lafayette St., Brooklyn, Tel. 718/636-4100
Carnegie Hall, 154 W. 57th St., Tel. 247-7800
City Center, 131 W. 55th St., Tel. 581-7907
Madison Square Garden, Seventh Ave. and 33rd St., Tel. 465-6741
Metropolitan Opera House, Lincoln Center, Tel. 362-6000
New York State Theater, Lincoln Center, Tel. 870-5570
Radio City Music Hall, 1260 Sixth Ave., Tel. 247-4777
Alice Tully Hall, Lincoln Center, Tel. 875-5050

This company produces four operas a year in the 400-seat Hirsch Hall at Temple Ansche Chesed. It also offers showcase productions, featuring rising opera talents, such as the recent staging of Donizetti's *Lucia di Lammermoor.*
Prices: Tickets $10; discount tickets available for children, students, and seniors.

MAJOR ORCHESTRAS

THE NEW YORK PHILHARMONIC, Avery Fisher Hall, Lincoln Center, Broadway at 65th St. Tel. 875-5030.

In 1991, the Philharmonic bade farewell to the legendary Zubin Mehta, and welcomed new music director Kurt Masur, who planned such performances as Dvorak's *New World Symphony* and Beethoven's *Eroica.* The 1991–92 season will be a prelude to the orchestra's 150th Anniversary Celebration. See also "Free But First-Class Entertainment" above for information on free concerts in the city's parks.

The Philharmonic's home, **Avery Fisher Hall,** also hosts the Great Performers series, which has included such notables as Itzhak Perlman, and the summer Mostly Mozart festival.
Prices: Lincoln Center tickets $10–$40; Philharmonic in the Parks series free.

THE TOP DANCE COMPANIES

DANCE THEATER OF HARLEM, 466 W. 152nd St., between Amsterdam and St. Nicholas aves. Tel. 967-3470.

The world-famous Dance Theater of Harlem was founded in 1969 as Artistic Director Arthur Mitchell's personal commitment to the people of Harlem after the assassination of Martin Luther King, Jr. It comprises both the renowned ballet company, which tours the world and performs at various New York theaters and the school. If you catch the company while it's in town, you're in for an impressive show. If you don't catch them, you might want to attend one of the school's open houses, which take place at 3pm the second Sunday of every month from November to May. Depending on who's in town at the time, students and company and workshop ensemble members perform.
Prices: Tickets $15–$30; open house tickets $5 adults, $2.50 children.

MARTHA GRAHAM CENTER OF CONTEMPORARY DANCE, 316 E. 63rd St., between First and Second aves. Tel. 832-9166.

The Center is home to the country's oldest dance company (founded in 1926 by the great lady herself) as well as to a school for international students. The company generally performs a fall season at the **City Center,** 131 W. 55th St., between Sixth and Seventh avenues, or a spring season at the New York State Theater. Studio performances—which feature students and company members—are occasionally open to the public.
Prices: Tickets $10–$40; studio performances free or $2–$3.

NEW YORK CITY BALLET, New York State Theater, Lincoln Center, Broadway and 65th St. Tel. 870-5570.

⭐ The New York City Ballet was founded by the renowned George Balanchine, and its *Nutcracker* performances are a December tradition. Recent performances have included *The Sleeping Beauty*, Balanchine's *Apollo*, and Jerome Robbins' *Dances at a Gathering*. The company's home is Philip Johnson's imposing New York State Theater, itself worth a look.

Prices: Ticket $7–$50; $5 standing-room tickets sold on the day of performance.

CONCERT HALLS & AUDITORIUMS

THE TOP VENUES

ALICE TULLY HALL, Lincoln Center, 1941 Broadway. Tel. 875-5050.

Alice Tully Hall, seating 1,000, is home to the Chamber Music Society of Lincoln Center and presents a variety of other concerts and performances. Its recent "Serious Fun" program, for example, included music by Philip Glass and performances by Rachel Rosenthal and Laurie Anderson. Jazz greats such as Wynton and Branford Marsalis have also graced the stage. Check with the box office for specific shows. The Film Society of Lincoln Center also holds its film festival here.

Prices: Tickets vary widely depending on performance.

THE APOLLO THEATER, 253 W. 125th St., between Adam Clayton Powell, Jr., and Frederick Douglass blvds. Tel. 749-5838.

At press time, the Apollo's future was uncertain, but the black community is rallying to save this Harlem landmark. Wednesday Amateur Nights (which you may have seen on television as *Showtime at the Apollo*) have seen the likes of the legendary Lena Horne and Michael Jackson wowing the raucous crowds on their way to superstardom. More recent performances have included Patti Labelle and Ladysmith Black Mambazo.

Prices: Tickets $5–$30.

THE BEACON THEATER, 2124 Broadway, at 75th St. Tel. 496-7070.

A major auditorium, yet small enough to offer an intimate feeling and good acoustics, the Beacon has hosted headliners like Suzanne Vega, the Replacements, Joan Armatrading, Sting, and Little Feat.

Prices: Tickets $22.50–$35.

BROOKLYN ACADEMY OF MUSIC [BAM], 30 Lafayette St., Brooklyn. Tel. 718/636-4100.

BAM, home to the Brooklyn Philharmonic, is well respected for its presentations of ballet, modern dance, and music. Recently, it's garnered national attention for its Next Wave festival—an October-to-December celebration of the new and avant garde in dance, music, and theater.

Prices: Tickets $15–$35.

CARNEGIE HALL, West 57th St. at Seventh Ave. Tel. 247-7800.

⭐ How do you get to Carnegie Hall? Practice, practice, practice! For decades, playing Carnegie Hall has meant "making it" for classical musicians. Fortunately for music lovers with more taste than money, the hall—which presents orchestras, instrumental and vocal recitals, plus jazz and pop music—offers student and senior rush tickets. Check that day with the box office to be sure tickets will be available.

To the left of Carnegie Hall is the former Carnegie Recital Hall, now called **Weill Recital Hall.** Beautifully remodeled and refurbished by its donors, it presents lesser-known artists than those featured in the main hall.

Tours: Sept to mid-July on Mon–Tues and Thurs at 11:30am and 2 and 3pm for $6.

Prices: Tickets $10–$80; $5 discount tickets may be available from 6:30–7pm for students and seniors on day of performance.

THE JUILLIARD SCHOOL, Lincoln Center, Broadway at 66th St. Tel. 769-7406.
Considered one of the best music schools in the nation, Juilliard offers a wide assortment of free concerts and recitals. Stars of tomorrow perform symphony, opera, dance, and chamber music from September to May.
Prices: Tickets usually free.

MADISON SQUARE GARDEN, Seventh Ave., between W. 31st and W. 33rd sts. Tel. 465-6741.
Aside from hosting the New York Knicks basketball games, the New York Rangers hockey games, and other sporting events, the Garden is a venue for big-name concerts—Janet Jackson, Sting, and Bruce Springsteen are some of the headliners who have appeared here.
Prices: Tickets vary widely with performer.

RADIO CITY MUSIC HALL, Sixth Ave. and 50th St. Tel. 247-4777 for information, or 307-7171 to charge tickets.
When the 6,000-seat Art Deco auditorium at Radio City isn't hosting the world-famous Rockettes or its annual Christmas spectacular, it's the place to catch big-name concerts by the likes of Liza Minelli, Aretha Franklin, or Natalie Cole. See also Chapter 7, "What to See and Do in New York City," for information on tours.
Prices: Tickets $20–$40.

DANCE VENUES

From the Rockettes to Nureyev, from Alvin Ailey to the Paul Taylor Dance Company, New York City is the apex of dance in the nation and the world. The city helped pioneer theatrical dance in the early 20th century and modern dance in the 1950s, and is still a beacon for the great names. A typically glittering season includes visits by touring international troupes, from the Royal Danish Ballet to the Paris Ballet. The American Ballet Theatre has a spring season here. And we have our own New York City Ballet and the Joffrey Ballet as well as many smaller companies, covering everything from classical to experimental.

CITY CENTER, 131 W. 55th St., between Sixth and Seventh aves. Tel. 581-7907.
Housed in a landmark building that was once a Masonic temple, the City Center is the place to see innovative American companies—our favorite, the **Paul Taylor Dance Company,** as well as **Alvin Ailey,** the **Joffrey Ballet, Merce Cunningham,** and many important companies from abroad. Subscription discounts are available.
Prices: Tickets $15–$45.

DANCE THEATER WORKSHOP, 219 W. 19th St., between Seventh and Eighth aves. Tel. 924-0077.
Serving as a performance space for established artists, the Workshop is also a forum for new choreographers and dancers (one recent offering was an African-American Women's Choreography Showcase). It offers regular performances year round, including "Fresh Tracks," a program of five or six new works by up-and-coming choreographers.
Prices: Tickets $12.

THE DANSPACE PROJECT, St. Marks-in-the-Bouerie, Second Ave. and E. 10th St. Tel. 529-2318.
The Danspace Project sponsors a variety of dance performances, usually experimental, in this historic corner church from September through June.

Prices: Tickets from $10.

JOYCE THEATER, 175 Eighth Ave., at 19th St. Tel. 242-0800.

⭐ The bright new Joyce Theater has given a boost to its Chelsea neighborhood and to the dance-going public. The theater stocks its fall and spring seasons with such performers as the **Feld Ballet,** the **Laura Dean Dancers,** and the **American Ballroom Theater.** Subscribers save 40% on ticket prices and also receive 2-for-1 discounts at Chelsea restaurants.
Prices: Tickets $15–$27.

THE METROPOLITAN OPERA HOUSE, Lincoln Center. Tel. 362-6000.

⭐ In May and June, the famed **American Ballet Theatre** has its New York season at the opera house. Under the direction of Jane Hermann and Oliver Smith, the ABT presents classics as well as ballets by such modern choreographers as Mark Morris and Twyla Tharp. While tickets can be expensive ($10–$80), there are budget alternatives. Top-of-the-house Family Circle seats require strong opera glasses. If you decide to try for standing room tickets, remember that many fans come at dawn to stand in the ticket line. Standing room prices are from $7 to $11, and are sold for cash only at the box office on the day of the performance, from 10am.

In July and early August, the opera house presents a varied selection of world-famous dance companies. Recent seasons have included England's **Royal Ballet,** the **National Ballet of Canada,** and the **Paris Opera Ballet.**

PERFORMANCE SPACE 122, 150 First Ave., at E. 9th St. Tel. 477-5288.

What was once P.S. (Public School) 122 now hosts mostly experimental works in dance, theater, and music. Current offerings are always listed in the *Village Voice.*
Prices: Tickets $5–$8.

ADDITIONAL OFFERINGS

ASIA SOCIETY, 725 Park Ave., at 70th St. Tel. 288-6400.

This nonprofit organization promoting a better understanding of Asian culture sponsors traditional and contemporary performing arts from Asia. Usually featuring visiting Asian artists or Americans of Asian extraction, the society's performances combine drama, dance, music, and even puppetry. Most performances run from September to June, but call for a current schedule.
Prices: Tickets $6–$25. Student discounts available.

BARGEMUSIC, Fulton Ferry Landing, Brooklyn. Tel. 718/624-4061.

What could be lovelier than watching the skyline of Manhattan as you listen to classical music? The enclosed concert space aboard a boat provides a delightful change of musical scenery. (The boat doesn't go anywhere, but it does bob up and down when the water gets rough.)
Prices: Tickets $15–$18; $13 students and seniors.

KAUFMAN CONCERT HALL, in the 92nd Street YMCA, 1345 Lexington Ave., at E. 92nd St. Tel. 415-5440.

This 900-seat auditorium hosts a wide variety of jazz, classical chamber music, and lectures, such as a recent comedy evening with P. J. O'Rourke and the "Jazz in July at the Y" series.
Prices: Tickets usually $25.

LIBRARY AND MUSEUM OF THE PERFORMING ARTS, Lincoln Center, Amsterdam Ave. at W. 65th St. Tel. 870-1630.

The Library offers arts-related exhibitions in its galleries, such as the recent "Mozart's World: The Images of His Times," held in conjunction with the Mozart Bicentennial celebrations at Lincoln Center. Its auditorium frequently offers artists' workshops and free concerts and performances featuring young or up-and-coming talents. You'll have to arrive a few hours before the performance to pick up your tickets to most events.

Prices: Tickets usually free.

THE KITCHEN, 512 W. 19th St., between Tenth and Eleventh aves. Tel. 255-5793.

The Kitchen presents an array of innovative and avant-garde dance, music, and performance art. Offerings include video screenings, poetry and prose readings from artists like Karen Finley, dance showcases from exciting new choreographers, theater performances, and concerts featuring contemporary composers.

Prices: Tickets $10–$15.

MANHATTAN SCHOOL OF MUSIC, 120 Claremont Ave., at 122nd St. and Broadway. Tel. 749-2802.

This highly rated music school offers free concerts and student recitals during the school year, from September to May. Call for current schedules.

Prices: Tickets usually free.

MANNES COLLEGE OF MUSIC, 150 W. 85th St., between Columbus and Amsterdam aves. Tel. 580-0210.

Performances by the Mannes faculty and students are open to the public, with performances several times a week from October to May.

Prices: Tickets usually free.

THE MEADOWLANDS, East Rutherford, NJ. Tel. 201/935-8500.

Byrne Arena (indoor) and Giants Stadium (outdoor) host big names—the likes of the Grateful Dead. If you're driving, take the Jersey Turnpike; otherwise, check the bus schedules from the Port Authority.

Prices: Tickets vary widely with performer.

MERKIN CONCERT HALL, Abraham Goodman House, 129 W. 67th St., between Broadway and Amsterdam Ave. Tel. 362-8719.

This pleasant, intimate new hall on the concert circuit hosts recitals, chamber groups, and other performances. It's closed in July and August.

Prices: Tickets $10–$30; student and senior discounts available.

92ND STREET YMHA, 92nd St. and Lexington Ave. Tel. 427-6000.

The 92nd Street Y offers a varied program of orchestral and choral performances, chamber music, and recitals throughout the year.

SYMPHONY SPACE, 2537 Broadway, at 95th St. Tel. 864-5400.

Symphony Space offers a grab bag of concerts—from classical to contemporary to gospel music—along with dance, literary readings, foreign films, and drama. James Joyce devotees will want to catch the annual Bloomsday celebration in June, which marks the anniversary of the day chronicled in *Ulysses,* with readings from Joyce's works by an all-star cast. The "Wall-to-Wall" concerts, usually held in March, feature a 12-hour marathon of free music honoring American composers.

Prices: Tickets $6–$25.

CHURCH CONCERTS

Many of the city's major churches, such as **Riverside Church,** 490 Riverside Drive, at 121st Street (tel. 864-2929); the **Cathedral of St. John the Divine,** Amsterdam Avenue at 112th Street (tel. 316-7400); and **Christ and St. Steven's Church,** 120 W. 69th St., between Broadway and Columbus Avenue (tel. 787-2755), sponsor free or low-priced concerts, as do a number of universities and libraries. Our favorite is **St. Peter's Lutheran Church,** 619 Lexington Ave., at 54th Street (tel. 935-2200), where the Jazz Ministry conducts Sunday-night vespers. Call or stop by for information.

THEATERS

Note: For a backstage tour of Broadway, see "Behind-the-Scenes Tours," in Section 6, "Organized Tours," Chapter 7.

BROADWAY, OFF, AND OFF OFF BROADWAY THEATER

Deciphering the New York theater scene can be a tricky business. Space is too limited for us to describe every Broadway and Off Broadway venue here, so we suggest that you check the ads and reviews in the *New York Times, New Yorker,* the *Village Voice,* and *New York* magazine. Refer back to the "Discounts" section at the beginning of this chapter for information on TKTS and other low-cost options for theater tickets.

Many of the Off Off Broadway theaters have gained reputations for producing excellent, innovative shows. Indeed, these theaters' departure from the slick Broadway tradition is considered a selling point by the most sophisticated theater fans. Though they work on very low budgets, out of about 150 tiny theaters scattered about the city, the Off Off Broadway companies are nurturing ground for up-and-coming actors, directors, and writers. Each year a few showcase productions move to Broadway, where they often achieve critical acclaim. If you're willing to experiment, you may be one of the first to see a Broadway hit or a new star at a relatively low cost.

SPECIAL THEATER OFFERINGS

AMERICAN PLACE THEATRE, 111 W. 46th St. Tel. 840-2960.

One inexpensive theater that gets kudos from savvy New Yorkers is the American Playhouse, located near Radio City. Since its inception in 1964, the theater has won almost 30 *Village Voice* Obies, awards for outstanding theater outside the mainstream. The theater produces plays by living American playwrights. Its talent list includes such recognized writers as Steve Tesich (who wrote the screenplay for *The World According to Garp*), Sam Shepard (John Malkovich starred here in his *State of Shock*), and John Leguizamo (who's had a hit on his hands here with *Mambo Mouth*).
Prices: Tickets around $25.

THE ARTISTS' PERSPECTIVE, performing in the Master Theatre, 310 Riverside Drive. Tel. 663-8893.

This new not-for-profit, Off Broadway theater company specializes in musical theater productions that deserve to be seen again. Performances are held year round Wednesday through Sunday, with a summer training program for young people.
Prices: Tickets $17–$25.

THE CIRCLE REPERTORY COMPANY, 99 Seventh Ave. South, at Sheridan Sq. Tel. 924-7100.

You don't have to endure the hustle-bustle of midtown to see some of the city's best theater. This theater has been delighting audiences with new American plays performed by its highly acclaimed company for 20 years. William Hurt, Christopher Reeve, and John Malkovitch have all been members of this seasoned family of actors. The recipient of over 90 major awards, Circle Rep has dedicated itself to rediscovering American theater. Landmark productions of plays by Tennessee Williams, Sam Shepard, and Lanford Wilson, among others, have gone on to enjoy extended runs on Broadway.
Prices: Tickets $22.50–$28.

ENSEMBLE STUDIO THEATRE, 549 W. 52nd St., between Tenth and Eleventh aves. Tel. 247-3405.

For almost 20 years, with a season running from October to June, this theater has been one of New York's greatest seedbeds for the development of new American playwrights. E.S.T.'s yearly season is capped with the marathon of one-acts. Each night from mid-May through mid-June you can see four from a roster of twelve new one-act plays from such notables as Christopher Durang and Horton Foote. While you're watching the offerings at E.S.T., don't be surprised if you see some of its more illustrious members at work. Richard Dreyfus, Kevin Bacon, and Andrew McCarthy are all former marathoners.

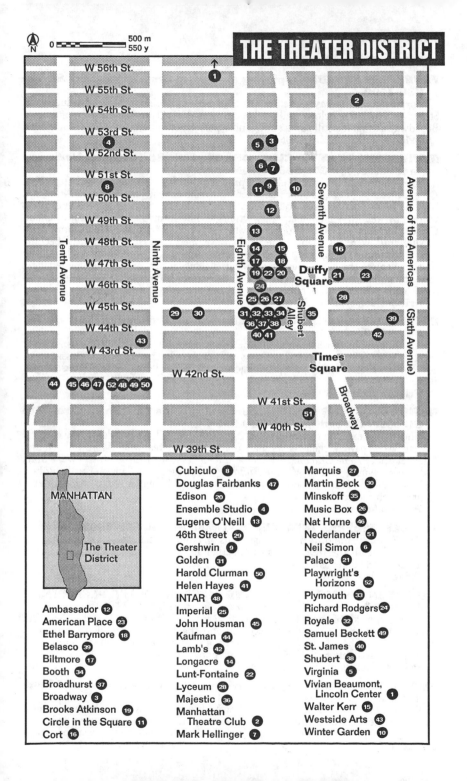

THE THEATER DISTRICT

Cubiculo 8
Douglas Fairbanks 47
Edison 20
Ensemble Studio 4
Eugene O'Neill 13
46th Street 29
Gershwin 9
Golden 31
Harold Clurman 50
Helen Hayes 41
INTAR 48
Imperial 25
John Housman 45
Kaufman 44
Lamb's 42
Longacre 14
Lunt-Fontaine 22
Lyceum 28
Majestic 36
Manhattan Theatre Club 2
Mark Hellinger 7

Marquis 27
Martin Beck 30
Minskoff 35
Music Box 26
Nat Horne 46
Nederlander 51
Neil Simon 6
Palace 21
Playwright's Horizons 52
Plymouth 33
Richard Rodgers 24
Royale 32
Samuel Beckett 49
St. James 40
Shubert 38
Virginia 5
Vivian Beaumont, Lincoln Center 1
Walter Kerr 15
Westside Arts 43
Winter Garden 10

MANHATTAN

The Theater District

Ambassador 12
American Place 23
Ethel Barrymore 18
Belasco 39
Biltmore 17
Booth 34
Broadhurst 37
Broadway 3
Brooks Atkinson 19
Circle in the Square 11
Cort 16

Prices: Tickets $15–$25.

FORBIDDEN BROADWAY, playing at Theater East, 211 E. 16th St. Tel. 838-7400.

Forbidden Broadway started out as a long-running dinner theater production at Steve McGraw's (see below), and has become a tradition, spoofing the current crop of Broadway shows. It's still going strong, now performed cabaret-style in Theater East.
Prices: Tickets $32.50–$35.

MANHATTAN THEATRE CLUB, 453 W. 16th St., between Ninth and Tenth aves. Tel. 645-5590.

The Manhattan Theatre Club now produces its shows at Stage I and Stage II at **City Center,** 131 W. 55th St., between Sixth and Seventh avenues (tel. 246-8989). It's one of the best buys in town. During its Mainstage Season, it premieres plays written by well-known contemporary writers and performed by such actors as Glenn Close, Bernadette Peters, and Sam Waterston. *Crimes of the Heart* and *Ain't Misbehavin'* were just two of the works developed here that went on to become smash hits; more recently *Lips Together, Teeth Apart* has won critical acclaim. The best way to see the club's plays is to become a subscriber, or member, by buying a series membership for the September-to-June season. Memberships go for as little as $115 (call 645-0905 for details).
Prices: Tickets from $35.

MITZI NEWHOUSE THEATER, Lincoln Center, Broadway at 65th St. Tel. 362-7600.

The tiny, intimate venue shouldn't be overlooked. Recently revived, this 299-seat theater presents contemporary works as well as new interpretations of classic plays. Some of its most notable past productions include Spaulding Gray's *Monster in a Box.*
Prices: Tickets $30.

NATIONAL ACTORS THEATRE, performing in the Belasco Theatre, 44th St. east of Broadway. Tel. 239-5134.

The newest exciting theater event in New York City, Tony Randall's new classical repertory company kicked off its inaugural season by featuring Martin Sheen and Michael York in *The Crucible,* Randall and Rob Lowe in *A Little Hotel on the Side,* and Earle Hyman in *The Master Builder.* Big names like Lauren Bacall, Robert DeNiro, William Hurt, Jason Robards, and Al Pacino have pledged to work with the company on future productions.
Prices: Series subscriptions $25–$95.

THE NEW FEDERAL THEATRE, 466 Grand St. Tel. 598-0400.

Specializing in minority dramas that focus on family, social, and community issues, the New Federal Theatre operates from September to June. Since they don't have a continuous schedule, call first.
Prices: Tickets $16.

NEW YORK PUBLIC LIBRARY AND MUSEUM OF THE PERFORMING ARTS, 111 Amsterdam Ave., at 65th St. Tel. 870-1600.

Another source of good, free theater, this Lincoln Center branch of the New York Public Library offers plays along with solo and chamber concerts, dance programs, musicals, and films from September through June. Information about current schedules is available at 870-1630 or at any public library branch.
Prices: Tickets usually free.

PLAYWRIGHT HORIZONS, 416 W. 42nd St., between Ninth and Tenth aves. Tel. 564-1235.

Playwright Horizons features new shows by American writers. Among its most notable successes was *Once on This Island,* which went on to enjoy Broadway success. Some plays in the process of being written are presented in workshops, free of charge.

Prices: Tickets from $22.

PUBLIC THEATER, 425 Lafayette St., south of 8th St. Tel. 598-7150.

When summer's over, the Shakespeare Festival returns to its permanent home in the East Village. The theater's six playhouses, and one cinema, offer high-caliber shows year round by a variety of companies. Notable productions developed here have gone on to become hits on Broadway (including old favorites like *A Chorus Line* and *Hair*). One-quarter of the seats are held to be sold at half price the day of the performance. These discount seats, known as Quiktix, are available at 6pm before evening shows and at 1pm on matinee days.

Prices: Tickets $25–$30.

REPERTORIO ESPAÑOL, 138 E. 27th St., between Lexington and Third aves. Tel. 889-2850.

For Spanish speakers and students, this theater company performs classic Spanish works and contemporary Latin American drama, comedies, and musicals. Some productions are now offered with English simulcasts. Twice a year the company, which performs in the Gramercy Arts Theater at the same address, features a performance of flamenco dance.

Prices: Tickets $15–$25, with $5 discount available to students and seniors.

VIVIAN BEAUMONT THEATER, Lincoln Center, Broadway at W. 65th St. Tel. 239-6200.

There aren't any bad seats in this smallish theater, which in 1991 hosted John Guare's smash hit *Six Degrees of Separation*, with Stockard Channing and Courtney Vance.

Prices: Tickets $35–$45.

WESTSIDE THEATER, 407 W. 43rd St., between Ninth and Tenth aves. Tel. 315-2244.

This theater is a good place for musicals, comedy, and drama. Recent productions have included *The Kathy and Mo Show, Only the Truth Is Funny,* and *And the World Goes 'Round.*

Prices: Tickets $25–$37.50.

2. THE CLUB & MUSIC SCENE

New York is a mecca for musicians, and the city is home to a plethora of clubs, bars, and cafés where you can hear them every night of the week. For the music lover, it's a feast. Some clubs charge no admission or minimum; others tack on a music charge that varies depending on who's playing that night. To be certain, phone ahead to ask what the cover or minimum is that evening.

It's all but impossible to list every club and venue the city has to offer—things change fast and there's a wealth of entertainment out there. We've listed what we consider the best and the most famous spots below. *New York* magazine and the *Village Voice* are good sources for current listings on who's playing in any given week.

NIGHTCLUBS/CABARETS

From glossy cabarets to Middle Eastern belly dancing, New York's nightclub scene has it all—read on.

THE BALLROOM, 253 W. 28th St., between Seventh and Eighth aves. Tel. 244-3005.

The Ballroom features cabaret acts, singers, dancers, and comedians such as Terry Sweeney from *Saturday Night Live*. Dinner is served, or you can nosh and nibble your way around a tapas bar. There are shows at 9pm most nights, with additional late performances on Friday and Saturday.

Admission: $15–$25, plus two-drink minimum.

THE BLUE ANGEL, 323 W. 44th St. Tel. 262-3333.

The Blue Angel is home to an eclectic mix of cabaret productions, and it's attracted lots of attention recently for its current production of *Pageant,* a screamingly funny musical comedy that should be around for awhile. Five lucky audience members are selected to judge the "Miss Glamouresse" beauty contest, complete with talent, evening gown, and swimsuit competitions. The twist? The contestants are all men in drag.

Admission: $32.50–$35; dinner-and-show packages $55–$60.

CHIPPENDALES, 1110 First Ave., at 61st St. Tel. 935-6060.

This 1980s phenomenon gives new meaning to the phrase "girls' night out." Whatever happened to mahjong and bridge? The club can accommodate up to 850 people, who sit on bleacher-style seats in this arena/theater where an all-male burlesque revue ultimately gets down to the bare necessities: their G-strings. The show is for women only, and reservations are required. The seats closest to the stage cost an additional $10 Wednesday through Friday, and an additional $10 to $15 on Saturday; they can be purchased only at the time of admission. After the show, at about 10:30pm, the club becomes a disco and the stage a dance floor. Men are allowed in for the disco. Shows usually begin at 8pm Wednesday through Saturday.

Admission: Show $20–$25; disco $15, or free if you've attended the show.

DANNY'S SKYLIGHT, at the Grand Sea Palace, 346 W. 46th St., between Eighth and Ninth aves. Tel. 265-8130.

The dress code here is casual New York style. Special attractions include a jazz cabaret and piano-bar entertainment with show tunes. Reservations are recommended, and music usually begins at 9pm.

Admission: Cabaret $10–$20, plus $10 drink minimum; piano bar no cover or minimum.

DON'T TELL MAMA, 343 W. 46th St., between Eighth and Ninth aves. Tel. 757-0788.

Anything goes at Don't Tell Mama—the piano bar may feature show tunes or oldies from the 1960s and 1970s, and the "open-mike" policy allows anyone to get up and sing. Music begins around 9:30pm. The back-room cabaret features two shows nightly.

Admission: Cabaret $7–$10, plus two-drink minimum; piano bar no cover but two-drink minimum at tables.

THE DUPLEX, 55 Grove St., between Seventh Ave. South and Bleecker St. Tel. 255-5438.

The Duplex presents a mixture of inexpensive entertainment. There's a piano bar, and upstairs, Thursday through Sunday, there are original and Broadway cabaret shows.

Admission: Cabaret $5–$10, plus two-drink minimum; piano bar no cover but two-drink minimum.

EIGHTY EIGHTS, 228 W. 10th St., between Bleecker and Hudson sts. Tel. 924-0088.

If you like to sing along with Broadway show tunes from today and yesteryear, the piano bar at Eighty Eights may be the place for you. Music starts at 9 or 10pm most nights. The casual upstairs cabaret highlights musical comedy shows, with two performances nightly, and might feature Broadway performers. The club sometimes offers a lineup of comedy acts. Reservations are recommended.

Admission: Cabaret $8–$15, plus two-drink minimum; piano bar no cover but two-drink minimum.

THE NILE, 327 W. 44th St., between Eighth and Ninth aves. Tel. 262-1111.

This Egyptian-themed nightclub offers a floor show with Middle Eastern–style dancers and musicians. You can take in the fun while enjoying their five-course dinner or stop in just for the entertainment.
Admission: $15, plus two-drink minimum; dinner-and-show package $49.

RAINBOW AND STARS, on the 65th floor of the RCA Building, Rockefeller Center, 30 Rockefeller Plaza, Sixth Ave. at 50th St. Tel. 632-5000.

It's way too pricey for the budget-conscious, but if you want to treat yourself to the splurge of a lifetime, the big-name talent, the Art Deco elegance, and the view will leave you breathless. Dinner is required at the early show, but there's no minimum during the late performance (although if you'd like a cocktail, you should be prepared to pay at least $6).
Admission: $35.

STEVE MCGRAW'S, 158 W. 72nd St., between Broadway and Columbus Ave. Tel. 595-7400.

A wonderful production of *Forever Plaid*, a musical full of laughs and 1950's-style music, has been wowing the crowds here for quite a while, and you can enjoy excellent continental fare while you take in the show. Performances run once or twice a night (the 10:30pm performances are usually cheaper), and reservations are recommended.
Prices: Tickets $30–$35; dinner-and-show packages $57–$62.

SWEETWATER'S, 170 Amsterdam Ave., between 67th and 68th sts. Tel. 873-4100.

This predominantly black supper club hosts blues, gospel, Latin, and funk acts. A back-up singer named Whitney Houston was "discovered" here by a record producer one night. You might catch Stacy Lattisaw, Gwen Guthrie, or the Ohio Players. Shows nightly except Tuesday, with two sets Thursday through Saturday.
Admission: $5–$10 Sun–Mon and Wed; $20 Thurs–Sat, with $10 minimum.

COMEDY CLUBS

CATCH A RISING STAR, 1487 First Ave., near 78th St. Tel. 794-1906.

As its name suggests, this is the place to see up-and-coming comics. There's a 9pm show Sunday through Thursday, with two shows on Friday, and three shows on Saturday.
Admission: $8–$12, plus two-drink minimum.

CHICAGO CITY LIMITS, 351 E. 74th St., between First and Second aves. Tel. 772-8707.

If you're interested in creative audience participation and improvisational comedy, check out Chicago City Limits. This nonalcohol club features improvisational actors and guest comedians. Reservations are recommended. Weeknight shows start at 8:30pm; weekend shows are at 8 and 10:30pm.
Admission: Weekdays $12.50, weekends $15.

THE COMEDY CELLAR, 117 MacDougal St., under the Olive Tree Café. Tel. 254-3630.

IMPRESSIONS

She has become a wicked and wild bitch in her old age has Manhattan, but there is still no sensation in the world quite like walking her sidewalks. Great surges of energy sweep all around you; the air fizzes like champagne. . . .
—TOM DAVIES, *OBSERVER*, NOVEMBER 11, 1979

★ You'll be packed in like a sardine, but you'll leave with your sides aching from laughter. We've never been disappointed with the lineup here. There's one show Sunday through Thursday, and two or three shows on weekends. Highly recommended.

Admission: $5–$12; plus $5 food-or-drink minimum.

THE COMIC STRIP, 1568 Second Ave., near 82nd St. Tel. 861-9386.

The Comic Strip features aspiring comedians. Reservations are suggested. There's a 9pm show nightly, with an additional 11pm show Friday and Saturday.

Admission: $8–$14, plus two-drink minimum.

DANGERFIELD'S, 1118 First Ave., between 61st and 62nd sts. Tel. 593-1650.

One of the best-known New York comedy clubs, Dangerfield's is owned by Rodney ("I can't get no respect") Dangerfield, who performs whenever he's in town. Other performers have included the late Redd Foxx, Red Buttons, Jackie Mason, and Robin Williams when he happens to be in the audience. Reservations are recommended, especially on weekends.

Admission: $10–$15, plus $7 minimum.

THE IMPROVISATION [THE ORIGINAL], 358 W. 44th St., off Ninth Ave. Tel. 765-8268.

The Improv is the city's premier breeding ground for new talent. This highly regarded restaurant/comedy club features a constantly changing lineup of performers. Famous alums include Rodney Dangerfield, Robert Klein, Robin Williams, Joe Piscopo, Bette Midler, Danny Aiello, and just about any comic you can name. Reservations are essential on weekends. The action begins nightly at 8pm, and with additional shows on Friday and Saturday.

Admission: $8–$12; plus $8–$9 food or drink minimum.

MOSTLY MAGIC, 55 Carmine St. Tel. 924-1472.

As its name indicates, Mostly Magic is a nightclub-theater-restaurant featuring combination or solo comedy-magic routines. Reservations are recommended.

Admission: $10–$15; plus $8 food-or-drink minimum.

STAND UP NEW YORK, 236 W. 78th St., at Broadway. Tel. 595-0850.

Modern and loft-like, this comedy club offers a light bar menu. There's one show most nights, with two or three performances on Fridays and Saturdays.

Admission: $7–$12; plus two-drink minimum.

COUNTRY

THE LONE STAR ROADHOUSE, 240 W. 52nd St., between Broadway and Eighth Ave. Tel. 245-2950.

This honky-tonk outpost of Texan esthetics is housed in a building that looks like a touring band's bus, with an airplane suspended from the ceiling. The Lone Star books top country, blues, zydeco, and rock-and-roll performers—Buckwheat Zydeco, the Neville Brothers, and Margareth Menezes have played here. Don't dare to order anything but a Lone Star beer.

Admission: $7–$20, depending on performer; plus two-drink minimum at tables.

O'LUNNEY'S, 12 W. 44th St., between Fifth and Sixth aves. Tel. 840-6688.

This is the place to come for pure country music and bluegrass. One of the oldest country-music spots in the city, O'Lunney's features local and big-name country bands and an occasional bluegrass group.

Admission: Free.

RODEO BAR, 375 Third Ave., at 27th St. Tel. 683-6500.

The Rodeo Bar, next to Albuquerque Eats, is fast establishing a reputation as the top spot for young, hard-rocking local country, blues, and rockabilly performers. The

place has real honky-tonk spirit, and you'd do well to check out the margaritas. Music daily from around 10pm.
Admission: Free.

ROCK

BLONDIE'S, 2180 Broadway, at 77th St. Tel. 362-4360.
If Blondie's isn't featuring a live R&B or rock band, there's usually a DJ. Atomic Wings is next door, and on Monday nights, there's all-you-can-eat wings for $8.50, with $1 draft beers.
Admission: Free.

THE BOTTOM LINE, 15 W. 4th St., corner of Mercer St. Tel. 228-7880.
The Bottom Line is the Village's premier showcase for top rock and jazz groups. The decor is mostly black, also the favored color of the crowd's attire. The stage is large (good views from every corner of the room), the sound system excellent, and the bookings are first-rate—The Roches, Doc Watson, or perhaps Buster Poindexter and his Banshees of Blue. Advance tickets are on sale at the box office or through the mail, and they are advised for the really popular acts. Showtimes are usually 8 and 11pm nightly.
Admission: $15–$17.50.

THE CAT CLUB, 76 E. 13th St., near Fourth Ave. Tel. 505-0090.
The Cat Club has ample dance room and bands that know how to make use of it. Inside businessmen in three-piece suits clink glasses with Village trendies in basic black. Hardcore, underground, and emerging acts like Damn Cheetah and Drugstore Cowboy appear most of the week.
On Sundays, the place completely changes character and hosts an evening of swing dancing to live big bands.
Admission: Up to $10; plus two-drink minimum at tables.

CBGB, 315 Bowery, at Bleecker St. Tel. 982-4052.
Still going strong, CBGB helped launch the New Wave and punk scenes in the 1970s, having hosted greats like the Talking Heads and the Ramones. It looks rundown, but is intentionally so, and the spirit lives on. It's located on the fringes of lower Manhattan—an area that should be approached with care. Music from 8:30pm weeknights, from 9:30pm Friday and Saturday.
Admission: $3–$8; plus two-drink minimum.

GONZALEZ Y GONZALEZ, 625 Broadway, between Houston and Bleecker sts. Tel. 473-8787.
A hopping bar and restaurant featuring local rock bands like Milo Z Steppin' Out or Felicia and the Hotheads, Gonzalez y Gonzalez boasts that it offers "homestyle Mexican food and music from both sides of the border." Lunch and dinner are served daily, and most shows start at 10pm. Look for the velvet painting of Elvis.
Admission: Free.

KENNY'S CASTAWAYS, 157 Bleecker St., near Thompson St. Tel. 473-9870.
Kenny's Castaways features young rock-and-roll bands who are on the way up, with music from 9pm nightly. On Monday there's a midnight jam session. Most drinks run from $2.75 to $4.50.
Admission: Free before 10pm; $2–$3 after 10pm weekdays, $5–$10 after 10pm weekends. Two-drink minimum per set.

THE MARQUEE, 547 W. 21st St. Tel. 929-3257.
The Marquee prides itself on featuring new and alternative bands like the LA's, the Meat Puppets, and Difford & Tilbrook (formerly of Squeeze).
Admission: Tickets $9–$10.

PYRAMID CLUB, 101 Ave. A, near East 7th St. Tel. 420-1590.
If you want to hear some of New York's hottest new bands, this is the place to go.

Although you might find patrons with shaved heads, the crowd is filled with more conservatively dressed types too, all dancing to a DJ or the likes of the Butthole Surfers.
Admission: $5–$10.

THE RITZ, 254 W. 54th St., between Eighth Ave. and Broadway. Tel. 956-3731.
For years, the Ritz has been booking bands on the cusp of stardom, like the Gipsy Kings, the diVinyls, EMF, or De La Soul. Buy your tickets ahead of time—most shows sell out. The box office only accepts cash, but you can charge tickets through Ticketmaster.
Prices: Tickets $12.50–$25.

SUN MOUNTAIN CAFÉ, 82 W. 3rd St. Tel. 477-0622.
In the heart of Greenwich Village, this venue features live up-and-coming rock bands. The bar carries a full range of imported ales on tap. Showtime is 9pm nightly.
Admission: $3–$5.

JAZZ

For jazz lovers, New York is paradise. Nowhere in the world will you find more jazz per square foot than in the Big Apple, and much of it is concentrated in Greenwich Village. We've listed both major clubs and those that are good bargains—happily, many places offer both good talent and low prices. For what's playing, check the weekly listings in the *Village Voice* or call **Jazzline** (tel. 718/465-7500).

June brings the **JVC Jazz Festival,** with special performances in various venues all over town by the likes of Michel Camilo, Wynton Marsalis, Ray Charles, and Syro Gyra. Write ahead for details to: JVC Jazz Festival, P.O. Box 1169, Ansonia Station, New York, NY 10023 (tel. 787-2020).

LOWER MANHATTAN

AMAZONAS, 492 Broome St., near West Broadway. Tel. 966-3371.
Quality Brazilian jazz and an exotic jungle decor create a unique ambience at Amazonas. If dinner is too pricey, try the bar, where there is no minimum. Or check out the restaurant's Sunday brunches, when you can take in the same music along with various Brazilian dishes at a more moderate price.
Admission: Free, but $7.50 minimum per person at tables, none at bar.

5 & 10 NO EXAGGERATION, 77 Greene St. Tel. 925-7414.
While this irrepressibly creative supper club specializes in live big-band-era music, their unique brunch on Sunday from 1 to 5pm, has live jazz accompaniment to silent movies. It also has a jewelry and antique shop and an art gallery, so you can dine, shop, and listen to bands playing oldies from Glenn Miller, Benny Goodman, and the Andrews Sisters.
Dinner items on the varied menu start at $5.50 for a half-order of fettuccine. There is no minimum. Reservations are recommended at all times; closed Monday.
Admission: $5, plus $10 minimum.

GREENWICH VILLAGE

BLUE NOTE, 131 W. 3rd St., off Sixth Ave. Tel. 475-8592.
This is one of the biggies. According to a jazz-knowledgeable bartender, there have been dozens of clubs at this address, going all the way back to speakeasy days. This wood-paneled, blue-carpeted beauty seems to be doing an admirable job of keeping up the tradition. The Blue Note books top jazz stars such as pianist Michel Camilo, Freddie Hubbard, Stanley Jordan, Herbie Hancock, Sarah Vaughan, and Herbie

Mann & Jasil Brazz. Two sets nightly Sunday through Thursday, usually three sets Friday and Saturday. Reservations recommended.

Admission: $20, plus $5 minimum.

BLUE WILLOW, 644 Broadway, at Bleecker St. Tel. 673-6480.

Along with sophisticated American cuisine for lunch and dinner, Blue Willow serves up live jazz. Reservations are suggested.

Admission: Usually free, with no minimum, but may vary.

BRADLEY'S, 70 University Place, between 10th and 11th sts. Tel. 228-6440.

Good conversationalists and all-star piano/bass duos are Bradley's hallmark. Musicians like Ron Carter, Tommy Flanagan, Red Mitchell, and Hank Jones play regularly in this clubby, wood-paneled room. Music nightly from about 9:45pm; call ahead for dinner reservations.

Admission: $5–$12; plus $8 food-or-drink minimum.

KNICKERBOCKER BAR & GRILL, 33 University Place, at 9th St. Tel. 228-8490.

One of the best places to hear jazz and blues coupled with the best T-bone steaks in New York is this pleasant restaurant and bar that's always crowded with attentive listeners and hungry patrons. Some of the most accomplished jazz pianists and bassists around play in the plush dining room. Judy Carmichael, Roland Hanna, Ron Carter, Walter Bishop, Jr., and Cecil McBee are just a few. Harry Connick, Jr., got his start here. Music from 9:45pm Wednesday through Sunday.

Admission: $3.50 in main dining room and lounge on music nights after 9:45pm; free, with one-drink minimum, at the bar.

SWEET BASIL, 88 Seventh Ave. South, between Bleecker and Grove sts. Tel. 242-1785.

With its exposed-brick walls and glass facade, Sweet Basil is one of the handsomer Village jazz haunts. It also books a wide range of top jazz groups, from mainstream small combos to avant-garde big bands. Monday nights usually bring the Grammy-winning Monday Night Orchestra, with Miles Evans conducting the music of Gil Evans. Reservations are recommended, and music usually begins at 10pm.

Admission: $12–$15, plus $6 minimum.

VILLAGE GATE, 160 Bleecker St., at Thompson St. Tel. 475-5120.

The famed Village Gate has been around almost as long as the Village Vanguard. In the past few years the Gate has been presenting more Off Broadway musical revues, such as *Prom Queens Unchained*, and cabaret and rock singers such as Dr. John. But jazz names, such as David "Fathead" Newman, are still its bread and butter. One of the best shows in town is the Monday-night "Salsa Meets Jazz" series. Each week two top Latin bands, such as Tito Puente's or Eddie Palmieri's appear with a top jazz soloist such as Dizzy Gillespie—the interaction is something to hear.

Admission: Varies widely with the performer and the night of the week; usually a two-drink minimum on the terrace.

VILLAGE VANGUARD, 178 Seventh Ave. South, at 11th St. Tel. 255-4037.

The Village Vanguard is the most famous jazz club in New York—and perhaps in the world. For more than 30 years, jazz aficionados have been walking down the long flight of steps into the Vanguard's smokey, dark basement room to hear the likes of John Coltrane, the late Miles Davis, Charles Mingus, Sonny Rollins, Pharaoh Sanders, and the Tommy Flanagan Trio. Today the Vanguard is as popular as ever, and it still attracts the biggest names in town. Unlike many other jazz clubs, the Vanguard treats both its audience and its musicians with respect. There are no ringing cash registers in the background or hustling for drinks; customers are invited to sit back, relax, and concentrate on the music. Musicians love the place: Dozens of live albums have been recorded in the club over the years, and any night's performance can

turn into a blistering set of jazz. Be sure to check out the Monday-night shows, with the Vanguard Jazz Orchestra. There are usually three sets performed nightly.
Admission: $12–$15, plus $7.50 minimum.

VISIONES, 125 MacDougal St., corner of West 3rd St. Tel. 673-5576.
Adventurous jazz and good Spanish-style food are offered at Visiones. The atmosphere is funky: Walls are decorated with record jackets and meals are served on hand-painted tiled tables. You might be treated to a headliner performance, such as Paul Motian, Dewey Redman, or Lee Konitz; other nights Visiones highlights up-and-coming artists.
Admission: $5; plus one-drink minimum at the bar, two-drink minimum at tables.

ZINNO, 126 W. 13th St., between Sixth and Seventh aves. Tel. 924-5182.
For good jazz and fine food, Zinno is the place. Dinners at this comfortable Italian restaurant are quite reasonable, and you'll be entertained by small combos, perhaps a piano-and-bass duo or the Joe Locke Quintet, while you dine.
Admission: Free, but $15 minimum at tables, $10 minimum at bar.

EAST VILLAGE

CONDON'S, 117 E. 15th St. Tel. 254-0960.
In this cozy restaurant, you can sit back and enjoy mainstream jazz from the likes of Arthur Taylor's Wailers, the Clifford Jordan Big Band, or the Jimmy Heath Quartet. The dinner menu here is available in five different languages, and offers a number of main dishes under $15. Two sets on weeknights, with dinner served until midnight; three sets on weekends, with dinner served till 1am.
Admission: $12.50–$20 at tables, no cover at bar, two-drink minimum.

GRAMERCY PARK/MURRAY HILL

FAT TUESDAY'S, 190 Third Ave., at 17th St. Tel. 533-7902.
For an evening with big-name jazz musicians in a cozy atmosphere, Fat Tuesday's is the place. This supper club has featured headliners such as Dizzy Gillespie, Les McCann, and Stan Getz, and since it only seats 100, the view and sound from anywhere are good. The Les Paul Trio plays every Monday night, and there's a weekend jazz brunch. Reservations are suggested.
Admission: $12.50–$15, plus $7.50 minimum.

ZANZIBAR & GRILL, 550 Third Ave., between 36th and 37th sts. Tel. 779-0606.
Hiram Bullock or Tom "Bones" Mallone and the New York All Stars are a couple of the names that have appeared in this swinging jazz supper club.
Admission: $5–$15.

CHELSEA

ANGRY SQUIRE, 216 Seventh Ave., between 22nd and 23rd sts. Tel. 242-9066.
A nautical-themed pub and restaurant, the Angry Squire has been a Chelsea fixture for many years. Featured are contemporary vocalists, pianists, and mainstream jazz bands, one of which includes one of our favorite trumpet players, Joe Magnarelli. Good food is served, and the atmosphere is warm and lively. Sets daily from 9:30 or 10pm.
Admission: $5–$7, plus $6–$8 minimum at tables; no cover but two-drink minimum at bar.

LOLA'S, 30 W. 22nd St., between Fifth and Sixth aves. Tel. 675-6700.
Lola's is a fine, upscale Caribbean restaurant, but don't let the pricey menu keep you from dropping in to hear some hot jazz combos. A gracious and glamorous

hostess, Lola greets you at the door and treats all her guests as if they're her good friends. The restaurant features a variety of musical entertainment on other nights of the week so call for information. There's usually a Sunday gospel brunch.
Admission: Free.

MIDTOWN EAST

MICHAEL'S PUB, 211 E. 55th St., between Second and Third aves. Tel. 758-2273.
Woody Allen sometimes plays Dixieland clarinet here on Mondays, but Michael's features good music on other nights, too.
Admission: $20; plus two-drink minimum.

MIDTOWN WEST

RED BLAZER TOO, 349 W. 46th St., between Eighth and Ninth aves. Tel. 262-3112.
Located in the theater district, Red Blazer Too is home to big-band, swing, and Dixieland enthusiasts. Live bands perform Tuesday through Sunday and usually attract an over-30 crowd to the dance floor. As a bartender noted, the theme of this very New York–style bar, with Tiffany-style lamps and pictures of celebrities along the walls, is nostalgia.
Admission: $5; plus two-drink minimum if you're not eating.

UPPER WEST SIDE

BIRDLAND, 2745 Broadway, at 105th St. Tel. 749-2228.
Named for one of the great nightclubs of the 1950s and 1960s, Birdland is a favorite Upper West Side jazz lair, presenting the likes of guitarist Freddy Bryant, Joe Chambers & the Jazz Connection, and John Hicks. (Pianist Renée Rosnes is one of our favorites.) A wide-ranging menu, including a selection of seafood and steaks, is offered on an upper tier overlooking the bar and bandstand, as well as on the main level. The Sunday jazz brunch is a real treat, as are the big-windowed views of Broadway. The bar crowd is often boisterous. Sets are nightly at 9 and 10:30pm and midnight.
Admission: $5 cover plus $5 minimum at bar; $10 cover plus $10 minimum at tables.

J'S, 2581 Broadway, between 97th and 98th sts. Tel. 666-3600.
Upstairs at J's is a comfortable, friendly, high-ceilinged restaurant and bar overlooking upper Broadway. The jazz is usually traditional and always top drawer, ranging from solo piano to 16-piece big bands. The continental dinner menu is served every day beginning at 7pm and running until 11:30pm Sunday through Thursday, until 12:30am Friday and Saturday.
Admission: Free, but $12 minimum at tables, $7 minimum at bar.

BLUES

ABILENE CAFÉ, 73 Eighth Ave., between 13th and 14th sts. Tel. 255-7373.
Have some Texas chili and listen to the blues—perhaps you'll catch Hubert Sumlin, the Voodoo Rhythm Kings, Snooky Pryor, or Charmaine Neville. This is the real thing.
Admission: Free–$10, depending on performer.

DAN LYNCH, 221 Second Ave., near 14th St. Tel. 473-8807.
Though the tunes can be soulful, the atmosphere is lively and friendly. The club is tiny, and the decor is down-at-the-heels, but you'll get a close-up look at some of the city's best blues musicians. Music starts at 9:30pm most nights, although local musicians have been known to jam here on weekends from 4pm.
Admission: Weekdays free, Fri–Sat $5.

MANNY'S CAR WASH, 1558 Third Ave., between 87th and 88th sts. Tel. 369-BLUE.
Junior Wells, Rod Piazza and the Mighty Flyers, or Commander Cody serve up the tunes here, with an emphasis on Chicago-style blues. White Castle burgers are available at the bar.
Admission: Free–$10.

MONDO CANE BLUES BAR, 205 Thompson St., at Bleecker St. Tel. 254-5166.
One of the newer venues for the blues is fast making a name for itself by booking such popular bands as the Spin Doctors, G.G.B., and 970-SOUL, and Pat Cisarano. On weekends this tiny bar fills up fast, so get there early. The music usually starts around 10pm.
Admission: $5–$10, plus a two-drink minimum.

TRAMPS, 125 E. 15th St., between Third Ave. and Irving Place. Tel. 727-7788.
 Tramps is one of New York's top blues club, featuring the best in Chicago and New Orleans blues acts. Luminaries in rock-and-roll, pop, zydeco, and rhythm-and-blues appear here frequently. (REM's Michael Stipe hosted a recent show highlighting new bands he discovered in Georgia.) There's also a Cajun-Creole menu, with most selections around $10.
Admission: $5–$15; plus two-drink minimum at tables, none at bar.

WONDERLAND BLUES BAR, 519 Second Ave., at 29th St. Tel. 213-5098.
This unpretentious spot for down-home blues, jazz, and R&B, serves dinner and drinks.
Admission: Free–$15, depending on performer.

MIXED BAGS

ASTI, 13 E. 12th St., between Fifth Ave. and University Place. Tel. 741-9105.
Join the singing waiters in opera or show tunes as you dine on northern Italian cuisine and watch the "flying pizza" act. Reservations are recommended, and Asti usually closes for a couple of months in the summer.

THE BACK FENCE, 155 Bleecker St. Tel. 475-9221.
Located near Kenny's Castaways, the Back Fence adds country to its repertoire of rock, blues, and folk. Sets start at 8:30pm, and the club stays open until 2am on weekdays, until 3am on weekends.
Admission: Varies with performer and night of the week; two-drink minimum at tables, one-drink minimum at bar.

THE BITTER END, 147 Bleecker St., between Thompson St. and LaGuardia Place. Tel. 673-7030.
The Bitter End presents a variety of rock, reggae, folk, jazz, and country acts; it's one of the few Village clubs that presents three or four bands a night. This is a good place to catch rising stars before they graduate to bigger (and more expensive) clubs. Open nightly, with about four shows each evening.
Admission: $5, plus two-drink minimum at tables, one-drink minimum at bar.

CAFÉ WHA?, 115 MacDougal St. Tel. 254-3630.
The music could range from the 1970s to the present, or you might run into special events like the "Best Singer in New York" contest or a classic rock and R&B night. The fun starts around 9:30pm most nights.
Admission: $2–$8; plus two-drink minimum.

CORNELIA STREET CAFÉ, 29 Cornelia St., between Bleecker and W. 4th sts. Tel. 989-9319.

This French country restaurant doubles as a cabaret and bar. While you're enjoying a reasonably priced dinner, you might be entertained by a comedian, a jazz artist, or a poetry or prose reading. We recently went there to hear one of our favorite trumpet players, Joe Magnarelli, who played with the swinging Keith Sanders quartet.
Admission: $5; plus $5 minimum.

DELTA 88, 332 Eighth Ave., at 26th St. Tel. 924-3499.

Blues, R&B, funk, zydeco, or rock—Delta 88 hosts them all, with performers like the Little Big Band, Urban Blight, Loup Garou, or Milo Z and Steppin' Out. Try the Sunday Gospel brunch.
Admission: $7; plus $5 minimum.

EAGLE TAVERN, 355 W. 14th St., between Eighth and Ninth aves. Tel. 924-0275.

⭐ If you love traditional Irish music, run, don't walk, to the Eagle Tavern. Stop at the bar up front for your drinks then head for the back room where you'll find a friendly, welcoming crowd sipping Guinness. Traditional Irish music, with musicians playing guitar, fiddle, and all manner of pipes, is the staple here, with comedy, acoustical music, bluegrass, rock, and poetry occasionally filling the bill.
Admission: Free–$7, depending on night and performer.

GREENE STREET CAFÉ, 101 Greene St., between Prince and Spring sts. Tel. 925-2415.

If you're feeling flush and in the mood for a splurge, this popular yuppie dinner spot in fashionable SoHo offers a multilevel entertainment complex. There's jazz nightly in the main dining room; a separate cabaret features, revues, comedians, jazz, or pop music, usually with three shows on weekend nights. Recently we heard a wonderful young singer, Carol Horn. Call ahead to make sure that what's scheduled suits you; reservations are advised.
Admission: $10–$12.50; plus $10 minimum.

INDIGO BLUES, 221 W. 46th St. Tel. 221-0033.

Call ahead to see who'll be center stage—you might catch Hiram Bullock, an evening of Brazilian music, or a blues jam session. There are usually two shows nightly.
Admission: $10.

THE KNITTING FACTORY, 47 E. Houston St., between Mott and Mulberry sts. Tel. 219-3055.

The Knitting Factory offers an eclectic variety of local and international talent ranging from poetry readings to folk music to modern jazz fusion. Two shows nightly.
Admission: $5–$12.

O'LONNIE'S, 915 Second Ave., at 49th St. Tel. 750-6427.

O'Lonnie's, designed as a Mississippi riverboat, offers an eclectic mix of local and international entertainment nightly. The food is your basic good-value pub fare, with superb Irish beers on tap, served by the imperial pint. There's also a full range of single-malt scotches available.
Admission: $3.

SPEAKEASY, 107 MacDougal St., near Bleecker St. Tel. 598-9670.

Folk lives and thrives in the heart of the Village. Walk right through the Greek restaurant in front to the darkened, intimate club in back. Operated by a local folk musicians' co-op in conjunction with the owner, this club features some of the strongest acts in folk music. The Washington Squares, Josh White, Jr., and Jesse Winchester are a few recent ones. The cover charge goes to the musicians. Greek and Middle Eastern cuisine is served.
Admission: $4–$10; plus two-drink minimum or dinner.

SYLVIA'S, 328 Lenox Ave., between 126th and 127th sts. Tel. 996-0660.

You may have seen Sylvia's featured recently in Spike Lee's *Jungle Fever*. It's a

Harlem institution that's been offering down-home soul food along with jazz, gospel, and blues since 1962. Dinner main dishes run from $6.50 to $10.95. Don't miss the Sunday gospel brunch.
Admission: Free; $3 minimum.

WETLANDS PRESERVE, 161 Hudson St., three blocks south of Canal St. Tel. 966-4225.
A downtown spot primarily for rock, Wetlands is a music club with a vaguely 1960s-style, sproutsy social consciousness. You might hear acoustic, country, R&B, reggae, funk, or world-beat bands. Healthy bar snacks are available.
Admission: $6–$15.

DANCE CLUBS

The dance scene in New York is not what it used to be: the beautiful people standing in line waiting to be chosen for admittance to outrageously expensive discos. A few of the really famous 1970s and 1980s discos are still around, but they've lost their luster as celebrity nightspots. These huge clubs need to draw large crowds, and coupons for discounted admission are available all over the city. Passes should be available at fashionable record and clothing stores. **Tower Records,** at 692 Broadway on the corner of East 4th Street, offers particularly good pass pickings.

Any printed guide to the "in" scene is inevitably out of date. Clubs open and close with a bewildering frequency. And fame, as Andy Warhol, the late patron saint of New York nightlife, so aptly observed, is a fleeting thing. Today's trendy clubs often last longer than 15 minutes, but rarely make it past 15 months. By the time this book is in your hands, nocturnal New York may have a dramatically different landscape. The really trendy, cutting-edge dance clubs go in and out of vogue (and existence) so quickly that if you're hell-bent on tracking the glitterati to the very latest locales, your best bet is to ask the locals and check the *Village Voice* when you're in town to find the hot club-of-the-week. And keep in mind that the more exclusive and expensive the club, the more "attitude" you can expect to get from an everpresent doorperson whose job it is to create the most interesting and stylish mix of people inside.

We've listed some of the tried-and-true spots below, plus some places where the music is something more special than your average DJ mix. Check also the listings above under "Rock," "Country," "Jazz," and "Blues," since many of these spots also offer dancing to live bands.

While New York's clubs generally open at 10pm, anybody who's anybody won't show up until well past 11pm. Clubs can stay open until 4am. Cover charges range from $5 to $20 and drinks can cost more than $6 at the more expensive clubs.

THE AMAZON CLUB, West Side Hwy. at North Moore St. Tel. 227-2900.
★ No, you're not in the tropics—you're in Lower Manhattan, despite the fact that you're surrounded by thatch-roofed bars, mini-waterfalls, a volleyball net, and, believe it or not, sand. Lots of young professional types head here after work for frothy daiquiris and reasonably priced light fare. The dance floor gets crowded early on, and occasionaly there's live music. Open nightly till 2am.
Admission: $5.

BAJA, 246 Columbus Ave., between 71st and 72nd sts. Tel. 724-8890.
The Baja is heavy on college students and surfer T-shirt types dancing to DJ mixes. You'll hardly notice the decor except for the beer on the bottom of your shoes.
Admission: $10 after 10:30pm.

BIG CITY DINER, 572 W. 43rd St., at Eleventh Ave. Tel. 244-6033.
You'll want to take a cab here—it's on the western fringes of Manhattan. This is Hell's Kitchen, though more desolate than dangerous. Once an eatery for cabbies coming off the late shift, it's now a restaurant/disco and the flavor of the month. The DJs usually get things cranked up around 10pm.
Admission: $5–$10.

CAFÉ SOCIETY, 915 Broadway, at 21st St. Tel. 529-8282.

✪ Café Society looks more like the set of an MGM musical than a place where mere mortals are allowed to tread. But take heart—you can live out your Fred and Ginger fantasies. On weekends this enormous restaurant with dramatic illuminated pillars and 50-foot ceilings pulsates with modern music. But on Monday and Wednesday from 8pm to midnight couples gather on the large dance floor while a big band plays Latin and swing music.
Admission: $10 after 10pm.

CARMELITA'S, 150 E. 14th St. Tel. 673-9015.
Carmelita's is a small upstairs hall rented out for weddings to a predominantly Hispanic clientele most of the week. But on Monday everyone can enjoy the kitschy disco balls and mirrored walls. The young, trendy crowd, with a heavy contingent of NYU students, sweats itself into a frenzy while dancing to vintage 1970s disco.
Admission: $5.

CHINA CLUB, 2130 Broadway, at 75th St. Tel. 877-1166.
MTV's Downtown Julie Brown has been spotted in this Upper West Side spot with an attitude. In the spirit of the Hard Rock Café, the China Club has introduced its own line of clothing and merchandise.
Admission: $10.

CRANE CLUB, 201 W. 79th St., at Amsterdam Ave. Tel. 877-3097.
There's no sign outside, but you probably won't miss the crowds lined up outside this newish dance club. The interior is plush, with dark wood accents and overstuffed booths, and the dance floor is kept hopping with the latest dance and house music tracks.
Admission: $5.

LIMELIGHT, 660 Sixth Ave., at 20th St. Tel. 807-7850.
An old church converted into a disco? Yes, it's true, and it's almost worth the trip just for the irreverence and the architecture, but this former hot spot has lost its chic. You'll find passes circulating all over the Village for discounted admission.
Admission: Around $15.

NELL'S, 246 W. 14th St., between Seventh and Eighth aves. Tel. 674-1567.
Nell's was *the* celebrity spot of the 1980s and it launched a wave of small, exclusive, comfortable clubs as an alternative to warehouse-sized discos. Inside, the well-dressed and well-turned-out mix with the trendy in an atmosphere reminiscent of a 1920s English gentlemen's club. A light supper is offered to the accompaniment of a jazz quartet. There are two rooms of overstuffed couches and chairs, and a dance floor. Admission is on a first-come, first-served basis, and reservations are strongly recommended.
Admission: $6–$15.

THE PALLADIUM, 126 E. 14th St., between Third and Fourth aves. Tel. 473-7171.
Housed in an incredibly well-designed and well-executed space, Palladium has the latest in acoustic and lighting technology. In its early 1980s heyday it was one of the hottest clubs going. Today it draws crowds by circulating lots of discount passes and by hosting occasional live performances.
Admission: $15–$20.

RED ZONE, 438 W. 54th St. Tel. 582-2222.
The Red Zone is a large open space packed with hi-tech lighting, video screens, and the occasional celebrity. Watch for special house music nights with top local DJs.
Admission: $10–$15.

ROSELAND BALLROOM, 239 W. 52nd St., between Broadway and Eighth aves. Tel. 247-0200.
If your tastes run to swing music, the dance floor at 65-year-old Roseland may be for you. You may also catch live Latin or rock bands.

Admission: $7–$10.

SHOUT!, 124 W. 43rd St., between Sixth Ave. and Broadway. Tel. 869-2088.

The crowd's a little older and a little less ferociously trendy here. The tunes are exclusively oldies from the 1950s and 1960s.
Admission: $5–$10.

SOB'S (Sounds of Brazil), 204 Varick St., on Seventh Ave. Tel. 243-4940.

One of the hottest places to dance in all of New York is tropical SOB'S. Calabash gourds and stuffed alligators adorn the walls. Onstage, the best international calypso, salsa, samba, reggae, and world beat music is played to a very knowing—and well-dressed—audience. You might catch such eclectic acts as Julian Marley, Junior Walker and the All-Stars, or Mory Kante. Tuesday nights are devoted to the down-and-dirty Soul Kitchen. Dinner reservations are accepted.
Admission: $10–$25.

TATOU, 151 E. 53rd St., between Lexington and Third aves. Tel. 753-1144.

One of the newer breed of restaurants with ornate decor and a dance floor, Tatou is oh-so-chic—and priced accordingly (scotches have been known to run $8). Try the Monday night variety showcase.
Admission: $10–$15.

WINDOWS ON THE WORLD, One World Trade Center. Tel. 938-1111.

If you're willing to spend more, you can "swing" to the sounds of a trio on the top floor of the World Trade Center, in the Hors D'Oeuvrerie section of the plush Windows on the World restaurant (see also "Rooms with a View," in Section 3, "The Bar Scene"). No jeans or sneakers are allowed, and men should wear jackets. There's no minimum, and a light menu is available until midnight.
Admission: $3.50.

3. THE BAR SCENE

On a weekend night in Manhattan, the bars and cafés are as seductive as anything in town. In the Village and on the Upper East and West sides they dot nearly every block; when passing by you can't help but be enticed by what's inside—chatter and music that spills into the street, and the glitter of the famous and high-powered that frequent many of them. There is a bar for everyone—for artists, actors, students, musicians, politicos, and business types. They are as much a New York trademark as the Stock Exchange and Broadway.

Expect to pay from $2.50 to $4.50 for a beer, and from $3.50 on up for a mixed drink in all the places that follow—we'll note any particularly cheap or expensive spots.

LOWER MANHATTAN/TRIBECA/SOHO

BROOME STREET BAR, corner of Broome St. and West Broadway. Tel. 925-2086.

This pub-style restaurant and bar in SoHo is popular among artists, writers, and musicians. There's an accent on tropical drinks, and jazz plays from the bar's sound system.

EAR INN, 326 Spring St., between Washington and Greenwich sts. Tel. 226-9060.

A neighborhood favorite, the Ear Inn offers a good jukebox, poetry readings, and for the creative customer, butcher-paper tablecloths and crayons for scribbling.

KATIE O'TOOLE'S PUB AND RESTAURANT, 134 Reade St., between Hudson and Greenwich sts. Tel. 226-8928.

Dozens of local musicians stop by this quaint Irish pub to play the blues almost every night. Have a burger or an authentic plate of bangers and mash with a pint of English ale while you enjoy the music.

MANHATTAN BREWING COMPANY, 40 Thompson St., between W. Broadway and Broome St. Tel. 219-9250.

The beer is brewed right on the premises, and the reasonably priced ribs draw hordes of hungry young patrons.

NORTH STAR PUB, 93 South St., at Fulton St. Tel. 509-6757.

One of the best places to hang out in the South Street Seaport area, the North Star Pub serves several varieties of ale to go along with your bangers and mash, in keeping with its British decor.

ODEON, 145 W. Broadway. Tel. 233-0507.

Odeon is full of sleek chrome and art deco set against a color scheme of black and white. It attracts painters, sculptors, entertainers, and assorted beautiful people; you may remember mention of this trendy TriBeCa bar scene in *Bright Lights, Big City*.

PRINCE STREET BAR AND RESTAURANT, 125 Prince St., at the corner of Wooster St. Tel. 228-8130.

For a warming hot toddy in winter or a cooling piña colada in summer in SoHo, you might make a stop at the Prince Street Bar and Restaurant. A popular hangout for the locals, it's open till 1 or 2am.

PUFFY'S TAVERN, 81 Hudson St., four blocks south of Canal St. Tel. 766-9159.

There's always a neighborhood crowd here for late-night drinks, socializing, and dart throwing.

SOHO KITCHEN, 103 Greene St., between Prince and Spring sts. Tel. 925-1866.

For wine connoisseurs, the SoHo Kitchen is a must. It serves over 100 varieties of wine and champagne by the glass or bottle and 12 different draft beers. Sit down by the open kitchen and try their tasting menu: 2.5-ounce tastes of four or five different wines.

THE SPORTING CLUB, 99 Hudson St., between Harrison and Franklin sts. Tel. 219-0900.

Sports fans will love it—the main draw is a 10-foot video screen and its companion, a computerized scoreboard, that tower above the oval bar.

211 WEST BROADWAY, at Franklin St. Tel. 925-7202.

This lovely, lofty place is typical of TriBeCa's warehouse-turned-bar/restaurants, with a pressed-tin ceiling and cast-iron columns.

GREENWICH VILLAGE

In the Village the bars tend to be more casual, less expensive, and livelier. In any one of a number of clubs and nightspots you can join an offbeat crowd of students, artists, musicians, and locals for music, a drink, and a good time.

ACME BAR & GRILL, 9 Great Jones St., near Lafayette St. Tel. 420-1934.

Have a beer to wash down your barbecued ribs or other Cajun fare. It's always a good time (if a rather loud good time) at this cheerful Village watering hole.

BAYAMO, 704 Broadway, between Washington Place and E. 4th St. Tel. 475-5151.

If you enjoy a funky Mexican/Caribbean atmosphere, you'll like the party at Bayamo. It offers big, bold decor and big, frothy tropical drink concoctions.

BOXER'S, 190 W. 4th St., between Sixth and Seventh aves. Tel. 633-BARK.

This large, lively old-time tavern in the heart of the Village sports an antique bar and a huge crowd. Burgers, chicken pot pie, and other American fare make up the menu (the kitchen is open till the wee hours). Look for the large pub-style sign outside.

CALIENTE CAB COMPANY, 21 Waverly Place, corner of Greene St. Tel. 243-8517.

You can't miss the loud and festive Caliente Cab Company—look for the huge margarita sculpture over the door. It's a bit touristy, but fun all the same. A waitress will probably come over to your table and cajole you into ordering a tequila slammer—if you acquiesce, she'll pound the tequila and soda mix on the table with a banshee yell.

THE CEDAR TAVERN, 82 University Place, at E. 11th St. Tel. 929-9089.

The Cedar Tavern, with a rich history as a Beat Generation hangout in the 1950s, is still popular, with a full bar and affordable food. The tavern offers a dark and cozy atmosphere and its century-old bar caters to a student, business, and neighborhood crowd.

CHUMLEY'S, 86 Bedford St., at Barrow St. Tel. 675-4449.

Chumley's is the quintessential Old Village bar. The entrance is unmarked, since it used to be a Prohibition-era speakeasy, and you'll have to be persistent to find it. This two-room basement establishment seems not to have changed a bit since the old days.

THE CORNER BISTRO, 331 W. 4th St., corner of Jane St. Tel. 242-9502.

This quiet, old-fashioned neighborhood bar will never be confused with a hot spot, but if relaxation, conversation, and a great hamburger are what you need, this is your place. Open daily to 4am.

COTTONWOOD CAFÉ, 415 Bleecker St., between W. 11th and Bank sts. Tel. 924-6271.

This place is Texas in Manhattan, serving up great Tex-Mex food, a can't-be-beat friendliness, and live folk and country-western music most nights.

FUDDRUCKER'S, 87 Seventh Ave. South, at Barrow St. Tel. 255-9643.

There are few places more crowded of a summer night than the patio area at Fuddrucker's; try to stake out one of the umbrella tables. It may be part of a nationwide chain, but Manhattanites aren't snobbish about enjoying the reasonably priced burgers and fries. The real draw, however, is the "Daquirita" bar, where a long row of see-through machines mixes up tropical drinks—from scorpions and strawberry margaritas to Lynchburg lemonade.

GOTHAM BAR AND GRILL, 12 E. 12th St., between Fifth Ave. and University Place. Tel. 620-4020.

Gotham is one of Greenwich Village's choicest restaurants. Its postmodern design, done in a pink-and-green color scheme, with cloudlike parachute lights, creates the ambience of an outdoor café. The spacious bar area provides views of the fashion-, music-, and art-world movers and shakers who come for the superb American fare. Usually closed before midnight.

THE KETTLE O' FISH, 130 W. 3rd St., between Sixth Ave. and MacDougal St. Tel. 533-4790.

It's an NYU dive—lots of beer in pitchers, pinball, video trivia games, and wooden booths.

THE LION'S HEAD, 59 Christopher St., just off Seventh Ave. South. Tel. 929-0670.

The cozy, pubby Lion's Head is one of the most famous writers' bars in the city, counting lots of publishing types among its regulars. Open most nights to 4am.

PANCHITO'S, 105 MacDougal St., at Bleecker and W. 3rd sts. Tel. 487-8963.

If you're craving Mexican food and want to choose one of 100 different kinds of fruit drinks, try Panchito's. Its drinks are pure and natural—no additives or premixes. Open to 4am.

PEACOCK CAFFÈ, 24 Greenwich Ave., off 10th St. Tel. 242-9395.

For a late-night espresso instead of a drink, the Peacock Caffè is a popular coffeehouse hangout. Its classical music and baroque columns provide a restful, pensive break from sightseeing or bar hopping. Open till 1am weeknights, 2am on weekends.

WEST 4TH STREET SALOON, 174 W. 4th St. Tel. 255-0518.

Also a restaurant, this casual spot couldn't be more centrally located in the Village. An inviting, warming fireplace crackles in the winter.

WHITE HORSE TAVERN, 566 Hudson St., corner of W. 11th St. Tel. 243-9260.

Dylan Thomas wolfed down 18 shots of whiskey in less than 20 minutes here, and died several days later. The White Horse is still host to writers and artists. It serves good hamburgers and omelets.

WOODY'S, 140 Seventh Ave. South, between W. 10th and Charles sts. Tel. 242-1200.

The mix of regulars and newcomers at this popular place creates a friendly and pleasantly rowdy atmosphere. You can sit at the glassed-in patio or take a seat at the 150-year-old Bavarian bar to try the unbelievable menu of international beers—91 at last count. An international beer tour of 28 countries is offered, or, if you try 50 different beers, you'll get a Woody's T-shirt. Those with true stamina, the ones who manage to sample all 91 varieties, get a sweatshirt, baseball hat, their own personal Woody's stein for the next visit, and a six-pack of their favorite beer (if they can still remember what that was).

YE WAVERLY INN, 6 Bank St., at Waverly Place. Tel. 929-4377.

This old and dimly lit tavern is perfect for a romantic date; it's been around since the 1920s, and you'll love the old-time Village atmosphere.

EAST VILLAGE

CONTINENTAL DIVIDE, 25 Third Ave., at St. Marks Place. Tel. 529-6924.

The bold, kitschy western decor in this always-crowded East Village watering hole will make you do a double take.

KING TUT'S WAH WAH HUT, 112 Avenue A, at E. 7th St. Tel. 254-7772.

If your revels take you out to the deepest, darkest parts of the East Village, know that King Tut's has been a favored New York spot of late, with lots of loud music and an imaginative decor.

SUGAR REEF, 93 Second Ave., between 5th and 6th sts. Tel. 477-8427.

We've already introduced you—in Chapter 6, "Where to Eat in New York City"—to the fabulous Caribbean eats to be had here, but don't overlook the bar. It'll take the indecisive among you a few minutes to choose your poison from the long list of exotic drinks. The bar is always crowded, but after a couple of daiquiris, you won't notice.

TELEPHONE, 149 Second Ave., between 9th and 10th sts. Tel. 529-9000.

You can't miss the facade—it's a row of bright red telephone booths imported straight from England (yes, they work). Come for dinner if you fancy Scotch eggs or shepherd's pie, and expect to get the same gruff service you'd get in an English pub. Open till 4am on weekends.

CHELSEA

CADILLAC BAR, 15 W. 21st St., between Fifth and Sixth aves. Tel. 645-7220.
You guessed it, it's a converted garage, attracting a youngish crowd of revelers with its margaritas and Tex-Mex menu.

EMPIRE DINER, 210 Tenth Ave., at 22nd St. Tel. 243-2736.
The Empire Diner is the pride of Chelsea. Ensconced in an old roadside diner, it was refurbished into a fashionable Art Deco restaurant/bar with chrome chairs, stainless-steel walls, and black tabletops. This is the place to go after the nightclubs close. It has countless brands of imported beer and serves everything from standard diner fare to elaborate meals. The atmosphere is one of candlelight and romance; a pianist performs from 7pm most evenings. Open 24 hours.

GRAMERCY PARK/MURRAY HILL

LIVE BAIT, 14 E. 23rd St. Tel. 353-2492.
The drinks are better than the Cajun-style food at this scruffy yet trendy bar. Quite a pick-up scene and always packed.

OLDE TOWN BAR & GRILL, 45 E. 18th St., between Broadway and Park Ave. South. Tel. 473-8874.
An old-New York kind of place, the Olde Town is a beautiful spot, with high ceilings and wooden booths.

PETE'S TAVERN, 129 E. 18th St., at Irving Place. Tel. 473-7676.
Pete's claim to fame? O. Henry wrote *Gift of the Magi* here. A former speakeasy, it maintains a down-to-earth pub atmosphere despite having hosted President Kennedy and the filming for some of the Miller Lite commercials.

RODEO BAR, Albuquerque Eats, 375 Third Ave., at 27th St. Tel. 683-6500.
There are live country tunes every night (see the listing under Section 2, "The Club & Music Scene"), but no cover. You'll feel as if you've been transported to the Wild West as you down a tequila shot.

23RD STREET BAR & GRILL, 158 E. 23rd St., between Third and Lexington aves. Tel. 533-8877.
A sophisticated spot, the 23rd Street Bar & Grill hasn't lost its neighborhood feel (and the food's not bad, either).

MIDTOWN WEST

Around Midtown West/Times Square, the bars and pubs attract audiences and performers from the nearby theater district, and if you're lucky you might just bump into a Broadway star.

HARD ROCK CAFÉ, 221 W. 57th St., between Seventh Ave. and Broadway. Tel. 459-9320.
If you've really got to have one of those ubiquitous T-shirts, join the other tourists in line outside waiting to be served burgers, fries, and all-American sundaes. Like its London counterpart, this Hard Rock is a museum of rock-and-roll memorabilia, including 100 gold records, Prince's jacket from the movie *Purple Rain,* Chubby Checker's boots, and the guitars of Eric Clapton and Eddy Van Halen.

JOE ALLEN'S, 326 W. 46th St., between Eighth and Ninth aves. Tel. 581-6464.
Joe Allen's sometimes star-studded bar still manages to remain down-to-earth as it hosts a friendly pre- and posttheater crowd.

LANDMARK TAVERN, 626 Eleventh Ave., at 46th St. Tel. 757-8595.

 For a romantic, steeped-in-history atmosphere, head west (way west) to this beautiful pubby spot. Take a cab: it's in the middle of nowhere. Open till midnight or 1am.

LAVIN'S RESTAURANT AND WINE BAR, 23 W. 39th St., between Fifth and Sixth aves. Tel. 921-1288.

Lodged in a historic oak dining room built by Andrew Carnegie, Lavin's is a relaxing place to educate your wine palate. The bar, with its cool white marble countertop and etched-glass lamps hanging overhead, is a genteel refuge on a hot summer day. The bar emphasizes California wines, though there are European wines available as well. Expect to pay anywhere from $3.50 to $12 for a taste of the grape.

B. SMITH'S, 771 Eighth Ave., at 47th St. Tel. 247-2222.

Former model Barbara Smith holds forth here and attracts the beautiful people; look for the sleek neon sign outside. The Caribbean and Cajun menu is only a tad above our budget.

TRIXIE'S, 307 W. 47th St. Tel. 582-5940.

There's no cover or minimum here, but you're likely to find talent nights or dancing here nonetheless. It's always crowded with those pursuing fun, libations, and southwestern-style food.

MIDTOWN EAST

MARGLO'S, 974 Second Ave. Tel. 759-9820.

Belly up to the bar in this New Orleans–inspired spot for a Dixie beer and a plate of spicy popcorn shrimp. Watch for drink specials.

RUNYON'S, 305 E. 50th St., at Second Ave. Tel. 223-9592.

Billing itself as "The Original New York Saloon," Runyon's offers sports TV, and a cute porch area with a couple of outdoor chairs, perfect for an intimate chat. There's a full dinner menu offered, to be enjoyed in charming, plant-filled surroundings.

UPPER WEST SIDE/LINCOLN CENTER

Head up Columbus Avenue, and your choice of watering holes will seem limitless.

THE ABBEY PUB, 237 W. 105th St. Tel. 222-8713.

A not-so-loud bar in the heart of Columbia University country, the Abbey Pub is a favorite with grad students and professors.

THE ALL-STATE CAFÉ, 250 W. 72nd St., between Broadway and West End Ave. Tel. 874-1883.

 This friendly, no-fuss spot has an elegant pub decor and a great CD jukebox. The fireplace makes it a warming place to catch a nightcap when the weather's right. The burgers are huge, but the pitchers of beer are on the expensive side.

AMSTERDAM'S, 428 Amsterdam Ave., between 80th and 81st sts. Tel. 874-1377.

Young neighborhood professionals flock to Amsterdam's, which is more upscale than the many pickup joints that surround it. It's usually crowded, so don't come looking for a table unless you plan to eat, too—but then again, the rotisserie-grilled chicken is worth it. Good jukebox.

BAMBOO BERNIE'S, 2268 Broadway, between 81st and 82nd sts. Tel. 580-0200.

There's no sign marking the entrance here, just a primitive painting, a corrugated-tin overhang, and a crowd that sometimes spills onto the sidewalk. Among other equatorial touches inside, there's a woven rattan ceiling and a tape of lively island music. So tiny that if more than 10 people come inside, it might explode. Open daily until about 4am.

COLUMBUS, 201 Columbus Ave., at 69th St. Tel. 799-8090.

Baryshnikov's place sports a logo meant to look like a Columbus Avenue street sign. Prepare to be overrun by a well-dressed clientele trying to catch a glimpse of him, or of Danny Aiello, who sometimes frequents the place.

DUBLIN HOUSE, 225 W. 79th St., between Amsterdam Ave. and Broadway. Tel. 874-9528.

The cheap pitchers of beer keep 'em coming back. It's often full of college kids, but that's never deterred a handful of neighborhood locals.

EMERALD INN, 205 Columbus Ave. Tel. 874-8840.

This is a quiet, comfortable, and casual pub with low, beamed ceilings. The Emerald Inn isn't usually very crowded, and it serves up substantial, filling fare along with the beer.

THE HI LIFE, 477 Amsterdam Ave., at 83rd St. Tel. 787-7199.

So hip that it hurts. At press time, this was a hot spot, although West Siders are notorious for turning fickle very quickly. There's a huge aquarium at the entrance, some interesting antiques scattered about in the quirky decor, and, the night we were there, some good background tunes ranging from Donald Fagan to a samba mix.

KCOU RADIO, 430 Amsterdam Ave., between 80th and 81st sts. Tel. 580-0556.

This bar competes with its neighbor, Amsterdam's, for the local young professional crowd. There's no food and no sign outside announcing it; just a streamlined look with touches of neon lighting, and a jukebox that features rock, rhythm-and-blues, and some campy tunes you thought went away with the 1970s. Open daily to 4am.

LUCY'S, 503 Columbus Ave., between 84th and 85th sts. Tel. 787-3009.

Hey, dude—pretend you're from Baja, California, and squeeze your way into this desperately overcrowded, trendy college pickup scene. Featured (and lampooned) in the film *Crossing Delancey*.

McALEER'S, 455 Amsterdam Ave. Tel. 874-8037.

Pitchers of beer flow freely in this pub that comes complete with dartboard. The menu offers all the cheese fries, chicken wings, and potato skins your cholesterol count can stand, to accompany your libations.

P&G, 279 Amsterdam Ave. Tel. 874-8568.

The neon sign outside looks like it stepped out of a 1940s movie. Inside this happy dive, you'll find friendly bartenders and an ambience that discourages raucous college-age crowds. Good cheese fries and jukebox.

PATZO, 2330 Broadway, at 85th St. Tel. 496-9240.

Patzo looks quite elegant, but it serves up Italian cuisine and a full range of bar drinks at reasonable prices. The bar can get crowded when people are waiting for a movie to start at the Loew's complex a few doors down.

SPORTS BAR, 2182 Broadway. Tel. 874-7208.
Even the most avid sports junkie will be satiated—there's screen after video screen to keep you posted on the sporting event of the moment. If there's nothing more exciting on the tube than lacrosse, this cavernous place might be deserted, but you can't hear yourself think in here during the NFL playoffs. Tear yourself away from the screen if you can to shoot some hoops at the miniature basketball game near the door.

WILD LIFE, 355 Amsterdam Ave. Tel. 724-3600.
Brought to you by alums of Lucy's (see above), Wild Life is brand new, serving dinner and keeping huge crowds of drinkers happy around its bar. Watch for the elephants, lions, and other safari creatures over the entrance.

WILSON'S, 201 W. 79th St., at the corner of Amsterdam Ave. Tel. 769-0100.
The trendy crowd that gathers in this elegant spot sometimes includes ABC soap stars. The revelers have been known to break out into dancing on occasion.

UPPER EAST SIDE

Along First Avenue in the 70s and Second and Third avenues in the 90s, you'll find bar after bar full of yuppies and college kids on the prowl. Many of these spots are interchangeable, and if a loud, raucous pickup scene is what you want, you're in the right place. Tuesdays are usually Ladies' Nights in many of these spots, with discounts or free drinks available.

We've also included a few spots where the decibel level is a bit lower.

AMERICAN TRASH, 1471 First Ave., between 76th and 77th sts. Tel. 988-9008.
A very, very loud, scruffy spot, with beat-up couches and video games.

BROTHER JIMMY'S, 1461 First Ave., at 76th St. Tel. 545-RIBS.
The food's better than the drinks in this BBQ joint, but no one crowding around the bar seems to mind. If you're at a table, you can feast on chicken wings or ribs; if you're standing, peruse the Duke, University of North Carolina, and Georgia Tech memorabilia on the walls. Try the Texas Tea.

P. J. CLARKE'S, 915 Third Ave., at 55th St. Tel. 759-1650.
Housed in a 19th-century red-brick building, Clarke's is a remnant of a time when bars, tenements, and antique shops gave this area a real neighborhood feel. Inside, blue-collar locals mix with the occasional young professional type. There's a dining room in back, and one of the best jukeboxes in town, with oldies by Sinatra, Peggy Lee, the Ink Spots, and the Mills Brothers. Open daily to 4am.

DRAKE'S DRUM, 1629 Second Ave., between 84th and 85th sts. Tel. 988-2826.
Rumor has it that English tourists are almost always directed to this low-key, tavern-style bar (owned by Englishmen) and that most regular customers have Cockney accents. British flags are stretched across the ceiling and the floor is covered with sawdust. Open daily to 4am.

ELAINE'S, 1703 Second Ave., between 88th and 89th sts. Tel. 534-8103.
It's legendary. For the price of a drink you can sit at the bar and watch for Woody and Mia.

JIM MCMULLEN, 1341 Third Ave., near 76th St. Tel. 861-4700.
A casual spot for the beautiful people, Jim McMullen's is lined in dark wood paneling and attracts a crowd that's outgrown the rowdier college scene. If you stick to the low side of the menu, you can enjoy well-prepared American specialties and an excellent dessert selection.

NAME THIS JOINT, 1644 Third Ave., at 96th St. Tel. 369-8600.
Along with your beer, you can sample the Atomic Wings—the spiciness, which ranges from mild to meltdown, is up to you.

OUTBACK, 1668 Third Ave. Tel. 996-8117.
Guess the gimmick. Australian beers, Australian memorabilia in the decor. . . . The college kids love it.

THE RAVELLED SLEEVE, 1387 Third Ave., between 78th and 79th sts. Tel. 628-8814.
The casual spot draws mainly an over-30 crowd, with its friendly atmosphere, its warming winter fireplace, and an American/continental menu.

RUBY'S RIVER ROAD CAFÉ, 1754 Second Ave., near 91st St. Tel. 348-2328.
The revelers are packed in like sardines, and the music's not bad. Come early for some Cajun fare, and watch for drink specials.

RUPPERT'S, 1662 Third Ave., at 93rd St. Tel. 831-1900.
Ruppert's 54-foot bar is stunning—a gleaming mahogany structure that spent its first 50 years in a newspaperman's bar downtown. The crowd of young professionals tends to sport polo shirts, crew-neck sweaters, and tweed jackets. A pianist performs most nights.

SAM'S CAFÉ, 1406 Third Ave., at 80th St. Tel. 988-5300.
Mariel Hemingway's place is jam-packed with lots of young suit-and-tie professional types who seem to have just gotten off work. A fun place for conversation and a happening bar scene.

SPANKY'S, 1446 First Ave., between 75th and 76th sts. Tel. 772-6597.
Spanky's, new to this location, offers a fun atmosphere and a small menu of terrific Caribbean food for noshing at the bar.

THE VICTORY CAFÉ, 1604 Third Ave., at 90th St. Tel. 348-3650.
A little nicer than most of the bars along this strip, the Victory, a restaurant serving good American fare, gets increasingly rowdy as the night wears on.

PIANO BARS

This is becoming one of New York's most popular scenes, and understandably so! Piano bars are more romantic, more fun, and more relaxed than singles bars. And since few piano bars have either minimums or cover charges, they tend to be less expensive than jazz clubs. (See also "Hotel Bars," below, and "Nightclubs/Cabarets," above, since several of these spots offer piano tunes, too.)

LA CAMELIA, 225 E. 58th St., between Second and Third aves. Tel. 751-5488.
You can expect live music by Clinton Hayes here daily from 10pm to 2am.

CAMEO'S, 169 Columbus Ave., between 67th and 68th sts. Tel. 874-2280.
This second-floor Art Deco piano bar serves a full dinner menu, with sophisticated show tunes to accompany your cocktails.

MIMI'S, 984 Second Ave., at 52nd St. Tel. 688-4692.
A pianist is on duty here every night, and you can enjoy reasonably priced Italian specialties (see Chapter 6, "Where to Eat in New York City").

ONE FIFTH, One Fifth Ave., at E. 8th St. Tel. 260-3434.
Most nights there's a jazz pianist performing in this classy little spot, and in

addition to the standard drinks and wine list, clams, burgers, and shrimp are available until the bar closes.

THE VILLAGE CORNER, Bleecker St. at LaGuardia Place. Tel. 473-9762.

⭐ The Village Corner is a good spot to escape from the hustle and bustle of Bleecker Street. Resident pianist Lance Hayward plays from 8pm to 1am most nights. On weekends there is a $6 per-person minimum.

THE VILLAGE GREEN, 531 Hudson St., between West 10th and Charles sts. Tel. 255-1650.

This is another highly recommended piano bar, open Tuesday through Saturday.

HOTEL BARS

You may not be able to afford a room in some of New York's posh hotels, but that shouldn't prevent you from enjoying their distinctive ambience or their cocktail hours.

ALGONQUIN HOTEL, 59 W. 44th St., between Fifth and Sixth aves. Tel. 840-6800.

⭐ For *New Yorker* magazine fans, or anyone interested in things literary, what could be more exciting than a drink at the Algonquin? The hotel was home to the magazine's celebrated "Round Table"—Franklin Pierce Adams, James Thurber, Dorothy Parker, Alexander Woollcott, and Heywood Broun. You can still see *New Yorker* writers and editors sipping drinks. Wednesday through Sunday nights, there's a singer-pianist entertaining from about 5pm on.

THE CARLYLE, 35 E. 76th St., at Madison Ave. Tel. 744-1600.

The Carlyle has its share of celebrity guests. You may glimpse a few in **Bemelmans Bar** (named after the illustrator whose delightful murals adorn the walls), a pleasing place with decorated columns, small dark tables, and a grand piano for the singers who perform nightly from 9:30pm. Adjoining the bar is the Gallery where you can sip your drinks while sitting on velvet couches and comfortable upholstered chairs. (In the afternoon—from 3 to 5:30pm daily—it's a tea room.) The bar is open nightly until 1am, and usually features a pianist or other entertainment.

Also in the hotel, the elegant **Café Carlyle** offers drinks and musical entertainment.

THE HOTEL ELYSÉE, 60 E. 54th St., between Park and Madison aves. Tel. 753-1066.

The decor in the **Monkey Bar** is reminiscent of Disney's *Jungle Book* and hasn't changed since the place opened decades ago. The leopard-spotted carpet, fake-lizard upholstery, and monkey lamps are a testament to kitsch. Monday through Saturday there are two sets of piano music. On Saturday they add a comedian and singer, and, depending on who's on the bill, a cover charge.

THE MILFORD PLAZA HOTEL, 700 Eighth Ave., between 44th and 45th sts. Tel. 869-3600.

The **Stage Door Canteen** piano bar features Mike Cossi playing show tunes and popular music.

THE NEW YORK HELMSLEY, 212 E. 42nd St., between Lexington and Third aves. Tel. 490-8900.

Harry's, named after the man who built the hotel, offers a lavish complimentary buffet served between 5 and 7pm, which includes shrimp cocktails, fresh vegetables, and quiches. A pianist entertains while you dine. Drinks are expensive, but anyone with a large appetite will make out fine.

There's another **Harry's** in the Helmsley Palace, 455 Madison Ave., between 50th and 51st streets (tel. 888-7000), where for $8 you can buy a glass of champagne and pretend you're staying at one of the world's most expensive hotels. The bar has a pianist between 6pm and 1am. Located in the adjoining Villard House, a landmark and the hotel's trademark, is the elegant **Hunt Bar.** Soft couches and corner tables offer privacy and piano music plays nightly until 2am.

THE PLAZA HOTEL, 768 Fifth Ave., at 59th St. Tel. 759-3000.
Stop in for a Bloody Mary and soak up the elegant atmosphere in the **Oak Room** or the **Edwardian Room**—it's the cheap way to see the Plaza.

THE REGENCY, 540 Park Ave. at 61st St. Tel. 759-4100.
A wood-paneled cocktail lounge with subdued lighting and dramatic red floral murals attracts an international crowd. For the price of a glass of wine, you can enjoy the nightly piano music.

THE ROYALTON, 44 W. 44th St., between Fifth and Sixth aves. Tel. 869-4400.
Across the street from the Algonquin, the Royalton is light years away in atmosphere. You've never seen hotel decor like this. It's sleek, stark, and terribly chic. Watch for publishing and music-biz types.

ST. MORITZ, 50 Central Park South, at 59th St. and Sixth Ave. Tel. 755-5800.
If it's a summery evening, you might sit at the outdoor **Café de la Paix**—this Parisian-style café offers the perfect setting for a romantic interlude as you gaze out onto Central Park.

WALDORF-ASTORIA, Park Ave. and 50th St. Tel. 355-3000.
An international clientele gathers nightly at the Waldorf's three distinctive and extravagantly decorated bars. **Sir Harry's Bar** has an African-safari motif with trophy heads and zebra skins on the walls. **The Cocktail Terrace** overlooks the exquisite Art Deco Park Avenue lobby and is open for tea from 2:30 to 10pm.
Peacock Alley is next to a 2-ton, 9-foot-tall, bronze clock that's capped with a miniature of the Statue of Liberty. The main attraction at this famous bar is songwriter Cole Porter's personal piano. Porter lived at the Waldorf for several years, and his tunes are played on the piano nightly.

ROOMS WITH A VIEW

The view from the top of New York's skyscrapers is overwhelming. It spreads across Manhattan to the outer boroughs, showing off miles of crowded avenues, massive buildings, and elegant brownstones. Viewing all of this can be done relatively cheaply—provided you limit yourself to one cocktail.

HORS D'OEUVRERIE, Windows on the World, One World Trade Center, 107th fl. Tel. 938-1111.
You'll find this bar with a 180° view at the top of the World Trade Center. The Windows on the World restaurant is way too rich for our blood, but in the Hors d'Oeuvrerie you can have afternoon or evening drinks, along with tasty international hors d'oeuvres ($4.75 to $15) while taking in the Statue of Liberty, Staten Island, or the Brooklyn Bridge and Queens. Hors d'oeuvres are served from 4pm to midnight. Men must wear jackets, no blue jeans are allowed, and there's a $3.50 cover charge. (See also "Dance Clubs," in Section 2, "The Club and Music Scene," above.)

THE RAINBOW PROMENADE, 30 Rockefeller Plaza. Tel. 632-5000.
The newly renovated 65th floor of Rockefeller Plaza rests about 850 feet above the city and the view from its three sides spreads at least 50 miles. You can see downtown Manhattan and Central Park directly below, and then as far afield as New Jersey. Meals at the Rainbow Room are very formal and expensive, and the Rainbow and Stars supper club charges a whopping cover (see "Nightclubs/Cabarets," in "The Club and Music Scene," above). Better to go just for the view and a drink at the Rainbow Promenade bar—the ambience and the view don't have to cost you an arm and a leg.

THE RIVER CAFÉ, 1 Water St., Brooklyn. Tel. 718/522-5200.
Housed in a barge that floats beneath the Brooklyn Bridge, the River Café has one of New York's best views of the river and lower Manhattan. This restaurant/bar is

elegantly simple with wooden floors, fresh flowers, and one wall made entirely of glass. Though it's way beyond our budget, you may want to drop by for a glimpse and a drink—the drinks are $5 or $6; the view is free. Open daily to 2am.

RUSSIAN TEA ROOM, 150 W. 57th St., between Sixth and Seventh aves. Tel. 265-0947.

This fabled lair of the beautiful people has a second-floor bar that's a perfect roost for watching the parade of celebrity diners. Sit back and watch the dealmakers wining and dining their clients (it's a favorite New York power-lunch spot). A favorite with Carnegie Hall concert-goers, the restaurant was refurbished in the red-velvet opulence of a czar's palace. This is not a place to come in jeans and T-shirts, especially if you expect to get good service. While you're here, you might try one of the vodka specials that go by names like Ivan the Terrible, the Ballet Russe, the Moscow Mule, and the Nureyev. Open daily to 11pm.

TOP OF THE SIXES, 666 Fifth Ave. Tel. 757-6662.

This skyscraper café is located on the 39th and top floor of 666 Fifth Avenue. The scenery through its large windows includes Central Park, downtown Manhattan, and parts of New Jersey—all yours for the price of a cocktail. Complimentary hors d'oeuvres are served during happy hour, from 5 to 7:30pm.

TOP OF THE TOWER, Beekman Tower Hotel, 49th St. and First Ave. Tel. 355-7300.

The view from atop the Beekman spreads from the East River to the Empire State Building and the United Nations. There's also an outdoor terrace from which the scenery is even more pleasant. There's no cover or minimum, but drinks are expensive. A pianist entertains between 9pm and 2am.

4. MORE ENTERTAINMENT

TELEVISION SHOWS

TV folks are always looking for audiences to fill up their studios. Unfortunately for us, Hollywood has lured a lot of the entertainment industry away from New York, so there aren't nearly as many shows to visit now as there were in the early days of television. Participating in a studio audience is always a fun way to see how a show is produced, so it's worth a try to find a show that's open. Unless you're very lucky and see a network employee handing out tickets in Rockefeller Center on a weekday afternoon (which has happened to us), your best bet is to write to the studios well in advance. And there's another attraction to these studio broadcasts—they're absolutely free!

Below are the procedures the networks have set up for obtaining tickets.

NATIONAL BROADCASTING COMPANY (Channel 4).

NBC, located at 30 Rockefeller Plaza with an entrance on West 49th Street under the familiar peacock sign (tel. 664-3055), asks that you write ahead because some shows have long waiting lists. NBC has several popular shows based in Manhattan: "Late Night with David Letterman," "Saturday Night Live," and "The Cosby Show." To write for tickets, address your request to NBC Tickets (name of show requested), 30 Rockefeller Plaza, New York, NY 10112 (postcards only). There is a limit of two tickets per request, and you must be at least 16 years old to get into the studio. NBC doesn't air many pilots, and tickets for those pilots are usually given out the day before airing.

AMERICAN BROADCASTING COMPANY (Channel 7).

ABC also asks for a written request as much as ten months in advance. Requests, with a specific date, should be sent to ABC Guest Relations, 36A W. 66th St., New York, NY 10023. At press time, ABC ticketholders were invited to watch "Live with Regis and Kathie Lee," a talk show with Regis Philbin and Kathie Lee Gifford, airing at 9am. You, the audience, arrive at 8am. ABC shoots its TV pilots in the summer. Call 887-3537 the day before you go, to see if there's a show.

COLUMBIA BROADCASTING SYSTEM (Channel 2).
    CBS, at 51 W. 52nd St., between Fifth and Sixth avenues, is housed in a black-glass tower sometimes called "Black Rock." CBS no longer tapes live shows in New York, but they still film many of their pilots before live studio audiences. Call 877-3537 for information about upcoming programs.

MOVIES

No city in the world has a film selection comparable to New York's. Not a week goes by without a special screening or event somewhere in the city—from the annual Animation Film Festival to the International Festival of Gay and Lesbian Films. Check the weekly listings in the *Village Voice* or the *Sunday New York Times* for information. You can also call 777-FILM, a free computerized service that can help you check what's playing nearby or find theaters playing a specific movie. Call from a touch-tone phone.

    Below we've listed a selection of museums, theaters, and other venues that show out-of-the-ordinary, avant-garde, classic, or foreign films.

American Museum of the Moving Image, 35th Ave. at 36th St., Astoria, Queens. Tel. 718/784-0077.
Angelika Film Center, 18 W. Houston St., at Mercer St. Tel. 995-2000.
Anthology Film Archives, 32-34 Second Ave., at 2nd St. Tel. 505-5181.
Bleeker Movie House I And II, 114 Bleecker St. Tel. 807-9205.
Donnell Library Media Center, 20 W. 53rd St., near Fifth Ave. Tel. 621-0609.
Eighth St. Playhouse, 52 W. 8th St., between Fifth and Sixth aves. Tel. 674-6515.
Film Forum, 209 W. Houston St., west of Sixth Ave. Tel. 727-8110.
French Institute, 22 E. 60th St., just east of Fifth Ave. Tel. 355-6100.
Japan Society, 333 E. 47th St., between First and Second aves. Tel. 752-0824.
Lincoln Plaza Cinemas, 63rd St. and Broadway. Tel. 757-2280.
Millennium Media Center, 66 E. 4th St., between Second Ave. and the Bowery. Tel. 673-0090.
The Museum of Modern Art, 11 W. 53rd St., just west of Fifth Ave. Tel. 708-9490.
New York Public Library, 42nd St. and Fifth Ave. Tel. 221-7676.
Public Theater, 425 Lafayette St., near Astor Place. Tel. 598-7171.
The Whitney Museum, 945 Madison Ave., at 75th St. Tel. 570-0537.

POETRY/PROSE

As one of the world's publishing centers, New York always has something literary going on, whether it be a poetry reading, a book signing, or a symposium. Often churches, major bookstores, and universities sponsor such events, and generally at little or no charge. The *New York Times* entertainment section, the *Village Voice,* and *New York* magazine are good sources to check for current happenings.

COOPER UNION FOR THE ADVANCEMENT OF SCIENCE AND ART, 41 Cooper Square, at Third Ave. and East 7th St. Tel. 353-4155.
    The Great Hall at historic Cooper Union was the site of the first free public lecture series in the nation. Its debates, speeches, and readings have seen the likes of Abraham Lincoln, Susan B. Anthony, Mark Twain, and Margaret Mead. Today the tradition continues, and the free or low-cost music, poetry, and lecture series continues to draw notable names.

NEW YORK PUBLIC LIBRARY, with its main branch at 455 Fifth Ave., at 42nd St. Tel. 221-7676.

Many branches of the New York Public Library sponsor literary readings. Usually the most famous writers can be seen either at the **Donnell Library Center,** 20 W. 53rd St., off Fifth Avenue (tel. 621-0618), or at the **Jefferson Market branch** in the Village, 425 Ave. of the Americas, between 9th and 10th streets (tel. 243-4334). Call or stop by any branch for information.

92ND STREET YMHA, Lexington Ave. and 92nd St. Tel. 427-6000.

The Poetry Center at the Y is a forum for highly regarded poets. Umberto Eco, Mark Strand, Harold Pinter, and Eugene Ionesco are among those who have read their work there. They follow Dylan Thomas, who made this theater the stage for his fabled readings in the 1950s. There is usually a large and interesting selection of poetry readings and lectures. Tickets sell on a first-come, first-served basis (unless you are a member, in which case they are reserved at the beginning of the season). Performances are usually on Monday nights from late September to early May.

A $95 membership fee includes admission to all 32 events of the season. On selected Sunday mornings, from October to May, the center also sponsors a lecture series, "Biographers and Brunch." For $14 you can enjoy bagels, cream cheese, and fruit salad while listening to literary biographers such as James Atlas, Justin Kaplan, or Ian Hamilton. For a current schedule, check listings in the *New York Times* entertainment section or write to the Poetry Center.

Prices: Tickets from $6.

PEN, 568 Broadway, near Prince St. Tel. 334-1660.

This writers' organization periodically sponsors literary events such as readings and symposia at its headquarters as well as at other locations around the city. There are no events during the summer months. Call for a current schedule.

Prices: Many events free.

THE WRITER'S VOICE, West Side YMCA, 5 W. 63rd St., between Broadway and Central Park West. Tel. 787-6557.

This literary program, sponsored by the West Side Y, offers authors' readings every Friday from October to December and March to May at 8pm. All genres from mysteries to poetry are featured. The admission price also includes a reception and book party afterward. A $40 membership fee includes admission to all events in either the fall or spring season.

Prices: $5–$10.

INDEX

GENERAL INFORMATION

SIGHTS & ATTRACTIONS

KEY TO ABBREVIATIONS: An asterisk (*) indicates an Author's Favorite.

ACCOMMODATIONS

KEY TO ABBREVIATIONS: *H* = Hotel; *Hs* = Hostel; *Y* = Y; *D* = Dorm; * = An Author's Favorite; *$* = Super Value Choice; *W* = Worth the Extra Bucks

RESTAURANTS

KEY TO ABBREVIATIONS: * = an Author's Favorite; $ = Super Value Choice; W = Worth the Extra Bucks; *24h* = Late night/24-hour

NOW, SAVE MONEY ON ALL YOUR TRAVELS!
Join Frommer's™ Dollarwise® Travel Club

Saving money while traveling is never easy, which is why the **Dollarwise Travel Club** was formed 32 years ago to provide cost-cutting travel strategies, up-to-date travel information, and a sense of community for value-conscious travelers from all over the world.

In keeping with the money-saving concept, the annual membership fee is low—$25 for U.S. residents and $35 for residents of Canada, Mexico, and other countries—and is immediately exceeded by the value of your benefits, which include:

1. Any TWO books listed on the following pages;
2. Plus any ONE Frommer's City Guide;
3. A subscription to our quarterly newspaper, *The Dollarwise Traveler;*
4. A membership card that entitles you to purchase through the Club all Frommer's publications for 33% to 40% off their retail price.

The eight-page **Dollarwise Traveler** tells you about the latest developments in good-value travel worldwide and includes the following columns: **Hospitality Exchange** (for those offering and seeking hospitality in cities all over the world); and **Share-a-Trip** (for those looking for travel companions to share costs).

Aside from the various Frommer's Guides, the Gault Millau Guides, and the Real Guides you can also choose from our Special Editions, which include such titles as **Caribbean Hideaways** (the 100 most romantic places to stay in the Islands); and **Marilyn Wood's Wonderful Weekends** (a selection of the best mini-vacations within a 200-mile radius of New York City).

To join this Club, send the appropriate membership fee with your name and address to: Frommer's Dollarwise Travel Club, 15 Columbus Circle, New York, NY 10023. Remember to specify which single city guide and which two other guides you wish to receive in your initial package of member's benefits. Or tear out the pages, check off your choices, and send them to us with your membership fee.

FROMMER BOOKS
PRENTICE HALL TRAVEL　　　　　Date_____
15 COLUMBUS CIRCLE
NEW YORK, NY 10023

Friends: Please send me the books checked below.

FROMMER'S™ COMPREHENSIVE GUIDES
(Guides listing facilities from budget to deluxe, with emphasis on the medium-priced)

☐ Alaska	$14.95	☐ Italy	$19.00
☐ Australia	$14.95	☐ Japan & Hong Kong	$17.00
☐ Austria & Hungary	$14.95	☐ Morocco	$18.00
☐ Belgium, Holland & Luxembourg	$14.95	☐ Nepal	$18.00
☐ Bermuda & The Bahamas	$17.00	☐ New England	$17.00
☐ Brazil	$14.95	☐ New Mexico	$13.95
☐ California	$18.00	☐ New York State	$19.00
☐ Canada	$16.00	☐ Northwest	$16.95
☐ Caribbean	$17.00	☐ Puerta Vallarta (avail. Feb. '92)	$14.00
☐ Carolinas & Georgia	$17.00	☐ Portugal, Madeira & the Azores	$14.95
☐ Colorado (avail. Jan '92)	$14.00	☐ Scandinavia	$18.95
☐ Cruises (incl. Alaska, Carib, Mex, Hawaii, Panama, Canada & US)	$16.00	☐ Scotland (avail. Feb. '92)	$17.00
		☐ South Pacific	$20.00
☐ Delaware, Maryland, Pennsylvania & the New Jersey Shore (avail. Jan. '92)	$19.00	☐ Southeast Asia	$14.95
		☐ Switzerland & Liechtenstein	$19.00
☐ Egypt	$14.95	☐ Thailand	$20.00
☐ England	$17.00	☐ Virginia (avail. Feb. '92)	$14.00
☐ Florida	$17.00	☐ Virgin Islands	$13.00
☐ France	$15.95	☐ USA	$16.95
☐ Germany	$18.00		

0891492

FROMMER'S CITY GUIDES
(Pocket-size guides to sightseeing and tourist accommodations and facilities in all price ranges)

☐ Amsterdam/Holland $8.95	☐ Minneapolis/St. Paul $8.95
☐ Athens. $8.95	☐ Montréal/Québec City. $8.95
☐ Atlanta $8.95	☐ New Orleans. $8.95
☐ Atlantic City/Cape May $8.95	☐ New York $12.00
☐ Bangkok. $12.00	☐ Orlando $12.00
☐ Barcelona $12.00	☐ Paris $8.95
☐ Belgium $7.95	☐ Philadelphia $11.00
☐ Berlin. $10.00	☐ Rio $8.95
☐ Boston. $8.95	☐ Rome. $8.95
☐ Cancún/Cozumel/Yucatán $8.95	☐ Salt Lake City $8.95
☐ Chicago $9.95	☐ San Diego. $8.95
☐ Denver/Boulder/Colorado Springs. $8.95	☐ San Francisco $12.00
☐ Dublin/Ireland. $10.00	☐ Santa Fe/Taos/Albuquerque. $10.95
☐ Hawaii $12.00	☐ Seattle/Portland $12.00
☐ Hong Kong. $7.95	☐ St. Louis/Kansas City $9.95
☐ Las Vegas $8.95	☐ Sydney. $8.95
☐ Lisbon/Madrid/Costa del Sol $8.95	☐ Tampa/St. Petersburg $8.95
☐ London $12.00	☐ Tokyo. $8.95
☐ Los Angeles $8.95	☐ Toronto $8.95
☐ Mexico City/Acapulco $8.95	☐ Vancouver/Victoria $7.95
☐ Miami $8.95	☐ Washington, D.C. $12.00

FROMMER'S $-A-DAY® GUIDES
(Guides to low-cost tourist accommodations and facilities)

☐ Australia on $40 a Day $13.95	☐ Israel on $40 a Day. $13.95
☐ Costa Rica, Guatemala & Belize	☐ Mexico on $45 a Day $18.00
on $35 a Day. $15.95	☐ New York on $65 a Day. $15.00
☐ Eastern Europe on $25 a Day $16.95	☐ New Zealand on $45 a Day $16.00
☐ England on $50 a Day. $17.00	☐ Scotland & Wales on $40 a Day $18.00
☐ Europe on $45 a Day $19.00	☐ South America on $40 a Day $15.95
☐ Greece on $35 a Day $14.95	☐ Spain on $50 a Day $15.95
☐ Hawaii on $70 a Day. $18.00	☐ Turkey on $40 a Day. $22.00
☐ India on $40 a Day $20.00	☐ Washington, D.C., on $45 a Day. $17.00
☐ Ireland on $40 a Day. $17.00	

FROMMER'S CITY $-A-DAY GUIDES

☐ Berlin on $40 a Day $12.00	☐ Madrid on $50 a Day (avail. Jan '92) . . .$13.00
☐ Copenhagen on $50 a Day $12.00	☐ Paris on $45 a Day $12.00
☐ London on $45 a Day $12.00	☐ Stockholm on $50 a Day (avail. Dec. '91) $13.00

FROMMER'S FAMILY GUIDES

☐ California with Kids $16.95	☐ San Francisco with Kids. $17.00
☐ Los Angeles with Kids $17.00	☐ Washington, D.C., with Kids (avail. Jan
☐ New York City with Kids (avail. Jan '92) $18.00	'92) $17.00

SPECIAL EDITIONS

☐ Beat the High Cost of Travel. $6.95	☐ Marilyn Wood's Wonderful Weekends
☐ Bed & Breakfast—N. America $14.95	(CT, DE, MA, NH, NJ, NY, PA, RI, VT) . . .$11.95
☐ Caribbean Hideaways. $16.00	☐ Motorist's Phrase Book (Fr/Ger/Sp) $4.95
☐ Honeymoon Destinations (US, Mex &	☐ The New World of Travel (annual by
Carib). $14.95	Arthur Frommer for savvy travelers) . .$16.95

(TURN PAGE FOR ADDITONAL BOOKS AND ORDER FORM)

0891492

☐ Paris Rendez-Vous . . . .$10.95   ☐ Travel Diary and Record Book. $5.95
☐ Swap and Go (Home Exchanging). . . . .$10.95   ☐ Where to Stay USA (from $3 to $30 a
                                                                           night). $13.95

FROMMER'S TOURING GUIDES

(Color illustrated guides that include walking tours, cultural and historic sites, and practical information)

☐ Amsterdam. . . . .$10.95   ☐ New York $10.95
☐ Australia . . . .$12.95   ☐ Paris $8.95
☐ Brazil . . . .$10.95   ☐ Rome. $10.95
☐ Egypt. . . . .$8.95   ☐ Scotland. $9.95
☐ Florence. . . . .$8.95   ☐ Thailand. $12.95
☐ Hong Kong. . . . .$10.95   ☐ Turkey $10.95
☐ London . . . .$12.95   ☐ Venice $8.95

GAULT MILLAU

(The only guides that distinguish the truly superlative from the merely overrated)

☐ The Best of Chicago . . . .$15.95   ☐ The Best of Los Angeles $16.95
☐ The Best of Florida . . . .$17.00   ☐ The Best of New England $15.95
☐ The Best of France . . . .$16.95   ☐ The Best of New Orleans. $16.95
☐ The Best of Germany . . . .$18.00   ☐ The Best of New York $16.95
☐ The Best of Hawaii . . . .$16.95   ☐ The Best of Paris $16.95
☐ The Best of Hong Kong. . . . .$16.95   ☐ The Best of San Francisco $16.95
☐ The Best of Italy. . . . .$16.95   ☐ The Best of Thailand. $17.95
☐ The Best of London . . . .$16.95   ☐ The Best of Toronto $17.00
                            ☐ The Best of Washington, D.C. $16.95

THE REAL GUIDES

(Opinionated, politically aware guides for youthful budget-minded travelers)

☐ Amsterdam . . . .$9.95   ☐ Mexico. $11.95
☐ Berlin. . . . .$11.95   ☐ Morocco $12.95
☐ Brazil . . . .$13.95   ☐ New York $9.95
☐ California & the West Coast . . . .$11.95   ☐ Paris $9.95
☐ Czechoslovakia . . . .$13.95   ☐ Peru. $12.95
☐ France . . . .$12.95   ☐ Poland $13.95
☐ Germany . . . .$13.95   ☐ Portugal. $10.95
☐ Greece. . . . .$13.95   ☐ San Francisco $11.95
☐ Guatemala . . . .$13.95   ☐ Scandinavia $14.95
☐ Hong Kong. . . . .$11.95   ☐ Spain. $12.95
☐ Hungary. . . . .$12.95   ☐ Turkey $12.95
☐ Ireland. . . . .$12.95   ☐ Venice $11.95
☐ Italy. . . . .$13.95   ☐ Women Travel. $12.95
☐ Kenya. . . . .$12.95   ☐ Yugoslavia $12.95

ORDER NOW!

In U.S. include $2 shipping UPS for 1st book; $1 ea. add'l book. Outside U.S. $3 and $1, respectively.

Allow four to six weeks for delivery in U.S., longer outside U.S. We discourage rush order service, but orders arriving with shipping fees plus a $15 surcharge will be handled as rush orders.

Enclosed is my check or money order for $_____

NAME_____

ADDRESS_____

CITY_____ STATE_____ ZIP_____

0891492